BERMUDA

TURKS & CAICOS ISLANDS

PUERTO RICO

BRITISH VIRGIN ISLANDS

ANGUILLA

BARBUDA

ST KITTS    ANTIGUA

NEVIS    MONTSERRAT

DOMINICA

ST LUCIA

ST    BARBADOS
VINCENT

GRENADA

TOBAGO

TRINIDAD

VENEZUELA

GUYANA

A

| Date Due | | | |
|---|---|---|---|
| FE 27 '70 | | | |
| APR 4 1973 | | | |
| MY 28 '80 | | | |
| JE 13 '80 | | | |
| NO 9 '82 | | | |
| | | | |
| | | | |
| | | | |
| | | | |
| | | | |
| | | | |

# THE GROWTH OF
# THE MODERN WEST INDIES

# The Growth of
# The Modern West Indies

GORDON K. LEWIS

NEW YORK AND LONDON

PUBLISHED 1968 IN THE UNITED STATES
BY MONTHLY REVIEW PRESS
116 WEST 14TH STREET, NEW YORK, N.Y. 10011
PRINTED IN GREAT BRITAIN

COPYRIGHT © GORDON K. LEWIS 1968

Library of Congress Catalog Card Number: 68–13657

FOR
SYBIL
*BELLE CRÉOLE*
OF MY
WEST INDIAN
SOJOURN

# CONTENTS

# PREFACE

I HAVE set myself the task in this book of undertaking a descriptive and interpretative analysis of the growth of the modern West Indian society, that is to say of the English-speaking Antilles, over the last forty years or so. It covers, then, the period that starts with the post-war years after 1918 and ends, for Trinidad and Jamaica, with the advent of national independence in 1962 and, for Guyana and Barbados, with independence in 1966. Inevitably, some attention is paid to the historically earlier periods, especially as they released forces helping to shape the contemporary society. But in general this essay concentrates on the modern formative period, starting at the point where most existing histories of the West Indies terminate. I am anxious also to insist that it does not purport to be an exhaustive study of West Indian life and society as they stand today. I do not, that is to say, include a thoroughgoing analysis of, say, the West Indian Negro family structure or the patterns of race-relations or the organization of political parties, on all of which there already exist detailed monographic studies by other Caribbeanists; rather, the mode of analysis here employed treats those phenomena, as it treats others, only insofar as they have contributed to the shaping of the society, both in its spirit and structure, as we know it today, and seeks, moreover, to treat them in at once a historical and sociological fashion. The book has been written, in one way, to clarify to myself, as an outsider, what have been the main currents in modern West Indian life. Having thus cleared the decks, as it were, I anticipate undertaking later a more detailed analysis of the contemporary society as it stands in the immediate aftermath of independence, probably to be entitled *Politics and Society in the West Indies*. This present volume must therefore be taken as the first of two volumes which together will constitute a prolonged examination of West Indian society both past and present.

An additional word of explanation seems in order. First, to the West Indian reader: it has been so much a part of the colonial burden for him to have to read about himself in books written by the expatriate and the outsider, in a relationship in which, to use Maunier's term, he is supposed to be civilized by those types playing the role of his *instituteur social*, that it seems inexcusable to add yet another title to the list. I can only plead in extenuation, without being apologetic, that a prolonged residence in the Caribbean area, along with a strategically located perch in Puerto Rico, gives me a right to be heard. Secondly, to the non-West Indian reader: it is curious that the avalanche of inquiry and reportage, both journalistic and academic, into the West Indian 'problem', particularly in Canada and Britain, seems to have failed to generate any real curiosity about the nature of the society from which the West Indian immigrant comes. This book, as best as it can, seeks to fill that gap.

A book of this kind has of necessity to come out of extensive research and travel over a period of years, covering so much territory as it does from the jungle-lanes of the Guyanese interior to the isolated 'out islands' of the Bahamian archipelago. That, in turns, requires time and money. I am grateful to all of the institutions that have helped provide me with both. The University of Puerto Rico has kindly granted me leaves of absence and reduced teaching loads. The Rabinowitz Foundation of New York and the Social Sciences Research Council in Washington have helped to cover various expenses with their grants. The major part of travelling expenses has been met by grants from the Institute of Caribbean Studies at the University of Puerto Rico; indeed, I am especially grateful to the Director of the Institute, Dr Thomas Mathews, for his unstinting aid throughout and for his genius for making help available with alacrity and without bureaucratic fuss. I must also express thanks to the two Puerto Rican friends, Marcos Ramirez and Raul Serrano-Geyls, who offered financial aid which proved their worth as patrons of the arts in a society where such patronage is on the whole of dismally small proportions.

Not least of all, of course, I am deeply in debt to all those very many West Indians, from Governors and Premiers down to cane-cutters and banana growers, some of them friends, many of them acquaintances, many more of them complete strangers, who have welcomed my intrusions with characteristic West Indian hospitality and good spirit and who, over the years, have helped me to understand both themselves and their society. A great deal of eloquent nonsense is uttered, in the West Indies as in other newly-independent nations, about the supposed 'sympathy' of writers on the society with the society's 'aspirations', and uttered, too, as frequently by the ingratiating expatriate ideologue as by the sensitive nationalist critic. To enter into such speculation seems to me to be worthless. What really matters is the ultimate quality of what the writer says. I merely express the hope, then, that all of my West Indian friends will accept this book as a small token of the affectionate regard in which I hold them and all things West Indian; and, more, as evidence of my surrender, like so many others before me, to the *magie antillaise*.

I avoid the invidious task of mentioning names. But the recent death of Harry Simmons in St Lucia calls for a note. To all of his friends Harry was St Lucia embodied. As artist, folklorist, historian and archaeologist he commanded an encyclopaedic knowledge of local conditions and always placed it, with his genial eagerness to please, at the disposal of the visitor. He had an imaginative range of interests unspoiled by a modern university education. He was friendly, garrulous, versatile, always a joy to be with. Most of all, he stayed in St Lucia throughout his tragic life to fight almost singlehandedly for the cause of aesthetic culture against colonial philistinism while others left. He spurned the 'pleasures of exile' to embrace the thankless task of bringing culture to the anarchy of a narrow-minded society that gave him back little but neglect and contempt. The new West Indian society of the future—which this book only implicitly describes—will, let us hope, one day pay him his full reward.

Christmas Day 1967
Trujillo Alto
Puerto Rico

# THE GROWTH OF
# THE MODERN WEST INDIES

# Chapter I

# THE WEST INDIAN SCENE

THE MOST striking single feature of the Caribbean chains of the West Indies society is, perhaps, their unique geographical position. Stretching from Jamaica on the western point of the northern Antillean range, through the groupings of the Leewards and Windwards islands, to Barbados and Trinidad at the southern tip of the eastern archipelago, and rounded off by the twin mainland territories of British Honduras and Guyana, they cover between them the four points of the Caribbean compass. Jamaica, on the one side, is the neighbour of Cuba; Trinidad, on the other, of Venezuela. In the north, the islands divide the Caribbean Sea and the Gulf of Mexico, in the east they divide the Caribbean Sea from the Atlantic. If, moreover, Bermuda and the great Bahama chain are included there is also an Atlantic outpost composed of those coral rock formations. Barbados, the 'Clapham Junction of the West Indies', faces the great trade avenues of the Middle Atlantic passage, while the Leewards do likewise further north. On the larger hemispheric canvas the islands, like the Caribbean as a whole, form a link between the two American continents, being at once a vital communications area and a strategic geo-political region between those two land masses. The very distances involved in all of this—Jamaica lies a thousand miles away from the eastern Caribbean—helps partly to explain the notorious insular prejudices still characteristic of West Indian communal psychology. Nor should the facts of geography be forgotten as contributing factors to West Indian political and economic development. The position of the area in the great trade wind belt gave it a massive pre-eminence in the era of the sailing ship, and with that era passed the trades serve as an essential ingredient in the new commerce of Carribbean tourism. Its climate determined the early growth of the region as a classic sugar area, along with the concomitant features of the slave trade and the slave plantation society, thus making it an integral part of the general American plantation regime which, as a massive socio-economic system, developed its characteristic institutions and social forms from Brazil to the Southern United States. The fact, finally, that the islands stretched like a line of watchdogs across the route between Spain and her seaborne New World empire laid down the pattern of West Indian politico-military history for more than three centuries, the scene of perennial warfare between each European colonizing power as it arose within the region and its emerging rivals eager to despoil it of its riches.

To the facts of geography, so imperious, there must be added the forces, at once powerful and dramatic, of Caribbean nature. Of the violent and magnificent beauty of the West Indian scene, the famous *magie antillaise*, there is, of course, a prolific literature. From the very moment of the Discovery conquerors and travellers alike built up that literature, half true, half legendary, starting with the conviction of Columbus himself that he had discovered there the Terrestrial Paradise. The extravagant view of the region as a delicious tropical garden, giving rise as it did to the fanciful *voyages imaginaires* that became, in their turn, the basis of the romantic myth of the 'noble savage', has perhaps only been matched by the equally extravagant view of the region as yet another white man's graveyard, what Lafcadio Hearn spoke of as the 'evil power' of the West Indian tropical climate. The truth, perhaps, lies somewhere in between. There is, indeed, a tremendous beauty of palm and beach, mountain and plain, that more than deserves the panegyric, 'personal islands', in the phrase of the West Indian poet, 'for which Gauguins sicken'. Mrs Carmichael reported in 1833 the poetic fancy of the Trinidadian Negroes that when God made the world he shook the earth from his hands into the water and thus created the West Indies;[1] and every new visitor, up to today, yields to the fancy. At the same time, there is an intimidating harshness that belies the sales-talk of the contemporary tourist literature. Geologically, the islands are in the main part summits of a range of submerged volcanoes that can terrorize and destroy as surely as Etna or Vesuvius. The dead city of St Pierre in Martinique can still be seen to testify to the destructive power of the great central cone of Mount Pélée. The almost total destruction of Kingston in 1907 by combined earthquake and tidal wave—only overshadowed by the San Francisco tragedy of a year earlier—demonstrates the grim hazards of West Indian city life; and if it was possible to see the earlier destruction of Port Royal in 1692 as divine vengeance for the sins of that Jamaican pirate stronghold it would have been more difficult to advance the same reason for the later destruction of the Victorian creole respectability of Kingston.

Above all, there is the brooding omnipresence, each season, of the hurricanes spawned somewhere in their breeding grounds east of Barbados. Every island population in the hurricane belt (Trinidad and the Guianas happily outside of it) lives, each summer and fall, in the dread fear of being struck, for the truly appalling force of the phenomenon has to be lived through to be felt. A typical Caribbean hurricane can destroy a whole city, like Belize in 1931, in the matter of a few hours; or shatter an island economy, like the pulverization of the Puerto Rican highland coffee industry in 1899 or of the Grenada nutmeg industry in 1955; or level every building, private and public, if the victims be, like Anguilla or Anageda, small, flat islets utterly defenceless against its onslaught. The toll of human life it exacts today is less, perhaps, than formerly, if only because of the improved detection and warning systems of modern technology, in which the United States meteorological and air patrolling services, centred in Miami and San Juan, play an important part. Caribbean nature, even so, still dominates Caribbean man, and no government in the area can afford to ignore the possibility, at some time or another, of a first-class natural disaster, such as, for example, the killer hurricane that ravaged Haiti and eastern Cuba in late 1963. Disaster might even drive a government to re-locate its capital city site, as in the British Honduran case after 1961.[2] The English-reading publics have been persuaded to see the region as a beautiful necklace of 'islands in the sun'. The realities are somewhat different. Life in the West Indian tropics, it is true, does not mean the daily struggle with unpleasant or hostile weather so characteristic of Anglo-American life. Yet tropical nature, at the same time, can be a harsh taskmaster when it decides to put aside its deceptive somnolence. The knowledge of that possibility is never far from the conscious surface of the West Indian mind.[3]

The real oppressions of West Indian life, however, have not been so much those of nature and geography as those of history and culture. If the region has been since slavery Emancipation (1834) nothing much more than a geographical expression, that has been due in the main part, to the legacy of its colonial history in all of its manifold forms. It is nurture, not nature, that has produced, from the historical beginnings, the Balkanization of the regional government and politics. The real barriers have been the artificial ones, linguistic, monetary, commercial, for the mutual ignorance and sometimes mutual hostilities of the various island populations, even when they all are English-speaking, stem from the fact that colonialism decreed that the avenues of communication should be between each individual West Indian fief and London rather than between the territories themselves. For the distances between the islands, going south from the Virgins group, are never very great and have certainly not prevented common action at critical moments as, for example, in the case of their resistance, under the old plantocracy, to the movement of slavery abolition or, more recently, in the case of their closer association in the field of modern higher education. 'A Jamaican,' wrote the Jamaican historian Frank Cundall over sixty years ago, 'sees more of his brethren of the other islands in six months spent in London and on shipboard between Barbados and Southampton, than in six years in his own island.'[4] That is still largely true even today and helps explain the notorious psychological alienation of Jamaicans from the eastern Caribbean populations. But this, clearly, is a matter of communications, not of geography. To blame geography is, in fact, to offer a spurious alibi for the British colonial failure to build up a sense of West Indian nationhood, a West Indian cultural identity, which could have been the fruit of a wise imperial statesmanship viewing the whole area as a unitary entity; as, indeed, it is, for there are general cultural regularities that transcend in many ways the continuing sense of separate identity in each island people. Much of the recent British literature on the area, official and unofficial, and especially that dealing with the short-lived West Indies Federation (1958–62), is full of ponderous homilies taking West Indians to task for their insularism, when in harsh fact the basic responsibility is that of the English themselves who kept the islands unnaturally apart from each other for three centuries or more and then expected them to come together in less than fifteen years. Political imperialism, in brief, explains, more than any other single factor, the present disunity of the region, the aimlessness so distressingly apparent since the collapse of the federal venture in

1962, with the resultant trend towards micro-nationalism. Cultural imperialism, in its turn, by seeking through education to convert the West Indian person into a coloured English gentleman produced the contemporary spectacle of the West Indian as a culturally disinherited individual, an Anglicized colonial set within an Afro-Asian cultural environment, caught between the dying Anglophile world and the new world of Caribbean democracy and nationalism seeking to be born.

The West Indian society that thus faces these issues—and, incidentally, comes more and more to a fertile consciousness of itself as it does so—is, as is well-known, one of tremendous ethno-cultural variety. It is biologically and culturally mixed. Sir Alan Burns has recorded looking on at a British Honduran schoolhouse in which German nuns were attempting to teach Mayan children out of an English textbook which they had to explain in Spanish.[5] The example is an extreme one, for colour heterogeneity varies profoundly; thus many of the smaller island communities, Carriacou and Barbuda, for example, are virtually homogeneous, being almost entirely Negro communities, while, on the other hand, the larger territories like Guyana, British Honduras and Trinidad exhibit a high degree of ethnic variation. Generally, however, racial purity is at a minimum. Thus, the last handful of pure Caribs are dying out; the Chinese in Trinidad are already nearly half mixed; and where racial endogamy is consciously pursued it tends to characterize marginal small groups like the Grenada and Barbados 'poor whites' or the French 'Cha-Chas' of St Thomas, whose anomalous position as lower class economically but upper class in race and culture drove them, understandably, into their present-day closed communities, and whose members exhibit, as the price for their attitude, a high degree of consanguine degeneracy. The East Indian elements in Guyana and Trinidad, it is true, may appear to belie this general argument. Yet their members exhibit more racial admixture than they sometimes care to admit; the practice of familially-arranged early marriage, itself a device to ensure a 'pure' union, is gradually breaking down as Indian youth revolts against it, and the Indian norms of feminine submissiveness and filial obedience thus are being constantly violated; and the more liberal Indian leadership is turning its attention increasingly to eliminating the continuing practice, albeit in truncated form, of *purdah* and the sexual subjugation of the Indian wife that it symbolizes. The average West Indian, this is to say, is a *sangmêlée*, the product of special West Indian historical-cultural trends, particularly (1) a matrifocal tradition which enabled the West Indian woman to put advantageous terms to her sexual 'friending' with the white father of her children and (2) more latterly, a liberal tradition of racial intermarriage. Whereas yesterday, then, sexual enterprise for the white man in the society meant the coloured mistress, today it means, more and more, the coloured wife. Correspondingly, the West Indian professional man who previously expressed his 'shade' prejudice by marrying an Englishwoman (and there are some well-known West Indianized English wives in the world of the arts and public affairs today) is now more likely to take a local bride. All this, of course, is not to say that the sense of colour shame is absent, for continuing marriage patterns based upon that shame and designed, as the saying goes, to put some cream in the coffee, testify to its continuing deep power in West Indian modes of thought. More correctly, it is to say that, granted the fact, obvious to all, that apart from a few groups, the Syrian and Lebanese mercantile families, for example, those West Indians who are not yet mixed will be effectively mixed in a few generations, the conclusion is unavoidable that miscegenation is not only the biological base of the society but must also assuredly become its operative ideal; the final point of the process being a genuinely Caribbean *mestizo* society much, indeed, as present-day Cuba is already.

Or, to put all this differently, the class-colour correlates of the West Indian social structure are real. But they are not the absolutes of a rigid caste system. Skin colour determines social class; but it is not an exclusive determinant. There are many fair-skinned persons who are not upper class, and many dark-skinned persons who are. The real divisions of the society are the horizontal ones of social class rather than the vertical ones of colour identification. The poet's 'third estate of colour' is there, certainly. But it yields, increasingly, to what is more and more, under the dual pressure of modernization and Americanization, a society of, first and foremost, class stratification. Nothing exemplifies this better than the growing anachronism, felt by West Indians themselves, of the bad variety of West Indian novel which melodramatically exploits the theme of racial violence for mercenary ends. That kind of book has its genesis, perhaps, in Alec Waugh's too-famous *Island in the Sun*. For that novel purveys an entire set of massive misconceptions about West Indian life. It successively depicts, among much else, the social stigma of an inter-racial marriage; a prominent island family shaken with horror at the discovery that it has a Negro ancestor; the impossibility of successful political candidacy on the part of white residents; a colonial Governor unseated by the force of critical newspaper articles written by a visiting American journalist; and middle class creole girls generally living a life of tropical leisure: all of them, it is safe to say, situations difficult to imagine occurring in real contemporary conditions. Nor is it at all likely that a 'white collar' office girl would dance indiscriminately with the street populace (Carnival time, of course, excepted); while as far as industrial relations are concerned it is far more likely that an island labour leader would address his followers in terms of class abuse rather than in terms of race conflict. The assumption common to all those imaginary situations is that of a society divided racially along North American lines whereas in reality the evolution of Caribbean race-relations has been along entirely different lines. That explains why Garvey's appeal to racial purity, as distinct from his message of Negro self-respect, has evoked little response, save for the marginal Rastafarian groups (many of whose West Kingston leaders, ironically enough, are themselves brown-skinned individuals), and why a volume like Dr Coulthard's *Race and Colour in Caribbean Literature* draws its examples of *négritude*, overwhelmingly, from Spanish and French Caribbean sources, a Jamaican poet like George Campbell being one of the very few English-speaking Caribbean poets to identify fully with that theme. The theme of Africa, again, to take a further example, is not a pronounced element in West Indian English literature, and the calypsonian's derisive piece on 'The Congo' speaks volumes for the attitude of the West Indian man in the street to the pro-Africa ideology. The Waugh novel fatally distorts all this. It only remains to be added that it was perhaps fitting that the actor chosen to play the role of the novel's hero-figure in the Hollywood film version should have been the Harry Belafonte (a calypso singer rather than a calypsonian) who has done so much to prostitute the art-form of the calypso for the Puritan American audience.

The emphasis on ethnicity, in fact, too easily encourages an over-pessimistic view of the society. Where every prospect pleases and only man is vile: there is a discernible tendency, especially in the professional academic literature on West Indian society and character, to see the matter in the light of the Augustan couplet. A whole body of culture-and-personality studies, for example—Hadley, Simey, Campbell, Kerr, Weinstein—has used the frustration-aggression hypothesis to build up a deeply pessimistic picture of West Indian personality deformation, just as other studies have tended to view the West Indian (particularly lower-class rural) family as 'deviant' or 'disorganized'. Both views are really posited upon a contrastive reference to the socio-psychological norms of middle-class Anglo-American individuals and families, which is valid if West Indian experience is seen as a derivative of that external experience: an assumption difficult, if not impossible to accept. To perceive the society in terms of general psychological characteristics may be more scientific than seeing it in terms of racial categories, yet it is noteworthy that much of the frustration-aggression thesis depends upon assumptions about the priority of racial feelings in the West Indian person. This is not to deny that the psychological burdens of slavery, race prejudice, colonialism and economic hardship are not real, but merely to insist that to seek to quantify their measurement in terms of concepts of 'normality' and 'deviance' raises important questions about what is, and what is not, 'normal' and 'deviant'.

For it is not necessary to accept the opposite extreme—that is, the view of the West Indian people as a 'happy-go-lucky' lot, the romantic concept of the 'colourful' West Indian ethnic mosaic of diverse groups, relatively equal in status and 'dwelling together in unity', sometimes accompanied by a sort of anthropological Rousseauism, especially when speaking of the Caribbean peasantries—to appreciate the remarkable qualities of tolerance, good humour, and sheer capacity for enjoying life, characteristic of the West Indian scene. The *comédie humaine* of the general West Indain life-style is too rich, too vital, too splendidly rumbunctious, to justify generalizations about a West Indian paranoia, either racial or cultural. This, after all, is a pre-industrial civilization (with the exception of certain oil and bauxite sub-economies); in terms of its economic development it is, on the whole, commercial rather than industrial; and its public opinion has grown up, historically, outside of the conventional structures of modern capitalist society. Until only very recently, it was a traditionalist society in which, as one observer a generation ago put it, the faded presence of the past helped to perpetuate the innate conservatism of the West Indian Negro and in which his remoteness from large countries and his lonely island life, combined with the fact that time had hardly moved since the days of slavery, made him hard to move and hard to change.[6] That, naturally, is no longer true, except for the smaller and more isolated groups. But it suggests the cultural roots of contemporary West Indian values and attitudes. In a society with such an extensive historical time-span, shaped by sources as diverse as Negro Africa and Elizabethan England—there are interesting anecdotes to be picked up in Montserrat attesting to the persistence of the Irish brogue among the Negro descendants of early seventeenth-century Irish emigrants to that island[7]—there is a variety, a vitality, of attitudes, a genuine eccentricity of character, the power to act, as it were, unpremeditatingly, and therefore to act naturally, a capacity for unselfconscious exhibition, 'making-style', that mark it off from the Anglo-Saxon Protestant bourgeois societies.

This can be seen everywhere. It is there in the way in which even a society as fiercely competitive as Trinidad, where the struggle to survive is accurately mirrored in the calypso's savagely cynical attitude to the troubles of life, can still manage to satirize the more avaricious of its members 'working for the Yankee dollar'. It is there in the splendid eclectic character of West Indian religion, for a society without a common tradition inevitably spawns an amoebic proliferation of street-corner sects; and even within the more ortho-dox framework of the more respectable congregations the expression of belief on the part of the West Indian common man has none of the deprecating, almost shamefaced, admission of faith so characteristic of more prosperous societies. It is there in the general 'promiscuity' of sex relations, for in a society where faithful concubinage, rather than marriage, is the most common form of family existence and where, too, legitimacy is the exceptional status and not illegitimacy, the traditional Judaeo-Christian view of sexual life is a minority view, and always on the defensive. The repercussions of West Indian sexuality, indeed, are far-reaching. So, in politics, it would be difficult to imagine a West Indian Profumo case; while in the area of West Indian-English social relations there is evidence to suggest—as Lord Kitchener's early calypso 'Norah' intimates—that the West

Indian migrant uses his alleged sexual prowess to meet, and defeat, the Englishman on a ground where the latter is notoriously vulnerable. All in all, it is not for nothing that the West Indian novel, since its remarkable beginnings in Mittelholtzer and Roger Mais, has been a picaresque literature full of social types, the 'saga boy', the West Indian 'spade', the cultist, the 'mystic masseurs' and the Rastafarian Jonathan Wilds, long since disappeared in the Anglo-Saxon societies under the weight of democratic standardization and social conformity. That quality, indeed, is even there in the work of a novelist like Naipaul who rejects his own society and whose novels are full of an atmosphere of melancholy negation which is, at bottom, the expression of the morbid self-contempt of which, perhaps, only the West Indian snob is capable. All of this, finally, receives its linguistic formulation, both in the world of the novel and in that of the West Indian street, in a language which swings with the response of all of the senses to the vivid quality of the immediate Caribbean world.

If, then, the society is to be characterized at all, perhaps not the least important interpretative principle must be that, quite simply, of territorial and, therefore, of social size. Most West Indians recognize the common parentage of their way of life; and central to the recognition is that all of them, even in Guyana and British Honduras, live in small communities in which the myriad ties of kinship, friendship, neighbourhood and associational membership bind everybody into an elaborate complex of mutual obligation. It is, in many ways, traditional village society with all of its features: the passion for intrigue; the malicious gossip, the famous Trinidadian *mauvais langue*; the enormous public importance that accompanies every private event, courtship, marriage, family relations, recreation; even death becomes an important social event and funerals important social symbols, so that, as one commentator has put it, a death notice in the *Trinidad Guardian* can cause more uproar and indignation than a Rudranath Capildeo statement from London; the public character of daily life that makes anonymity almost impossible, so that the habit of spiteful scandal-mongering, of the *gazette nèg*, the backyard talk, leaves almost nobody untouched, at any social level; and the same quality explains why a well-kept secret is a West Indian rarity, Dr Williams's success in keeping his second marriage a secret for one whole year being not the least of his remarkable successes; and, not least of all, the readiness to take offence at real or imaginary slights to one's dignity, perhaps the best known illustration of that particular defensive psychology being the ritualized pattern of 'eye-pass' disputes in Guyanese Indian village life, although there is also another variant in the form of Trinidadian 'fastness'. Nor are all these merely features of the more isolated villages separated from the larger centres by lack of transport and characterized by a tenantry-life of enforced idleness, with no electricity and no cinema, whose inhabitants perforce have to await a visit by a Government film unit or by a lecturer of the local Extra-Mural Department of the university for any form of entertainment. They are, equally, the defining characteristics of life in both the small towns and even the few larger West Indian cities, and if Ronald Firbank's early (1921) uninhibitedly malicious study of that way of life, *Prancing Nigger*, reveals them at the level of the small town petty-bourgeois elements of Jamaican life, a later book like Naipaul's *Miguel Street* reveals them at the level of big city street life in Port of Spain. It is—as is, notoriously, village society—a lifestyle of tremendous snobbery. It perhaps takes a visit by one of the members of the British Royal Family to bring it out in all of its splendid vulgarity. If the more lively imaginary descriptions, on the part of the West Indian journalistic wits, of what is likely to happen on such an occasion to all those who feel they have a natural right to discuss their intimate family affairs with the royal visitor seem to be excessive caricatures,[8] it only requires a reading of the lengthy and indignant correspondence let loose by the actual visit of the Duke of Edinburgh to St Vincent in 1964 to be made aware of its essential verisimilitude.[9] Sex, politics, neighbours: everybody has their own private little gossip about them all. Everybody, too, expects the audience to take the game seriously: 'if I lie, I die'.

It is another way of saying all this to say that the society is a popular society. Social pretensions receive short shrift, although that of course does not make them disappear. No social rank, not even that of the Governor, is privileged against sharp comment. The temper was noted by early visitors. 'Almost as a matter of course,' wrote an English resident-observer in 1852, speaking generally of the Negro mass, 'the West Indies have become extremely democratic.'[10] The context of the remark makes it evident that it was meant to apply to social manners rather than to social or political structure, being employed, that is, in the de Tocquevillian sense of the word 'democratic'. In part, as already noted, this quality was born out of the special character of West Indian race-relations, for the fact that the West Indian Negro, unlike the American Negro, was never a minority meant that he never accepted the classic minority-group psychology, the highly oppressive sense of being a Negro. His very numerical superiority, that is, gave him a relaxed self-confidence, a freedom, after Emancipation, from physical fear. This, even today, is the real difference between the West Indian Negro and the American Negro. What strikes, particularly, the American visitor is, first ,the calm self-assurance, void of either subservience or arrogance, of the upper-class coloured West Indian groups, so different, in at once their old-fashioned manners and their sense of dress, from the American 'black bourgeoisie'; and, secondly, the breezy self-assertiveness of the West Indian man in the street, only attenuated in those islands, like Barbados, where 'white ascendancy' has been more pronounced or, like Bermuda, where the white-Negro ratio is much more evenly balanced. In the phrase of one observer of all this, speaking even of Victorian Bermuda, a century ago, instead of being, as in the United States, a redundant portion of the community, the 'people of colour' in the West Indies filled a place of the utmost importance.[11] It is in this sense that, paradoxically, social democracy antedates political democracy in the society. This, of course, does not reconcile the subterranean social civil war of 'shades', of colour rankings, against each other; but it contains it within a consensus of common social views. It is at least significant that all of the various socio-ethnic groups share together not merely the general liberal values of constitutional democracy but, even more, collectively embrace a common image of West Indian personality. 'I think that when I was a boy,' Sir Arthur Lewis has told a University of the West Indies graduating class, 'the image of the West Indian was that he was a happy-go-lucky character. A good cricketer by nature, and not because he took the game seriously. A good dancer, and a wonderful companion at a picnic. Irresistible to women and proud of his string of conquests. I think we took a certain pride in understanding that life was meant to be enjoyed, and not meant to be taken seriously.'[12] The new slogans of work and discipline of the new nationalist political task-forces put this image on the defensive. But it is as yet problematical whether they will manage seriously to change it.

Until they do, the West Indian society continues to be immensely gregarious. There is a common passion for sports. There is a vigorous private house *fiesta* tradition, heir to the old plantation house social round, and there are standing invitations with most families to 'drop in' for drinks. There is an energetic, pulsating public style of living—in the street, going to church, in the market, on the beach, in the popular movie houses; for if in American life noise is the noise of machinery, in the West Indies it is the noise of people. It is, especially, the gregariousness of the West Indian populace, since the visual impression of the West Indian scene is one of a vast social canvas overshadowed by the faces of the friendly crowd. For the fact that the majority, in most cases, is at once Negro and proletarian reinforces the 'democratic' social climate already noted; because it means that although the white and mulatto groups effectively control the economic and political apparatus of rule they live, nevertheless, from the psychological angle, on sufferance, genially tolerated by the mass majority; and a minor variation on that theme is the confrontation between the expatriate liberal, or the returning Creole liberal, and the majority groups with whom they attempt to identify, so much so that it can become, as in John Hearne's novels, the separate material of one element in West Indian literature. Even the term 'middle class', so honorific elsewhere, can be used as a term of social abuse rather than of social praise for the reasons that (1) the 'middle class' elements, who are mostly professional and commercial people, constitute only a tiny percentage of the population, especially in those territories, like Guyana or St Kitts, that are characterized by a social polarization between what Martin Carter has aptly called the traditional house-slave culture and the majority field-slave culture, and (2) even where the class-structure is less rigidly stratified, as in Trinidad, the proportionately larger middle class groups have not yet managed to make of their type the model image, the representative man of the national community as a whole. The general result is that if in the future some West Indian historian comes to write a book on English culture and West Indian anarchy he will have to take note of the fact that West Indian society is not, as yet, anyway, a generally bourgeoisified society and its 'white collar' types—the lawyer, the doctor, the civil servant—are popularly regarded as individuals, the 'big boys', who jeopardize the national interest by foreign travel or conspicuous consumption despite the fact that, in many instances, they are subsidized out of public resources.[13]

This can be seen best of all, perhaps, in the folklore of West Indian popular entertainments. For if there is a common 'West Indian culture' it has been created, first and foremost, by the social classes at the bottom of the West Indian social compost, 'the view from the dunghill'. They, more than any others, have been the culture carriers, for the higher rung groups have been inhibited by the hybrid forms of European culture they have imbibed from playing that role. The bias of colonial education engendered a snobbish hostility to the popular art-forms, even to the very idiom in which they were couched, for as a person rose in the social ladder he has been expected to 'improve' his language and speaking style. Even the language of social protest has been that of the lower classes, and the interesting decline of French creole as the vehicle of political agitation in later nineteenth-century Trinidad, and its supersession by 'calypso English', reflected the decline of the French creole whites in the area of Trinidadian progressive reform politics, certainly after World War One. The post-1945 debate on 'West Indian culture', then, has really been a debate about social class functions. For the traditionalists, West Indian culture must be seen as an integral part of Western European culture, but possessing an organic relationship to the West Indian environment. The absorption of folk-culture elements is possible, in this view, but the leading offence of colonialism was not that it neglected and despised, as it did, those elements but that it failed to give West Indians full opportunity to inherit the culture of Western civilization and especially its English sector. For the radicals, on the other hand, the common experience which infects any cultural manifestation of genuine vitality in the West Indies is the special inheritance of the masses, who have created, and defended, their own art-forms as against the sterile borrowed culture of the educated classes.

The radical thesis, as the record shows, is undoubtedly the correct analysis. Much of the popular folklore, of course, has died from official hostility, as in the case, for example, of the *jamèt* bands of Trinidad Carnival, or of the ceremonial Moon Dance in Carriacou. Much of it has withered away under the pressures of modern times;

the Jamaican John Canoe tradition of old Christmas mummery has thus long since declined from its original rich spontaneity of Set-Girls and Grand Masters, as described in the 1830's in Belisario's colourful prints, into a pathetic survival of commercial-minded masqueraders not far removed from mendicancy. Much, again, is peculiar to individual islands, for the West Indian linguistic map shows a regional unity, based on the common acceptance of English, along with a variety of sub-regional patois dialects; thus, Selvon's portraiture of the racy, Damon Runyonesque Trinidadian dialogue can be read by all, whereas Louise Bennett's pithy pantomine verse is a closed book to all save Jamaicans. At the same time, much remains, as vigorous as ever. There are the 'Island Maroon', the Dance of the Cakes, the Parents' Plate of the wedding festival tradition of the Grenadines. There is the remarkable Big Drum Dance of Carriacou. There are the Christmas Cowboy and Indian plays of Nevis, the latest addition to the local indigenous folk-dramas which reflect the diffused influence of the post-war export of old Western films from the United States. There are, all over, the *embarass de richesses* of the popular folk-songs: the Shanto and Queh-Queh songs of Guyana, the Honduran 'breakdowns', the prayer-songs of the various cult-religions, the Jamaican market calypsoes, the Barbadian hymnology. There are the St Lucian Flower Festivals, especially the *Fête La Rose* and the *Fête La Marguerite* of the rival Roses and Marguerites societies, at one time invested with a political character. There is the dance tradition, so heavily documented, both before and after slavery, as to suggest a historical continuity unbroken by the great oppressive forces of economic and political organization. There are, finally, the religious cults, the Afro-Trinidadian *Shango-obeah* complex and the Afro-Jamaican Rasta-farian and *pocomonia* followings, providing as they do emotional release from the ordinary frustrations of lower-class life and from the special frustrations that accompany economic and political in-feriority; and, even more, providing, especially for the 'Rasta' brethren, a coherent world-view, at once social and theological, that rationalizes their view of themselves as 'black Israelites' living out their life of exile in the Babylonian Captivity of the Jamaican Egypt. It is possible to argue, as the well-known Herskovits thesis argues, that much of all this is evidence of African survival forms in Caribbean life. It would perhaps be more valid to say that they reflect, in their mere capacity to survive, the presence of continuing forms of economic and social slavery from which the West Indian common man must find relief and escape. They are a function, that is, of presently-felt socio-economic deprivations rather than proof of ethno-historical continuity. The fact is that, all in all, the West Indian person has been deprived of a meaningful kinship with his origins and has sought relief in sheer movement—dance, cricket, carnival, activist religion, migration itself. The outlets, in their turn, have taken on qualities of intimacy and spontaneity arising inevitably from the social traffic of small populations living an open street life in the sun-drenched luminosity of the Caribbean atmosphere. For the Creole respectability it was, until only yesterday, a world apart, to be viewed with suspicion through their half-closed Demerara shutters.[14]

The supreme example of all this, beyond doubt, is Trinidad Carnival. For what passes for Carnival, elsewhere, as in St Thomas, is mostly tourist gimmickry. The Trinidad event, by comparison, is a tremendous bacchanalian folk-fiesta drawing its vitality from at once a long historical background and the living processes of contemporary West Indian experience. From its opening moment of *jour ouvert* and the 'ole mas' costume bands to its finale, forty-eight hours later, in the dusk of Mardi Carnival, the Trinidadian populace gives itself up to the 'jump up', the tempestuous abandon of Carnival (to use the Anglo-West Indian term) or the Masquerade, the earlier Creole French connotation. The massive spectacle of it all— dance, design, colour—stuns the imagination as much as it exhausts the body, for its essence is participatory movement, so that merely to 'observe' it, without joining in—as a Barbadian, bereft of the capacity for *fiesta* by his Cromwellian-Puritan background, might do—is to miss the sheer madness of it all, the fact that it is, above all else, what Derek Walcott has aptly styled a theatre of the streets. From Marine Square to the Savannah, Port-of-Spain becomes a panic of mob art: the Sailor Bands, sometimes of five thousand or more masqueraders apiece, with their subtypes of 'bad behaviour' sailors; the Seabees groups, mocking their original United States Navy inspiration with their exaggerated high-ranking officer titles and overblown campaign ribbons; the impish humour which converts the Trinidadian coloured face into impertinent personifications of, variously, Texas Rangers, French Foreign legionnaires,

British Palace Guards and Nazi High Command officers; the fantastic costumes and headgear of the large 'Wild Indian' warrior bands; the more individualistic single or small group masqueraders like the 'Coolie Devils', the *Pierrot Grenade*, the Yankee Minstrels, the King Clowns, the Tennessee Cowboys; the tremendously elaborate historical bands, organized by their creative artist-leaders like Bailey and Saldenah, portraying, with an amazing historical accuracy based upon research that would put a Ph.D candidate to shame, the 'Grandeur that was Rome' or 'Zambesi' or 'Custer's Last Stand' or 'Genghis Khan and the Mongol Hordes' or 'Gulliver's Travels'; and accompanying all this, and much more, the strident musical confusion, with the emphasis more and more since the war upon the highly organized and fiercely competitive steel bands, their 'pan men' beating out the hypnotic spell of the 'road march', the crowd's favourite calypso of the year, the 'leggo', to the step of the characteristically arrogant strut of the calypso dance form, not unlike the preening shuffle of the mambo; not least of all, the beauty of the Trinidadian girl as she joins in all of this in her typical Carnival costume of tights, jacket and sailor hat. 'Mama, "dis is Mas" ': it is indeed.

For the social historian of the Southern Caribbean the import of all this is far-reaching. From the very beginning the pre-Lenten festival was the voice of the common Negro folk, thus following closely the South American pattern where, as in the Brazilian festival, a strong Negro influence reflected the great degree of social equality enjoyed by the minority Afro-Brazilian population and thus, too, being different from the Louisiana festival tradition where New Orleans carnival was maintained mostly as a European custom. So, although the Trinidad event was, almost certainly, of French origin, the fact that the planters and European officials did not care to identify themselves with the emancipated Negro celebrants left the door open for the African elements to become increasingly the major component, as the incorporation of the old slave customs, such as *Cannes Brulées* and the stick-games, emphatically shows; and despite prolonged efforts to Europeanize them, and notwithstanding that some of them have by now almost completely disappeared—the *chantrelles*, for example, the snake dancers, the Midnight Robbers and the formidable bands of the famous stick-men—there still remains a powerful undercurrent in Carnival of *shango*, *bamboo-tamboo*, *canboulay*, of the secret Negro cults of the Americas. It was the *jamette* class of backyard society that thus became and remained the custodian of Carnival. Similarly, the calypso art-mode arose out of social adversity, for the typical calypsonian, the *kaisonian extraordinaire*, sprang from the working class and the class viewpoint was pointedly evident in the calypso's general character. So much so was this the case that the appearance at the turn of the century of a great calypsonian, the 'Lord Executor', in the form of a white-skinned 'store clerk' of Venezuelan parentage was a rarity all the more remarkable since he was, by all accounts, the greatest of them all. The steel-band, finally, emerged in the post-1945 period from the social recesses of the Laventille shanty-towns, to become, as it is today, a new status symbol for its aspiring members. There is, then, no need to accept the pleasing local myth that Carnival 'breaks down social barriers' to see in it the brief annual revolt of the Trinidadian masses against a society which, for the rest of the year, has held them captive. The calypso themes, over the years of the modern century, make this clear enough. There was, to take random examples only, the caustic reply of 'Attila the Hun' to the Englishman who wrote a slanderous letter to the *Trinidad Guardian* in 1944 attacking Trinidadians as 'slackers' in the war effort. There was the admonition of 'The Roaring Lion' to Trinidadian girls to give up their partiality for the free-spending American soldier. There was, again, earlier on, the 'Lord Executor's' support of Captain Cipriani as the people's champion in the first really representative local elections in 1925, all the more noteworthy since, in the later period, the development of popular party politics and trade unionism have provided other outlets for social self-expression and thereby en-couraged the decline of the political calypso. The best calypso, then, was, and still is, the *chanson* that seizes hold of a broad social pheno-menon or a raffish social type or a piece of social injustice, and annotates it without vulgarizing it, mercilessly 'ragging' its victims but always, in the West Indian fashion, with singular unvindictive-ness: 'Sparrow's' *Benwood Dick*, or 'Lord Brynner's' *Rich Man, Poor Man*, or 'Melody's' *Ice Man* or, again, 'Sparrow's' satirical piece on colonial education, *Dan is the Man*. The poetic impulse of the calypso thus, is the proverbial folk-wisdom of the masses, achieving its end by irony, self-mockery or sheer irreverence.[15]

Yet since Carnival, and its accompanying *motif*, calypso, are essentially art-forms adapting themselves to the new social conditions of each generation, their history is, in itself, a commentary on those changes. The two great changes of the post-war period have been (1) the effective 'nationalization' of Carnival and (2) the increasing 'Americanization' of the Carnival-calypso complex, both in structure and theme. The first process started, probably, during the nineteen-thirties, when, having been until that time dominated by the barrack-room society, Carnival began to attract the 'better' elements, with their menfolk attending the calypso 'tents' *incognito*, and thus helping to break down the traditional barrier of the *Rue des Anglais*. The war of 1939–45 accelerated the process and unleashed forces—the economic emancipation of colonial women, liberalizing ideas about sexual freedom, the idea of nationalism—which helped produce changing attitudes to the Creole bacchanal on the part of the coloured middle class. The new respectability of the event, com-bined with 'clean' calypsoes and, after 1956, the official recognition of Carnival by the Peoples' National Movement Government as a national cultural heritage, all helped to break down the pre-war image of the 'jump up' as a despised, although secretly envied, lower-class black activity.[16] This has meant, among other things, a curious resurgence of the European element, evident in the privately-sponsored Chamber of Commerce Carnival production which, with its lavish shows, emphasizes the period costume, the fancy dress *tableaux*, in short, the genteel aristocratic European tradition of Schumann's *Carnival* piece; and, not without significance, the winner of the accompanying Beauty Queen contest is invariably a white or near-white girl. The new 'national' emphasis even reached out—although with, so far, indifferent success—to incorporate the marginal Indian and Chinese ethnic groups, an effort early on anticipated in 'Lord Kitchener's' *Double Ten* calypso (incorporating Chinese rhythms into the calypso structure) and 'The Mighty Killer's' *Grinding Massala* (incorporating Indian rhythms).

The second process, of 'Americanization', must be noted because it exemplifies, with special reference to Trinidad, a general process affecting all of the contemporary Caribbean: the diffusive influence of the American 'way of life'. The American military-naval presence in wartime Trinidad, as well as the post-war influence of the Holly-woodian spectacular-extravaganza type of movie, introduced into Carnival the heavily-financed and over-organized 'grand production',

2

like *Dimanche Gras*, in which the producer, like his Hollywood counterpart, enslaved himself and his cast to massive regal and statuesque crowd scenes, sacrificing movement to posed stillness. The sea of Carnival magnificence has thus become, increasingly, a showplace for the history, ancient and modern, of every country except Trinidad itself. 'Research is right', a local critic has aptly argued, 'but not into the decline and fall of the Siamese dynasties or the authentic choreography of American Indians in a war dance or, worse yet, the artistic canons in the proper stage production of stills.'[17] Under this weight, the satirical, the grotesque, the clownish, the witty, all get lost or diminished in importance. They still peer out, of course: the band that takes a hard look at Californian justice of the nineteen-fifties as it parades the Chessman case, the imaginative portrayal of Trinidadian birds and flowers, the steel-band which by its very name, 'The Johannesburg Fascinators', sticks out its tongue at the Boer Fascism of South Africa, the droll caricature of the famous Trinidadian murderers like Dr Dalip Singh and Boysie Singh. But they rarely get the big prizes, giving way to the big historical bands that are, in the same critic's words, merely pale exhumations of bygone ages.

A not dissimilar change has affected the calypso and the calypsonian. The new wealth of the mid-century period has revolutionized the economics of calypso. The sweet smell of success—which now means the lucrative recordings by the American record companies, the paid trips abroad, the Carnival money prizes—has converted the calypsonian into a performer, developing a Hollywoodian 'star personality'—'Lord Brynner's' shaved head, 'Sparrow's' Bogart-like controversies. He no longer has to suffer prolonged exile abroad, as did 'Lord Kitchener' a generation ago. Originally the lyrical satirist openly chastizing the economic system, he has now himself become a part of the system; and, inevitably, the gift for successful satire falters. The original folk-calypsonian, like 'Kitch', passes away. The melodic, delicate wit of a great artist like 'The Mighty Spoiler' gives way to the aggressive exploitation of the sex theme—the public controversy surrounding 'Sparrow's' *Mae-Mae* is suggestive. In part, this is the Americanizing influence, the confusion of bigness with greatness, the conviction that big money can produce great art, evident enough in the fact that a choreographer like Bailey or Wallace or Bobby Ammon will spend 30–40,000 dollars on the year-round preparations for his grand scenario. In part, it bespeaks the impact of the new nationalist spirit upon West Indian folk art and entertainments. The calypsonian, like the steel-band leader, becomes a symbol of the new national pride, the new national culture. A new state cultural apparatus appears, to organize cultural standards. He is told that he is important to the tourist industry; that he personifies the West Indian cultural identity abroad; that he must improve his public manners. He must strive to become a progressive element in the national life and not remain the 'antithesis of refinement and ambition'.[18]

To the degree that this *credo* prevails, the calypsonian might rapidly cease to be the wandering troubadour, licensed by popular will to comment as he pleases on social life—the idyll of 'Houdini's' calypso, *Arima Tonight, Sangre Grande Tomorrow Night*—and become more and more the money-making public idol, subordinating his anarchism to the pressure of what appear to be two contradictory forces: the aesthetic appeal of the higher Creole nationalism and the materialistic appeal of the American-style world of 'show business'.[19] Only the fact that the final judge of his competence is the street folk audience will perhaps offset those pressures. But whether that will be so depends, obviously, upon how those forces manage to reshape the character of that audience itself. A positive West Indian nationalism could make of him a vitalizing anti-American force, fostering a needed anti-American spirit as his predecessors created a popular spirit against English colonial politics. Conversely, a nationalism that was itself more political than aesthetic—and there is much, for example, of the Fabian spirit of cultural philistinism in the new nationalist oligarchy of the Trinidadian People's National Movement, not to mention a new official Jamaican nationalism which sees the international reputation of its Millie Small, a working class 'pop singer' from rural Clarendon, as the greatest of all testimony to the Jamaican 'image abroad'—could reduce him to the degrading status of a patriotic culture-salesman. How far West Indian individualism can resist those pressures, or at least adapt itself to their demands without being submerged by them, remains not the least seminal problem of the contemporary West Indian scene.

It has been argued in the most recent theoretical discussion of the

West Indies, that it is a 'plural society' in the sense in which that concept was originally used by Furnivall in his work on the colonial Far East societies, that is to say, a society characterized by sharp polarities of ethnic differentiation between its constituent sub-groups, those sub-groups constituting, in effect, separate socio-cultural worlds that, in Furnivall's phrase, may mix but do not combine or, as M. G. Smith, the leading Caribbean exponent of the thesis, puts it, constituting a culturally divided society in which 'each cultural section has its own relatively exclusive way of life, with its own distinctive systems of action, ideas and values, and social relations'.[20] The debate unleashed since 1960, after Smith's extensive formulation of the thesis in that year's Conference of Caribbean scholars on social and cultural pluralism in the area, is important, first, because in itself it embodies perhaps the first attempt by indigenous Caribbean scholarship itself to comprehend the society in terms of first principles (an attempt hitherto made impossible because of the paucity of intellectual life in the colonial society) and, secondly, because the applicability, or the non-applicability, of the Furnivallian thesis has important practical consequences for the future development of West Indian society.[21]

The difficulty with this theory is that as an explanation of the complex interaction between class, race and culture in West Indian society it fails at too many points to fit the observable facts. Based as it is, in one way, on a Malinowskian view of social institutions, it exaggerates the concept of society as a set of clusters of institutional sub-systems incapable of generating, at the general territorial state level, a harmoniously integrated whole. There is, presumably, a sort of progression from separatism to integration; but the argument provides no method of how it is possible to determine the point at which, on this socio-geometrical scale, variations within one institutional sub-group or sub-system become important enough to assume the effective development of integration with a rival sub-system. Quantitative measurement of such a process is, in any case, difficult if only because it concerns subjective phenomena of thought, attitude, feeling, imperceptible elements not easy to assess. The thesis is only persuasive if one accepts its inarticulate major premise that, in terms of a model, a completely integrated society can exist. Yet the difficulties Smith has in deciding what are the necessary criteria of 'pluralism' indicate that all societies, in some sense, are pluralistic;

the contradictions of his position are thus made evident in the fact that he denies that an advanced industrial society like the United States is pluralist, although he concedes that it is 'heterogeneous', despite the fact that, as Vera Rubin points out, all of his own criteria of plurality—racism, charismatic leadership, religious escapism, instability—all flourish vigorously in American life. [22] The dichotomy this is to say, between assimilated (integrated) and non-assimilated (pluralist) societies is artificial. Reality is more complex; cultural diversity between sub-groups can co-exist with institutional unity; incompatibility between groups, conversely, does not necessarily prove the existence of that 'absence of social will' which the Furnivallian thesis sees as basic to colonial societies; heterogeneity does not necessarily imply pluralism, and the failure adequately to define the two concepts confuses the issue; while the inherent tendency, as the thesis sees it, of the colonial societies to run to social atomization and political conflict once the hand of the metropolitan power disappears can be seen—since such conflict and atomization strikingly occur even in the so-called 'integrated' societies, as contemporary America demonstrates—not as the absolute axiom it seeks to announce itself as but as, perhaps, the rationalization of European observers, like Furnivall himself, as they suffer 'culture shock' in the presence of 'native' economies. The very measurement itself of concepts such as 'atomization' and 'conflict' (quite apart from the consideration that conflict can be either destructive or creative) is not subject to objective estimate. Different observers see the same things differently; so, as Braithwaite has noted, observers from the United States see the situation in the British Caribbean as one of relative peace, whereas observers from the United Kingdom perceive it as racial conflict. [23] There is also at play here the bias of professionalism, for if the West Indian cultural anthropologist, like Smith, tends to view the social pyramid from the bottom level of local community and kinship structures, the American political scientist, like Ayearst, tends to view it from the top level of the state political machinery; with inevitable distortions of emphasis in both cases.

These general considerations receive rich documentation from the empirically-observed data of the West Indian situation. There are, indeed, sub-groups of markedly different cultures. But they are not so much separate monolithic entities within a Hobbist 'state of nature' environment as they are sub-cultures increasingly subjected to formidable acculturative and assimilative pressures and gradually accepting a set of transcending common values. The continuing presence of hostile stereotypes that some members of groups hold about other groups has not prevented the growth of an all-embracing nationalism, as in Trinidad and Jamaica, of a peculiarly marked intensity. A process of 'creolization' takes place in which marginal groups, hitherto kept outside of the 'national' community by the colonial economy, gradually incorporate themselves into the emergent Creole culture, although it remains, as yet, a process pretty well confined to the educated, professional persons of those groups who accept the competitive norms of the class stratified society. Nor is this a relatively new process. The literature documenting it goes back, some of it, some fifty years or more: Clementi on the Chinese in British Guiana (1915), Luckhoo on the East Indians in the same territory (1919); while a great deal of it goes back at least twenty-five years or more: Andrade on the Jewish community in Jamaica (1941), the volume edited by Horton on the Chinese community generally in the Caribbean (1941), the work of Ruhomon (c. 1938) and Nath (1950) on the Indo-Guianese sector.[24] What emerges from the literature is the picture of the rise of a commercial and urban bourgeoisie of a mixed cultural character, its members merging with each other in social intercourse, frequently, it is true, for reasons of survival as economically privileged groups of long standing (Jamaican Jewry) or as *nouveaux-riches* immigrant families making their way in occupations, like trade and commerce, in which their alienism was a distinct advantage (Chinese and Indians); but sharing, nonetheless, a universe of common discourse, especially in matters of economic philosophy. They became a distinct class of professionals and merchant capitalists in West Indian life: the Chinese grocery and merchandise families; the Indian family dynasties of professional practitioners like the Luckhoos in Guyana, descended from the old patriarch J. A. Luckhoo, the great criminal lawyer and first Indo-Guianese be to made a King's Counsel; similar family dynasties, like the Sinaanans, in Trinidad; the Portuguese business families in Guyana like the Camachos, Pimentos, Santos and d'Aguiars; the Jewish-Jamaican business magnates, those, to take an example only, of the formidable de Cordova family, originally founded by the remarkable Jacob de Cordova, co-founder, among much else, of the *Gleaner* newspaper in 1834.

It is true that this assimilative process was unequal. The Jamaican Jewish *élite* remained throughout a high prestige group, as the frequent occurrence of its well-known names in the history of Jamaican public office shows. The Trinidadian French Creoles, on the other hand, after holding political leadership in the aristo-cratic anti-English politics of Port of Spain for nearly a century, dropped out after 1918 with the growth of a more popularly-based democratic politics. The Chinese, again, especially in Jamaica, remained throughout a physically distinctive group, failing generally to force an entry into public affairs or the higher reaches of business life; while on the other hand the Guyana Indian group successfully managed to go beyond the first historic phase of migrant-assimila-tion—the drift from plantation labour to commercial pursuits— and to enter the later stages of success in upper-class patrician business enterprise. The degree of social acceptability also varied. The unfortunate remark of the Anglican Bishop of Jamaica in 1959, in which he advised his congregation to 'go into a Chinaman's shop and make him a Christian', was proof that even many educated Jamaican creoles still accepted the stereotype of the lowly, unchris-tian 'John Chinaman' shopkeeper whose 'conversion' was a social duty somewhat comparable to the 'rehabilitation' of a 'Rasta' man.[25] The entrenched position of Jamaican Jews in the rigidly stratified Jamaican society, on the other hand, would make it unthinkable for an Anglican dignitary, least of all a coloured one, to publicly contemplate their 'conversion' to Christianity or, indeed, to any other rival religion.

It is another way of saying all this that there has occurred, as against the 'plural society' thesis, a remarkable breaking down of sub-cultural values in the 'minority groups' of West Indian life. The process, as here suggested, is most apparent in the upper social reaches, for nothing corrupts custom more than wealth and economic power. The best example, on that level, is, perhaps, that of the Jamaican Jewish community. For, like French creoles in Trinidad, these were the 'first families' of the society, and early on developed a powerful sense of Jamaicanism, even although passing episodes like the fight against civil disabilities might at times have retarded the process. The result was a gradual attenuation of Jewish faith and tradition. The historian of the group noted, in 1941, that there was only one copy of the Talmud in the whole island, owned by the widow of the late Hazan Solomon, and that so weak was the group's sense of international Judaism that there was no branch of the Zionist organization on the island; indeed, merely to read the list of the business activities and honorific public service appointments of a magnate like Charles de Mercado is to realize how fully creolized the group had become.[26] But cultural assimilation (not to be mistaken for racial admixture, although both processes sometimes coincided with each other) has taken place at all socio-economic levels. The very fact of having to work and live side by side in a new land forced the Indian indentured worker and the Negro creole, from the beginning, to accommodate to each other, just as, in a different environment, Mexican and American were forced to understand and accept each other in the United States-Mexican border areas. The general result has been that despite continuing 'in-group' attitudes in matters of dress, diet and family patterns, in other areas like attitudes towards government, education, leisure and the acquisition of wealth, the groups move more and more towards assimilated patterns. The development of the Trinidadian steel-band movement into a respectable middle-class youth activity is well-known; not so well-known is the gradual entry of creolized Indian youths into the movement.[27] All this, of course, is a process frequently best described by the imaginative eye. Thus, Naipaul's large novel, *A House for Mr Biswas*, is an extensive portrait of a Trinidadian East Indian property-owning family, the Tulsis, unable to stand by any original Oriental conviction, vulnerable, because of their colonialist credulousness, to the latest social or mental fad that they encounter, incapable of making out of their Hindu faith an effective defence-mechanism against cultural fusion, leaving their 'Indianism' to become, indeed, as it is with so many Indians in Trinidadian society, simply an occasion for 'making style', in the best creole competitive fashion, and a stick with which to beat offensive Creoles.

Even in the case of Guyana, where recent racial violence might seem to validate the 'plural society' thesis, the situation is a little more complex than that. Ruhomon, celebrating the first century of Indian life in the colony, perhaps failed to appreciate how much of the Indian tradition had in fact been retained, how, indeed, the general erosion of the caste system under the pressure of harsh economic necessity had not prevented its perpetuation, in attenuated form, in the continuing religious antagonism between Hindu and Mōhammedan. Certainly, too, he was excessively optimistic in his general conclusion that the growth of Indo-Guianese professional men and their various associations had brought about a 'denationalization' of Indians, fostered in turn by a 'community of mixed races where Western cultural standards prevail'.[28] At the same time, it was at least true that the two separate culture-spheres were breaking down, with the new competitive drive of the urbanized professional and clerical East Indian evoking, on the part of the Georgetown Creoles, a new racialism aggravated by what they saw as a threat to their traditional monopoly of certain areas of the national economy. The record since 1962, then, can be seen not as a widening of cleavages but as a discovery of them. It can be seen, paradoxically, as in itself evidence of fusion. For economic development and upward-branching social mobility in a relatively open society is certain to disturb the sort of factitious inter-group peace which in itself has in fact resided, in part, upon a high degree of social rigidity, in which relatively few people move out of their class-occupational niche and therefore present no felt threat to others. The Puerto Rican who told a recent observer that 'on the (United States) mainland there has always been a lot of social mobility and a lot of colour discrimination, here there has been little social mobility and little colour discrimination',[29] indicated the real key to the problem, that is, the fact that cultural disturbance flows from economic change and in colonial societies, where the democratic tradition has been either absent or at best fragile, may, in the early stages, generate social and political violence. Furnivall's 'plural society' thesis, it is worth adding, posited the continuing existence of a static colonial economy, the concept of Boeke's 'dual economy', the latter, in its turn, having been influenced by Sombart's theory of economic types. The thesis becomes increasingly difficult to apply—as a theoretical tool and as a measure of reality—to a West Indian economy increasingly dynamic under the pressures of modern development.

In the contemporary West Indies, indeed, there is, patently, a complex pattern of parallel social hierarchies—Negro, Indian, Chinese, Portuguese, European—each with its own upper, middle and lower classes. But cross-fertilization takes place by means of inter-connecting bridges between the classes corresponding to each

2*

other in the various hierarchies, bridges built out of economic interest, political affiliation, social intercourse, to a lesser degree, family life and religious practice, even surreptitious sexual relations. The older close relationship, in the earlier stages of the West Indian economy, between occupation and ethnic origin also imperceptibly breaks down. For it was an accident of colonial history, not a law of human nature, that the Asiatic immigrant groups, for example, entered the field of business enterprise and became identified with it in the popular mind. Barred from education, government and 'respectable' social life, the only escape from estate labour was the field of business entrepreneurship neglected by the other groups, and it was not surprising that the Asiatic, with the helpful tradition of the organized, patriarchal Oriental family structure behind him, seized the opportunity to full advantage. He and his kind were, and still much are, the object of great ridicule in the West Indies. It was only natural that, in the face of the contempt and ridicule, he should retreat more stubbornly into the protective cocoon of Indian or Chinese or Syrian ghetto life. Inevitably, the stereotypes shaped by all this stubbornly survive: that the Asiatic has an innate capacity, the Negro an innate incapacity for business, that the one is the 'economic man' with all of the petty-bourgeois acquisitive instincts, the other the spendthrift of the well-known West Indian creole 'personality image'. Sometimes, too, the stereotypes, inevitably, contradicted each other: so, at times, the Oriental is blamed because he is 'clannish' and 'won't mix', at other times he is criticized for his 'aggressive' intrusion into areas where he 'doesn't belong'. Sociological investigation has by now fully catalogued the gross obsolescence of the stereotypes, as the work, variously, of Broom, Lind, Crowley, Skinner and others makes evident. The 'minority groups' are being more and more absorbed into the general permissive Creole culture. Isolationism becomes increasingly difficult, more difficult to defend. Traits becomes less and less intrinsically 'Negro' or 'Indian' or 'Chinese', more and more hallmarks of the social ranking of the individual person; the quality of the Caribbean personality more and more grows out of the social relations set by the economic system. That this is, as yet, only imperfectly understood by the public opinion of the society is due, in part, to the continuing power of vested interests that seek to gain by racial prejudice, in part to the notorious inability of people willingly to embrace realities that, although existing under their very noses, violate every-thing that they have been taught to regard as part of the immutable order of things.

If, then, it is true that it is the criteria of class, wealth, education and general life goals, and not those of ethnic affiliation that come to shape West Indian life more and more, it follows that pluralist theory is applicable less in the anthropological sense and more in the older political science sense in which analysis is directed to the relationship of the sovereign state power to the non-localist associa-tions and institutions of the general secular experience. But this means that the alternative to the 'plural society' proposition is not to be seen, as some of its critics sometimes imply, in an effectively unified society transcending the divisional sub-group differences, but in a class structure held together, as Smith sees, by force and not by will. For to say, as proponents of the class-stratification thesis like Braithwaite[30] and Cumper[31] tend to argue, that the society is held together by a common loyalty to the values of the creolized British parliamentary tradition is to overlook the fact that, as Lowenthal points out, such a loyalty, even when in fact it exists, does not so much indicate that all share a basic way of life or common institutional systems as that each strives to advance by emulating the perceived behaviour of the ruling section and by discrediting his own way of life.[32] It is the weakness of studies like that of Bell on *Jamaican Leaders*[33] that they seek to prove the commitment of West Indian ruling *élites* to the general ideology of eighteenth-century liberalism and egalitarianism by using 'egalitarianism' in a politico-constitutional sense, rather than in a positive social sense, so that the deep power of class prejudice in those *élites* is deceptively underestimated. The fact, after all, that Mr Abe Issa is a dedicated federalist in an isolationist Jamaica only means that, as a business tycoon with extensive tourist hotel interests in the other islands, he naturally thinks in federalist terms; and the fact that Mr Pat Delapenha is known as the 'Prince of Monticelli' in his Mandeville bailiwick does not mean that he is likely to become the Jefferson of a new Jamaican Revolution. At times, indeed, the objections to the Smith 'plural society' thesis seem to be born merely of a sense of outrage that it emphasizes the things that divide West Indians and not the things, as the critics see it, that ought to unite them. The truth is, frankly, that West Indian society is based, primarily, on class oppression and paternalism (whether within or outside of the graded culture-class hierarchies) in all of its strategic ateas: government, education, the police system. Social bullying and economic intimidation are pretty much the order of the day in the life of the masses. Especially in the smaller islands, life is divided between a tiny *blasé* middle class and a broken and docile indigenous majority of peasants and workers. Nor does the political fact of independence in the larger units necessarily change the social system. It merely transfers its control from the metropolitan masters to the local ruling class groups. And because those groups understand the majority better than did the expatriate officials they might be able, indeed, to tighten up the psychological screws that hold the majority in their prison.

If, this is to say, the academic debate on the character of West Indian society is to be polarized between the twin concepts of (1) a plural society based on sub-cultural separatism and (2) social stratification based on social class organization, the socialist observer must enter a demurral. For to accept that form of the discussion is to embrace what G. K. Chesterton once termed the argument of the suppressed alternative. A genuinely harmonious society is only possible within the framework of a real equality, social as well as political. That requires the abolition of class privilege as surely as it demands the removal of ethnic prejudice. For, from this viewpoint, class feeling is as 'rational' or 'irrational' as race feeling. The 'minority group' individual who retreats into the shell of his culture group, in face of the difficulties of life in a hostile world, may, indeed, be acting as 'rationally' as the person who utilizes class prejudice in a similar manner. In a society like the West Indian, still full of rural poverty, urban rootlessness, mass unemployment and social insecurity, the haven of race, as much as class, frequently remains the only known and available hiding place. To which hiding place people turn will depend, clearly enough, in particular, upon the specific conditions of each separate territory and, generally, upon the capacity of West Indian society to solve those social and economic problems. Failure to solve them will inevitably lead to intensified resort to those defence-mechanisms, essentially sterile as they are: intensified class war, along Jamaican lines, or intensified race war, along Guyanese lines.

A society that manages in the future to tackle those problems with energy and determination, and within a framework of real and not just bogus social equality, would then be more ably equipped to confront its problems of cultural differentiation. The trouble, in one way, is that so far West Indian discussion has failed to identify with any clarity what functional role it wants its minorities to play. The confusion springs, in turn, from the larger failure to think out in broad terms what kind of society in general it wants to be. As Martin Carter has aptly put it, it is not only that the society is out of joint, but our idea of what West Indian society should be is also out of joint.[34] It is possible that since American social influence is the predominant influence in the region the American 'melting pot' thesis will gain popularity as the proper guideline to be followed. The consequences of such a choice would surely be disastrous. The subordination of ethnic differences to an American-style cult of democratic standardization would mean that the society would lose the tremendous richness that comes from ethnic variety. A local observer noted this a generation ago. Speaking of the Jamaican Chinese group in particular, but inferentially for all such minority groupings in the Caribbean as a whole, the ideal, H. P. Jacobs noted, should be the encouragement of 'that vigour which we so often find in minorities which decline to be "assimilated", yet do not regard the majority as enemies. A man should be able to feel that, if his physical type is different from that of the majority, the difference of physical type represents a new and special contribution to the mental and cultural achievements of the whole mass.'[35] The quality of West Indian civilization can only be enhanced by the acceptance of such an ideal.

For it is the mixture, both of individual person and general type, that remains the final fascination of the vital and handsome peoples of the West Indies. The mixture has led, generally, to mutual tolerance, if only because all types have had to learn the common devices of colonial survival, to live with each other. Their criticisms of others, even of the old imperial masters, has rarely been translated into personal bad manners. It would be surprising to hear of Englishmen treated in the West Indies as rudely as West Indians are treated in the United Kingdom. Even a Rastafarian radical who might 'curse out' an American tourist because he has read in the morning's newspaper about race riots in Harlem or about an insult offered to a West Indian visitor in a Washington hotel (a type of incident frequently reported in the West Indian press) will usually be his ordinarily inoffensive self the following day. A sense of social propriety is always present, so that even in the midst of the Guianese race-killings of 1962–63 it was possible for Indian and Negro villagers to organize an orderly system of house exchange with each other. Only the small groups of recalcitrant whites, particularly in the smaller islands, who are blindly prejudiced are immune to this quality, being capable of reprehensible behaviour, such as request-ing visiting English Test cricket teams not to embarrass them by permitting themselves, as visitors, to be defeated on West Indian soil by coloured local teams. And all of this goes along with a physi-cal presence, especially in the West Indian woman, of remarkable vivacity and beauty. Madame du Barry was so impressed with it that she devoted an entire chapter of her *Mémoires* to an eulogy of the beautiful Haitian creole Isabeau who so stirred up the court of Louis XV. The Rabelaisian eye of Père Labat likewise saw it and in a lyrical passage of his *Nouveau Voyage aux Iles de l'Amérique* (1722) used the beauty of the Caribbean *belle negresse* to support his grave plea for the rhythm of history which, as he saw it, held all of the islands together in a common destiny. 'I have travelled everywhere in your sea of the Caribbean,' he wrote, '. . . from Haiti to Barbados, to Martinique and Guadeloupe, and I know what I am speaking about . . . You are all together, in the same boat, sailing on the same uncertain sea . . . citizenship and race unimportant, feeble little labels compared to the message that my spirit brings to me: that of the position and predicament which History has imposed upon you . . . I saw it first with the dance . . . the merengue in Haiti, the beguine in Martinique and today I hear, *de mon oreille morte*, the echo of calypsoes from Trinidad, Jamaica, St Lucia, Antigua, Dominica and the legendary Guiana . . . It is no accident that the sea which separates your lands makes no difference to the rhythm of your body.'[36] That splendid invocation, today no less than in Père Labat's eighteenth century, remains the ultimate *raison d'être* of the West Indian scene.

# Chapter II

# THE CARIBBEAN BACKGROUND

THE HISTORY of the British West Indies is, of course, intimately related to that of the larger Caribbean region. The sweep of historical forces that since the Discovery have shaped the archipelago—colonization, slavery, the plantation system, sugar, Emancipation —has also shaped the West Indian society. The particular impact of each particular force has naturally been different in each island society, since the region's anomalous decentralization has worked to isolate island from island, island-group from island-group. That explains, still, the absence of any real Pan-Caribbean consciousness and the continuing political Balkanization of the area. At the same time, even so, the massive forces at play over the area have at least left a common historical experience and a common imprint upon its peoples.

The region, to begin with, possesses at once a great historical antiquity and a rich and brilliant variety. Its historical span stretches over four centuries. The first three great voyages of Columbus had ended before the close of the fifteenth century; Cortes entered Aztec Mexico in the same year, 1519, of Charles V's accession to the Spanish imperial throne; and by 1700 the four great powers of Caribbean economic and military aggression—the French, Dutch, Spanish and English—had established flourishing island and mainland colonies when the Atlantic seaboard colonies of Massachussetts and Virginia were hardly beyond the first stages of settlement. The consequent Europeanization of the islands and of the Spanish Main area produced in its wake large cities rivalling those of Europe in size and magnificence; the loot that Caribbean buccaneers like Morgan were able to take in their capture of cities such as Puerto Bello and Panama equalled the booty of contemporary European warfare with ease. The enormous racial and cultural variety of the area, still its ultimate fascination, stems from the fact that at one

47

time or another practically every European nation has joined in the scramble for the control of the region. Apart from the major powers —including the Portuguese in Brazil—the lesser European kingdoms also left their mark. The Danish kingdom ruled the Virgin Islands group for more than two centuries before their sale to the United States in 1917. The Dukes of Courland once occupied Tobago. Sweden ruled the island of St Barthelemy from 1784 to 1877. The Order of St John of Jerusalem, under its Grand Masters in Malta, ruled in St Croix for a brief generation in the eighteenth century.

Some of the Caribbean atmosphere, again, owes its origin to the European refugee. Barbados, after 1650, welcomed the English Royalist fleeing from the Protectorate. Jamaica, in the same period, was partly colonized, under Cromwell's Great Western Design, at once by Puritan and Jewish emigrants. The Portuguese Jewish refugees from the Spanish Inquisition likewise became active colonists in the American colonies, taking advantage of the great Dutch tradition of religious toleration as they entered Brazil and the Guianas. The influence of the American Tory refugees after 1785 in the Bahamas is well-known. During the nineteenth century British Trinidad and Spanish Puerto Rico, in their turn, became centres for Spanish conservatives fleeing the national liberationist movements in the imperial mainland colonies. To all this there must be added the impact, from the beginning, of every type of European adventurer eager to obtain his share of the legendary spoils of the New World and, in the case of the non-Spaniard, to despoil the hated Spaniard of his Catholic empire overseas. The Welsh Royalist, the Dutch Jew, Cromwell's transported Irish prisoner, the obscure Spanish soldier, the Puritan merchant-adventurer, the Catholic friar, all crowded into a society of brutal vigour and tropical brilliance in which personal greed and cupidity could assert themselves free from the caste and class restrictions of Europe. Esquemeling's famous account of the organized pirate society of Tortuga—*The Buccaneers and Marooners of America* (1684)—is, indeed, a perfect description of Hobbes's 'masterless man' in a social order that had hardly begun to control his instinct of anarchy. Most of the descendants of these early adventurers, of course, have been absorbed into the racial melting-pot of the island life. But the 'Redlegs' of Barbados, the 'poor whites' of Grenada and St Vincent, white descendants of transported Royalists, and the 'white zombies' of French Guiana, the liberated prisoners of the evil fortress of Cayenne, survive into the twentieth century as bizarre relics of the chaotic and brutal history of the region. And all of this, finally, has taken place in an arc of islands so overwhelmingly beautiful in its gifts of nature that from Columbus himself on its discoverers have been tempted, like the Lotus Eaters, to yield up the rest of their lives to its allure. The record of its enchantment, already manifest in the remarkable auto-biography of Père Labat, has produced its own unique literature, Lafcadio Hearn's appealing *Two Years in the French West Indies*, for example, or, more latterly, fictional reconstructions of the Caribbean Golden Age in novels like Patrick Leigh-Fermor's *The Violins of St Jacques*.

It would be easy to make out of all this a romantic saga of tropical paradises, a historical canvas of sex, piracy and slave revolt in the manner of books like those of Alec Waugh and German Arciniegas. There already exists a large tourist-oriented literature of that sort, perhaps the most dangerous being the type of lurid account of Haitian *vodou* that goes back to Sir Spencer St John's *Haiti : or the Black Republic* of 1884. The sentimental novel of an earlier literature did much the same thing for the European Romantic audience, St Pierre's famous *Paul et Virginie*, for example; while a novel like Michael Scott's *Tom Cringle's Log* preserved a genial and romantic vision of a splendid English Jamaica for whole generations of English schoolboys.

The reality behind the romantic myth could hardly have been more different. For Caribbean history throughout has been, first, the history of European imperialism and, second, the history of slavery. With variations from island to island the characteristic West Indian economy has been that of the extensive sugar plantation worked by forced coloured labour under European supervision for the ultimate benefit of an absentee ownership, a classic combination, that is to say, of white capital and coloured labour. The introduction of sugar superseded the earlier efforts to create a small settler economy, and the change, pregnant with so much evil, can be read in the description (1673) of Ligon's early *History of Barbados*. It immediately required a large and cheap labour task-force capable of heavy, unremitting work under brutalizing tropical conditions, and the demand was met, for two hundred odd years or more, by the slave trade. During that period probably some ten million Africans were transplanted, *via* the horror of the Atlantic passage slavers, to the American and West Indian colonies; and even now it is impossible to read the record, summed up most recently in the volume *Black Cargoes* of Mannix and Cowley, without a sensation of shame at the capacity of men to dehumanize themselves in the service of profit. The supreme offence of the crime could only be matched, perhaps, by the cruelty with which, earlier, the Spanish and Portuguese settlers and soldiers had systematically exterminated the original Arawak Indians by means of forced labour in the New World mines. The social organization of slavery, in its own turn, meant in effect the quasi-militarization of the plantation economy to apprehend the ever-present danger of slave rebellion. One has only to read a document like Lady Nugent's *Diary* written in her years as Governor's wife in Jamaica during the period of the Napoleonic Wars to be made aware of how much the fear of revolt was a brooding omnipresence in the daily lives of the planter class, requiring the almost continuous presence of a friendly naval squadron or of reliable 'home' regiments to allay its terrible pressure. Nor did the formal abolition of slavery in the nineteenth century release the Caribbean Negro masses from servitude in any real sense. It merely replaced the whip of slavery with the prison of low-cost agricultural 'free' labour. The ex-slave became, even at his most fortunate, a *petit proprietaire* growing tropical commodities—cotton, rice, coffee, tobacco—the demand for which was controlled in the world market by economic forces beyond his control. European capitalism withdrew its investments in order to redirect them to the more profitable fields of Africa and Asia. The Caribbean plantocracy, in its turn, sacrificed by its European protectors as Free Trade destroyed the privileged status of West Indian sugar on the world market, either sold out or stayed on to symbolize the decayed gentility of a depressed economy, dreaming of a 'golden age' that would never return.

Certain leading features about all this help to explain the contemporary crisis of West Indian society. In the first place, the society emerging after 1700 was a society of slaves and masters. The relationship, frankly, was one of an open exploitation of the slave as a chattel by the combined forces of planter and merchant, estate overseer and the overseas 'West India interest'; for, legally, he was an item of capital equipment only, not a labourer with personal status, and therefore—to use Edmund Burke's phrase about him in that statesman's speech in the 1789 House of Commons debate on the slave trade—dead as to all voluntary agency. Inevitably, the relationship brutalized both sides. It made impossible, as always with slavery, any spirit of mutual trust or devotion between the two sides. For a slave society, in the words of a West Indian apologist concerned, on the whole, to defend the institution, is one based on fear, and fear supersedes right.[1] The dictum of an old Antiguan planter—'The worse you behave to a Negro, the better he behaves to you'[2]—was only one of the cruder rationalizations invented to justify the system; the rest followed easily, to compile the well-known directory of myths about the Negro 'character' which survived even Emancipation. In such a world there was little room, on either side, for the serious cultivation of the social or intellectual arts; indeed, the art of combining slavery with the arts is a Graeco-Roman achievement the Caribbean planter class never learned. The testimony of every observer—Père Labat, Lady Nugent, Bryan Edwards, Père du Tertre, Humboldt, 'Monk' Lewis, Schomburgk—agrees in painting the portrait of a society of West Indian 'great houses' whose masters led lives fixed upon drinking, dancing, insipid conversation and sexual excess. John Luffman noted in the Antigua of the late 1780s the languid conversation of the women of the class, the rascality of managers, the opulent eating and drinking, as well as the moral blindness created by the ownership of slaves.[3] Schomburgk corroborated the general picture for the life of Georgetown society in Guiana sixty years later; where, indeed, ostentatious luxury had become so much the rule that the society, in his words, retained an extraordinary large amount of ceremonial stiffness and something in the way of unnaturalness and affectation.[4] Nor is it without significance that, later still, most nineteenth-century travellers in the area agreed in the observation that drunkenness, when it existed, was a vice of the white group, not of the coloured or Negro. There was, of course, the occasional master whose conscience got the better of him—Thomas Humphreys, for example, the Tortola Quaker whose money helped found the Institute for Coloured Youth in Philadelphia, the elder and younger Codringtons in Barbados, the Antiguan Nathaniel Gilbert whose conversion to Methodism in 1757 marks the real beginning of Methodist

missionary endeavour in the West Indian field. But these were exceptions, clearly enough. The master who attempted to be humane
to his slaves, like 'Monk' Lewis in his Jamaican estates in the years
following the Napoleonic Wars, rapidly discovered that he would
be vilified by his fellow planters as dangerously Jacobinical and that
his society would be shunned.

   Nor was the dream, in the British Caribbean case, of the rise, as
an early Guianese account saw it, of a colonial gentleman class
developing the life-style of the English territorial baronage overseas,
any nearer the mark of what actually took place.[5] Everything about
plantation society militated against such dreams of *noblesse oblige.*
The slave was compelled to live in a world of his own, a world
despised and feared by others, half-African, half-westernized, all
the more threatening to the master class because they were so ignorant of its real character. The forces of official society—law, religion,
government—were organized in such a way as to prevent his dissatisfaction from erupting into revolt. Home governments, no doubt,
attempted to enforce humane legislation to protect the slave; in
the Spanish case, to take an example, the comparative liberalism
of the legislation, culminating in the great Code of 1789, had its
roots in the mediaeval legal precepts on slavery. But the combination
of local interest and geographical distance made evasion relatively
easy. And even at that the various codes passed by the different
home governments were mild only in a comparative sense, for all
of them permitted various forms of physical mutilation as modes
of punishment against disobedience. Nor was the growth throughout the seventeenth and eighteenth centuries of ideas of constitutional liberty in the Caribbean calculated to aid the slave for these
ideas in large part were the vehicle of the planter class and its allies
in its self-interested struggle against the metropolitan executive and
legislative bodies. The fight of local assemblies against the imperial
powers, indeed, was calculated as much in pre-emancipation West
Indian societies as in the later Kenyan and Rhodesian colonial
societies to serve the narrow interests of the creole master classes
rather than those of either the slave class or the class of 'free coloured'
persons. Altogether, the slave lived under a tropical feudalism tempered only either by the individual owner's sense of humanity or
by the effective power of the home government to interfere. His
sole hope lay in servile revolt, and a reading of Captain Stedman's

account (1796) of the savage Dutch repression of the revolt of run-away slaves and 'bush' Negroes in the Surinam interior in the 1770's provides some appalling evidence of the fate that awaited the re-captured slave who had deserted his master. But revolt, nevertheless, was always around the corner, and the Abbé Raynal, in a famous and prophetic passage in his great history, wrote of the terrible retribution that would overtake the Caribbean slave society if the Negroes ever were to find a leader sufficiently courageous to lead them into a racial civil war of vengeance and slaughter.[6] The passage was originally penned in 1770. It was fulfilled, a generation later, with the emergence of the black Spartacus, Toussaint L'Ouverture, and the explosion of the great Haitian war of black liberation.

The second characteristic of the society, apart from this fact that it was a house divided against itself, was the steady resistance that it evinced, both before and after slavery emancipation, against out-side liberal influence; or, in other words, the intractable parochia-lism of its governing climate of opinion. Outside influence made its mark, of course, most notably in the prolonged humanitarian cam-paign for abolition. And, too, there were not wanting local liberal forces to help that influence; it was the astonishing fact, for example, that slavery abolition in Puerto Rico stemmed in large part from the remarkable Report presented to the Spanish Crown in 1867 by a local commission of eminent creole liberals, supported by the slave-owning class itself. On the whole, however, liberal influences were resisted fiercely by Caribbean reaction. Every liberal voice seeking to defend the Indian or the slave or even the emancipated Negro has been systematically vilified by that reaction's representa-tives. The great work of Las Casas, early on, in defending the origi-nal Indian populations of the islands against Spanish brutality was traduced by later Spanish historians as a 'black legend' purveyed by a traitor to the Spanish cause. The attack launched upon slavery by the French *philosophes* after 1750, summed up in the Abbé Raynal's magistral *Histoire philosophique et politique des établissements et du commerce des Européens dans les deux Indes* (1770), earned for its protagonists the bitter hatred of the white societies of the French Antilles. Similarly, the plantocracy of the British islands saw in the efforts of the Baptist and Methodist missionaries to offer a rudimen-tary education to the Negroes nothing less than an attempt to sub-vert the social order. The most that could be expected of any champion of the local vested interests was a recognition of the evil of slavery when it appertained to the members of a rival national group; thus Bryan Edwards, the 'moderate' voice of the English planters, could find no language sufficiently violent to denounce the Spanish extermination of the Arawaks in Hispaniola and Puerto Rico while he could conveniently forget the same humanitarianism when he came to discuss the slave institution in his own contemporary Jamaican society. Nor is all this of historical interest only. For the phenomenon continued on into the post-emancipation period. Lord Olivier, as a Governor who was also a Fabian Socialist, was not too kindly accepted by the conservative elements, expatriate and West Indian alike, in Jamaica after the turn of the century, and it is only necessary to read Governor Tugwell's account in his autobiographical volume, *The Stricken Land*, of the hate campaign unleashed against him by the 'better elements' of Puerto Rican society after 1941 because he refused, unlike his predecessors, to fit into the mould of a pliable and 'non-controversial' governor to realize how much of the historical exclusivism of the area has been able to survive into the middle of the twentieth century.

One corollary of this situation was that both under slavery and emancipation the world of the Caribbean masses remained a dark, unknown void. Transplanted forcibly from his African tribal culture the slave became, in the new milieu, a deculturated individual. Losing one world, he was driven to create a new one. The work of the cultural anthropologists has by now fully documented that truth, and it is reasonably certain that the survivals of the African transplantation, despite the famous thesis of Herskovits, were extremely small and scattered. In their place, slave society produced its own new cultural amalgam of African and Caribbean, the *Vodou* world of rural Haiti, or the great religious Myal movement of which present-day religious cults like the Shouters of Trinidad are probable survivals. But it is symptomatic that this Afro-Antillean 'new world', both in its folklore and its linguistics, was in large part ignored by the region's historians, with exceptions, in the British islands, of writers like Long and 'Monk' Lewis. There was a temptation to see that world either as a new multi-racial community moving, under the wise guidance of the slave owners, to a fuller civilization (the theme of a work like the *Annals* of the cleric-historian Bridges) or as, once the distorting element of slavery had been removed, a Victorian class society tempered by the civilizing influence of Christianity (the theme of a work like Gardner's *History of Jamaica*). And if, as in those two cases, the local resident historian knew little at first hand of the world of the masses that was even more so in the case of the creole planter class and the European humanitarian. The first rationalized his ignorance by embracing the myth of the Negro saved from the hell of neo-mediaeval Africa, the second by developing the myth of the 'noble savage', neither of which came anywhere near to a recognition of the anthropological realities. The truth is that even today very little is known of the thought patterns of the Caribbean Negro during his centuries of bondage, with the exception, perhaps, of the hints contained in the Anancy stories and the Maroon legends.

It is another way of saying all this—and this constitutes the third leading characteristic of Caribbean history—that not only the dominant institution but also the controlling attitudes of the society have been shaped, to a great extent, by the white European influence. Its ethnic composition has been basically Negro. But its social and political directions have been European. And, moreover, selectively European. For whatever the great European achievements since the century of genius may have been in art, technology, and science, it must be remembered that for the Caribbean, as for most other colonial areas, there has been little chance of access to their enjoyment. European control has meant, on the contrary, exposure to the less attractive attributes of Europe, its lust for adventure, its drive for expansion, its search for quick profits, not least of all the racialist arrogance and pride of the European man as he made himself, after 1500, the conqueror of the universe. From the very beginning, then, the Caribbean was carved up among the rival European state systems with scant regard for its own permanent interests; the Papal Donation of 1493 set the pattern of deciding Caribbean destinies by the power politics of European chancelleries. The consequences have been deep and far-reaching. Apart from the well-known economic and political consequences there was the fact that the European mind, in general, failed to apply the idea of equality—so much at the centre of European liberalism—to the subject Caribbean peoples. There is hardly a single outstanding mind in the history of that liberalism which felt able to accept the Negro as the equal of the white person. The reading public of Victorian

England received its impressions of the West Indian Negro from writers generally hostile to him. Carlyle's venom on the 'nigger question', Trollope's ingenuous paternalism mixed with undertones of anti-semitism, Froude's bitter Negrophobia, the latter serving the additional purpose, as one of his West Indian critics pointed out at the time, of an attempt to fight against the extension of democratic government in Britain itself[7]—all of them equated the Victorian moral ethic with white supremacy; all of them, too, contributed to the popular image of 'Quashie', the freed slave whose habits of laziness and irresponsibility were supposed to have been the major causes of the decline of the sugar industry in the British islands after 1834.

The attitude even pervaded, one way or another, the mental atmosphere of the friends of the Negro. There was real nobility of will and motive in the great humanitarians like Clarkson and Wilberforce in the British case, in the great liberal statesmen like Jefferson and Lincoln in the American case. But of the former, and especially of Wilberforce, it must be said that their concept of the Negro hardly went beyond that of a social child who should be protected against the power of his masters. And of the American group it must be said that its members had little insight into the cultural or anthropological roots of the 'race question'. Both Jefferson and Lincoln, of course, rejected the white master-black servant image. But Jefferson, following David Hume, believed in the racial inferiority of Negroes and penned, in a passage of his *Notes on the State of Virginia*, one of the most offensive pieces in the literature of racial animosity. Lincoln, in turn, was only slowly and reluctantly driven by events to replace his earlier concern with the salvation of the Union, even at the price of compromising on the issue of slavery with the slave-owning states, with his later acceptance of full civic equality between Negro and white. Later on, even the most liberal of American popular movements, the Social Gospel movement, for example, and the movement of literary naturalism, uncritically accepted the presumption of hereditary racial inequality. All in all, whether the prejudice has been racial or cultural in its roots, the white man, in the history of the long debate on the Negro 'problem', has rarely been able to divest himself of an inborn assurance of his own superiority.[8]

The ownership and control of the Caribbean and its peoples by

the outside colonial powers did not exist, of course, without a history
of effort to clothe it all in the protective aura of a philosophical
system. With the Americans, confronted particularly with the glaring discrepancy between empire and democracy, it was to take the
form of the argument of Manifest Destiny. But, before them, Europeans had established the popularity of the effort. The early Christian writers on the subject, both Catholic and Protestant, easily
accepted the classical view that slavery, as a condition, was the
consequence of either natural inequality or conquest in war. The
Deists agreed, here, with their orthodox opponents, so that Locke's
argument justifying slavery as a right of conquest was able to bypass the moral challenge to the institution implicit in the Lockeian
natural law theories, and influenced later writers like Paley. Other
British apologists, like Robertson in his once-famous work on the
*History of America*, adopted the view, promulgated by Montesquieu,
that slavery was a system made necessary not so much by racial as
by climatic factors. Clerical apologists were fond of invoking the
obscurantist argument of a divine will that imposes slavery upon
the world for purposes inscrutable to man. For those who could not
accept supernatural reasons (increasingly the case after 1750) there
was the semi-sociological argument of a 'dark Africa' from whose
heathenism the Negro had been saved, precariously based upon
dubious travellers' tales of the eighteenth-century kingdoms of
Dahomey and Abyssinia. Others, again, who could not accept the
argument of innate nature managed to defend the system on the
ground that it could be ameliorated by legislation and goodwill,
although they failed to demonstrate how a recalcitrant planter class
might be persuaded to accept amelioration; the argument received
a well-known expression in the *Account of the European Settlements in
America* published at the time of the American revolutionary war
and popularly supposed to have been partly written by Edmund
Burke in a moment of financial embarrassment.

The nineteenth century saw the rise of new and more sophisticated
rationalizations. An entire offshoot of social Darwinism came into
being to justify racialism in the name of eugenics and social evolution.
The idea of unequal social evolution was especially appealing, for it
was able to dispense with arguments about individual merit and bypass the compulsive logic of natural law. There was something of it
in Froude's *The English in the West Indies*, (1888), in, too, a book like

W. P. Livingstone's *Black Jamaica* (1899), the latter book indicating how deeply this line of argument had managed to infect the educated West Indian mind itself. But one of its more emphatic statements appeared in Benjamin Kidd's essay on *The Control of the Tropics*, published in the same year of 1898 that witnessed the entry of the American presence as a world power in Caribbean colonialism. The rule of the white man in the tropics, for Kidd, was justified not by innate superiority but by the cultural fact that the higher 'social efficiency' of the European and North American states alone could ensure the rational exploitation of the tropical economies. 'The first step to the solution of the problem before us,' he wrote confidently, 'is simply to acquire the principle that in dealing with the *natural* inhabitants of the tropics we are dealing with peoples who represent the same stage in the history of the development of their race that the child does in the development of the individual.' 'If we look,' he continued, 'to the native social systems of the tropical East, to the primitive savagery of Central Africa, to the West Indian islands in the past in process of being assisted into the position of modern states by Great Britain, to the Black Republic of Haiti in the present, or to modern Liberia in the future, the lesson seems everywhere the same; it is that there will be no development of the resources of the tropics under native government.'[9]

The most formidable presentation of all this, of course, was the American contribution in the years after the Civil War, laying the ground for the processes that finally converted the Caribbean into an American Mediterranean. Dr Weinberg's definitive analysis has listed them in tremendous detail. There was the argument that it is a 'law of nature' for a people to expand or, alternatively, that if expansion ceases, death supervenes. Or there was the argument of 'natural right', which then justifies claims to expansion by fiat of geographical propinquity, or by fiat of national security, or for the purpose of preventing the possible accession of a dangerous neighbour. Or, again, expansion could be justified by a theory of predestined geographical use, so that the alleged superior ability of the American to 'use' the territory he covets becomes, as in the case of the American Indian, a sufficient rationalization for expropriation. Even the dogma of the 'white man's burden' was taken over to do service, so that, from this viewpoint, it became the moral duty of America to civilize the 'backward' peoples, to spread Christianity, to prevent the sacrifice of native peoples to Catholic 'barbarism', like the actions of Spain in the Philippines. The religious argument was a powerful one with the American Protestant mission boards that entered Puerto Rico after the cession (1898) of the Spanish Antillean possessions and it suffered there, as elsewhere, from its naïvely demonic view of the Catholic power.

As far as Caribbean expansionism was concerned two further ingenuous rationalizations were invoked, to become the basis of a Caribbeanized Manifest Destiny. One was the thesis that the American nation was justified in territorial seizure where the occupying country hindered the interests of 'collective civilization' by its refusal or inability to cultivate the potential of the area under its jurisdiction, a thesis made more urgent by the fear that rival nations, like England, for example, with reference to the early case of Yucatán, might themselves undertake the task. This was the official justification, later on, for President Roosevelt's actions with reference to the Panama Canal issue. According to this thesis, the United States holds a vague mandate from world civilization to coerce a nation which by its selfish policy (in this case, Colombia) stands in the way of measures that will benefit the world as a whole. It was anticipated as early as 1826 in Representative Cambreling's observation, with reference to Cuba, that 'The right of Spain once extinguished, from the nature of our position, and our peculiar and various associations with that Island, our right becomes supreme; it resists the European right of purchase; it is even paramount to the Mexican and Colombian right of war.'[10] The argument applied, moreover, not only to the original use of virgin soil but also to the technical and economic development of already established communities. Thus, President Taft could speak of the necessity of remembering, when dealing with the Caribbean, that 'it is essential that the countries within that sphere shall be removed from the jeopardy involved by heavy foreign debt, and chaotic national finances, and from the ever-present danger of international complications due to disorder at home. Hence, the United States has been glad to encourage and support American bankers who were willing to lend a hand to the financial rehabilitation of such countries.'[11]

The other rationalization used to justify American action, apart from this one of world trusteeship, concerns the self-conceit of

Americans as the greatest exponents, as they have viewed themselves, of 'democracy' that the world has seen. In peculiarly American fashion the argument has seen democracy not merely as a system of civil government but also as a moral condition, and it becomes the duty of America to export it to other societies. That representative institutions of the liberal type were the expression of a particular set of socio-historical conditions in the industrially advanced societies of the nineteenth century rather than springing from a moral absolute of politics seems not to have been appreciated by most American leaders, and even a mind as sophisticated as Wilson was able to combine a theoretical perception of that truth with a passionate belief in the obligation of America to impose 'good government' on less fortunate peoples. His remark to Sir William Tyrrell— 'I propose to teach the South American Republics to elect good men'[12]—meant, in effect, as it was bound to, American intervention in the internal affairs of those countries and American sponsorship of leader-candidates who satisfied the definition of 'goodness'. The spirit no less than the purpose of this type of compulsory democracy was illiberal, for it had about it a self-righteous condescension to those supposed to benefit from it, the worst example, of course, being the arrogant contempt of the opprobrious epithets hurled by President Roosevelt against the Bogota politicians who resisted American pressure throughout the Panama affair. Yet even when a more cultured mind, such as Root's, was at the helm in the State Department, the open contempt was replaced, not by a new friendly spirit but by a secret patronizing tone; and the Secretary's remark that the people of Central America 'are perfectly willing to sit at the feet of Gamaliel if Gamaliel won't kick them or bat them on the head'[13] was no less an expression of Anglo-Saxon arrogance. Franklin Roosevelt, it is true, repudiated the idea, behind all this, that the United States had a right through a doctrine of paramount interest to act alone as the policeman of the hemisphere. He insisted that 'when the failure of orderly processes affects the other nations of the continent . . . it becomes the joint concern of a whole continent in which we are all neighbours'.[14] But that was in 1933, before the new president had had a chance to invent institutional methods more appropriate to a foreign policy of genuine collaboration.

The later post-1945 period, under the clamant pressures of Cold War diplomacy, finally shattered that idea. The tragically short-lived Kennedy experiment of the Alliance of Progress over, the American power succumbed to the temptation to revert to the 'big stick' methods of the earlier period, and the massive intervention in the Santo Domingo affair of 1965 added a new weapon to the armoury of Manifest Destiny thought, the doctrine of 'preventative intervention' to forestall the growth of possible left-wing revolutions in the region. In the light of that record, coming fast on the heels of CIA-sponsored insurrectionist plots against the Cuban regime, it becomes laughably implausible to argue, with the later emendators of the Manifest Destiny doctrine, that the doctrine has never been supported by majority American opinion or that a distinction can be made between Manifest Destiny imperialism and a national sense of mission in which the United States sets itself forth as a model for less-favoured nations and as the champion of international public philanthropy. There is, in grim truth, little evidence to suggest that either American public opinion or American leadership understands or accepts that distinction.[15]

Two footnotes ought to be added to this account of European and American theories of colonial justification. The first is that, with the possible exception of the Quakers, the organized churches of the Western metropolitan culture rarely challenged in their official capacity the depressed status of the Caribbean native peoples. They undertook no root and branch onslaught upon slavery; the British Society for the Propagation of the Gospel even had its own slaves, albeit under trust, in the West Indies. It was the deist Assembly of the French Revolution, not the Christian nations, that first abolished slavery in 1791, forty-three years before England and eighty-two years before Spain. And even the Quaker record was a hesitant one. Its influence in the region probably started with the visit of George Fox to Barbados and Jamaica in 1671. But that great stalwart contented himself, at this time, with meeting-house sermons admonishing the owners of slaves to treat them as human beings, to inculcate in them respectable habits of marriage and to set them free 'after a considerable term of years, if they have served them faithfully'.[16] Religious enterprise in the colonies, in any case, like economic enterprise, was hardly calculated to attract the best of men, despite the noble work of the Methodist, Baptist and Moravian missionaries. Hurrell Froude's Puseyite *cri de coeur*, uttered from his position in exile as mathematics master at Codrington College—

'Negro-land is a poor substitute for the threshold of the Apostles'—was the more standard reaction of clerical England in the West Indian vineyard.[17] Altogether, the influence of organized religion was thrown into support of the *status quo*, as reflected in the 1816 instructions given to the missionary John Smith, that he was sent out not to relieve the slaves from their servile condition but to afford them the consolations of religion.

The second additional point to be noted is that the alignments of attitudes in the imperial centres during this prolonged debate did not always reflect the traditional liberal-conservative dichotomy. The prevaricating attitude of the Enlightenment has already been noted, witness as one further example the fact that Montesquieu could pen a celebrated passage in the fifteenth book of his great work in which he justified slavery by denying common sense or moral sentiment to the Negro. On the other hand, writers usually conservative in their attitude to domestic topics could be surprisingly humanist on this issue; thus, Dr Johnson could oppose the system of slavery on grounds of natural liberty and could even utter, while on a visit to Oxford, a toast to 'the next insurrection of the Negroes in the West Indies' which Bryan Edwards reported in tones of scandalized horror. Later on, the picture became somewhat more logical, so that whereas Froude's angry tract against West Indian society was all of a piece with his conservative position in domestic English Victorian politics, Kingsley's sympathetic book on the other hand—*At Last: A Christmas in the West Indies*—was directly related to the roots of his liberalism in his earlier Christian Socialist period.

The apologetic literature, both European and American, was thus lengthy and formidable. Yet it was curiously ineffective. In its European manifestations especially, when it dreamed of the imperial regeneration of the colonies, it struck foundations of sand, for the reason that by 1850 most of the European 'mother countries' had decided that West Indian enterprise was a losing concern, thus making it all the easier for the United States to step into the void, especially after 1898. Writers like Froude dreamed, Carlylean-wise, of a benevolent imperial paternalism coaching the colonial peoples into a fuller maturity, protecting them at once against their own weaknesses and the shortcomings of the merely utilitarian system of commercial empire. The realities were far different; and Tory

Democracy succeeded no more in the colonies than it did at home. For as the twin gospels of Free Trade and domestic free enterprise came to dominate European policies both the Caribbean planter and the Caribbean peasant were compelled to shift for themselves. That Emancipation and the withdrawal, later, of Protectionism should have been seen as the beginning, and not the end, of a positive philosophy seeking to reconstruct Caribbean society on new developmental principles was an insight unappreciated by economic individualism. 'The gift of freedom,' a recent student of the matter has concluded, 'could not by itself transform the recipients or endow them with a nineteenth-century European conception of utility as the proper test of progress.'[18]

The subsequent history of the region graphically illustrated the truth of the remark. By the end of the nineteenth century, as a result, the Caribbean had become, in place of its once splendid tradition, a forgotten derelict corner of the world, a condition that remained, indeed, until the strategic imperatives of the Second World War brought the area back into the limelight. The occasional literature produced upon it was by the occasional traveller who almost stumbled upon it, as had done Columbus in the beginning, by accident. It became a precarious 'windfall economy', dependent upon intermittent bursts of activity like the construction of the Panama Canal. As the metropolitan mercantile houses withdrew their capital from the islands the latter declined into a state of somnolent stagnation. Nevis, once the Saratoga of the older class of West India gentry, degenerated into a forgotten outpost, as it still remains; the Bahamas, once the rich centre of the Civil War blockade runners to the Confederate ports, declined equally catastrophically; while it is almost possible to read Froude's indignant chapters on the scandalous neglect of Dominica as a description of that island's contemporary state. Changes of technology helped to accelerate this process. The growth of the steam ship and the replacement of coal with oil dealt a sharp blow to those ports, like St Thomas, that had been the important terminal points of the transatlantic commerce, and to those ports, like Castries, St Lucia, that had been prosperous coaling stations for maritime traffic. The concomitant decline of sailing traffic, along with greater safety at sea, also helped to eliminate the old 'wrecking' industry of the Bahamas, as well as that of small islands like Barbuda which had lived for generations off that unhappy trade.[19] The general indifference of the 'home' governments to all of this was only emphasized for what it was by the spasmodic interest of an energetic Colonial Secretary, Joseph Chamberlain, for example, in the British case. The Caribbean thus slipped away quietly from the notice of the world. It is no exaggeration to say that as late as the 1930s, on the eve of the general political awakening of the West Indian peoples, the sociological discovery of the area was at pretty much the same stage that its geographical discovery had been four centuries earlier, the publication, indeed, in 1929 of Maria Beckwith's *Black Roadways* constituting, perhaps, the first serious attempt to comprehend the life and thought of the West Indian masses from the viewpoint of the professional social-sciences disciplines.

The Caribbean has thus been throughout its history the pawn of European and, later, of American power struggles. It provided a theatre for the display of imperial sea power, and if the battle of Waterloo was won on the playing fields of Eton it is certain that the victory at Trafalgar was guaranteed in the waters of the Antilles. That is why it has been so easy for English popular writers on the region to see it as primarily the nursery of the British Navy and the scene of Homeric encounters with the traditional French enemy. The kaleidoscopic fortunes of the islands have been made and unmade by the treaty arrangements of European congresses or, more latterly, as with the 1940 Anglo-American bases-destroyers deal, of British Prime Ministers and American Presidents. Just as the commercial revolution of Europe after 1600 made their fortunes, so after 1800 the industrial revolution of Europe unmade them. The European progressive elements, it is true, devoted great idealism to the native Caribbean cause, as Wordsworth's noble *Sonnet to Toussaint l'Ouverture* testified. But the decline of revolutionary fervour in Europe after 1848 meant, correspondingly, a decline in that interest. As with all societies in decline, the genius and talent of Antillean life were driven abroad in search of opportunity and recognition: Alexander Hamilton in the eighteenth century, the Dumas family in the nineteenth, the young artists and writers of the present day. The modern revolutions of nationalism and democracy by-passed the region, only to catch up with it haltingly after 1918 and with increased momentum after 1945.

The society, as a result, has rarely been seen in its own light and on its own terms. It has been seen, rather, by friend and foe alike, through the naturally distorted perspective of the imperial governing class or of the traveller in a hurry or of friends in metropolitan capitals. The early Spanish and French writers saw it almost exclusively through the mirror of Catholic Christianity. An entire library of histories and travel tales retailed the region to the European reading publics as the *locus* of fantastic legends and heroic adventures clothed in an imaginary West Indian chivalry, from Sir Walter Raleigh's dream of the fabulous Guianas and the New World sections of Rabelais' great picaresque novel, to *Robinson Crusoe* and *Treasure Island*. The later literature of the academic historians, in its turn, has been composed from the expatriate viewpoint, seeing developments within the Caribbean as simply appendices, one way or the other, to the histories of the respective 'homelands'. Books like Mary Proudfoot's *Britain and the United States in the Caribbean* and Sir Harold Mitchell's *Europe in the Caribbean* are examples; while even an author as sympathetic as Sir Alan Burns can make of his *History of the British West Indies* a narrative, on his own account, concentrating on the white conquerors and settlers since the Negro masses had 'little to do' with the shaping of events: a thesis only tenable within the narrow framework of a Whig historiography of Churchill-like 'events'.[20] The economic dependency of the societies of the Middle American district on absentee-owned capitalist enterprise has thus been echoed in their intellectual dependency, until only very recently, on absentee-sponsored academic enterprise.

What all this has meant for the *homo caribiensis*, both in terms of socio-economic oppression and psychological deprivation, it would, even now, be difficult to estimate. The fact that so much of the regional history has been a reflection of the struggles between rival overseas powers for the massive profits of sugar and slavery has tended to obscure the graver social and psychological consequences of the situation. Yet those consequences are, in large measure still, the key to the contemporary West Indian society. Forcibly uprooted from his African cultural *ambiente*, first detribalized and then deculturated, the Negro slave was compelled to adjust to an utterly alien life-style. His descendants, both black and coloured, have inherited the tortured ambivalence of his position. They have lived in, first, the slave society and, second, the creole society controlled by ruling groups resident in the tropics only so long as they could

3

reap a profit. The creole concept of 'home' has thus suffered from a snobbish attachment to the 'mother country', thereby seriously inhibiting the growth of an effective local sense of citizenship. The alienation of government from the popular life left behind a popular suspicion of all government, so that the West Indian of today is almost a natural anarchist. The classic heritage of slavery—the identification of manual labour with a status of social degradation— has managed still to survive, so that the region's agricultural industries continue to suffer from occupational preferences for 'white collar' jobs; likewise, the 'go-slow' tactic evolved by the slave field-hand as his only defence mechanism in the plantation regime, has remained to condition continuing popular West Indian attitudes to work. The luxuries of existence—fine houses, good food, travel— have been reserved for the white ruling group and the coloured middle class *élite* in the civil service and commercial enterprise. The average labourer of the society, as the Moyne Commissioners of 1938–39 noted in the British case, has been more strictly confined to his own island than the English village labourer of the eighteenth century was tied to his parish in the most rigid phase of the Settlement Laws. Nor has the educated West Indian successfully identified himself with Caribbean values, for he has been shaped by a process of pedagogical indoctrination in which the 'pleasures of exile' have been seen as more desirable than the responsibilities of local life; so that Caribbean society has become well acquainted with the psyche of his cultural maladjustment. The general historical experience of the Caribbean Negro peoples, all in all, has not been unlike that of the European Jew. Both of them have been uprooted peoples at the perennial mercy of the forces of migration and accident. 'Like the Jews,' a Jamaican observer noted in 1899 of his own folk, 'they have had unforgettable experiences. They have come through the wilderness, through a land of drought and of the shadow of death, through a land that no white man has passed through, and where no white man has dwelt, and the misery and loneliness of it all is still with them. The more they evolve and the more they know, the more the heritage of the race becomes a mystery, strange alike in its origin and in its intolerable pressure upon every moment of their lives.'[21] The analogy explains why so much of Caribbean literature, like Jewish literature, has been a literature of exile: Zobel's *Fête á Paris*, Selvon's *The Lonely Londoners*, Cotto-

Thorner's *Tropico en Manhattan*. Not the least of the promises held out by the achievement of national independence will be, perhaps, the final termination of the West Indian *diaspora*, to be replaced with the West Indian homecoming.

As the Caribbean thus entered the twentieth century it was a society of poverty, neglect, despair, devoid of any real community consciousness. The mutual distrust of transplanted black and expatriate white, as Philip Curtin's book *Two Jamaicas* has shown in the case of Victorian Jamaica, perpetuated disharmony in a society where perhaps only the intermediate group of 'free coloured', the *affranchis*—the only group created whole out of the Caribbean environment—felt in any real sense at home. Colonial government, in turn, placed a premium upon that disharmony, since it divided local opinion by attaching to itself local elements, usually from the lighter 'shades', whose advancement then lay in the art of pleasing the imperialist ruling group. And even when colonialism was replaced with independence, as in Haiti, the Dominican Republic, and the Central American states, it turned out to be a Pyrrhic victory, inasmuch as the external struggle against the European powers merely gave way to an internal class-colour struggle between mulatto middle class and black rural masses. For although 1789 ended the aristocracy of white economic power in the case of the politically free islands, it did nothing to prevent its supersession by the aristocracy of colour.

It would, indeed, be a Herculean task to estimate the terrible ravage worked by colour-psychology in Caribbean life, both past and present. It is true that the barriers between white master and black colonial did not grow into rigid caste lines nor, indeed, generate the brutalizing hatreds of racial-colonial violence; Fanon's thesis of the moral necessity of violence as the purgative of colonialism, if it applies to the Caribbean at all, applies more to the special case of Haiti than it does to the English-speaking territories. At the same time, however, the disease of racialism took on other, more subtle forms. A value-system grew up emphasizing skin-colour and ethnic affiliation as the badges of social respectability. A complex system of social stratification compelled a vast and disproportionate volume of individual thought and energy to be consumed in the search for acceptance by the light-skinned and white groups. A coloured middle group distrusted the European whites, but it feared the black mass even more; and the awful fate of the Haitian coloured group as it suffered periodical attempts at extermination at the hands of the Negro majority did little to allay the fear. Energy and talent that should have gone into creative social activity thus got wasted in the personal struggles of men and women who had been taught by everything in their society to be half-ashamed of their colour. Bitterness, frustration, chauvinism became the dominant elements of their existence. Social pressures either produced, on the one side, an art of evasive deference to superiors, the famous Puerto Rican docility, for example, or, on the other, an aggressive individualism, the defiant contempt for authority so much a part, to take another example, of the Trinidad calypso. Those defence mechanisms were then invoked by the dominant groups as evidence to justify resistance to each successive popular movement for reform, slavery abolition, economic emancipation, universal suffrage, political independence. All in all, it is not too much to say that by 1900 the European liberal spirit had succeeded in releasing the Caribbean peoples from the more onerous of their objective burdens but had done little to relieve them of the equally oppressive subjective burdens laid upon them by colonialism. That task remained, still, a task for the future.

# Chapter III

# BRITISH COLONIALISM

## THE SOCIAL LEGACY

THE English Antillean society has thus to be seen as an integral part of the larger Caribbean society. At the same time it possessed, of course, its own distinctive features. For each metropolitan culture-system left its special mark upon its colonial subjects, the French in Martinique, the Dutch in Surinam, the Spaniards in Cuba. The English in the West Indies did likewise, creating a local culture almost utterly derivative of the most suburban of English values, even although geographically remote from the ancestral sources. They did this the most successfully in those islands, like Barbados and Jamaica, where a cultural *tabula rasa*, as it were, awaited their imprint; a society like Trinidad, with some two centuries of Spanish and French occupation preceding the English ownership, did not so readily surrender itself to a complete Anglicization. That, as much as anything else, explains why, even today, to pass from Bridgetown to Port of Spain is to pass from a tropical English market town to a bizarre and Byzantine city life, and why the centre of West Indian society as a culture *sui generis* is Trinidad and not Jamaica. Even in Trinidad, however, the main directive force has been English, so much so that the territory's physical contiguity to the Latin American mainland has had surprisingly little effect upon its socio-cultural development. West Indians, then, as a people, have been shaped mainly by England, and they are indeed not the least English when they are in revolt against the system England has created. That is why even the radical nationalist, like Dr Williams, can at the same time be an ardent Oxonian; why the literary native son, like Vida Naipaul, can describe, Dickens-like, his own local culture at the same time as he reveals his own rejection of it in favour of an East Indian Englishness; and why the professional West Indian Trotskyite insurrectionist, like C. L. R. James, can at the same time constitute himself the fulsome Victorian-like eulogist of the English gentleman class. It has been rare even for the West Indian intelligentsia, who might have done better, to look beyond the horizons of their society as an English cultural dependency, and an exception like the late Adolphe Roberts, whose book *The French in the West Indies* marked him off as a romantic Jamaican nationalist of the Latin rather than of the Anglo-Saxon persuasion, only proves the general rule.

The character of the old West India society before 1834 has already been noted. It was replaced, after that date, by the post-abolition society which prolonged itself, with unimportant changes, until the advent of cataclysmic events—the widespread riots of 1935–38, the outbreak of the Second World War, the break-up of the old colonial empires after 1945, the growth of nationalism—forced upon it revolutionary changes that have still (1968) not yet run their full course. For a whole century, that is to say, the new free-labour tropical society established by Emancipation developed along lines set by Victorian Christian bourgeois modes of thought. It was, almost completely, a unilateral relationship, since, as minor colonies, the West Indian local capitals stood little chance of influencing the metropolitan culture or politics. The crisis over the Jamaican constitution that precipitated the downfall of the Melbourne government in 1839 marks the end, in fact, of serious West Indian influence on British politics, a fact finally demonstrated by the failure of the London Jamaica Committee nearly thirty years later to embarrass in any serious way the Derby government of 1865 on the occasion of the Jamaica Morant Bay 'rebellion' of that year. Cultural influence was even less apparent, and the image of the West Indies that flourished in England was somewhat that of the Jamaican passages of *Jane Eyre*, a sort of sinister Gothic background productive of miscegenation and madness; notwithstanding the fact that the Antigua of Jane Austen's Sir Thomas Bertram and the St Kitts of Thackeray's 'woolly Miss Swartz' were regular mines of wealth supporting dozens of Mansfield Parks all over England. It must also be noted that the final success of the abolitionist movement terminated the popularity of the West Indian theme embodied in the English anti-slavery literature of the Augustan age and ably documented in Wylie Sypher's *Guinea's Captive Kings*. That explains why, even up to the present day, the average Englishman's conception of things West Indian has been a mixture of uninformed prejudice and paternalist condescension, so that even as late as the 1940's Lord Olivier could complain that his own authoritative books on Jamaica had been received in the London journals as if they were merely guidebooks for the West Indies as a charming residence and not a studied defence of the West Indian subjugate native peoples against colonial capitalism.[1] And not the least ironic aspect of the Englishness of the West Indies was the fact that West Indians for so long preserved among themselves a Victorian Anglophilism, an almost imperialist chauvinism, and an uncritical loyalty to the Crown long after those attitudes had waned in Britain itself. Only the more recent *risorgimento* of West Indian nationalism promises perhaps finally to terminate that climate of opinion.

In the meantime, that climate of opinion can only be understood if the major factors that shaped it are understood. The post-emancipation society has been called a 'new order'. To some extent, of course, it was. Abolition of chattel slavery precipitated a real property revolution, with the master-slave relationship being replaced, however slowly, with an employer-tenant relationship; and the misconceived apprenticeship system, an experiment adopted in all of the islands except Antigua and Bermuda, only served to generate additional popular resentment against the alliance of planters and colonial assembly politicians who had hoped by that means to maintain the spirit of slavery under the letter of freedom. The tactic of the slave revolt was replaced with refusal to continue working on the plantation system or, as in Jamaica, with flight from the plantation into the hills. The economic struggle between former master and slave continued, but in new forms, so that the labourer came to depend more and more upon his new power to influence wage rates and the estate proprietor upon his power over rent, accompanied by the power of eviction. The basic maxim of slavery—that, as Cairnes put it, the most effective economy is that which takes out of the human chattel in the shortest space of time the utmost amount of exertion it is capable of putting forth—disappeared forever, to be replaced with the capitalist principle of supply and demand, albeit within an underdeveloped semi-feudal West Indian framework. The history of West Indian labour disputes, indeed, begins at this point; and the record of those disputes during the early apprenticeship period, fully described in W. L. Burn's *Emancipation and Apprenticeship in the British West Indies*, makes it clear how much the new instrumentality of the stipendiary magistrate gave to the freed slave a bargaining power and an independent legal representation quite unknown in the slave economy.

All this, furthermore, was accompanied by deep changes in the structure of society, for 1834 without doubt marked the beginning of a new societal phase in which the old groups of planter, merchant monopolist, and white colonial official were gradually superseded, both in economic power and social status, by the new groups of creole cultivator, peasant farmer, and native politician. The decline of the old planter class, well under way long before Emancipation, has been catalogued in Ragatz's classic volume. The decline was accompanied by the rise of the class of 'freed coloured', recruited from the growing body of peasant Negroes who had benefited from the process of manumission, the solicitous care of white fathers, and special economic conditions, and who rapidly became urbanized town and professional people. This was a general process itself well under way, too, long before 1834. The Jamaican historian, Edward Long, noted as early as 1774 the virtual monopoly of slaves in the Jamaican internal marketing system, and the memoirs of missionaries and the reports of stipendiary magistrates indicated, sixty years later, that by the time of abolition there existed in that leading island a body of coloured people with the financial capacity to purchase land and the initiative to build homes and chapels; while a generation still later the introduction of the banana as an economic crop gave new opportunities to this class of peasant cultivator, the economic energy of the type being attested to by the growing prosperity of the Jamaican banana parishes after 1870. The West Indian custom of inter-racial sexual liaison, inevitable in a sex-slavery situation, at the same time conferred economic security and social placing upon the woman of colour who consorted with a white man; and half a dozen or more phenomena—the racial statistics of the 'free schools', the figures of land sales, especially of ruinate estate property, the construction of Nonconformist churches and chapels, the growing liberality of wills, entries into journalism and the law— attest to the social advancement of her children. Practically every traveller's report on Victorian West Indian life noted the existence of a flourishing coloured 'society' in the regional towns, whose members were at once the most fully creolized group of the colonies in their general life-style and the most Anglophile in their political and social attitudes. Thus, to take the case of Grenada only, an English resident in the late 1820s noted approvingly how the grant system had enabled the class of 'free coloured' to become well-to-do merchants, as well as occupy prestigious posts like the editorship of the *St Georges Chronicle*, and that many of them were better educated than the class of white managers and overseers.[2] By the time that Froude came to compose his slanderous volume (1888) the growth of these liberalizing forces, as well as the development of more liberal attitudes both in the local coloured group and in the group of the imperial administrators, had made his racialist authoritarianism quite obsolete, and the English groups to whom he made his appeal were, in fact, as one of his critics noted, a very different body of men from the old slave-owners and planters whose disappearance Froude so much regretted.[3] 'We hear ceaselessly,' wrote the same critic, 'of the ruin of the West Indies; but this simply means the break up of the old order of things. The new order of society which is being evolved contains elements of stability which were missing. The establishment of a large body of peasant owners and a number of middle class cultivators alongside a few great proprietors cannot reasonably be accounted a calamity in any country . . . In the new and better order that is being established in these dependencies the old notions will happily find no place; the usual gradations of society found in every advanced community will be established.'[4]

That sentiment—the ideology of a rational liberalism in a rational class-oriented society—was indeed almost the official creed of West Indian society in the century between 1838 and 1938. But when all is said and done its 'new order' was in reality new more in degree than in kind. The class-colour alignments shifted; but they did not disappear. The more odious of post-Emancipation injustices—a repressive legal system, for example—disappeared with the Morant Bay affair of 1865. New occupational opportunities, true enough, emerged for the ex-slave; Phillippo described in his book of 1843 on Jamaica how much the native leader and lay agent system in the popular churches became a training ground for Negro leadership and Negro entry into occupations such as confidential servants in mercantile houses, subordinate estate managers, governesses, and schoolmasters.[5] But all this, at best, was simply the effort of the emancipated slave to raise himself in a slowly-changing society. It was not a fundamental reconstruction of the society, any more than

3*

*post-bellum* Reconstruction in the United States a generation later meant the growth of a new, free society in the Deep South. 1834 removed the gross features of the slave system without basically upsetting the underlying class-colour differentiations of the society. The three hierarchically ordered sections—white, coloured, and black—remained as solidly entrenched as ever. The changes that took place were changes, albeit important for understanding the new internal dynamics of West Indian life, within the subworld of their organized interrelations.

The white group, as already noted, accepted the end of slavery without open counter-revolutionary activity (as in fact did occur in Hispaniola). But it was a long, reluctant process. Caste prejudice declined; and a brief generation after Emancipation both black and coloured men had obtained positions of prominence, not only as merchants and landed property owners, but also as clergymen, barristers, schoolteachers, magistrates, and members of Assembly, the Jamaican leader Gordon being the son of a slave-woman and her white master and rising, through the position of justice of the peace, to membership of the House of Assembly. But race prejudice remained; and Dr Elsa Goveia has demonstrated in her exhaustive *Historiography of the British West Indies* how long it took for the ex-aggerated racism of the pro-slavery creed to disappear from nine-teenth-century literature. The plantocracy in a comparatively unimportant island like Antigua sought to give Emancipation a fair trial. But in the more important territories like Jamaica and Bar-bados they met it with systematic opposition, and some of the harshest passages of Sewell's remarkable volume, *The Ordeal of Free Labor in the British West Indies*, published as a warning to the Ameri-can Southern plantocracy on the very eve of the Civil War, were reserved for the Bourbon intransigeancy of the Barbadian white oligarchy in whose field of values, as he remarked, even remote descent from an African ancestor made some unhappy creature a pariah in that island's little world. Those reactionary attitudes held up progress for a generation and more, and in Jamaica, the leading West Indian island, it was 1865, not 1834, that marked the end of the full reign of the planters and the beginning of the ascendancy of the Negro. As a body, the whites clung to their traditional pre-judice that rum and sugar were the only economic cultures per-missible to the tropics. They consequently failed either to encourage more productive varieties of cane through more efficient production methods or through more intensive research (which did not come to Barbados, indeed, until the great work of John Redman Bovell towards the end of the century) or to develop the cultivation of other cash crops. The abandonment of properties—the well-known scene of West Indian ruinate—was more their fault than that of the ex-slave population, and Sewell demonstrated conclusively with a wealth of statistical data how far more productive free labour was as compared to slave labour and how much the decline of the sugar estates, especially in Barbados and Jamaica, was the result of a general entrepreneurial lethargy pre-dating 1834 by some thirty years or more.

To all that there must be added the fact that the general refusal of the white aristocracy to work out new terms of social coexistence with their former serfs was accompanied, in Trinidad and British Guiana, by the new policy of the importation of East Indian indentured labour (lasting until 1917) which had the fatal consequence of producing racially dualistic societies divided into mutually antagonistic groups of 'coolies' and 'niggers' (the very epithets themselves testifying to the general contempt in which both were held by the *élite* groups) ; and the subsequent history of those two colonies was one of the disruption of effective national community arising out of the presence of groups of radically different cultures and languages, with fundamentally different traditions, and existing, until well into the twentieth century, at different economic levels. It is enough to read, for example, Peter Ruhomon's centennial *History* of the British Guianese East Indians (1838–1938) to realize how the 'new slavery' of contract labour effectively stifled, until the period after the First World War, the growth of either civic consciousness or political awareness on the part of that ethnic group. What power, altogether, that there was was left to the white group to be used for its own narrow purposes. 'Theirs,' concluded Sewell in his book, 'was not the broad, grasping selfishness of a powerful oligarchy wise enough to combine their own aggrandizement with that of the nation at large; but it has been from first to last a narrow-minded selfishness that pursued crooked paths to accumulate gain at the expense of the public weal, and to the infinite detriment of the colonial credit.'[6] Nor has the effort of modern historians—Professor Douglas Hall's argument in his *Free Jamaica, 1838–1875*, for example—to be kinder to the record been very successful, depending as much of it does upon reviving, in a way, one of the most famous arguments of the old pro-slavery apologetics, that the West Indian slave was better off than the English labourer. For if, as Hall argues, things were not much better in a mid-Victorian England dominated by *laissez-faire* capitalism, the comparison still fails to answer why the West Indian ruling class failed to produce its own Shaftesburys and Disraelis.

The truth was, of course, that the social contradictions first, of slavery and, secondly, of a post-Emancipation society still deeply imbedded with the spirit of slavery precluded a positive leadership-role for the ruling white group. Theoretically, it could have led a West Indian popular revolt against British mercantilism, after the American fashion; but the fear of slave rebellion at home and, after 1834, the failure to forge a new *modus vivendi* with either the enfranchised coloured group or the vast mass of freed slaves stifled that possibility. It chose, therefore, to share its power with the metropolitan centre, and, humiliatingly, on the punitive terms set by the metropolitan centre. The supine character of this group, on into the twentieth century, must be related to this social source. 'The North Americans indeed were too much for us,' an English observer noted in 1825, 'the West Indians may be crushed by a wave of Mr Canning's hand.'[7] The creole power-groups thus preferred the colonial relationship rather than face the growth of democracy at home. The high-handed treatment of the region by British official-dom was thus given fresh encouragement, lasting up to the present time. If, too, West Indian national independence today has little about it of the mass enthusiasm that comes from a prolonged and militant struggle to wrest it from the colonial power, the phenomenon likewise has its roots in the leadership vacuum of the nineteenth-century creole society. All that, finally, must be seen within the context of the fact that, ironically, there was not absent, indeed, a real influence in that society of the democratic ideas of the American republican tradition, as the work of scholars like Kerr and Siebert has shown.[8]

Effective leadership, then, for what it amounted to, passed increasingly to the coloured intermediate group. Its members had economic power and social influence long before they obtained enlarged political power. Not as exile-conscious as the whites in the hermetic West Indian society, since they were the most fully creolized of all groups—that is to say, the most fully acculturated in the direction of the dominant Creole-European tradition—at the same time their pro-British alignment, combined with their anxiety to deny their African heritage, made them into the social and political enemy of the black masses, a few liberal individuals excepted. They were the carriers, perhaps more than any other group, of the 'white bias' of the society. When the desire was frustrated it generated, frequently, a pathology of self disrespect so deep that they rejected even sexual contact with each other, a phenomenon which persuaded the eighteenth-century historian Edward Long, in the case of Jamaica, that the male and female members of the group were biologically incapable of procreation one with the other. They yearned for social acceptance by the whites; and the pathetic contradictions that they thereby embraced can be seen, to take an early example only, in the bitter complaint that the author of the early West Indian novel *Marly* (1828) put into the mouth of a cultured Jamaican coloured gentleman who had graduated from Edinburgh University, only to come home to a 'white gentleman' society that rejected him and his type.[9] Thirty years later, in the 60s Grant Allen's satirical romance, *In All Shades*, showed how colour still remained as a valid standard of value accepted by all groups in the white-black colour scale; for all of the figures in that novel were the well-known stereotypes of the West Indian racial character enmeshed in a tragi-comedy from which they could not escape: the educated mulatto son returning to vulgar family surroundings after being socially spoiled in England; the young English wife of the brown professional husband treated as a moral leper by the local whites; the affected and stupid 'Hottentot Venus' of the brown middle class daughter anxious to marry an English officer of good connections if only the shame of her racial identity can be long enough hidden; the visiting English aristocrat whose own identity as a 'throw back' to unsuspected coloured ancestors is readily exposed in a society which, unlike the English, has a fine detective instinct for the recognition of traces of miscegenation.[10] In varying forms, they are all to be met with in West Indian literature, and so frequently that, clearly enough, they more or less accurately reflected the class-colour structure of the servile colour-variable West Indian society of the nineteenth century. Only the itinerant visitor could afford to satirize the general picture, as did Trollope. The local resident could hardly afford that dangerous luxury.

At the bottom of the social ladder there were, of course, the ex-slave masses, reinforced by East Indian and Chinese immigrants in, variously, Jamaica, Trinidad, and British Guiana. Where they were not harassed by white and brown-controlled machineries of law and government, and by oppressive land tenure systems, they were openly neglected. Nothing was done to train them in the new duties of citizenship. The slave regime was dead. But it was replaced by a regime almost equally oppressive, imbued still with the slavery spirit. For while British capitalism killed slavery once slavery turned out to be unprofitable, it continued to nurture the colonial mono-polistic commercial system as a continuing profitable enterprise. The economic power of the plantocracy declined. But that of the colonial mercantile class continued, became even stronger through-out the rest of the century. Salmon's book of 1884, *Depression in the West Indies*, cogently criticized the system from the viewpoint of Free Trade economic liberalism. Restricted inflow of capital; ex-cessively high customs tariffs benefiting a closed monopoly of local merchant houses; a heavy burden of colonial revenues carried by taxation upon local necessities such as corn, flour, rice, fish, and meat; the failure of local real and personal property to share in the tax burden; the excessive costs of colonial administration: all of these, Salmon argued, had produced a maladjusted economy in which the West Indies bought their foodstuffs dear and sold their produce low, and from which both planter and worker suffered. 'It is obvious,' he concluded, 'that a great injustice has been done to these islands; they have been handed over, as it were, to a power-ful corporation, and the consequences of this monopoly are seen in that want of development and that stagnation which is the only end possible to such a state of things.'[11] The criticism was composed in 1884. But the conditions it described remained virtually unchanged right up to the period before World War II; nor, indeed, has the advent of labour governments since that period done much to curb the stranglehold of the 'powerful corporation' that Salmon des-cribed. More than any other group, the West Indian peasant and worker masses paid a high price, in their generally depressed living standards, for that situation.

All of these different groups, conceivably, could have combined in a united front against Britain. But, frankly, there was little to unite them. There were, of course, odd alignments of common interest as, for example, the common eighteenth-century sexual code, reflected in the habits of consensual cohabitation and extraresidential mating, shared by both upper-class whites and lower-class blacks as against the Victorian respectability of the missionary societies and Nonconformist churches, not to mention Victorian England itself. But mutual distrust of each other precluded active union. The belief, expressed in much of the literature of the time, that exposure to the 'civilizing' European influence would fashion out of them a homogeneous body of people with uniform social values turned out to be unfounded, for even a group as pro-English as the ruling whites maintained their English customs only with important modifications specifically West Indian.

The general outcome was that the society remained, after 1834, and well on into the modern century, a basically disorganized society, with very few common values rooted in common experience. The social differentiations, based partly on property, partly on colour, remained fairly static for nearly a century, with the tempo of slow change quickening somewhat during the 1920's and undergoing marked acceleration during the 1930's. Each group 'knew its place'. There was, increasingly, free acceptance in business circles and politics—a black candidate, Alexander Dixon, was returned to the Jamaican Legislative Council at the turn of the century—and also widening social recognition, especially on the official level under more liberal colonial Governors like Sir Henry Norman and Sir Sydney Oliver. Competitive examinations for the Jamaican civil service, established in 1885, opened up a new gainful 'white collar' occupation for the Negroes. Yet at the same time there was widespread social ostracism based on colour. A dark person with a flair for 'society' might be admitted to the homes of whites or reputed whites, but difficulties arose if he aspired to marriage. A coloured doctor or lawyer (particularly in the country towns) might live down his disability by sheer merit; but his type would not be readily accepted in the more exclusive clubs. The club, and the club snob, indeed, became expressions of subtle segregationism. And there were few places of public resort, which made segregationism even more effective. In Jamaica at the turn of the century, for example, there were only certain restricted balls in Kingston society, the Caledonia Ball promoted by Scottish residents, for instance, or the Queen's Birthday Party at Government House, while the first public subscription dances only came into existence after the establishment of the Myrtle Bank Hotel.[12] Around the same time Barbadian social life, as described in a Diamond Jubilee directory, centred around the five 'gentlemen's' clubs, that is, the white clubs, plus the Masonic Lodges, the Benefit Societies, the Barbados Auxiliary Bible Society, and the Bridgetown Circle of the National Home Reading Union aiming 'to encourage the reading of the works of good authors'.[13] The divisions of Trinidadian society, likewise, reflected the ethnic separatism of its polyglot character, so much so that even its fiction reflected that fact, Negro Trinidadian life finding its voice in a novel like C. L. R. James' *Minty Alley* and the life of the Portuguese Creoles in a novel like Alfred Mendes' *Pitch Lake*. Unity in this kind of society, finally, was made impossible by the fact that, being intellectually depressed communities, there was no play of common ideas, no educated and at the same time socially conscious class ready to take the lead in nationalist assertiveness. Thus the English Guianese resident Henry Kirke, speaking of British Guiana in the last twenty-five years of the nineteenth century, could observe that the only material difference between society in the colony and in Great Britain was in the absence of the leisured and literary classes and that although there were Guianese classical and mathematics scholars, and erudite botanists and zoologists, they were a very small minority and had no influence upon the general lump.[14] It was highly unlikely, in the face of all this, that West Indians would unite in a war of national liberation (as happened in Haiti and, later, in Cuba). The relative cultural antiquity of Barbados, of course, made its servility to English social values the most pronounced of all. But all of the colonies, in varying degree, exhibited the same character.

By 1900, then, the West Indies, altogether, were a bizarre mixture of racial discord, crass commercialism, and cultural imitativeness. Some relaxation in racial matters took place after 1920 by reason, mainly, of two factors, one being the fillip given to new sports, especially tennis and golf, the other being the progress to adult life of old school friends of various shades, coupled with the outstanding personal achievements of men of colour. A widening educational pattern also helped; it is worth noting here that in Barbados where, unlike Jamaica, agriculture and commerce remained throughout this period the stronghold of the resident white aristocracy, education provided about the only safety valve against brown-Negro frustration, as the careers of Sir Grantley Adams, Hugh Springer, and Dr H. G. Cummins amply prove. But this was amelioration only, and the Moyne Commissioners of 1938–39 felt constrained to report, in that section of their great report dealing with colour prejudice, that although prejudice was deplored by every witness who gave evidence about it all responsible quarters in the region shared a widespread feeling that it was seriously on the increase, especially where economic differences between white employers and black employees inevitably became transmuted into racial differences. The result was a continuing racialist sentiment, taking the expression, in the social lowly, of extreme sensitiveness to ridicule, and in the more well-to-do of a delicate touchiness where their ethnic *dignidad* was concerned. Nor were there any powerful institutional traditions to lend support to individual identity. For the established institutions were imperial and therefore unreachable, while those created out of crystallizing local forces were constantly vulnerable to the jealousy and distrust of the colonial spirit. Just as slave revolts bred the defecting informer so the trade union, the benefit society, and the political party bred, later, the disruptive adventurer. Local institutions have got broken up, as one West Indian union leader has noted, speaking from a lifetime of experience, because people feel they cannot trust each other or themselves: 'One has only to raise a finger and say, "You see so and so has a new car; you know where your money is going" and such insidious aspersions tend to break up the institution.'[15] That kind of suspicion naturally arises with ease, moreover, in a society of mass poverty in which the mere ownership of a car evokes popular suspicions against its user as a member of the 'motorized salariat'; and for years any sort of collision between a pedestrian and an automobile in any West Indian town would almost precipitate a minor street riot, with racial overtones should the driver—as was mostly the case in the early days—be white or near-white.

Nor were the materialism and moral hypocrisy of colonial society —nicely satirized in their Jamaican expression in Herbert de Lisser's novel *The Cup and the Lip*—seriously mitigated by the rise, in the twentieth century, of the slowly expanding coloured educated *élite*. It is true that that *élite* produced individuals in every territory who stood out, in their time, as persons of unusual merit—in Jamaica, for example, the Rev. A. A. Barclay, father of the Jamaica Agricultural Society, and Dunbar Wint, ardent champion of the depressed teacher class; in Barbados, politicians like H. W. Reece, the only self-acknowledged person of Negro blood in that colony's House of Assembly fifty years ago; and in Trinidad the galaxy of brilliant men who, as Island Scholars, made their name, like Sir Henry Pierre, in tropical medicine or, like Sir Courtenay Hannays and Sir Hugh Wooding, in law. There were individual women, too, of outstanding ability like the Audrey Jeffers in Trinidad who, through the Coterie of Social Workers, taught a whole generation of Trinidadians a new concept of social responsibility. But whether due to the general social environment or inherent tradition the scope of influence of such individuals was generally restricted to the narrow sphere of their own circles. To the general public they were little more than legendary figures, seldom reported, and usually denied widespread recognition by means of opportunities of public service at the top levels. It is true, too, that in the fifty years after 1900 new occupational avenues opened up for the full-blooded Negro, so that the traditional opportunities of schoolroom and pulpit were replaced by the wider ones of the civil service and other professions. But the low repute in which the West Indian civil servant, even today, is held in popular public opinion, and the fact that, also as even today, the majority of West Indian professional men are content to occupy an honourable position and make a comfortable living without curtailing their pleasures or indulging in undue exertion, suggest that the new openings were used mainly for selfish personal purposes. The West Indian churches also came to provide better career opportunities for the coloured candidate, although the vast personal popularity of an expatriate minister, like Cowell Lloyd in the East Queen Street Baptist Church in Kingston, might delay the process for a generation or more in certain denominations. Yet it tells volumes for the light in which the local candidate saw his opportunites that when John Joseph Purcell reached a high post in the Catholic hierarchy in British Guiana he used his power, not to undertake a social Gospel movement, but to conduct violent theological disputes with his local Protestant enemies, almost as if inviting the colonial white congregation to admire the Newmanite zeal of a coloured priest.

In general, then, the West Indian middle-class groups had little to do but to endure the ennui of colonial existence. The *cri de coeur* of one of them summed it up for all: 'Look at my existence extending over twenty years. Work from 7.30 am to 4 pm, dull and uninspiring. Then home, and, if equal to it, sport. Otherwise literally nothing, except the banality of the cinema, or social grumperies.'[16] For the lower middle groups, at the same time, a commercial clerkship came to be regarded as almost the only worthwhile existence, and the history of the West Indian *Kipps* has still to be written; although Mittelholtzer's early pioneering novel *A Morning at the Office* described something of the inter-personal tensions of office life as they arose between the classic Trinidadian character-types of the Negro office boy, the sexy Chinese stenographer, the fawning Indian clerk, and the supercilious English 'bosses'. Most people retreated into their private worlds or their own social games, frequently operated under complicated rules; the Trinidadian creole world, for example, characterized by the ironic contradiction between a national capacity to laugh, play 'picong' and produce insulting calypsoes and, on the other side, groups of people who took refuge in pomposity and verbosity as a safeguard against ridicule. A laconic self-derisory sense of humour, clearly enough, did not easily flourish in the social climate of colonialism. It was the same, essentially, in every colony; van Sertima's account of respectable social life in British Guiana at the turn of the century thus portrays accurately the emptiness of a social routine of carriage expeditions to the Sea Wall and the Botanic Gardens, only relieved by the spurious excitement of gambling in the Chinese *chéfa* houses.[17] Leadership from the top and middling ranks was thus not readily forthcoming. Leadership from the bottom, on the other hand, was frustrated, in part, by the fact that the West Indian masses, of all ethnic strains, exhibited throughout a diffuse sense of immigrant mentality, as the history of the idea of East Indian communal representation in Trinidad and British Guiana shows. Groups either looked outwards for help, as East Indians looking back to 'Mother India'; or they retreated in upon themselves, turning their back on movements of national unification, the most famous example of that exclusivist psychology being, of course, the history of the Jamaican Maroons. It was as true in 1938, all in all, as it had been a century earlier, when Lord Harris uttered the phrase, that a race had been freed but a society had not yet been formed.

The most complete evidence for all this, of course, is to be found in the monumental *Report* of the West Indies Royal Commission of 1937–38, summing up in magisterial form as it did the record of West Indian life and society as they had grown up during the century since abolition. It was the supreme achievement of that *Report* to annotate, in damning detail, the social and economic servitude of the West Indian proletariats, thus providing a welcome change from a situation in which most reports on the region, being the diaries of travellers, had concentrated almost exclusively on describing the pleasant, if futile, life of the whites and Anglo-West Indians. Along with other documents such as the various reports of the Committee on Nutrition in the Colonial Empire and Major Orde-Browne's report on *Labour Conditions in the West Indies*, the Moyne report, composed by conscientious Commissioners who insisted on seeing things for themselves, provided an astonishingly comprehensive portrait of West Indian life and experience; for, as the Commissioners themselves remarked, few Royal Commissions could ever have had to cover so wide a field of subjects, the West Indies Royal Commission of 1899–97 having been concerned principally with the plight of the regional sugar industry, as was also the case with the later Olivier-Semple inquiry of 1929–30.

In general cultural terms, the *Report* saw the West Indian society as basically embryonic. 'One characteristic of the West Indies,' it noted, 'is the regrettable absence of those factors and traditions which elsewhere make for social cohesiveness and a sense of membership of a community . . .' 'The whole West Indies,' it added, 'are practically devoid of all the multifarious institutions, official and unofficial, which characterize British public life and bring a very large proportion of the population into some living contact with the problems of social importance.'[18] In more particular terms, the *Report* meticulously catalogued the items of that general social malaise: a declining sugar industry supporting an estate labour force by means of an exploitative task work system and with wages so low that in many cases, St Kitts and St Vincent, for example, the wage level had barely advanced beyond the daily shilling rate introduced after Emancipation; gross malnutrition and chronic

sickness in the people generally, made worse by a general medical
education, of exclusively overseas character, which emphasized
curative rather than preventive medicine, with the result that
bitter resentment against the medical profession was evident in
many of the colonies; a housing picture characterized by decrepit,
verminous, and insanitary 'houses', with the barracks or 'ranges'
system of the Guianese East Indian estate peasantry providing
some of the worst examples; a 'working class', when it had work, in
a state of economic servitude to a well-organized employer class,
while the defence mechanism of a strong trade union movement was
stultified by the existence of punitive legislation, British Guiana
alone of all of the colonies having passed legislation to protect unions
against actions for damages consequent upon strikes; a status of
women so low that the Commission heard of only one woman who
was a member of a West Indian municipal council; children, the
most exploited of all West Indian persons, denied opportunity for
the healthy development of either mind or body since they lived in
small, unlighted hovels with wooden shutters tightly closed at night
in order to shut out evil spirits or thieving neighbours; an
educational system characterized by serious absenteeism, obsolete
curricula, a cheap teaching staff, mainly of pupil teachers, and dread-
fully inadequate school buildings, reinforcing the findings, here, of
the West Indies Education Committee of 1931–32 that had quoted
an experienced observer of education all over the world as declaring
that primary education in the West Indies was the least progressive
of any that he had encountered in the British Empire; and much
else. 'If,' wrote the Commissioners generally of the life expectations
of even the lucky West Indian child, 'he has been fortunate enough
to continue his education until school-leaving age, which is usually
fourteen in the towns and twelve in the rural districts, he enters a
world where unemployment and under-employment are regarded
as the common lot. Should he find work as a manual labourer, his
wages often provide only for bare maintenance and are far from
sufficient to enable him to attain the standard of living which is set
before him by new contacts with the outside world. If he is fitted
by education and intelligence for clerical posts, competition for
which is intense, he will have the prospect, at best, of a salary on
which, even in Government employment, he will find it a serious
struggle to keep up the social position and appearances which he

and his friends expect. He will have leisure hours but few facilities for recreation with which to fill them.'[19]

That kind of destiny—a general alliance of gross poverty and low cultural attainment—was not, of course, the same for all West Indians. Trinidad, for example, with its prosperous oil industry, and Jamaica with its large independent peasant class, were far ahead of the others. But that only meant that there were even lower levels of poverty in the other islands, not that Trinidad and Jamaica were not themselves full of social material that made them into slums of empire. It is true, too, that within the interstices of a relatively rigidified social structure there existed opportunities, at times, for social manœuvrability. Even in Barbados, with its settled Victorian ideas about social station, peculiar social mechanisms made some degree of elevation possible; in particular, in the nineteenth century the emergence after Emancipation of a remarkable Barbadian newspaper journalism provided an outlet for bright poor young men, as the early journalistic careers of both Samuel Prescod and Conrad Reeves show, who could not hope to enter the closed world (closed, indeed, until the 1950s) of executive and managerial personnel in mercantile commerce; while in the twentieth century the equally remarkable revolution in the social foundations of Barbadian cricketing power, transforming the game, through devices like the 'Frame Food' League, from the exercise of small privileged minorities to the national pastime for literally almost everybody, gave to the Barbadian working class the opportunity to shape the famous line of great Barbados batsmen and fast bowlers, culminating in the superb figure of Gary Sobers.[20] Even so, such social phenomena elevated favoured individuals, not social classes as a whole, and perhaps only the famous Barbadian complacency could exaggerate their importance. As far as the pre-Moyne period was concerned, nowhere had the West Indian masses risen much above conditions of life so depressed that, as the Commissioners themselves reluctantly agreed, the widespread habit of gambling in the society was the result of 'a natural craving for excitement in lives whose amusements are few, and an expression of the dream of pennies from heaven so appealing to those whose best efforts fail to provide them with a tolerable competence'.[21]

Two further aspects of this general character of West Indian life deserve emphatic mention. First it was made worse by the particular character of the British colonial service. Its bias was political rather than social or cultural, so that it was, in terms of its personnel in the colonies, strong on the administrative side and weak on the scientific and technological side. There was, significantly enough, no organization whatsoever in the colonial empire which viewed the problems of science as a whole; the technical officer's status was usually lower than that of the administrative official, who usually despised or, at the most, tolerated him, and he was usually condemned to stagnate in small and isolated departments; the bold initiative earlier on of Sir Joseph Chamberlain, when Colonial Secretary, of establishing the London School of Tropical Medicine had not been followed up; and expenditures in fields as varied as entomology, mycology, soil science, and plant genetics were pitiably small compared to what countries like Egypt or the United States were spending.[22] The people who suffered most from this type of administrative conservatism were, naturally, the subject-races of the Empire. They turned, understandably, to the obeah-man or the 'water-people' medium or the 'bush-doctor' for the help they could not get from officialdom.

There was, secondly, the special character of West Indian education in its social aspects. The exclusion of the masses from anything save a rudimentary primary schooling, following the class bias of the British metropolitan model, has already been noted; suffice it to add that contemporary West Indian educational enterprise still inherits the legacy, so that, to take an example only, in 1960 more than fifty per cent of the total working population of Trinidad and Tobago comprised persons whose formal education went no higher than Standard VII of the primary school level.[23] But even more dangerous was the general fact that, being based on the prevalent snobberies of race and class, the West Indian school conspired to perpetuate the distrust and jealousy of the colonial social climate. The scholarship system, in particular, by its competitive character, was profoundly anti-social and the scars left behind by the old Island Scholarship system can still be seen in West Indian life. It was a grinding, merciless system that each year, or sometimes biennially, let one favoured candidate through the escape-hatch from the colonial prison; and it would be difficult to estimate who was damaged most, the winners who themselves frequently collapsed from tension and exhaustion of new studies, or the losers who gave up hope as marked 'failures' and settled down desperately into the familiar routine of early marriage, a large family, debt and heavy drinking on the West Indian cocktail circuit. Not the least of its total irony was that it was fiercely accepted, with all of its anti-democratic bias, by the Creole society itself, so that there grew up the amiable local tradition that to win the Island 'Schol' was to achieve the best any colonial boy could do, even although the winner might, on occasion, be, like Sir Robert Scott in the Trinidad of the 1920s, an expatriate Scotsman who barely stayed long enough in the colony to win it or, like Sir Frank Newsam in the Barbados of the pre-1914 period, the son of a colonial civil servant who, having won it, left the colony never to return.

All this provided the backdrop for the 'disturbances' of 1937–38. There were, of course, particular and local reasons behind the movement, reduction of wages in the Jamaican sugar estates, for instance, and punitive methods of worker regimentation such as the 'red book' system in the Trinidad oilfields. But the underlying causes lay in the nature of the colonial economy itself; as the Moyne Commissioners (hardly fiery revolutionaries) themselves noted, the disturbances represented no longer a mere blind protest against a worsening of conditions, but a positive demand for the creation of new conditions that would render possible a better life; and, further, as the 1937 Commission that reported more particularly on the Trinidadian explosion noted, the demand had been made possible, in part, by the recent formation of a Trinidadian working-class opinion increasingly affected by the Great War experiences of West Indian soldiers, industrial unrest in the United States and the spread of elementary education in the colony.[24] The demand, thus, was the revolt of West Indian peasant and worker against a society in which, despite formal emancipation, they were still regarded merely as supplies of cheap labour to sugar kings and oil barons in search of quick fortunes. Slavery had been abolished; but the economic foundations of slavery, especially in the general picture of land ownership, had remained basically untouched. New social classes, it is true, had emerged to ameliorate the gap between the 'haves' and the 'have-nots', yet the social pattern of slavery—the vast masses labouring in poverty on the property of the minority—remained stamped on West Indian life. On the industrial side, the power of the local business class was strengthened by the virtual absence of effective trade unions, and the general inadequacy of industrial law. Up to 1938, indeed, the economy hardly knew the meaning of the phrase 'industrial legislation', and wage agreements, workmen's compensation, health insurance, restriction of child labour, factory inspection, old age pensions, and collective bargaining were matters practically unknown to the colonial statute books. The Moyne Commissioners only timidly hazarded the guess that powerful vested interests had stood in the way in these matters; but they were at least emphatic in their assertion that they had met no evidence that any active steps had been taken by West Indian governments to encourage the formation of trade unions either inside or outside the Civil Service.[25]

On the agricultural side, however, there was no doubt at all of employer oppression, and even the special Blue Books of the period were outspoken on the issue. For some three centuries labour shortage had been seen by the West Indian planter as his most acute problem, and he had throughout fought fiercely against the extension of the independent peasant class as a threat to his control of the labour supply. By 1938 the final battle in that social civil war between planter and peasant had yet to be fought. Hence the special importance of the history of the peasant proprietary class, both as an idea and as a socio-economic fact. From 1900 onwards, certainly with the championship of the idea by the 1897 Royal Commission, shocked by the social consequences of retaining the plantation system, local governments had begun actively to foment the creation of such a class. But the main motive, throughout, perhaps, was the fear of a labourers' revolt; and little enough had been achieved by 1938. For such a policy required that West Indian governments (1) open up undeveloped Crown Lands on easy purchase terms and (2) undertake systematic land settlement by means, in part, of breaking up the large plantations. But planter-controlled governments were unlikely to do either; and in fact did not. In the case of Barbados, for example, the Olivier-Semple Report on the sugar industry observed (in 1930) that no attempt had been made in that island from the date of the last Royal Commission report (1897) by either the Government or the local Agricultural Society to organize any kind of popular associations for the encouragement and improvement of peasant and labourer's garden agriculture,[26] with the result, as the report added, that the Barbadian labouring population resided clinging on to the fringes of cane fields and perched on the banks of the highway; a condition, incidentally, that remains almost unchanged up to the present time.

West Indian literature, of course, is full of the ideology of this particular dream; the dream, in the words of a frequently quoted passage from Sir Sydney Armitage-Smith's financial report of 1931, of 'a numerous, prosperous, happy and healthy peasant population, protected against plague pestilence and famine, living in decent dwellings on holdings which, as the result of their own labour, wisely directed by Government, become their own property in their own lifetime; *adscripti glebae* not by any harsh constraining law, but by the operation of their own unfettered choice, cherishing the land which offers to them generous nourishment, and enriching the commonwealth by the fruit of their labours'.[27] But apart from the fact that West Indian colonial governments were at no time genuinely paternalistic regimes governing utopian commonwealths, there was the ultimate realistic consideration that the idyll of a pastoral society, of a serene past with its polite, contented peasantry, was the kind of feudalism the West Indies had never experienced; and looked even less like experiencing in the period after 1918. The main features of West Indian agriculture, indeed—shifting cultivation, low technical knowledge, indebtedness, reluctance to try new methods combined with over-sanguine adventurousness when a cash crop had a good year—all testified to the truth that the average West Indian peasant's attitude to the land was that it was something to be used to scrape together a bare living until something better turned up. The ownership of land, in its turn, immensely fragmentalized, constituted, most of all, a sort of status symbol in the village social struggle, and a play like E. M. Roach's *Belle Fanto*, set in Tobago, illustrates accurately all the rage and indignity of the West Indian peasant family's squabbling over property. There was little room there, obviously, for agricultural reform dreams based upon the English attitude to gardening.[28]

The strength of the Moyne Report, of course, was the remarkable candour of its examination of West Indian society. It is worth noting that the social liberalism of its members was far more capable of appreciating West Indian discontents than, by contrast, Lord Olivier's Fabian Socialism in his volume of 1936, *Jamaica: The Blessed Island*, for the basic assumption of that volume was that

Jamaican society on the whole was a well integrated society in which smooth change could successfully take place, a view quite discredited by the events of 1937–38. The weakness of the *Report*, on the other hand, was the general timidity of its recommendations. Since the underlying economic assumption of British colonial rule was that the colonies were best suited for producing agricultural products, it was perhaps inevitable that the Commission's sole reference to the possibilities of West Indian industrial development should have been disparaging in tone; but the prejudice was noted by West Indian progressive commentators at the time.[29] The social welfare recommendations, which gave birth, in 1940, to the Colonial Development and Welfare organization situated in the area itself, were more positive and wide-ranging. But at least two things must be said of them in criticism. First, they were so very much like the programme advocated by West Indian Labour parties and politicians for the previous twenty years that they came as no surprise; and the only change lay in the fact that, now coming from a high-powered Royal Commission, they stood a chance of being received by West Indian officialdom in terms other than the hostility and abuse with which Colonial Office and local government houses alike had met the similar schemes of West Indian political leaders and social workers. Secondly, and more fundamentally, the bias in favour of social welfare conspired to prevent any bold attack upon the more basic problems of economic development, for the West Indian problem, then as now, was not so much one of obtaining more financial assistance from London as of making the West Indian economy self-supporting so that, with the termination of metropolitan grants, it could continue to finance the new public services of a West Indian welfare state out of its own resources. The *Report*, it is true, at times seemed to be demanding a rebuilding of West Indian society, but in terms of concrete suggestions the demand too frequently subsided into limited specifics, buttressed by homiletic passages to the West Indian peoples to become morally rehabilitated; and the successive biennial reports of the new C.D. and W. organization after 1940 tended to carry the same note.

It is suggestive that Professor Simey's influential volume of 1946, *Welfare and Planning in the West Indies*, profoundly sympathetic as it was to the social welfare movement in the region, nevertheless constituted a severe criticism of the welfare phobia of the Commission report and of the subsequent work of the C.D. and W. experiment. The commission wanted to repair the social fabric of colonial life; it failed to see that the social fabric itself needed replacement. It assumed that the basic need of the West Indies was the growth of a socially conscious middle class, hitherto conspicuous by its absence; it failed to appreciate that it was the class system, not merely class relationships, that needed attention; and that perhaps explains why it paid so little reference to the need for economic equality in West Indian life and so much attention to things like an organized campaign against 'immorality' in sex relations. Inevitably, then, the work of the C.D. and W. organization exhibited the same limitations. All of its projects had a marked rural bias. They were piecemeal improvements of social services and agriculture rather than an attempted re-orientation of economic life; as well as a multitude of minor schemes: agronomical demonstrations in Barbados, books for the Antigua grammar school, training of district nurses in Grenada, cotton variety trials in St Vincent, a new jetty in Barbuda. The C.D. and W. leaders believed, theoretically, in West Indian 'self-help', but it was symptomatic of the colonialist assumptions of the organization that the Comptroller and his very comprehensive staff were almost all imported Englishmen, despite the fact that any number of West Indians were qualified to hold most of the posts with distinction. The history of the organization, therefore, was the history of its English administrators and specialist experts: Briarcliffe, Hammond, Wakefield, Ibberson, Benham, and Beasley; on which the proper comment was, of course, Marryshow's tart remark in 1945 that he would have confidence in C.D. and W. when he saw a West Indian on its executive staff. It was an outfit, altogether, with a marked consumption rather than production bias, so that its schemes had little, if anything, to do with the major task of net capital improvement. They were, rather, schemes on which the recurrent costs of upkeep would fall upon the shoulders of the West Indian taxpayer, public works programmes, construction of reservoirs, school buildings and medical centres, adult educational projects, the reconstruction of Castries after the great fire of 1948, land settlements, in the main abortive, for small settlers, and so on. 'There has been too ready an assumption in Great Britain,' observed Simey acidly, 'that a pattern of social life has been achieved in the past which, given a few administrative reforms, is adequate for the needs of any people; that if troubles arise anywhere, all that is necessary is that the British way of life should be more fully understood and more closely followed.'[30] The Moyne Report had talked, boldly, of constructive efforts to provide a satisfactory alternative to the original cultures now lost to the West Indian peoples. But, in practice, that grand concept declined into the game of administrative reorganization so beloved of the colonial civil service mentality. 'It is impossible to deal with the social problems of the West Indies,' concluded Simey, 'without first inventing new tools to facilitate the task, or, in other words, without first promoting advances in the applied science of social engineering.'[31] But such a recipe of cure was novel even in Britain in 1946. It was even more impossibly novel in the colonial dependencies.

This, altogether, was the condition of the West Indies as they stood on the eve of the Second World War, and of all the tremendous changes unleashed by that event. They were a decadent backwater, neglected by the British and overlooked by the Americans; for American liberal opinion had throughout been so much concentrated on India that it had paid little attention, by comparison, to the British colonial debris on its own Caribbean doorstep. British progressive opinion was occasionally jolted out of its traditional disinterest in colonial matters, as far as the West Indies were concerned, by the publication of notable books, W. M. MacMillan's *Warning from the West Indies* of 1935, for example, a cogently argued exposé of West Indian social disorganization and economic retardation; and an effective antidote to the Bloomsbuty cult of the simple and healthy savage that infected so much of the thinking even of the British Left, and which was largely responsible for the cult of peasant ownership in the more liberal-minded of British officials in the Caribbean area, from Sir Henry Norman to Lord Olivier. But even that noteworthy book was limited by the fact that it was almost as much about Africa as about the West Indies and by its assumption that progress in the area would come, if at all, from re-invigorated official policy and not from the revolt of the West Indian masses. Throughout all of the literature on the colonial society at this time, indeed, there was a startling contrast between the magnitude of the social evils it unveiled and the pedestrian ordinariness of the prescriptions of cure it advanced. That, once again, was the defect of the Moyne Commission analysis, for it seriously underestimated the importance of developing a trained West Indian leadership which would learn to manage its own affairs, a deficiency strikingly illustrated by the fact that although the Commission cited the need for special institutions—an educational institute, an agricultural school, a centre for training social workers, a school of hygiene—it made no mention at all of the tremendous contribution that a local university could have made to West Indian social and intellectual life; a contribution envisaged, much earlier, by the resident white minister James Phillippo in the case of Jamaica (1843) and the Keenan Report on education in the case of Trinidad (1869). The social legacy of colonialism—the deep-rooted social implications of colonial rule which have tended to be obscured by viewing colonialism as a political fact—would clearly have to be tackled by other forces and other means.

# Chapter IV

# BRITISH COLONIALISM
## THE POLITICAL LEGACY

THE POLITICAL government of the West Indian territories was exercised, classically, through the instrumentality of the Crown Colony system. That system, with individual variations, characterized West Indian political life certainly from 1878 onwards, when the process of replacing the old constitutions, based on a narrow and almost exclusively white suffrage, had been virtually completed; although the Bahamas, Bermuda, and Barbados retained the old regime, undisturbed by that process. An entire chapter of the regional political life, of course, relates to the extended history of the old regime, with its basic feature of perennial constitutional conflict between imperial Governors and local 'representative' Assemblies, the oldest of the latter legislative bodies being those like Barbados, St Kitts, Nevis, and Antigua, which went back to the early formative period of the 1630s and 1640s. The planter historians, indeed, like Long and Bryan Edwards, developed a whole political theory, founded on Lockeian grounds, of the colonial Assemblies as the guardians of popular rights against an overweening alien executive in the form of Governors and their Executive Councils, and much even of contemporary political attitudes in Bermudian and Barbadian political circles can be traced to that old Whiggite tradition. The realities, of course, were somewhat different. For although—as F. G. Spurdle has shown in his book, *Early West Indian Government*— there did take place a running fight between the legislative and executive powers, it was no more a struggle between a popular parliament and a tyrannical executive than was the case in the more famous English constitutional struggles of the same period (although the Whiggite fiction continued to permeate the history books read by West Indians in their English-formed schools). For the assemblies were based on a fantastically limited franchise; they represented, at best, only the planter, merchant, and legal classes; and the moral

95

bankruptcy of their membership, with individual exceptions, was equal to that of the Governors whom they attacked as enemies of the liberties of West Indians as fellow English subjects. 'The British West Indies,' wrote Sir Charles Lucas at the end of the nineteenth century, 'enjoyed representative institutions, but the colonial assemblies consisted of slave-owners; consequently the slaves lived under an exclusive oligarchy bred and born in  local prejudices. Again and again the history of colonization has shown that the safeguard of coloured races consists in a strong Home government outside and beyond local influences, and that Home rule for a dependency, where the white men are few and the coloured many, has in past times meant for the majority of its inhabitants not so much the gift of local freedom as the withdrawal of Imperial protection.'[1]

That the indictment was justified is evident enough from the historical record. The assemblies were the tools of the Creole ruling classes; and they were used as such. They were reactionary on every seminal West Indian issue: slavery emancipation, religious toleration, economic improvement. It could, perhaps, be plausibly argued that since in legal theory the colonies were communities of white emigrant settlers the assemblies were more or less representative bodies. But Emancipation, and its accompanying social changes, robbed the thesis of any validity; and, suggestively, even later West Indian historians as Christian-conservative as Gardner could dismiss the old constitutional system as obsolete and undesirable; while, equally suggestively, Froude's famous argument in favour of the authoritarian Crown Colony system successfully made the assumption that the conservative interests of the old West Indian ruling groups could now be institutionalized in forms other than those of the old representative system, hitherto regarded as being indispensable to the protection of those interests. Both friend and foe, this is to suggest, had little to say in defence of the system as the new post-Emancipation society more and more exposed its grotesque obsolescence. That they were right was proved, in the last analysis, by the fact that when the old system did finally reach the end of its tether a morally bankrupt oligarchy could offer no rational alternative to replace it. In the Jamaican case, indeed, the governing *élite* permitted their fear of constitutional reform, brought to a head by their panic-stricken reaction to the Morant Bay 'rebellion' of 1865, to surrender up the old system and let it be replaced by the autocratic Crown Colony regime, rather than embrace the dangers, as they saw it, of extending political participation to the black masses. In the case of Barbados—where the old proprietary system of a settled colony had created a different political climate—the entrenched plantocracy, threatened in 1876 by a British-sponsored federation plan, were not above promulgating the lie that federation would mean a return to slavery, in order thereby to muster popular support for the defence of their privileges under the ancient Barbadian constitution. There was, in truth enough, a struggle against the imperial power, often with justifiable cause. But it served, overwhelmingly, the oligarchic interests. Hence, paradoxically, as Adam Smith pointed out in his famous book, the condition of the slave was generally better under an arbitrary government, as in the case of the French West Indian islands, than it was under a free government, as in the British islands, since in the latter case the power of the colonial state was in large part coincidental with the interests of a class of slave-owners who also were controlling forces in the colonial legislative assemblies.[2]

From the mid-Victorian period on, then, up until only recently, West Indian government was Crown Colony government. The component parts differed in different colonies. But they all had one feature in common, the common denominator, as it were, of the system: the fact, as the Secretary of State for the Colonies put it in 1868, that the power of the Crown in the local legislature, if pressed to its extreme limit, would avail to overcome every resistance that could be made to it.[3] It was not, admittedly, an openly repressive system, like Spanish rule in Cuba and Puerto Rico, if only because the 1865 Jamaican affair cured the Colonial Office of tolerating, if it ever felt so inclined, the Governor Eyres of the service. It was profoundly constitutionalist, in theory if not always in practice, evidenced by the fact that no people today are more stout constitutionalists than West Indians. It believed passionately in the rule of law; and nothing was more English than the constitutional methods the West Indian militant forces used in their historic struggle against British rule. It says much for British colonial administration that the British islands witnessed sporadic outbreaks of violent protest but did not spawn, as did Puerto Rico in the 1930s, a terrorist-nationalist movement in open rebellion against the whole system. Governors and Administrators were by no means pure autocrats

4

as they were benevolent despots, frequently open to influence by public opinion or at least by what they liked to term 'responsible sections' of public opinion.

Yet that was about all that could be said in favour of the regime. It was, after all, a colonial administration, the rule, that is, of a subject people by a superordinate power; and that the English official could see nothing seriously wrong with it was shown by the interesting fact that as late in the modern day as 1940 the approbrious adjective 'colonial' could be given to the instrument set up by London to implement the Moyne Commission recommendations, and that, eight years later, the same adjective could be included in the formation of the Colonial Development Corporation. Final power, always, lay in the hands of the executive and, within the executive, in the hands of the Governor and, through the Governor, of course, in the hands of the distant Colonial Office. The one great constitutional defect of the old representative system—the failure to locate power as between executive and legislature—had been remedied since, under the reformed system, gradually introduced into most of the colonies—although only as late in the day as 1928 in British Guiana—the executive could always stamp out legislative opposition. But the remedy was as undemocratic as the disease it replaced. The official executive was fully independent, like the Crown in England before the development of the Cabinet system, and its discretionary and reserve powers survived every reform absorbed by the system, from Major Wood's Report of 1922 to the constitutional recommendations of the Moyne Commissioners. The local Executive Council was invariably filled with official members, plus a few unofficial advisers, and with no elected members from the Legislative Council. It owed no responsibility to the legislative body except where, as in the case of Barbados, a mixed body like the Executive Committee brought legislators into the policy-forming side. It is true that, in theory, the power of the Governor to nominate —that is, to appoint in his own discretion—an unofficial element made it possible to widen the popular base of government by bring-ing in representatives of all important sections of the community. But in practice most Governors played it safe by selecting men from the dominant groups, and the Moyne Commissioners (whose own constitutional proposals simply amounted to a loud enthusiasm for an insignificant reform measure, the introduction of a limited committee system to afford selected legislative members an insight into administrative business) bluntly noted that of only one Executive Council in the area in 1938–39 could it be said that it contained any representative of the interests of labour.

The Governor, then, was in fact an American President rather than a British Prime Minister, and the only remedy—that of the collective responsibility of a genuine cabinet, through the legislative body, to the electorate—was inevitably ruled out by the continuing refusal of London to grant responsible government based on political parties. True enough, he was, again in theory, accountable to the Secretary of State for the Colonies. But in practice that meant accountability to the permanent officials of the Colonial Office, granted the low prestige of the Colonial Office in the politics of British domestic government, and they, in the nature of things, could exercise only a shadowy control over public officers scattered throughout the Empire and, in any case, believed in the fetish of supporting the 'man on the spot'. Much of the adverse comment on the Crown Colony system has emphasized the irresponsibility of the legislative oppositions. But the executive was equally irresponsible; and it bred an arrogance of attitude on the part of the official side towards the nominated unofficials and the elected politicians that was peculiarly characteristic of government in the smaller islands. Quite justifiably, then, one of Froude's most able critics could point out that, for all of Froude's strictures on it, the existing Crown Colony system was in fact very little different from the Indian autocracy that Froude wanted and, with one or two exceptions, was only different in name.[4]

The legislative side was hardly in better shape. There were differences, early on, between the pure Crown Colony system, as in Trinidad and St Lucia, in which the whole legislature was nominated, consisting of both official and unofficial nominated individuals, and the semi-representative system, in which a part of the legislature was chosen by election, as in the Court of Policy in British Guiana and in Jamaica after 1884. The reforms initiated in the 1920's, however, following the Wood recommendations, produced a more or less uniform system in which the popularly elected element, either as a majority or a minority, played an increasingly active part in the legislative area. With the exception of Barbados, where the old House of Assembly was fully elective, the legislatures were mixed bodies in which the official view could invariably prevail by means of the gubernatorial veto; or, as in Jamaica, by the use on the Governor's part of the doctrine of paramount importance; or, finally, by the deployment of the official majority. Major Wood's note, in his Report of 1922, on the use of the official majority indeed made it brutally clear that the Colonial Office would never surrender its ultimate power to control both legislation and administration, so much so that the sole concession that Report recommended— that in the case of unanimous unofficial opposition against an official proposal the dissentient minority should have the right to forward a statement of their views to the Secretary of State—was an empty gesture since it presumed, contrary to all that was known of Crown Colony rule, that the Colonial Office would be willing to overrule its local representative. The legislative machinery of the system, then, in effect constituted legislation by officials voting to orders and abetted by ostensible representatives of a limited elec-torate selected and nominated by the government. It is small wonder that all self-respecting West Indians despised it.

As a system, indeed, it robbed all who participated in it of self-respect. The *ex-officio* member, required to support policy whatever his own opinion might be, was in a cruelly humiliating position. Professor Hume Wrong noted the dilemna in his book on the system, as it stood (1923) immediately prior to the implementation of the Wood reforms, and urged, by way of alleviation, that official mem-bers should be left free to vote according to conscience, with power reserved to the Governor to disregard the decision of the Council by means of a special declaration;[5] but nothing ever came of the suggestion. The system remained, in Wrong's phrase, humiliating to the conscientious official, and galling to the other side. The situa-tion was even more humiliating for the nominated unofficial group. Its members were beholden to the Crown for their appointments; they sat for limited periods only; and they had no constituents behind them to support an independent stand. As a result, their reputation for being official 'yes men', a set of colonial Quislings, was justified. Their epitaph, long overdue, was composed by the codicil in favour of a bicameral legislative structure written by Vincent Harlow and Rita Hinden for the 1950–51 Constitutional Commission report on British Guiana. Noting, generally, that the device of the nominated class was a relic, now utterly anomalous, of a Crown Colony system which had originally been devised for the government of the Caribbean settlements entering into British jurisdiction in consequence of the Napoleonic Wars, the two critics recognized the implausibility of the theoretical 'independence' of the nominated set. 'If the nominated members,' they wrote, 'operate as a disciplined bloc to prevent unwise legislation, all protestations about their freedom and independence go by the board. Inevitably, they come to be branded as "King's Friends". Such a situation would be invidious and distasteful to the persons concerned, for many nominated members at the present time are scrupulous in maintaining an attitude independent of that of the government, and it is this doctrine of independence (to which His Majesty's government in the United Kingdom has frequently and fully subscribed) which often alone persuades public-spirited men to accept nomination. If, however, they are prepared to surrender their independence and act as a group, the stultifying idea is perpetuated that "government" is something extraneous and imposed, which, since it alone wields the power, can be left to carry the responsibility.'[6]

Not the least of the system's evils, finally, was the moral havoc it worked on the elected members' side of the legislative assemblies. For responsibility belonging to the official side, the popularly elected element was unavoidably cast in the role of an opposition whose factious behaviour would never be quelled by the requirement, and the opportunity, to take responsibility itself. There was a constant temptation to make extravagant electoral promises the failure of which to materialize could always be blamed upon the hostility of the nominated members. The system at this point, as Mr Manley said of its Jamaican manifestations, was a perfect instrument for the degradation of political life, for it gave the illusion of power without the reality of responsibility, and turned decent men into rancorous critics.[7] Colonial government, seen thus, was negative government. Its institutional arrogance bred popular irresponsibility. It precluded effective co-operation between the executive and legislative branches. Local officials might from time to time invoke the image, so pleasing to the English public-school mentality, of colonial government as a polite football game played by gentlemen who understood each other,[8] but the image broke down once it was realized that it was a game between unequals in which one side had the exclusive power to construct all the rules. The report of the 1932 Dominica Conference of West Indian progressive leaders pinpointed the weaknesses of the system with fine clarity. 'Instead of a fundamentally harmonious and fruitful co-operation between government and governed,' it wrote, 'there exists in most of the West Indian islands two hostile camps: one displaying an arrogant and calculated contempt of popular desires and opinions, and the other a sullen and suspicious resentment of all the acts of Government, a state of affairs which, inevitably, reacts unfavourably on both camps to the detriment of the peace and progress of the community as a whole.'[9] Opposition for opposition's sake naturally became the rule. The average popular assembly felt that its privileges were sufficiently vindicated by fierce resistance to all official demands for rates and taxes; and, suggestively, many of the political crises of the Crown Colony period—the St Vincent riot affair of 1935, for example, or the more famous Trinidad water riots of 1903 —exemplified that general truth. There was also the fact that the general insecurity of the elected members was sharpened by (1) the absence of any party structure to contain their individualism, each of them becoming, therefore, an 'independent' responsible only to the handful of taxpayers in his parish or district, and (2) the extremely narrow electoral base on which they relied for support: in Jamaica, politically the most advanced of all the units, only one-twelfth of the population qualified for the taxpayers' franchise, while in all the colonies high property and income qualifications restricted candidacies for election to the legislative councils to the small groups of the well-to-do classes. The West Indian electoral system, as a matter of fact, was not much more advanced in 1938 than the electoral system had been in Great Britain before the Reform Bill of 1832. Professor MacMillan remarked, in his book, upon the curious fact that most of the elected political class in the region, even those who professed Socialism, were at most old-fashioned Radicals, emphasizing abstract political rights rather than matters of social and economic reconstruction. He might have added, however, that that was so because so many of West Indian social conditions at the time were a pathetic Dickensian parody of the older English conditions that had originally inspired the old Radical tradition in England itself.

In all this, inescapably, the key figure became that of the Governor. The Executive Council, not being directly responsible to the legislative body, was his creature. He was a virtual autocrat within the limits of his instructions from London. The working of the system, therefore, much depended on the individual style of individual Governors. What 'H. E.', His Excellency, said and did became the touchstones of colonial daily life. Three centuries or more of colonial rule naturally produced a wide variety of character in individual officers. But the long tradition of metropolitan equation of the West Indian colonies with naval bases and military outposts catering to 'home' interests meant that security considerations invariably preceded welfare considerations in the minds of most Government House occupants. The Colonial Office wanted no 'trouble'. The first instinct of the typical Governor, therefore, in the face of 'trouble', was to act autocratically, as, indeed, did Sir Arthur Richards as late in the colonial day as the 1940s in his high-handed treatment of Jamaican critics of British war intentions like Roger Mais. Recruited almost invariably from the career overseas service, and often prejudiced by previous African tours of duty, they usually came from the less scholarly elements of the English gentleman class. They had, then, some of the virtues, and all of the defects, of that class.

There was the usual quota of eccentrics, like the Viscount Gormanston who, as Governor of the Leeward Islands after 1885, allowed his Irish landlord's fear of the Sinn Feiners to drive him into self-appointed exile at his West Indian country seat, guarded by the Antigua Yeomanry Cavalry.[10] Or, again, like the Governor Swettenham who, in the years before 1914 as Governor in British Guiana, undertook a campaign, doomed to failure, against the planters' habit of taking a mistress; or the Governor who in nineteenth-century Nassuvian society saw fit to assume the etiquette of the Vice-Regal Court of Dublin.[11] There was, too, the usual handful of Governors and Administrators genuinely interested in West Indian life who wrote authoritative books on its various aspects, men like Sir Reginald St Johnston, Sir Henry Hesketh Bell, Mr Gideon Murray, Sir John Lefroy, and others; and special mention ought to be made, at least, of the efforts of Sir Gordon Lethem, in British Guiana, to appoint and encourage the local committee which produced, in 1948, the exhaustive *Bibliography of British Guiana*, a mine of information for the serious student of Guyanese history; as well as the tremendous work, nearly destroyed at the very end by hurricane, that went into Sir John Burdon's monumental treatise on British Honduras which, as Governor after 1925, he undertook in collaboration with local enthusiasts. Yet even this, to a great extent, was more the interest of the historical antiquarian than anything else and, indeed, gave rise to a particular brand of popular West Indian history writing usually associated with the name of Sir Algernon Aspinall. At times, even more, there was the occasional Governor who shared none of the Kiplingesque idolatry of the Empire enshrined in the Colonial Office and who could take a sceptical view of official instructions; and when such a man appeared it is worth noting that his scepticism was frequently heightened by the fact that, as with Olivier in Jamaica, he was of Huguenot ancestry or, as with Pope-Hennessy in Barbados, of Irish ancestry, and not likely, then, to share the typical upper-class Englishman's conviction of the sanctity of all things English. Generally speaking, however, such conviction was the unwritten rule of West Indian Government Houses.

It was at this point, the apex of the system, that the British political legacy joined hands with the social legacy. There was underlying political tension between government and people because government, for the most part, was not on the side of the people. The theory of the system, true, postulated a Governor and his fellow officials fighting the local vested interests on behalf of the people. After all, it was because those interests, historically, had stood in the way of general progress that the Colonial Office, earlier on, had fought to abolish the old constitutions. But the grim realities of trusteeship were widely removed from the theory. For the individual Governor, like all colonial officials, was usually a member of the English middle or upper classes, with the social bias of those classes. He came to a community, in the West Indies, where white men were social aristocrats merely by token of their skin colour, and where his official position gave him an importance unrelated to any personal merit. He discovered a local white society whose members were eager to welcome him as their ceremonial head and as their most prominent social exhibit. To join with them meant a pleasant tour of duty, to fight them meant, as Administrator Des Voeux discovered in St Lucia after 1869, political conflict and social ostracism. So, inevitably, with few exceptions, he passed smoothly into the union, political and social, of government and vested interests, even to the point

of sometimes marrying into a prominent local family. The exceptions were at least honourable ones. Olivier, following the positive
record of Sir Henry Blake, was keenly aware, as a Fabian Socialist,
of the socio-economic war between white capital and coloured
labour in the colonies. Sir Robert Neville opened up the social life
of Government House to the coloured element in the Bahamas, to
the dismay of the white oligarchy. Sir Eustace Fiennes, as Governor
in Antigua after the First World War, was that rare oddity, the
genuine aristocrat who did not feel obliged to associate with white
people in the tropics whom he would not have recognized socially
at home.

But where such types managed to do good it was because of
peculiar circumstances not germane to the system as a whole. Thus,
the reform programme pushed through the Jamaican legislature
by Sir John Peter Grant after 1866, finally granting to the Jamaican
Negro masses the full benefits of the Emancipation measure, was
only made possible by the willingness of the old Jamaican ruling
class to co-operate with a strong Governor in the aftermath of the
panic set loose by the Morant Bay 'rebellion'. Other liberal-minded
Governors elsewhere were less successful, as, for example, the brief
struggle of Pope-Hennessy in Barbados in 1875–76 on behalf of the
unenfranchised majority which ended in his early evacuation of
the post under the pressure of the hostile 'Bims'. All in all, the average Governor or Administrator was not of the calibre to lead the
'have-nots' against the 'haves'. Policy, consequently, was settled
over a chat at Government House, or a cocktail at the club, or over
a round of golf. Its terms were set, overwhelmingly, by the white
social-economic caste, with its few selected coloured favourites,
which surrounded the Governor and his officials. The occasional
ADC who wrote a memoir on his experiences, like James Pope-
Hennessy's *West Indian Summer*, invariably managed to see it in
those terms. For years it was the fixed belief of the ordinary Guianese
citizen that a Governor who attended the Georgetown Club had
thereby sold out to the local gentry; and the suspicion was echoed,
in varying degree, in every territory. In theory, all this is to say,
the ideal Governor, as A. R. F. Webber said in the case of British
Guiana, should have been a man who said to the Colonial Office
that, as a Guianese, he was on the side of the Guianese, for a Greater
Guiana.[12] In practice, he adopted such an attitude at the peril of

4*

being 'promoted' to another place by an embarrassed London bureaucracy, as, indeed, the Swettenham record in British Guiana itself showed. The average occupant of Government House, then, was on the side of the colonial ruling groups. He would, of course, be diplomatic about it; not every Governor crudely intervened with local estate managements, as did Sir Frederick Hodgson in British Guiana in 1905, to persuade them to rescind wage increases lest such increases cause 'trouble' throughout the sugar industry.[13] But his sympathies, nonetheless, were known; and taken for granted. The end-result of that situation was the general social picture painted by the Moyne Commission; and it explains why, up to the very end, the cost of the administration of the Crown Colony system fell mainly on the poor, since the rich managed throughout to avoid the imposition of direct taxation.

It is essential to note what exactly had happened to West Indian government after 1865. With the decline of the planter class at that time, and the vacuum thus created, the imperial government had been faced with two alternatives. It could have retained the embryonic democratic structure of the old representative system but with an extension of its political base, through franchise enlargement, to the colonial masses, or it could abrogate the existing political rights and itself assume direct and full responsibility for the colonial administration. It chose, perhaps inevitably, the latter course; and the measure of its subsequent failure, in the following seventy-five years or so, was summed up in the ironic fact that the very constitutional instrument, the Crown Colony regime, which was originally introduced in order to defeat the West Indian vested interests had become, certainly by 1922—as a reading of Major Wood's report on the political thinking of the mercantile class at that time shows—the cherished darling of those same interests. The choice, of course, stemmed from the fear of the masses imbedded at the heart of Victorian liberalism, so that to Victorian governments, however liberal, the idea that agricultural labourers, and Negro at that, should be granted political power must have seemed the height of absurdity. Even the most Benthamite of liberal Colonial Office officials shared that class prejudice, graphically evidenced in the remarkable advisory Minute written for Lord Glenelg by Henry Taylor in 1839. Anticipating by a generation the collapse of the old Jamaica Assembly, Taylor argued that the sole alternative was direct imperial rule. The only other choice, as he saw it, was a 'black ascendancy'. 'A black oligarchy,' he wrote, 'will certainly oppress a white minority of the people, but it will not protect the population at large; for no irresponsible oligarchy of any colour will ever do that'. Such a situation, he firmly believed, would produce another Haiti in Jamaica. 'But if we are looking,' he therefore concluded, 'to the establishment of a polity in Jamaica which shall be adapted to the circumstances of the years to come, we must contemplate the possibility of having to thwart the coloured and black interest as well as the white.'[14] Fear of the Negro masses, this is to say, combined with a conviction that they could never look after themselves, lay at the heart of British policy. That combination of class and colour phobias dominated the official outlook for the next one hundred years. It was, of course, grievously wrong. It is worth noting that George Price penned, a little later than Taylor's outburst, in his *Jamaica and the Colonial Office*, a documentary account of conscientious and successful Negro self-government in the Jamaican parish vestries and their various boards.[15] But British officialdom preferred Taylor's erroneous thesis, based as it was upon a naïve acceptance of the Haitian legend. Not the least ironic aspect of all this was that a genuine identification of colonial policy with the black majority would have found more than a ready response in the West Indian Negro, who had become accustomed to regard the British government, sometimes even Queen Victoria personally, as his protector against the predatory local interests, and who consequently lacked confidence in the idea of national independence which, as he saw it, would only mean the unbridled rule of those interests; that attitude being so deeply felt that it survived in Jamaica even up to the 1945s.

That was so all the way, until the global progressive forces unleashed by World War Two finally precipitated the grant of universal suffrage and, later, independence. In Colonial Office theory, West Indians were at school, gradually being groomed for self-government, when they were 'ready'. But both the pace and the terms of the 'advance' were set by the imperial power; and the glacial pace and restrictive terms of each successive small dose, rationalized by the very ambiguity surrounding the term 'self-government', rapidly induced disgust and scepticism in West Indians. The Colonial Office theory, quite frankly, was a complete myth.

For the history of the West Indian movement for self-government and representative institutions, especially after 1918, shows decisively that (1) Colonial Office policy, in practice, was to grant miniscule reforms at the last moment, discriminating between different territories, and seeking every way to delay the inevitable; and (2) progress, in any case, was the result of the struggle of the militant progressive forces in each colony, extracted from London through protest and agitation, led by liberal-minded coloured professional middle-class men in the beginning and, increasingly after 1935, by the Negro working class through the medium of its emergent trade unions. Just as earlier on, Dr Williams showed in his minor classic, *Capitalism and Slavery*, it was the pressure of economic forces, including the lessening profitability of slavery as an economic institution, and not English humanitarianism, that was mainly responsible for abolition, so, correspondingly in the later period, it was colonial class militancy and not British goodwill that secured the politico-constitutional advances of the time. Nor was the fact lost upon West Indians that British colonial policy operated a vicious double standard, with dominion status as the accepted goal for the white colonies and the Crown Colony system for the Negro colonies.

Political domination and economic exploitation, indeed, were accompanied by moral and intellectual rationalizations seeking to justify them. Both English writers and academic historians have contributed to the literature, frequently scandalous, of that *apologia*.[16] It is evident enough, reading that literature, that the majority of the English educated class, as well as its expatriate bureaucrats in the colonies, believed, as an article of faith, in the cultural, sometimes the racial inferiority of the West Indian person. The real offence of Froude's book, in the light of the record, was not that it was full of English Negrophobia *in extremis*, but that it gave open and unashamed expression to prejudices that the English official mind, with typical hypocrisy, preferred to keep *sub rosa*. How deeply imbedded all that was in the inarticulate value patterns of the English mind shows in the fact, frequently insufficiently noted, that it informed the attitudes and policies of the British Left almost as much as it did those of the British Right. The Moyne Commissioners themselves were a remarkable liberal group, including Sir Walter Citrine and Dame Rachel Crowdy. But they could not agree on universal suffrage, and their leading recommendation—the estab-

lishment of a development and welfare scheme—really amounted
to a suggestion that the fate of the West Indies should fall into the
hands of yet another set of British officials subject to no overriding
West Indian political authority, and failing thereby to recognize
or appreciate the political implications of the administrative federalism they had in mind. Dr Williams, again, quite rightly concedes
that no colonial Governor wrote as sympathetically and as pene-
tratingly as Olivier of the Negro people and of their problems and
potentialities.[17] Yet Olivier insisted, in his book of 1936, that the
Jamaican political community was not yet adapted for the satisfactory working of responsible government, while his complacent
eulogy of the Jamaican Crown Colony constitution at that time was
an astonishing exercise for a confessed socialist.[18] Shaw's later
account of his talks with Olivier in Jamaica leaves no doubt that
Olivier's attitude here—including his refusal to persist with his own
Fabian Society's recommendation that colonial government should
be democratized by the formation of local councils, with the Governor working with them as a Prime Minister rather than as a despot
—was not caused by racial prejudice as it was by the typical Fabian
preference for bureaucratic rationality as against democratic politics;[19] yet it had the consequence of relegating the Jamaican Negro
to the status of a second-class citizen.

Professor Simey's book of 1946, finally, although a strong plea
for the rebuilding of West Indian society, and a much-needed
warning against the dangers of the uncritical 'Westernization' of
colonial peoples, ended with a demand not for the abolition of
empire but for merely a 'new outlook' in the empire, to be formu-
lated by a new type of colonial civil servant trained in planning,
anthropology and the newer social sciences. The social welfare
enthusiast of the Moyne Report, that is to say, was to be replaced
by the scientific sociologist of the Simey variety. But in both cases
the argument assumed a continuing British control of subject
peoples deemed to stand in need of guided development towards
higher things. The 'responsibilities of empire', according to Simey,
had to be thought out anew in Great Britain. But he did not specify
how that was to be done; nor did he seem to consider that West
Indians, by this time, might be themselves wondering whether it was
not the imperial system itself, rather than the varying degrees of
'responsibility' which it might care to exhibit, that was on trial.[20]

Up until the last, in brief, educated English opinion, of all political complexions, although frequently opposed in real sincerity to Froude's racialism, tended to accept his ideal of continuing white imperial trusteeship. And a final illustration of that attitude could be seen in the Evans Settlement Commission of 1948 which advocated for the economic rehabilitation of British Guiana and British Honduras an extensive resettlement and immigration policy to be administered by the officials and experts of the Colonial Development Corporation, with the individual colonial governments playing a minor participatory role only.[21]

The sad fact was that trusteeship, as an operative reality, never really got off the ground. Originally enunciated by Burke in 1783, it was the stated first principle of British colonial rule. But the date of slavery emancipation (1834) almost exactly coincided with the year (1832) heralding the victory of *laissez-faire* in English life, involving, pretty rapidly, the application of that dogma to a West Indian post-Emancipation society which required planned social reconstruction and vast economic expenditure if trusteeship was to mean anything. Hence imperial policy became an absurd effort, as in the case of the misguided 'Queen's Advice', sent to Jamaica in response, indirectly, to the famous Underhill letter of 1865, to apply the *laissez-faire* economic virtues of industry and prudence to a poverty-stricken peasant-planter economy for which they were hopelessly inappropriate.[22] That did not sound like a Colonial Office eagerly protecting the West Indian peasant masses against their master-class. And even when there were Colonial Office policy makers, most notably James Stephen, who sought that role—Sir Henry Taylor observed in his *Autobiography* that by his genius Stephen virtually governed the colonial empire for more than twenty-five years—their dream petered out because its only condition of success, an organized alliance between the imperial guardians and a supporting West Indian social force, necessarily that of the peasant mass, was never seriously investigated, let alone created. The lag in West Indian constitutional progress, consequently, was throughout a sorry commentary on the liberal ideal of those British writers—Professor Zimmern's *The Third British Empire*, for example—who imagined that the various territories of the Empire were members of a procession marching along the high road towards responsible self-government.

From time to time, it is true, an alliance of sorts did grow up between the more liberal of white officials and the politically conscious local groups. But it never had full metropolitan support, without which, of course, it rapidly withered away. Even as late as 1937 it was possible for the Colonial Office to remove the Governor of Trinidad, Sir Murchison Fletcher, because of his speech to that colony's Legislative Council chastising the Trinidadian white employer class for their narrow-minded policies and regretting that the earnest sincerity of the Butler revolt in the oilfields, as well as the personal sincerity of its remarkable leader, had not been properly appreciated.[23] Trusteeship, in other words, presupposed the existence of British governments ready to send out strong Governors and Administrators to the islands to keep in closer touch with local conditions. It demanded, that is, a faith both in the good will and in the power of the Colonial Office bureaucracy to overrule local vested interests, a faith it was difficult to summon up in the light of the record. The battle of the West Indian peoples, clearly, could only be won in the West Indies, not in Church Street or Downing Street. Once West Indian leadership came to see this, as it did after 1935, the function of the Colonial Office was to acquiesce, as graciously as it could, to the terms of a changing situation. The function of the liberal-minded Governor, likewise, became that of presiding over the liquidation of the Crown Colony system, as with Beetham in Trinidad and Foot and Blackburne in Jamaica. For the Governor in the colonial setting, however much he might personally identify himself with what he liked to call West Indian 'aspirations', was the agent of the supreme imperial power. His destiny was to protect, above all, the interests of that power ; rule conscientiously, as being usually an English gentleman, he would ; then retire to compose a volume, usually dull, of his memoirs, secure in the knowledge that he had done his duty ; as indeed, within the limits of the system, he had.

A genuine trusteeship, what is more, would have required ties between London and the island capitals far more intimate and creative than in fact existed. The Colonial Service, unlike the Home Civil Service, developed only very late a sophisticated career sentiment. There was no organized system either of recruitment or of training until the end of the First World War. The story of the nineteenth-century Governor of Bermuda who was, on his own account, simply a hardworking soldier and who was chosen by the Secretary of State to go to Hamilton merely on the basis of the fact that his book on the *Law of Storms* had been read with interest by that august personage,[24] was typical of the way in which people got appointed. And even when a system of more rational selection developed it remained the wholly undesirable one of continuing selection by the Secretary of State on the advice of the Private Secretary's (Appointments) establishment and thus avoided the democratic method of open competitive examination; a system which even an official committee of inquiry termed, in 1930, a system of patronage that, 'if seriously challenged . . . could not in theory be defended' and that ought to be replaced by a selection process 'at once more authoritative and more independent'.[25] Appointments to the *élite* Administrative Services, moreover, were almost the exclusive monopoly of the two ancient universities, thereby ensuring the rule of the 'old school tie' ideology in the commanding heights of the colonial administration. The average administrative officer only too painfully reflected the inadequacies of the traditional Oxbridge mentality, for he knew little of economics, labour, nutrition or social welfare, while his knowledge of the later social sciences was usually absolutely nil. Living abroad for such lengthy service periods as he did, he was usually abysmally ignorant of public opinion at home, and especially of public opinion outside the ranks of the Establishment. He was, then, an expert neither on the colonial situation nor on the 'home' situation, and thus merely served to render their mutual ignorance of each other even more dense.

All of this was stated with admirable frankness in the remarkable *Memorandum* by Sir Ralph Furse, published in 1943, on the need for radically new training and recruitment schemes for the post-war service. 'The Englishman,' he wrote, 'especially that type of Englishman who is mainly representative of the Colonial Service, has been, on the whole, brilliantly—even uniquely—successful in his dealings with what is called the unspoilt native. So far he has shown himself much less successful in dealing with the new native intelligentsia.' The meaning of that observation for the West Indies was, of course, that its trusteeship assumption was wholly out of place in a society where the African-type 'unspoilt native' was quite unknown, small pockets of Mayan Indians and Guianese Amerindians excepted. The Caribbean colonies, again, had suffered much from the cultural parochialism of their English ruling *élite*, and would have benefited tremendously had Sir Ralph Furse's ideal of a finely trained official been the real thing. That ideal, as the 1943 *Memorandum* put it, would be 'to send the given officer wherever in the world he can best study the subject matter he has chosen, whether it were advanced anthropology at some British or continental university, the agricultural development of Java, the organization and methods of a shipping firm or business house, American town planning policy in Puerto Rico, economics or problems of population and census at London University, Russian policy in relation to the backward people of Kazakstan, social welfare at Liverpool, or the policy of foreign administrators of genius like General Wood or Marshal Lyautey and their effect on the Philippines and Morocco.'[26] The sentence had peculiar relevance to the Caribbean area, where the British colonies were in close proximity to the French, Dutch, and American possessions. But, as a policy, it was too late by 1943 to undo the damage done by generations of 'educated' English officials who knew practically nothing, and rejoiced in knowing nothing, of colonial problems in Martinique or Surinam or Puerto Rico.

The official, of course, was the servant of London, and appeal to London was always possible. But granted the traditional reluctance of the Colonial Office mind to take sides against its own men, appeal, usually made at West Indian expense by means of costly visiting delegations 'up to England', very rarely paid off. At the same time, Governors on the spot became adept at all the little diplomatic tricks of keeping agitators quiet, including the use, if the tricks failed, of deportation powers, prohibition of 'subversive' literature and, in the last resort, detention and imprisonment. From time to time recommendations were made for improving the channels of communication between the centre and the circumference, the interchange of officials, for example, between London and the individual colonies, or the Moyne Commission idea of colonial representation in parliamentary committees at Westminster, after the fashion of the rights of access to United States parliamentary bodies enjoyed at that time by elected members of the municipal councils in the United States Virgin Islands. Invariably cold-shouldered as such ideas were, the colonial interests could only present their grievances to Westminster at second-hand through the good services of friendly House of Commons members. Not, indeed, that the House of

Commons was itself an ideal forum for expressing colonial discontents. Sir Stafford Cripps described its defects, as such, in his speech to the historical inaugural meeting of the Jamaican People's National Party in Kingston's Ward Theatre in 1938. 'It means,' he said, 'that if something exceptional occurs in Jamaica it may be that for one hour or one hour and a half during the course of twelve months a discussion will ensue and questions will be put in the House of Commons. During that period of time the Colonial Secretary will be armed with particulars from the Colonial Office obtained from the local government and he will courteously assure everybody that their facts must be wrong. And as he has the assurance that he is always right, and as no vote of any effectiveness can take place on supply at the termination of the question, the interests of Jamaica will be put to bed for twelve further months. And if you will add to this picture a true picture of the administration of colonial affairs of empire—the Parliamentary discussion of affairs—there will probably be present in the House of Commons no more than 40 people, not half a dozen of them having the slightest knowledge of what they are talking about, you will appreciate that the Imperial administration by the Imperial Parliament can hardly be looked upon as an effective or constructive method of managing colonial dependencies.'[27]

The Fabian Colonial Bureau helped in some way to counterbalance all this, publishing, as it did, a multitude of informed and critical books and pamphlets on the colonial problem, while books like those of Olivier and MacMillan and Simey enabled many West Indians to see their problems afresh, in much the same way as Leyburn's *The Haitian People*, published in 1941, had a profound influence upon the Creole intellectuals of the Haitian *mouvement indigène*. Yet, even then, it is urgent to remember that Fabianism, essentially parochial, was preoccupied from the beginning with domestic, industrial and political issues and was only reluctantly driven, early on, to state its position on colonial problems, by way of the pamphlet *Fabianism and the Empire*, because the pressures of the South African War of 1899 forced it to do so. That explains why Olivier found it difficult to get his Fabian friends in London to take his Jamaican interests seriously, just as, later in the century, Governor Tugwell in Puerto Rico found if difficult to persuade his Washington New Deal friends that Puerto Rico was important. It explains, too, why Fabian interest in the colonial empire, when it did materialize, offered little in the way of fundamental politico-constitutional change, for its bias in favour of the rule of the expert reinforced, rather than challenged, the benevolent autocracy of the system. That explains, why, finally, the Fabian suggestions made from time to time to improve the system, the recommendation, for instance, of a parliamentary committee on colonial affairs, dealt with the administrative symptoms rather than the basic causes of the colonial problem. The Fabian attitude to that problem, in brief, was frequently more English than socialist. As late as 1951 the Guianese popular leadership could say of the Waddington Constitution of that year that it was an insipid document 'written by an old colonial Governor accustomed to the sweets of domination, a professor of history who said British colonial pirates were motivated by a "spirit of adventure" and a Fabian socialist who believes that only gradually, step by step and inch by inch, must any progress come about'.[28] The upshot of all this was that whereas the propertied interests in the area had the West India Committee to look after their concerns in London the progressive Creole forces had no such agency. Those forces had to fight the Colonial Office as best as they could, and more often than not on their own.

The political legacy the British left behind them, in brief, was highly Roman. On its positive side, it was incorruptible, highly motivated, passionately conscious of duty and conduct. It was determinedly constitutionalist, although the Crown Colony system placed severe strains upon constitutionalism. It cared for civil liberties; and it must mean something that a recently published (1964) book on public liberties in the new states does not contain a single reference to the West Indies.[29] It was not even afraid to declare its own faults and its West Indian critics have perhaps not sufficiently appreciated the fact that most of the ammunition they have used in their indictment of colonialism has come from the voluminous Blue Books of innumerable official reports. In that sense, it is patently wrong to say, as Blanshard says in his book of 1947, that the neglect of the social sciences in the West Indian educational system is due to a deliberate attempt to perpetuate the colonial status by withholding knowledge that might lead to rebellion against the colonial power.[30] What has been done, indeed, by British colonialism itself in furnishing material for the massive indictment of its critics, West Indians and others, is itself proof of the honesty of British intentions; and the reports of British officials play the same role in the anti-colonial literature that they had earlier on in illustrating the argument of Marx's *Capital*. It is the weakness of books like Dr Williams's *History of the People of Trinidad and Tobago* that, conceived more in a spirit of hatred rather than of anger, they consistently underestimate the contribution, however minor, of the best of the British spirit to West Indian life, so that in that particular volume there is only one brief mention of the Moyne Commission Report; while in a subsequent volume, *British Historians and the West Indies*, Dr Williams is so anxious to paint everything the British have done in the blackest possible colours that he fails to mention British liberal writers on the West Indies such as Coke and Southey, while the work of Olivier and Pares is discussed only cursorily, thus enabling the author to concentrate, at the cost of a proper perspective, on the imperial historians like Freeman and Seeley, who in fact showed little interest at all in the West Indies but are vulnerable targets because they wrote offensively about the 'native' peoples of the Empire. The British, in all conscience, were colonialists. But it is at once historically inaccurate and psychologically unconvincing to write about them as if they were devils in human form.

Having said that, of course, it remains true that, on its negative side, British colonialism, measured by any lasting standard, was found wanting. It cared little about the artistic and aesthetic background of colonial life and experience (the official suppression of Carnival in Trinidad was a case in point). It concentrated almost exclusively on political institutions, inadequate even as the final record in that area was, being certainly far behind the granting to all West Indian territories (as the 1945 Conference of the Caribbean Labour Congress demanded) of wholly elected legislatures based on universal adult suffrage, with policy-making executive councils responsible to the legislatures, and of wholly elected local government authorities. It lacked something, as Sir Ralph Furse noted, of the Greek spirit, and in that sense was far inferior to French colonial administration. It prided itself on its imperial manners, the moral code of the English gentleman as idealized in Burke and Newman, and, indeed, imparted the code to the small groups of the educated West Indian classes, the West Indian gentleman, as he is known, of the 'old school'. But that simply meant, in the political sphere, the incorporation of those groups into the local colonial Establishment, struggling for their own limited political rights and leaving the popular social base comparatively untouched; although later, as is well known, that acceptance of the British constitutional system and its scale of values would help lay the foundations of a wider West Indian democracy. At their best, then, the British evoked respect and even loyalty from the majority of their West Indian subjects. By comparison with the American colonial record there were advantages to the British style. 'On first acquaintance,' observed an American traveller in 1936 of his fellow Americans in Puerto Rico, 'we become warmly personal, and then paternal. The British are different. They are coldly impersonal; they go out to rule and nothing swerves them. In their code there is always socially an abyss between natives and rulers, yet they will die for each other. Time and time again, in our colonies, we have seen the American contact grow into something like a canker sore, a form of social indigestion, as it were, from too much sweetness.'[31] But to urge that British colonialism avoided those cruder excesses of the American brand was, at best, a negative compliment only. It did not absolve the British record from its own basic failure, from the fact that by 1939 most West Indians had become thoroughly disillusioned with protestations that Britain held democracy in store for them as their ultimate status. Henceforward, they would expect immediate action; or, denied it, move to demand it.

# Chapter V

# THE INCUBUS OF CROWN COLONY

## THE LEEWARD ISLANDS

THE GENERAL neglect of the West Indies was worse, of course, for the smaller units of the Leewards and Windwards, due to the comparative smallness of their constituent communities, the tiny scale of their economic activities and their distribution over an oceanic area large enough to make frequent communication a fairly expensive matter. Their earlier importance, especially in the case of the Leeward Islands, as the first of the English colonizing efforts and as the birthplace of early West Indian government by means of the old proprietary system, was rapidly superseded, after 1763, by the new ceded territories and by the larger territories, so that even today most English people identify the West Indies with Jamaica. The written literature about them is scanty to a degree. Much of it, suggestively enough, belongs to the earlier period when they were better known: Atwood's *History of the Island of Dominica* (1791), for example, or Breen's *St Lucia, Historical, Statistical, and Descriptive* (1844); while the later literature frequently carries the stamp of the official mind, like the 1924 *Handbook of the Leeward Islands*, published by the Crown Agents for the Colonies. Or, again, there was the occasional memoir published by the liberally minded resident magistrate or medical doctor, like Dr S. B. Jones' *Annals of Anguilla* (1936), that particular volume being published as a gesture of admiration for the courage of the Anguillan folk during the harsh drought years after 1918.

Their general decline throughout the nineteenth century continued into the twentieth. Once prosperous economies like Nevis, for example, fell into oblivion, only to be remembered, even in modern times, when sentimental Americans organize (as in 1957) a series of events commemorating the bicentennial anniversary of Alexander Hamilton's birth in the island. The evacuation of the British Navy from its old-established West India stations—as from

118

Nelson's Dockyard in Antigua in 1899—stripped such islands almost overnight of a vital source of income, to provide historically-minded English governors later with pet schemes of antiquarian renovation, like Sir Kenneth Blackburne's patronage of the fund launched in the 1950's for the rehabilitation of the same Nelson's Dockyard. Smaller islands, again, like Barbuda and Anguilla, whose economy for a long time had been in fact that of the notorious 'wrecking' system, rapidly went downhill with the decline of West Indian maritime shipping and the improvement of navigational aids; but not before, be it added, 'wrecking' had left behind it a rich folklore, like the marching songs of the Anguillan liquor smugglers, commemorating, some of them, the famous West Indian rums:

> *All hail the power of Cockspur's Name*
> *Let drunkards prostrate fall*

Apart, therefore, from the more general causes of West Indian decay analysed by Ragatz in his classic study, additional particular factors aggravated the Leewards situation. A diversified agriculture did not grow up as extensively as it did elsewhere so that, especially in St Kitts, the large corporate sugar estate utilizing the labour of a landless sugar tenantry has remained, up to the present time, the controlling feature of all Kittitian life. Migration patterns were accentuated by the lack of employment opportunities generally, so that they oscillated between a heavy exodus in the 1920s to the United States, Santo Domingo, Costa Rica, and Cuba and a mass return in the 1930's; while later in the 1950s the small economy of Montserrat lost some fifty per cent of its population in emigration to the United Kingdom. Nor was any of this offset by counterbalancing forces, for, being of small size, the islands did not attract, until very recently, the notice of the modernizer; and even then modernization, as with the burgeoning tourist industry in Antigua, has taken the form of a notoriously vulnerable investment sector.

Whereas, therefore, the history of the larger units—Guyana, Jamaica, Trinidad, Barbados—during the post-Moyne period has been that of a slow but sure growth of a consciously felt local nationalist spirit, culminating in national independence for Jamaica and Trinidad (1962) and for Guyana and Barbados (1966), that of the smaller Eastern Caribbean territories has been one of a prolonged stalemate within the vise of the Crown Colony system. In terms both of economic progress and politico-constitutional development they have consistently been twenty years behind the larger entities. That is why, even today, their politics still revolve around open or covert war against the Colonial Office and its local representatives; and why, too, the tactics of that struggle remain much what they were a generation ago. There is still the organized demonstration, sometimes a monster torchlight parade, against Government House, practically unchanged as a mode of orderly protest from the Grenada episode of 1931 to the 'Operation Blackburne' organized by the St Kitts labour movement in 1950, and defended by its organizers, in 1950 as much as in 1931, by archaic references to the traditional English constitutional struggles from the Provisions of Oxford, through the Pilgrim Fathers, to the seventeenth-century regicides,[1] rather than being set within a West Indian reference frame. There is the method, long since of historical interest only in England, of the petition of subjects to the Crown, such as the petitions to the Queen, pleading against the proposed introduction of legalized casino gambling into Antigua, prepared by the Antigua-Barbuda Democratic Movement and by the Antigua Christian Council in 1962.[2] The myth that the Queen governs as well as reigns dies hard in the West Indian popular imagination, going back, as it does, to the conviction that Queen Victoria 'freed the slaves'. There are the official trips of island political leaders to London to improve the terms of metropolitan grants-in-aid, success in which is always a prime source of local popularity. It should be noted on that point that St Kitts has been the only Leeward-Windward territory able to do without grant-in-aid, with its concomitant humiliating surveillance of daily expenditures by the United Kingdom Treasury. A local economy like the Montserratian may become almost completely dependent on metropolitan financing, with the resultant exacerbation of the general tension and ill-feeling prevailing between the elective and the official sides of government, not to mention the fact that Treasury control effectively impedes the usage of the tax power by local governments for purposes of economic development. The grant-in-aid economy thus breeds the typical London psycho-complex, with all of its debilitating consequences. The more sophisticated of the small island leaders, of course, have insisted that they are fighting the Crown Colony system, not the individual persons of Governors and Administrators. But such a nice separation has always been difficult to maintain, and especially in tiny circumscribed island societies. Person and office are bound to get mixed up with each other. So, finally, there was the tactic of abusing the Administrator, sometimes his wife and family, in the diatribes, often inventively scurrilous, of the local market square political meeting. Hence, generally, the melodrama, only too often, of the small island power struggle: Governor Williams becomes 'an animated condition of delay'; Colonel Howard's marital life becomes cocktail party gossip; Mr Turbott is an 'Africa man' who is pilloried in the local press because he allegedly refuses to have local photographers take shots of visiting Princess Margaret dancing at Government House with coloured partners; Mr Rose is an imported Guianese who, it is said, uses his Leeward Islands appointment as a safe refuge until new conditions in Georgetown permit him to return home to a handsomely remunerated public appointment. Only too often, in response, the official side took to an attitude of, at best, genial contempt for their elected opponents, in the manner of the language put into the mouth of a mythical small island governor in Alec Waugh's novel: '. . . they are all of them comics, these West Indians, even or rather especially my legislative councillors; and like all true comedians they behave with the utmost seriousness. One must never let them think that their acting has not convinced one. And it is not only the coloured West Indians who behave in this way; the "sugar barons" have caught their tempo.'[3]

What officialdom failed to see, of course, was that such behaviour was not intrinsically West Indian but the outcome of the reactionary Crown Colony system. The basic premise of the system, that English guardians were looking after West Indian wards, was gall and wormwood to West Indian pride, for even in the most liberally-minded of Government House occupants it sustained the attitude that local leaders were 'my legislative councillors'. The leading fact about it all was that, throughout all of the gradual steps of constitutional reform that took place slowly after 1925, and with increasing momentum after 1945, that premise was never in any real sense relinquished. The pace of reform, of course, was glacial and almost certainly in the later period the result in part of the growing pressure of American liberal opinion. Universal adult suffrage had to wait until 1951; while through the next fifteen years or so there were a series of piecemeal measures—the introduction of the committee system, the cutting down of the power of the nominated members in the legislative councils, the ministerial system, the introduction of the office of Chief Minister—which, even when all put together, still left untouched the real power of the imperial agents. Nothing was granted willingly, no large gesture of magnanimity made. Each little concession was the end-result of interminable agitation. The class bias of the Colonial Office mentality infused all of its West Indian policy; it granted concessions only when 'responsible opinion' or 'substantial elements'— phrases that abound in Major Wood's 1922 report— supported concessions. The basic dishonesty of the Wood report, indeed, was that, in general, it wrote against reform when 'responsible opinion' in any particular territory was against it, as was the case at that time in both St Kitts and Antigua, but that, when in the particular case of Dominica (at that time united with the Leewards) it unfortunately found that 'responsible opinion' was for reform, it casuistically shifted the line of argument and justified its refusal to meet the Dominica demands on the ground that to do so would stimulate fresh 'agitation' in the other islands; so that the reformist case lost either way.[4] Metropolitan timidity, in turn, was aided by the fact that until the late 1930s leadership of the various island Representative Government Associations and Reform Leagues was in the hands of middle-class professional people who were concerned with limited reforms centring around the increase of the elected element in the legislatures, and whose outlook was perhaps most fully expressed in the report of the Dominica Conference of 1932 which only endorsed the adult franchise as the 'ultimate aim' of a new West Indies Federation and was content to leave the matter of immediate reform of voting qualifications to the local legislatures. It is suggestive, then, that London began to grant something like real reforms only after 1945, when the pressure of American opinion already noted, plus the growing influence of progressive West Indian groups living abroad in London and New York, combined with the rise of militant trade union organizations, changed the colonial climate, with the initiative passing from the brown middle class to the black working class. St Kitts had the honour, in that development, of forming one of the first of those progressive organizations, the Workers League, in 1932, which in turn stimulated the formation of the Trades and Labour Union in 1940; while Antigua followed in 1939 with the formation of its own organization of similar title, being inspired, incidentally, in large part by the lecture on the history of the British working class movement delivered at the St John's Anglican Cathedral schoolroom in January 1939 by Sir Walter Citrine during his short stay in the island as a member of the West Indies Royal Commission.

Individual Administrators, it is true, were frequently, though covertly, on the side of local progressivism, for, after all, it did not require much of a liberal spirit to condemn the primitive mentality and antediluvian social ideas of the West Indian white employer class. In societies like the smaller islands, where there was little of widespread consultation between government and representative associations, the influence, by means of personal contacts, that a liberal-minded Administrator could bring to bear upon recalcitrant local conservatives, might, indeed, be of vast importance. Even so, apart from occasional homilies in Legislative Council, his hands were tied by official instructions, and their general conservatism. He ought to have been able to form local alliances with the progressive forces. But that would have necessitated imperial willingness to accept the two leading principles of change demanded, for example, by the Kittitian labour leadership in the 1950 crisis: first, the right of the local colonial peoples to be consulted about the appointment of Governors and, second, the principle that West Indians should become candidates for the appointments.[5] But neither principle was accepted by London. To the last, British officialdom believed, as Sir Henry Taylor had put it a century earlier, that there was a natural disposition in the colonies to be governed by an English aristocratic personage, and, if not that, at least a metropolitan person. What that meant in practice, only too often, as the West Indian press was not slow in pointing out, was the use of the colonial appointments power for the purpose of finding hiding places for embarrassing skeletons from the closets of noble families, who rarely turned out to be young men whose intellect and clarity of judgment could assist the colony's advance unaffected by social distractions and by the urge to calculate their personal recognition.[6]

Reform, then, in both Leewards and Windwards, was throughout too little and too late. Major Wood, in his report, had wanted the Colonial Office to avoid the mistake of 'withholding a concession ultimately inevitable until it has been robbed by delay of most of its usefulness and all of its grace'.[7] Yet, during the next forty years, that was, indeed, the cardinal mistake committed by official policy, leading directly to the present parlous state of the smaller islands. Each concession, as it was made, was followed by constitutional quarrels serving to illustrate its obsolescence even before it could expand into something else. Adult suffrage pushed further along the development of mass party organizations, replacing the old middle class independent politician with the new labour leader, so that, in St Kitts, Bradshaw and Southwell replaced Seaton and Manchester, in Antigua, Bird and Hurst replaced men like the adopted Barbadian planter and editor Harold T. Wilson, also at one time founder and editor of the old *Antigua Magnet*. But the new men were denied the logical concomitant of adult suffrage, popular government in its fullest form. They were given, instead, an elective majority in the legislative councils and an increased number of elected members, albeit still a minority, in the executive councils. The introduction of the committee system at much the same time, whereby certain elected members of the executive councils became chairmen of departmental committees, breached the hitherto solid wall of separation between the legislative and administrative arms of colonial government. But such chairmen had no responsibility for departmental policy, being associated in name only with the departments assigned to them, the real policy-making power remaining still with the Directors of the departments, usually Englishmen. The final power of the Governor, or Administrator, and his senior officials, remained, somewhat obscurely but none the less real, in the background; while the power of the purse remained untouched in the hands of the Financial Secretary, always a close associate of the chief executive. This was followed, in 1956, by the introduction of a quasi-ministerial system in which, the Executive Council now having a majority of elected members, three of the latter were permitted to hold ministerial portfolios—Trade and Production, Communications and Works, and Social Services. But that, at best, was a pseudo-cabinet without a head, and the effectiveness of the system, from the popular viewpoint, depended solely upon how much of a united front the ministers could present against the official and nominated sections. If, in fact, the elected members, whether of the legislative or of the executive councils, were politicians of different party allegiances that would result, as the Antigua Labour

Party pointed out early on in its first manifesto attendant on the adult suffrage regime, in a perpetual squabble between those who should be looking after the community interest while Government and the nominated element would gladly take advantage of the division and continue to rule in the old imperialistic way.[8] It was fortunate that in all three presidencies of the Leeward Islands— St Kitts, Antigua, Montserrat—that danger was avoided only by the fact that, even before adult suffrage, organized labour had dominated their political life and that, after the conferment of adult suffrage, it held, and continues today to hold, a virtual monopoly of the elected seats. Finally, in 1960 the institution of the office of the Chief Minister, along with the recognition of the constitutional principle that the Administrator would appoint as Chief Minister the member of the legislature most likely to command a legislative majority and that, further, other ministers would be appointed on the Chief Minister's advice, made possible the growth of at least an embryonic cabinet system based on the collective responsibility of its members for policy.

But all that constituted an embryonic cabinet only, and not the real thing. For the real thing requires, as Trinidad and Jamaica full national independence. The constitutional development of the smaller island, in truth, has been a development in which the British have given up, step by step the forms of power while retaining its substance. As a federal colony, the Leewards were ruled—until the dismantling of the Leeward Islands Federation, with defederalization, in 1956—by a Governor with wide reserve powers in the fields of defence and foreign policy, as well as of domestic matters touching upon imperial interests. The senior officials, both at the federal and presidency levels, retained the strategic portfolios of law, finance, and control of the police, away from popular control. Defederalization, it is true, which also meant the abolition of the office of the Leeward Islands Governorship, ended the life of the general legislative body and executive councils of the 1871 Federation, a dissolution demanded for years by the Leewards labour movements. But even then the office of the general Governorship was retained, between 1956 and 1960, for a further humiliating period; and when it did finally disappear most of its vital reserve powers were delegated to the individual island Administrators. It is worth noting that, in the twilight of the unpopular federal period, the Governor's reserve power to certify bills above legislative council objection was used with increasing frequency against the local labour blocs—the fight in 1943 with the Montserrat legislature over the key issue of the police force, for example, and the overriding of the St Kitts-Nevis-Anguilla legislature in 1952 on the matter of single-member constituency districts, a move designed to cut down Labour's chances of electoral victory. The individual Administrator, in his turn (or, as in the case of Montserrat and the British Virgin Islands, the Commissioner), became, after defederalization, the main figure around whom constitutional and political dispute continued to rage. There was a contradiction involved in the anomalous status he enjoyed, since he was at once leader of the administrative government and President of the Legislative Council and it was not until the early 1960s that he was finally replaced by an elected Speaker in the legislative body, a change demanded in the 1957 motion on Constitutional Reform introduced by Mr Bradshaw in the St Kitts Council. It has now become conventional for his annual address to the legislative councils to be a sort of Throne Speech, outlining the Chief Minister's policy programme, after the Westminster fashion.

But the continued presence of official and nominated members on the executive council level continued to symbolize Labour's failure fully to democratize the 'cabinet' administrative system, frustrating the development of the councils into genuine cabinets based on full accountability to the popular electorate (not to mention the quite different problem of the 'democratization' of a civil service which, on the whole, was anti-Labour in its sentiments, constituting not so much a politically neutral instrument of public administration, as its British architects liked to believe, but a thinly-disguised interest group tending to view the new class of popularly-elected ministers as upstarts encroaching on the powers of the civil bureaucracy). The most outstanding example of the impasses thus created in the machinery of government in the Leewards case was the 1958 struggle between the Administrator of St Kitts-Nevis, Colonel Howard, and the St Kitts Labour Party over the matter of the nominated member of the Executive Council representing the separate Nevis constituency. For a situation in which an 'independent' member of the Council, in that particular case, the Hon. Eugene Walwyn, could vote against legislation supported by the legislative majority, be evicted by them and, in turn, be renominated to the Council by the high-handed action of the Administrator acting on the basis of discretionary powers conferred upon him by Royal Instructions, the necessary amendment to those Instructions having been arranged in the Colonial Office without consultation with the local Kittitian leadership—clearly underlined the dangers of a constitutional instrument in which an Executive Council member could remain as an enemy of the majority leadership within the very citadel of policy formation. Furthermore, the justification put out at the time by the federal Governor constituted a grave assault upon the emergent principle of collective responsibility, since it in effect argued that three members of Council—the statutory member for Nevis, the nominated member, and the official member—were exempt from the application of the principle since they were responsible neither to the Legislative Council nor to the electorate; and what that meant, frankly, was that they were made privy to the most intimate of 'cabinet' discussions and were then free, if they desired, to use that privilege as a means of opposing 'cabinet' decisions. Nothing could have illustrated better the fatal divorce between power and responsibility so much the chief defect of the Crown Colony system.[9] A genuine cabinet system, granted the continuation of the Crown Colony regime, at the least required, as the St Kitts leaders argued at the time, a non-voting Crown Attorney, an Administrator stripped of the power to assign subjects to 'ministers' as he pleased, the control of finance to pass to an elected member and, in general, a cabinet responsible to, and removable by, the Legislative Council.[10]

'There comes a time in the life of an emergent people,' the St Kitts leaders told the Secretary of State, 'when the penultimate stage to self-determination is no longer tolerable because of its own political and psychological limitations and because of the accentuated zeal with which the subject people must naturally press onward to the visible goal.'[11] At such a stage, obviously, the play of personality, based upon personalist power, must yield more and more to the general demands of that goal. So, an illiberal Administrator can make things worse. But a liberal Administrator cannot make things much better. Colonel Howard, in the St Kitts-Nevis situation, generally sought to co-operate with the new Labour forces, a disposition reinforced by his own local experience; his refusal to be elected to the all-white local Tennis Club was symptomatic and no one realized better than he how the 'black-balling' that went on in clubs like the St Christopher Club kept the more able and liberal type of West Indian coloured civil service officers away from service in the Presidency. Lord Baldwin's brief tenure of the Leewards Governorship (1948–50) likewise showed how sympathetic a radical English socialist, albeit eccentric, in the rather tired Edwardian manner, could be to the West Indian tragedy. Yet the Baldwin governorship ended in forced resignation since, for all his patronage of the local steel-bands and friendship with the Bird forces, he still retained, under the epidermis of kindness and sympathy, the assumption of the English gentleman that he was always, in the last resort, to be in command, so that in the end he lost the confidence of both of the local political factions.[12] In St Kitts, again, Colonel Howard's aplomb may have managed to control the characteristic outbreaks of social aggressiveness on the part of popularly-elected ministers at Government House cocktail parties—for such ministers could never afford to be suspected of too close a relationship with the colonial officials, however friendly—but it could not avoid the built-in conflicts of a constitution the Administrator himself disliked. Nor were matters made any better by the tendency to hand over responsibilities in the smaller islands to the expatriate West Indian civil servant group from the larger islands, many of whom came with a sort of Harrison College, Barbados condescending attitude to their 'small island' fellow West Indians.

The smaller islands, altogether, have been held back by colonial rule. They must now make up for lost time. Their problem, at bottom, is economic. But the Colonial Office prescriptions of cure have generally been of a constitutional character, so that there has been a history of ill-advised constitutional schemes such as the recommendation of the Closer Union Commission of 1933 for the inclusion of the Leewards, along with the Windwards, into one large colony, to be ruled by a new Governor conceived of as a miniature Viceroy of India.[13] There have been too many attempts to apply British constitutional norms to West Indian conditions totally different from those prevailing in the United Kingdom, in particular, the 'rule of obligation' enunciated by successive Secretaries of State for the Colonies concerning political ministers who concurrently held acting trade union appointments; an attitude which failed to appreciate that in small tropical economies the trade union has been the traditional doorway to political eminence and rarely possesses sufficient leadership talent to tolerate complete loss of trained personnel to the political side; not to mention the fact, of paramount importance, that united political-cum-industrial action on one single front of battle has been a basic minimum rule of organization necessary to challenge a bitterly reactionary sugar plantocracy. For monolithic employee units are only a response to monolithic employer units. In these small sugar islands the plantation came to constitute at once a powerful social system exerting a high degree of influence over the family and social life of the plantation workers, and a political subentity all of its own. This produced the characteristic situation in which, as in the Antiguan situation of the 1950s, the most powerful single man in the island life was Moody Stuart, at once managing director of the great Antigua Syndicate Estates empire and leading member of both Legislative and Executive Councils, thus constituting in his own person a 'conflict of interests' rarely, if ever, noticed by the various despatches from the Colonial Office that warned of the dangers of 'conflict of interest' in the trade union area. There is also the consideration, peculiarly West Indian, that union leaders who, on becoming ministers, resign from the trade union run the risk of losing their union support to those who take their place; as in fact happened with Grantley Adams once he resigned the Presidency of the Barbados Workers Union in 1954 in a characteristic act of Barbadian deference to English rules. [14]

Worst of all, perhaps, there has been a fatal indecisiveness about the ultimate political status of the islands. They have never had constitutional parity with the larger units. They have never known, constitutionally, where they are going. Dominica has been shunted around, between Leewards and Windwards, without any apparent logic. The dismal experiment of the West Indies Federation constituted, in retrospect, a blind alley and diverted attention away from the struggle for full internal self-government for each island to a sterile preoccupation with federal issues; and the smaller islands did not get back on the right path until the final dissolution of the Federation in 1962. It had been confidently expected, as the old Standing Federation Committee had recommended, that each unit territory of the Federation would have pressed onward as far as possible to full self-determination; it had been equally expected by the unit governments that the Federal Government would have become

5

their champion in that fight. But one of the many anomalies of the federal constitution was that it left the constitutional advancement of each unit to be decided still by the Colonial Office; while the Colonial Office, in turn, delayed reform with the specious plea that constitutional progress in the Leeward and Windward units must go together, which meant in effect that the more progressively-minded units were sacrificed to those units less interested in reform. Not surprisingly, then, when federally-sponsored recommendations for reform were finally made, through the Windward and Leeward Islands Constitutional Conference of 1959, they were fantastically timid, for they retained the system of nominated members and the continuing presence of the individual Governor in the Executive Council, left untouched the power of the Crown to refuse assent to bills, to disallow legislation and to legislate itself by Order in Council, and at best merely advised that Governors should not possess powers of certification.[15] It is true that the proposals were drafted and accepted by the small island leaders themselves, with the sole exception of Mr Joshua's spirited Vincentian dissent. Yet the fact remains that (1) those leaders received little help from the larger units whose leaders were preoccupied at the time with their own constitutional development and (2) the collapse of the federal structure itself, a few years later, was caused in the main, not by them, but by Jamaican secessionist sentiment, aided and abetted by Colonial Office refusal to stand up against its destructive force. The small island leaders, like the Jamaican, were hostile to a strong Federation with strong central powers, although they might have benefited immeasurably from such a scheme. But at least they were ready to fight for a weak federation, a stance that the Jamaican leaders and, later, the Trinidadian rapidly abandoned.

In the end-result, the dissolution of the experiment left the small islands feeling that they had been betrayed both by Great Britain and by their West Indian brethren in the larger territories, a feeling vividly expressed in the 1962 *Memorandum* of the 'Union of Students of the Little Eight' at the St Augustine campus of the University of the West Indies, criticizing the Trinidadian proposals of a unitary state between Trinidad and any small island interested in the idea, and strongly advocating a new federation of the Eastern Caribbean. The unitary state idea, the *Memorandum* argued, would impose upon Trinidad the same economic burden of carrying the small island economies as was objected to in the original Federation; and what would happen, in reality, is that Trinidad would go ahead with her own development and the attached smaller units would suffer the neglect that Ireland suffered under the terms of the unitary alliance of 1800 with England. The idea constitutes simply a vicious attempt to rule the Eastern Caribbean from Port of Spain and ought not to be countenanced. At best, it can only be seen as a vague offer of help motivated by the Trinidad Prime Minister's awareness of his own failure towards the Eastern Caribbean peoples.[16] Nor have later proposals from London been much more encouraging. For the leading idea of the 1966 proposals—that the small islands should be converted into home rule states 'associated' with Britain, after the model of the new Cook Islands relationship with New Zealand, with the right to declare themselves independent by unilateral vote should they so wish—is no more satisfactory. That the British Government, under that scheme, will retain responsibility for the Eastern Caribbean external powers and defence matters means, in fact, a continuing British influence in the area, nor is it clear what criteria would be used to distinguish 'external' from 'internal' matters. The Puerto Rican experience with the 'association' concept since 1952, in any case, has proved emphatically that there can be no real equality or partnership between states that are grossly un-unequal in economic and military power; not to mention the prac-tical difficulties that arise in finding the appropriate institutional machinery for joint consultation inevitably made necessary when two states formally associate with each other. The 'association' idea, in brief, looks suspiciously like yet another British device to promote West Indian unity on the cheap.[17]

British neglect and West Indian betrayal have thus created the impasse of the contemporary situation in the Eastern Caribbean. It is important, here, to note the continuing emotional force of the 'small island' complex in the West Indian communal psychology. The Trinidadian attitude to the 'small islands' has been one of genial contempt, the Jamaican attitude one of sheer disinterest, compounded by gross ignorance. Sir Alexander Bustamante's re-mark at the time of the 1958 federal election campaign—'How can people who are very near Treasury control and no future economi-cally help to build a nation?'—was typical, as was the scurrilous abuse by the Democratic Labour Party in the same campaign, featuring the smaller islands as 'parasites', with the further dramatization of 'poor little Montserrat' as the prime example of what awaited Jamaicans should they remain within the Federation; all of which culminated in the xenophobic hate campaign against the smaller units unleashed by the Bustamante forces in the later 1961 Jamaican referendum campaign. But the complex infects the 'small island' mind itself. Each island distrusts its neighbours, a rivalry that has its historical roots in the traditional fear that the planter class of one sugar island had of competition from its neighbours. 'Never yet,' comments the foremost of all British military historians, 'had the Leeward Islands suffered from a foreign foe but Barbados had rejoiced over the weakening of a commercial rival.'[18] The best known historical example of that mutual distrust in the Leewards is the long-standing jealousy between St Kitts and Nevis, as can be seen in the Nevisian struggle against Governor Shirley in the years 1782–84, resisting demands for sharing the expenses of the military and naval campaign in St Kitts against the French.[19] But there is a modern illlustration, for the constitutional crisis in St Kitts in 1957 was brought on by the attempt of the Basseterre politicians to impose fresh taxation upon the Nevis agricultural community, which has always been treated as a source of cheap labour for the St Kitts sugar factory and as a source of market gardening foodstuffs for the St Kitts sugar estate labourers. That, indeed, is the economic base for the continuing struggle of the Nevis representatives to have their constitutional relationship with St Kitts fundamentally rewritten.

More generally, the discussions, since 1962, on the question of a new Eastern Caribbean Federation have exhibited once more the peculiar virulency of small island *insularismo*, for few of them are reluctant to surrender up their tiny sovereign worlds, with their costly and top-heavy administrative structures, to a strong central government which would govern more rationally what is already a single culturally homogeneous region as a single administrative unit; not to mention the fact that from the viewpoint of its migration patterns the region is in fact a single area with its centre in Port of Spain. Antigua, with its more developed economy already freed of grant-aided status, seems about to become the protagonist of a states-right mercantilism as protection of her burgeoning oil and tourist industries against any new federal government that might one day appear. Significantly enough, too, all of the islands, except

St Vincent, voted in 1959 in favour of an Australian-like federal system in which each of them (none of which have a population exceeding 90,000 persons) would have its own Governor, exercising in his own little sphere functions analogous to those of the Australian Governor-General, plus its own Premier and separate legislative and executive establishments; thereby exacerbating an already critical situation in which the archipelago is perhaps the most over-governed area, for its size, in the modern world, with as many politicians to the square mile, in the words of one critic, as there are oil derricks in Texas. 'Antigua and the other islands in the group', wrote an observer more than fifty years ago, 'have been simply sinking into the sea under the weight of useless official salaries and the Gilbertian arrangements of elective government. Even Froude, superficial and rather narrow-minded as he showed himself to be in his book of the West Indies, saw this clearly, especially when he kept himself apart from the talk and good-fellowship of the clubs.'[20] The British colonial maxim of 'divide and rule', thus taken over and assimilated by the West Indian political class itself, remains behind to stand in the way of the rational organization of the area.

The socio-economic development of the islands, as a result of all this, has depended upon the separate growth within each of a social-political force working largely on its own. The achievement of those local labour-trade union parties, over the last twenty-five years, has been remarkable. They started, as embryonic organizations, in societies brutally feudal, in which the estate labourer worked for a pitiable wage of a shilling a day under execrable conditions and in which all the institutions overlooking his existence—government, church, sugar factory—were more or less controlled by a plantocracy mediaeval even by the West Indian standards of a generation ago. At no time in the Leewards history had that plantocracy evinced any temptation to adopt humane attitudes, not to mention the sort of romantic advice that James Grainger, for example, offered to the St Kitts planters in his Goldsmith-like poem of 1766.[21] Today, after years of struggle, the labour parties constitute the official governments, with Vere Bird in Antigua, Paul Southwell in St Kitts, and W. H. Bramble in Montserrat leading, as respective Chief Ministers, teams of devoted colleagues in the work of social and economic reconstruction. They will no doubt remain solid Labour bastions for some time; the ease, for example, with which

Southwell succeeded Robert Bradshaw as leader of the St Kitts organization, despite his handicap of being an outsider born in Dominica, indicates a strongly entrenched political unionism based on wide mass support, with little of the factionalism so pronounced in the Windwards.

Much of Labour's task, of course, has centred around the humanization of the sugar industry. For apart from Anguilla, with its fishing and boat-building, and Nevis with its mainly peasant economy, the Leewards have been a low-efficiency sugar estate economy saddled with excessively heavy populations (the legacy of the old colonial sugar regime which generated artificially high population levels through the slave trade), with those populations at once dependent upon the sugar industry but by now psychologically averse to cane-cutting as a physically back-breaking task and an occupation—like coal mining traditionally in Great Britain—of low social status. Over the years, the St Kitts labour union has fought for overtime pay, guaranteed sickness benefits, and old age pensions for estate workers; pensions and retirement bonus schemes for sugar factory workers, as well as regaining the concession of the yearly bonus payment after some eleven years of struggle; a 44–hour week for Government non-establishment employees, as well as things such as protective clothing and boots for sanitary gangs; and, among much more, the equalization of employment opportunities for waterfront workers by means of a registration and rotation scheme. The successive Reports of the Annual Conference bear testimony to the hard organizational and bargaining work put in by the union officialdom, covering a remarkable variety of schemes, from the securing of protective goggles and helmets for loader operators and tractor drivers in the field to the promotion of a pension scheme for hospital domestic staff and the payment of members' expenses while attending trade union seminars, to negotiations with the Leeward Islands Air Transport Company for an agreement covering wages and work conditions for airline attendants at the local airport.[22] Beyond that, there has been support of the Frampton Plan for the rehabilitation of Nevis, especially urgent in the light of the fact that for years the junior island was governed by means of the unsatisfactory device of Wardens appointed solely by the Administrator in Basseterre. It has been a heroic battle against sometimes impossible odds, for in an economy in which the whole cost of public administration is borne by a budget depending for over 90 per cent of its revenue on its sugar exports, and where that cost, in turn, is triplicated between three separate island communities no government, however progressive, can hope to do any more than introduce ameliorative reforms. Full employment, to take an example only, is extremely difficult, if not impossible, to organize in an economy whose chief industry provides only seasonal employment.

The Antiguan record has been more hopeful, as the statistics of its economic growth in the decade of the 50s amply show. In part, that has been due to a more diversified economy, cotton, tourism and, more latterly, oil refining facilities helping to break the earlier stranglehold of the sugar mono-culture. In part, it has been the modernizing influence of the Americans, whose military presence after 1942 accustomed Antiguans to high entrepreneurial and operational standards in, for example, the area of well-boring for new supplies of fresh water, the success of which no doubt encouraged the local government to go ahead with the Martin-Kaye survey of existing and potential water supplies. In part, again, it stems from the fact that, psychologically, Antigua is an open society whereas St Kitts is a closed society, made evident, for example, by the rapid tourist development in Antigua compared to the St Kitts failure to promote tourism even on a limited basis, due largely to the hostility of the Kittitian lawyer-planter class to 'damn tourists' and the modernizing tendencies they allegedly bring with them. The hostility has an interesting historical comparison, for it is not unlike the hostility shown by the old planter-class of the slave period to the missionaries. In both cases, the local ruling groups were suspicious, perhaps rightly so, from their viewpoint, of the damage, albeit not deliberately meant, that the visiting outsider, whether missionary or tourist, must inevitably do merely by the fact that he brings with him a different, and frequently a wider way of looking at things. The difference here noted between Antigua and St Kitts must also note the influence, early on, of English Harbour, for naval officers who passed through that station must have done something, merely by the fact that they were educated men, to stimulate the thought processes of the upper-crust whites who entertained them. The mental consequences of the presence of the tourist, even although he is, in the main, not a mentally active type, must have somewhat similar results in the modern picture.

There has been, consequently, more experimentation in the Antiguan economy. There is the tree-planting programme as a means of rehabilitating the local supply of mango, breadfruit, coconut and citrus; the attempted restoration of the pineapple industry on a commercial basis; the establishment of a Port Labour Committee to put an end to the old days when spiteful 'bosses' victimized workers with large families so that, today, to use the dockworkers' slogan, the 'waterfront is watertight'. There is the anti-mosquito spraying campaign, supervised by World Health Organization personnel, for a 1953 *aedes aegypti* survey disclosed an extremely high incidence of the fever-carrying insect throughout both Antigua and Barbuda. There is the reorganization of the Spring Gardens Teachers' Training College, designed to improve its professional standards and to rescue it from its sad deterioration from its earlier Caribbean-wide reputation. There is the device of the Village Council, introduced during the 1940's, to awaken popular interest in government affairs; and it is worth noting that Labour's traditional belief in democratic education was aptly expressed in the party's Education Committee's suggestion that the Workers Welfare Fund in the sugar industry should be used to set up some twenty secondary school scholarships for selected children from poor families. There is, again, the attempted rehabilitation of de-pressed Barbuda, that island ward being known, indeed, until the Labour government's programme there, chiefly as the favourite hunting and fishing spot for retired Englishmen visiting as guests of the Governors of the Leeward Islands.

Above all, there is the remarkable Peasant Development Scheme. Since its inception, it has done much to develop a peasant proprie-tary as yet practically unknown in St Kitts and only of recent growth in Montserrat where the long-established sharecropping system, used by the Montserratian planters as a means of retaining owner-ship of their estates during periods of economic depression, has militated against the easy emergence of a class of independent peasant farmers. The Antiguan scheme emphasized the values of such a class by means of loans, new technological methods, com-munity ownership plans and village extension programmes. The agricultural credit scheme, in turn, sought to break down the old evil system of shop credit. 'Land settlement of peasant allotment in Antigua,' wrote the Special Agricultural Emissary of the Colonial

Office in a report, 'is in marked contrast to that seen in most other islands. The view that a man will not work his acre or two of cotton, cane or vegetables satisfactorily, because he has a job somewhere else, simply does not hold good. The farmers seem to be imbued with the will to work and they do produce crops. I visited most districts of the island, saw estate work and peasant settlement, and in nearly every case the standard of agriculture of the peasants was little below that of the Antigua Syndicate. I can only infer that Antigua is blessed with a first class team who have secured the confidence of the peasantry.'[23] That may perhaps be excessive optimism, for the later emphasis of official policy on industrialization and tourism is certain to stimulate rural depopulation tendencies. At the same time, it is true to say that, on the general level, there have been new stirrings of self-consciousness on the part of the Antiguan masses making themselves felt over the last twenty-five years, stirrings which, as Vere Bird has properly noted, have too often been dismissed as signs of lawlessness and irresponsibility.[24]

In Montserrat, finally, a somewhat different social process took place during the period. Even more isolated than Antigua or St Kitts, its peasant population was divided between sharecroppers burdened by a system in which the small cultivator assumed all the risks and the estate managers all the control, and peasant proprietors whose economy exhibited all the pathological weaknesses of unaided peasant farming; both of them combining to produce the social atmosphere of claustrophobic frustration, despair, peculiarly embittered class relations and a corroding self-doubt in all individual Montserratians which has been noticed almost unanimously by all visitors to the island. That atmosphere, in its turn, has been reinforced by the tremendous drainage of human wealth occasioned by massive emigration, with all of its calamitous social effects: the loss of trained personnel to government and private business, a high turnover rate in government departments, the evil of multiple office-holding, the growing depletion of a middle class already infinitesimally small, the chronic suspicion of the 'outsider' which discourages the able expatriate from staying, so that, in W. H. Brambles's plaintive cry, 'we can't get out bad people from Montserrat, we can't keep in the good ones'. Not the least of all this is the fact that the local Labour Party has been unable to attract the more gifted or educated of the upper groups so that there is nothing in its

5*

history to compare with the group of public-spirited professional and business men who early on, after 1945, openly espoused the working class cause in Antigua: Reginald Stevens, the jeweller, the Rev. Charles Francis, R. H. Lockhart, the lawyer, the English-man Major Hugh Hole, and others. It is possible to argue that much of this is compensated for by the moral character of virtuous self-sufficiency that comes from small island isolationism, so that every-body has to pull together, everybody has to learn to do without. That may be so. But the fact still remains that, in this sort of Robin-son Crusoe economy, most people seize the opportunity to escape when it presents itself.[25]

The general record of the Leeward labour forces, clearly, is im-pressive enough. Yet it still remains true that, today, the Leeward societies are sick societies. They are not integrated communities bound together by the social cement of common ideals, not to speak of a vibrant national consciousness. For all of their embryonic welfare state apparatus, they still remain socially polarized systems, with the planter aristocracy at one extreme and the working people at the other, with a hard-pressed and psychologically insecure middle class group in between. Unionism has been accepted, albeit after a generation of fierce struggle in both field and factory. But effective resistance has throughout been put up, both by estate managements and sugar factory syndicates, against any kind of positive union participation in matters regarded by labour as perti-nent to its interests: the financial relationship, for example, between the St Kitts Sugar Factory company and its London parent company; or the allocation of percentages of estate land to food production purposes; or the alienation of estates to absentee owners, like the sale, without any consultation with the local work force, of Wade Plantations Ltd., in St Kitts to the National Trust in Great Britain; or, finally, the structural imbalance of the sugar industry, exempli-fied—as the St Kitts union testified in its memorandum to the 1961 Commission of Enquiry—in the estates policy of hiring attorneys, managers, deputy managers and overseers in excessive proportion to their employment of sugar technologists. The effect of expatriate ownership, in particular, is disastrous: 'large absentee land owner-ship,' argued the memorandum, 'tends to create a lackadaisical attitude with respect to the plantation, and this usually results in

inefficiency and low productivity. The social impact, too, of a landless mass dwelling in an area of large land ownership is degrading.
Human beings tend to assume secondary values and develop a
gradual and uncompromising resentment against a life which con-
demns them to perpetual servitude as is the case with the industry.'[26]
One outcome of this, among a great deal else, is that the insular
politics becomes little more than an open civil war between capital
and labour, as the protracted struggle over the years between the
Antigua Labour Union and the O'Neill business enterprise in St
John's illustrates.

In similar fashion, most insular problems come back, in one way
or another, to the three-cornered fight between union, estate owners
and factory management. Much of this, too, is racial, for the rigid
social hierarchy is based on local white endogamy. The white planter
families continue to send their children to England or at least to the
Lodge School in Barbados. They are hostile to the mixed groups,
and have attempted, for instance, to get rid of those few coloured
men who were appointed to estate managerial positions during the
war when the manpower shortage necessitated that step. It is worth
noting that the massive three-volume work of Oliver, published in
1894, on *The History of the Island of Antigua*, was, in effect, simply an
anthology of the pedigrees of the great Antiguan proprietary families,
a sort of colonial Burke's Peerage, in which any reference to colour
was discreetly avoided.[27] There is, of course, the occasional liberal-
minded young planter, like the Cambridge-educated Mr Wigley
in St Kitts. But, as a group, the class remains almost as reactionary
today as it was a generation ago when it ostracized Manchester, the
*doyen* of the Workers' League. For the common labourer, then, the
Leeward societies still remain something to escape from, if it be only
a seasonal contract job in the United States Virgin Islands or, better
still, the United States itself. For the light-skinned *élites* they become
an overseas colonial England jealously guarded, and a visiting
Canadian scholar has recently described how young white Kittitians
out on Sunday afternoon picnics on the green slopes above Basseterre
amuse themselves by competing among themselves in naming the
English public schools.[28]

Nor is there a proportionately sizeable middle class possessed of a
professional ethic and a social consciousness capable of leading a
local nationalist movement as in Trinidad and Jamaica. The lawyers

and the merchants are tied, by economic interest, to the estates. For many years doctors, on one pretext or another, settled in the towns with their more remunerative practices, to the neglect of the outlying districts, and only labour's policy of building doctors' houses in those districts has helped stay the process. Yet it is still difficult to get medical men to serve in the dependent islands like Barbuda and Anguilla, while the tendency to resign, often unexpectedly, from government appointments creates constantly recurring crises in the campaign to establish a stable medical service. What social conscience there is belongs to individuals, not to the class as a whole: Dr Wynter's record of public service in Antigua, for example, or Mr Willie Herbert's valiant campaign, as Social Welfare officer of the St Kitts Sugar Factory, to set up welfare service facilities for factory workers against both a conservative management and an unsympathetic trade union officialdom. With again the occasional exception like Reginald Stevens, early on, or, later, Maurice Davis, political leadership has remained the monopoly of the old-style small island labour politician and the trade-union graduate, not of the new style professional leader, not to mention the university graduate; for men like Bird, originally a Salvation Army drummer boy, or Lionel Hurst, a professional carpenter, or Robert Bradshaw, a former machinist in the St Kitts sugar factory, or Paul Southwell, an ex-shopkeeper, have no pretensions to a conventionally sound education. The figure of Maurice Davis, indeed, which is that of a bitterly disappointed political aspirant, shows how difficult it is, in such an embittered class environment, for even the progressively-minded professional man to break down the traditional hostility of labour to his class. The figure of Novelle Richards in the Antigua Labour Party is proof, perhaps, of a larger class tolerance than that existing in St Kitts, probably due to the fact that the social frustrations of the Antiguan peasantry are finding more escape valves than is the case in St Kitts, as a rapid drift takes place, in the Antiguan employment structure, from the fields to the Public Works Department, the sugar factory and the new tourist hotels, the latter particularly offering employment opportunities at once more comfortable, more exciting and more socially prestigious, than work in the agricultural sector. As, indeed, the 'white collar' occupational preference scales of Antiguans in favour of becoming a clerk or a teacher or a nurse—statistically examined in the Rottenberg-Siffleet Report on unemployment of 1951[29]—are reinforced by the possibility of becoming a bartender or a cook in the new hotels, to join in the new 'native' game of 'fleecing' the tourist, they will help to strengthen the upper working class and lower middle class levels of the society.

Not, of course, that that process is altogether admirable. For it is already bringing about its own new social dislocations. It enlarges the divorce between the status of manual work and that of mental work, noted recently by the *Antigua Star* in its remark that 'The machinery of education is geared with the object of producing men for the medical and legal professions, the Church and Agriculture, but little, if anything, is being done for the youngster who has the creative urge, and who wants to look with pride and joy on the work of his hands'; and the same editorial adds, suggestively, that the prejudice is all the more surprising when attention is drawn to the elegant standards of public architecture in both church and state buildings set by the West Indian craftsman a century ago.[30] Nor is a tourist economy necessarily more trouble-free than a sugar economy; at least the 1962 Report of the Board of Enquiry on the recurrent labour relations crisis in the new hotel industry noted the growth of a spirit of paternalism and anti-union prejudice on the part of the new employer and management class and opined that 'we should not like to think that it has become necessary to fight in Antigua in 1962 battles which were begun in 1938 and to all appearances long since won'.[31] But that, surely, is a pious hope, for tourism is in fact producing those new lines of battle, bringing in its wake the influx of new American wealth, new acquisitive instincts, new predatory social attitudes as they are portrayed, for instance, in Herman Wouk's description of them in the Virgin Islands in his novel *Don't Stop the Carnival*. New social inequalities flow, in turn, from all that, so that it is naïve utopianism to say, as the historian of the Antigua Labour Party claims, that Antigua is 'fast becoming a society of equals' as a result of the welfare state programme of the party.[32] The remark, indeed, reflects the new complacency of the Labour politicians as they settle down into their new role of administrative oligarchs dependent, increasingly, on American investment and the class of rapacious 'big business' operators that investment brings with it to the islands.

Not surprisingly, in conclusion, all this bespeaks a continuing culturally philistine way of life. There is practically nothing of a local intellectual life that might become the basis of an energetic local patriotism and a pride in local achievement. Leeward Islanders know practically nothing of their history; nor does the occasional publication, for example, that on Antiguan Governors put out by the local historian like Miss Bessie Harper, do much to fill the gap. There have been experiments in adult education, but always of a markedly Victorian tone. The General Improvement Society, started in Antigua years ago by P. A. W. Gordon, as well as the Spartro movement, aimed to provide some limited mental occupation for the ordinary elementary schoolboy debarred from secondary education and therefore debarred from civil service employment (except in the category of 'Petty' Officer), and from the better paid posts in local business concerns; but the 'social welfare' touch was always there.[33] The Mutual Improvement Society of St Kitts, likewise, founded in 1901, struggled over the years against public indifference to act as a sort of local Chatauqua movement, but its membership was always tiny, never rising above seventy, while the tone of its work can be gauged from its boast that for years it was the only institution in the Presidency that observed Empire Day by the holding of patriotic concerts.[34] All of those efforts, brave as they have been, have been little more than Creole celebrations of a borrowed English literary culture, based on the uncritical assumption that 'Chaucer is one of us', and often in a style long since disappeared in the metropolitan society itself. Mr Southwell, for example, is proudly known as a Shakespearian *aficionado*. But it is doubtful if his literary appreciation goes beyond that once made popular by the school of Sir Arthur Quiller-Couch. The fragment of colonial autobiography, again, composed by Charlesworth Ross, one-time Administrator of Montserrat, is the sort of club chit-chat characteristic of gubernatorial memoirs, while its section on the once-famous Antigua Grammar School reads like a colonial echo of *Tom Brown's Schooldays*.[35]

All in all, genteel respectability reigns supreme. There is the same song recital by the local soprano; the same church bazaar opened by the Administrator's wife; the same choral competition under official patronage; the same lecture on Keats or Shelley by the visiting American eminence; the same newspaper stories about the upbringing of the children of the Royal Family; the same ceremonial opening of the Legislature; the same state dinners and garden parties at Government House, religiously noted by the local newspaper gossip writers. Nor is it likely that the small enclave of English refugees from the British welfare state in Nevis or the rich 'jet set' of the American residential colony of Mill Reef in Antigua will do much to improve upon all this. The Extra-Mural Department of the University of the West Indies has introduced a new professional, West Indian note since its resident tutors set up shop in the islands after 1949, and it is only necessary to note the West Indian quality of the Leeward Islands drama festival sponsored by that department in 1956 or to read the anthologies of local authors and of historical writings on the colony compiled by John Brown as one of those tutors, to realize the value of the new note.[36] But that, again, like the work of the British Council, is the work of an outside force. The domestic force which will convert anarchy into culture has yet to appear.

# Chapter VI

## THE INCUBUS OF CROWN COLONY

### THE WINDWARD ISLANDS

THE FATE of the Windwards has been no more fortunate than that
of the Leewards. The same factors accounting for the decline of the
northern island chain were present in the southern chain. But there
were additional aggravating causes, in particular, the general
sociological fact that whereas the Leewards have been more or less
a homogeneous single community, with frequent inter-island visiting
taking place, the Windward units have had little in common and
communications between them have been more difficult. They were
all ceded territories: Dominica, Grenada, and St Vincent in 1763
and St Lucia in 1814. So they did not have behind them the long
British tradition of, say, St Kitts. There was, and still is, immense
cultural diversification, so that while Grenada and St Vincent
rapidly became Anglicized, St Lucia and Dominica remained in
large part linguistically and culturally French, as the continuing
usage of French *patois* language forms in their peasant populations
shows. An English social pattern, that is, was superimposed upon
existing French social patterns. The division within St Lucian
society today between Catholicism and Freemasonry is only one
example of the consequences of that fact. It is hardly surprising,
then, that whereas a federal system, albeit unpopular, managed to
survive in the Leewards it never developed in the Windwards.

The politico-constitutional development of the Windwards followed much the same pattern as that of the Leewards. In the early
years after the Great War there was the same gradual liberalization
of the Crown Colony system by means of miniscule increases in the
elective side of the island legislative councils, which was inspired
(as was the case, from the very beginning, with the Wood Report
of 1922) by the Colonial Office desire to win over the local middle
class speaking through the various Representative Government
Associations, and thereby, incidentally, to help stifle the incipient

revolt of the masses. In the later period, as that revolt did in fact materialize, there was the same official effort to buy it off with belated concessions, such as the Secretary of State's 1945 proposal for a federated Leewards-Windwards group, that offer being in fact a timid response to the more radical demands of the Windward Islands Conference held earlier in Grenada in the same year. This was followed by the grant of universal adult suffrage in 1950–51, only made possible, of course, by the presence of a Labour Government in London. Mass suffrage elections, in their turn, gave birth to the same victories of the new labour-based parties, less spectacular, perhaps, in Dominica than in Grenada and St Lucia, but everywhere bringing about the replacement of the older moderate politicians by the new Labour radicals : Gairy, Loblack, Joshua, Charles. There was the same leisurely pace of constitutional change, in which the initial step of permitting an elected majority in the legislature was followed by various schemes to solve the problem of how that majority was to control or influence the executive arm of government : the Committee system, the acceptance of unofficial members into the Executive Council, the quasi-ministerial system, the replacement of the Administrator with an elected Speaker as presiding officer in the legislative councils, the establishment of an embryonic cabinet system by virtue of setting up the office of the Chief Minister ; and so on. Constitutional growth was held back, in particular, by the fact that (1) before the Federation experiment, the Colonial Office made the smaller islands wait on the advances granted to the larger units, the Jamaica Constitution of 1944, for example, while (2) after the Federation London made them wait upon the constitutional advances granted, with equal tardiness, to the Federal Government. The general upshot was that, as Mr Gairy noted in his 1957 communication to the English Chairman of the Standing Federation Committee, all the islands suffered from a wide and marked disparity in constitutional status, a condition that ought to be remedied before the individual units actually entered the Federation.[1] The subsequent demise of the Federation meant, of course, the end of any federal championship of such remedies—the demand, for instance, of the federal programme of the West Indies Federal Labour Party in the only election, that of 1958, held during the Federation's brief lifetime, for the achievement of full internal self-government in all the unit territories.[2] That meant a return, for the small islands, to the old West Indian pattern of each territory being governed in isolation away from the others and having to fend for itself in the general Caribbean anarchy.

Even more than the Leewards, the Windward Islands group has been, and still much is, an almost classic *mîse en scène* of the myriad consequences of this general condition. There has been the ever-lasting struggle between the official and the popular sides. 'You are English,' wrote George Marecheau candidly to the Governor of the group in 1931, 'and I appreciate that it is difficult for you to rid yourself of the famous notion of privilege and prestige. Against that notion you will be confronted by the rising tide of the opposition of those who feel that they possess a greater right to order their own destiny than one who is sent to them from outside their ranks'.[3] That sentiment has flavoured all of the constitutional encounters of the period, for it was fed by the fatal division of authority which every constitutional panacea short of independence—a word almost unknown to the official British literature—exhibited. Before the office of the Chief Minister was set up—speaking, that is of the post-1945 period—the conflict usually took place between the Administrator and the local Minister of Trade and Production, regarded by convention as 'leader' of the Government, but in reality lacking any power to enforce his will upon colleagues who were independently accountable to the Legislative Council; and the case of the expulsion of L. C. J. Thomas from the Grenada Executive Council by a power play on the part of defecting allies revealed the fragility of the arrangement. After the establishment of the office of Chief Minister it became an equally bitter fight between the politician holding that office and the Administrator, as the epic struggle between Mr Gairy and Mr Lloyd, again in Grenada, between 1960 and 1962 amply demonstrated. For the Chief Minister was such in name only since he had to share fiscal control with the Administrator, while the latter retained the effective supervision of the civil service by means of his continuing appointive power to the local public service commissions. So-called Ministers, as one local critic put it, could have very little authority while an iron hand was allowed to the Governor, or his agents, with his veto in all matters, and such a ministerial system would simply be a very broken reflection of the United Kingdom system.[4] The elected members in that system, anyway, were, constitutionally, individuals only, so that even when they entered the assemblies as a party team the system rapidly encouraged them to behave as irresponsible individualists. The collapse of the legislative members belonging to the United Workers Union in the case of St Vincent after 1951, splitting into the rival camps of the 'big four' and the 'small four', and ending ingloriously with the ridiculous eviction of Mr Joshua from the Executive Council in 1954 by an opportunistic alliance of the official bloc and his erstwhile labour colleagues, nicely illustrated how the system worked to break the unity of the local progressive forces.[5]

It is essential also to note that this was not simply a struggle between West Indian patriots and alien British officials. For the accident of a Catholic Administrator, the Earl of Oxford and Asquith, in a Catholic territory like St Lucia did not prevent a St Lucian variant of the encounter. Nor was it simply a racial struggle, although the pathology of skin-colour certainly played a role. For the Gairy-Lloyd affair raged as acrimoniously as any other despite the fact that Mr Lloyd, as Administrator, was himself coloured, a Jamaican civil servant on secondment (i.e. on approved loan) to St George's; just as, at much the same time in the case of the United States Virgin Islands, the appointment of Gordon, a Negro as Governor did not still in any way the fratricidal strife between presidentially-nominated chief executive and locally elected politicians which is still, even now, the leading permanent feature of Virgin Islands politics. The Windwards situation, rather, was the result of the built-in defect of the Crown Colony system and its separation of powers between the legislative and executive arms. Yet, albeit, an intentional defect, for it was part and parcel of the 'divide and rule' maxim of metropolitan imperialism, whereby fifth columns were created within the colonial societies to ensure 'stability', that is, a clash of local interests profitable only to the metropolitan ruling force.

Constitutional retardation, of course, had its own particular socio-economic setting. The Windwards, it is true, have been far more diversified economies than the Leewards, witness the cocoa and nutmeg peasantries of Grenada, the original nutmeg introduction in 1782 having been the achievement of Sir Joseph Banks, the great Botanical Adviser to George III, also responsible in large part for the creation, as director of the Royal Gardens at Kew, of the famous West Indian botanical gardens. There is also the significant fact that both St Lucia and Dominica, and especially the latter, possess vast untapped Crown Lands areas, saving them from the unbalanced land-people ratio that afflicts the Leeward territories. Yet today they are still relatively poor economies. All of them are grant-aided, and therefore controlled in their daily fiscal policies by the United Kingdom Treasury; and even when one of them, like Grenada, has been in the past a relatively strong economy, its recent budgetary history shows that a high rate of growth in the cost of government services, plus the almost complete destruction of its tree crops due to hurricane damage (in the Grenada case, hurricane 'Janet' of 1955), can rapidly work to put it back into a grant-aided status. What there is of a sugar industry is stagnant, so much so that recently both St Vincent and St Lucia have ceased sugar production; and it is worth noting that the basic causative factor, here, has been the technological conservatism of the local plantocracy, so much so that an authoritative expert noted in 1947 that the 'glaring economic defect of West Indian populations' was deficient entrepreneurial ability, so that there was 'too little competition between managers of agricultural and industrial enterprise and too much competition among the wage earning labourers. As a result, the earnings of managers are high in relation to the services they render in making their business ever more efficient, as judged by European standards; the wages of the workers judged by the same standards are low for their services in sweat and toil.'[6] The St Vincent arrowroot industry is a case in point, for despite a series of critical reports on its structural and managerial inefficiency, from the Robinson Report of 1944 to the Courbois Report of 1958, nothing was done to implement the various recommendations for improvement, largely because the people who suffered most under the system, that is, the class of small peasant growers, were not the people who had the most influence on the structure of the industry, the strategic directive group being, in fact, inadequately educated planters and planters' sons, with very little, if any, training in tropical agriculture and whose life-style is that of the idle rich.[7] Both employer and worker mentalities, indeed, have been shaped by the perennial dream of 'bonanza' crops, so that the temptation with both of them to put all of their effort into immediate cash export crops has worked to prevent serious investment in local food production or even more moderate earning export crops. That is why the history of such crops in the Windwards—sea island cotton, cocoa, arrowroot, citrus—has been marked by failure related to continuously present and endemic limitations: inadequate marketing arrangements, praedial larceny (the practice of stealing produce from vegetable and fruit plots which is not so much a habit as an ingrained way of life in the West Indian rural proletariats), insufficient feeder roads, absence of cheap credit facilities; so that a grave export-import imbalance afflicts all of the island economies, importing, as they do, expensive food items that should be replaced by locally-grown foodstuffs, and thereby reinforcing the economic stranglehold of the local dry goods merchants and import mercantile houses. The recovery of credit grants, where they exist, is always difficult, as the history of the post-1955 hurricane relief credit arrangements in Grenada shows. Such credits, in any case, are intermittent, not continuous, for an expatriate-owned banking system operates to the crass neglect of the 'small man' in the colonial economy.

The panacea of rural co-operatives has also been a comparative failure in practice, if only because nothing in West Indian economic history has prepared the small farmer to understand the concept and implications of unlimited liability. The absence of a fully trained leadership has also been a factor, the early movement in St Vincent, for example, having been largely the product of the enthusiastic efforts of interested clergymen and schoolmasters, who undertook the duties of 'honorary' secretaries but left no trained personnel behind them to carry on.[8] It is true that, since 1953, the new popularity of the banana as a profitable cash crop has brought prosperity to the Windwards, notably St Lucia. It is only necessary to read the various dismal reports on the pre-banana St Lucian economy, the 1951 report of the team of visiting experts, for example, and then compare them with later reports such as the 1963 report of the Commission of Enquiry into the banana industry, to be made aware of how much the 'banana revolution' has helped the economy to get away from its earlier notorious artificiality, relying precariously on the coaling trade, or the American base, or the post-1948 reconstruction of Castries.[9] It has brought in its wake, too, a healthy minor social revolution, for to sit in on a branch meeting of small banana growers in a roadside 'trash hut' or to look at the renovated peasant cottages with their new tin roofings and linoleum floors is to be in the presence of social phenomena that were never possible in the brutally feudal conditions of life in the old sugar villages, as, for example, in the notorious 'Korea' district of the St Vincent Mt Bentinck sugar barony. Even so, notwithstanding all that, the replacement of sugar with bananas does little to change the basic mono-product character of the economy, and there is nothing to protect the Windward Islands banana adventurer, the typical small grower, from at some time meeting the same fate as his Jamaican counterpart in the earlier period between 1900 and 1929, when attempts to create a permanently assured market for the Jamaican small farmer finally lost out to the hostility of powerful interests and the collapse of the world market. The recent so-called 'banana war' between Jamaica and the Windwards, which is really a struggle between two different groups of imperially-owned buyers and shippers, also indicates that the habit of inter-colonial economic rivalry exists as vigorously as ever in the absence of effective regional economic planning in the interests of all.

The social and economic history of the Windwards, as a matter of fact, has been in large part the history of an oppressed peasant proprietary class fighting to maintain its precarious existence within a hostile environment. For it is true to say that up until the 1950's the Windward territories were semi-feudal economies in which the merchants, the large landowners, either personal or corporate, and the middle class civil servants ruled the inarticulate peasant and worker with an iron hand. To see the growth of 'labour relations' within such a context in traditional English terms is, then, profoundly misleading, for worker grievances were not simply bread-and-butter grievances so much as a revolt, perhaps felt only half-consciously, against a repressive social order; as Rottenberg points out in the Grenadian case, a reference by a popular leader, in open meeting, to a planter who is 'playing white', or to the reserving of office employment for children of the 'better' families, or to claims that land planted in cocoa by the workers' forefathers should by right belong to their descendants, will evoke more emotional response than a reference to the insufficiency of the daily wage rate.[10] The class separatism reflected itself in a social separatism between town and countryside. A recent commentator has feelingly summed up the situation in its St Lucian locale. 'The poor, barefoot, uneducated, unsophisticated, shy people in the out-districts,' he writes, 'looked up with awe and fawning respect to the well-dressed, well-spoken and better read city folk—the people who could boast of electricity, who met and hobnobbed with people from abroad, who went or probably might have gone to college. Castries was St Lucia in every way. Administrators and Governors without end continued to tour the island exactly twice during their tenure of office—once when they assumed and once when they shed the mantle of office. The out-districts were a Never-Never land where people walked silently and uncomplainingly in misery and neglect, where people waited hand and foot on leadership and direction, and the occasional word of wisdom from the city folk of Castries. That was St Lucia only twelve years ago. It is still the image of St Lucia that innumerable city folk still believe represents the real St Lucia today.'[11]

The passage aptly summarizes the social history of the last thirty years. In every island, peasant farmer and estate tenant suffered from its consequences. It can be seen, to take examples only, in the victimization of estate labourers in Grenada by means of summary eviction from house lots they had occupied for thirty to forty years,[12] dramatizing, as such actions do, the decline of the old paternalistic relations characteristic, in the past, of the Grenadian family-owned plantation economy;[13] although it would be easy to romanticize those relations, for the 1896 Report of the local Agricultural Commission appointed to investigate the cocoa crisis prevailing at that time made it abundantly clear that the small household owner was offered no help by the state against bankruptcy, despite the eloquent pleas of his defenders in the Legislative Council at the time who saw him as being as vital to the island economy as was the backbone to a vertebrate animal.[14] It can be seen, in another example, in the transition in Dominica from the rule of the old white plantocracy to that of the town merchants who supplanted them after the First World War, with the scions of the old families living on declining incomes, men who cannot work living on the coloured women who love them, a social process lovingly traced, with nostalgic regret, in Phylliss Allfrey's *The Orchid House*; a process that created generally in all of the territories a new form of internal absentee estate ownership, that of the merchants and lawyers whose interest in the land rests solely on its economic profitability or on the social status that it confers in a traditionally land-conscious society. In the case of St Vincent, again, it is enough to read the

Legislative Council debate of February 1954 on Mr Joshua's motion
to control the reckless use of child labour on the estates to realize
how a socially unconscionable planter class was always ready to use
cheap juvenile labour instead of more highly paid adult labour when
a morbid social climate and a deficient educational system allowed
it to do so; and one planter-nominated member's remark that
children 'make much better citizens when they learn to work' was
symptomatic of the attitudes the Vincentian labour movement has
had to combat.[15] It should be noted, in passing, that the Vincentian
problem was aggravated by the failure to produce, over the years,
local growers' associations after the Jamaican fashion, so that defence-
mechanisms were weak when, for instance, the arrowroot producers
were threatened by new competition in the open world market
consequent upon the production of corn starch and potato starch
in Canada and the United States;[16] just as, earlier on, the decline
of the old lime industry in Dominica due to the development of new
technical processes for the manufacture of citric acid from cheaper
materials, notably exhausted molasses, had caught both planter
and peasant smallholder unprepared;[17] and just as, to take one
further example, the small growers of the Grenadian nutmeg industry had had their interests subordinated to those of the local dealers
and the American buying interests, giving rise, finally, to the establishment in 1947 of the Co-operative Nutmeg Association, although
the co-operative principle has subsequently been somewhat fragile
in the actual working arrangements of the Association.[18]

The general result of all this, in all of the islands, has been a dual
migratory movement of dispossessed tenantry and unsuccessful
peasant growers: (1) internal migration from countryside to town
and (2) external migration, either to the United Kingdom or to
Trinidad *via* the famous 'rat passage'. The remittances sent home by
migrants thus become a further example of the financial dependence
of the island populations upon external aid, for they constitute an
extremely important factor in local household income, as high as
15 per cent or more in the Leewards territory of Montserrat. If the
islander stays at home, then, he can easily become a rural proletarian
living on subsistence or near-subsistence levels. If he migrates he
becomes an uprooted nomad facilitating, in the phrase of an official
St Lucian report of 1959, a concomitant break in the agricultural
tradition of the people. Nor is it enough to blame peasant land-

tenure systems such as the old French 'family land' joint ownership system prevailing in St Lucia, for although such fragmentalized holding systems undoubtedly hinder the development of rational standards of soil use[19] at the same time they constitute, from the anthropological viewpoint, institutional supports without which he would be naked against the blasts of life. Nor is it reasonable to expect him to surrender such supports to governmental development programmes so long as such programmes fail to include suggestions for an equitable land tax or for land development authorities with real powers ready to be used against the large landowner as well as the small holder.[20]

Crown colony government naturally facilitated much of this. Since each territory was governed by London as a separate microscopic sovereign entity and not as a unit in a confederationist group it was saddled with all of the paraphernalia of sovereignty, with comic results. This produced the well-known imbalance, still continuing, of local governmental structures, with poverty-stricken populations paying for costly administrative superstructures they cannot afford and would not need in a rationally organized group system. The 'Little Eight' territories thus pay the astonishingly high figure of some 60 per cent of their revenue on costs of administration, which includes an abnormally high level of civil service salaries in relation to the national income, that latter fact helping to explain why popular Labour governments, seeking a fairer wage-salary structure, rapidly run afoul of their civil servants.[21] Nor should the fact be overlooked that below a certain population level the costs of administrative services per individual person become excessively inflationary. What is worse, the resultant heavy tax load has borne down most of all upon the working classes. Colonial governments habitually increased consumption taxes or import duties on necessities instead of demanding more from the higher income-bracket taxpayers. The entire revenue-expenditure system, in the phrase of one Windwards politician, went back to the days of Morton's Fork. Even a Spartan austerity programme, however, could probably not manage to finance the fundamental planned reorganization, on a regional basis, the area so urgently requires. That can only come from external fiscal sources. That was the premise of the Colonial Development and Welfare legislation after 1945. Yet the C. D. and W. expenditures in the West Indies as a

whole—some 29 million pounds in their first decade up to 1956—
hardly began to scratch the surface, concentrating as they did on
social service schemes many of which, once initiated by a C. D. and
W. grant, became recurrent expenditure items on local budgetary
resources. A typical C. D. and W. report—that of Miss Ibberson on
St Vincent in 1945, for example—thus included proposals for a
model poor relief scheme, a cottage industry in straw and fibre
work, a series of community halls, the construction of cottage homes
by the Anglican Church, hostels for 'loosely attached young people',
all of them exemplifying the naïve optimism of the professional
social service worker mentality about the success of merely ameliorative measures in stagnant unemployment economies.[22] What the
region needed, and still needs, is a comprehensive plan for its
economic rehabilitation, in which the individual territories play com-
plementary, and not competitive, roles, so that the smaller agricultural islands could become the prosperous food producers for the
industrializing larger units, and the sparsely populated areas absorb
the surplus population of the high density areas; the idle lands of
Dominica, as it were, absorbing the idle hands of Barbados and St
Vincent. Both the erstwhile Federal Government and the Government of Trinidad have published such plans, both of them, for
different reasons, stillborn, while the more recent pre-federal report
of Dr O'Loughlin on the Eastern Caribbean area estimates that
such a plan would cost over some three hundred million pounds.
Nor is that kind of aid likely to come from British governments,
including Labour Party governments, anxious to retrench on their
colonial expenses and totally unwilling, as the futile 1966 constitutional talks between the Colonial Office and the Windward Islands
delegations brutally showed, to assure guaranteed markets for
Windward Islands exports in the United Kingdom or freedom of
migration for Windward Islands citizens to the metropolitan employment market, despite the fact that Great Britain enjoys a
protected high-cost export market in the Windwards to the extent
of some fifty million pounds, plus continuing Treasury relief as the
energy of Windward Islands governments and farmers produces
higher *per capita* incomes in the territories.[23]

In the meantime, the absence of any kind of planning along these
larger lines means that grandiose schemes collapse for want of money
—the bulky volume of some 800 odd pages, for example, that the

St Vincent Government published in 1947 as a Master Plan for guided economic development over the next ten years.[24] In the meantime, too, the smaller territories remain comparatively stagnant, reflecting a dual colonialist process in which (1) their own fiscal economies, under United Kingdom Treasury control, are ruled by an external authority, while (2) they themselves rule, perforce with an equally cheeseparing outlook, their own smaller dependencies, so that the Grenadines, under Vincentian jurisdiction, remain today a cultural and economic backwater lagging far behind the living standards, low as they are, of the Vincentians. Nor should the significance be lost of the fact that newly-independent Trinidad spends upon its island ward of Tobago, as part of its new development programme (if the 1960 budget year is taken as a yardstick for measurement) amounts of some 50 percent more than the United Kingdom grants to the three territories of Dominica, St Lucia and St Vincent, covering essential services such as water, electricity, telephones, and port services.[25]

A Crown Colony economics breeds, of course, a Crown Colony politics, the legendary West Indian politics of the small islands. What Governors liked to call 'irresponsible' politicians were, after all, only local expressions of an irresponsible system. That was seen clearly enough by the Dominica Conference of West Indian leaders in 1932. 'Powerless to mould policy,' their Report noted of the general type, 'still more powerless to act independently, paralysed by the subconscious fear of impending repression and therefore bereft of constructive thought, the West Indian politician has hitherto been inclined to dissipate his energies in acute and penetrating but embittered and essentially destructive criticism of the government on which, nevertheless, he has waited for the initiation of all policies intended to benefit his people, and which he has expected to assume the full responsibility for all necessary decisions. His political life has been overshadowed by a government too omnipotent and too omnipresent, and has had little opportunity for independent growth'.[26] That, generally, has been the definition of Windward leaders like Marryshow and Paterson, MacIntosh and Duncan, Joshua and Gairy, Charles and Jn. Baptiste. Only more recently has the type of the London School of Economics graduate, as in the figure of John Compton, begun to replace those older types. Even when, as with Marryshow, they were sometimes willing to be seduced by invitations to Government House—Marryshow often boasted that the Governor of Trinidad, Sir Bede Clifford, had been the first person in the colony to invite the Grenadian labour leader to his house—they were forced, on the whole, to fight the office of the Governor because, quite simply, it was a political and not just a constitutional office. The liberal-minded Governor who advised West Indian leaders, over cocktails, to attack the 'real' problems was assuming, grossly mistakenly, that his office, in Bagehot's terms, was a dignified and not an efficient element of the Crown Colony constitution; whereas, in reality, he was not so much a small island monarch as he was the local powerful agent of a powerful Colonial Office, a truth amply demonstrated by the fact that if, like Lord Baldwin in the Leewards, he was tempted to espouse the local labour cause against the plantocracy he was rapidly disciplined by his commanding officers. He was caught in a cruel dilemma: if he was too friendly with labour the employers lobbied against him in London; if he tried to be 'statesmanlike', holding the balance between the opposing local elements, he soon lost the confidence of labour, as Lord Baldwin lost that of Bird in the Antiguan situation. And when, to all that, there was added an explosive social situation in which a depressed peasantry was in incipient revolt and, in turn, their mood coincided with the grant of universal adult suffrage in the 1950's, the battle was inevitably joined. Small island politics, then, were strongly personalist, and if the Governor or Administrator was not the target it was likely to be one of their subordinates, the Financial Secretary, or the Colonial Secretary, or the Police Commissioner. The acrimonious struggle in St Lucia between 1960 and 1962, for example, between a heavily disaffected local police force and an English Commissioner who was an old Kenya hand gave rise, indeed, to the appointment of two commissions of inquiry within a brief period of four months. [27]

But the *cause célèbre* of the battle in the Windwards was, of course, the phenomenal rise of Gairy, and Gairyism, in Grenada after 1950. A West Indian political scientist has attempted to see the movement in Weberian terms. [28] But it is doubtful if a schematic analysis that sees Gairy as the Weberian charismatic leader and the Grenada Government as the embodiment of rationalistic bureaucracy does anything more than describe the institutional superstructure while ignoring, except for a brief description, the social class struggle out of which Gairyism emerged; not to mention the fact that the procedure attributes motivational factors to the actors of the drama and thereby seriously distorts the meaning of what actually happened. For *charisma* is not a self-generating first cause; it grows out of deep social crisis. Gairy's providential return to Grenada in 1946 from the Aruba oil fields—the nursery of West Indian agitational leadership—did not create the crisis. It merely provided the crisis with its appropriate leadership. To be properly understood, it must be seen in terms of (1) its socio-cultural environment and (2) the old-style Grenadian political leadership that preceded it.

The first point springs from the general cultural fact that, as elsewhere in plantation America, slavery and the estate economy destroyed the possibility of a cohesive community tradition in West Indian life, in fact, more positively, actively promoting social disorganization. That explains why the West Indian riots of the 50's occurred most heavily in plantation areas, like the North Windward Coastal area in St Vincent and, in Grenada itself, the area of the southern coast. The 'little man' lived in a world of squalor, disease, and ignorance. It was only with the remarkable WHO-UNICEF penicillin injection campaign of 1956 that any serious attack was made upon the dread afflictions of yaws and venereal disease; and the failure of any of his various successive governments in St George's to harness the waters of the Grand Etang and the Great River meant that in most of the country districts the average Grenadian citizen was without light and power. There were no co-operative defences to protect the masses, for the associative principle in the nutmeg industry only started in 1947, while it was not until 1958 that the Grenada Farmers' Club co-operative was formed under the influence, mainly, of the visits of Mr Eddie Burke from Jamaica. The plantocracy was feudal in its social attitudes, as always, with the odd exception like Mr Lionel Alexis; although it is doubtful if the real reason for that could be traced, as Mr Alexis himself suggests in his little book of essays on Grenadian agriculture, *Agricola*, to the absence in Grenada of a Barbadian-like set of old-established white families. Gairyism, then, was the politics of a peasant *jacquerie* feeding on all of this.

With reference to the second point, it is true that Gairyite politics were traditionalist, being in line with the traditional small-island style, the particular brash forcefulness, half confident, half petulant, so characteristic of the political condition that lies halfway between unadorned colonial status and complete independence. For it was, in effect, Trinidadian Butlerism coming late to the 'spice island', with its street violence, its demagoguery, its curious mixture in its ideological content of God, Marx, and the British Empire. But it was also, in large part, a fundamental breakaway from the old school of politics to which Gairy's predecessors belonged. There was F. B. Paterson who, although an avowed socialist, allowed the family conservatism of the old estate at Belvedere to condition his outlook on life, so that he was always known to his Carriacou constituents as 'Mas' Fred'. There was the lawyer-politician like F. B. Renwick, whose record as planter, lawyer, and newspaper proprietor pro- bably helps to explain why a Grenada reporter could say that the presence of a lawyer on a public platform, addressing schoolchildren and their parents on their duty to society, despite his vast knowledge of the law of Torts, would cause the same amount of fear and speculation as the visible approach of a hurricane.[29] There was, above all, Marryshow himself, whose great record of public service commenced when, as a young reporter for the old *Federalist and Grenada People* some seventy years ago, under the aegis of the patriot- editor William Galway Donovan, a Negro of Irish extraction, he was outraged at the short shrift given by a reactionary Council of nominated members to a motion to aid the impoverished workers of the colony; and it continued throughout the thirty years of his long legislative career. But, for all his noble gifts, Marryshow, at the most, was a West Indian Fabian, a Royalist-Loyalist whose staunch Whig constitutionalism never permitted him to fight the colonial power except on its own polite terms. It was perhaps wise, as he was fond of repeating, to see that it is better to light a little candle than to curse the darkness. But a stage arrives in every colo- nial freedom movement when the darkness must be cursed, the entire system engaged; and Marryshow's vanity, his enjoyment of Buckingham Palace garden parties and parliamentary receptions at Westminster and his comic pursuit of royal personages all made it impossible for him to lead that open fight.

This special temper of West Indian 'radicalism', with its com- bination of borrowed Labour Party rhetoric and domestic social paternalism, naturally had its examples in the other islands. The

Barbadian variant is well known. In St Vincent there were union leaders like the venerable George MacIntosh who, for all his defiant radicalism—he kept a portrait of Stalin prominently displayed in his small druggist shop in Kingstown until the end—was certainly no Leninist insurrectionist, as the facts brought out at his 1935 treason trial clearly show.[30] Or there is Mrs Phylliss Allfrey, Labour Party stalwart in Dominica, granddaughter of the famous Sir Henry Nicholls, whose Fabian Socialism has not stifled in her an obvious pride in belonging to the 'Royal Family of Dominica' and whose battle against her own class, the 'bourg high-life', in Dominican parlance, has been entirely English in its style, with the exception perhaps of her clever use of *patois* as a mode of communication with her Dominican peasant following. Or, finally, it is only necessary to read the various brochures put out by the West Indian middle class leaderships celebrating the twenty-fifth anniversary (in 1950) of elected representation in the island legislative councils to appreciate their essential respectability, Mr. Duncan's commemorative paper on the St Vincent story even going so far as to quote, without a murmur of criticism, the inane observation of the Administrator of the day that 'what is essential in this mechanical, money-loving world is a sober, God-fearing, law-abiding, hard-working people.'[31] Of none of this could it be said that it was the first blast of the West Indian trumpet against the colonial class society.

What Gairyism did was to call this elaborate bluff. Gairy, in his own flamboyant person, represented the Negro of working class origin and limited education who has reached eminence through union leadership and mass voting, bitterly hostile to the white plantocracy and the brown middle class, not overly concerned, even when he becomes Chief Minister, to maintain intact the conventions of the established legal-political order. There is a strain of ribald irreverence in West Indian life; Gairy brought it into the open with his guying of prominent local personalities, the 'big boys'—merchant princes, rival politicians, civil servants—in his inventive market square orations. Not only did he raise wage rates for his followers through stubborn trade union pressure—after all, an old and recognized tactic—but he helped break down the rigid class barriers of Grenadian life by teaching his followers a new class self-respect. When he took a group of terrified estate workers into the Santa Maria tourist hotel and demanded they be served a meal, or told domestic servant girls to revolt against a system of minor slavery which required them to work from 6 a.m. to 9 p.m. so that they had no time even for a bath, he was helping to destroy their ingrained deference to their 'betters'. He gained from them, in return, a fanatical hero worship men like Marryshow did not get. Marryshow's strength, in any case, had been in the St George's urban district, while Gairy's was in the country districts, and the 'harvest festivals' that he regularly celebrated were part of the rural folklore. His famous boast, that if he wanted he could send a crapaud or a ground-dove or a lizard to represent them, 'my dear people', in Council, made it clear that it was to him, and not to the constitutional order, that they gave their fealty. And they were ready to give it because they saw in him all the tongue-sticking defiance of the master class they themselves could not afford to take on. So while the St George's respectability shuddered, the rural masses applauded each Gairyite indiscretion: the gaudy vanity of his appearances at meetings of the Standing Federation Committee, his unashamed enjoyment of his various secretaries as physical architecture rather than clerical aid, his preening self-esteem—'if Purcell can be nominated for the District Board why can't I be nominated as Federal Prime Minister?'—his final disenfranchisement for leading a steelband through an opponent's political meeting. 'Every time they say Gairy, a woman send me a fowl,' he was fond of saying; no political setback, like those of 1957 and 1962, could destroy this radical political theatricalism since it fed itself, with tropical virility, upon the social conditions of small island life. It can only be ended, of course, by a genuine social radicalism that makes its *sansculottisme* the beginning, and not just the end, of real change.

Gairyism is also typical, however, as proof of the fragility, almost the irrelevance, of constitutional conventions in societies where universal suffrage is only something more than a decade old. The damage done by the Gairy governments in Grenada itself to those conventions has been set out in the *Report* of the 1962 inquiry which precipitated the British Government's suspension of the local constitution: the deliberate and systematic violation of financial regulations, the browbeating of public servants, the illegal purchase with public monies of luxury items, including an expensive piano and a radiogram for the Chief Minister's residence, the deliberate destruction of the morale of the civil service.[32] All in all, it was a systematic assault upon the canons of constitutional government quite different from the more normal politics of small island Public Works Departments, the comparatively minor pecadilloes, for example, of Mrs Joshua as Minister in charge of the St Vincent Public Works Department, not going much beyond illegal methods of employing and paying members of road gangs.[33] But to express horror at it all, on the basis of textbook maxims about public administration drawn from the British experience, is in part to miss the point. The real point is that the record illustrates virtually the helplessness of small communities when they are thrown on their own moral resources, when they are obliged to act out the Colonial Office theory that each territory preserves a theoretical sovereignty it never, in reality, possesses. Such communities do not have the complex, impersonal, institutional life which makes possible, elsewhere, the separation of politics and administration or the anonymity of the civil servant. In Jamaica or Barbados, even, a weak civil servant can find refuge in a strong professional association or, alternatively, can find employment in some large business firm or even in the public service of another territory (there is, incidentally, a widespread anti-'foreigner' feeling against Barbadian government appointees in the smaller islands). His counterpart in Roseau or Castries has no such refuge. No better argument exists, perhaps, for the incorporation of the smaller territories into larger administrative regional units. A federal government with a federal public opinion behind it, would do much to cut down the local bossdoms, especially if it was accompanied by a real development of federal social services and economic planning to deal rationally with the regional problems. It would certainly end the sort of *opera bouffe* politics in which 'Uncle' Gairy, having violated every principle for which rational federal government stands, could decide after his local disenfranchisement that the best way to rehabilitate himself was to apply for the post of Labour Adviser to the Ministry of Social Affairs of the then-existing Federal Government in Port of Spain.

Therein, of course, lies the rub. For Gairy-like politics thrive, in part, upon the continuing confusion about ultimate political identity. As things stand presently, the Eastern Caribbean is trapped within a veritable maze of confusing and conflicting alternatives. The discussions between Trinidad and Grenada on the unitary state idea have not yet proceeded beyond the stage of preliminary

6

reports by committees on the economic and administrative problems involved.[34] To remain with the present Crown Colony system will certainly mean that the islands would rapidly revert to the status of the Virgin and Caymen Islands. To 'go it alone' into separate independence, without any guarantees of economic aid or military defence from friendly regional sources, could easily reduce them to a Haitian position. The continuing discussions on the possibilities of a new and smaller regional Federation has revealed, as already noted, the prevalence of the same insularist psychology that marked the first federal experiment, and the old Trinidad-Jamaica quarrel over a strong central government versus a loose confederationist association has repeated itself in a new quarrel over the same issue between the St Lucian view and the Antiguan view. There is the same jealousy, the same suspicion of others' motives, the tendency of the smaller islands—if the Barbadian official view is to be believed —to be motivated by the desire to organize a power bloc, in federa- tion or out of federation, against Barbados.[35] There is the same temp- tation of the colonial mentality to look for some protector from outside; so, there is little difference between the Dominica Confer- ence's weak admission in 1932 that 'the stage has not been reached when the Crown's veto can be regarded as one of the vestigial preroga- tives. In short, the demand is not for Dominion Status as described in the Balfour Declaration and embodied in the Statute of West- minster, but rather for Dominion Status as featured in Lord Dur- ham's Report on the affairs of British North America,'[36]—and in the argument of the St Lucian Chief Minister in 1963 in favour of the idea of association with Canada after the United States-Puerto Rico model on the ground that a West Indian federal enterprise cannot succeed.[37] It is worth noting that leading circles of Canadian capitalism have recently spoken openly about the possibilities of a customs and monetary union with the Eastern Caribbean West Indies, along with a political arrangement in which Canada would be responsible for External Affairs and Defence, all for the purposes of 'protection of the Canadian dollar, more effective development of the Canadian defence policy, and vital aid to a deserving people'.[38] So long as such thinly-disguised neo-imperialist ideas gain a wel- come in the West Indies it is evident that the pathology of colo- nialism, the absence of a strong local pride, the failure of nerve in political leadership, are all still endemic in small island life. The sardonic comment of one Trinidadian PNM chieftain on all of this—'you can't impose Independence on a grant-aided mentality' —is, regrettably, all too true.

Not only are there inter-island divisions of this sort. There are, too, intra-island divisions that make effective choice difficult. Barbadians themselves were divided on the issue of separate independence. To come back to the Grenadian case, the discussions in St George's on the unitary state proposal only serve to illustrate how divided the local public opinion is on that controversial and novel idea, a division, indeed, that goes back some forty years when the idea was broached by the Wood Report and discussed favourably by the then Governor of the day with the respective legislative councils of the Windwards group.[39] It remains to be seen whether the many family ties between Grenadians and Trinidadians—many Trinidad families are descended from French planters who left Grenada in 1783 to grow sugar in Trinidad—will be sufficiently strong to bring Grenada into the Trinidadian fold. The state of local opinion, in turn, naturally varies in relation to what can be expected, at any time, from Great Britain. It is possible that the growing harshness of British attitudes will have the result, in the long run beneficial, of breaking the colonial mentality. The bitterness engendered in West Indians by that harshness may become the stimulus for a new and vibrant nationalism looking more to the West Indies and less to the Commonwealth. For, frankly, British interests and West Indian interests more and more diverge, and it is enough to read the accounts of the 1966 constitutional talks to realize that there was a conflict, only half-recognized, of basic values, the British thinking in terms of a continuing custodial politics, the West Indians in terms of a developmental economics.

The growth of nationalism and democracy will serve to make this more and more a self-evident truth to West Indians. Certainly, the general cultural life of groups like the Windwards, characterized by moral and intellectual depression, awaits the liberating breeze of those forces. It is true that in some ways it is a more homogenuous culture than that of the larger groups. Small island pride, strong feelings of localist loyalty, keep people together remarkably well. There is no colour problem of Barbadian dimensions, no ethnic-group problem of Guyanese dimensions; mainly because, as in the case of Grenada, sugar cultivators disappeared early on to make

room for the class of small holders and because, too, the original
white planter class was early on in part supplanted by a Creole
mulatto group, a process culminating in the evacuation of the last
of the 'old' English families under the pressure of Gairyism in the
1950's. But class snobbery remains still a potent force. Small island
social history has been the history of class struggle. The sense of class
oppression is keen; a Vincentian labourer's remark—'if a man stand
up for his rights in this country he get hated by the above people'—
is amply borne out by the record of victimization of union members
by estate and factory managements.[40] Nor is this as yet ameliorated
in any way by the growth of a political-cultural nationalism seeking
after the fashion of the Trinidadian PNM to heal the wounds of
colonialism with the new medicine of assertive nationhood; and,
significantly, small island attempts to emulate the PNM—Mr
Dupigny's short-lived movement in Dominica and the rise of the
Comptonite 'intellectuals', as they are known, in St Lucia—have
so far not been very successful. The Grenada National Party styles
itself 'national', but has little to say about what nationalism means
for Grenada; its programme follows that of the PNM but lacks the
stimulating quality of PNM literature; while it has failed to construct
for itself, as over against traditional British history attitudes, a new
nationalist history which, for example, would acclaim Julien Fédon,
the Creole mulatto leader of the insurrection of 1795–96 against
the British, as one of the first national patriots rather than what the
British history texts term a 'brigand'. Until such a spirit of positive
nationalism emerges the radical movement in the smaller territories
will remain racked by institutional weakness, fratricidal persona-
lism and factionalism. It is no accident, then, that the breaking up
of the labour organizations in the Windwards group—noteworthily,
in the Dominican and St Lucian Labour parties over the last few
years, and dramatized in the Dominican case by the arbitrary expulsion of Mrs Allfrey from a party which she herself had done so
much, and through great personal sacrifice, to found in 1955[41]— has
been caused not by ideological differences but by personal rivalries.

There is, of course, a brighter side. There are resident professional
students of Windwards anthropology like Douglas Taylor in Dominica
and knowledgeable amateur local authorities like the late Harold
Simmons in St Lucia and Alistair Norris-Hughes in Grenada. But
they are exceptional, often isolated, sometimes persecuted indivi-

duals, not members of groups actively inseminating the social body with aesthetic values. The annals of the insular histories are full of liberal minded individuals who have been socially punished or economically ruined for their views. Mr Duncan has listed them in his little volume, *Footprints of Worthy Westindians*, from the Claudius Adams who promoted Sunday school work in the Vincentian country districts to the Gertie Wood who fought in British Guiana for equal pay for women.[42] The McCarthy-like witch-hunting of Mr Joshua in St Vincent merely because of his attendance at a Russian-sponsored trade union conference in Vienna is symptomatic. A respectable social climate has throughout assumed that it is more permissible to be interested in the genealogy of the European crowned families than in local working class conditions, as the comic disproportion of the space allocated to those two topics in the small island Handbooks illustrates.[43] That all 'unrest' is the fault of the 'agitator' has of course been the cardinal conviction of the Caribbean ruling classes ever since slavery. It speaks volumes for the mental climate of the smaller islands today that the conviction, increasingly discarded elsewhere, still thrives there. Hence the continuing use of long-standing colonial legislation against the importation of 'subversive' literature, and the deportation of 'undesirable' persons, as in the Kelshall case of 1964 in Grenada. The pervasive influence of the Catholic Church, staffed by expatriate European orders, explains much of all this. It is at least suggestive that two of the best-known books on Windward Islands history, Father Jesse's *Outlines of the History of St Lucia* and Father Devas' *Concepcion Island*, are written from an orthodox Catholic viewpoint untouched by the modernist spirit; so that the first title records the French Revolution in St Lucia as an encounter between 'heroic' British troops and a collection of 'slaves, demagogues, virulent Republicans' in a style long since departed from English Catholic scholarship, while the second title is simply a vigorous priestly defence of Catholic schools in Grenadian history in their struggle against the developing idea of secular state education, a struggle, as the author sees it, between Protestant 'bigotry' and Catholic 'education'. The real truth, of course, is that in all of the Catholic islands the Roman Church has throughout bitterly opposed educational reform. The Church cannot prevent the rise of non-Catholic politicians, Mr Compton, for example, who is Anglican, and Mr Maurice Mason, who is Methodist.

But it can still effectively sabotage any direct challenge to its power, a state programme of birth control, for example, or an outright secularist scheme of state education putting an end to the old dual educational system in the West Indies; Trinidad excepted. How it does that could only be told if a record could be obtained of what goes on in the audience chambers of the various bishops' palaces in the island capital towns.

The intellectual life of the smaller Windward units, this is to say, remains still pretty much a dialogue between the liberal and conservative wings of a tiny urban *élite*, with the masses as yet playing an inert part. That it was so in the Victorian period is clear from the role that George Charles Falconer played in Dominican politics during the middle decades of the last century as liberal gadfly against the local Establishment; as well as from the role that J. R. H. Bridgewater played, in a more Booker T. Washington sort of way, at a later period in the fields of public service and constitutional reform agitation.[44] And that it remains much the same, a century later, was made clear by the 1958 episode in which the Vicar-General of the Catholic Church in St Lucia killed the possibility of Roderick Walcott's play *The Banjo Man* being presented at the West Indies Arts Festival on the ground of its 'immorality'; as if, as the author protested, a play about a Creole country festival could be written in anything but the Rabelaisian manner: 'the work of the late Diego Rivera, the Western Hemisphere's greatest painter,' he added defiantly, 'although filled with agnostic propaganda, could not be retouched by the Pope and all his Cardinals to comply with a pastoral letter.'[45] Until they are emancipated from this ecclesiastical authoritarianism the Windwards will remain something less than genuinely liberal societies.

# Chapter VII

# THE EMERGENCE OF NATIONAL SOCIETY

## JAMAICA

I T I S no accident that Jamaica should have been the first British West Indian territory to gain independence (1962). For throughout the regional history her size, historical antiquity (having been in continuous English occupation since 1655), population (comprising roughly one-half of the total West Indian figure) and economic importance as a leading sugar colony, have combined to give her a paramount position in the Western colonial empire. The Emancipation controversy, as its voluminous literature shows, was largely a Jamaican controversy. A series of Jamaican events—the slave revolt of 1831, the Morant Bay affair of 1865, the Frome riots of 1937-38—have been the catalysts, for good or ill, of new social and political phases in the history of imperial policy in the area as a whole. West Indians elsewhere have automatically assigned a leadership status to Jamaican politicians, a pre-eminence only recently surrendered as a result of Mr Manley's retreat from federalist ideology. The politico-constitutional changes of the last twenty-five years or so started in Kingston with the grant of the 1944 constitution; while today, along with Trinidad, Barbados and Guyana, the territory has become the testing ground for the thesis that the territorially tiny West Indian societies can carry the burden of sovereignty. Jamaica likewise plays a leading role in the popular British image of the West Indies and it is perhaps fitting that the long residence of Ian Fleming, the Hemingway of Jamaica, in the island should have finally produced a posthumous volume, *Ian Fleming Introduces Jamaica*, which is full of the English myths about Jamaica of the old 'pink gin and verandah' colonial atmosphere. More seriously, Jamaica, as Lord Olivier claimed, has a prerogative; the privilege, in particular, of furnishing the leading case as to whether mixed poly-ethnic societies that have lost their original cultures can become healthily inclusive communities. Here, more than anywhere else in the English-speaking Caribbean, emergent national society leaves the old world and enters a new.

The story of modern Jamaica starts, of course, with the upheaval of the 1930's. Its background was that of the long period after 1866 of the modified Crown Colony regime. It can be argued, however, that the struggle towards nationhood had its genesis earlier in the pre-1865 agitation, arising out of the political implications of Emancipation and based on the new group of coloured freeholders, from whom Boyle and his leading associates in the 1865 'rebellion' came; or indeed that there was an earlier genesis even before that time in the form of the effort of the Jamaican settler-historians of the eighteenth century, particularly Long and Edwards, to give a coherent Creole philosophical foundation to the struggle of the colonists against the absentee metropolitan power. Neither of those movements, naturally, was a democratic nationalism. For the historically earlier movement was no more than an expression of the white planter interests, gradually becoming eroded as its wider and deeper growth within Jamaican soil was frustrated by the white distrust of the 'persons of colour' and by the joint insensate distrust that both white and coloured had for the black majority; so that Long, for example, could combine a Lockeian assault upon imperial dominance with an almost morbid Negrophobia. Similarly, the localist loyalism of the great coloured population of the later period was an expression, likewise limited, of the continuing struggle against the social supremacy of the whites after their legal supremacy had been broken. Because, then, of its strong pro-British loyalties, working to the exclusion of a Jamaican nationalism, the coloured group failed to become a rallying point for the revolt of the masses. That explains why, among other things, its leaders never overcame their crippling ambiguity towards the colonial power, for the colonial power, as they saw the matter, would in fact save them from such a revolt. So, it is not astonishing, as an instance, that Edward Jordon believed that pre-1865 Jamaica was not fit for responsible government, or that Gordon's letter to his wife on the eve of his execution was a model of Christian resignation, or that a characteristic expression of late Victorian Jamaican middle class solicitous concern for the moral welfare of the masses, in the form of W. P. Livingstone's *Black Jamaica*, should conclude that the 'desolate tranquillity' of their lives could only be ended by their being brought into the broad life of the Empire under the 'wise guidance' of the white British race.

Yet it is true, even so, that both of those movements testify to the slow, tortuous growth over the centuries of a powerful local sentiment, of a Jamaican sense of being. They were reinforced, after 1900, by the new voices of a more widespread protest. To begin with, there was the agitational work of individual men like Sandy Cox and 'Jag' Smith, both of them socially conscious civil servants (at a time when the service was an exclusive club almost impossible for the average Jamaican youth to get into) who, later as barristers, devoted their lives to fighting the legal and political battles of the poor. Theirs, inescapably, was a limited work, for they had no party structure to give them an institutional support. They were lone 'independents', disliking the Crown Colony system but with no clear ideas of what ought to replace it. Men like 'Jag' Smith, accordingly, like the coloured politicians who, earlier on, had come to prominence after 1830, waged an essentially negative battle whose weapons, the refusal, for example, to attend social functions at Government House, were of necessity weak and ineffectual. Yet they managed to produce a fully reasoned case for radical change, as is evident enough from the conversations with Jamaican Negroes of radical persuasion reported in the Forrest-Henderson travel book of 1906, conversations all the more illuminating since the author of the text was himself a reactionary white who believed that Negroes were incapable of self-rule and that no white people could ever live in a country ruled by black men. He was impressed, nonetheless, by the quality of the radical argument: neither the Imperial Parliament nor a short-term Governor could properly understand Jamaican needs; the system of Jamaican representative government was a fantastic caricature of law-making; it was a fine thing to be part of the Empire, but a finer thing to be a free nation and independence was inevitable, maybe by concessions to be made by the new force of the renovated Liberal Party in British politics; for the weakness of English rule in Jamaica was that the island was governed by those who were merely paid to govern; in the mass, the Jamaican people compared favourably with the agricultural workers of England or France and were capable of self-rule; and, in any case, the local coloured population shared the same ideal and, in an independent

6*

Jamaica, would play, as it were, nothing more dangerous than the role of 'our Irish'.[1] There was an obvious ambiguity about the argument, for it oscillated between the idea of a local liberationist movement attaining all this and the idea that it would be the result of Imperial magnanimity. At the same time, the note of Jamaican nationalism, albeit not fully spelled out in theoretical terms, being more of a list of moral declarations, was strong and pervasive.

What it was up against, of course, was the blind hostility of the Jamaican colonial system and its controlling forces. The same Forrest-Henderson book recorded something of this, too, in its chapter on 'The White Man's Politics'. If the report is true, the Jamaican English of the pre-1914 period, and supposedly later as well, still thought in terms of 1865 and Governor Eyre. The 'black fellow' had not forgotten the lesson he was taught after Morant Bay, so the argument ran. The 'black Tommies' in Up-Park Camp and the white troops at Newcastle would have something to say if Jamaicans started talking again about the rubbish of freedom. The 'blacks' were utterly incapable of self-government; if they came to rule the island not one white man would remain; it would become a 'lawless republic' like Haiti. What the island needs is a solid population of 'solid white men', not the migratory English adventurer who looks for a fortune in ten years and then a suburban home near London. Labour difficulties would disappear under the rule of such a new settler type, for the 'black man' is very much what his white employer makes him. Any ideas apart from that were the impossible ambitions of 'scheming gentlemen of the coloured class'.[2] The desperate quality of the argument, even envisaging the use of force against even mild ideas of constitutional reform, makes it clear that the possibility of compromise with those ideas was pretty remote. The lines of the general struggle were thus clearly drawn. Only the outbreak of the 1914 war perhaps made an open confrontation between the two opposing arguments impossible. It goes without saying, of course, that a Jamaican Negro gentleman with radical ideas who looked to the Liberal Imperialism of the 1906 period in British politics for their fulfilment would have been unlikely to have had any criticisms about Britain's role in that war.

It is not surprising that Major Wood found, in the postwar situation, that demands for reform were 'fairly general', despite the absence of a defined concensus of opinion as to what the reforms should be. Men of independent views refused to accept appointment of nominated members since they would be, in Major Wood's own phrase, legislative dummies with votes that had to be recorded automatically. Jamaican politics at the time revolved in great degree, however, around the unsatisfactory relations between the central Government and the elected Parochial Boards, the old stronghold of Jamaican popular localism; so much so indeed that the elected members to the Legislative Council tended in many ways to be more disturbed by the grievances of those Boards than by the reform of the colonial constitution. For the Boards were subject to the control of the colonial Treasury and, even more humiliatingly, were subject to dissolution by the Governor and replacement by a Commissioner: an evil habit so deeply ingrained that it survived even the colonial period, as the Jamaican Government's dissolution of the Kingston and St Andrew's Corporation in 1964 shows. The political struggles of the 1920's tended to revolve around that issue. The decade of the 1930's, of course, introduced a more radical, a more socially inclined note. A new preoccupation with the 'condition of the people' question made itself felt. There was the birth of things like the Jamaica Welfare community development scheme, initially based upon Mr Manley's pioneering agreement of 1937 with the United Fruit Company, which did much to foster in the years to come a virile welfare movement independent of official agencies, and a middle class group willing to staff it, both of them conditions absent in the smaller islands. The contrast here, indeed, with the Trinidadian situation is instructive, for in Trinidad such organizations, as well as the entire trade union movement, grew up, when they did, with practically no support from a socially-conscious middle class group. By comparison, there grew up, early in Jamaica, a whole corps of such people and their names testify to the influence in the colonial life of the Fabian-Oxford tradition of social obligation of the metropolitan society—Eddie Burke, Leila Tomlinson, Art Carney, Philip Sherlock, Lenworth and Beth Jacobs, Mrs Manley herself. They were expressive of a social awakening on the part of an entire social section, not just a few isolated individuals. They dramatized, too, the value of indigenous leadership, for the organizations they variously created avoided, for example, the artificiality of groups such as the later Jamaican Federation of Women arising as such groups did out of the patronage of an active

Governor's wife like Lady Molly Huggins and of the snob value that accompanied any interest from King's House.

Concurrently, there flowered a variety of new political groups, all more or less nationalist in temperament: the Social Reconstruction League, whose secretary at one time was the odd Barrington Williams who, almost alone of them all, managed to write a book about the period; the collection of writers—MacFarlane, Domingo, Roberts—appearing in the new progressive magazines like *The Outlook*; the short-lived National Reform Association founded by Ken Hill; above all, the Jamaica Progressive League, founded in 1936 mainly under the inspiration of the Harlem group of ultra-nationalistic Jamaican exiles and inspired more immediately by the 1937 visit of Adolphe Roberts to the island, centred around the patriotic insistence, as the very first issue of its news-sheet stated it, that 'Edward Jordan outweighs a dozen Governors. Thomas Henry MacDermot, patriotic journalist and first Poet Laureate of Jamaica, is more to us than all our imported Directors of Education put together'.[3] To that there must be added the contribution to Jamaicanism, the 'greater Jamaica' philosophy, of the long drawn out struggle of professional organizations like the Jamaica Union of Teachers and the Jamaica Agricultural Society. For by some strange quirk the colonial power in Jamaica did little to interfere with the right of teachers to engage in political activities, a privilege unknown elsewhere in the British Caribbean, so that for half a century after its foundation in 1894 the JUT acted as the focal point for a special Jamaican struggle against colonialism, including campaigns in defence of teachers' rights against school management boards, the setting up of vocational schools, methods of teacher payment, and so on, not to mention its function as a training school for a whole new crop of Legislative Council politicians—G. L. Young, H. E. Allan, D. Theodore Wint, and others—and public figures like Mrs Dalton-James and the late H. Anglin Jones.[4] The JAS, likewise, despite its being partly government-subsidized from the beginning (1895), and therefore suffering from an illogical duality of role, helped create an independent bloc of farming opinion, ready to defend itself at any moment against government bureaucracy, so that for years, and continuing up to the present time, its half-yearly conferences at Ramson Hall saw both departmental officials and government ministers compelled to defend their policies against that opinion. It would indeed be difficult to overestimate the importance of such professional associations in the pre-independence period when the Crown Colony machine, even when modified as it was after 1944, meant practically unmixed official rule by expatriate departmental heads uncurbed by any form of a national will; inevitably, then, in the absence of other platforms those organizations became the natural platform for the nurture of such a will, became, that is, politicized bodies as a consequence. Not must it be overlooked that both the JUT and the JAS were organs of the 'little man', for although the JAS started off as a large landowners' lobby it soon became the voice of the small owners as they emerged from the thraldom of mountain tenancy into freehold ownership; while the JUT, from its inception, was the vehicle of a prestige profession which almost alone among the professions of colonial Jamaica provided an avenue of social-occupational mobility, at the level of the primary schoolteacher, for the enterprising children of the lower middle classes. They were, in effect, political party and trade union before the 1937–38 events, with the birth of the modern Jamaican union-party structure, ended their usefulness as such.

Nor, finally, in all this must the contribution of the press be overlooked. For although it is true that from its beginnings the *Daily Gleaner* was the mouthpiece of Jamaican conservatism under its authoritarian editors like Michael de Cordova and Herbert G. de Lisser, there was always an independent journalistic tradition. Thus, most famous of all, the beloved Tom Redcam created a popular journalism at once Jamaican in theme and professionally ethical in tone, first in the old *Jamaica Post* and later in the *Jamaica Times*. Likewise, the English expatriate editor William J. Makin made himself, during the 1930's, into what one local admirer termed the economic abolitionist of the downtrodden people of Jamaica. Not least of all, O. T. Fairclough's formation of the weekly journal *Public Opinion* in 1937 provided a forum for the publication of every progressive idea. All of these, indeed, gave a new life to a radical journalism of some standing in Jamaican life, certainly going back to figures like Dr Robert Love who, as editor of the old *Jamaica Advocate* around the turn of the century, had employed the *Negritude* that he had learned in a prolonged Haitian residence in the service of the idea of black representation in the Legislative Council of that period; as well as figures like the educated Jamaican Negro Dr T. E.

S. Scholes, whose remarkable books written on the colonial problem at much the same time, *Sugar and the West Indies*, for example, and *The British Empire and Alliances*, have not received the attention they deserve. The general intellectual ferment of this later period of the 1930's could likewise be seen in the appearance of novels, like Adolphe Roberts' *The Single Star*, dramatizing the theme of the anti-colonial struggle of a nationalist liberalism; in books like Nembhard's *Jamaica Awakening* (1943); in the poetry of social protest of Campbell and Mckay. There was, too, the lifework of the feminine patriots, Una Marson, for example, who among much else pioneered popular literary publication in Jamaica, including her editorship of the *Pioneer Press* volumes. And last but certainly not least there was the special contribution, more subtle and indirect but nevertheless powerful, of the new Jamaican scholarship of the gentleman-scholar Frank Cundall whose creative work in Jamaican historical studies and bibliography, starting with his *Bibliographia Jamaicensis* (1902), was proof to West Indians—just as was C. L. R. James' pioneer study, *The Black Jacobins* (1938) in the Trinidadian case—that they, as much as the British, had a genius for scholarship that only awaited a structure of higher West Indian education to bring it to full fruition.

Even so, much of all this was at best, middle class protest, seeking, to mend, not end the system. Even the Jamaica Progressive League, forerunner of the People's National Party, only wanted self-government within the Commonwealth, as its early pamphlets, like Roberts' *Self-Government for Jamaica*, Domingo's *The Case for Self-Government* and James O'Meally's *Why We Demand Self-Government for Jamaica* fully show. It was, throughout, a middle class leadership accepting, more or less, the Jamaican class divisions into what an early publicist, writing in 1919, had termed, in a morally prescriptive fashion, the lower class, the better class, and the best class. 'The better class,' he wrote grandiloquently, 'cannot advance without the basic labour of the lower class; nor can the lower class be inspired in spirit, enthused in heart, marshalled in companies, maintained in motion, directed in aim, sustained in effort, encouraged in delays, restrained in triumphs, without the teaching, influence, guidance, cheering, controlling leadership of the better class.'[5] This was class fear, not social analysis. It blandly overlooked the fact that the Jamaican 'lower class' had in fact never been that inert. From the colonial beginnings it had been, as a slave class, an assertive independent force, as the history of its slave revolts, detailed in Richard Hart's *Out of the House of Bondage*, amply shows. The protracted guerrilla warfare of the Jamaican mountain folk, the Maroons, ending in 1738, testifies likewise to that social truth; a truth only obscured for present-day Jamaicans by the legend, prevalent now that independence has become a respectable idea, that the national freedom struggle has been mainly one of the free coloured group. The truth of the matter is, of course, that whereas the 'better class', in McLarty's phraseology, has regarded self government—or representative government, or responsible government, there being a changing fashion of polite terminology in these things—as the final cause of political activity, the basic struggle which has engaged the attention of the 'lower class' has been the search for a better social life. That truth once appreciated, it becomes clear that 1938 was not, as the Jamaican popular mythology now believes, a completely new dispensation but the final flowering of an already well established way of life in the mass population.

The best known earlier examples of the popular Jamaican struggle in the twentieth-century period are those of Bedwardism and Garveyism. The first movement had its genesis, as far as is known, in the quixotic figure of 'Shakespeare' Woods, who organized a following after 1876 in the August Town area, centring around the two doctrinal elements of the vow ceremony and the strict observance of fasting. He was followed by Bedward himself, born a labourer in the Mona estate and founder of the Native Baptist Free Church. The accounts of his activities in the camp he set up point to the existence of a large unemployed army of rural and urban labourers in the districts adjoining Kingston that could have become, with less otherworldly leadership, a serious threat to the colonial establishment. It is worth noting the essentially proletarian character of the movement, something in itself traditionally Jamaican, for early local Baptist leaders had come, like George Lisle, from the slave class. Bedwardism, even so, was essentially anachronistic, more an apocalyptic survival into the twentieth century of the great Jamaica Revival of 1860 than a secular revolt of the modern style, a fact dramatized by Bedward's final bizarre attempt at celestial ascent.[6] The impact of Garveyism, by its very nature, was immeasurably more profound, although because it was a world movement rather than just a Jamaican episode it is difficult to separate its effect upon world Negro opinion from its more specific effect upon the growth of Jamaican society; and indeed, Garvey himself, after his disastrous flirtations with Jamaican colonial politics in 1929–1935 turned his back on his homeland to concentrate on more sympathetic Afro-American audiences abroad; as Sandy Cox, before him, tired of his battling with Lord Olivier, had left to practise law in Boston. The story of Garvey's struggle with the Jamaican official society, and its ruthless persecution of his efforts, both by its political and judicial machinery, is well known, equally so his rejection by the Jamaican coloured middle class—as evident in the attitude of Wint, his opponent in the Legislative Council election of 1930, and summed up in the denunciatory letter against Garvey and the United Negro Improvement Association which a West Indian who was also a naturalized United States citizen forwarded to all colonial Governors in 1920; the inherited slave complex of telling the master what was happening on the plantation, Mrs Garvey acidly comments in her book, dies hard with some of us.[7]

Nor is it likely that the return in 1964 of Garvey's ashes to Jamaica and his elevation by the Jamaican Government to the status of an official national hero proves anything except the need of every newly independent nation to create its own national Pantheon of father figures. Indeed, the controversy let loose by that action served to show that for a substantial portion of Jamaican 'respectable' opinion the core of Garvey's message—the physical return to Africa—is unacceptable, even in its diluted form of a psychological return to the African tradition as against the imported Europo-centrism of the colonial heritage; and it was left to a handful of liberal journalists to remind their fellow countrymen that Garvey's greatness lay in the massive psychological warfare that he deployed to wipe out the inherited inferiority complex and the facelessness of the Negro in a white world.[8] The proper commentary upon the real official Jamaican attitude to Garveyism could be seen in the dismal fact that it was left to his widow, with no financial aid from any Jamaican institution, government, university or business, to undertake the real tribute to his memory in the form of writing up his biography and that the final product of her labour passed by almost unnoticed when published. The intellectual push of the movement was felt more deeply overseas; Nkrumah has acknowledged his debt to

Garvey's books, just as, earlier, the great Latin American liberator Bolivar claimed to have learned much from the Maroon leader Cudjoe's guerrilla strategy against the British regimental troops while he was resident briefly in Jamaica.

There is little doubt, even so, that Garvey's Jamaican episode left a lasting, though hidden mark upon the national spirit. He openly challenged the reigning false standards of racial values. Equally, he was the pioneer of organized political party life, for he demonstrated, in Kingston as in Harlem, that the Negro could be organized and that he was eager to repose confidence in and support sincere Negro leadership. The launching of his People's Political Party in 1929 emphasized the bankruptcy of the rule of the elective independents in the Crown Colony system, a condition of things that extracted the usually complaisant Major Wood, in his 1922 Report, the tart comment that the government of Jamaica would seem largely to consist in a series of efforts to avoid a contest between the Governor and an unknown nine out of fourteen men in the Legislative Council. Garvey's American experience enabled him to educate his Jamaican following in the meaning of organized political activity and coherent party programmes, including his own election programme of 1930, containing, among other items, the suggested compulsory employment of a higher percentage of local labour enterprises, including government service, a suggestion that only became statutorily recognized by way of the Foreign Nationals and Commonwealth Citizens Act of 1964. To speak—as does Dr M. G. Smith[9]—of the 'tragic escapism' and 'social withdrawal' of Garvey's Jamaican period is to ignore the fact that his party offered, for the first time, a reasoned programme for Jamaican social development; and it is very possible that Garvey would have remained in Jamaica, as his continued active service as a member of the Kingston and St Andrew's Corporation suggests, had he not been forced out by continuous harassment. For it is a grim commentary on the Crown Colony regime that his political movement at its height in 1930 could not sweep him into power as Bustamante's later movement swept 'The Chief' into power in 1944. A genuinely democratic system, with the popular franchise, would have had a similar result as in the case of the Bustamante Labour Party landslide of that later year, made possible by the new quasi-parliamentary constitution. In that case, the development of modern Jamaica might have

been fundamentally different, with the Garveyite Rastafarians playing the role, as it were, of the Levellers of the Jamaican Revolution
and not, as they now do, the role of its Fifth Monarchy men.[10]

Garveyism, this is to say, contributed at least two of the ideological pillars of that 'revolution'—racial self-respect and organized
political party. They were liberating forces, despite the theoretical
weaknesses of Garveyism as a whole, its failure, for example, to
understand the economic roots of race prejudice, its anti-scientific
concept of 'Negro' traits, its own inverted segregationism, its general
Africanist orientation which did not perhaps sufficiently appreciate,
as an Anglican critic noted, that it is impossible to restore a racial
and tribal continuity violently broken for more than two hundred
years, so that whereas the African native might have conceivably
been made a Christian without being Europeanized, the West Indian
Negro had been Europeanized long before he was converted.[11] The
other two elements in the Jamaican general developments of the
modern period—working class consciousness and nationalism—it
was the special task of the new groupings after 1938 to contribute:
the People's National Party and the Jamaica Labour Party, along
with the unique politico-labour union structure that they both set
up in the subsequent period; as well, of course, as consolidating
the political party segment.

The period 1938–62 is, in essence, the gestatory period in the
growth of those twin forces of class awareness and nationalism. The
first grew out of the history of working class struggles, going back
at least to the great railway strike of 1919 and rapidly accelerating
with the riots and general strike of the 1937–38 confrontation. Its
economic base was a loose alliance of workers and peasants, but
particularly the growth, in the inter-war period, of an increasing
proportion of the working class as an unemployed and underemployed industrial army dependent entirely for its livelihood on
wage labour (unlike the small cultivator class of the rural economy),
concentrated in the Kingston slum areas and therefore capable,
once energized, of having the greatest possible impact upon government. That is why, once started in the Westmoreland Frome district,
the central stage of the 1937–38 politico-economic drama soon
shifted to the capital.[12] Once thus finding itself, working class militancy created, almost overnight, its own new organizational forms
in the shape of the new trade unions (although unionism certainly

goes back to at least 1918 in the economy) and political parties, and of the new party-union structures that have since then joined the two together. The central figure in that development has, of course, been that of Bustamante, perhaps so by historical accident but, nevertheless, even more than Manley, the central figure. There were many others: H. C. Buchanan, Ken Hill, Richard Hart, Ferdinand Smith. The dominant form of political unionism, in which the Jamaican unions have come to be run by the political parties as vote-catching annexes instead of being controlled by the workers, has inevitably taken the edge off the militancy; as distinct from the Trinidadian experience, where the fact that the labour movement antedated the national political movement instead of accompanying it, as in Jamaica, has meant that organized labour has enjoyed a more independent role. That is why, among other things, union leader names like Manley and Shearer are respectable Establishment names in the Jamaican situation today, whereas names like Sutton and Weekes in the Trinidadian situation signify powerful personalities leading independent entities, frequently *personae non gratae* with the political Establishment and having little of the social respectability of their Jamaican counterparts.[13] At the same time, the class militancy of the Jamaican crowd unleashed by 1938, although thus somewhat muted, has basically remained as a permanent element in Jamaican society. The old habit of class deference has gone for ever, as testified, indeed, by the way in which bitter complaint about the 'bad manners' and the 'abusive' language of the street populace has become, over the years, the stock in trade of the middle class and its communications media.

The raw material of the working class struggle lay, of course, in the general labour conditions of the Jamaica of 1937–38. The Orde-Browne Report listed them in an extensive section. There was, at best, employment that was discontinuous, ill-paid, and featuring excessively long hours of work, frequently at the request of the employee who jealously guarded the little work he could get by willingness to work incredibly long hours calculated to achieve his own physical exhaustion with reduction of efficiency, the Kingston dockworkers providing the worst example of that evil system; the exploitation of a surplus labour economy by the socially unconscionable employer, the plight of women workers in the urban establishments and in domestic service being grim evidence of that situation;

the evil of the rotational employment system which simply served to exacerbate the real problem of intermittent employment; bad housing conditions made worse by the absence of any body of legislation—such as accompanied indentured labour in British Guiana—obligating the estates to certain standards of housing; the growing degeneration of most forms of Government employment into a thinly veiled relief system and having among other consequences the result of making urban living conditions even more wretched by attracting new rural migrants who, in their turn, once they adopted town life, abandoned it with reluctance; and all of this not made any better by an almost complete absence of any labour organization or industrial relations administration, despite the fact that the Royal Commission that had investigated the 1865 'rebellion' had asked for such a machinery.[14] The way out of all that seemed to Major Orde-Browne to be (1) the reduction of unemployment by means of land-settlement and swamp-reclamation schemes and (2) the growth of trade unions under the benevolent direction of a well-qualified officer who would supervise all questions affecting labour. In fact, of course, it was the two national union power-structures affiliated to the two major parties which, in the next twenty years, led the workers' struggle against those conditions, achieving, in the end-result, a real redistribution of economic and social power within the Jamaican class system.

Some of this is traceable to the tremendous impact of the 'Busta' personality. For that personality, with its raucous and bogus radicalism, its tremendous braggadocio, its personification of the Jamaican folk-hero, the spiderman Anansi who survives in a hostile world by cunningly exploiting the weaknesses of his enemies, symbolizes the profound change that took place in Jamaican inter-class relations after 1938. He had, it is true, massive defects. He has never understood the democratic ideal. He has always been against the idea of shared collective leadership in party life, and that he attempts to justify that attitude by reference to the archaic structure of the British Conservative Party only shows that, for all his terrorizing of colonial Governors, he has had his full share of the colonial mentality.[15] His temperament is messianic, living on mass emotion; he has none of the 'patient equanimity' which Bagehot, in his essay on Gladstone, noted all great orators lack; for, as Bagehot also noted, with men of this style the tranquil deposit of ordinary ideas is interrupted by the sudden eruption of volcanic forces. Yet it was those defects, mirroring as they did the weaknesses of the colonial society, that accounted for 'Busta's' success and Manley's comparative failure. His appeal to the unlettered crowd, like Gairy's, was that they glorified in him the poses and perquisites they felt they could never obtain for themselves. The witness who, after listening to one of the early 'Busta' speeches to the Kingston dockworkers in 1938, remarked to a companion, 'that man is the uncrowned king of Jamaica for the next ten years' was prophetically right.[16] Up to independence, and even beyond, 'Busta' seemed, much more than his arch rival, to embody the self-image of the Jamaican populace.

With regard to the other constituent element of Jamaican development, that of a national spirit, the fertilizing agent, by comparison, was the People's National Party and its predecessor, the Jamaica Progressive League. Walter G. MacFarlane has described the genesis of the League in his valuable account written years later in 1957; and it is of special importance to note how the League, after 1939, moved (as a body now affiliated to the PNP) to undertake the task, in MacFarlane's phrase, of Jamaicanizing Jamaicans. We ought to begin, as MacFarlane again summarized it, to look more realistically to Jamaicans who believe in the process of national self-government instead of those who seek to promote personal self-government.[17] That became the note, in turn, of the new PNP under Manley's leadership. With its advocacy of full self-government, its crystallization of latent political interest into a militant political party, its organized research, through planning committees, into all aspects of the Jamaican problems, and its propaganda effort it generated, altogether, a vast volume of political consciousness, of inestimable importance as a prerequisite to the advent of universal suffrage in 1944. Events between 1939 and 1944 helped to push the movement into a more militant posture. For originally a reformist party waiting upon the publication of the Report of the Moyne Commission, it was shaken out of that passive attitude by the realization that the Report, when in fact finally published in abbreviated form, was nothing more—as the second Annual Conference report put it—than a futile proposal to make charitable social services do duty for economic, political and social reform, and finally demonstrated the truth that Jamaica's hopes would depend on Jamaica's own efforts.[18] The struggle to survive as a progressive movement committed to leading moral ideas in an apathetic colonial society naturally strengthened the awareness of that truth.

There was the struggle, to start with, against the reactionary plantocracy and its 'Uncle Tom' political 'yes-men' in the structure of colonial government. For there was much truth in Manley's early remark that there was no real upper class in Jamaica, only an essentially alien group of colonial Jamaican elements in parasitic relationship to the British colonial officialdom.[19] The parasitism, it should be added, was in large part attributable, of course, to the weakness of the manufacturing principle and the strength of the trading principle in the colonial economy, for the merchant is tied more closely to imperialist connections; and with the decline of sugar and coffee in nineteenth-century Jamaica, indeed, the ideas essential to manufacturing organization disappeared. It was therefore logical that the leading political expression of the dominant economic groups at this time should have been the short-lived Jamaica Democratic Party, started outside Kingston by the big landowners and pen-keepers but rapidly falling into the hands of the Kingston merchant group led by Abe Issa. Added to that particular struggle there was also the continuing struggle against the colonial power which, in the shape of Sir Arthur Richards' administration, became more authoritarian than ever under the pressures of the war after 1940, characterized by wholesale internment—the arbitrary arrest of Walter Domingo as he stepped off the plane from New York was particularly scandalous—repressive censorship legislation and the use of the law of seditious libel to silence outspoken critics. With the PNP the new spirit, as it fought this battle on two fronts, centred around the constitutional struggle, of concern, in the beginning, only to the PNP educated elements, but later extending to the workers. The widespread popular acceptance of the self-government idea—a tribute in itself to PNP missionary enterprise—was no better illustrated than in the fact that whereas Bustamante was able openly to oppose the idea in the 1944 general elections and win support on the ground that self-government would bring 'brown man rule', in 1949 he did not dare to do so and later, indeed, embraced the idea himself.

These, then, were the integral components of emergent Jamaicanism in the thirty years or so leading up to independence. Their collective achievement, seen in retrospect, was slowly to foster the general idea of a Jamaican national consciousness, replacing, as best it could, the traditional alienation to their own country which the majority of Jamaicans had usually felt; it was revealing that the main point of Mr Manley's inaugural speech to the newly-formed PNP in September 1938 was an emphatic insistence upon the importance of that new nationalist sense despite the unfortunate connection of the word 'national' with the ugly nationalism of the European Fascist powers of the time.[20] Because independent Jamaica has been made by these elements, transforming the country from a static, placid colonial community into an expanding society of raucous vigour, it is essential to note how much they achieved and their final relationships, as a parallelogram of forces, one with the other.

Of the success of the national enterprise in strictly political terms there can be, to begin with, little doubt. For it is idle to say, as some of the younger present-day leftists charge, that there has never been a real Jamaican nationalist movement, only an imperial transfer of power.[21] That is to be unjust to the older figures like Mr Manley who, for all his defects—his vanity, his legalist frame of thought, his inability to master what Lord Rosebery called the Tom, Dick and Harry aspect of the business of politics—devoted a lifetime of superb talents to the nationalist cause. The end-result deserves more than a radical sneer. There has been a comparatively untroubled transition from colonialism to independence. A remarkable two party system grew up, almost overnight, with the two mass parties practically monopolizing the electoral loyalties, and the complete failure of third party movements during the period to intrude upon that monopoly, whether on the Right, like Kirkwood's Country Party, or on the Left, like Millard Johnson's 'black man's party', only served to emphasize the strong social foundations of that political stability; not to mention the significant fact that all of those third parties, including even that of the Rastafarian chieftain Sam Brown, as a candidate of the 'only party, the suffering party',[22] elected to try their luck within the framework of the constitutional system. After 1949 there was a basic PNP–JLP agreement on what form developing self-government should take, so that in effect the political status of the territory, the Federation issue excepted, was taken out of the area of party politics. The twin factors of historical continuity and relative population homogeneity helped to entrench the habits of parliamentary life and convention originally implanted by English colonization. What the Jamaican political force did after 1944 was to provide that skeleton of constitutional ritual with the living flesh and blood of a vigorous two party system. That system, in turn, helped create an agreement on fundamentals, for it is true to say that although the PNP styled itself socialist, while consistently refusing to give it a Jamaican definition, and the JLP styled itself the defender of capitalism without comprehending the implications of *laissez-faire* economics in an immature tropical economy, both of them, when saddled with the responsibility to govern, adopted roughly similar methods to attain roughly similar ends. Nor must that ideological similarity be obfuscated by the fierce partisanship of the mass party followings—few things in Jamaica are more comic than the fury with which the PNP black proletarian will assault the JLP black proletarian, as the ridiculous travesty of the local Labour Day celebrations illustrates—for Jamaican politics have been, and still are, essentially a Dickensian mock-encounter between Tweedle-dum and Tweedledee. The destruction of working class unity caused thereby, with its chief architect undoubtedly being Bustamante, essentially negative and sterile as his politics have been, has had tragic consequences. But on the credit side the total process here described has, in the end, provided the society with a truly national policy, claiming with some exceptions the full loyalty of the electorate. Thus both parties, although divided on Federation, joined together, once Federation was over, in a common front at the final Independence conference in London in 1962 and on the terms of the Independence constitution.[23] Merely to look at the signal failure of such a process in Guyana, with the collapse of Indian-African *frentismo* after 1955, or at the crippling effects that profound disagreement on basic political status can have on the life of a society, as in the case of neighbouring Puerto Rico, is to place the proper value upon the Jamaican achievement.

At the same time, let there be no doubt, Jamaicans have paid a heavy price for their bargain. For it involved not only the breakup of working class unity but also the jettisoning, over the years, of both of the ideological elements of positive nationalism and racial pride. The dynamics of nationalism were lost early on. For Bustamante, of course, it was easy. His pseudo-radicalism had no place for political theory of any kind, so that he could ridicule not only socialism but also nationalism; he could even suggest at one point the replacement of the Jamaican native police force with English police. For the PNP, originally a genuinely national alliance, it was a gradual surrender of its early anti-imperialist stand in favour of a policy of collaborationism with the British ruling class. The surrender took time, it was never, of course, a modern 1865; for PNP militancy remained steadfast during the war period, based on the dual argument of the 1940 conference that (1) since it was Britain's declared aim to grant self-government to the colonies a colonial struggle seeking the same end ought not to involve conflict with any imperial interest and (2) the danger of the West Indian territories being taken over by the United States, due to the concentration of British efforts on the European war front, required the existence of a strong local nationalist movement to take care of Jamaican national interests in case of such a catastrophe.[24] What went wrong? Essentially, that, the war over, the PNP elected to continue following the British lead in peacetime as well, no doubt influenced by the expectation that a Labour Government in London would support its colonial Fabian friends in Kingston. The argument advanced in support of that decision was that although each new concession from London was not in itself good enough to deserve acceptance nevertheless it might contain such good elements that it should be accepted, provided certain modifications were agreed to.[25] That meant, in effect, accepting the pace set by London, so that every concession, as it came—adult suffrage, the Committee system, the ministerial system, the transformation of the Executive Council into a more representative Council of Ministers, the abolition of the post of Colonial Secretary, the introduction of cabinet government, the new constitution of 1959, the convention (1960) that Governors should be appointed only after prior consultation with the Premier, the gradual relinquishment of certain of the Governor's powers—inevitably took on the aspect of yet another generous gesture from the imperial centre, not of a new victory on the part of the nationalist task force. Jamaicans might boast that as the first of the 'black' colonies to obtain adult suffrage they were at the head of the class. But they were still in the class, under continuing British headmastership. And even the final Independence constitution came as yet another 'grant' by way of Royal Orders in Council, a Jamaican graduation ceremony, as it were, marking her final success in the British honours school. It was, true enough, the growth of a democracy. But, throughout, it was a tutelary democracy. The shadow of power, at every step, was yielded up, but the substance retained. It was a march towards self-government. But it proceeded so slowly that, as the PNP itself prophetically stated in its early 1941 declaration, it could turn out to be a hindrance rather than a help. Each step, too, was grandiloquently announced as the 'final' step of the process so that in the end Jamaicans became apathetic, even sceptical, towards it all. It was hardly surprising, then, that the island entered its independence stage in a mood of half-hearted, simulated enthusiasm, hardly filled with any real passion for its achievement. Colonialism, for Jamaicans, ended not in a bang but a whimper.

A vibrant nationalism hardly thrives in such an environment as this. Its decline, in the case of the PNP, could be attributed, as some disappointed party stalwarts saw it, to the desire of the leaders simply to become heroes in colonial garb, a situation only to be remedied, according to them, by a new appeal to all Jamaicans of 'goodwill' both at home and abroad.[26] Others, like the spokesmen of the powerful Jamaican lobby in Harlem, traced it, with some justification, to the fatal decision after 1945 to embrace the federal idea, an idea at once alien to the Jamaican psychology and sponsored by Britain as a devious means of abdicating her continuing obligations to the West Indian peoples.[27] It is certainly true, to say the least, that the PNP *élite* seriously divorced itself from Jamaican realities by championing that idea, for they thereby overlooked the psychological isolationism of the Jamaican public mind and its corollary, the smug self-satisfaction and conviction of superiority which are, to others, the least attractive facets of the Jamaican character; the overwhelming popular vote in the 1961 referendum showed that the Jamaican national spirit, in its more negative embodiment, was solidly secessionist. The PNP failure, even more, to think out the proper relationship between Jamaican nationalism and the new federal forms generated a fatal ambiguity of attitude and a loss of purposeful direction ultimately sapping its capacity for militant leadership. Or, again, it could be said that the PNP decline was caused by 'Busta', Manley's *bête noire*, for both in 1944 and 1962 Manley sowed and 'Busta' reaped. But that is to mistake symptom for cause. For—and this is the real explanation—the apologetic character of what passes for Jamaican nationalism is traceable to (1) the insular social structure insofar as it was responsible for the growth of particular political attitudes and (2) the heritage of metropolitan colonialism.

The Jamaican social structure, in the first place, has been, and still largely is, a pyramidal mound of three separate social tiers: the white upper class, comprising the older rural squirearchy and the top mercantile families; the urban middle class groups; and the great Jamaican working class, both rural and urban. By comparison with, say, Trinidadian society, it has been a rigidly stratified structure, for it has lacked, until only recently, any of the special phenomena which have loosened the structure in Trinidad, creating whole new layers of rich people who did not belong or fit into the traditional colonial society: the discovery of oil, the introduction of Indian indentured labour, the Second World War period and its invasion of American forces and influences. The social upheavals that stem from heavy migration movements have been minimal; there has been a relatively stable age structure and ethnic composition structure, with the single exception of the rapid increase in the size of the Chinese foreign-born section; and what important changes there were in the structure of the labour force were almost exclusively the result of internal forces, the decline, for example, of female employment in agriculture and the concomitant increase of female employment in domestic service, reflecting rural economic decline and urban economic growth.[28] The general upshot of all this was that whereas a certain type of Horatio Alger 'rags to riches' myth has flourished in Trinidad it has always been conspicuously absent from the Jamaican mind.

With a few exceptions, the top class has been socially and politically reactionary; in economic terms, the junior partners of expatriate financial enterprise; and therefore mentally colonialist. Their leadership role, therefore, has been a restrictive one, confined to the honorific office like that of the Custos or nominated appointment in the old Crown Colony system, the high percentage of prominent Jewish names in both elective and nominated offices in the period between 1884 and 1935 testifying to a real sense of public service in the members of that particular segment.[29] Generally speaking, however, they were, and still are, in Sir Robert Kirkwood's phrase, 'the rich Jamaicans in the commercial, financial and indus-trial world, men who keep in with both political parties'.[30] As a class in Jamaican history, they controlled everything behind the scenes until only yesterday, silencing the Negro 'agitator' like Garvey with open persecution, buying off the colonial expatriates with the open hospitality for which they have been so famous; it is significant that with exceptions such as Sir Henry Norman and Olivier most of the executors of the British power passed under their influence. Even in their own professional fields, they have rarely been inno-vators or great captains of industry, technical and managerial advances having been generated, in the main, by the overseas investment companies; the typical Jamaican figure in that alliance being that of the wealthy lawyer or business executive with the vital local contacts, Lewis Ashenheim, for example, in the pre-war period, the D'Costas and the Matalons in the post-war period. Not un-naturally, they have been hostile to political change. When a mem-ber of their group entered politics he was rarely a success, and Abe Issa in Kingston was no Abe Lincoln in Illinois. Just as their class brothers in 1834 had seen Emancipation as the harbinger of social chaos, so they saw the changes after 1944 in the same light.

The cruel pressures that make daily life so much of a misery for the general West Indian middle class, deliberately avoiding identi-fication with the black majority yet never really accepted by the white *élite* that it seeks to be, and masking its frustrations with the invention of new and ingenious colour schemes, like 'Trinidad white' and 'Jamaican pink', are well known. The Jamaican middle class has felt this tragic duality of attitudes as much as any other, perhaps even more so, since, unlike, say, Grenada, the population-structure has a higher percentage of white persons to give the *malaise* more point, while, unlike the situation in Barbados, a policy of social withdrawal has been more difficult to adopt. As a con-sequence, lacking at once the national pride and the racial self-respect so necessary for progressive political participation, the Jamaican middle groups, in the 1938 beginnings, clung stubbornly to their political atheism, so that both PNP and JLP had to be content with what material they could get as party workers. It is true that, as already noted, there was a real strain of social consciousness in the more educated sections, as the contribution that was made to the early PNP by, variously, Nethersole, Arnett, King, Jacobs, and the Hill brothers, very well shows. But the general body retreated into what Paul Blanshard, writing somewhat later (1947), aptly termed the 'absenteeism of the verandahs'. When they did emerge from that shell it was, in the main, to support the JLP, driven by the fear, perhaps quite unfounded, that a PNP victory would usher in the socialist commonwealth. But once the PNP, especially after its 1952 'purge' of its more left-wing element, begun to shed its socialism— a process applauded by the English residents in books like Mrs MacMillan's *The Land of Look Behind*—the middle class, including the bulk of the civil service salariat, turned to the PNP as the logical vehicle of at once their social respectability, which was outraged by the 'vulgarity', as they saw it, of the Bustamante style, and of their new-found nationalism. They were joined, after 1948, by the new element of educated professionals out of the new University College of the West Indies. Yet it is revealing that that new element, on the whole, preferred merely to inherit the new social comforts created out of the struggle of the 1940's rather than to continue the struggle, as can be seen in the fact that the new UCWI faculty-intelligentsia made little contribution to the Jamaican public debate, preferring to retreat into the coma of professional academic research; a situation only changed with the emergence, after Independence, of the *New World* group of younger faculty members.

The final outcome of all this was—as it is, today, the general truth of political Jamaica—a two party system in which both parties, although necessarily structured on a mass basis, are fundamentally bourgeois in spirit, led by a foreign-educated middle class leadership. The leaders, of both persuasion, must, it is true, continue to tease the middle class, hardly at any time a popular group in West Indian life; Mr Wills Isaacs' 1958 tirade against 'those foolish middle class people . . . those Jamaican mulatto people believe anything you tell them' is symptomatic.[31] But that is a small enough price to pay for the real control that the middle class Jamaican civilization now finally exercises over both parties. The PNP can no longer claim to be the party of middle class 'intelligence', any more than the JLP can claim to be just the party of middle class 'property'; the distinctions of policy, as a reading of party platforms makes evident, are of degree, not of kind. That is why, in both parties, there was, as Independence approached, a shifting away from the earlier type of demagogic candidate. Thus the JLP hierarchy, now as fully bureaucratized as its rival, retained men like Barrant simply to prove it had not forgotten its street origins, while the replacement in the PNP of the type of 'Slave Boy' Evans with the younger professional men like David Coore and Vivian Blake emphasized the final victory of the Kingston organization men. The 'Father Coombs' episode of 1961, indeed, showed how newly respectable the PNP had become, for the decision to drop an old trade union stalwart symbolic of the 'common man', as an act of punishment for a few financial peccadilloes, not to be compared with the old infamous practices of Trinidadian 'bobol', was generally seen at the time as proof that, with the changing climate of opinion—in which nationalism, of a sort, had become the fashionable thing—the type of the Montego Bay old warrior was expendable.[32] There remained, of course, the personal rivalry of the two magnetic leaders, often degenerating into childish name calling, as, to illustrate only, the astonishingly abusive exchanges between the two in the Cocoa Marketing Board debate of June 1957, leading to the unceremonious and hasty adjournment of the House by a frightened Speaker.[33] But even that rivalry could be seen, by critics, as a not too elegant façade behind which an increasingly conservative Jamaica was governed by the great cousinhood of Manley and Bustamante.[34] It is true that the PNP went on record, in 1965, as the champion of a revitalized socialist programme designed, by means of a radical land policy, once and for all to smash the plantation system in Jamaican life, and, by means of tax and development policies based largely upon the experience of Israel and the Eastern European socialist economies, to promote economic growth without surrendering the control of the commanding heights of the economy, in Puerto Rican fashion, to the powerful expatriate forces of international capitalism. But it remains to be seen whether that 'turn to the Left' will carry the powerful conservative elements of the party with it or whether, even more, it can ever be acceptable to the dominant power complex of the American and Canadian commercial and industrial companies, with their local Jamaican allies, that has filled in the vacuum left by the stagnation of the sugar-citrus-banana-rum economy.[35]

All of this has left the Jamaican masses as nothing much more than the darkened theatre audience that alternatively applauds and hisses the actors on the national stage. The salient point to note, with reference to their particular role in the emergence of a national society, is that since Jamaica is an overwhelmingly Negro community apart from a few amorphous groups whose identification is Jamaican almost, as it were, by default—for the island population was pre-dominantly African as early as 1700—any national consciousness, to be real, must perforce be racial consciousness. The one cannot be divorced from the other. Yet an attempted such divorce was, throughout, the hallmark of Jamaican leadership, both govern-mental and party. The Garveyite strand of racial affirmation was sacrificed to the idea, which rapidly acquired the status of an official myth, that race did not really count in the harmoniously inter-racial Jamaican community; Peter Abrahams' book *Jamaica* is a typically exuberant expression of this romantic view, while, suggestively, there was only one brief mention of Garvey, noting his electoral defeat, in Adolphe Roberts' book of 1955.[36] The grim reality of Jamaican life was different, that of a racial separatism, undeclared yet virulent, that infected every nook and cranny of inter-personal and inter-class relationships, based on a social system characterized by strongly entrenched class-colour correlations. The characteristic disease of 'shade' prejudice, whereby colour discrimination was so ingenuously practised that specific degrees of discriminatory treat-ment were frequently prescribed with reference to even marginal differences in pigmentation, ensured that in that struggle everybody, discriminator as well as victim, would suffer from a profound irresolution about racial identity. Garvey's mistake was to see it as consciously motivated evil behaviour on the part of evil people, instead of seeing it as something people were driven into, frequently without knowing why, by the system.

It is true, of course, that much of the resultant ill feeling between white, brown, and black takes on class rather than race forms. For in a society where, to speak particularly, such prestige-carrying Establishment posts as those of Lord Bishop of Jamaica, the editor of the powerful *Gleaner* newspaper, and the Governor-Generalship itself, are filled by extremely dark men and where, to speak generally, a whole range of political occupations has emerged since 1938 in which high prestige accompanies a dark skin, there is no room, obviously, for overt racialism of the American variety. 'Whereas,' a recent observer has noted, 'the Southern Negro is treated as a second-class human being because his skin is black, the lower-class

Jamaican is treated as a second-class human being because he is poor and ignorant. In the mind of the upper-class Jamaican, poverty and lack of culture have taken on the same connotations of disgrace and shame as Negro blood has in the Southern United States.'[37] So, when Jamaicans discuss this problem, as they do quite openly once discussion is provoked, it is usually in class rather than racial terms, as the lively 1961 correspondence in the *Gleaner* shows, pointing out, as did that correspondence, that the fact that there are rich Negro persons and poor Chinese persons in the social picture makes it difficult to accept the thesis of rigid class-colour correlates.[38] The Kingston riots of 1965, likewise, ostensibly anti-Chinese, could be seen not so much as racial as socio-economic in their roots, expressing popular resentment against the sub-group of small Chinese shopkeepers, conspicuously visible in those working class districts where the pressures of an inadequate economy are felt most acutely, and whose growing economic strength has not as yet been accompanied by the moral legitimacy of the older European business enterprises they have been replacing over the years.[39]

That, so far, the inter-class tensions embodied in all this have not yet received open political expression in racial terms, with the single exception of the Millard Johnson third party, is perhaps accidental and, from the viewpoint of the Jamaican respectability, providential. It only requires, perhaps, continuing economic distress and the appearance of, as it were, a Jamaican Malcolm X, combining the racial appeal of Garvey with the assured erudition of Manley, to provoke a black revolt against the PNP 'brown man's party'— which is, after all, only the successor of the old 'Coloured Party'— and against the 'Busta' leadership, which has exploited race feelings tactically but has never used them in terms of first principle. In the meanwhile, it is only fair to note that despite all of the massive vilification with which the Jamaican ruling class has treated them over the years, the Negro proletariat responds still with inborn resignation, even good humour. Jamaican society, as a local student has put it, remains still a society divided into three categories— 'those who make things happen, those who watch things happen and those who do not know that anything is happening.'[40] It is a society of repressed violence in which the real threat to the carefully nurtured image of inter-racial fraternalism comes, not from the mass, but from the top groups placed on the defensive by the advent of independence. 'It is important,' a local journalist has warned, 'that we recognize the suppressed violence in our society at the moment; it is equally important for us to recognize that most of this violence simmers on the verandahs of upper St Andrew and not in the shacks of Western Kingston.'[41] It is worth adding that a professional study of Jamaican social attitudes undertaken at the time of independence concluded that the traditional middle-upper class stereotypes of the lower-class Jamaican as an individual filled with class hostility were in fact not supportable on the evidence; those stereotypes, presumably, were a myth that the upper groups needed in order to justify their own class feelings.[42]

For, to sum it all up, independent Jamaica, despite the formal transfer of sovereignty, remained at heart a society still shaped by the colonial heritage. Katrin Norris' critical pamphlet, published in the year of independence, portrayed a society still full of self-rejection, lacking as yet the new motive energies to replace the old which, naturally enough, had been derived from the post-1938 struggle. Its values were still imported; for all of the ideas the new national bureaucracy praised—fair play, the rule of law, parliamentary government, and the rest—were ideas imparted by the colonial pro-consuls, as was sufficiently and painfully demonstrated in the abject vote of thanks passed by the local Chamber of Commerce in 1962 to the new British High Commissioner.[43] It could be argued, indeed, that of all the principles of the British way of life left behind only one had grown out of indigenous Jamaican experience, that of the right of wage earners to organize in trade unions in their harsh struggle for survival. The motto of 'Jamaicanization', as the Foreign Nationals bill of 1964 showed, could be no more than the exercise of the new state power in the interest of the socially comfortable groups, the lower bourgeoisie of mixed blood, extending into the worlds of commerce and business a principle already firmly established in the world of the civil service. There was no common cause, no new and real sense of being Jamaican, to offset the social alienation engendered by Anglophilism. The Rastafarian cult was, of course, only the extremist manifestation of the quite different alienation of the Jamaican crowd. 'One of the visible results of this confusing social climate,' a Jamaican educator has noted, 'is the absence of any real sense of "belonging", either to the country or to one another. People still speak of Jamaica as "de wuss place", and

7

of one another in such opprobrious terms as "naygur", "red-'kin", and what have you. The term "we" is singularly rare in our vocabulary, while "me" is repeated *ad nauseum*. The extent to which rows, abuse, and litigation enter our national life is an indication of our belief in individualism and separatism.'[44]

The most favoured *nostrum* for all this, from the viewpoint of the new official and semi-official Jamaica, is, apparently, the development of a social welfare *élitism* in which the new ruling groups cater as guardians to the 'lower classes'. The Report of the 1961 Conference on Social Development, published on the eve of independence, was a representative expression of the attitude. For, after a full examination of the Jamaican social ills (many of them only 'ills' if seen from the viewpoint of the social worker mentality) the Conference ended with the pious hope that the answer lay in widespread changes in religious values or, alternatively, in some cohesive force operating as the personal conviction of a national purpose;[45] yet failed to demonstrate how those recipes could have any meaning for the vast mass of the Jamaican common people who live, most of them, in rural or quasi-rural communities lacking at once the community spirit of the English village and the communal tradition of the African tribal system. It may be true that what the society needs is, as the Report puts it, a collective new direction in which everybody subordinates immediate personal satisfactions to the greater social good. But it is incredibly naïve to imagine that a middle class characterized by a pathological insensitivity to the mass social world,[46] can provide the leadership of such a direction, or that orthodox Christianity can provide its ideological motor power.[47]

For, frankly, as far as religious Jamaica is concerned, a wide gulf separates the world of official Christianity from the world of popular belief. It is true that, earlier on, somewhere between 'Monk' Lewis's description of 1819 and Phillippo's description of 1843, a semi-pagan populace gave way to a Christian one. But it was, and still remains, Christianity with a difference. The real religion of the masses, today, whether in its urban manifestations, as described in Orlando Patterson's *The Children of Sisyphus*, or in its rural manifestations, as described in Sylvia Wynter's *The Hills of Hebron*, is the shamanistic fervour of revivalistic cults splendidly immune to the middle class goodwill of either social worker or church minister, and certainly immune to an Anglicanism which, in Jamaica as in England, is the faith of the established interests: the judiciary, education, medicine, political leadership and the economic *élite*.[48] It is apparent that a very real ferment of ideas has taken place in the underground world of mass belief, much of it bearing evidence of Garveyite influence; to read, for example, a book like the Rev. Samuel Lord's *The Negro and Organized Religion*, published in Jamaica in 1935, is to be made aware of the deep influence of American cultist ideas upon West Indian belief-systems, combining Garveyite *négritude*, quasi-theocratic humanism, half-baked sociology and the demand for a new Negro church movement that will concern itself with the economic bondage of the masses.[49] And even when religion has been more or less orthodox, as with the Baptist groups, it has been frequently esoteric, even heretical; so, a book like Smith's *Conquests of Christ in the West Indies*, also published in Jamaica, in 1939, has much to say about the bitter fight of the local creole Fundamentalist teachers of Calabar College to protect their narrow scriptural evangelism against the intrusion of the Higher Criticism in the persons of liberal-minded presidents sent out from London, and invoking the aid of Southern Baptist fundamentalism from the United States in their struggle.[50]

The social divisions of Jamaican life clearly enough are reflected in its religio-cultural divisions. Although not as absolutely as in the case, say, of Grenada, there is a real chasm that divides the folk-culture from the *élite*-culture. The *élite*-culture has throughout looked upon the folk-culture with distaste, even fear, and it is suggestive that the history of the study of Jamaican folklore is the record of 'eccentric' Englishmen, from 'Monk' Lewis to the Walter Jekyll whose remarkable *Jamaican Song and Story* has only recently been re-edited, whose enthusiastic interest in the popular art forms was not inhibited by such phobias. It is true that, with the advent of independence, such an interest has become fashionable. But even then it is frequently tinged with considerations of social utility. So every so often a Rastafarian 'outbreak' will galvanize the churches and their allies into the hasty formulation of a new and well-publicized 'crusade', the particular recommendations, for instance, of the 1961 Jamaica Christian Council Consultation.[51] But, the scare once over, such recommendations remain a dead letter, save for the work of the occasional pries who takess his social Christianity seriously. For the rest, there is the easy rationalization that the social infection is the work of 'religious fanatics and Communist agitators';[52] or the usual diatribe about the 'dangers' of democracy; or a romantic nostalgia for the 'good old days' when the Jamaican populace was 'by nature and instinct a smiling, gentle, kindly people' which, by the inference of the argument, they now are not.[53]

Independence, of course, like Emancipation before it, must make a difference. It is worth remarking that, with Anglophilism on the defensive, a tendency has grown up in cultured professional Jamaicans to repudiate the British cultural image, even to reappraise the historic African connection. Yet this is a minority movement only and, understandably, is accompanied by a corresponding anti-Jamaican sentiment on the part of the masses. As the classes claim the 'new' Jamaica for themselves, the masses instinctively move against the claim. As new pseudo-theories emerge to justify the claim—the growing popularity of the theory of *élites*, essentially anti-democratic as it is, as used in volumes like Wendell Bell's *Jamaican Leaders*, is symptomatic—the masses tend to retreat to their own inner socio-religious sub-worlds, following a traditional Jamaican tendency, as the history of the Maroons most famously illustrates, to turn away in crisis from the official world, to become a 'land of look behind'. So long as that temper prevails the capacity of Jamaicans to make their own rich contribution to New World civilization will be stultified. For the truth is that if there is a recognizable Jamaican community it has been created, over the last century or more, by the social *mores* and culture of the black-brown masses, arising out of the historic formation, after Emancipation, of the 'free village' system and of the system of a popular, creolized Jamaican Christianity as it was described in the books of Phillippo (1843) and Underhill (1862). That alone can be the foundation of a new cultural nationalism on native grounds, rooted firmly in popular experience and serving popular needs.

# Chapter VIII

## THE EMERGENCE OF NATIONAL SOCIETY

### TRINIDAD AND TOBAGO

THE LEADING significant fact about Trinidad and Tobago is that they entered the West Indian 'family' at a comparatively late date (1802). That has meant a number of things. It meant the survival of a certain Franco-Spanish cultural imprint, not least of all the tradition, in the form of the *cabildo*, of a local government system which, albeit weak, laid the foundations for a virile municipal politics in the later English Crown Colony period; the failure, by comparison, of the Spanish Empire to leave any cultural imprint behind it in Spanish Jamaica helped to make the process of Anglicization easier in that island than in Trinidad. The comparative shortness, again, of the slavery period meant that the Trinidadian Negro, unlike his Barbadian or Kittitian brothers, escaped the debilitating effects of centuries of bond slavery, which perhaps explains today his style of raucous ebulliency as compared to the social deference of those others. The general Trinidadian eudaemonism—invariably the first impression of visitors—certainly lends itself to some such interpretation. The history of English settlement was therefore different, so that Trinidad did not produce the special social structure of Barbados and Jamaica, anything comparable, for example, to the resident white squirearchy of Barbados or the retired army officers and professional men who form the 'English' ghetto of property owners in the St Ann parish districts of Jamaica. The earlier pre-English settlements, indeed, left behind important groups of French and Portuguese creoles to constitute many of the Trinidadian 'first families'. As a result, Trinidad has played a far lesser role in the shaping of the West Indian image than most English people have. The English literature on Jamaica, thus, is lengthy and voluminous, going back at least to Sir Hans Sloane's great work of 1707 while, by comparison, books on Trinidad did not begin to appear until the last quarter of the nineteenth century. There were, as a matter of fact, no proper histories of Trinidad, the ancient 'histories' of Borde and Fraser excepted, until the very recent publication of Gertrude Carmichael's *History of Trinidad and Tobago* and Dr Williams' own *History of the People of Trinidad and Tobago*. The attention of most Englishmen, including the scholastic sort, has been given to Jamaica and Barbados in preference to Trinidad, whose un-English quality has apparently put them off, as it put off Trollope who only spared it a brief two days' visit in 1859 and left it convinced that, since it was French in language and habits, and Roman Catholic in religion, and populated by 'French Negroes and hybrid mulattoes', it would make an even worse hash of self-government than Jamaicans in Jamaica.

The emergence of a national spirit out of this colonial obscurity began, in earnest, with Captain Cipriani and his labour movement after the First World War. The society that Cipriani sought to reform has been described in detail in Dr Williams' portrait of Trinidadian life in the years immediately preceding 1914.[1] It was, in almost every sense, the perfect model of a colonialist body politic. The politico-constitutional structure was even more autocratic than that of Jamaica, since the colony had passed almost instantaneously, *via* the brief unhappy experiment of commission government by a triumvirate of military and naval officers between 1803 and 1804, from Spanish rule to the British colonial system, without the intervening experience of an elected self-governing legislative body controlled by the planter class and its allies; with the general result that the Trinidadian free 'people of colour' were denied any opportunity to prove their capacity for self-rule. There was thus no Trinidadian equivalent, for example, of the brief experiment in cabinet government that Jamaica enjoyed between 1854 and 1865. There was, instead, a Governor with near absolute powers, whose autocracy was reinforced by the inherited despotic character of the old Spanish governorship and the old French notion of paternal government; a nominated legislative council comprising official and 'unofficial' members—the very nomenclature, as Dr Williams observes, constituting a solecism in the philosophy of democracy, since it confused the opposed natures of administration and legislation[2]—of which body the 'unofficial' members were, in fact, nothing much more than members representing the special 'electoral colleges' of sugar, cocoa, commerce and the professions; an administrative system staffed, in its higher and more lucrative offices, by colonial Englishmen who, as a rule, were petty bureaucrats thoroughly contemptuous of the 'unofficials' and whose social relations were restricted to the more wealthy element of the white creoles; and all of this topped by the distant authority of London, so that even the Governor, a despot locally, was simply, in the irreverent language of a daringly outspoken nominated member at a later period, a functionary regarded by the Colonial Office merely as the servant of the centurion. The system's philosophical basis—if one can speak of a philosophy of colonialism—was the British conviction that, as an English Director of Public Works once put it, the people of Trinidad were not fitted by their personal qualities, character and education to exercise such an important privilege as self-government on English lines. Not the least unhappy quality of the system was the way in which so many of the Creole legislative group accepted that insulting alien estimate of themselves, so that their own contributions to Council debates during that period aped the pattern of the English members of that body in which, to take an example only, the English Attorney-General of the time could employ the opportunity of the Council debate on proposed marriage legislation to discourse learnedly upon the topic of Henry VIII and the history of the English ecclesiastical courts. The exceptions, remarkable Creoles like Prudhomme David or Sir Henry Alcazar or Dr Prada, only served to emphasize the servile mentality of the majority of the coloured group of legislative members whose sole bond of unity, as C. L. R. James wrote some twenty years later in his study of the system as it remained in 1932, basically unchanged except for the introduction of an elected element, was their mutual jealousy in their efforts to stand well with the governing officials.[3]

The political arrangements, it goes without saying, reflected the economic and social system they were intended to protect and perpetuate. The dual character of the colonial economic structure— local economic interests pitted, unequally, against British economic interests—took the form of an agricultural sector of cocoa, coconut, and small food-crop local farmers and an industrial sector of capitalist-style sugar estates and burgeoning oil well investments owned largely by absentee English investors, with the import and export

channels controlled, in turn, by the Port of Spain mercantile capitalist class, the majority of whose members, apart from the Chinese,
Portuguese, and Indian retail shopkeepers, were likewise wealthy
Englishmen. Despite the fact that, by 1914, a dying sugar industry,
as the 1897 Royal Commission had seen it, was, in terms of output,
less important than cocoa agriculture to the economy, the history
of economic legislation under a planter-controlled system was one
of vigorous support of the sugar interests and of indifference, even
hostility to the small farmer. The classic epitomization of that bias,
as is well known, had been the history of indentured Indian immigration between 1844 and 1917, only finally terminated at the urgent
request of the Indian Government. Initially consented to by the
British Government as a consolation to the West Indian planter
interests for having been abandoned to the free trade interests of
the British consumer, the Colonial Office had permitted the local
legislatures to make the scheme a public enterprise at general expense, so that, in Lord Harris' words, colonial finances were allowed
to be consumed in a most extravagant and only partially successful
immigration system to which everything had been sacrificed, for
the sake of getting an extended cane cultivation about in any case
to be abandoned.[4] Thus, for some seventy-five years or more, the
Trinidadian tax-payer, like the Guianese, was compelled to subsidize a scheme which, by providing a new source of cheap and
manageable competitive labour, permitted the planter class to defer,
once again, facing up to the issue of adopting planned estate husbandry and rational utilization of existing labour resources as the
proper means of economic rehabilitation. That class was accustomed,
in the phrase of the British historian of the scheme, to the role of
recruiting labour by purchase, and working it under limits only
imposed by exhaustion and incapacity.[5] Their control of the colonial
political machinery permitted them to continue that habitual practice in the form of the harsh servitude of the indenture system, at
once technologically inefficient and socially degrading. Neither the
device of the office of the Protector of Immigrants nor the passage
(in 1899) of an immigration Ordnance to control wages and working
conditions gave the 'coolie' any real protection; and the Colonial
Office consistently refused to intervene. To read Sir Henry Alcazar's
attack on the system in his evidence before the 1897 Royal Commission, or the Report of the Indian Government's own separate

inquiry of 1915, or the speeches with which Prudhomme David, as a minority of one, opposed the annual immigration vote in the Legislative Council of the period, is to be made forcibly aware of how the indenture system operated as a cheap labour-recruiting scheme, creating over the decades an ill-paid labour army under-cutting the wage levels of the non-agricultural working class groups. Its social effects were equally debilitating, even monstrous, for from the beginning it engendered deep racial group animosities between Negro and Indian, still flourishing today in the widespread usage of the opprobrious epithets of 'nigger' and 'coolie'. Its effect on the Trinidadian employer class was equally disastrous, for, in the words of Sir Henry Alcazar, since the system had only substituted the jail of indenture for the whip of slavery its effect had been to keep the Trinidadian educated classes at the moral level of slave owners.[6] It was as true in 1917 as it had been in 1834 that, in Canning's famous phrase, the West Indies thought too much about sugar, and too little about strength. On every issue of the period—the Canadian reciprocity question, the graduated income tax, the release of Crown lands for peasant development—the Trinidadian governing class provided fresh evidence of that truth.

In a society so divisive to speak of Trinidad as a whole was difficult, if not impossible. It was symptomatic of the absence of any deeply felt all-Trinidadian sense that it was not the plantocracy nor the mercantile-professional groups but the colonial working class that became after 1918 the chief element leading the self-government movement. That Trinidad was, as Major Wood noted, the one community appearing largely to lack any homogeneous public opinion was, in fact, the grim harvest of indenture, since that system not only created racial separatism but also proletarian disunity as low-cost Indian labour drove the Negro labourer into the ur-banized areas of Port of Spain commerce and Southern Trinidad oil; and early on Sewell had noted the consequent disproportion of freed Creoles entering the world of urban commerce.[7] Hence, in 1921, Major Wood met a Chamber of Commerce and an Agricul-tural Society fiercely hostile to reform of any kind, their reasons being the intellectually arid considerations that existing prosperity afforded adequate representation for all views and that in any case the demand for reform was largely inspired by outside influences,

7*

not specified. In addition, he encountered not only a sharp division between Negro and East Indian but also a split in the Indian ranks themselves, between those who wanted outright communal representation and those claiming an increase in the nominated member system over the one single representative that Indians had at that time on the Council.[8] The treatment of the Indian group as social pariahs, of course, was only the most glaring illustration of the national disunity; it is worth adding, as testimony to the continuing strength of anti-'coolie' prejudice that if, before 1914, the Indian ghetto of Port of Spain 'Coolie-Town' was advertised to the visitor as the place to visit in order to see 'the Son of India in all his phases of Oriental primitiveness', in 1956 the same vilification was evident in the calumny of the British Federal Site Commission Report that the Indians were a 'disturbing element' in the national life, presumably because, as a local radical newspaper caustically headlined it, the Indians 'can't be loyal Trinidadians if they take off their shoes to go to their Muslim Temple'.[9]

As for the *élites*, the French, both white and coloured, were perhaps the most creolized of all, having been resident in the colony ever since the period of the Spanish Bourbon rule, and their members figured predominantly in the earlier struggle against the Crown Colony system, as the well-known names—de Boissiere, Guppy, Agostini, Lange, de Verteuil, as well as journalists like Billouin and de la Sauvegere—testify. Yet, like the white colonial masters, of whom they were in large part the phenotype, they were culturally Europo-centrist, and they sent their children to be schooled in England, like the rest. Their struggle, at best, was that of the French creole 'old families' against the 'upstart' English party. Their sense of racial and social exclusivism was summed up as late as 1936 in Frederick de Verteuil's defiant assertion that, as 'a respecter of old blood', it ought to be remembered that 'without your aristocratic Mirabeaux your plebeian Marats would never have left the gutter'.[10] The ruling *élites*, that is to say, both in the past and the present, as social and economic power groups, were naturally the guardians of the *status quo*. At best, they gave individual names only to the national struggle—Sir Gaston Johnston, for example, the *doyen* of the legal profession and loyal supporter of Cipriani in famous struggles like the divorce legislation crisis of 1930–31, or Sir Lennox O'Reilly, who frequently said of himself, also as an independent

Cipriani supporter, that he was not a socialist but an intellectual of the Left. Or, again, they gave individual families, people like the Grants and the Mortons who, along with the Canadian Mission, were the first to undertake the education of the children of the Indian indentured workers. Beyond that, however, they did not, perhaps could not go.

The history of the Trinidadian national affirmation against all this in the period between the two World Wars was, in effect, the history of Cipriani. Himself descended from Corsican immigrants, his social background, incongruously, was that of the old racing set of estate proprietors of Edwardian Trinidad, and his political awakening was occasioned, quite fortuitously, by his experiences during the 1914–18 period with the British West Indies Regiment, beginning with a local meeting in 1914 to help the Trinidad Breeders' Association, hardly a politically minded body, in their effort to purchase cavalry horses for the British Army. His prolonged fight with the local colonial government, which looked upon the mere idea that West Indian troops should fight for the Empire as palpably absurd, and with the British War Office, which considered such troops, once they were recruited, as being only fit for the menial job of labour battalions in Egypt, sharpened the Captain's latent powers of leadership and brought him back to Trinidad, after demobilization, to become the leading spirit in the rehabilitation of the old Trinidad Workingmen's Association. From then onward 'the Captain', as he was generally known, as champion of the 'barefoot man', became, like Franklin Roosevelt in New Deal America, the hero-figure of the masses, probably the most beloved of all West Indian popular leaders, then and now; and it was no more out of place, on the occasion of his death in 1945, to quote Whitman's moving lines of grief on the slain Lincoln in the City Council spoken obituaries of his friends and colleagues than it would have been to have quoted them in honour of President Roosevelt who died in the same year.[11]

His platforms were the mayoral office of the capital and, after 1925, an elected seat in the Legislative Council. But his real strength lay in the Workingmen's Association, later named the Trinidad Labour Party, with its forty-two affiliated sections in Trinidad and thirteen in Tobago (1930) and its total membership (in 1936) of some 125,000 workers, peasants, and small business people. While not strictly, like the later People's National Movement, a trade union movement so much as a political educational movement, it nonetheless gave him a mass support that other independents in the colonial politics neglected to fashion for themselves. In return for their support he gave to the masses their first real lessons in courageous opposition to colonialism, in the growth of national pride, in the art of directing social discontent into rational political activity. For a whole generation political life in the colony revolved around his slogan of 'agitate, educate, confederate'.

It was a brave record. There was the struggle for workmen's compensation, for a minimum wage, for the eight-hour day. There was the fight to secure statutory restrictions upon the use of child labour, especially in the Indian areas of the sugar estates. Cipriani led the agitation in favour of compulsory education, and was the champion of the local teachers who resented the fact that Government treated them as Civil Servants for disciplinary purposes but not for the assessment of salaries. He exposed the system whereby the annual military vote for the Volunteer Force was in reality support for a battalion of employees intended to be used against industrial 'unrest'. He campaigned endlessly for priority of local men over expatriates in the public service. A white man himself, he opposed all forms of discrimination, as his stand on the matter of discrimination against coloured candidates for the Imperial College of Tropical Agriculture well illustrated. He was in favour of local democratic control of native economic resources; it was he who, as Mayor of Port of Spain, successfully pushed through the purchase of the absentee-owned electricity undertaking, albeit at the expense of a costly delegation of the Council to London. He launched the beginnings of the lengthy campaign to force the foreign-owned oil industry to accept heavier taxation rates noting *en passant*, that if the colony had been allowed to make more advantageous use of its mineral resources there would have been no necessity to ask the Imperial Government for financial assistance to the sugar industry. As a self-confessed socialist he supported all sorts of social reform measures at a time when social reform was viewed as outright subversion and when, too, the social values of the Crown Colony System were such that the colonial Government regarded the construction of a golf course as more important than the building of a badly needed tuberculosis sanatorium. As a Catho-

lic, he defended the religious character of Trinidad against a Pro-
testant-minded Colonial Office as, of course, the famous episode of
the Divorce Bill demonstrated, as it also demonstrated how tactless
British colonialism could be in the treatment of subject peoples
whose cultural *mores* were alien to the parochial English mentality.
Finally, he unequivocally supported the twin ideas of compulsory
education and universal suffrage, going back at least to his speeches
to the 1926 British Guiana and West Indies Labour Conference,
and he perceived, acutely, that the one could not succeed without
the other.

Much of all this, in retrospect, seems respectable enough. But it
must be remembered that Cipriani had to fight with at least two
grave handicaps working against him. First, there was the handicap
of the Crown Colony system. Geared to getting things not done,
rather than done, it was no vehicle for any kind of reform programme
such as Cipriani's, least of all a socialist programme. Apart from the
fact that his legislative seat gave him privilege of speech, there was
little else it could do to help him. The nominated member was tied
to Government policy, as Sir Gaston Johnston's failure to be renominated after his vote against the Divorce Bill graphically showed.
The elected member could do only a little more, for the solid phalanx
of the official bureaucracy was against him; and, in any case, the
official theory of his position, as an English official had anticipated
years earlier, was that he would voice the wishes of the people, and
in return would 'receive and pass on to the people full explanations
of the questions brought before the Council'.[12] The elected member
gained entrance, as a minority group, to the Executive Council
in 1931. But his power was advisory only, and Cipriani himself
resigned in 1943 because he did not like the atmosphere of the
Council. There was the semblance of consultation, as in the Finance
and Estimates Committees. But the decision-making power still
remained unilaterally with the Governor. As with Garvey in
Jamaica, Cipriani's tragedy was that his great gifts were denied
their full expansion by a restrictionist constitutional regime.

But his second handicap was perhaps even more grievous, for it
stemmed from the hostility of some of his fellow-Trinidadians. As
one of his chief lieutenants put it, years later, if Cipriani did not
sufficiently clear the way for his successors it was because the two
forces of the Colonial Office and the local Chamber of Commerce

stood up like Rocks of Gibraltar in his path.[13] The local employer class, indeed, was myopic to a degree. It resisted the elimination of child labour practices in a manner reminiscent of the fight of the early Victorian factory owners against Lord Shaftesbury, typically expressed in the view of one of them that to educate the whole mass of the agricultural population would mean the deliberate ruin of the country. It used terror, intimidation and victimization against workers suspected of trade union or labour sympathies. It tried to 'buy off' the government bureaucracy including Governors, and frequently succeeded: it was a well known fact that the alienation of the important asphalt deposits of the famous Pitch Lake to an American company early on had been accompanied by the appointment, on his retirement, of the then Governor of the day to the post of the company's London director. This combination of enemies, local and imperial, defeated Cipriani practically all along the line. He died with the Crown Colony system still basically intact. After all of his agitation there was still, up to 1938, no general labour code to give legal protection for ordinary trade union activities. Even in areas especially dear to him, such as the military and the police, it was the final commentary upon his struggle for their West Indianization that it was not until 1943 that the first local man, Inspector Arthur Johnson, was appointed a commissioned police officer from the ranks.

In one way, of course, he was the architect of his own defeat. For he had all the defects of his virtues. He was not so much a socialist as he was an old style Tory Radical speaking in socialist language. He was, as it were, a West Indian Cobbett, hating the 'system', but vague about the sort of social order that should replace it. He lacked the intellectual's capacity to set the problem in terms of historical perspective or first principles, and his opposition was founded less on the reading of books than on harsh personal experience, reinforced, perhaps, by the French Creole's traditional antipathy to the 'English party'. It is true that, as his early biographer C. L. R. James put it, he expanded our conception of West Indian public personalities. But his chief error was to believe in the ultimate moral rightness of the British Empire and of the English governing gentleman class. He fought them on their terms, not on his, with the result that he never called the massive moral bluff of English colonial rule. If it is true that he was fond of saying that he could cause a riot

simply by lifting his finger, he failed to realize—as 1938 showed—
that it was only riot, and not appeals to the Englishman's 'sense of
fair play', that could move an Empire determined, as it was not so
determined in the later period of the PNM, to hold on to its own
at any cost. It seemed at times indeed that he was not so much
against colonialism as such but merely unenlightened colonialism,
as his remark in 1933 to a visitor that 'if the Mother Country would
send us her best brains to govern us we should have nothing to say;
but she does not' would appear to indicate.[14] His dependency on
the British Labour Party was part of the same general error, for
there was nothing either in Fabian Socialism or in the calibre of
'socialists' like Ramsay MacDonald or J. H. Thomas to suggest
that they would ever help establish an independent socialist West
Indies. Cipriani's perhaps most famous speech, indeed—at the
Labour Commonwealth Conference of 1930—challenged the seem-
ing temptation of British Labour to be content with the old hackneyed doctrine of colonial trusteeship, and at the same time bitterly
complained that the metropolitan Labour Government of that time
had refused permission for the introduction of trade union legislation in Trinidad; and the remark that Labour in opposition gave
Trinidad much more help and support than Labour in power attests
to the general dismay he must have felt. The constitutional methods
successful in a matured democracy like Great Britain were not of
necessity the appropriate methods for serious change in colonial
societies, where the democratic tradition was practically non-
existent. Cipriani, then, was inevitably superseded after 1938 by
more militant leadership of the Butler type with whom he had little
sympathy. His failure was the price he had to pay for the fatal
ambiguity involved in trying to be Empire loyalist and West Indian
patriot at one and the same time.

The period 1938–56 witnessed the nadir of Trinidadian life. The
Butlerite type, like the 'Chief Servant of the Lord' himself, were
street agitators necessary at that stage in the development of the
national movement. But they lowered the tone of political life by
their bombast and buccaneering. They had no coherent programme:
Butler's contribution to Trinidadian political thought was his promise in the 1950 election that if returned to power he would abolish
dog licences, while the oddly-assorted Political Progress Group in
the same year could do little more in its own platform than call for

a strong and efficient police force. They operated on the assumption, rapidly losing any validity at that time, that the way to advance things was to frighten colonial Governors; and they completely lacked any understanding of rational insurrectionary strategy designed to bring the mass movement into power. Their basic achievement, seen in retrospect, was twofold: first, they precipitated the rise of trade unions that proceeded to become independent forces of their own and, second, they engineered the direct entry of the working class into colonial politics. But they had no theoretical framework whereby they could see the full significance of that achievement, and what to do with it. They fought zealously for temporary issues, not for permanent principles. They failed to see that the union struggle needed the complement of a political struggle waged by political parties themselves gaining new strength from union affiliation, so that for the entire period the local political scene was a wild circus of electoral independents and trade union 'czars' having nothing to unite them in a national front (despite the so-called United Front of the 1946 campaign) save a common passion for the spoils of office.

The detail of that record is well known; so much so, indeed, that the flagrant immorality of the local political life, the widely-publicized Trinidadian 'bobol', became a byword in the Caribbean. The three elections held in 1946, 1950 and 1956 under the new full suffrage constitution provided a wealth of tawdry evidence of that general truth. It was the heyday of the political adventurer who, as an 'independent', promised the moon to a gullible electorate, from increased old age pensions, more scholarships for civil servants, more taxi licences, 'good and plenty water' and a promise to 'demobilize unemployment' to promises galore for a 'better' Carnival (always good for a laugh in Trinidad); all of it accompanied by shameless protestations of personal talents and past records, from the candidate who boasted that he had been instrumental in restoring Carnival after the wartime ban to another who recalled his connection with a hurricane inspection committee back in 1930 notwithstanding the fact that Trinidad, with rare exceptions, lay outside the hurricane zone; and possessed of no coherent pattern save the eagerness of the candidate, uncontrolled by any party discipline, to become a colonial legislator and possibly, after the quasi-cabinet system was introduced, a minister. It all portrayed a scandalously low level of political intelligence and a complete failure to think out in any coherent way long-range answers to the colonial problems, and it cried aloud to be replaced with a rational party system based on mass political education, firm discipline and clear-cut ideology after the fashion of the Jamaican PNP.[15]

It was the Eatanswill election regime, colonial style, encouraged in its turn by a venal press and a sort of bogus radicalism in which it was assumed that the more unlettered a candidate was the more capable he was considered of representing the electorate, as figures like Chanka Maharaj and A. P. T. James, 'Governor Fargo of Tobago', aptly illustrated. It was colourful enough, with its Creole Beau Brummels, its 'Bengal Leopards' and its calypsonian-politicians. To read the biographical sketches of its leading figures for the decade after 1946, with their opportunism, their playing to the gallery and their unprincipled perambulations from one 'party' to another is to realize how it all accurately reflected the local racial and religious divisions, for many of them nursed the support of those divisions: Victor Bryan nursing the small farmers of the Eastern counties, Butler and John Rojas the Negro workers of the oil belt, Roy Joseph the teachers, Ajodhasingh and the dynasty of the Sinanaan brothers the East Indians. There was, again, in the person of the almost legendary Bhadase Maraj the American-style ward 'boss' with his political strength in at once his fabulous wealth and his control of the Sanatan Dharam Mahasabha; the astute politician like Norman Tang whose success seems to have come from his ability never to reveal his inner thoughts, thus making it possible for him to develop the reputation, completely negative as it was, of being the only minister never accused by the Civil Service of political interference; and, of course, the irrepressible 'Bertie' Gomes who despite his capacity, as someone said, to look like a genial photographer was in fact a *politico* whose *forte* was the raucous browbeating of his opponents and the habit of finding new scapegoats every so often for Caribbean ills, ranging, variously, from the American troops, the East Indians, and the 'Reds' in Jamaica. In such an environment and with such a cast, the overnight formation of new 'parties' and the empty gesture of 'resignations' by peeved candidates (one candidate in the 1956 election resigned from the curious Party of Political Progress Groups merely because, as a taxi driver, he resented the fact that the Arima Borough Council had given permission to a bus company to use his own familiar route) became the order of the day.[16]

Naipaul's novel *The Mystic Masseur* describes the birth of such typical colonial politicians, in that particular case the Indian pundit who comes to power by exploiting the awe that the rural Indian labourer has for those with pretensions to learning; while the same author's other novel, *The Suffrage of Elvira,* describes the grim price paid for it all by a community ignorant of the true nature of democracy and corrupted by bribery, blackmail, racial prejudice, and racial isolationism. West Indian scholarship has yet to document all this. But it is worth noting that Albert Gomes, the most famous of all the gallery, has recently described in an autobiographical series of revelations how he first learned the deadly arts of Trinidadian politics in his 1938 struggle for a seat on the City Council, including the necessity for any candidate who was anxious to win to accept the paid services of professional canvassers who by reason of an illogical voting system had both the vote and the voter in their possession.[17] In all of this, as a result, there was little room for parties, like the West Indian National Party (1942) and the Caribbean Socialist Party (1947), advocating reasoned ideological positions, nor for the occasional candidate imbued with real social ideals, like Quintin O'Connor or Dr Patrick Solomon who was first precipitated into public prominence by his support of the 1946 waterfront strike or David Pitt who, defeated and disillusioned, finally left for England to use his gifts in the service of the British Labour Party.

All this, in one way, was only the political expression of social reality, a truth perhaps only obscured by the fact that Trinidadians tend to use their politicians as penance, in much the same way as they use their calypsonians as celebration. Political individualism reflected social individualism. The political charlatan was simply the social climber of the Trinidadian *picaroon* society operating in the political field. The national character was notorious, even in the other West Indian territories, hardly themselves models of social rectitude, for its raucous egocentrism. The typical Trinidadian was the *homme moyen sensuel*, living 'now for now', what one local commentator termed the gay troubadour of the West Indies, for whom 'rum, fashionable clothes, a quatro, the races, the thrill of illicit amorous liaisons, the rhythm of dancing and a precarious modicum of lightly earned dollars, would constitute the perfect existence'.[18] Such moral condemnation, of course, perhaps failed to appreciate how much those traits had been shaped by the various forces that had gone to create social Trinidad. There was, of course, first and foremost, a colonial system which traditionally allowed only a singularly emasculated form of public service via the nominated member system, so that the great names of that regime—McShine, Laurence, Kelshall, O'Reilly—never had a chance to carry their powers to the peak of the machinery of government. There was, after that, the fact of cultural and ethnic heterogeneity, so different from the relative cultural homogeneity of Barbados and Jamaica, for the mosaic of the Trinidadian types—French creole plantocrat and Chinese merchant, Spanish cocoa farmer and Grenadian oil worker, English expatriate and mulatto professional, Negro urban worker and Indian peasant—had had little time, historically speaking, to jell into a felt sense of overriding common identity. That is why, in the 1937–38 period, the Jamaican intellectuals and professionals had rallied to the cause of the new Jamaican labour movement and why, by contrast, no such process took place in Trinidad, so that the strident anti-intellectualism of the Trinidadian popular movement—

*We never went to college*
*But Butler gave us knowledge—*

held the field until the 1956 PNM 'revolution of intelligence'. There was, too, the dangerous imbalance of city and countryside, expressed in the domination of Port of Spain over the rest of the country; a phenomenon, again, not nearly so pronounced in Jamaican life.

Finally, there was the disastrous impact of the American occupation of the colony in the 1940's, following the Anglo-American bases-destroyers deal. Many of the modern Trinidadian types—the sophisticated prostitute, the 'saga-boy', the gang leader—are direct creations of American influence, of 'working for the Yankee dollar', and Derek Bickerton's study of the most famous of all Trinidadian criminals, Boysie Singh, has described how American capitalist culture, funnelled through the filter of the occupying American troops, facilitated the transformation of a small-time hoodlum into the king of the Port of Spain underworld, Chicago-style.[19] That influence also helped create the money basis of the local politics, for the new wealth that men like Norman Tang and Bhadase Maraj brought into the game was originally amassed by its owners as clever business operators servicing American needs, Tang in the trucking business with American contractors, Maraj in the sale of land and surplus equipment. The natural anarchism of the colonial society was thus reinforced by the disruptive influence of Americanization. In the end-result contemporary Trinidad, twenty years later, has become a roughly-hewn combination of British snobbery and American vulgarity. The state of its politics was only a consequence, not a cause, of all that.

How that politics was superseded, after 1956, by Dr Williams and the People's National Movement is a well-known story. The political history of the territory since that time has been the PNM's effort, first as government under the modified Crown Colony regime and then as the first government of the independent nation (1962) to fulfil its promise of building up a 'democratic party of men and women of honesty and incorruptibility, of all races, colours, classes and creeds, with a coherent and sensible programme of economic, social and political reform aimed at the development of the country as a whole, dedicated to its service, appealing to the intelligence rather than to the emotions of the electorate whose political education it places in the forefront of its activities'.[20] Looking back, of course, the victory of the new force takes on the aspect of a certain historical inevitability. But at the time it looked like, and indeed largely was, the almost singlehanded achievement of the remarkable personality of Dr Williams. A brilliant Island Scholar, an outstanding West Indian Oxonian as his autobiographical sketch, *A Colonial at Oxford*, shows, faculty member at Howard University and, later, research secretary of the Caribbean Commission, his academic record as the outstanding authority on Caribbean history fitted him perfectly for his final entry into politics; an entry partly the result of choice, partly something forced upon him by the hostility shown towards him, as a West Indian, by the expatriate officials of the imperialist body of the Anglo-American Caribbean Commission, described in his public lecture of 1955, *My Relations with the Caribbean Commission, 1943–1955*.[21] The long scholarly training and rigorous intellectual discipline, combined with the opportunity his strategic position in the Commission gave him to study the Caribbean economy at close hand (a position similarly enjoyed by the American liberal publicist Paul Blanshard), found their logical home in his grand attempt, after 1955, to guide the Trinidadian polyglot society towards a new civic nationalism.

For he was, above all else, Burke's definition of the politician, the philosopher in action, bred out of the radical intellectual's conviction that the cloistered virtue of academic life becomes sterile save as it seeks to translate its knowledge into social purpose, bred, too, out of his professional historian's conviction that, as Lord Acton put it, the historian must be judge as well as witness. The constituent elements of his programme, national pride, party discipline, morality in public affairs, were not in themselves earth-shaking ideas and certainly were common to other colonial nationalist movements. Dr Williams' more unique contribution was to engineer a remarkable marriage between the creole intellectual and the colonial crowd, founded on his belief that in colonial societies searching for a new identity politics and culture must travel hand in hand, so that the political leader also feeds the infant indigenous culture. It was a conscious return, that is to say, to the grand tradition of classical politics before it was destroyed by the rise of capitalist individualism.

To watch the Political Leader, 'the Doctor', undertake that task in his mass lectures at the 'University of Woodford Square' is to appreciate how, first, he managed to invest the dullest of facts and figures with a life of their own, italicized by the measured metronome of his dry, deliberate delivery and, second, how he forged between himself and the popular audience a bond of deep feeling and mutual respect which no hostile force, always readily present in a colonial society where everybody, traditionally, was ever ready to tear down any one of their number who had any sort of success, could pollute. Then, and later as Premier, he brought style, wit, learning to the office of politics, in much the same way, indeed, as the Kennedys managed, for a brief while, to bring together government and the arts into a new and deeper relationship at the White House. Almost by himself, he educated the popular crowd on the elements of political science, on Federation, on the Burkian gospel of political party, on the economics of nationhood. It would be difficult, certainly, to think of any recent British Prime Minister who could celebrate the act of national independence by the composition, in the manner of

Dr Williams' *History of the People of Trinidad and Tobago,* of a textbook of independence or who could celebrate the centenary of the Indian poet Tagore by a scholarly address in which that great humanist's supreme achievement was seen as the attempt to blend European intellectual independence with Indian mental tranquillity and in which that achievement was at the same time identified as being immensely important for the development of the contemporary West Indian nationalist development.[22]

One footnote is necessary to complete this biographical sketch. The difference between the PNM and the other progressive West Indian parties like those in Barbados and Jamaica, was not only that those parties were pre-war movements while the PNM was post-war but also that whereas the Manley-Adams outlook had been shaped by the English academic tradition the Williams outlook was shaped, after Oxford, by the American. The difference was important. For it helped Dr Williams to see things within an American perspective, to call the bluff of British imperial manners because he did not share their underlying presumption about the moral pre-eminence of all things British. More particularly, as C. L. R. James has pointed out, the American experience helped Williams (1) to absorb the American qualities of dynamic energy and rapid movement, of the urge to get things done, so much opposed to the traditional caution of the British national outlook and (2) to learn at first hand about the race question in a society where the phenomenon could be seen in all of its nakedness and its deep historical roots, and in its tremendous effect on racialists and anti-racialists alike. That first item gave the PNM then, when it started, the proper attitudes with which to meet the urgency of the local stiuation, while the second item enabled it to comprehend scientifically the multi-racial Trinidadian community in a way that neither the British experience nor the British academic tradition could do.[23] The Williams concept of a university, likewise, was shaped by the American pragmatic and egalitarian tradition. If, then, Dr Williams, as his critics averred, was anti-American, he was so only to the degree that he opposed those elements in the contemporary American civilization that played traitor to the leading humanist ideals of the Jeffersonian liberal tradition.

The period between 1956 and 1962, including the subsequent general election of 1961 in which the PNM consolidated its earlier victory and in which, too, the local conservative forces that had been openly anti-PNM in 1956—the French and Portuguese Creoles, the white English enclave, the Chamber of Commerce, even the Catholic Church—were now only lukewarm in their opposition, witnessed the mushroom growth of the new nationalism which became, in typical Trinidadian style, the new fashion of the day. Dr Williams saw it in its positive sense as being simply the public spirit of the good citizen in the classical Periclean manner. But since the presence of hostile forces always gratuitously feeds national feeling he was too good a political tactician not to take advantage of those forces in the Trinidadian situation. The story of his governments is thus, in one way, the record of the struggle against their opponents. Essentially, those were three: the West Indian Federal Government (after 1958), the Colonial Office, and the Americans. And if, again as his critics averred, Dr Williams fought those opponents like a man who had a 'chip on his shoulder', that was nothing more than the easy rationalization that the more cautious types in the colonial society developed in order to make their own accommodating inaction more palatable to themselves.

The struggle with the Federal Government, and its Premier, Sir Grantley Adams, was, in part, the debate between the Adams embodiment of a Crown Colony type of federal constitution and the Williams theory, stated most fully in his government's brief, *The Economics of Nationhood*, in support of a strong central government with full powers of independent taxation and a genuine customs union to undertake that full scale planned development of the region which alone could (1) end the economic status of the West Indies as a satellite economy, and (2) lay the foundations, through the common allegiance of the individual unit territories to such a government, of a real West Indian nation.[24] There were, of course, other facets of the struggle: the Trinidadian claim, possibly *ultra vires*, to separate authority in the external affairs field, especially with regard to the protection of Trinidadian citizens in the Netherlands Antilles and to the resolution of various disputes with Venezuela; the defence of West Indian preferences in the United Kingdom market in the light of possible British membership in the European Common Market, and which Adams, not being an economist, did not perhaps fully appreciate; the question of United Kingdom economic assistance to the new Federation, meagre as such assistance had always been; above all, the protection of

Trinidadian interests against the possibility of increased intra-Federation migration pressing upon the territory's embryonic social services, revolving around the discussion of the principle of the freedom of movement of persons within the Federation. In all of those problems, Dr Williams adopted the stance of the belligerent federalist confronting a timid Federal Government. The Federal Prime Minister saw the Federation as a young infant protected by its fond British parent; Dr Williams saw it as an artificial entity born of the British post-war desire to contract out of their continuing obligations in the Caribbean. Dr Williams saw Sir Grantley as the 'stooge of the Colonial Office'; Sir Grantley viewed him, in turn, as a pertinacious troublemaker.

In part, all this was the conflict between federal centre and local unit power characteristic of all federal enterprises; in part, it was a personal feud between a Barbadian constitutionalist cast in the Anglo-Saxon mould of Sir Conrad Reeves and a trained political scientist seeing problems primarily in terms of their economic meaning. Much of the Williams attitude, then, was federalist, not just parochially Trinidadian. But the fact that it was persistently put forward to publicize the image of Trinidad as the leading champion of the federal idea had the general result of fomenting the Trinidadian national sense. Nothing better illustrated that than the ease with which the Trinidadian populace gave up the federalist sentiment in 1962, at the command of Dr Williams. 'Federation mash up': the sentiment, as they put it, showed that the Political Leader could as easily kill the sentiment as, earlier, starting with his Public Library lectures in 1955, he had created it. Jamaican nationalism, true enough, was likewise given new strength in the similar conflict between the Federal Government and Jamaica on the separate issue of retroactive federal taxation and freedom of intra-federal trade. But the Manley thesis of a weak Jeffersonian Federation was not, in any case, as susceptible to ready dramatization as was the competing Williams thesis of a powerful Hamiltonian Federation. Nor should the additional fillip given to Trinidadian national pride by Dr Williams' success in obtaining the federal capital site for Trinidad in 1957 be overlooked in this discussion of the contribution of the federal issue between 1956 and 1962 to the growth of the Trinidadian national spirit.[25]

The fight with the Colonial Office was all of a piece with this.

In the main, it concerned the development of the colonial constitutional forms. Adult suffrage (1946) and the rudimentary ministerial
system (1950) did not do much to end colonial control. The retention of a mixed legislative council, with its bloc of nominated members, worked as always to weaken the elective element; for although
that element (unlike its Jamaican counterpart) had a clear majority
the absence of strong party support ensured that its individual
members, beholden to no group ideas or discipline, would turn to the
support of the official side; as indeed happened. The result, in
Gomes' phrase, was a bastard coalition in which normal personal
rivalries were exaggerated and in which the Governor expected all
elected Ministers to emulate his easy conformity to Colonial Office
edicts.[26] The so-called Chief Minister, as Gomes found out, was
that in name only. He had to work with colleagues chosen by the
Legislative Council, whom he could not remove save by an impro-
bable two-thirds vote of that body. Such a Chief Minister, in a
country without responsibility, was, in the phrase of Dr Solomon's
trenchant Minority Report on Constitution Reform of 1948 (a
report that was regarded from the day of its publication as a treatise
on all future constitutional advances) a King without a throne.
There was adult suffrage. But its logical sequence, a fully democratic
executive-legislative structure directly responsible to the popular
will, was withheld. Both of the majority reports of the two locally
appointed reform committees of 1948 and 1955 had turned in mild
recommendations that left the balance of power still intact, with
real authority remaining in the hands of the government bureaucracy and its nominated officials. Local timidity, here, reflected
Colonial Office caution. 'People grow accustomed to authority by
the exercise of authority,' was the reply of the four Butler Party
members who signed a pungent dissent to the 1955 deliberations,
'and the constant harping on the immaturity of our people, the
social stresses and the pains consequent upon the birth of a nation
does not give confidence either to our legislators or to those who
look to our role in the coming federation of British Caribbean territories. We can learn from our mistakes. Britain, great as she is, has
learnt by trial and error, and even now her political education is
far from complete. Let us, if we must, make our political mistakes
early, so that we can correct them early.'[27] But such radically simple
thinking was too much for the Colonial Office. Apart from the

shopworn rationalizations torn to shreds by Dr Solomon in 1948 and Dr Williams in 1955 London fell back on the alibi that constitutional reform must await the growth of an effective party system, a specious argument in the light of the fact that, as both Barbados and Jamaica showed, organized parties were the consequence of rational constitutions, and not their cause. It was the final commentary on the traditional faith that all the progressive forces in Trinidad before 1956 had in the goodwill of the British Left that that particular argument (which confused cause and symptom) found its most emphatic expression in the 1949 Despatch of a Labour Colonial Secretary, Mr Creech-Jones, one-time militant chairman of the Fabian Colonial Bureau; along with the astonishing assertion that the termination of the nominated element system would seriously disturb confidence in the economic and financial stability of the colony.[28] The general effect, all in all, was to stifle the growth of a healthy party politics, as the fate of the Butler Party illustrated.

The PNM inherited this struggle; and completed it. There was, in 1956, the successfully pressed demand that the Colonial Office accept the request that two of the five nominated members should be selected as party nominees by the Chief Minister; a precedent which, among other things, incidentally robbed the nominated system of any further logic. There was the introduction in 1959 of the cabinet system, with the Premier possessing the power to select and remove ministers and parliamentary secretaries. There was the accompanying whittling down of the powers of the Governor as well as the final recognition, by means of the appointment of Sir Solomon Hochoy, of the principle that the governorship should be filled by local candidates. The role of the officials was further diminished by the transformation of the Attorney-General into a political appointee from either of the two houses.

Two points are noteworthy about this process. First, there was its usual character of piecemeal measure by piecemeal measure, each of them the result of prolonged local struggle, thus making nonsense of the official Britain fiction of subject peoples being gradually groomed for self-government by a wise paternal leadership. Thus, the colony was supposedly unfit in 1957 for the local control of the police by means of a Ministry of Home Affairs, but became fit in 1959. Thus, again, the legislative powers of the United Kingdom, by means of the imperial power to disallow laws and the retention of control over the external affairs area, were retained throughout the period—despite the fact that the prevailing assumption underlying those retained powers, that there was a recognizable line of demarcation between 'internal' and 'external' affairs, was quite untenable, as the Venezuela and Chaguramas issues palpably demonstrated—and then abruptly surrendered in 1962. Or, again, the nominated system was seemingly viewed as inviolate in 1955, but by 1959 the PNM Government had been conceded the power to replace it with a fully elective popular house and a nominated Senate; although it should be noted that the change in part was nominal only since the new second chamber was set up on a principle, that of the collegiate representation of the local religious denominations and of the 'principal economic interests' of the country, likely to produce as many problems as it solved, and arising as did out of the PNM desire to conciliate powerful groups that could do damage if hostile. The second point to note is allied to the first: after decades of stubborn resistance to reform the imperial power, almost overnight, surrendered completely to the nationalist movement, for the grant of independence conceded every point over which, previously, the Colonial Office constitution makers had petulantly haggled. The abolition of the system, this is to say, was not so much the single-handed victory of the nationalist assault movement as it was the fruit of British retreat from empire. But the PNM naturally claimed credit for the achievement. In fairness, though, the truth is that they reaped, here, from the labours of others: not only Cipriani, but after Cipriani movements like the West Indian Nationalist Party which could justly claim to have been, before the PNM, the first organized attempt at party politics in the colony, having convened, indeed, an important conference of all local progressive groups on the demand for a new constitution as far back as 1945, thus anticipating the PNM device, in 1962, of the Queen's Hall consultation with different groups of local public opinion on the Independence Constitution issue. In addition to this, there were all the other progressive groups which, for example, penned vigorous minority reports and advisory memoranda to the 1955 Report of the Constitution Reform Committee—the Butler Party, the Socialist Youth Party, the Trinidad Labour Party, the Trinidad and Tobago Trades Union Council and the Independent Labour Party.[29]

As the British moved out, of course, the Americans moved in. They thereby set the scene for the PNM's third characteristic struggle in which the Chaguaramas Naval Base became the final symbol of local nationalism, not unlike the role of Guantanamo in the growth of Cuban nationalism. The original humiliation of the 1941 bases-destroyers agreement whereby West Indians, without consultation, had become the victims of an Atlantic system of control by London and Washington, had evoked open resentment as early as the British Guiana and West Indies Labour Conference of 1944.[30] The reopening of the question by the new Trinidad Government was based on the principle that the paramount reasons justifying the alienation of local territory in 1941, along with the various extra-territorial rights claimed by the Americans, could no longer be invoked in peacetime to justify the continuation of a 99-year lease by the Americans of areas now vital to the expanding social needs of the Port of Spain urban populations. There followed, in rapid succession, the selection of the disputed Chaguaramas site by the West Indies as the best location for the site of the proposed federal capital, the appointment of a joint commission, including the Trinidad Government as well as the American, British, and West Indies Federal Governments, to consider alternative sites, and the final convening in 1960 of a four-power plenary conference in Tobago, ending in a new agreement. What is vital to note here is not that the Trinidadian demands for a radically revised agreement, including the idea of joint administration of the base, did not carry the day, but that throughout the negotiations the Trinidad Government gained an enhanced international personality as the chief protagonist of the West Indian interest, as against a timid Federal Government and a British Government anxious not to upset its American friends. The result, again, was a new nationalistic assertiveness on the part of the Trinidadian man in the street, aptly exemplified in the story of the local citizen who justified his presence at the base gateway with the claim that a landlord is entitled to look over his property from time to time. And the hero-figure of that achievement, once again, was Dr Williams, whose articulate pertinacity and ceaseless dynamism kept the high principle and necessity of Chaguaramas as the federal capital in the forefront of the regional problem.[31] That the end-result of the struggle was, in effect, a retreat from the original PNM demands may be seen, it is true, as a betrayal by a timid leadership of the radicalism inherent, potentially, in the nationalist *credo*.[32] It could be seen, just as easily, as an object lesson in the harsh truth that no one single West Indian territory, however radically motivated, could be expected successfully to put a hook in the nose of Leviathan. The West Indian democracy, here, was up against the massive power of the American 'warfare state', along with its crass monetary values, appropriately expressed, in the matter of the Chaguaramas issue itself, in a petulant American mass magazine editorial declaring that 'Our not too-educated guess is that the best way to end the agitation would be to make it unmistakably clear from the start that if we are eased out of Trinidad in disregard of our plain rights under the lease, we are going for keeps, payroll and all.'[33]

All of those struggles, along with the less dramatic planning of the domestic economy, contributed to the promotion of the Trinidadian national community. Yet there is the danger of seeing it all as the grand conquest of the PNM 'revolution'. So to see it, as the PNM image of the corrupt 'old World' versus the bright 'new World' suggests, is to invite historical distortion because no society experiences, as if overnight, dramatic spiritual conversions like St Paul on the road to Damascus. For much of what the 'new world' signified preceded 1956, just as much of the 'old world' survived it.

Apart from the specifically political element of the numerous progressive groups and parties which, as already noted, did so much to prepare the groundwork for the PNM before 1956—even the much-maligned 'Bertie' Gomes had had an earlier period of vigorous criticism of Anglo-American imperialism, as his characteristically belligerent speech of 1944 at the Georgetown Labour Conference on the vexed question of the American bases sufficiently showed[34]— an embryonic national consciousness had long been pregnant within the Trinidadian socio-cultural world. There had been in process of development, that is to say, certain norms of common cultural allegiance transcending the separate framework-references of the different groups comprising a colonial society that was at once (1) divided vertically in terms of social class and (2) divided horizontally in terms of ethnic groups, in particular, the creole Negro majority as against the Hindu and Muslim minorities. The traditional prestige norms, those of the 'white' upper class society, had been increasingly under attack since at least the 1930's. That could be seen in a number of ways. It was there in the new writing, on native grounds, of Mendes and James, the influence of James, indeed, despite an egocentrism reaching almost paranoic dimensions, being of particular importance. It was there in the growth of a nativist painting and theatrical tradition, institutiona-lized after 1945 in the form of the Art Society. It was there in the long and bitter personal struggle of the *danseuse* Beryl McBurnie to foster West Indian dance as against the legacy of the Scottish reels and Highland flings she herself had been compelled to learn while a young girl at Tranquillity. It made itself evident in the history of the struggling obscure cultural clubs and little magazines, from the Maverick Club after World War I in which families like the Procopes, the Worrells and the James educated themselves by read-ing widely, among much else, in the new post-war literature of the American Negro movement, to the magazines of the 1940's in which many of the famous names of the later West Indian literary re-naissance started their work. It could be seen, again, in the growing revolt against the Anglophilism of the British Council and Dr Achong has described how, as Mayor of Port of Spain, he told the British Council representative in the territory that the notion of a cloistered British culture for the Trinidadian community had to be ruled out as a paradox since the component parts of that community had had cultures of their own long before William the Conqueror had landed in England.[35]

Nor was all this simply the preserve of the colonial *literati*. The same spirit infected the realm of entertainment. It could thus be seen in the struggle of great cricketers like George John and Learie Constantine to break out of an evil local club system in which the clubs were organized across the colour spectrum, a struggle, there-fore, in which the possession of an individual skill became trans-formed, willy-nilly, into the championship of the game as a carrier of national culture. It could be seen, too, in the way in which after 1945 the changing attitudes of the middle class towards the grand creole bacchanal of Carnival converted that event into a national occasion; likewise, the slow transformation, under the same pressure, of the calypsonian from being simply the court jester of the society, tolerated with bemused condescension for the period of *Mardi Gras* only, into the national hero of the new national feelings, somewhat

like the status of the man of letters in the French Republican tradition, was symptomatic. The calypsonian, indeed, by his very character, became a symbol of an independent local culture and therefore
a progenitor, himself, of the national feeling; in the words of the
Guianese poet addressed to his type:

> *While you stand singing your merry mood*
> *You're singing us all into nationhood.*

Yet there was more to it even than that. For to the degreee that
Carnival embodied economic values different from those of traditional Protestant capitalism, and in which a Port of Spain shopgirl
would arduously save a few hundred dollars throughout the year
in order to purchase the brief two days' glory of being a Cherokee
squaw or a Nubian slave in one of the splendid historical bands,
Trinidadians could feel that they were capable of enjoying themselves in spendthrift pageantry in ways denied to the 'cold' English
or the 'materialist' Americans and could thereby feed the sense of
distinctiveness, of being different from others, which is of the
essence of nationalism.

All of this, naturally, was a slow, imperceptible process. It did
not triumph overnight. It had to meet the resistance of the entrenched Anglo-Saxon values of the respectability, fearful of a
native culture identified, ever since slavery, with social degradation,
an attitude neatly summed up in the words of an official functionary
of the time that, in the context of a youth displaying 'anti-British
tendencies, an attitude of being hypercritical of Great Britain, and
a disposition to poke fun at things British', the people he spoke for
looked forward to the time when youth, on the contrary, would
'at least appreciate Shakespeare, the New Testament and Prayer
Book as much as they delight in listening and dancing to the ribald,
sensuous, and suggestive melodies of Attila, Lion, King Radio, my
Lords Executor and Caresser, and others of the hierarchy of pseudo-
nobility of the Carnival Tents.'[36] That such conservatism did not
die hard, indeed is still very much alive, especially in the expatriate
groups of the society, can be seen in the fact that Mrs Carmichael,
in her 1961 *History*, could devote an equal amount of space to the
topic of Carnival and to the royal visit of Prince Albert and Prince
George in 1880.[37] By 1956, however, the cultural-nationalist movement had advanced so far as to permit the PNM to take it over and

give it some sort of philosophical clothing. Thereafter, the Anglo-phile spirit, embodied in the Farquharian cult of the adoration of the English gentleman, was increasingly on the defensive.

Correspondingly, and in a reverse process, much of the 'old world' continued after 1956, and still continues, to infect the 'new'. Any portrait of Trinidadian society after independence supports that view. Political opportunism still characterizes the opposition groups, so that the Democratic Labour Party can stand unswervingly for 'free enterprise' in 1957 and for 'democratic socialism' in 1964.[38] The perennial leadership crises that afflict that party, springing in large part from an amateurish leadership conducted by Dr Capildeo from the odd haven of a mathematics professorship in London, exemplify its essential anarchism, while the decisive split of 1965, in which the Indian political 'boss' Stephen Maharaj joined hands with C. L. R. James to organize a new anti-PNM force, graphically illustrated how the passion for power can bring together strange bedfellows. That split also illustrates how easily the national political life may slip back into the opportunistic adventurism of the pre-PNM age.[39]

In social life many Trinidadians, despite the PNM moralism, still continue to 'play the fool' rather than 'play the game'. That fact, generally, reflects the absence, still, of any widely accepted code of ethical conduct. The trade union field remains as anarchistically individualist as ever, and the typical trade union leader is not so much the genuinely radical idealist, like the late Quintin O'Connor, as the union 'czar' like the John Rojas who in his public life over the last generation has travelled the whole gamut of Trini-dadian political attitudes from neo-communist demagogue to McCarthyite 'anti-Red' Senator.[40] Racialist feelings likewise still survive the PNM dogma of inter-racial solidarity, even running to a revival of the communal idea in certain members of the Indian political set;[41] while the DLP ran on a ticket of open racial chauvinism in all of the elections of the period, including the federal election of 1958.[42] It is true that the old dream of the Indian home-land, so much an evasion of West Indianism, and finely drawn in the figure of the fiercely unreconstructed old Pathan *emigré* grand-father in Ismith Khan's novel *The Jumbie Bird* is slowly becoming anachronistic, racial differences being ironed out as modes of life become less differential; and the cultural process of the creolization of the more modern-thinking East Indian is fully annotated in novels like Selvon's *Turn Again, Tiger.* Yet there is a long way to go before genuinely national allegiances completely supersede ethno-centred feelings; the 1965 Carnival episode, in which Hindu leaders successfully protested against a proposed Indian *motif* in one of the Carnival bands, served to emphasize the fact that although the official theory of Carnival is that it is a national festival a large percentage of East Indians do not so regard it and, in fact, hold it in disdain. The failure of the PNM, so far, to bring the Indian masses of the rural subculture into the fold only serves to underline that particular truth of minority alienation. Trinidadian East Indians, this is to say, remain a group still on the defensive; and it is suggestive that, so far, there is no written history of their contribution to Trinidadian life comparable to the work of the Indian historians of Guyana. All in all, it is still too early to say that the danger is past. Racialism could easily rejuvenate itself if economic development of the PNM style fails or lags.

The very frequency, finally, with which their Political Leader has to castigate PNM members for their indiscipline and habits of intrigue and personal careerism suggests how deep the social cancer of selfish individualism runs in the body politic. Dr Williams himself sees that cancer as the main problem of the new Trinidad.[43] Yet it is doubtful if in tracing its roots unilaterally to colonialism he properly estimates how much it is a matter of class ambitions and, therefore, how much it is fed, after independence, by the continuing class character of the social structure. That class character, in turn, is encouraged, not diminished, by the PNM acceptance of the Puerto Rican model of economic development in which the main appeal is to the cupidity of the outside investor and of the local business groups who become his allies. It is difficult, if not impossible, to have an acquisitive society based on the private profit motive without at the same time having its logical consequence, a pervasive social climate of predatory individualism; which then adds new fuel to the Trinidadian legacy of Byzantine hedonism. The PNM 'revolution', so far, seeks only amelioration of that social and economic structure. It has yet to move forward to its abolition. Slavery has gone. But capitalism remains.

# Chapter IX

# THE EMERGENCE OF NATIONAL
# SOCIETY

## BARBADOS

It is difficult to speak of Barbados except in mockingly derisory terms, whoever the writer may be, as Paul Blanshard's chapter on the island in his 1947 book and Patrick Leigh-Fermor's shocked remarks on the 'unpolluted Bims', both of them writing from quite different viewpoints, make evident.[1] Even more intractably English than Jamaica, it has been a tropical society modelled on the sort of English life that passed away in 1914. If Trinidad is West Indian Byzantine, Barbados is an English market town, Cheltenham, as it were, with tropical overtones; and if the terrible rococo beauty of the line of Savannah villas in Port of Spain reflects the polyglot Trinidadian colonial tradition the Barbados manor houses are proof, in their solid comfort which excited the envy even of Père Labat in 1700, of the strength of the English domestic civilization transported overseas. An almost pure sugar plantation economy, preserved more completely than in any other West Indian island, produced in its turn a white plantocracy proverbial for its reactionary conceit. Barbados, along with Bermuda and the Bahamas, thus became notorious for its entrenched system of racialist prejudice, and at times it seems that almost every coloured West Indian one meets elsewhere has a half-bitter, half-hilarious story of what happened to him when he visited 'Bimshire'. The ancient constitution of the island, never subjected to Crown Colony rule, gave birth to a spirit of Blackstonian conservatism untouched, until only recently, by any spirit of Benthamite reform. The educated Barbadian, under the pressure of a powerful population-occupation imbalance, became, as it were, through emigration the teacher of the West Indies; and, frequently, be it said to his honour, a zealous reformer, like Thorne in British Guiana and Richards in Bermuda.

All of this, together, gave rise to a temper in all classes of a smug self-satisfaction so pervasive as almost to constitute a national spirit. 'No people,' observed Trollope, 'ever praised themselves so constantly; no set of men were ever so assured that they and their occupations are the main pegs on which the world hangs.' So, West Indians make jokes about Barbados in much the same way as do Americans about Boston and Englishmen about Wigan Pier. A famous West Indian joke, in which England is supposed to have carried on in 1914 only because of a cablegram of Barbadian support against the enemy, sums up the attitude. Probably apocryphal— for Trollope repeated the joke, in a different context, as going back to the period of the Napoleonic Wars—it nonetheless testifies to a temper of glorious self-congratulation most outsiders find amusing, sometimes intolerable. When, therefore, Barbadians do write about themselves it usually turns out to be, like Louis Lynch's *The Barbados Book*, an odd assortment of items, from historical details about the local churches, through a large section for the tourists, to an anti-quarian nostalgia for the old folkways and pastimes losing out, as the author sees it, to a loose materialist age. Thus does the Barbadian climate of opinion live under the omnipresent shadow of a roman-ticized past.[2]

The social and political modernization of Barbados—to the degree that it has been at all possible to modernize a society so deeply traditionalist—goes back, as elsewhere, to the inter-war period. Overwhelmingly an imperialist sugar economy, the divorce of the people from the land continued in an aggravated form, with all of its evil consequences, unlike other West Indian economies, such as neighbouring Grenada, where the introduction of cocoa, and then nutmeg, created the economic base for the rise of an independent peasant proprietary, an end similarly achieved in Tobago through the successful survival of the *meyatage* regime of cultivation. The Barbadian working mass remained, therefore, a permanently dis-placed population, tied to the estate economy and denied, by reason of geography, the escape to the mountains or the 'back lands' that occurred in the post-emancipation period in Jamaica. Trinidad, to make another comparison, was an economy of sparse labour and cheap land, while Barbados was an economy of dear land and over-abundant labour. This did not absolutely prevent the growth of a small proprietary class. But it made it infinitely more difficult, and the economic and social subserviency of the black majority remained intact to a degree unknown elsewhere. How intact can be seen from the general observation of the Semple-Olivier report of 1930 that whereas, on the one hand, the white residents lived agreeably by means of large investments of income overseas and many of the coloured residents benefited from remittances from kinsfolk working abroad, no such considerations applied to the labouring classes who depended entirely upon wages.[3]

The particularities of that general truth were ominous. There was the primitive housing, with chattel houses built on land rented from the estates, but since the structure was in most cases the property of the occupier it relieved the estate management of any responsibility for the primitive and unsanitary accommodation; so that the growth of a free tenancy based on an equitable system— a reform regarded by Sewell as far back as 1859 as being urgent —still remained in large part an ideal only. There was the terrible toll of killer diseases: the local committee which reported on nutrition in 1939 noted that, with the lack of milk, eggs, and fresh vegetables, many households lived on the borderline of extreme poverty and that many children had no regular meals after Wednesday in each week; while the local annual report for the same year noted an appallingly high infant mortality rate occasioned chiefly by infantile diarrhoea, congenital debility and congenital syphilis. It was hardly surprising, then, that Bridgetown at that time had neither the necessary organization nor the equipment to adhere, as a port, to the International Sanitary Convention (Paris).[4] The Orde-Browne report on labour conditions at the same time noted how, in the non-agricultural sector of the economy, the imbalance between a high-density population pressing upon limited resources produced a system of sweated labour for shop assistants, low wages for schoolteachers, and unduly long hours of work for waitresses, laundresses, bakery employees, bus drivers and conductors. All this was made worse, first, by the particular factor of the decline of employment opportunities in the outside world after 1929, a serious blow to the Barbadian person-exporting economy, and the decade of the 1930's witnessed a flow of returning emigrants home to exacerbate the situation. Secondly, there was the more general factor of the social climate of indifference to mass suffering. The Duke of Devonshire's well-known Despatch of 1923 on the unsatisfactory state of health and sanitary conditions in the colony had been cavalierly ignored by the local press, save for the small radical *Herald*, while the low level of social thought in the sugar plantocracy can be guaged from the assurance given by one of its members to the Deane Commission of Enquiry of 1938 that the Barbadian plantation worker did not take milk in his tea because he did not like milk. There was also the shallow complacency of the myth, clearly a rationalization of the upper classes, that, as the Minister of Health noted as late as 1964, the diseases which plagued Latin America, Africa and Asia could have no calling in Barbados because the sea and the sun protected Barbadians from them.[5]

These, of course, were only symptoms of the Barbadian class system, so rigid as almost to constitute a caste structure. More than any other West Indian territory Barbados society re-created the structural configuration of Victorian England, modified, of course, even in 'little England', by the social fruits of slavery, concubinage, and colour, but at the same time intensified by the fact that the island was a cramped and introspective community. It was a familiar hierarchy: at the top, the white economic oligarchy, along with the professional echelons of law, church and state; in the middle, the various grades, nicely demarcated by income indices, of the 'middle classes'; at the bottom, the heavily Negro proletariat. Nor was this softened by any real inter-class mobility; at the most, there were minor movements of status-placing, such as the process which put the group of salary-holders, especially civil servants, in a comparatively 'low income' category in the decade after 1938, occasioned by the fact that their incomes rose much less during that period than the income of the professional and business communities. The stranglehold of the resident whites, not only in estate agriculture but also in commerce meant that it took years after 1940 for a coloured outsider family like the Wilsons to break into the trading monopoly of the famous 'Big Six' in the Bridgetown shopping emporia; the coloured middle group, that is to say, could not enter the commercial field as tranquilly as they did elsewhere, so that whereas the world of trade took on an Indian image, for instance, in British Guiana, in Barbados it retained throughout an upper-class white image. For the mass of the common folk life revolved around the daily drudge of village experience, living under the shadow, as Lamming's autobiographical *In the Cattle of My Skin* portrayed it, of the 'big house' from which the white landlord and his coloured overseers exercised their social and economic authority, the physical embodiments of a world of inter-class relationships in which although there was little of chronic racial hatred there was nothing much more than suspicion and mutual distrust.

Each group lived away from the other, feeding the distrust with gross stereotypes that they had of each other. The situation was reinforced by an openly class-prejudiced and class-ordered educational system. For the Barbadian pride in that system was in reality the pride of a snobbery that graded the school pupil on the educational ladder in terms of his class position, based on the assumptions of the seminal Mitchinson report of 1875: that the purpose of primary education was to create an obedient and honest working class; of middle class education, via the first and second grade secondary schools (that peculiarly Barbadian distinction in itself being a reflection of the snob value that attached itself to 'white' foundations like Lodge and Harrison), to aim at an education set within the external terms of the English public school; and of 'higher' education, by means of the glittering prize of the Barbados Scholarship, to work up, by attendance at Oxford or Cambridge, as the Report put it, 'the very best raw material' of the island into 'a cultivated article'.[6] Educational culture, in this context of values, meant, as in England, the ornamental development of the privileged individual, not the general enlightenment of a community; and in its colonial manifestation it meant the subjection of the school population to a murderously competitive regimen, with pupils exercised like race horses in a steeplechase only a chosen few could hope to win, and producing, in those few, the well-known phenomenon of the colonial Oxonian only too often made unfit, by experience, for creative service to his own community. Nor should the general fact be overlooked that although official aid to education was a real thing—the Barbados Legislature made its first grant in support of schools operating under the Negro Education Grant as early as 1846—the spirit that guided such aid was conservative enough, and even official educators anxious to educate the masses tried too hard to accomodate the planters' notion that formal education at any level would make children indisposed to join the labour force as manual workers; so that even today much is still done to instil into the mind of Barbadian youth the virtue of manual labour and the impropriety of entertaining social aspirations.

The 'Bajan' traditional ultra-conservatism in matters educational, then, meant that the perennial current of reform, evident enough in other fields, somehow tended to bypass the school system; so that one of the ironies of colonialism in Barbados was that, proudly English to its roots, it always remained a generation behind the actuality of its metropolitan model, thus producing the comedy in which, every so often, an enraged local Establishment saw its cherished institutions pilloried by expatriate Englishmen who knew better. That, certainly, was the record of the great 'heads', set in the Elizabethan prototype of the Anglican schoolmaster-bishop of Victorian England, who in the century after Emancipation came to the island to undertake reforms in the teeth of stubborn opposition from the Barbadian vested interests—Coleridge, Rawle, Mitchinson, Anstey, Hughes. It was, as a matter of fact, grim testimony to the continuity of Barbadian life, of which the 'Bajan' spirit has been so inordinately proud, that the harsh strictures that Mitchinson passed on the local upper class in the mid-Victorian period—castigating its members for their lack of 'that higher culture which develops breadth of thought and largeness of view, and the absence of which exhibits itself in an almost odious self-complacency or narrow prejudice, the offspring of a besotted ignorance[7]—could be repeated, nearly a century later, in the now famous Farewell Sermon of Bishop Hughes in 1950. For, starting off with the admonition to his Anglican audience that it would be foolish of them to believe that English bishops were waiting in a queue to come to Barbados (a deadly thrust at the Barbadian heliocentric self-image) that address launched into a bitter Christian Socialist denouncement of the Bourbonese mentality of the mercantile-planter interests, and of the Anglicanism they controlled. Clergy and leading laymen, the Bishop told them, knew nothing of the social and political awakening of the West Indian masses, for they lived, cyst-like, in a little world in which the local Anglican Church Act contained fifteen sections dealing with the subject of pew rents, as if the Christian message meant sorting themselves out on a cash basis every time they attended church.[8] Nothing could have better illustrated the crass philistinism of a colonial ruling class posing as a metropolitan aristocracy without possessing any of the liberal qualities of the English gentleman class it professed to adore. The effects of that pretence in a mixed community like Barbados, whether in politics or religion or education, were tragic.

It was the same story, more or less, in the politico-constitutional field. The literary theory of the famous Barbadian constitution was that, in the words of Sir Conrad Reeves, 'here in Barbados all our institutions are framed to meet exigencies of a single community, though made up of different classes, and to fit them for enjoyment of that self-government which is the common right of the entire colony'.[9] Early on, it is true, the claim had been sincere and perhaps valid enough, for it had been based upon the conviction of the early English settlers, enshrined in their colonial Whiggism, that their position as an English community overseas entitled them to all the rights and liberties of Englishmen; and Davis, in his book *The Cavaliers and Roundheads of Barbados*, has described how in the 1650's that feeling of a separate and equal Barbadian identity gave rise to a social truce in which the local planters, of both Royalist and Parliamentarian persuasions, joined together to prevent the extension of the English Civil War to the colony, thereby showing, too, incidentally, how early in the colonization process a Creole society had been formed which, while not yet culturally homogeneous, was already oriented in terms of separate colonial life.[10]

But with the development of a slave majority that theory of an English community rapidly became invalid and anachronistic. It degenerated, inevitably, into a defence of the classes against the masses. Every attempt to give some concrete embodiment to the Reeves ideal met, as a matter of fact, with tenacious opposition: Robert Bowcher Clarke's defence of the apprenticed labourers after 1834, the long struggle of Samuel Jackman Prescod, himself the first coloured member of the House of Assembly, the 'O'Connell of Barbados', to integrate the free coloured people into the political system, the efforts of Reeves himself to liberalize the franchise, the fight of Sir Herbert Greaves to humanize the administration of justice, Charles Pitcher Clarke's championship of income tax as a necessary principle of public finance. It is possible to argue that in opposing the Colonial Office scheme for Federation in 1876 the Barbadian oligarchy were defending the vital principle of representative government against the attempted imposition of Crown Colony government.[11] But it remains true that in that fight the oligarchy were thoroughly unscrupulous, even going so far as to compound popular ignorance on the subject of federation by telling the workers that the scheme, if successful, would mean the restoration of slavery. The depths of Barbadian reaction can be gauged from the fact that none of the liberal leaders who opposed it were in any way extremist. Sewell, in insisting that the free coloured population of the post-1834 generation ought to obtain political ascendancy as the logical sequence of Emancipation, abjured any intention of upholding the 'absurd pretension of social equality'.[12] Likewise, every Barbadian liberal took for granted the colonial social structure, seeking solely to soften its harsh edges. That they were vilified by the oligarchy only testifies to the deep power of the reactionary spirit in the insular life. The conclusion—as it was drawn by an English visitor as early as 1825—was inevitable, that although Barbados appeared externally to be governed on the English model, in reality it participated only to a small degree in the genuine spirit of the mother country. The forms of the mother-Parliament were thus too gigantic for the capacities of such little islands; the colonists were not elevated by the size, but lost in the folds, of the mighty robe which was never destined for their use.[13]

That, all in all, remained the position until the period after the First World War. It was critically summed up in the *Sketches* of 1921 of Clennel Wickham, whose editorship of the *Herald* newspaper, until it was crushed by the vindictive judgement of the Barbados Grand Jury in 1930, made him the militant voice of the Barbadian masses. Penned in the Walter Bagehot manner, those pieces of sardonic observation exposed the hypocrisy of Barbadian government and politics under the old 'rotten borough' system on the eve of its slow transformation. 'The purpose of their presence in the chamber,' opined Wickham generally of the House of Assembly members at that time, 'is not satisfactorily established in their minds. There is no sense of duty to the individuals of the island as a whole. There is no sense of responsibility for broad and reasonable treatment. There is merely a sense of class.' The particular individual examples of that general truth did not make for edifying reading, nor did Wickham intend them to be so. The character of Sir Fred Clarke suggested the ease with which any man could be placed on a pedestal of public office without any qualification save that of being a bogus aristocrat. The quality of the ruling families could be seen in the character of S. C. Thorne, 'coarse of appearance and

8*

brusque of manner, with the soul of a vulgarian looking through the face of a prize fighter, reckless and ready of speech and regardless of the truth'. There were the vapid talkers, members like Dr E. G. Pilgrim, who suffered from Johnsonian ponderosity, or like Washington Harper, retaining too much 'the manner of debating societies where youthful aspirants declaim with anachronistic disregard of times and manners'. There was the occasional *emigré*, like the Jewish E. I. Baeza, whose wealth went hand in hand with illiberal prejudices; or, again, the cricketer-politician, like Harry Austin, who merely proved that the gifts that made a great cricketer always revered in Barbados—were not those that necessarily made a great statesman. It is true that there was the rare genuine liberal, like the Douglas Pile of one of the old and respected English families in the island. But he could do little in the face of colleagues who, in the main, viewed their seats as pieces of private property and appeared to believe that they were conferring an honour on the electorate by condescending to be members. The general temper, altogether, of the Barbadian governing class was that of the professional lawyer and constitutional legalist, rarely, by their nature, radical social types. Their very preoccupation with Barbadian constitutionalism made them parochial in outlook; for, as Wickham concluded in an acid sentence, 'the constitutional history of Barbados is not more than any forward fifth standard boy could assimilate and master during an ordinary school term, without prejudice to his other studies.'[14]

The foundations of contemporary Barbados, what the most industrious of the local historians has called the 'assault on the oligarchy', were laid in the years after 1918 and with gathering force in the years after the watershed of the 1937–38 West Indian riots. Its leadership was that of Grantley Adams and his colleagues in the two-pronged movement of the Barbados Labour Party and the Barbados Workers' Union. Others came before, of course. There was the work of Negro educators like Rawle Parkinson who gave a new self-respect to the educated coloured Barbadian at a time when educational reform tended to be the preserve of the Barbadian white emulators of the Arnoldian public school ideology. There was the work of the liberal editors, Valence Gale and Charles Chenery, and of the more radical editors who attached themselves to the developing popular democratic movement, Clement Inniss and, of course, Clennel Wickham. There was even the occasional socialist like Charles Duncan O'Neale, who brought back to his island home the revolutionary ideas of Keir Hardie and the Independent Labour Party that he had imbibed in his English stay during the first decade of the century and went on to form, in 1924, the Democratic League as the immediate precursor of the later movement. Yet all of those, great names as they were, were individuals, except O'Neale, working for the masses rather than with the masses. They fought for single causes rather than for a complete reconstruction of Barbadian life. In different ways, they opposed the oligarchy, but they had no clear idea of what they wanted to replace it with. That their Barbadian historian should tell their story in terms of the old-fashioned 'leaders of men' school of history indicates how much they were individualists with a social conscience, but individualists still.[15]

All this became a more general and directive social force with the foundation in 1938 of the Progressive League, under the impetus of the riot movement (to become, later, the Barbados Labour Party) and with the establishment of the Barbados Workers' Union in 1941. The monolithic organization thus created recognized two basic truths. The first was that the Barbadian problem was primarily economic, a truth which the League successfully persuaded the Deane Commission of 1938 to accept, as evident in that body's conclusion that the large accumulation of explosive material in the colony, of which the Payne incident had only served as a detonator, owed its existence to economic conditions. The second truth was that any real solution necessitated the united front of both political and economic agitation, for a political leadership, however radical, which lacked a union base would assuredly decline, as the Cipriani record in Trinidad showed. The Barbadian leadership had the additional advantage of a united, Owen-like type of a general union —on the advice, interestingly, of Sir Walter Citrine—thus avoiding the fratricidal rivalry of different warring factions so characteristic of the Trinidadian labour scene. When the Labour Party became the Government, in 1946, it was thus assured the support of the union force under the able direction, first, of Hugh Springer and, after him, of Frank Walcott; and the later estrangement between Walcott and the party leadership, with all of its consequences, in part, the opposition of the seceding Democratic Labour Party, has only served to illustrate the tremendous boon that the alliance was. For the oligarchy, with the exception of the occasional sympathetic employer like Sir Dudley Leacock, or the exception of the remarkable gentleman politician of the 'old school', possessed of a real sense of *noblesse oblige*, like 'Josh' Haynes, was unrelentingly hostile to reform of any kind and was ready at any time to do what it could to destroy the reform movement. Its confident belief that the movement would of itself disintegrate—'let them strike', as one of its planter members is reported to have said, 'these fellows are like chubbs, they can't keep'—could only be proven wrong by an effective unity of the political and industrial arms.[16]

It was a battle, then, conducted by a unified command on two fronts. The first front was the political and constitutional. The official British thesis, accepted by Barbadians, that there were two sub-levels of government within the Caribbean hegemony, the Crown Colony regime and the surviving old representative system, as in Barbados and the Bahamas, was exposed for the constitutional fiction it was by the fact that in Barbados after 1938 the system, as elsewhere, stood in need of drastic overhaul. The subsequent history of the reform movement showed how empty was the distinction, proudly advertised by Barbadians, between a Crown Colony system that could be changed unilaterally by Orders in Council and an ancient constitution that required the consent of the metropolitan Parliament for proposed changes; for in both cases imperial parliamentary sovereignty remained supreme over colonial claims, and in both cases, too, the colonial Governor remained the powerful agent of that supremacy, the sole important difference being that in the Barbadian case he lacked the power to certify legislation defeated in the legislature. So, almost as much as in the Crown Colony territories, there was the reluctant grant of individual constitutional 'advances': the reduction of property qualifications for voters, the enfranchisement of women, the so-called 'Bushe Experiment' of a quasi-ministerial system, adult suffrage, the payment of legislators, the introduction, in 1954, of a full-scale ministerial system, along with the new office of the Premier, the attempts, finally, to whittle down the powers of the nominated Legislative Council. And, as elsewhere, there developed a continuing climate o, frustration as the defects inherent in each individual 'step forward' became painfully apparent almost before the Governor of the day had completed the usual smug address complimenting the colonials on their loyal devotion to British constitutional precedents and the British on their generosity in granting to their subjects a fresh part of 'the best system that the world has ever seen'.[17] It is true enough that the changes, collectively, had the effect, over the decade between 1944 and 1954, of replacing the old executive machinery of the Victorian period (basically unchanged since 1881) with a modern cabinet system worked by elected ministers accountable to the popular house and based on organized party support (for which the British could take no credit) ; and that those ministers became individually responsible in Executive Committee for propounding departmental business and collectively responsible in the House of Assembly for the public defence of government policies, with administration concurrently passing from the old colonial secretariat to the new cabinet body. It is true, too, that the new machinery undoubtedly enabled the Labour Governments after 1946 to push through their welfare programme much more expeditiously. Yet, with all that, Barbados still remained *in statu pupillari* to the Colonial Office. The dignity of the new title of Premier—the first such office in the West Indies did not lessen the fact that the Governor retained the ultimate power in the areas of foreign affairs and the administrative establish-ment. Neither did the change of title from Colonial Secretary to Chief Secretary disguise the fact that that British official, accountable to the Governor, continued to control, among other things, the areas of defence and security, the police, and the ceremonial and administrative work of the Executive Committee.[18]

That this was so became clear from the series of constitutional crises that took place during this period. The 1946 fracas over the anomalous status of the Attorney-General; the difficulties created by the continuing presence of nominated officials in the Executive Committee; the prolonged struggle to clip the wings of the Legis-lative Council, the Barbadian House of Lords; and the 1959 crisis over the question of the Governor's appointive power with respect to the nomination of aldermen to the newly created Bridgetown City Council: all of them were proof of the emptiness of the Bar-badian claim to be the pace-setter in West Indian constitutional development, the image of *Barbadoe duce et auspice duce*. That was particularly so in the vexed issues of the second chamber and the role of the Governor. The Legislative Council, throughout its life, had been almost wholly a reserve of the upper class white sectors of sugar and commerce, placed there by a gubernatorial power of unilateral appointment that was only qualified, late in the day, by the right conceded to the Premier to nominate his own candidate to act as Leader of Government business in the upper chamber. A thoroughly reactionary body, it consistently opposed the introduction of the ministerial system, paid legislative service, and universal suffrage, all on the inarticulate major assumption that, in the words of R. G. Mapp, the 'coloured boys' could not run anything.[19] It laid claim to extravagant powers, even going so far as to argue that, as a delaying and revising chamber, it could (1) amend or reject any measure, 'of whatever nature it might be', coming to it from the House, and (2) insist that a rejected measure, before being returned for further consideration by the Council, should become the subject matter of a new general election or of a special referendum; powers long ago abjured by the British House of Lords.[20] It must be noted, as a footnote to those claims, that the 1963 controversy over the Council's attitude to the legislation concerning the right of peaceful picketing in industrial disputes only avoided a head-on clash by the pretence that the Government party's promise, in its 1961 election manifesto, to revise the then existing Trade Union Act in effect constituted such a popular mandate.[21] It still remained true, despite such minor retreats, that the members of the upper house, including its sole trade union member, were possessed of an anti-Jacobinical mentality so morbid that they could not even entertain the mild suggestion of some representation of the official opposition (after the fashion of the British House of Lords they affected to adore) in their set-up. That such a measure of institutional conservatism could grow up in a body which, having only been established in 1874, was a comparatively modern item in the Barbadian constitutional scheme, speaks volumes for the deep power of tradition in the Barbadian political mind.[22] It is not surprising that, in 1964, it was replaced by a more up-to-date Senate.

It could of course be argued that an unrepresentative second chamber, being present in many independent countries, is not in itself evidence of colonialism; although the fact of its being recruited, in the Barbadian variant, by the nominating power of a colonial Governor weakens the analogy. Even in its successor-body, the new Senate, the Governor continued, anachronistically, to wield a power of discretionary nomination of a certain percentage of the membership. If, in any case, the matter of the bicameralist structure was a struggle between Tory Barbados and its own domestic critics, such was certainly not the case in the 1959 episode concerning the newly-formed Bridgetown City Council. Arising out of the Labour Government's drastic reform of the old vestry system of local government (which in itself, with its political churchwardens, like Mottley, building up a 'boss' system on the basis of colossal poor relief expenditures, constituted a superb example of Dickensian Barbados) that crisis brought into question the constitutional convention, accepted in 1954, that the Governor in Executive Committee would accept in legislative matters the advice of the Ministers except in the event of 'grave or exceptional circumstances'. Sir Robert Arundell chose to believe, in 1959, that the appointment of aldermanic members to the new Bridgetown municipality constituted such circumstances; with the result that whereas, in 1954, he could announce that new system as the latest development in a process whereby the elected Cabinet took up the reins of government with 'dignity and assurance', by 1959 he was being pilloried, by the same Cabinet, as a hypocritical villain assaulting the spirit of the constitution. Nothing could have better illuminated the dangers secreted in the West Indian tendency to embrace uncritically British constitutional conventions, as if a colonial Governor, however liberal, could be reduced to the ornamental status of a constitutional monarch; and the very vehemence of the response of the Barbadian politicians to the 1959 episode indicated, perhaps, the extent of their naïveté. It was probably true that, in the words of one of them, the Governor had so acted because he was mortally afraid of making it appear that he was attempting to upset the equilibrium of the Bridgetown financial magnates.[23] But it was equally true that in their conviction that their Premier enjoyed a relationship in Barbados with the Governor akin to that of the British Prime Minister *vis-à-vis* the Queen, the Barbadian political leadership had allowed its Anglophilism to get the better of its sense of colonial realities. Nor was the answer to their dilemma the introduction of a written and rigid constitution after the American fashion, as some of them sternly demanded.[24] Only independence (which finally came in 1966) could put an end to such constitutional storms in colonial teacups. Only independence too, perhaps, could put an end to the more general contradiction of the Barbadian political spirit, between an inordinate pride in an immaculate constitution and the continuing need, as each succeeding storm exposed its weaknesses, to reform it.

The second front of the Labour Party struggle, in the heyday of its freedom march between 1945 and 1961, was the socio-economic. Union and party, working hand in hand, slowly put together the rudimentary welfare state of contemporary Barbados. The period of the first Parliament under Labour control, that of 1946–51, saw the beginnings of that policy. There was the revision of the tax structure so as to alleviate the heavy pressure of indirect taxation, via the old customs duties legislation, upon the middling and lower income groups; and for the first time, with that end in view, a trained statistician was added to an Income Tax Department which, as the Howie Report of 1944 pointed out, was so inadequately staffed that five of its eight officers were not yet fully trained in their specialized duties and even lacked a typist so that typing had to be done by clerks normally engaged in other duties.[25] There was the organization of new loan and credit facilities to push forward the silent revolution by which one-fifth of the arable land in the island, according to the party election literature, passed gradually into the hands of the smallholder class. There was the modernization of hospital conditions, starting with the taking over of the old General Hospital by government and the construction, completed years later, of the new Queen Elizabeth Hospital: the naming of which, incidentally, gave rise to yet another typically Barbadian controversy. There was the introduction, after the experience gained in a number of pioneer schemes, of the Provident Fund for Sugar Workers, a vital insurance measure in a seasonal employment industry and a new source of help under distress to a working population that has relied, traditionally, for help on its own inventive savings resources, as in the well-known local institution of the 'sou-sou', what Barbadians call the 'meeting turn'. As early as 1951 the Labour regime could boast of an impressive record of legislative achievement. 'In the field of social services,' its Manifesto of that year stated, 'the Labour Government can claim an impressive record in the recent session. It increased Old Age Pensions. It enlarged and increased the scope of the Social Welfare Department. It extended the Domestic Training Centre. It increased family allowances in the assessment of Income Tax. It led the way in the British Empire by passing legislation to provide holidays with pay for all workers. It extended the provisions of Workmen's Compensation. It extended the scope of the Trade Union Act by allowing for peaceful picketing. It made the notification of accidents and occupational diseases compulsory. It enacted legislation to provide for the safety of quarry workers. It pushed forward with the programme to provide playing fields throughout the island. It took steps to safeguard by law the wages of manual workers.'[26] All of this, of course, was ameliorative only. It did little, save for the inauguration of the United States Farm Labour Scheme and the training scheme for domestic servants going to Canada, to solve the desperate unemployment picture of an economy that has traditionally been an emigration-economy urgently requiring outlets abroad. What it did do was to begin the planned amelioration of general living conditions, including low wage standards, which, in the words of the Deane Commission, had made decent living impossible for the Barbadian masses. Not least of all, by the practice of appointing union members to the various boards and committees of the public administration structure, it began the recognition of the working class as a partner in community life and not simply as a group of employees existing merely to carry out the orders of a feudally-minded employer class.

Yet much of all this would have been impossible without the mass support engendered by the dramatic entry of the Union into the daily life of the Barbadian worker. From the beginning, the Union faced the harsh brutalities of an economic system in which, because of its high population density, there was the tendency for workers to be exploited on the altar of the maxim, 'If you do not accept, someone else will.'[27] The casual character of Barbadian employment along with its high proportion of unskilled labour, made the Union, when it came on the scene, inevitably a general union embracing categories of workers difficult to define into sections; and so it remained for the period as a whole. The stevedore, the tally clerk, the cane-cutter, the bus driver, the telephone worker, the Broad Street shop assistant (who for so long resisted unionization because of the element of paternalism shaping his social attitudes), all came under the general umbrella of the most remarkable of all West

Indian trade unions. The engineering strike of 1944 secured the claim of the Union to be a bargaining unit recognized by the employer class; while the Lewis episode of 1949—in which 'T. T.' Lewis, the generally beloved white Barbadian socialist, was victimized by his employers of twenty-eight years' standing for his radical views, and received full retribution only after a mass demonstration of both Union and party provoked an official inquiry—finally served notice on the Bridgetown mercantile oligarchs that the days of easy victimization were over once and for all. 'The merchants got the money, but the Union got the men': the refrain, sung to the tune of the American *Battle Hymn of the Republic*, testified to the 'new day' of working class solidarity in support of new social principles. The rest was consolidation: a guaranteed daily wage for the sugar workers, the organization, along with government, of the Labour Welfare Fund, workmen's compensation schemes, holidays with pay, the 44-hour week, the acceptance of the check-off system, and much else. In more general terms, the Union became an overall defence mechanism of the Barbadian Negro proletariat.

For before the Union's advent on the scene, Barbadian life was that of the three-dimensional class world portrayed, as already noted, in the Lamming novel of tropical childhood, the Negro villagers ruled by the estate overseers, the overseers ruled by the white owners, little social universes sealed off from each other as much by class prejudices as by racial animosities, reflecting the astonishing combination in Barbadian life of tiny geographical distances and immense social distances. The Union, of course, did not destroy that way of life. But it helped smooth its rougher edges. It championed the cause of freehold occupancy, for the phenomenon of large labour forces resident with their families on the estates, prevalent elsewhere, has not been the practice in Barbados. It helped give a new social status to the working class woman, especially by way of its fight against the scandalously low wages of the town shopgirls (seven dollars a week as late as 1957), a situation facilitating the exercise of a sort of *droit de seigneur* on the part of the Swan Street merchant employer. There was the fight for the union shop in collective bargaining, a process still incomplete. Not least of all, the Union sought to teach its members to help themselves, particularly by encouraging the savings habit; and the sugar 'windfall' issue of 1963 fully illustrated how, in that effort, the Union was struggling against the traditional tendency of the worker to use the savings habit, as in his Friendly Societies, not so much as a long-term insurance device but rather as a means of getting an annual Christmas bonus. The 'bonus' psychology, indeed, figures heavily in a consumer population whose living costs have been seriously inflated because of the enormous middleman profits exacted by the monopolistic three-tiered distribution system of commission houses and importers, wholesalers, and retailers.[28]

The superior quality of Barbadian unionism has been noted by outside professional observers.[29] The quality is noteworthy in at least three respects. In the first place, the Union, as a national institution, has been throughout a school of industrial democracy, both by means of its branch meetings and its annual conferences. The real importance of that contribution would be missed if one neglected to note that, by comparison, the local Labour Party initially lacked such grass-roots democracy, not, indeed, convening its first annual delegate conference until 1958, and for a considerable period not even possessed of a written constitution or organized constituency groups. The party, in fact, was a loose association centred around the dominant personality of its leader Grantley Adams. It reflected the old colonial politics in which the party legislator was more important than the constituency unit. It was the chief merit of the Union that it counteracted the individualism of the colonial politician—the figure, for example, of Mr Slime, the schoolteacher turned politician, in the Lamming book—with a vigorous organizational life. For most of its period in power the Labour Party continued to use the mass meeting, with all of its shortcomings, as its chief contact with the masses. The Union added the regular delegate conference and, more latterly, its General Secretary's weekly press conference.

Secondly, the Union, in typically Barbadian fashion, placed a high premium on education. Most of its members, being working-class, would have been barred from the closed world of Barbadian secondary school education, training an *élite* minority group of scholarship boys, as that system did, on an outmoded eighteenth-century classical curriculum.[30] The Union's contribution, here, was twofold. One, it began to use the local intellectual in the adult education of its members, and only one instance of its progressive attitude was its scheme, drawn up in consultation with Dr Rawle

Farley, for the organization of a trade union educational course.[31] Two, it emphasized from the outset the absolute necessity for an imaginative policy of technical-vocational education. The old education, increasingly anachronistic in a popular democracy based, since 1950, on adult suffrage, was seen as an inexcusable burden upon limited fiscal resources, and illogical in a scientific age—the observation of the Petter Report that it was only possible to teach chemistry, physics, and biology beyond the very elementary stage in Harrison College and Lodge School and that, further, it was rare to find outside the first grade schools a teacher of modern languages with any substantial qualifications for the task,[32] showed how much the system was in thrall to an outmoded past. So, the working-class majority who entered employment—if they could find it—at the age of 14, unskilled and eking out a low-wage exis- tence in a high-cost domestic market, was ruled by an educated *élite*, both white and 'pass as white', as the Barbadian saying has it, that knew little of the new technological age it lived in. Merely to read the Union's General Secretary's speeches of 1963, in his legislative capacity, on the need for industrial training, is to be made aware of how much the Union wanted, and still wants, to change that situation. The old snobbish contempt for the worker by hand, the general argument runs, must go. The unemployed youth whose only skill is that at games of chance must be taught to become a skilled labourer, for the sad fact is that no girl has ever become trained in Barbados to become a maid, nor has a boy ever been trained to become a waiter. So, the economy is a half-baked one, with every kind of service basically inefficient and characterized, in a happy-go-lucky fashion, by market square attitudes. Nor is emi- gration necessarily the complete answer, for Barbados is not a settler economy, and the island's population pressure could in fact be seen, not as a liability, but as itself a stimulus for vigorous economic expansion. But it has to be a trained population, which means a new type of education, technical, popular and, not least of all, compulsory. There must, finally, be a revolution in social attitudes, so that the average Barbadian can be persuaded to give up his idea that the best way to prove his manhood is to breed children like flies.[33]

The third point of the Union's general contribution—arising out of that second point—was its insistence upon the need to recognize the social consequences of technological change in the local territorial economy. Trade unions in 'backward' economies are notoriously hostile to technological change, as the smaller Caribbean islands show. Barbadian union leaders like the remarkable Frank Walcott saw, more perceptively, that the problem called for not a Luddite opposition to change but a planned effort to control the pace and the scope of its application to historically vulnerable labour-oriented economies. Whether it was the question of the profound changes in the employment structure arising out of the new methods of bulk loading of sugar in the new deep water harbour; or of the need to recast industrial negotiation techniques on a scientific basis of full statistical knowledge of operating costs, frequently withheld from the union side by obscurantist employers; or of proposals for a sugar workers' rehabilitation and welfare fund; or of the submission of a memorandum to the 1962 sugar industry Commission of Enquiry so wide in its scope as to force re-examination of practically the entire economic structure of the island, including the question of the sociological consequences of the possible centralization of the unique family estate system of Barbadian sugar; or of the establishment of a National Productivity Centre for the study of all the factors, sociological, economic and technical, that impinge upon productive efficiency: all of them were treated in the same spirit of a passionate concern on the part of the Union leadership to lift the working class from the era of a Victorian *laissez-faire* plantation economy into the modern atmosphere of an intelligent popular participation in the creation of higher living standards. There was, even more, an equal concern for the general welfare as a whole, of which the Union saw itself, as much as the Church or even the political parties, as a self-appointed conscientious custodian; the outcome being that, today, the General Secretary of the Union—like the President of the newly enlivened Junior Chamber of Commerce—is accepted as a public figure with a right to comment on public affairs, a privilege reserved, until only yesterday, to figures like the Governor, the leader of the Legislative Council and the Bishop of Barbados. The Union, all in all, has done much to changed the brutalized lifeways of the Barbadian labourer; so much so that a piece of fiction such as Austin Clarke's *The Survivors of the Crossing*, which purports to describe a Barbadian village in 1961 in search of a socialist Utopia, is dangerously anachronistic in its assumption that, at that late date, a canecutters' strike, called without benefit of the Union, could be put down by a Simon Legree type manager along with guns and bloodthirsty Alsatian hounds.[34]

Yet the name with which modern Barbados is most famously associated is, of course, that of Sir Grantley Adams, so much so that his biographer sees the rise of the modern Barbadian democracy as the story of its great Labour leader.[35] Undoubtedly an exaggeration it is true, even so, that Adam's decision, after 1934, to join up with the local progressive movement marked a turning point in its history, for that act, so startling a break with the placid conservatism of the coloured professional class, and earning for its author, as it did, the dangerous reputation of being a traitor to his class, marked him as the Barbadian statesman of the age. Notwithstanding his eclipse after 1961 his personality and philosophy did much to make Barbados, warts and all, what it is today.

It was typically Barbadian that his progress towards socialism was a lengthy and cautious odyssey. As a young student in the Oxford of the First World War period, the earliest and perhaps the most lasting of the intellectual influences upon him was the liberal humanism of Gilbert Murray and T. R. Glover, and he came down in 1925 a confirmed Asquith liberal. As such, it took years of painful experience for him to discover that colonial liberalism had little of the real metropolitan spirit in it. His literary controversy with Wickham revealed him as the anti-socialist; while the acrimonious debate with Father Besant over the divorce issue showed him as the anti-ecclesiastical rationalist, spending his powers on a matter hardly calculated to appeal to a mass population most of whom have never experienced marriage, let alone divorce (it is odd to note the frequency of the colonial echoes of intellectual controversies long since dead in the metropolitan intellectual circles). It was not until the mid-1930's that, with the aid of white individuals like E. T. Cox and Dr Eustace Greaves, he finally identified himself with the radical forces; and the events of 1937–38 cemented the alliance. His 1937 visit to London added the new influence of the West Indian groups there and of the Fabian Society, and on his return home he almost automatically assumed the leadership of the local movement, as against all other possible candidates—Seale, Clement Payne, 'Chrissie' Brathwaite. What Wickham had called 'an inarticulate majority brooding over unredressed wrongs and unventilated grievances' had at last found their chosen leader.

Yet, notwithstanding his splendid record, it is open to grave doubt as to whether Adams, any more than his contemporaries Cipriani and Marryshow was socialist in anything except the idiom that he borrowed from the British Labour Party. The 1938 programme of the British Guiana and West Indies Labour Congress, including proposals for nationalization of the sugar industry, limitation of plantation ownership of land, and government operation of purchasing and exporting processes, to this day remains an ideal only in Barbadian realities. The Labour Party cabinets in practice did not go beyond the acceptance of union bargaining rights and limited consultative rights, as in the 1951 sugar agreement, and, generally, a policy of mutual respect and accommodation between capital and labour: a far cry, certainly, from the classless society its pamphlet literature bravely talked about.[36] It is true that Frank Walcott has more recently speculated about a land 'take-over' policy, but the remarks were clearly *obiter dicta* occasioned by their author's irritation in a moment of difficulty with the employers' organization and, in any case, did not reflect any deliberate group or party opinion.[37] There was, under Labour, an important redress of the balance of social and political forces, for what it achieved, broadly speaking, was the conquest of the citadel of political power in the interests of the rising educated professional coloured group. But there was no fundamental reshaping of the structure of society. The Adams leadership apparently accepted the widespread Barbadian belief that a radical stance on the sugar question destroys a political career; it apparently also accepted the belief, sedulously spread by the plantocracy, that a nationalization policy would lead to economic disaster and social chaos. Adams, in any case, was first and foremost a liberal constitutionalist, convinced of the primacy of politics: 'when the political fight is won, economic ills will disappear.'[38] Major emphasis was laid upon constitutional advance, in willing co-operation with liberal Governors. That explains why, on the economic-social side, little was done to set up a modern comprehensive social security scheme under central control, and only in the very last few months of the Labour Party regime was the International Labour Office requested to report on the feasibility of such a scheme.[39] That explains why, on the political side, no thoroughgoing campaign for independence was undertaken, as in the PNM fashion, for the *bona fides* of British governments were accepted uncritically, and Adams' real tragedy was not, as the Hoyos book suggests, the dissolution in itself of his dream of West Indian Federation, but the fact that a Colonial Office for whom he had played so long the role of its West Indian darling (including his gratuitous defence of the British colonial empire in the United Nations 1948 session) should, in the end, have so callously helped destroy his handiwork. The upshot was that, on the domestic scene, the 'assault on the oligarchy' left the commanding heights of the economy still in oligarchic hands and that, on the external scene, the struggle for independence was abandoned by default. The Barbados Labour Party, in brief, was the vehicle of colonial socialism, just as the work of Sir Conrad Reeves had been colonial Whiggism. Its essential respectability was summed up in the assurance of one of its ministers, Mr Cox, to the Annual Conference of the Barbados Workers' Union that May Day was a Soviet Russian invention with which honest Barbadians, presumably, should have nothing to do. Credence was thereby lent to the legend of the perdurability of the 'sacred cows' of Barbadian life: the Church, the professions, the *élite* schools, sugar estate capitalism.

It is not surprising, then, that the Grand Old Man was so easily supplanted by the Young Turks of the Democratic Labour Party in 1961. Yet even then it was not, in any real sense, a new ideological direction that took over, for the new Premier, Mr Errol Barrow, and his colleagues sought less to socialize the economy than to modernize it, which is not necessarily the same thing. The sugar question was met by the standard device of appointing yet another commission of inquiry whose recommendations referred more to the managerial and organizational aspects of the industry than to the problems of ownership and control. The new Development Plan, with its attempt to avoid the new economic imperialism of the foreign investor—so harshly apparent in Puerto Rico—brought new ideas to the discussion of Barbadian economic problems, hardly the strong point of Adams; but it remains to be seen whether government shareholding in key industries, the acquisition of plantation tenantries for resale to tenant occupiers, the encouragement of local banks so as to counteract the colonial banking system in which credit policy and interest rates, as well as the effective use of internal savings, have been determined from outside, will be enough in themselves, short of an outright socialist policy, to prevent the growth of a Puerto Rican-style neo-colonial capitalism. The historic agricultural base of the economy, certainly, is both psychologically and financially inadequate and, being already fairly fully developed, cannot hope to expand commensurately with a growing population. There remain tourism, light industry, emigration. Of those, tourism creates its own special problems, as local legislative debate illustrates.[40] Emigration, in its turn, depends so much on good relations with the receiving countries that Barbadians of all shades of opinion become alarmed when emigrants, as in the United States Farm Labour Scheme, renege on their contractual obligations in the typically Barbadian conceit, utterly misconceived, that Americans anxiously wait upon Barbadian workers to perform tasks for them.[41]

Trapped within this framework, the main concern of the Barrow modernizing *élite* has been their effort to strike a new note of urgency against Barbadian complacency. Basically, they seek to create a revitalized infrastructure necessary to economic growth, a task traditionally neglected by the usual United Kingdom aid programmes more concerned with social welfare purposes than with new productive projects. There has been a ruthless re-examination of a variety of defects: mediaeval work practices in an economy of casual labour; an internal trade structure that sacrifices the labourer, living on credit, to local shopkeeper, middleman, and Bridgetown merchant; an educational snobbery which encourages in all social classes the anti-social conviction that a child must attend a snob secondary school even it if only comes out with a certificate in Scripture studies; Civil Service lackadaisical work habits; and much else. A new emphasis has been placed upon the urgent need for the Barbadian labour task force, at every level, to acquire new skills by which it can begin to command the external market, after the fashion of the modern Swiss and Israeli economies. Along with that there has gone a campaign to modernize the machinery of government. At the local government level, there are the inefficiency and excessive administrative costs of the relatively recent (1958) council system, a system possibly without justification in a tiny body politic with a population of less than 250,000.[42] At the island-wide level, modern-minded Barbadian leadership faces the task of revamping a public administration structure designed for colonial ends; the office of the Premier, to take an example only, today imposes upon its occupant a complex of duties fifty times greater than those that confronted the former British officials who, for themselves, enjoyed the support of a staff four times the size of the one that the Premier presently uses.[43] More generally, there is a new official spirit of dissatisfaction with the Barbadian self-congratulatory ethos of 'muddling through'. That spirit is ready to learn from models other than the British. Men like Barrow, Crawford and Walcott are modernists striking a new note in the territorial life. By any genuinely socialist norms, it is not revolutionary. After all, what it stands for is essentially what a progressively-minded local business-man like K. R. Hunte stands for. It sees government, basically, as a galvanizing pacesetter to the private sector, not anything more. But for Barbados, which moves slowly at any time, it is perhaps all that can presently be absorbed.

For it would require a *fidelista* hurricane to change Barbados over-night. It remains, despite the Democratic Labour Party 'wind of change', a mixture of class privilege, genteel respectability and Trollopian institutional conservatism, with a new element of in-truding American wealth. If one accepts Mr Dooley's witticism that the Americans defeat their enemies while the British disqualify them, Barbadian society could be seen as a collection of various disqualification exercises, an exemplar of games theory, English style. Subtle discriminatory walls continue to separate whole groups from each other. For the Negro populace there are the rum shop and the pentecostal meeting hall; for the middle bracket people the secrecy of home life, for their public expressions are still hesitant, constituting, in Judge Vaughan's phrase, 'a series of angry mutter-ings behind closed doors', the well-known Barbadian middle class tactic of withdrawal; while the top *élites*—British demi-residents, Creole upper class whites, the merchant princes—occupy select areas like the St James 'Platinum Coast'. The easy victimization of the employee in industrial and commercial life is perhaps gone forever, and the sort of shameful episode that used to occur—the employee fired from his job after being accused of passing a director of a big concern in Bridgetown without taking off his hat, or the plantation 'head-row' man prosecuted for absenteeism after taking a day off for urgent medical attention[44]—is unlikely to mar social relationships again. At the same time the habit of social deference remains pretty firmly entrenched. It is surprising, too, that despite the fact that the period of the 1920's and 30's witnessed the rise of peasant farming and an increase in the number of professional men, creating thereby community sections not entirely dependent upon the plantation-merchant house regime, there did not emerge, as in Jamaica, a movement of protest in the middle class as a whole; and protest, when it did make itself felt in that class, was the work of individuals only, not of the group as a whole. The rigidity of the Barbadian social structure obviously accounts for much of this. There has been little in the history of the Bridgetown commercial and industrial firms to equal the story, say, of J. T. Johnson in Port of Spain, the one-time clerk who rose to become the dry goods king of Frederick Street, so that Barbadian class relationships have not been loosened up by the liberalizing attitudes that such stories engender.

Nor does a sense of colour fraternity transcend these essentially class barriers based on economic considerations, for it is doubtful, speaking now only of 'white' Barbados, if the white English engineer, out on contract, living the sort of dull expatriate life described in Derek Bickerton's *Tropicana*, would ever get to mix with either the local planters or with members of the 'jet set' of wealthy British refugees like the ex-Ranee of Sarawak; it is equally doubtful if any well-to-do white person would dream of mixing with the Barbadian 'Redlegs', the 'poor whites' of St John's Parish who, as they cling to their pathetic snobberies of race, constitute one of the saddest anachronisms of the local scene. And there are other social *curiosa*. There is the sartorial snobbery of the Barbadian gentleman, including the Labour persuasion; embodied, as a St Lucian critic put it with reference to the Grantley Adams period, in the 'quite ludicrous sight to be seen on certain occasions celebrated by morning parades on the Garrison, when the Cabinet of the Socialist Government of Barbados is to be seen in the heat of a tropical sun, freely sweating in striped trousers, morning coat and top hat.[45] There is the mental snobbery of the Barbadian royalist; to read the radio address in which the Minister of Education, in 1964, announced the impending arrival of the Duke of Edinburgh to the island, like nothing so much as a West Indian John the Baptist preparing the way for the royal English Christ, is to be made aware of a Barbadian reverence for the monarchy long since in decline in England itself.[46]

Not least of all, there is the snobbery, with all of its complex ramifications, of the local club system. In part, it is purely a social snobbery, not the least virulent in the innumerable fraternal organizations, frequently obligated to some grand body in the United States, that cater to a gullible labouring class and the quarrels of whose leaders reach the Registrar of Friendly Societies with monotonous regularity. It is worth noting, here, that the predecessors of those organizations a generation ago, the Barbadian 'land ship' societies—described in George Bernard's *Wayside Sketches* at that time —likewise catered, with their comic emulation of the elaborate naval ritual of the British Navy, to the same popular passion for empty form. In part, the snobbery here being discussed is, however, a racial snobbery, for there are still places of amusement that invoke their dormant legal status as 'clubs' at the sight of coloured clients; while the nasty Adie affair of 1957, in which a British official was pilloried for sending his daughter to a segregated private school, sickeningly revealed how Barbadians were prepared to use an unsuspecting white visitor as a scapegoat for a problem created by their own cowardice and evasiveness. Barbadians exercise a vast deal of ingenuity in the pretence that colour prejudice does not exist or that if it does it is of little account. But the fact that the Government party felt constrained in its 1961 Manifesto to announce open war on all the myths of colour superiority that promote the degradation of the social scene—to use the words themselves of the document—suggests that if, as the local self-image boasts, the matter is dead it refuses, oddly, to lie down.[47] And not the least pathetic footnote to this is the curious observation of one local writer, undoubtedly reflecting the subserviency of many coloured elements, that the best solution to the colour problem 'appears to be the emergence of enlightened white leaders, which is almost impossible'.[48]

Visiting American sociologists, Mack for example, have argued, more optimistically, that as a new emerging class structure, reflecting the new political dominance of the educated coloured group in the society, solidifies itself it obliterates the old meaning of race as a defining boundary line.[49] To a great extent that, of course, is so. What has taken place, as Mack points out, is the emergence of status aggregates, composed of persons similar in income, education, religion, and amount of social power, which cut across the old racial boundaries. But two critical points must be made about this line of argument. In the first place, the process can hardly be said to have completed its course, any more than integration has been completed in American society. Much of it, in Barbados as in the United States, is a token integration only, so that the decision of one of the last white clubs in Bridgetown to invite the Premier, as a coloured person, to membership by no means signals the end of the club system. Secondly, it is difficult to accept the thesis, advanced by Mack, that all this is part of a 'democratic revolution'. For a process that gives the privilege of class categorization, as distinct from racial categorization, only to those persons whose income or educational qualifications can effectively claim the privilege is, in effect, a process of gross social inequity and, in the Barbadian environment, nothing much more than a process for promoting the transformation of the small percentage of educated professional mulattoes into an 'in-group' in alliance, for all of their radical political rhetoric, with the older established interests. It may mean, certainly, the decline of racial discrimination. But it is arguable as to whether discrimination based on social class considerations can be considered more morally reputable or socially equitable. It leaves the social and economic subjection of the Negro mass virtually unchanged. From their viewpoint, indeed, barely clinging to the bottom rungs of the social ladder, the new coloured presbyter is but old white priest writ large.

In many ways Barbados is not unlike Hawaii. Both are geographically tiny tropical territories beset by chronic land and population problems—the family estate system in the one, the old royal estates in the other. In both cases commercial life has been dominated by closely-knit business leader groups descended from the 'old' families; and in both cases a rigid economy has been successfully changed over the last twenty-five years by militant union movements, the Barbados Workers' Union and the Hawaiian branch of Harry Bridges' powerful West Coast union empire; and, indeed, there is a marked similarity in personality between Frank Walcott and the Hawaiian union 'boss' Jack Hall. The general history of the two societies, since 1940, has been that of an emancipatory movement against white supremacy, for the Oriental groups in Hawaii, for the Negro majority in Barbados; and the *causes célèbres* of that struggle, in both cases, have concerned the once exclusive aristocratic clubs, the Savannah in Barbados, the Outrigger Canoe Club in Hawaii. The political aspect of the struggle was fed, in the Barbadian case, by the return of young leaders like Errol Barrow from a well known World War Two career in the Royal Air Force, just as the Democratic Party in the Hawaiian case received new blood from the much-decorated young Japanese of the 442nd Regimental Combat Team, including the Senator-to-be Dan Inouye. The cultural face of both societies was shaped by the religious heritage of Anglo-American Puritanism so that, in both cases, although there are indigenous cultural resistants to the Puritan repressive psychology there is little of the neo-pagan popular culture that makes Trinidad Carnival, by contrast, so much a theatre of the streets; notwithstanding the massive ballyhoo propaganda that has paraded Hawaii as the fun-centre of the world. The Puritan heritage perhaps also explains the cultural backwardness of Barbadian life, for there is no adequate civic centre, no modern museum, no evening newspaper, no good theatre (for years the only theatre in Bridgetown was the Green Room theatre club, founded by and relying on 'white' patronage). The literary culture has also been deficient, for Frank Collymore's remarkable editorship of the pioneer journal *Bim* has been a personal odyssey rather than a national achievement, as can also be said of A. J. Seymour's editorship of the journal *Kyk-over-al* in the Guianese case. It is suggestive, all in all, so pervasive is 'Bajan' provincialism, that a novelist like John Hearne can enlarge his creativity in Jamaica while George Lamming feels that his genius would be stifled in Barbados. In Barbados, finally, as in Hawaii, there is not so much a homogeneous world as a hierarchy of semi-segregated social worlds: the tight little group of 'old families'; the newcomers who fail to get on to the 'inside track' and whose resultant discontent takes many forms from the desire to see snow to a yearning for a London show; the middle class groupings with their militant philistinism; and the Negro working class majority, its womenfolk, in one observer's phrase, 'rigid with starch and Anglicanism', but not so rigid that they do not possess a healthy resistance against the Judaeo-Christian fear of the sex life. It remains to be seen whether the recent advent of academic centres to both societies—the Liberal Arts College in Barbados, the East-West Centre of the University of Hawaii—will help in any way to break down those barriers.

The analogy collapses, of course, at the point of political identity. Hawaii launched a militant campaign for statehood. Barbados, by contrast, undertook no similar campaign for independence. It took, rather, the line of least resistance, founded on the Adams deference to Colonial Office 'leadership'. Membership in the West Indies Federation made, as with others, for further delay, while after 1962 time was wasted in the continuing futile effort to organize, once again under British guidance, some sort of Eastern Caribbean federal structure. It was only in 1965 that the Barbadian leadership finally released itself from that thralldom to demand outright independence alone,[50] posited on the general principle that the contrivance of federal constitutions had been for the past one hundred years an inevitable act of final absolution performed by departing British officialdom and followed, almost without exception, by the subsequent collapse of the schemes.[51] The London psycho-complex of the Adams school has finally given way to a new note of nationalist self-help; men like Barrow, Crawford and Walcott use a language of cosmopolitan reference quite new, whether they are debating the 'small island' complex, the need to take non-British small economies as models for economic development, British immigration policies, the continuing mercantilism of British trade policies or the question of Caribbean unity; the remark of the late 'T. T.' Lewis, that in Barbados the sincerity of a white man's behaviour is rarely taken for granted, clearly looks like becoming part of the burgeoning Barbadian foreign policy. It would certainly be difficult to imagine Mr Barrow repeating Sir Grantley's observation, when he was in power, that the visit of Mr Harold Macmillan, as British Premier, to the island constituted the greatest event in West Indian history since Emancipation. At the same time, the new leadership helps create a new political style, so that the malicious scandal mongering of Barbadian political meetings, encouraged as it has been both by the cultural and political illiteracy of the mass audience and the peculiar double-member constituency system, is gradually giving way to the PNM mode of serious political discussion.

There is, finally, a new note of self-confidence. Barbadians increasingly believe that they can 'go it alone', that they can now manage on the basis of Sir Keith Walcott's observation that it is better to govern yourself badly than to be governed by somebody else. There is a new conviction, summed up in the important speech of the Leader of the House in August 1963, that Barbados already possesses the four essential prerequisites to independence: a sense of national unity, political experience based on democratic foundations, administrative capacity in the form of a seasoned civil service structure, and a sound economy.[52] Barbadian conservatism will certainly continue to resist that line of argument. But theirs is certain to be a weak minority outlook especially as local public opinion begins to realize that the 'mother country' is increasingly disinterested in filial affection. In that respect, the local reaction to the racialist immigration regulations promulgated in 1965 by the British Labour Government suggests that Barbadian public opinion is rapidly shedding its traditional Anglophilism under the pressure of unpleasant realities. It is a harsh medicine. But in the long run it can only do good. Deprived of the British protective umbrella Barbadians will learn to fend for themselves under the Caribbean sun.

# Chapter X

# THE EMERGENCE OF NATIONAL SOCIETY

## GUYANA

FEW CARIBBEAN territories have exercised such a potent hold over the English imagination as Guyana, as the literature from Ralegh's early panegyric of 1596 to W. H. Hudson's *Green Mansions* and Conan Doyle's *Lost World* sufficiently testifies. The vast hinterland of jungle, savannah, and river—geographically, constituting a part of the enormous watershed system of the Amazon-Orinoco river complex—has excited its own special library written by the earlier missionaries and the later travellers, including the work of the curious band of creolized English exiles—Michael McTurk, Barrington Brown, Sir Everard im Thurn, Walter and Vincent Roth—who, variously as magistrates, government surveyors, museum curators, and Indian Commissioners, have contributed so much to the scientific understanding of the interior regions and their Amerindian folk-culture. Ever since the Elizabethan exaggerations of Ralegh's account, who dreamed that he could subjugate the mysterious Empire of Guiana as Cortés had subjugated the Aztec Empire, the myth of the Guyanese El Dorado has enslaved both expatriate and creole, and its most recent manifestation, the cult of 'continental destiny', explains much of contemporary Guyanese political attitudes. That they are a people apart from the West Indian islands has become a fixed article of Guyanese national faith—the refusal to enter the Federation was symptomatic—despite the general economic fact that Guyana, in essence, is itself, with its heavily populated and intensely cultivated coastal strip, a West Indian-type sugar economy the thralldom of which may, in some problematical future, be ended by a rational exploitation of the interior resources; but this, so far, is a dream only. Guyana, indeed, is a fascinating complex of strident paradoxes: the paradox between the overdeveloped coastlands and the underdeveloped hinterland; between the continental dream and the 'coastal mentality'; between the two sub-economies, whose mutual isolation from each other is only now breaking down, of an Indian agriculture and a Negro commercial urbanism; between the theory of a Pan-American fraternal alliance with the Latin neighbours and the brooding omni-presence of the Venezuelan threat to Guyanese territorial integrity in the form of the famous boundary dispute; between, all this is to say, a denial of West Indianism feeding on the obsessional dream of massive interior development, and an actual attitude to the in-terior which is compounded of fear and ignorance, summed up in one observer's remark that 'although man has carved out this little kingdom for himself, yet crouching all around, ready to pounce and regain what it had lost, was the spirit of that great impenetrable bush with its hostile denizens'.[1] It is perhaps not too much to say that the outsider's own attitude to Guyana might often depend upon what particular school of the various authors on the country he reads, those for whom Georgetown is the centre of national life and those for whom it merely constitutes a necessary and irritating way station on the road to the inland paradise.

This pervasive feeling, that Guyana is geographically and econo-mically different from the other Caribbean lands—the leading Opposition point in the Legislative Council's debate on Federation of March 1955[2]—has tended to obscure the general truth that the historical development of the Guyanese society has been shaped by the same forces shaping the development of the island colonies— colonization, slavery, sugar monoculture, the Crown Colony system. There was the same diffusion of English culture forms which made it so difficult for Guyanese, as for island West Indians, to build up the inborn sense of cultural tradition so essential to self-confidence; and, surprisingly, that process was not countermanded by any continuing Dutch cultural influence after the transfer of 1803, save, perhaps, for the continuing influence of the unique cultural abilities of the Dutch to deal with the problems of water control. For the resident Dutch population dwindled away so rapidly after the transfer by 1916 there was no difficulty in the final displacement of Roman-Dutch law by English law as a result of the seminal Report (1914) of the Commission of Enquiry two years earlier (quite unlike the different process that took place in Franco-British St Lucia).[3] There was the same transcending fact of race admixture carried on between resident ethnic stocks over a period of centuries and all of its tragic results, classically annotated in the great saga of Mittel-holzter's Kaywana series of novels. There was the same transition, with all of its difficulties, from a slave system to a free society after Emancipation; a transition, indeed, so traumatic that present day Guyanese, like Barbadians or Jamaicans, continue to refer to a slave past abolished over a century ago as if it were a continuing factor in their present discontents; as if, in Dr Raymond Smith's apt phrase, one were to attribute Britain's balance-of-payments problems to the Napoleonic Wars.[4] There was, finally the same Crown Colony system of government, only modified by the peculiarly Guyanese incorporation of the old Dutch institutions of the Court of Policy and the Combined Court as legislative-cum-executive bodies into the British colonial framework. Geographical size, perhaps, did affect somewhat the working of the system, exemplified for example in the need for the Legislative Council to go on tour to the more isolated districts, the 1952 trip, for instance, into the Essequibo and North West districts graphically described by Vincent Roth.[5] But it was the same Crown Colony regime, in which the Governor, as elsewhere, was the lynch-pin of an autocratic machine of government. The psychological consequences of the system, especially as they affected the Guyanese politician type, were also the same as elsewhere and are not to be regarded, as some English writers too readily assume, as peculiar to the Guyanese psychology.[6]

Even so, of course, within the general framework there are always individual idiosyncrasies. For in degree, not so much in kind, it is true that Guyanese development was in many ways quite special. It would, indeed, have had to be special in order to explain why the breakdown of the British imperial system after 1953 took on forms that it did not take on elsewhere: the collapse of the local political consensus on fundamentals, the growth of politicized racism, the decision of the imperial power to withdraw its traditional tolerance of national independence movements, the eruption of violence of a kind quite different from the usual West Indian street violence, which is contained by a ritual all of its own, the final demoralization of the society itself between 1962 and 1964. The basic constructs in that general process—Negro-Indian conflict and the rise, after 1950, of the People's Progressive Party—had their genesis, after all, in the historical Guyanese society. The peculiar factors that helped shape the society were, perhaps, three in number. There was, first, the racial divisionism arising out of imperial population policy; secondly, the big plantation system fostered by the peculiar demands of Guyanese geography; and, third, the domination of the small colonial economy by a few giant firms, notably the mammoth Bookers' organization which penetrates into almost every nook and cranny of the Guyanese economy and the Guyanese communal psychology alike.

For if today the chief problem is that of the successful integration of the various ethnic groups into a common Guyanese culture it is urgent to recall that the problem arises from the system of Indian indentured contract labour permitted by the British governments of the nineteenth century to a planter class anxious to find a cheap labour source and reluctant to come to terms of reasonable accommodation with the newly emancipated Negro labourer. The result was the well-known pattern of Indian, Chinese and Madeiran Portuguese immigration from 1838 to 1917. The terms of the process were set almost exclusively by the planter interests, resisting as they did any metropolitan supervision, and using the most reprehensible weapons in that fight, including the traditional device of stopping the supplies of the local government structure. The planter wanted only male labour; so the recruiting agencies, neglecting the familial character of Indian life, helped create the sexual disparity in the plantation life which played havoc, even into the modern period, with Indian family organization. It is worth noting that in the separate Chinese immigration scheme, between 1853 and 1879, the planter likewise adopted policies—the cancellation, for example, of the allotment system, so much a bond of connection between the emigrant and home, and the refusal to guarantee a paid return passage—which exposed the essentially dehumanizing character of 'free' emigration.[7] The sort of life that awaited the contract immigrant is fully attested to in the documentation of the period: Beaumont's *The New Slavery*, the Des Voeux Enquiry of 1870, the Report of the Pillai-Tivany Delegation of 1922; not surprisingly, Indian educated opinion finally secured the termination of the traffic in 1917. The later post-war efforts of the Guyanese planter class to secure a free emigration scheme collapsed due to their characteristic parsimony and the fact that they wanted cheap estate labour while the Indian Government was only interested in genuine settlement schemes, always the pet aversion of the sugar barons. The planter mentality was exemplified for what it was in the abortive attempt, at the same time, to obtain immigrants from the Indian Native States, 'whose princes exercise autocratic sway within their own domains, so that it would not be necessary to secure the favour of either the Government of India or the extremist Indian politicians . . .'[8]

The transplanted Indian labourer, altogether, lived a degraded life just above the poverty line, enjoying a theoretical equality but, for all practical purposes, disenfranchised because illiterate, and illiterate because denied equal access to educational opportunities. The characteristic separation of town and countryside, so typically colonial, thus became transformed into a racial separation between Negro and Indian. For that process of racial-economic polarization was not in any way offset by the perennial dream, as in the Veness book of 1866, of colonization by English small farmer emigration, sabotaged as it was by the official policy of keeping Crown Lands so expensive as to make them unavailable for settlement schemes that might depopulate the coastal area and thus embarrass the planter.[9] Nor did the Portuguese and Chinese immigration streams seriously alter the situation. For the Portuguese early on became the base of the small shopkeeper class in the country districts (whom not even the later Chinese could oust), earning the hostility of both of the major ethnic groups because of their anomalous position as racial whites with a relatively low ascriptive status; while the Chinese rapidly deserted the estates to organize their strategic control of the town grocery trade or to become, like the notable John Ho A-Shoo, a pioneer in the exploitation of the shopping business of the emergent gold-bearing districts of the interior. Neither of them came to constitute, like the Javanese group in Surinam, a middle section that could play the role of broker between Indian peasant and Negro urban worker. So, since those two racial groups had been thus originally introduced into the colonial life with specific occupational roles they came to constitute two separate worlds. It was the breakdown of that separatism, increasingly evident after 1945, under the pressure of new occupational and geographical mobilities that set the stage for the present-day ordeal of Guyana.

The second general explanatory factor is the character of the Guyanese dualistic economy, with its tragic contrast between the advanced technical endowment of capitalist export production and the stagnation of the domestic sector. More than Trinidad or Jamaica, this has been the colonial export economy *par excellence*. The absentee character of English colonialism, as compared with the Dutch residential temperament, was noted early on by the eighteenth-century travellers to the Guiana settlements,[10] and it became the economy's leading feature after the transfer of sovereignty. The typical sugar estate came to be part of a highly centralized operation run by a managerial class for absentee share-holders; while the industry as a whole, under the rule of the Sugar Producers' Association, was characterized, unlike the multiple ownership system of Barbados, by intense corporate concentration. For the extraordinary hydrographic character of the territory— Guyana is essentially an aquatic country—has required, throughout, enormous capital outlays on drainage and irrigation schemes which only large operating units have been able to finance. The consequences of this seminal fact of the economy have been serious and far-reaching. It meant that, in the absence of government plan-ning, lines of development were left to the sugar interests, and it is worth noting that up until certainly the pre-war period before 1939 no complete survey of the national drainage, irrigation and navi-gational system had ever been made, by either private or govern-mental agencies, the colonial Government even admitting to the fact that it had not been official policy even to draw up a long range agricultural plan that would have included such a survey.[11] When, as in the modern post-war period, there have been, by contrast, massive modernizing schemes put under way, they have been the fruit of large scale colonial-capitalist technology. A further con-sequence of this was that at the same time the failure of a small scale peasant farmer class to grow up, along Jamaican lines, aggra-vated the sharp dualism of the system. The exception, of course, was the growth of the Guyanese rice peasantry. Yet the point to note there is that the growth was only made possible, against the hostility of the sugar interests, through the development after 1953 of government-financed irrigation, mechanization, milling and marketing schemes. Quite clearly, economic development in such a situation, whether it be large scale expansion of the present drainage-irrigation complex, the opening up of the interior, the exploitation of latent hydroelectric power or the provision, long overdue, of a modern communications system, requires organizational and financial resources on a scale comparable, say, to that of the TVA in the United States. The only question is whether such development will take place under corporate-private or public auspices. That question, so far, is unresolved. But what is certain is that if, as Ragatz asserted, the Guyana-Trinidad region constitutes a sort of West Indian frontier area in the American sense, at the same time it has so far signally failed to produce a frontier mentality in the Turner sense.

The social consequences of the plantation system were perhaps even graver. For plantations, classically, are culture regimes in which economic and technological forces shape an entire compendium of socio-cultural phenomena: housing, family patterns, recreational styles, the general life-style itself of the resident labouring population. In the Guyanese case, there was a comparative failure to develop a vigorous creole business class in other than the traditional lines of enterprise, in contrast to the growth of such a class in the Jamaican and Trinidadian economies. Thus there was less effective challenge to the system; and the recent Dumont Agricultural Report has noted how, despite modernization, the plantation mentality still survives to perpetuate the unhealthy contrast between the high technical level of sugar cane cultivation and the low level of rice cultivation, the small man's economy.[12] So, the social effects were correspondingly of a grossly disproportionate character. For a century or more, not only the industrial organization of the plantation, but the social life of its labour army, was controlled by the managerialist *élite* whose attitude, at the worst, was one of repressive harshness, at the best of condescending paternalism. The general picture, as late as the 1930's and 40's was a dismal one, that is, up until only recently, before new liberal policies were set in motion by what has been called the 'Georgetown outlook' of the new centralized bureaucratic headquarters of the industry.[13] The Report of the 1949 Commission of Enquiry, despite its exaggerated optimism, itself invoked the picture of the average sugar estate as a military organization run by the manager as its commanding officer; yet it envisaged the continuation of managerial control with only a few modifications, and offered no criticism of the significant fact, as it itself noted, that overseers and managers were, overwhelmingly, white ex-servicemen in whom the military caste of mind must have been dominant.[14] A reading of the *Report* of the Labour

Commission appointed by the local Government in 1935 or of those parts of the evidence relating to plantation problems presented to the visiting Moyne Commissioners in 1938 reveals a sugar economy characterized by exploitative wage levels, substandard 'range' housing, harsh overseers and deputy managers, the abuses of the system of the 'boy gangs', the indignities visited upon women as members of the estate working gangs and, not least of all, a diet so defective as to produce massive malnutrition and general sickness. The 1935 hearings annotated a primitive class struggle in company estates where trade union activity was virtually forbidden, so that grievances exploded, ultimately, in trials of brute strength characterized by intimidation wrought by roving gangs of strikers against 'blackleg' labour, the cutting of telephone wires, the erection of barricades against police brought in by estate management, and so on.[15] The truth was that the estates were private compounds in which the worker was dependent for almost all of his needs on management; one Moyne Commission witness reported that he had even been refused permission to take an official representative of the Government of India on to the estates.[16]

The demands of the British Guiana Labour Union and the British Guiana Workers' League at the time—a minimum wage, a contributory old age pensions scheme, slum clearance, an eight-hour day and security of tenure for estate workers—told the story.[17] The workers and their champions felt, not surprisingly, a deep distrust of the veracity of the evidence of the Sugar Producers' Association in the 1938 hearings; a perhaps natural distrust in the light of the arbitrary insertion into that evidence of rather fanciful descriptions of the make-up of the sugar worker as a person, clearly designed to serve as rationalizations for employer obscurantism, culminating in the citation of a description from, of all sources, a Jamaican conservative magazine in which the West Indian worker was described as 'essentially a gay, light-hearted, emotional person, fatalistic in his attitude to life, and as a rule taking no thought for the morrow ... His main requirements are food, shelter, bright and attractive clothing, a little spare money for gambling, and the opportunity for easy love-making'. How Sir Walter Citrine, as a member of the Commission, compelled the Sugar Producers' Association witnesses to withdraw that gratuitous piece of class mythology makes, even today, instructive reading.[18]

The plantation economy has also frequently become, everywhere it has existed, a political sub-entity, exercising political power in varying degree. In the Guyanese case the well-known expression of that phenomenon has been the amazing dominion of the Bookers' empire which, in its enormous ramifications, with its vital base in its sugar holdings—the company itself has claimed that it controls, directly and indirectly, the lives of some eighty per cent of the population, and it is a local axiom that Bookers will do everything except bury you—has become a veritable state within the state. The extractive and importation components of the colonial economy, separated elsewhere, were united in Bookers, so that an expatriate organization, controlled by a London directorate and accountable to British shareholders only, at one and the same time exported sugar to be refined elsewhere and helped import consumer items manufactured elsewhere; thus, the twin sides of the 'colonial pact', whereby the colonial economy produces what it does not consume and consumes what it does not produce, became centralized in a vast capitalist enterprise whose very efficiency, especially in the post-war period, merely served to aggravate the basic defects of the situation. Those defects—a highly mechanized sugar industry providing less and less employment, and a high propensity to import— thus became symbolized by Bookers; and if outside visitors deplore the emotional fixation that Guyanese public opinion has for the organization they fail to appreciate that the phenomenon has real economic foundations. The architecture of post-war Georgetown in itself symbolizes the realities of power secreted in the bitter national joke about 'Bookers Guiana', for the new Bookers' headquarters complex dominates that architecture, to the detriment of Government buildings.

The results of that situation have been almost endless. Recruitment to the managerial echelons of the organization, particularly since 'Guyanization' became official policy,[19] became a political weapon, especially as a means of anti-Jagan operations, and the exchange of correspondence between Sir 'Jock' Campbell and his American critic Philip Reno on that point did nothing to answer the charge that the officially declared policy of political neutrality has been grossly violated, and the violation condoned, by the activities of officials like Miss Anne Jardin; not to mention the earlier example of radicals like Robert Hart.[20] It is clear, indeed, that the pressures of political life in Georgetown have frequently inhibited the application by a local reactionary managerial group of policies fashioned by liberal directors in London. Apart from all this, Bookers symbolizes the 'coastal mentality'. It may be wrong to say, as Dr Jagan asserts, that the sugar empire has actively sabotaged schemes like the Hutchinson project for the opening up of the riverain lands. But it is certainly true that it has never enthusiastically supported them. It is equally true that, so far, the Bookers' leadership has shown little inclination to follow the advice of outside competent critics, so that, responding to the general fact that the old imperial framework within which Bookers grew up is now quite obsolete, the organization could conceivably become a miniature development company using its capital wealth to stimulate a vast programme of industrial diversification in co-operation with a local nationalist political regime.[21] Finally, there is the fact, of tremendous social importance, that Bookers became, in itself, an almost separate sovereign kingdom, undertaking and controlling an extensive set of essentially public services which the political state, for want of organizational skills and capital revenue, was unable itself to provide for its citizens. This produced the peculiar oddity of a society in which, as the authoritative Marshall Report of 1955 on local government put it, solid blocks of population received without charge social services frequently better than those provided by the local government authorities and were thus without any experience of some sort of self-government. The termination of this paternalism, whereby the sugar producer would be relieved of his special responsibility for public services on his terrain and would become subject, as he is not now, to normal taxation, both central and local, will be made especially difficult, the Report added, by the dependent mentality the system has produced in its recipients, which might necessitate intensive 'missionary' work to make local government palatable to them. In any case, the system must go, as assuredly as the equally undemocratic system of the District Commissioner must go.[22]

All of these factors helped turn out, in sum, the British Guiana of the immediate post-1945 period, on the eve of its continuing (1967) era of crisis. They were accompanied, naturally, by the usual system of Crown Colony government. The situation at the time of the prewar Moyne Commission hearings was typical. Under the 1928 constitution the colony, in effect, was ruled, in Daly's phrase, by the industrial government of sugar, by sugar, for the benefit of sugar. That constitution, it must be remembered, was itself the outcome of the 'rape of the constitution' in 1928, when, against the forceful 'Grand Remonstrance' of the elective members at that time, the old dual legislature with its popular control over finance, had been arbitrarily replaced with a legislative council controlled by an official majority and special reserve powers in the hands of the Governor. Care was always taken that the nominated members of the Executive Council represented the twin leading estates of Bookers and La Penitence, while the two elective members at that time, typically, were a legal adviser to Berbice sugar estates and a professional man out of touch with popular opinion. No provisions were made for the representation of labour, an omission severely criticized by the Moyne Commissioners in their subsequent Report. The Sugar Producers' Association and the Chamber of Commerce were always consulted, as a matter of course, when Government contemplated financial legislation. Likewise, in the lower level of local government, the spirit of the earlier 1914 changes—that the Government nominees to the Georgetown Town Council would always be technical men—had been perverted, so that by 1939 those nominees were representatives of financial interests. With notable exceptions, Swettenham, for example, and later Lethem, both of them enthused with the great Storm van 's Gravesande tradition, the average Governor took the *status quo* for granted, a process facilitated by the celerity of changes in the appointment: 'Each one,' observed a Moyne Commission witness acidly, 'prefaces his first year's stay with the remark that he must get acquainted with the problem, then in the second year he leaves and another man comes to get acquainted with the problem.'[23]

Continuity of imperial rule, of course, was provided by the permanent administrative bureaucracy, wholly expatriate at the top and imbued with a 'See, I am boss of my department' mentality.[24] Most of its members shared, perhaps unconsciously, the sugar industry values, so much so that a Commissioner of the Interior genuinely interested in the interior came to be a nine days' wonder. There was, naturally, the occasional exception. Thus, the great Guyanese hero of the doctrine of imperial responsibility is the figure of James Crosby, the most famous and most able of all Agent-generals for Immigration; but there has been no Guyanese Sanders of the River to give equal care to the Amerindian peoples. The English officials were 'little tin gods' in an authoritarian system. For the civil servant under their rule to criticize his department, or make a statement to a legislator, or write a letter to the press, was truly dangerous, while internal defence-mechanisms were absent due to the attitude of superior officers that employees were nonentities who had no right to form trade unions.[25] At his best, naturally, the English official could be superb, witness the remarkable Bain Gray report on education, a veritable state paper on colonial education. But even then the best was only made possible by an autocratic regime in which a strong-minded officer, like some other Macaulay, could impose his will against local professional opinion. The rule of that kind of officer, then, lasted until only very recently, as the 1959 fracas over the Postmaster General appointment of that year illustrated. This was a society, altogether, in which the economic power of the sugar complex and its mercantile offshoots impregnated, unwittingly, the total social and political ideology of the Guyanese public mind. It is suggestive, to take only a final example of that truth, that the leading private library in Georgetown today is still, that of the Royal Agricultural and Commercial Society, reflecting in its name, since its foundation in 1844, the pre-eminence of the planter and merchant cliques in the colonial life.

The present discontents of Guyana flow from all this. But it must be remembered, even so, that the struggle against the system pre-dated the contemporary struggle of the People's Progressive Party after 1950. The 1891 constitutional reforms had signalled, in fact, the emergence of a new political group comprising the 'coloured', the Negro professionals and Portuguese businessmen elected (as elective members) by a narrow electorate mainly Negro. For fifty years or more that group was the vanguard of the colonial resistance. The story has been told, in a racy and violent prose, by the Guyanese journalist-historian P. H. Daly[25] in the third volume, *The Assimilative State*, of his remarkable series. There was A. A. Thorne, whose fierce radicalism fought for progress through a continuing series of *causes célèbres*: the liberalization of Queen's College, the improvement of the Island Scholarship system, the attack, in the Bishop Swaby episode, upon the disgraceful discriminatory practices of the Anglican Church, the exposure of the public hospital scandals, the struggle, only fulfilled after his death, for a local university. There was A. R. F. Webber who, in his adventurous life as editor, party organizer and Council member, fought with a defiant pertinacity equal to Thorne's all the evils of colonial government and wrote, unusual for a coloured author, a minor classic on the life of the East Indian immigrant, *Those That Be in Bondage*. There were the other politicians who led the Opposition group to government— Edun, Eleazer, Lee, Jacob, Sir Alfred Crane. All of them kept alive the oppositionist spirit in a system that so easily stifled it by elevating the potentially dangerous elective member to membership of the Executive Council where, in Daly's phrase, his lips were sealed as firmly as a confessor's, as, indeed, happened in the case of the lawyer-politicians of the remarkable Luckhoo dynasty.[26]

Yet this was a limited struggle only. For the group, altogether, was at best a small *élite* of educated Creoles seeking, as they saw it, a legitimate share in government rather than the complete over-throw of colonialism, as, indeed, was evident enough in their 'Grand Remonstrance' against the constitutional changes of 1928. Thorne, like Cipriani, accepted uncritically the assumptions of British Labour Party thought. Edun wrote a curious book on the ideals of the British Empire. They fought, generally, the abuses of colonialism rather than the idea of colonialism: Governor Guggisberg's hare-brained scheme of 1929, for example, to replace the elected local councils with an African-style Commissioner system, or the astonishing Jewish immigration fiasco of 1938, in which the British Government proposed to set up an autonomous Jewish refugee settlement in Guyana, including separate representation of the domiciled Jews in the local legislature, a reform measure hitherto denied to Guyanese themselves. They were political independents, for the old Popular Party was less a mass action party than a Georgetown electoral machine. Culturally, they were British, an attitude summed up in Thorne's observation, with its fatal presumption that Guyanese Africans only had the British cultural model to look up to, that 'We would be lacking in gratitude if we cut loose from the West Indies with their British outlook and declare ourselves a separate unit where we have the two major races at each other's throat, and where one race would say, "We look to India", and the other, "We look to Great Britain".'[27] They wanted universal suffrage, it is true. Yet even there the father of Guyanese unionism, Hubert Critchlow, whose British Guiana Labour Union had advocated the reform as far back as 1925, himself came to feel some wavering doubts late in the day about giving the vote to people who might be fooled, as he saw it, by any kind of thing.[28]

They sowed where others later reaped. For it would be idle to deny their achievement, whatever its ideological ambiguities. It was, as Daly insisted, summing it up in 1943, the first upsurge in a great psychological movement of national consciousness. They were producing genuinely 'representative men' who, already ascendant in industrial government, would inevitably rule the political government. They forged a new public opinion compelling the colonial masters, over the years, to behave more circumspectly.[29] Not least of all, Daly's volumes themselves bespoke a minor revolution, for they were books written by Guyanese journalism for a Guyanese audience, replacing the earlier tradition, as seen in Bryant and Rodway, of books written for a scholarly audience abroad. And they successfully challenged the prejudices of those earlier writings, especially the calumny of the 'despised races', African, Indian, Chinese, Portuguese, penned by the slavery bias of Rodway.[30] By 1945, all in all, it was time for a new movement to build anew on those foundations.

The salient facts of the post-war Guyanese 'permanent crisis' are well known: the rise after 1950 of the bi-racial People's Progressive Party (PPP), replacing the old racialist organizations of the East Indian Association and the League of Coloured Peoples; the electoral victory of 1953 and, in the same year, the suspension of the constitution by a characteristic act of Churchillian gunboat diplomacy; the subsequent interregnum marked by the split between the Jaganite and Burnhamite factions leading, almost inexorably, to the growth after 1962 of widespread racial-political violence; the imposition of the Sandys formula of proportional representation designed, as actually occurred in 1964, to overthrow the Jagan Government under a thin guise of constitutionalism; the emergence of Forbes Burnham as the 'favourite son' of the Anglo-American alliance seeking to bring Guyana into the fold of the 'free world'; and, over all, the final and almost total demoralization of the society, making of the act of independence (1966) simply one more step in the complex power play at once cause and effect of that demoralization. And all of this, be it noted, has been reported in the world press in generally paranoiac Cold War terms as a struggle of 'freedom' against the rise of 'communism', with Dr Jagan and his wife cast in the role of the villains of the piece; so that it has been almost impossible for the foreign reader to understand the concatenation of forces seeking to break out of the shell of the Guyanese colonial framework, whether that framework be seen as the old British regime or the new American neo-colonial regime.

For what the arrival of universal suffrage in 1953 did was to precipitate the cardinal element of the situation: the direct entry of the masses into the state electoral machinery—from which, as colonial subjects, they had hitherto been alienated—and the progressive direction given to their new social energy by a single popular political organization, the PPP, enjoying as it did the support of the sugar worker, the rice farmer, the small shopkeeper, the waterfront worker, the small businessman and the young professional. In the light of what subsequently happened it is vital to remember that movement was united in its socialist ideology (even after the 1955 split, as the 1961 election literature showed, the Burnhamite People's National Congress (PNC) agreed at least on ideological fundamentals with the Jaganite PPP); it was thoroughly constitutionalist, being willing, in 1953, to seek to work a clearly unworkable constitution; and if Dr Jagan's socialism was Marxist it was a Marxism, after all, picked up from an American and not a Russian experience. The charges brought against the movement's short-lived Government of 133 days to justify the British suspension were pitiably unconvincing. That the Cabinet sought to set up a monolithic Communist state, to be prefaced by the planning of a general conflagration in Georgetown (a shrewd charge since West Indian populations, in their wooden house towns, live in constant fear of fire) was supported by supposed evidence of police informers that was never released for critical examination. Alternatively, the Government's proposal to remove ecclesiastical control of the schools (a principle long since accepted in the United Kingdom itself), or its removal of repressive legislation against the importation of radical literature into the colony (a liberal measure more than a Marxist one), or the decision of the political leaders to remain, while in office, the heads of their trade unions (a practice, after all, made sufficiently respectable by Bustamante in the Jamaican setting), all were cited as evidence of insurrectionary plotting. The Report of the 1954 Commission of Enquiry indeed, was replete not with concrete evidence but with the dubious doctrine of tendency. 'Worry and apprehension as to what might happen at any time'[31] was the leading note of its essentially Mc-Carthyite logic, descending into a comic vein when it recited, as 'evidence' of ministerial malevolence, the 'insolent and insulting references' made by the ministers to the Governor and his *ex-officio* aids, as if such public language was not a standard feature in the turbulent politics of all of the West Indian Crown Colony islands. So fictitious, indeed, was the 'plot' attributed to the elected majority members, and the atmosphere of 'violence' it was supposed to have engendered, that when British combat troops disembarked to put an end to it all they found nothing more insurrectionary than an inter-island cricket match—the final ironic British touch—in progress. As a piece of Churchillian *opéra bouffe* politics the whole episode took its place with the Siege of Sidney Street and the Napoleonic antics of the 1926 General Strike. It is difficult not to read the White Paper and not become aware of a serious decline in the traditional veracity and fearless respect for the facts usually associated with British official documents, not least of all in the field of the colonial empire. If, indeed, 1953 saw Georgetown in a 'state of turmoil', full of 'tension' and 'distinct danger of real trouble'—all of them terms loosely used in the Report—it would require some imaginative ingenuity to discover language sufficiently appropriate for the state of the capital city in the years after 1962.[32]

The truth is, indubitably, that 1953 can only be understood in the light of the environmental factors, internal and external, at work at the time. The internal factor was the special character of the PPP. The real offence of Dr Jagan, apparently, was that, simply, he meant what he said when, with his colleagues, he declared open war upon the colonial economic-political alliance that dominated the territory. He organized what Janet Jagan called a politics of exposure. His was, almost for the first time, the raised voice of the rural disinherited traditionally forgotten by a class of Georgetown politicians who, as the Waddington Commission of 1951 pointed out, possessed no roots in their constituencies and professed, when elected, little active care for the interests of the constituents.[33] As the new leadership saw the problem, it was open to serious doubt as to whether a constitutional instrument like that of the 1953 reforms, in which they held the shadow of power while British officialdom held the substance, could either facilitate or permit the fundamental changes they wanted. As, indeed, they really did want; this was not a case, Barbados-style, of colonial 'labour' parties using a left-wing phraseology in the service of mild reform. They inevitably collided, then, with the unwritten rules of British colonial cricket in which the native political class enters into a 'partnership' with a benign officialdom which means, in effect, partnership on imperial, not local terms, that is, terms envisaging not the socialist elimination of the colonial 'enclave economy' but its continuing existence with minor modifications. In such a relationship, the local leaders are expected, in Governor Renison's phrase in the Guyanese case, to be men of 'the required balance', wise enough to embrace the 'spirit of a new Elizabethan Commonwealth'.[34] Professor Smith has suggested that 'any sensible politician' would have accepted this line of action since, in the end, it is his royal road to political independence.[35] Yet both the Manley forces in Jamaica and the Williams forces in Trinidad having taken that path find themselves today with a hollow victory in their hands, with their societies still unnaturally bifurcated between a local political power and an expatriate economic power. The PPP, in brief, was interested primarily in the total transfer of power, less so in implementing its reform programme. The British political mind, basically gradualist, could neither understand nor tolerate such an unpardonable violation of its democratic mythology.

The external factor at work was, of course, the climate of international affairs in the 1950's. For Guyana was, in effect, the victim of the Cold War. Churchillian romantic imperialism, less ready than its Labour predecessor to promote the liquidation of the empire, rapidly relinquished the traditional benignity of British governments to the colonial people's movements. Even more, it relinquished its own imperial pride as it became the junior partner of the new Atlantic alliance. Seen from this angle, 1953 was an explosion marking the direct confrontation of two basic forces: (1) a local nationalist movement seeking to call the bluff, as its leaders saw it, of the British and (2) the new American global imperialism taking over the defence of the Western social order from a bankrupt British imperialism. In the Guatemalan affair of 1954 that meant open American intervention openly confessed by the President.[36]

In the Guyana case it meant, starting after 1953 and increasing in intensity during the 60's as the Cuban Revolution shattered American nerves, a clandestine interference never openly acknowledged but, by now, sufficiently attested to by much evidence. The claim to a 'new Elizabethan Commonwealth', in the light of this, was a mockery of words. The British Labour Party, in whose goodwill Dr Jagan mistakenly chose to believe, shared in that mockery. It refused its official aid to the ousted government and, in fact, actively facilitated the subsequent disintegration of the Guyanese popular front by encouraging the Burnhamite secession. Patrick Gordon-Walker's efforts to promote that secession make revealing reading.[37] No less revealing for the unconscious racial snobbery that is latent even in British socialists was the Rev. Donald Soper's vapid reference, after a flying visit to Georgetown, to 'these simple Africans and kindly Indians' misled by 'Marxist agitators'.[38]

Imperialist culpability, here, is undeniable. Much of 1953 and after was caused by the imperialist need to smash the remarkable unity of the Guyanese African-Indian majority, a unity beyond the genius of the PNM to accomplish, by contrast, in Trinidad. At the same time, of course, the disintegration of the popular movement, precipitated by the imperialist interventionism, had its own roots, *sui generis*, in the nature of Guyanese society. The theories seeking to explain this internal factor are varied and rarely persuasive. There is the theory of 'politics', that racial disharmony has been visited upon a once peaceful community by power-hungry 'politicians', put forward, for example, in the various pamphlets of Norman E. Cameron. Any virtue the thesis may have disappears once it is noted that it is usually advanced either, paradoxically, by men who are themselves political aspirants,[39] or by the economic oligarchy: the remark of the usually liberal-minded Sir 'Jock' Campbell— that Bookers' acceptance of Guyanese nationalism must not mean that 'we must help to throw the people to a pack of political wolves who wait with slobbering jaws to strengthen themselves upon their unsuspecting prey'—is suggestive.[40] Allied to this is the related theory that, granted the legitimacy of politics in a free society, the game has been compromised in Guyana by inflexibly-minded leaders, on both sides, who should now resign; the theory is especially popular with Guyanese groups abroad frequently out of touch with the local realities.[41] Or, more generally, there is the theory of an ideological split between Burnhamite socialism and Jaganite communism. Yet, programmatically, as all observers have noted, there has remained throughout the continuing power struggle a very real unanimity about the final goals of independence, socialism and a planned economy. Even the principles of strategy have been roughly identical for both sides inherited the constitutionalism of the original parent body of the national movement. It was only after 1961, as a matter of fact, that the PNC abandoned the cloak of constitutional legalism and resorted to the street violence of the February 1962 riots; while the PPP throughout accepted the electoral framework, thus incidentally exploding the American myth that no Marxist party can come to power in a Western society by benefit of free elections. Traditional constitutional theory, as a matter of fact, has little real applicability in the Guyanese colonial setting where, against all the Cold War myths, it is the 'democratic socialist' group that has stepped outside of the constitutional framework and the 'communist' group that has remained within it.

The most satisfying theoretical explanation, almost certainly, is that posited on the recognition of Guyana as an unintegrated poly-ethnic society. For the split of 1955 was a clear-cut racial division, with the PPP base in the rice farmers, field sugar workers, and the Indian middle class, and that of the dissident PNC in the African elements of the working class, mostly urban workers, and the Negro middle class groups that had supported, often clandestinely, the original PPP. It could be argued, indeed, that it was a fictitious split in the sense that, as the incisive 1963 analysis of the *New World* group interpreted the situation, there had never really been a real unity. The original coalition, that is, represented only an advance along the road to unity; it was not itself the embodiment of that unity. What happened is that, for the first time, the society saw its unintegrated condition, that is to say, realized the full significance of the group differences in terms of political action and public policy. But the condition, of course, had been there all along.[42] Seen from this viewpoint, it no longer becomes a question of the personal faults of the individual leaders, Jagan's 'inflexibility' or Burnham's 'opportunism', for the dual charisma of Jagan-Burnham only reflects the play of those deeper forces. The thesis of 'politics', among others, thus collapses, for it fails to see that the political difficulties are themselves part of the cultural condition and serve only to indicate the particular point that has been reached, at any one moment, in the trajectory of cultural evolution.

Indian fear of the Negro, Negro contempt for the Indian, had long since become deeply imbedded attitudes. It may be true to say that most of the stereotypes thereby let loose—that Indians are provident and Africans profligate, that Africans are gregarious and Indians clannish—were gross prejudices purveyed usually by outsiders, summed up in the slanderous comment of a British agricultural 'expert' of 1927 that 'contact with the African races has led to a more thriftless and indolent mode of life (in the East Indians) and the temperate habits enforced in India by the struggle for existence, the joint family system and caste scruples no longer exist'.[43] But it is true, nonetheless, that the stereotypes have had powerful indigenous psychological roots. There was a marked sense of physical aversion between the members of the two groups, as the low rate of inter-racial marriage perhaps reflects. There was the feeling that, as indentured low-wage labourers, the Indians had 'destroyed' the economic position of the Negro worker; conversely, the pro-Indian apologetics insisted that the Indians had 'saved' the economy by their willingness to accept sacrifices the Negro spurned to make: a thesis that ignored, incidentally, the rise of a distinctly Negro peasantry in the post-Emancipation period. The differences between the groups, concededly, were at bottom economic, for the Africans, in the main, were an urban mass hating the land and its slave memory and identifying itself with its middle class brethren who had become the white collar proconsuls of the colonial structure, while the Indians were a rural mass trapped in the sugar estate prison. But the differences came to express themselves in racial terms. The Marxist language of the original PPP united front, itself an imported ideology, had little power to withstand the pressures of that situation, and the Left Creoles, like Sydney King and Martin Carter, significantly failed to breach those cultural barriers in their doctrinal struggle after 1955, first with Burnham and then with Jagan.

The society, all this is to say, was more divided vertically along racial-cultural lines than it was divided horizontally along class lines; or, more exactly, being in fact divided in both senses, it was to the racial-cultural identity that the masses turned as they were driven to find some sort of haven from mutual division and self-contempt. This, of course, was not always easily recognizable. Both the knowledgeable outside observer, like Dr Raymond Smith in 1962, and the local analyst, like the *New World* group in 1963, were optimistic, even in the early 60's, that racism would not become a leading and permanent factor, the latter even envisaging, on the very eve of the 1964 racial warfare, a new bi-racial coalition which would regroup the latent national forces into a final united push for independence.[44] To see the problem, almost equally optimistically, in Marxist terms of economic rationality, as in the Philip Reno pamphlet which almost manages to say nothing about the racial element,[45] is to fail to appreciate how brutally powerful racial group feeling must have been to so completely destroy the original proletarian unity of 1950. And, one may add, to so completely destroy the hope of its resuscitation, not to mention the re-emergence of new political alignments along economic interest lines; certainly as late as 1966, at the time of independence, there was little evidence to indicate that the Left element of the PNC would seek out its ideological counterparts in the PPP or that there was any move to the PNC on the part of conservative Indian elements.

The ordeal of Guyana, rather, has been that of the shock of self-recognition. The breakdown of the old imperial system laid bare, in all of its nudity, the hitherto repressed conflict, at once racial and economic, of the society. Yet it has to be noted that it was not so much the ethnic division of the society as it was, ironically, the accelerating collapse of the division, that brought on the crisis. What some Guyanese nostalgically remember as the 'good old days' of racial harmony was, frankly, a 'harmony' only made possible by the physical separation of the races. The Georgetown Negro could afford to take a tolerant view of the rural Indian, like the northern American liberal being broadminded about the American Negro of the Deep South, because he never, or rarely saw him. The most important single fact of the last twenty-five years, perhaps, has been the rude shattering of this complacency by (1) the increasing social and occupational mobility of the educated Indian, and (2) the drift from the land under the pressure of labour-saving technical changes in the sugar industry. The first process was well under way even at the end of the First World War period and by the time that one of its leading personal embodiments, the aged patriarch of the Luckhoo family, Joseph Alexander Luckhoo, died in 1949 it had become a minor social revolution. The voluminous mass of evidence offered to the International Commission of Jurists that investigated the 'imbalance' problem in 1965 attests to its present dimensions. By that date Indians accounted for nearly 35 per cent of posts in the public service as a whole, with an even higher percentage in the professional technical grades; there were more Indian male primary schoolteachers than Negro or mixed, despite the popular belief that it is the Negro who has been the traditional teacher of Guyana; the Public Health Department of the Georgetown Town Council had more than 50 per cent Indian employees; the Police Force was still, as always, predominantly Negro, but in the new Special Service Unit (1964) some fifty-six Negroes had been recruited to some sixty-nine Indians; whereas in 1938 the highest posts reached by Indians in the public service had been as medical officers or magistrates, by 1965 there obtained no barrier to the highest positions, evidenced by Indian occupation of such varied appointments as Chief Justice, Commissioner of Titles, Commissioner of Inland Revenue and Chief Works and Hydraulics Officer; while if, as a final example, the Civil Service Association presently had no Indian members on its executive that was because of political withdrawals during the 1962–63 crisis and not because of discrimination, the Association in earlier years having had, in fact, a number of Indian presidents. All in all, there could be no foundation in 1965 for the notion that Indians were under-represented in the major sectors of governmental activity. What the evidence in part did suggest, in fact, was the presence not of ethnic but sexual imbalance, and within the Indian group itself, where the continuing under-representation of female East Indians both in the public service and in the teaching profession as a whole reflected the legacy of early marriage and a male-dominated family life leading to the seclusion of its female members.[46]

The second process—the desertion of rural occupations—was, in part, a corollary of the first. For as the Negro monopoly of the school system gave way to make room for Indian children hitherto discriminated against both by reason of parental conservatism and official discouragement (it was not until 1933 that compulsory education for Indian girls was accepted, thus ending the long scandal of the Swettenham Circular that had in fact made possible official connivance at Indian parental reluctance to use the school system), the educated young Indian moved away from the traditional occupation of farming and small business into those of the civil service and the teaching profession. The old regime, then, in which, to use Daly's phrase, the Indian was economically strong and educationally weak and the African educationally strong and economically weak, thus gave way as the Indian intellect struggled to recover its self-respect. This left behind, of course, an additional crop of ethnic stereotypes, including the argument, popular as late as 1965 with many of the ICJ witnesses, that the Indian, being 'acquisitive', did not 'want' education; the truth being, of course, that, as the British Guiana Teachers' Association pointed out, these Indian attitudes had been shaped, overwhelmingly, by economic forces, not by natural laws, the terrible struggle, for example, for economic survival in the estate system, a struggle which, in turn, had not been alleviated by any real attempt of either plantocracy or Government to help.[47] As the Indian, in any case, thus belatedly took advantage of educational opportunity he was enabled, as much as the Negro, to escape the prison of agricultural toil. Just one example only of his new freedom is to be seen in the fact, on reading the two accounts of Guyanese boyhood, Jan Carew's *Black Midas* and Lauchmonen's *Guiana Boy*, that both of their hero-figures, in a sort of Huckleberry Finn fashion, finally leave the ancestral land, the Negro boy leaving his Negro coastal village for the life of the interior 'pork knocker', the quasi-legendary Guyanese gold-digger, the Indian boy leaving his Berbice sugar estate home for Georgetown.

The end-result of these two processes was, as of today, a society in which the old rigid correlations between occupation and ethnic origin have increasingly broken down. The breakdown precipitated a mutual confrontation of both ethnic groups on a common ground. The post-1953 period, and especially the events of 1962–64, may be viewed, in one way, as the social and political expression of what for many Guyanese must have been a traumatic experience. The Negro and mixed groups rationalized their fears in terms of a theory of Indian communal 'aggressiveness'. But the very ambiguity of the charge proved how pathological it was for if, on the one hand, it was charged that Indians wanted to build a 'new India' in Guyana, on the other hand it was charged that they never looked to Guyana as their home. Ruhomon's centennial history is cited as evidence of an Indian 'plan of conquest'.[48] Yet that book, a typical expression of Indian cultural pride, evinced not a separatist tendency but, rather, a search for Indian equality within a Guyanese universe. It concluded, indeed, with a rapturous eulogy of the 'new freedom' that the Indian immigrant had found in Guyana, exaggerated perhaps, as Ruhomon noted of Kirke's earlier romanticized description, but real nonetheless.[49] The leading feature of the Indian story, indeed, is one of a steadily increasing absorption into the cultural mainstream of people who, because of historical circumstances, retained a greater cultural residue than their urban fellow Guyanese. The recent evidence of that process has been noted by Dr. Smith.[50] How little ground there is to fear the process is palpably evident in the light of the fact that, in the first place, it has been characterized by a positive deculturization of the rising Indian *élite* and the loss of the 'old' Indian customs, attenuated in any case, as those customs were, by the egalitarian pressure of Westernized life; early on, observers like Bronkhurst noted the absence of traditional Brahminical ritual in the religious life of the estates.[51] That denationalization has continued apace, unavoidably so, as Ruhomon admitted, in a community of mixed races where Western cultural standards prevailed, with their urge towards unity and uniformity.[52] In the second place, this process of integration was essentially non-revolutionary, being spearheaded by the new Indian middle class professional group combining cultural radicalism and social conservatism in their outlook; Ruhomon's account, for example, of the various riots of Indian labourers on the estates from 1872 to 1924 was couched, suggestively, in terms of 'law and order' challenged by the 'mob'.[53]

Yet the superordinate Creole culture chose to see all this in racial, not economic terms. It saw it as an Indian revolt, not as the creolization process of potentially new bourgeois allies in the class struggle. The attitude was expressed, early on in 1929, in the leading newspaper's editorial opinion that 'It was a mistaken policy to convey to the Indian community, undoubtedly a useful asset to the colony, the impression that they were indispensable to its future well-being and so produce that inflated spirit which led them, despite every concession made to them, to ask, like Oliver Twist, for more.'[54] Instead, then, of seeing the process, in Martin Carter's apt dualogy, as the demand of the agricultural sector, the 'field slave culture', for entry into the modernizing sector, the 'house slave culture', the Guyanese social-political Establishment preferred to see it as a slave rebellion, thus giving the lie, incidentally, to the later rationalization that it was opposed to the movement because, after 1950, it was 'communist'. The stage was thus set, by 1960, for open conflict. Not the least tragicomic aspect of it all was that the Negro urban groups, embracing the excuse of the 'aggressive' Indian, were accepting an excuse similar to that of the 'uppity nigger' theme directed against the Negro freedom movement in the United States.

The catastrophic deterioration of the Guyanese political order after 1960 has been fully described elsewhere.[55] It would be easy to interpret it all as a consciously engineered plot of imperialist villainy, as the official PPP theory argues. A large part of the African-Indian problem is indeed the direct creation of British colonialism. But it is not wholly its creation, and a long period of developing employment opportunities, probably only possible through a full industrialization programme, will be required to mitigate its acerbities. Guyanese politicians of all sides have shamelessly utilized the racialist appeal, and to argue that British Royal Commissions have 'set out to lay the foundations for suspicion and animosity between the Indian and African races' in order to buttress the declining influence of the 'European class' is to overlook the fact that those foundations existed long before the open conflict of the 1950's and 60's.[56]

Having said that, it remains true that British Tory policy, whether consciously seeking all that flowed out of the policy or not, was primarily responsible for the decision to get rid of Jaganism and that the Guyanese Negro leadership, along with the propaganda arsenal of the local ruling class, eagerly exploited the situation once the 1955 split in the PPP, actively promoted by the British-American alliance, assumed the proportions of a full-scale racial cleavage in the community. The 'communism' of the PPP was a pretext only, just as earlier in 1928 the British argument that the bankrupt condition of the colony was due to the old constitution, whereas in fact it was due to the collapse of the post-war world price-structure of sugar, had been used as a pretext to impose the full Crown Colony system upon the colony. 1953 was thus the beginning, whether consciously planned or not, of a counter-revolution in which all the forces of reaction—the Ishmael type of labour 'boss', the Portuguese businessman, the Negro civil servant, the American *agent provocateur*—joined in a unholy alliance against the PPP. The events of February 1962—the 18th Brumaire, as it were, to the 1848 of the proletarian drama of the early PPP achievement—were, in grim fact, an attempted *coup d'état* against a democratically elected government which included, among much else, the odd spectacle of businessmen closing their shop premises in order to permit their employees to riot in the streets, and of civil servants going on strike against the urgent appeal of the Governor to remain loyal to British norms of constitutional legality which, traditionally, the West Indian civil service mentality has slavishly copied and defended. The official Commission of Enquiry, despite its failure to comprehend the deeper implications of the situation, clearly defined its precipitating agents as (1) the political ambitions of the PNC, whose leader saw in Dr Jagan's downfall the opportunity for his own elevation, and (2) the class fears of the business forces, led politically by the United Force of the 'beer baron' D'Aguiar and blindly opposed to a government fiscal policy which, in its proposals for the reform of an obsolete tax system, the effective taxation of capital profits and the rational utilization of local savings channelled customarily into the socially unrewarding areas of real estate, moneylending and speculation, constituted a model of the fiscal proposals generally being urged at the same time by the American Alliance for Progress scheme upon Latin American governments.[57]

In 1963 the struggle shifted to the industrial front with trade union and business leaders organizing a fully politicized general strike, once again using a comparatively mild piece of proposed government legislation—a labour relations bill seeking to put an end, among much else, to the artificial power of the Man-Power Citizens' Association as a 'company union' operating as a right-wing political party in the sugar industry and patterned, in its leading clauses, after the New Deal Wagner Act—as a pretext. What was noticeable in that second stage was the growing anti-communist paranoia of the Georgetown business and professional classes and the open interference of the American trade union and State Department forces, including various formidable expenditures in support of the strike action. Neither of those anti-communist forces seems to have asked itself whether, in reality, it would ever have been possible for the Jagans to sovietize a social class as property-conscious and socially conservative as the Indian peasantry. The story, all in all, is bizarre. So much so that when a Guyanese playwright puts together, as in Slade Hopkinson's *Fall of a Chieftain*, a fictional account of a West Indian radical leader destroyed by a variety of factors, the fiction pales in comparison to the tremendous realities of the actual Guyanese situation.[58]

The poison released by all this has, by now (1968) deeply infected the bloodstream of Guyanese society. The society becomes polarized, in effect, into two clandestinely armed camps adopting, in Hobbes' phrase, the posture of armed gladiators one towards the other. Both sides create, secretly, their extremist echelons of thugs, always in the name of self-defence, who become, as it were, political expressions of the Georgetown 'choke and rob' boys. A political martyrology grows up in which the PPP names its bookstore after one of its Negro heroes and the PNC annually commemorates the 'Son Chapman' riverboat tragedy. The 'displaced person' emerges as the pathetic symbol of forced evacuation of Indian from Negro village and Negro from Indian village; and that, in turn, becomes the basis of a new physical separation of the races half-legitimizing, in its turn, the defeatist ideology of partition. There takes place a re-emergence of racial or neo-racial organizations, as each ethnic group, feeling itself defenceless in the face of near anarchy, feels compelled to build up new defence-mechanisms, which in turn feeds the habit of sectionalism. Hence the United Force as an alliance of Portuguese wealth and Amerindian 'backwardness', Sydney King's African Society for Cultural Relations with Independent Africa, the Guyana All Indian League, the Maha Sabha (Hindu) and the Anjuman (Muslim). Rudy Luck's effort to teach Cantonese at his high school indicates a possible Chinese development; while even a Black Muslim movement, which looks like a half-plausible solution in an Islamic-Negro Christian society, gets started. As general ideas rapidly wither in such an environment they give way to an increasing personalization of politics. Whole groups become known as 'Cheddi's boys' or 'Sydney's boys' or the Bhagwan entourage. Entire problems are left untouched and unresolved since, as each side becomes more and more dependent upon communal support, it becomes reluctant to deal with many of its own serious issues, whether it be the problem of the subjection of the Indian woman to Indian male conservatism or the existence of racial segregationist practices between white Canadian administrative staff and coloured workers in the Canadian-owned MacKenzie bauxite compound.

On a more general level, what has taken place is in fact the dis-integration of national consensus. The constituent elements of the national debate—socialism, independence, the possibility of coalition government, the very nature of Guyana itself—are seen by the opposing sides in completely different ways, so that while a Negro analyst can see the events after 1961 as evidence of a deliberate Indian plan of racial genocide the PPP Marxist sees them as evidence of imperialist subversion.[59] The efforts of groups like the Guyana Group for Social Studies to bridge the gulf fail because they are small middle-class groups reaching no wide audience and tempted, in any case, to take a literary rather than an anthropological view of the general Guyanese 'culture' they invoke.[60] It is little wonder that caught in all this, increasing numbers of Guyanese begin to believe that the only way in which they can live together is by a system of 'balance' in which each group is guaranteed participation in every institutional activity on the basis of population percentage quotas; which, if in fact accepted, would entrench a pattern of communalism alien to the Guyanese historical experience and constituting in the obvious difficulties of its administrative application something too ludicrous for serious consideration.[61]

But the most depressing example of all this has been, perhaps, the steady decline, in the years since 1955, in the quality of Guyanese political thought. The original Marxist ideology of 1950, so potentially creative as a tool for fashioning a truly Guyanese socialist analysis, rapidly became diluted under the pressure of events, both within the PPP and the PNC. This was so for a variety of reasons. First, there was the fact that the Marxism, filtered through the strainer of Russian Stalinism, was of a rigid and doctrinaire kind and never really faced up to the special dialectics of Guyanese reality, the difficulties, for example, of sovietizing a rice peasantry thoroughly individualistic in its thinking, or of applying the Russian nationalities policy to a colonial polyethnic society neatly balanced between two equal groups. The Jagan-King exchange of 1956 exposed that weakness, for the Jagan Congress speech of that year, as King pointed out, discussed the United Front concept as if the position of Stalin on that question for the China of 1925 was equally valid for the Guyanese situation a generation or so later; and, more generally, the speech quoted large doses of Stalinist *obiter dicta* to an audience composed mainly of agricultural workers and peasant women utterly untrained to appreciate them. The critics within the PPP, in similar neo-totalitarian fashion, were dismissed as 'left-wing deviationists or 'ultra leftists' instead of having their arguments rationally analysed as serious intellectual contributions. Nothing illustrates so much the Jaganite temptation to use Marxist terms as political slogans rather than as tools of social-science analysis than the dismal fact that each such group of critics—from the King-Westmass-Carter group of 1956 to the Bhagwan Progressive Youth Organization group of 1965—was treated with the same barrage of sterile name-calling. It is suggestive that the tremendous upheaval in the world of international Communism following the de-Stalinization era in Soviet life seems almost to have by-passed the Guyanese Marxist leaders, and there are not wanting critics who argue that the death of any real intellectual debate within the PPP is to be traced to the fact, in part, that those leaders, unexpectedly swept into office in 1953, have too readily embraced, as a political bureaucracy, the prestige that comes from holding a seat at the horseshoe table of the Legislative Council. Be that as it may it is beyond doubt that the PPP record, certainly after 1955, became a combination of 'revolutionary' Marxist utterances and unimaginative action. For the PPP ideology, in truth, was an imported article as much as the Anglo-Saxon cultural norms that, theoretically, it attacked as imperialist. It may well be that this defect can now only be remedied by a new leadership nurtured from 'home-grown' Marxists as distinct from 'foreign-trained' Marxists.[62]

The second factor explanatory of the decay of theory is, of course, the intrusion of racialism. For the truth is that after 1955 all parties surrendered, willy-nilly, to the racialist appeal. That they all put forward multi-racial 'slates' of election candidates was a crass voter device that deceived nobody. With the PNC and the UF it was, beyond doubt, a conscious exploitation of race. Their electoral alliance, after all, revealed their basic opportunism. With the PPP it was a more complex matter. Whether the search after 1955 for a broader support among the ranks of the Indian merchants, big landlords and ricemillers was a freely chosen strategy of Dr Jagan's or whether, as some assert, he was reluctantly driven to it as the racial consequences of the political division of the society made themselves felt is, by now, an academic question only, although what is known of Dr Jagan makes the latter interpretation psychologically more plausible. The point is that once the process was under way it led inescapably to the capture of the party by Indian cultural and social conservatism. Dr Jagan's important speech of 1956 treated the West Indies Federation issue from a racial and not a class point of view, citing the supposed general hostility of Indians to the matter and coming dangerously close to the old Russian Menshevik position that, such things being a 'bourgeois' issue, the proletariat had no obligation to accept them or take part in them; and Lenin's classic exposure of the 'left-wing infantilism' of that attitude has been echoed, in the Guyanese case, by those critics who see in the Jaganite invocation of the middle-class character of the Federation an excuse for not seeking, as any really revolutionary party should, to change that character by direct participation in the venture.

In order, then, to rationalize the trend to a racial party base it was necessary to invent the thesis of an oppressed Indian community as a cultural proletariat denied entry to the national life. Yet the answer to that thesis is that, important half-truth as it is, it distorts reality since it fails to take into account how much the general creolizing process had in fact created a new middle-class urban Indian group whose members had little sympathy with the Indian rice and sugar proletariat. The Jaganite temptation thus to see 'Indian' and 'working class' as synonymous terms leads to a dangerous optimism about the social attitudes of the Indian landlord and businessman.[63] That this general pro-racialist shift in the PPP has not always been clearly recognized is due to the fact that it has throughout been expressed by the PPP theoreticians in terms of pseudo-Marxist doctrine. Thus it was argued that, as a 'native' capitalist class, the anti-imperialist feelings of the Indian business group made them potential allies in the colonial struggle. But the argument was fatally weak because (1) it imputed to the members of that group feelings that in fact they did not much entertain and (2) it overlooked the vital fact that they were willing to help finance the PPP in order to better their own class position and to anaesthetize any possible move against them by a future PPP government on the ground that they constituted, as in fact they do, some of the worst employers in the economy. Dr Jagan could argue, of course, in reply, that the revolutionary movement, having used the group, could later abandon it; in much the same way as Mr Burnham presumably hopes—and especially after independence with his new power as Premier—that, having gained office with the support of the D'Aguiar local conservatives and their American friends, he can at some point in the future reassert his independent authority against them. But this, in both cases, is an enormous gamble. In both cases, it probably underestimates the residual power of the Right in the total situation. The remarkable growth, indeed, of that power, in large part made possible by the tragic disintegration of the Left, is one of the most salient features of contemporary Guyanese politics. Both the PNC and the PPP leaderships have thus decided to play with fire; and each side hopes that the fire will consume its enemy. They may well find out that it will consume both of them.[64]

Theoretical weakness produces, inescapably, a politics of opportunism. In the last few years that has become the chief element of the situation. Both parties, seeking their respective middle-class 'national' extensions, fostered a diluted socialism. Each was for independence while in office and against it while out of office. Both were guilty, in face of crisis, of bankrupt leadership, most noticeably in the abject surrender of the infamous joint letter of November 1963 to the Colonial Secretary leading, as it did, to the fiasco of proportional representation. Both became, increasingly, import agencies for borrowed ideologies. Both allowed the cult of personality to develop a dangerously concentrated leadership style. Both used their trade union sections as political weapons, thus creating the chaotic confusion of the contemporary trade union situation. Both proclaimed multi-racialism while in fact making it difficult for their ethnic minority members to stay within their ranks, as the cruel dilemma of Mr Benn in the PPP illustrated. Hence, too, the cultural appendages of the parties, all of them, with the exception of ASCRIA, significantly conservative in tone. Progressiveness, all in all, gives way to respectability. It is noteworthy that in the case of the Indo-Guyanese section this means the betrayal not only of the socialist ideals of 1950 but of the earlier Gandhian-liberal ideals of the Indian Congress movement which reached the colony in the inter-war period by means of the visits, for example, of the English missionary disciples of the Mahatma like the Rev. C. F. Andrews whose visit in 1929 was remarkable for the liberal quality of his public lectures.[65] Nor is this poverty of philosophy alleviated by any sort of articulate intellectual debate outside the political arena, for any institution that essays such a debate finds, like the University of Guyana, that it becomes itself embroiled in the political maelstrom. It remains to be seen whether the new note of the group of New World Associates will manage to fare any better.[66]

Only long-term social processes will perhaps end all this. As occupational mobility increases the old economic dichotomy between Indian agriculture and African urban labour should disappear, as is already apparent in the entry of African artisans and skilled workers into the new government agricultural settlements. Similarly, when the new Indian middle class in the towns becomes large enough to build up a sense of cultural security away from its rural kin its class interests will become more important than its blood ties. The natural pull of class identity may thus reassert itself, undistorted by race. For that identity, however much submerged, is there. The burdens of the territory are common to both groups. Both African and Indian worker came to the 'wild coast' for the same purpose, as a source of cheap labour for the planter class, and they shared a common history of revolt, whether it was the Berbice slave rebellion of 1763 or the East Coast riots of 1826. Should, however, no such new class alignments thus materialize, racialism, what one Guyanese publicist has termed the insular imperialism of race, will conquer, made even more virulent by the advent of independence. In that case, the Guyanese future will become more and more like that of the American society of the 1850's, moving forward inexorably to an 'irrepressible conflict' culminating in civil war. Merely administrative devices, like the office of the Ombudsman contained in the 1966 Independence Constitution, will be of little avail against the terrible pressures of that situation.[67]

# Chapter XI

## THE LATIN ENCLAVE
### BRITISH HONDURAS

BRITISH HONDURAS has been perhaps the most neglected of all the British Caribbean possessions. Its geographical location in the Central American strip, the dismal reputation of the Mosquito Shore climate, the long struggle of the settlement to become recognized as a colony against British official disinterest, bad communications, the ever-present shadow of the colony's doubtful political status due to the Guatemalan claims, all have contributed as factors and help to explain the traditional Honduran sense of grievance against the 'mother country'. From its very beginnings the territory was a frontier settlement of the logwood cutters, the 'Baymen of Belize', deep in the heart of Spanish territory and therefore the victim of British official reluctance to offend Spain by showing anything except covert encouragement to the colonists. The right to territorial possession, the necessary basis for any sort of creative civic develop-ment, was thus left in doubt for a period, literally, of centuries. In the early beginnings protection came by way of self-help as the pioneers turned buccaneers against the Spanish enemy, a period described in the vivid pages of Dampier's account of 1690. Later on, as the Jamaican 'protectorate' began to take definite shape, some-time after 1764, protection came from Kingston, and the famous battle of St George's Cay of 1798, the anniversary of which has long been celebrated as a public holiday in the colony, showed how impor-tant Jamaican naval and military aid was to the survival of the Yucatán settlements. That period ended, belatedly, with the grant of colonial status in 1862 and the final separation from Jamaica in 1884.

Throughout it all the colonists learned to look after themselves, even maintaining their own crude frontier government in the form of an elective magistracy accountable to a primitive democracy of annual public meetings, not unlike the old New England model.

Not the least of the ironies of the anomalous 'constitutional develop-ment of the territory is that, as it gained the legal colonial status it had so long demanded, it was forced to accept the destruction of that popular democracy as the price for official metropolitan recognition. So ended, as Hume Wrong put it, the history of a free democracy set up by a few hundred sturdy adventurers in the land of Spain.[1] The general upshot of it all was that British Honduras came to be the least British, culturally, of all of the West Indian possessions. It is not surprising, then, that colonial Governors found their appointments to Belize, on the whole, disappointing and would perhaps have enthusiastically welcomed any local political move to get rid of them; as, indeed, actually occurred in the case of Sir Alan Burns in an amusing episode of his gubernatorial incumbency in the years before 1939.[2] The English official would enjoy, in the beginning, the novelty of white-sail fleets, woodcutters' Christmas revelling and logwood camps, but would rapidly find that general atmosphere demoralizing, as did Olivier in his first West Indian appointment as Colonial Secretary in Belize in 1890.[3]

Basic to the Honduran problem, then, has been, and still is, the territory's isolation, both geographical and psychological. A country of mangrove swamp, rain forest, and bad internal connec-tions rarely attracted either immigrant or tourist; significantly, the history of Honduran immigration is one of forced immigration, of shipwrecked British sailors, deported Sepoy soldiers of the Indian Mutiny, Indian refugees fleeing from the caste war of Yucatán, deported Black Caribs from St Vincent, Africans liberated from slave ships, Mennonites from Mexico, and even the subgroup of Mayan Indians were originally re-migrants from the neighbouring territories who entered the colony after British settlement. The very ethnic variety induced created its own drawback, for it precluded, as constrasted with what took place in the more homogeneous West Indian island societies, the growth of a vigorous civic unity, the sense, so powerful in the islands, that everybody is in the same boat, whatever his particular interests may be. This, in turn, helped to perpetuate the loose relations with Britain, while Britain, in its own turn, reciprocated with a tendency, as the Evans Commission pointed out, to treat the colony as a special case which could not easily be assimilated to the general programme of colonial advance. That splendid isolation also had its economic roots, for so long as

the peculiar Honduran economy of extremely profitable exploitation of the forest industries continued, along with the concomitant
features of a high wage structure and negative social attitudes
towards agriculture, the Honduran working types, the woodcutter
and the *chiclero*, declined to see themselves as in any way part of the
general West Indian scene; that is to say, of an economy of peasant
producers tied to a world market structure. The Guyanese economy,
by contrast, was essentially, in its coastal strip, a West Indian
economy; and its working types, the estate worker and the
rice paddy farmer, were part of the general West Indian production scene. The Honduran forest worker, as distinct from that,
was cast more in the mould of the frontier backwoodsman one
reads about in the Bret Harte stories of the American lumber
camps.

All of those factors helped to encourage Honduran separatism.
Their political expression in the continuing contemporary local
debate on external affiliations, whether to join up with the West
Indies or with Central America, has been fully described in the
work of scholars like Waddell and Humphreys. Their more general
cultural expression is to be seen in the fact that the Honduran story
of the post-1945 period has been in large part that of a crisis of
national attitudes as the economic foundations of the traditional
communal psychology have been steadily weakened by new forces.
Looked at from a slightly different angle, it has been the story of a
collision between, on the one hand, the social individualism bred
by the 'robber economy' of remorseless exploitation of natural
resources bound at some point to reach its terminating point and,
on the other, the recognized need for national planning to meet
that economic dilemma; a need that can perhaps be dated at least
from the date of the Evans Settlement Report of 1948, with its
revolutionary proposals for a planned plantation economy operated
by large multi-purpose combines, replacing the indigenous agricul-
turist with the paid wage-earner of a mechanized plantation agriculture, so startlingly different were those proposals from the earlier
recommendations of the Moyne Commission Report in favour of
mixed peasant farming. The proposals remain stillborn to the present day. But the challenge they originally presented still remains
as a definitive statement, for all of its more doubtful aspects, of the
task of organizing the transformation of the Honduran way of life,

which has by now long since ceased to be a pioneer settlement of mahogany and logwood cutters.

The socio-economic development of British Honduras thus travelled along lines different from those of the development of the islands. There was the *laissez-faire* economics, making possible the continuation of a class of small tradesmen and craftsmen that elsewhere disappeared under the weight of the sugar plantation economy. There was the relative unimportance of slavery, evident in the archival records describing the traditional good comradeship that existed, before Emancipation, between the logwood cutters and their slaves. The fact, indeed, that slavery, when it existed, had no economic basis in a plantation regime meant that the social culture was not shaped in any serious way by the functional requirements of plantation life. The unique settlement history of the colony thus had unique results. There was, first, the excessive imbalance of town and countryside, with Belize finally embracing, in 1946, almost 37 per cent of the total population, a phenomenon generated, in part, by the fact that the Negro woodman was a migrant labourer generally resident in town. There was, second, the excessive degree (by island standards) of ethnic heterogeneity, producing an astonishing mosaic of Negro, mixed, Maya Indian, Carib, white and Asiatic, further complicated by the division between the pure Amerindian element and the Hispano-Amerindian *mestizo* element. This produced, as a corollary and, third, the phenomenon of an advanced linguistic differentiation, the polite fiction that English was the official language only faintly disguising the fact that Continental Spanish, Maya and Carib were all important idioms. The linguistic geography of the society, even today, reflects the resultant fragmentalization, for only to take the ride from Belize to Corozal is to start in a Creole-English speaking bus and end up in Corozal, on the Mexican border, in a Spanish speaking bus. The growth of a national tradition of independence, consequently, apparent enough in English-speaking Hondurans, was complicated by Maya and Spanish 'problems'. The Spanish element came to be defensive about its cultural identity. The Maya Indian, as a quite different 'problem', was a latter-day survival of the once-great Mayan Old Empire, unassimilated in the modern Honduran society, lost forever to the influence of his pre-Colombian ancestry and tending, in any case, to become hispanicized rather than anglicized. The con-

sequences of the society's failure to afford him normal social participation were fully catalogued in the 1941 Report of the Interdepartmental Committee on Maya Welfare.[4] The relative success, by
contrast, of Carib assimilation seemed to indicate, at least, that the
reserve policy, officially accepted in British Guiana, had serious
defects and could only serve to freeze the depressed status of a
minority group, the grim lesson of the Indian reservation policy in
the United States. The upshot of all this, in any case, was a society
impregnated with a West Indian atmosphere in the capital city and
its environs and with a markedly Central American atmosphere
beyond that enclave.

There was, finally, the excessive (again by island standards)
vulnerability of the Honduranean economy. All of the colonial
economies, of course, were vulnerable. But the Honduranean
sample, as a dependent economy, was, as Professor Carey Jones'
national income structure analysis shows, almost a classic of
colonial exploitation, of taking away and not giving back,
so that its natural wealth was in no way utilized for permanent
improvement and capital development.[5] All the elements of the
colonial economy were present on an exaggerated scale. There
was the reckless alienation of the land by means of large concessions to expatriate capitalist groups, most notably the Belize
Estate and Produce Company (the Bookers of Honduras), concerned
only with lumber extraction and deliberately preventing any cultivation of the soil in order to retain the limited supply of available
labour for their lumber camps. Any progressive government seeking
to implement the Evans scheme of massive agricultural rehabilitation would rapidly be driven to the necessity of extensive compulsory
acquisition.[6] Such a programme, too, would inherit the retrogressive
social attitudes bred by this monocrop culture. For if, in the sugar
islands, the plantation regime alienated the peasant from agricultural pursuits, in British Honduras the social prestige of the lum-
berjack generated an even more intense alienation, reinforced by
the fact that the main proprietor of the subsistence farming sector
was the Amerindian farmer, so that occupational prejudice was
compounded by racial disdain; to be a farmer, thus, was not only
socially inferior, it was also racially degrading. The colonial anomaly
of a potentially productive agricultural economy importing, at
excessive cost, its basic food items was also present, engendering a

dietetic snobbery despising local produce of all kinds, so that, to take an example, the Creole Honduran came to believe that fresh milk was a tasteless liquid as compared with sweetened condensed milk. Not least of all, the Honduranean primary producer was subject, in a marked degree, to the vagaries of taste and fashion in the metropolitan buyers' market. Thus the decline after the war of 1914 of mahogany furniture as a Victorian *haut-bourgeois* status symbol played havoc with the Honduranean employment structure, as, later, the *chicle* industry was hard hit, after the war of 1939, by competition from synthetic substitutes and Oriental varieties. The social satirist of colonialism would see nothing but ludicrous comedy in the spectacle of an entire colonial society depending for its daily existence upon the Victorian passion for the mahogany bed and the American habit of gum chewing.

A century of all this spawned, in the end, the sick Honduranean society of the 1930's. In its economic and social aspects it consisted, in the leading forest industries, of a migratory labour force working seasonally and precariously for corporate employers whose grip on the land was made even tighter by scandalously low tax rates. The lumber camps in which the force worked and lived were severely criticized both by Major Orde-Browne's Report and the Moyne Commission Report. The pernicious system of advance payment which in effect, although popular with the worker, placed him in a position of indebtedness to the contractor; a penal legislation system of fines and imprisonment for the defaulting payee which ought to have been replaced long ago with a modern labour relations code with the trade union as the accepted bargaining agent of the worker; a food commissary system that amounted to truck payment—i.e. the forced acceptance of part wages in kind; the absence of anything except rudimentary medical services: all in all, it was the picture of an employment system characterized by chronic indebtedness and widespread fraud and the consequences of which were visited upon the woodcutters' womenfolk and children.[7] That, in sum, was the semi-serfdom of the Belize forest-Creole, far different from the romanticized versions of his existence that cropped up periodically in the British colonial travel literature. The plight of the Maya worker in the *chicle* industry was even worse, so much so that the Moyne Commissioners were persuaded to recommend the creation of a post of Special Commissioner for Mayas similar to the post of

Agent-General for Immigration in British Guiana. Nor did the war of 1939 work the minor revolution in social services that it worked elsewhere in the West Indies, and the Evans Commission called attention once more to the depressing list of social evils: the low standards of community hygiene and preventive medicine, the widespread illiteracy, the prevalence of malarial diseases unchecked by anything comparable to the remarkable work of the great malariologist Dr Gigliogi in British Guiana. The relative absence of any kind of large middle class professional group after the Jamaican manner meant that no local leadership emerged to elevate the moral and intellectual culture of the society. What passed for such a group in Belize was in fact a semi-urban, semi-rural *petit-bourgeois* small merchant and trader element whose members believed, as Major Orde-Browne put it, in Latin grammar or pianoforte playing as the fine flower of education. Hence the dull social life, even today, of Belize, made even worse by the strict licensing laws which effectively curbed all entertainments not connected with the churches; and leaving a Belizean popular culture in the precarious custody of the now half-forgotten Christmas holiday bands of the woodcutters, with leaders like the dynamic Alonso Schultz, along with the improvised song-parodies of the famous 'breakdowns'.[8] Nor should the fact be overlooked that the more powerful members of the tiny middle class, as local bankers and export consignees, exercised a tight grip over the logwood contractors by means of exorbitant interest rates on loans, unrelieved by any outside banking facilities that might have made capital advances on more civilized terms. At the same time those people also fiercely resisted any programme, such as Sir F. P. Barlee's scheme for regular steamship communications with New Orleans, calculated to challenge their monopoly over the supply of imports.[9]

Not the least disturbing result of this, as already noted, was the fatal division between town and countryside. The ruling economic forces, both resident and abroad, throughout refused to undertake capital expenditure on a road system when their own profits rested upon a riverine transportation system. Their standing reluctance to let out their large land tracts for agricultural purposes—recommended as a policy as early as 1879 by a Legislative Council select committee—lasted well into the twentieth century.[10] So, up to 1931 not a single road linked Belize with the rest of the country, while as late as 1953 a country member of the Legislative Council could charge that the Colonial Development Corporation would only build feeder roads for expensive pipe dreams that never materialized, while the small people got nothing.[11] Thus, city and countryside existed in mutual ignorance of each other; the out-district minorities lost out to the urban groups in educational provisions and social services; political apathy reigned supreme outside of Belize; and the 1951 Commission of Enquiry on Constitutional Reform discovered that witnesses in the capital knew little or nothing of conditions outside and frequently confessed, with charming candour, that they had not given any thought to the matter.[12]

Politically, the Crown Colony regime at once reflected and reinforced the social condition. The 1871 surrender of the predominantly elective assembly by the white leadership of the day had delivered the state power into the hands of the Governor and a completely nominated Council. In theory, the grant of gubernatorial reserve powers required legislative consent. But the 1931 incorporation of those powers, exacted from a reluctant Assembly as the price demanded by the British government for grant-in aid-status, demonstrated where the real power lay. The powers thus granted included gubernatorial control of the colonial finances so long as colonial indebtedness to the Imperial exchequer existed; and since it did exist most of the time Belize was, in fact, the resentful prisoner of the British Treasury mentality. It was a vicious circle: London denied the colonial Assembly power either to reform a grotesquely outmoded taxation system or to exact more equitable tax returns from the expatriate business empires and then cited the low revenue level caused by that denial as the excuse for continuing Treasury control. The restoration in 1935 of an elected legislative element belatedly terminated a process in which, over the years after 1870, a direct democracy of the old *folkmoot* kind had been superseded, *via* the Old Representative System, by a purely official autocracy limited only by a handful of nominated unofficials. But the new elective element, both in the Legislative Council and in the Belize City Council, were mostly respectable middle class members, typical in their outlook of pre-depression West Indian politics. They could never make up their minds whether they were national patriots or British parliamentarians. Their dilemma was nicely exemplified in the fact that whereas in 1949 they felt that they were mere puppets

in the hands of Downing Street, that feeling being their response
to the incipient devaluation crisis, in 1951, under the pressure of
the Belize Town Council activities of the younger and more radical
elements, they surpassed each other in their declarations of loyalty
to the Crown.[13] It was symptomatic of their basic Anglophilism
that they saw the famous battle of St George's Cay of 1798 as an
English victory over the Spanish enemy which even the Spanish-
speaking Hondurans ought to celebrate and not, as the later nationalist movement has seen it, as the first historic event in the growth of a
separate Honduran nationalism.[14] It was hardly surprising, in the
light of this, that this group remained to the last sceptical about
universal suffrage and, indeed, as the 1951 *Report* of their legislative
group indicated, were prepared to recommend an unusual electoral
college system to qualify the democratic principle of popular
government.[15]

As politicians, however, they could do little, even had they been
ideologically so disposed, to break the influence of the big interests
on the governmental process. That influence was evident enough,
to take an example only, in the fact that timber exports were consistently undervalued in customs declarations, with consequent
loss to colonial revenue. Local opinion was openly flouted in such
a system, the most famous example, of course, being the arbitrary
devaluation of the Honduran dollar in 1949, a perfect illustration
of how, in the economic arrangements of colonialism, local trading
interests were subordinated to metropolitan commercial considerations. Treasury control, altogether, meant the sacrifice of any chance
of large scale planning to the fetish of budget balancing; and just a
year before the explosion of the devaluation struggle the Evans
Commission sympathetically noted the local irritation and political
frustration brought about by the system.[16] The general consequence
was, in the language of a spokesman for local liberalism at the end
of the war in 1945, an inferiority complex in Hondurans so gnaw-
ingly persistent that it sapped the psyche of the community and for
which the political system was a contributing cause only.[17]

The wave of anti-British popular feeling provoked by the devaluation affair crystallized, with the formation in 1950 of the People's
United Party (PUP), into the creation of coherent party politics.
From the beginning the party became the vehicle of a radical
10*

nationalist movement. no better exemplified than in the fact that, as with the PPP in Guyana, the only serious opposition that grew up in later years arose out of its own bifurcation. Its mass support, made possible by the close relations with the General Workers Union, gave it a popular basis, a support conclusively ratified by its victory in the first adult suffrage general elections of 1954. The days when the popular interest could only be defended openly by the Senior Medical Officer or the Bishop of British Honduras were over, to be replaced by a modern popular secular leadership owing its success to the mass electorate and even injecting a new idiom into the political debate: from now on the typical political meeting, held on the Belize 'battlefield', was instinct with open hostility to the colonial power. The British, in the beginning, openly fought it, using, among much else, 'subversive control' legislation to imprison its leadership. But imprisonment, added to the dissolution of the City Council because of its refusal to hang a portrait of the King in the City Hall, only served to enhance the party's position. The Governor, having gone through the prescribed ritual of ostracizing the party leaders, accepted them as members of the Executive Council and, after the constitutional changes of 1960, as ministers in a quasi-ministerial system. They will become, as elsewhere, the new governing class, sooner or later, of an independent Honduras.

The anti-British position of that class has been much seized upon, usually by British writers. Thus one author refers to George Price's 'doctrinaire anti-British policy' which achieved nothing 'constructive';[18] while another refers to 'agitators who would stir up the people to clamour for unqualified universal suffrage in the name of "Democracy"': the proper comment upon the latter jejune observation being, of course, that it was composed in 1951, just a brief few years before the British government, ignoring the author's advice, granted universal suffrage to the colony.[19] Yet the PUP philosophy was only anti-British in the sense that it expressed a natural indignation at British failure to deal seriously with any of the local problems. Apparently what bothers the critics, since they harp unceasingly on the episodes, are the PUP demonstrations of 'disloyalty', the protests, for example, against the proposed visit of Princess Alice of Athlone which compelled the local Administration to submit to the indignity of putting forward a compromise proposal whereby 'God Save the King' would not be played during her stay on condition that the Belize crowd would not sing their favourite 'God Bless America'. Yet those episodes were far short of constituting communist conspiracy, any more than the Guatemalan visits and connections of the leading PUP figures constituted treasonable activities.[20] At their worst, the episodes were a deliberate effort to tease the English, psychologically a clever tactic, for nothing upsets the English official more than calculated affronts to members of the Royal Family; and, perhaps more important, the damage that they do to the myths of British Royalty that have served the colonial power so well in the Caribbean. They were, of course, no substitute for a coherent policy; and the Trinidadian labour leader who at much the same time reminded the Jaganite leadership in British Guiana, on the occasion of their refusal to send an official delegation to meet the Queen on her Jamaican visit, of the remark of the great Irish agitator Daniel O'Connell that it might be a question of the Queen against O'Connell but never of O'Connell against the Queen, might have had a point. But the British in Honduras surely deserved that response to their dismal treatment of a colony that had been kept waiting for a century or more, against its own ardent wishes, for Imperial recognition. Even a British author concerned to defend the British record against the propaganda of 'irresponsible demagogues' is constrained to admit that, notwithstanding the contribution to the Honduran economy of 'hard-working, hard-headed business men', the same problems of the colony that had been dissected in official reports before 1914 were still being dissected in the official reports of the 1940's.[21]

Certain aspects of the PUP outlook are worth noting, for they illustrate the special peculiarities of the Honduran problem. Its architects were a group of young Catholic radicals imbued with the ideals of Catholic Socialism, as could be seen in the elaborate system of consumer and producer co-operatives of their programme. They possessed, in their persons, and especially in George Price, who emerged in the 50's as their leader, qualities of rigid Catholic morality, social zeal and private asceticism ideally suited to a missionary politics in a Catholic community. All educated at the Jesuit St John's College with its American Jesuit faculty, they were strongly influenced, as indeed are most Honduran attitudes, by the American system, an influence naturally buttressed by the long-standing commercial ties with the United States economy. The popular songs of political rallies are American, not British or West Indian, just as the popular games are American.[22] There is, then, a Honduran national patriotism of American style being viewed as being in conflict, perhaps incompatible, with loyalty to Britain. The PUP educational programme was orthodox, unlike many of the West Indian island progressive movements which see the traditional dual system of state and denominational education as socially divisive. The things to be proud of, the PUP told the Honduran school child, were the fact that his country had the highest literacy rate of any country from the North Pole to the Magellan Straits, that there was no struggle between church and state in his community, that there was no religious or racial hate, that there was political stability and that, generally, the true patriot was the worker who gave a full day's pay and the employer who did not cheat his employees.[23] The same Christian-democratic ideology infuses the Premier's speeches as of today, often uttered in accompanying English and Spanish versions and frequently embroidered with elaborate political verse making. Living near the geographical navel of the Americas, the general tenor of the argument goes, the new Belizean patriotism must seek to build a new nation living harmoniously with its Latin neighbours. It must abjure the colonialist veneration for the world outside and devote its reconstructive energies to the full utilization of its own resources. It must search out its own Belizean values based on Christian Democracy. It must breed a new Belizean citizen who turns once again to the heroic virtues of the early American pioneers described in great novels like José Eustacio Rivera's *La Voragine*. It must dedicate those virtues to new purposes: the modernization of agriculture, the rationalization of industry and greater efficiency in the welfare state services. In that struggle, the argument proceeds, the nationalist leader plays a vital role, for he is not, as his enemies say, a dangerous fanatic but the dynamic force that awakens a people to the positive benefits of independence.[24] It is worth noting that the Opposition group, the National Independence Party, agrees, ideologically, with much of all this, save for its own more emphatic insistence upon development within the Commonwealth, its real quarrel with the Premier being not that he is a Communist (the chief accusation against Dr Jagan) but that, as the NIP sees it, he is a secret Guatemalan agent intent on handing over the new nation to a new and worse overlordship.[25]

The question of national survival thus works to inhibit ideological maturity.

The programme confronts a multitude of problems. There is, to begin with, the complex ethnic problem. It could be true that 'a race of British Central Americans', based on widespread racial integration, is in the making.[26] It is certainly true that talk, usually by visiting American reporters, about possible racial violence is irresponsible exaggeration possibly generated by a morbid regret for the absence of a 'white settler' influence in the national life.[27] Yet the four-tiered Honduran cultural pyramid, Creole, Amerindian, Spanish and Carib, certainly still awaits a hard social cement to hold it together. A common colour prejudice may unite the light-skinned Creoles and the Spanish urban *élite* in the old citadel of the Pickwick Club. But the group prejudices still remain, and if the Negro Creole accepts the social rise of the Spanish-speaking Honduran it is probably because he seeks allies against the Carib and Mayan minorities; just as in nineteenth-century Jamaica the white group repressed its incipient anti-semitism and subordinated it to the more vital strategy of accepting the Jewish group as an ally against the Negro masses. The Civil Service in Belize still remains the stronghold of one group, and even when it is penetrated by a Carib professional person like C. P. Cacho the fear still remains that he will use his position to recruit his 'own kind' into the service. There is a great deal of occupational integration at the lower levels, as the urbanized life-style of the 'black Caribs' of the Stann Creek area shows. Yet the fact that the 'black Caribs' are a Negro people speaking a Carib language-form and retaining many of the cultural traits of the Indian folk they have absorbed has helped sustain their old hostility to the Creole Negro group whom they regard, in part, indeed, as the authors of their own 'spoiled' racial character. The remark of a young Carib schoolteacher, quoted by Taylor in his 1951 study—'I could go and kill every Negro in Africa for having spoiled our race'—speaks volumes for the sense of shame and frustration that consumes many of them. The Mayan Indians, in their turn, have long been in close contact with both *mestizo* and Negro elements, and their resultant acculturation, in sexual habits, for example, was noted by Gann as far back as 1918. But their full social assimilation, not to mention political, as already noted, remains incomplete as yet. Nor in all this is there much of a pattern of ethnic inter-marriage, inter-marriage in any case furnishing evidence of barriers already broken down and therefore of little value as a weapon in breaking down continuing barriers. Nor have any of these various groupings been bound together by any feeling of common hostility that might have united them against a powerful and conspicuous creolized white group, for all schemes advocating white immigration—Morris's book of 1883, for example—have always failed to produce any response from the class of young English adventurers to whom they have been addressed.[28] This, altogether, is the general ethnic balance, unlikely to be much altered by, for example, the recent government-sponsored influx of white Mennonite farmers from north of the Mexican border.

The Honduran cultural situation, perhaps, is at the point where the Guyanese stood a generation ago, in which a more or less rigid separation of the different cultural sections precedes an open con- frontation arising out of developing social and occupational mobi- lities. What is different, of course, is that the effective creolization of elements such as the Spanish and the Mayan faces the obstacle that, geographically, they exist in easy contact with the Central American 'mother' civilization. The Indo-Guyanese, by contrast, isolated from India, must be content with lectures by visiting pan- dits. He can nurse his romanticized dream of the lost homeland, overlooking the very different reality of contemporary India. He rarely makes the costly pilgrimage back, to meet, like some other Naipaul, the trauma of disillusionment. The Spanish-speaking Belizean, by contrast, lives on the doorstep of Guatemala and Mexico. The mass media he hears are Spanish; there are even Spanish language sections in his own newspapers. He may not read Spanish literature, it is true, or even holiday in Mexico City. Cer- tainly, too, there is no real equivalent of the class of intelligentsia, centred around the life of a flourishing university, who carry the torch for a Hispanic culture under severe assault from the Ameri- canizing process, as in the case of Puerto Rico. Even so, the contact is there, and a process of cultural feeding takes place, helping to neutralize fusion into an amalgamating cultural mainstream.

The problem, as in Guyana, has nearly intractable elements. The answer may depend upon the Honduran ability to organize success- fully the reconstruction of the economy. In that reconstruction the lines of cultural change can in some measure be shaped by the growth of a full employment economy, replacing once and for all the long obsolete forest economy run by private interests for private profits. The place of the timber industry, then, will be paramount in such a programme. A radical revision of the land-tax structure will have to be the minimal demand, nationalization of private holdings the maximum demand. Even the mild Report of the 1954 development programme oultined by the International Bank of Reconstruction and Development recommended, short of nationalization, that the present under-utilization of large holdings should be met by a 'development area' programme imposing minimum standards of husbandry on private owners; failure to meet the standards to be followed by compulsory acquisition with compensation.[29] An openly socialist development is not unthinkable. The large-scale plantation system envisaged by the resettlement Commissioners of 1948 was, at bottom, a collectivist scheme socially organized and centrally planned, its only defect being its assumption that the administrative framework of the scheme should remain colonialist, resting, as they saw it, in the control of the expatriate Colonial Development Corporation. That assumption, today, is naturally obsolete. But a Honduran administrative direction of such a scheme, at the same time, would require, in the long run, a massive revolution in both educational theory and practice to produce the skilled manpower it would necessitate. The need was painfully evident in the fact, for example, that in 1954 only one British Honduran had managed to qualify for a senior post in the strategic Forest Department establishment, the expansion of that Department being an urgent matter in the light of the need to speed up programmes such as tree planting, conservation, Crown Lands protection and fire protection, hitherto signally neglected.[30] As late as 1964, to take another example, there were only five trained surveyors to undertake the appalling task of implementing the technical side of proposed legislation facing up to the fact that the vast majority of fertile lands were owned by corporate absentee landlords possessed of neither the will nor the intention of developing them.[31] The traditional Colonial Office thesis that it 'trained' colonials for the 'transition' to independence clearly did not apply to British Honduras. In the absence of its own local technical and administrative *élite* the PUP Government is driven, in the meantime, to embrace the entry of new private expatriate corporations, as in the 1964 banana agreement with the United Fruit Company, with all the problems such a policy creates. The truth is, of course, that with a population of only some 100,000 persons the potential taxable capacity—excepting, now, the possible revenue arising out of rational taxation of expatriate economic forces—does not generate sufficient revenue to maintain a modern state administration with all of its overhead costs. Only large scale immigration, combined with collectivist economic planning, can perhaps meet the issue.

It is at this point that the argument meets the problem of Honduran political status. For British Honduras cannot decide its long term policies until it decides the character of its state power, that is, whether, having gained independence, it will elect to remain a separate national entity or accept incorporation into a larger regional unit. That is, essentially, the heart of the long-standing question of Guatemalan annexation. That most of the literature on British Honduras deals with this question testifies to its seminal importance; and rightly so, since no people can set to work out its national problems until the basic instrument of the state, and its territorial integrity, is put beyond all doubt. The gravity of the problem is further indicated by the fact that the question is the most controversial one in the domestic politics. It led directly to the 1956 split in the PUP between its pro-Guatemala and pro-West Indian factions. So urgent is the matter, indeed, that party positions on the question even get themselves inserted, as binding agreements, into constitutional documents like the pro-Commonwealth preamble inserted into the 1960 agreement with the British government, an item inserted at the express request of the unofficial members of the Honduran delegation.[32] Every domestic issue, it is not too much to say, depends for its solution upon a final political settlement on the sovereignty issue. Every such issue, too, so long as such a settlement is missing, gets embroiled in the debate on the international dispute. Dispassionate discussion of any issue, this is to say, becomes increasingly difficult as it gets enmeshed in that atmosphere of fear; the Legislative Assembly debate of June 1962 on the question of a permanent national defence force is only a case in point.[33] Even the national commemoration of the 1798 battle with the Spaniards becomes a politically disputatious issue.[34] The society thus lacks, all in all, an effective concensus even about its own juridical identity, the PUP seeing the future as rooted in the ancestry of the indigenous Mayan people, the Opposition seeing it in an emotionally less compelling West Indianism.

The growth of a viable Honduran national spirit has thus been tragically frustrated by the problem. It destroyed the original PUP unity and generated a poisonous political climate in which the Price forces saw their opponents, later incorporated into the National Independence Party, as British 'colonial stooges', while they, in turn, saw him as a traitor seeking Guatemalan annexation with secret funds provided by official friends in Guatemala City.[35] It produced, in fact, a conspiratorial politics, the best known example being the 1957 episode in which Price and his colleagues met clandestinely with the Guatemalan Minister in London while carrying on talks at the same time, as members of an official delegation, with the Colonial Office; an episode viewed by British officials and domestic opponents alike as a violation of the traditional rules of British constitutional government.[36] Inevitably, then, the domestic ethnic problem became involved, for the Spanish-speaking group identified itself with the Guatemalan side and the Creole Negro majority took a stand on the pro-Commonwealth position. The local debate on the West Indies Federation also crystallized around racial fears, for the Spanish element viewed large scale West Indian immigration, generally imagined as likely to occur as a consequence of federal membership, as a threat to their internal status and power. Similarly, annexation to Guatemala, in any form, would confront the Creole Negro majority with a serious problem of social integration into a Latin American country which has made a conspicuous failure of resolving its own character as a dual society. The Honduran Mayas could conceivably become a new support for incorporation into Guatemalan overlordship. But the historical status of the Indian peasant majority in Guatemala itself, characterized by a history of brutal exploitation on the part of a ruling *élite* of whites and *ladinos*—graphically portrayed in Norman Lewis' *The Volcanoes Above Us*—is not reassuring. The British-Guatemalan dispute, altogether, has helped politicize the communal differences of the society. The resultant discord, likely to grow worse, is evident enough in the street violence set off in the summer of 1966 by the publication of reports that the British government was preparing to recognize a limited Guatemalan jurisdiction over the areas of defence and foreign affairs without proper consultation with British Hondurans. The analogy, here, with the Venezuelan land claims against Guyana is instructive. As with the Guatemalan claim, the Venezuelan demand for supposed territorial rights in the north-west region of Guyana goes back far into colonial history. But no party in Georgetown accepts or condones the demand for there is no ethnic group of Spanish origins likely to be sympathetic to Caracas problems; it would be difficult to imagine Deoroop Mahraj or Balram Singh Rai as *venezolano* Fifth Columnists. In Belize, quite differently, the Spanish element is powerful and Spanish is an important minority tongue, whereas in Guyana English is both the vernacular and the prestige language of the educated. A Venezuela-Guyana boundary war would most certainly meet with a Guyanese united front; a Honduran-Guatemalan war could conceivably widen the incipient rift between the two major ethnic groups. At that point, of course, the basic similarity between the two situations would make itself felt. For both Venezuela and Guatemala are Latin American societies torn asunder by class civil war; the Caracas regime faces a rising *fidelista* movement, the Guatemala urban-military clique faces a growing peasant guerrilla movement. In both cases, an embattled ruling class might at some point decide upon a boundary war against a weak neighbour as a diversionary exercise. Faced with such a threat, both Guyana and Honduras, being internationally fragile, and unable to face the problem alone, would be compelled to seek the aid of a more powerful national system equipped with the military power to meet the threat or seek refuge with the United Nations Organization. Few things could better illustrate how dependent colonies, once they have become independent nations, inherit the grim legacy of the diplomatic tergiversations of their former masters.

Internal and external problems are thus deeply enmeshed with each other in British Honduras. Whether the PUP appeal to a higher Honduran unity can heal the domestic wounds remains to be seen. In political terms, that ideology of a new Belizean patriotism seeks to raise politics to a new level, to get away, for example, from the old district parish-pump politics of Honduran experience. That political parochialism has perhaps been inevitable in a community so little tied together by proper communications; so, as late as the 1957 elections the Honduran Independence Party could put out a programme mainly concerned with what its 'native son' candidates had done for their local districts; comfort stations for the Tower Hill ferry, helping to drain lands for *milperos* in the El Cayo district, the organization of hurricane relief in the Corozal district.[37] It is still too early to say whether a politics of national patriotism can override that legacy. In religious terms, the patriotic theme seeks a new and transcending church-state concordat. Religious divisions, certainly, could easily be exaggerated. For in a community in which to be a Catholic still has real social status the fact that both Price and Goldson, the Opposition leader, are of the faith (albeit Goldson is a convert only, not quite the same thing as being born to the Church) must have some significance. Even non-Catholics in Belize will readily acknowledge the energy and devotion of the Roman educational mission in the colony. It is possible, indeed, to see the Price image as that of a young ascetic who seeks to apply the Catholic missionary spirit to politics, in the tradition of the young priests like William Stanton at the turn of the century who spent his short life in the terrifying loneliness of the interior river missions among the spiritually immovable Mayan tribes.[38] In racial terms, finally, the nationalist spirit seeks mutual reconciliation. It is possible that there, too, the lines of division could be exaggerated. It is at least worth noting that the sweeping capture by the PPP of the Belize City Council in the elections of December 1965 was accomplished with a 'slate' of overwhelmingly Negro candidates, names like those of Lois Encalada and Homero Escalante excepted;[39] thus indicating that the party may have a national following beyond the sectional support of the Spanish-Ladino-Indian elements. It may well be that all of those lines of division—political, religious, ethnic— will become blurred or, alternatively, become hardened depending upon the degree of pressure that is brought to bear upon them by the external problems of the society.

# Chapter XII

# THE ATLANTIC PERIMETER
## BERMUDA AND THE BAHAMAS

THE TWO Atlantic outposts of Bermuda and the Bahamas have traditionally been shaped by most of the same forces shaping the West Indies proper—English colonization, the implanting of English political institutions, slavery and Emancipation, the post-Emancipation decline. Yet they have always seen themselves as apart from the West Indies and West Indians, in turn, have not accepted them as members of the family. In part, it has been a matter of poor communications; in part, of the commercial rather than agricultural character of their economies; in part, of their proximity, as twin Atlantic bastions, to the United States; and, in part, of their bad reputation as centres of excessive racial discrimination: the important West Indian personage who, stranded overnight, has been unceremoniously shunted by a local officialdom to a third rate hotel in Nassau or Hamilton because of his skin colour has always been assured of a full and indignant report in his home press. The result has been that it is only in the geographical and historical sense that the island chains may be considered part of the West Indies (Watling Island in the Bahamas, after all, has always generally been considered to be the location of the first landfall of Columbus on his historic voyage). In the social and economic sense they have been influenced, overwhelmingly, by the traditional colonial English way of life brought over by the Loyalist refugees fleeing the American Revolution, with its sense of property and the psychology of Southern slavery. Barbados, it is true, was equally conservative to begin with. But its proximity to the more progressive islands and their more progressive streams of thought finally compelled it to break out of its Blackstonian Tory shell. No such modernizing process took place in the northern colonies until, that is to say, only yesterday. They remained strongholds of conservatism in the Caribbean ferment of the inter-war period. They stand today, therefore, as citadels of the Caribbean *ancien régime*. By force of contrast they illuminate much of what has happened to West Indian society during the last forty years.

From the earliest beginnings after 1620 or so the Bermudian-Bahamian developments departed radically from those of the islands properly West Indian. Their productive system, after a false start in tobacco growing, was essentially mercantile. The genesis of the New Providence colony, so deeply rooted as it was in the growth of its pirate economy, placed a maritime stamp upon the original settlers, not to mention a collective psychology of hardy individualism which remained with Bahamians even after the famous gubernatorial regime of Woodes Rogers finally terminated the existence of the pirate base. The piratical outlook tended to remain, founded as it had been upon a succession of early Governors, before the reforming Rogers' period, who had openly profited from the reckless sale of privateering commissions. The art of piracy, even so, was merely followed by the art of 'wrecking', the organized depredation upon shipwrecked vessels which, from a moral viewpoint, was hardly an improvement. Both piracy and 'wrecking' flourished on the geographical character of the Bahamian archipelago, with its hazardous sea passages and the virtual impossibility of imposing any kind of effective control over islands such as Grand Bahama and Inagua isolated, until the communications revolution of the twentieth century, from the capital centre. Bermuda, in its turn, the original colony from which the Bahamas were settled in the 1650's by religious independents turned out by the Bermudian Royalist counter-rebellion, rapidly established itself as the entrepôt of the American carrying trade. At the same time the control of the salt-ponds of the Turks Islands, treated in the beginning as a dependency, gave to the Bermudian merchant adventurers and their sailing crews the command of a commercial staple.

In such colonies the conditions did not exist which led, in the West Indies proper, to the development of a fully fashioned slave society of the plantation type. The slave population was proportionately smaller, relative to the demographic character of the sugar islands, and the seafaring life—always, sociologically, an anti-authoritarian existence—gave the coloured people a degree of freedom which would have been unattainable had they been tied strictly to the

land. The characteristic figures of social life came to be the 'Eleutherian adventurer', the self-sufficient tradesman, the skilled sailor,
the almost Elizabethan-style sea-captain, giving individual support
to the famous slogan of 'salt, cedars and sailors' which for so long
expressed Bermudian superiority on the high seas. The racial ratios
of the population revealed how, unlike neighbouring Jamaica, there
was a large 'white settler' population for whose members trading
and sailing were congenial occupations, and giving rise to the
characteristic prototype of the Bahamian 'poor whites' in the settlements of the lonely 'Out islands', jealously maintaining their racial
integrity well into the twentieth century: the 1903 survey team of
the Geographical Society of Baltimore noted in their report the
consequent ravages of family in-breeding in 'all white' townships
like Spanish Wells and Hopetown that actually outlawed Negro
residents.[1] Plantation agriculture was clearly impossible, and social
conditions in fact were far more akin to those of the continental
colonies than to those of the West Indian islands. The American
influence, too, was made more emphatic by the continuous intercourse taking place between the continental mainland and the
Nassau-Hamilton complex; the history of the early Bermuda Company was closely tied to that of the old Virginia Company, while
both sides in the prolonged Puritan-Royalist struggles of the early
period received aid from their respective co-religionists in the New
England and Atlantic Shore provinces.

Economic interest reinforced religio-political predilections. The
twin economies were, to all intents and purposes, annexes of the
continental economic system of the United States. They depended
on that system in a providential, even parasitical sense. At every
crisis in their history they have found salvation in their strategic
position *vis-à-vis* that system. That was the case, early on, with the
influx of new wealth brought by the rich royalists fleeing the American Revolution. It was the case, later, with the massive illicit wealth
spawned by the rise of Nassau and St George's as the centres of the
blockade runners penetrating the Northern blockade of the Confederate ports during the Civil War period. It was the case, finally,
with the Prohibition era of the 1920's when Nassau, along with
Havana, became the headquarters of the 'bootlegging' syndicates
pumping contraband liquor into an American acquisitive society
in no mood for an experiment in national austerity. All of

those episodes, all of some international notoriety in their day, exposed the accidental character of Bermudian and Bahamian prosperity, existing on factors arising out of circumstances alien to the island peoples and over which they exercised no control.

Certain leading features characterized this economic history. The history of essentially 'bonanza' economies gave birth to the 'bonanza' adventurer type: the counter-revolutionary American exile, the blockade runner, the Prohibition gangster, the amoral Hemingwayesque soldier of fortune who would do anything for a 'fast buck', usually on the wrong side of the law. It is difficult not to read the accounts of the social upheavals in the decades of the 1860's and the 1920's without feeling acutely how commercial greed saps the moral fibre of a society, especially when its indulgence brings, as it brought on those two occasions, fabulous profits. The Civil War 'bonanza' broke down the old Tory order of the colonial Regency period; the Prohibition 'bonanza' finally destroyed any element of it that might have been left. Both English colonial official—whose Government, in both cases, connived at illegal trafficking—and local Creole gentlemen might have thought that they were aiding and abetting the Confederate gentleman's cause against the 'damn Yankees' of the Northern business civilization. But what they accomplished, in grim fact, was the consolidation of capitalist business ethics in the Bermudian-Bahamian society. For, to make a second point, the ultimate beneficiaries of the 'bonanza' periods were, first, the foreign commercial agents, captains, pilots and gang leaders who left as soon as the brittle affluence of the Atlantic bubbles burst and, second, the Bermudian-Bahamian merchant class whose brief, lucrative careers as cotton and liquor magnates provided the financial foundations of their status as the social and political ruling class of the island societies. For the island masses it was all, at best, a brief and illusory prosperity; the high wages disappeared with the collapse of the 'bonanzas'; and as late as the 1920's it was possible to find both in Nassau and St George's traces of the financial demolition which came about when Richmond and Wilmington were lost to the Confederacy.

And the third point to underline is that the American influence throughout has been that of the more socially retrogressive elements of American life. The American adventurers who flocked to the islands were basically anti-democratic: the Tory Royalist of 1776, the Southern secessionist, the Chicago-style 'bootlegger'. There had been early expectations on the part of the American revolutionary leaders that the Bermudian colonists would join them, as General Washington's letter of 1775 to the inhabitants of Bermuda testified.[2] But the appeal underestimated the deep conservatism of the white colonist mentality, and every crisis thereafter in the American democracy found that mentality on the wrong side. Hence, out of all that, the phenomenon of the famous 'Bay Street boys', the Nassau mercantile oligarchy whose life style was the resultant mixture of the luxuriant vulgarity of American wealth and British social snobbery, with the first the controlling element. In the post-Emancipation society, with the onset of the prolonged nineteenth-century depression which, except for the Civil War interlude, lasted well into the twentieth century, that oligarchy ruled over the Negro majority in a manner that marked it out as perhaps the most narrow-minded ruling class in the entire English-speaking Caribbean.

The machinery of class slavery that the Bermudian and Bahamian oligarchies put together, untouched in its essentials until the 1960's, offers a fascinating study in the mechanics of colonial society. In its economic aspects the oligarchies, by means of their stranglehold on both the import-export trade and the credit system, held the majority at their mercy. Their members, through their ownership of shipping, controlled the vital industries like the Bahamian sponge and turtle enterprises, both ship captains and crews being bound by a repressive contract system, including an 'advance' system, leading to widespread indebtedness, not unlike the results of the 'advance' system of the Honduran lumber camps. Likewise, in the 'wrecking' industry, to which the islanders reverted after the Civil War débâcle, the ordinary sailor embraced all of the hazardous risks while the shipowners garnered the best of the profits by means of the iniquitous percentage system. The old Caribbean story of the commercial control of agriculture repeated itself here, so that the Bermudian small vegetable grower, for example, depended at once upon the town merchants for credit and upon the American-controlled steamship transportation system; for, unlike his American competitor, the Southern truck grower, he could not take advantage of fast freight train services to get his produce to the New York

markets. Likewise, the Bahamian pineapple industry finally collapsed because the Nassau shippers were unwilling to invest capital
in modernizing their packaging and shipping operations. More
generally, the rehabilitation of fishing and agriculture, the mainstay
of the economies in between the 'bonanza' episodes, was sabotaged
by a commercial mercantile class that found it more profitable to
import foodstuffs from the United States than to subsidize the local
food economy, and they justified their policy on the ground that the
island populations were 'lazy' and 'unproductive'. The truth was,
of course, that the entire communal psychology of the island communities had been shaped for so long by the adventitious event and
the spurious prosperity it generated, that its victims tended, Micaw-
ber-like, to wait always for something to turn up; and the attitude
precluded the development of any sort of rational economic planning
as insurance against hard times. It was small wonder that, in the
Bahamian case, the 'Out islands' suffered from the neglect and
disinterest of the mercantile group centred in Nassau. Lacking
bold leadership from their ruling classes the twin economies thus
stagnated for a century or more; Bacot's description of Nassau in
1869 was not very different from the description of the same town in
1917 by Defries. All in all, the legend of the Atlantic tropics as
idyllic, primitive and happy societies—immortalized in Marvel's
early *Song of the Emigrants in Bermuda*—was an empty fiction.
The reality, for Negro and 'poor white' alike, was altogether
different.

All this was cemented, politically, by the remarkable survival of
the archaic constitutional system of the Old Empire up until only
yesterday, with only minor changes taking place, like the 1841
bifurcation of the old Nassau Council into separate Legislative and
Executive Councils. In both societies the eighteenth-century *ancien
régime* survived intact into the modern period: an ancient Assembly
exercising its petty privileges; a restrictive electoral system weighted
heavily in favour of propertied interests; a corrupt vestry system as
well as an equally corrupt voting system, especially before the introduction, in Nassau, of the secret ballot in 1949; an inequitable constituency distribution penalizing the outer islands and the more
distant parishes; the pocket borough and the plural vote: all in all,
a regime serving the white rich minority interests, inevitably so,
once granted the close relationship existing between ownership of

land and ethnic grouping. Theoretically, it was pure representative government, for the Assemblies enjoyed ancient privileges long since lost in the Crown Colonies: the right of private initiative in financial legislation, for example, and the curious system of administrative boards in the Bahamian system whereby the elected members exercised a real authority over administrative departments. In practice, it was a 'rotten borough' system protecting vested interests under the guise of defending 'ancient liberties', and resisting all liberal reform measures, from income tax to electoral reorganization. 'This mockery of representation,' wrote the observer L. D. Powles in 1888, 'is the greatest farce in the world. The coloured people have the suffrage, subject to a small property qualification, but have no idea how to use it. The elections are by open voting, and bribery, corruption and intimidation are carried on in the most unblushing manner, under the very noses of the officers presiding over the polling booths. Nobody takes any notice, and as the coloured people have not yet learnt the art of political organization, they are power-less to defend themselves. The result is that the House of Assembly is little less than a family gathering of Nassau whites, nearly all of whom are related to each other, whilst the coloured people are ground down and oppressed in a manner that is a disgrace to the British flag.'[3]

The Atlantic West Indies thus entered the modern period politi-cally antiquated, culturally depressed and psychologically retarded. Their white oligarchies, of the 'Forty Thieves' in Hamilton and the 'Bay Street boys' in Nassau, presided over a socio-economic power structure in which they controlled the economic-financial apparatus by means of family-type interlocking directorates and the political apparatus by means of their personal occupation of the strategic members' seats in the House of Assembly, the Legislation Council and the Executive Council. Their social climate was a Dickensian mixture of American crass acquisitiveness and British snobbery, and not the least fascinating aspect for the social psychologist was the way in which, despite their efforts to draw social lines, the 'best people' finally accepted the newly-rich liquor families whose wealth they coveted as they despised their manners. Their intellectual life, such as it was, consisted of a historical antiquarianism that could become much more excited about the insular history under the old proprietary system than about contemporary politics or economic problems. At its best, it produced the scholarship of Sir John Lefroy's *Memorials*, at its worst the sort of book that rhapsodized about anti-quarian history like Sister Jean de Chantal Kennedy's *Bermuda's Sailors of Fortune* or Major Bell's *Bahamas: Isles of June*; the latter book, indeed, including a curious preface by Sir Bede Clifford in which that famous Governor managed at once to praise the English 'racial virility' of the Bahamian pirates and, irrelevantly, to malign the general character of the conscientious objectors of the First World War. That sort of literature, apart from reflecting the dismal social values of colonial life, was further encouraged by the fact that in Bermuda—like Gibraltar, a fortress colony—the Governor-ship was traditionally held by a high military officer, a tradition only finally broken by the appointment of Viscount Knollys in 1941 as the first civilian Governor. Nor has there been wanting the sort of 'blood and thunder' historical novel, like Christopher Nicole's *Blood Amyot*, which creates a vast panoramic melodrama out of the more flamboyant elements of the island stories. If to all this is added the paternalism of the social climate, viewing the behaviour pat-terns and folk beliefs of the Negro working masses as 'quaint' and 'childish' forms of 'superstition'—the attitude of a book like Robert Curry's *Bahamian Lore*—the general picture takes shape of incredibly archaic societies resting on parasitic forms of wealth, racial *apartheid*, political apathy and economic *laissez-faire*. That this was not appre-ciated on the outside was due to a carefully cultivated isolationism on the part of the ruling groups, combined with costly propaganda campaigns portraying the islands as veritable Shangri-la elysiums; a strategy so successful that the Moyne Commission of 1938 seems not to have even considered the possibility of visiting them.

In all this the Bermudian pattern, being more intractably British and less influenced by American forces, was perhaps more benign than the Bahamian. But it was sufficiently reactionary at that. Its parliamentary institutions, at the beginning of the modern period after 1918, remained much the same as they had been at the time of the abrogation of the old Bermuda Company's charter in 1684. Ultimate political power, in theory, lay with the elected House of Assembly. But in practice it lay with an Executive Council of nominated members and a Legislative Council—the upper house of the legislative branch—of nominated and ex-officio members,

including the powerful offices of the Chief Justice, the Colonial
Secretary and the Receiver General. The executive was responsible,
through the Governor, only to London, the legislature to (in 1918) a
miniscule group of freehold voters (some 1,413 voters out of a total
adult population of just over 20,000 persons). It was a potentially
explosive condition of things, had the Colonial Office decided at
any time to intervene as a trustee of the general welfare; which, of
course, it never had done since the Emancipation controversy.

The social structure, in its turn, was semi-feudal, with its economic
base in the merchant community and their control of the banking
system and strategic private companies like the Electric Light Company and the Bermuda Telephone Company. An American-type
race bar shaped social life, symbolized in the segregated entertainment institutions of the Royal Bermuda Yacht Club, the Mid-Ocean
Golf Club and the Bermuda Hunt Club, in all of which the well-to-
do American tourist, the local white *élite*, and the officers of the
British garrison fraternized in a secluded world closed to the coloured
majority. The cricket world was divided between the white elevens
and the coloured elevens; and it was not until 1961 that the Social
Welfare Board finally managed to provide the first golf course open
to the general public. The racialist spirit even entered the Bermudian
war effort, with whites joining up in the Volunteer Rifle Corps and
coloured in the Militia Artillery; and it was typical of Bermudian
conservatism that the segregation did not produce a Bermudian
Cipriani to challenge its arrogant stupidity. There was, in addition,
a racialist educational system, compounded by the peculiar Bermudian dual system of 'vested' and 'non-vested' schools, and even
further compounded by the distinction, officially recognized by the
Schools Act of 1949, between free schools and fee-paying schools.
British Governors, with honourable exceptions, countenanced the
general evil, although as time went by the racial exclusivism of
Government House began to meet a rising critical public opinion,
culminating in the widespread indignation let loose by Sir Alexander
Hood's failure to invite any of the coloured citizenry to the state
dinner of welcome for Queen Elizabeth during the 1953 royal visit.

The inter-war politics were thus the almost exclusive monopoly
of a deeply entrenched oligarchy, allowed to do as it pleased by a
complacent British government. The suppression of any kind of
free trade unionism stifled the possible growth of any union-based

opposition parties. Their absence, along with the smallness of the electoral body, fortified an individualistic politics in which members of the House, in the naïve judgment of one apologetic observer, were free to serve their constituents without interference from partisan sources.[4] Political life thus remained the private game, with all of its antiquarian mumbo-jumbo, of the Assembly parliamentarians. The political 'issues' were the picayune matters that affected their constitutional 'dignity' or their commercial interests, generating factional passions that left the inert majority unmoved; the prolonged struggle, for example, between the pro-automobile and the anti-automobile cliques and its continuation, later, in slightly different form between the advocates of the new railroad scheme and its Dickensian opponents. The final commentary upon the romantic fiction of the House of Assembly as the watchdog of popular liberties was its abject surrender to the hard 'Yankee trade' of the 1941 bases-destroyers deal between Britain and the United States and its failure to prevent the destruction by the new American base of a whole way of life in St David's Island; just as, indeed, a century before, official Bermuda had had nothing critical to say about the colony's status as a centre for the British system of penal exile or about the barbarous conditions of the 'convict hulks' described at the time in John Mitchel's *Jail Journal*.[5] On the eve of World War Two Bermuda was thus a society in which, on the credit side, a high wage structure and almost full employment provided living standards decidedly higher than those of the West Indian economies to the south; but in which, on the debit side, trade union law had progressed no further than the friendly society stage, there was no provision for workmen's compensation, any sort of industrial inspectorate was non-existent and, generally, in which there existed a precarious situation dependent on the burgeoning tourist trade and any adverse conditions could easily reveal the presence of the hardhearted or merely bankrupt employer.[6]

The post-1945 period seemed, on the surface, to perpetuate that somnolent condition. But only on the surface, for subterranean social forces were working to generate the revolt of the masses that had taken place years earlier in the West Indian islands. Until 1960 or so, the Bermudian leadership in that struggle was that of the coloured professional group whose independent members like E. T. Richards and G. A. Williams waged war in the Assembly against things like the infamous Hotel-Keepers Protection Act which since 1930 had granted legislative sanction to racial discrimination in the hotel industry; in addition, there was the work of the individual professional radical like the Trinidadian Dr Gordon. The prolonged struggle for franchise reform, finally ending in 1962 with the introduction of universal adult suffrage, was mainly their handiwork through the Committee for Adult Universal Suffrage. The second stage occurred with the more militant strategy of the Bermuda Industrial Union and its remarkable Secretary-General, Dr Barbara Ball; as elsewhere, the pattern of imperialist disengagement threw up a leader at once white and feminine, in this case a small, pleasantly nervous professional woman doctor—not unlike Mrs Allfrey in the Dominica situation—whose early secluded education in the all-white Bermuda High School, added to a McGill University residence, laid the foundations for a passionate concern for the Bermudian masses, sentimental in its character rather than ideological, that rapidly earned for her the deep hatred of her own class and her own race. Merely to hear her speak, without any trace of bitterness, of the victimizing pressures brought to bear upon her by the official institutions of the society—the police, the law courts, the Church, her own medical profession, not to mention the loss of most of her white friends—is to be made aware of the general climate of fear and intimidation in which the mass of Bermudians have traditionally lived. The strike activities of early 1965, as well as the direct appeal to the United Nations Anti-Colonial Committee, indicated a readiness to employ modern tactics in the struggle; thus going far beyond the old political ritual in which agitating coloured Assembly members were for years appeased by being made members of special committees that kept explosive items trapped within the parliamentary machinery. The organized political party also finally made its appearance under these pressures: on the Conservative side, the United Bermuda Party with its leader, Sir Henry Tucker, being at once a leading Assembly dignitary, a powerful banker and director of numerous companies; and on the radical side, the Progressive Labour Party, mainly led by liberal-minded lawyers, since only the professional barrister—like the dynamic Lois Browne in the Bermudian situation—is sufficiently financially secure to be immune to the economic victimization of the oligarchic forces. It remains to be seen whether future developments will take place along Barbadian lines or along lines more genuinely radical.

The modern stage of the Bahamian situation goes back to the period after the rum-running 'bonanza' when, with the official termination of Prohibition, American capitalists entered a new field, that is, descended on the island to acquire large land tracts on the west end of New Providence, thus bringing about the real estate boom and thereby reinforcing once more the rule of the Bay Street oligarchy whose members shared in the expansion. With stringent metropolitan laws restricting foreign purchase and investment, the ranks of the new liquor magnates had been filled from the existing Bahamian merchant class; and the subsequent development of a highly capitalized tourism added force to the process; so that the social and political life of the colony became that of the Bethells, the Christies, the Sands, and the Symonettes.

Their rule, at that time as before, remained as unenlightened as ever. The record in education alone was symptomatic: as late as 1957 the ratio of primary schoolchildren to those in secondary schools was a scandalously high 67 per cent, even worse than in Haiti, while of the total of 770 'teachers' in the system some 628 were totally untrained. As in Bermuda, in fact, the educational needs of the many had throughout been principally met by religious private enterprise, and the great names of Bahamian educational progress, especially in the earlier period, had been, significantly, those of the devoted Anglo-Catholic bishops and missionaries: Venables, Churton, Shedden, Weigall, and Matthews. Up until the 1960's, indeed, anything in the nature of a modern welfare state, in education or any other field, was conspicuously absent, and even then something was finally done only as a result of the combined pressure of local liberal opinion and belated Colonial Office investigations. Health and welfare services as known in Jamaica were practically non-existent, and the British official reports, the Houghton Report on education and the Hughes Report on medical services, painted a black picture. The Houghton Report noted how the board system meant running essential services by amateur politicians, to the exclusion of the professional person, with all of its fatal consequences; while the Hughes Report noted that the temptation of the medical profession to deal with the more wealthy patient had produced a general situation in which some twenty-one inhabited islands had to do with the services of only seven qualified practitioners.[7] In effect, the Bahamas government was deliberately kept a poor government in a rich economy. Denied the weapon of direct taxation and almost solely dependent upon an import duties revenue that could not hope to keep pace with the fantastic revenues of the private tourism and foreign investment sectors, it declined into virtually a parish-pump state power surrounded by tremendously wealthy private empires. Even more than in the United States, the resultant contrast between private affluence and public squalor, between the elegant hotels and gift-shops of Bay Street and the shacks of the Negro proletariat that works in them 'over the Hill', belied the official propaganda; in 1959 this was the only government in the British Caribbean lacking any scheme designed to solve the housing problem; New Providence had no adequate sewage system or water supply; there was no public bus service; there was no museum to compare with those even in Bridgetown or Georgetown; and the Public Works Department spent a meagre budget repairing pothole-ridden public roads—as compared with the modern roads of the private developments—that excited the derision even of the conservative *Nassau Guardian*.

The official theory of the constitutional regime behind all this was that, although not responsible it was representative.[8] In reality, of course, it was representative of the ruling group, no more. Almost every single member of the House, theoretically representative of all of the islands, could be found in person either on or around Bay Street as a prominent merchant or lawyer. An almost completely white legislature, it only recognized, even more than the Barbados House of Assembly, the imperatives of its own class interests. It rejected the Colonial Development Fund because acceptance would have been conditional upon the passage of up-to-date social welfare and trade union laws it did not want. It resisted the Duke of Windsor's pleas, when he was Governor during the Second World War period, for tax reforms that could have become the basis for a positive government programme, still lacking twenty years later, of slum clearance, low cost housing schemes, improved educational and agricultural services. In Nassau, indeed, the Duke confronted the most reactionary group of businessmen in the colonial Caribbean, and encounters with typical Bahamian Tories like Sir Kenneth Solomon must have made Stanley Baldwin appear, in retrospect, as positively Jacobinical; and his wife's contented carrying out of her duties as President of the Red Cross and honorary President of local Daughters of the British Empire can have been little consolation, not to mention her quaint belief that political differences were peculiarly male infantile prejudices that could be assuaged by meeting at cosy dinners at Government House.[9]

Reforms, when they did come, were minor structural repairs only forced upon an obstructionist House by events, the 1942 riots occasioned by the gross inequity of the wage rates paid to American white workers and local Negro workers by the American contractors building the wartime airbase and, later, the series of strike movements snowballing from the 1958 clash between the taxicab union and the wealthy Playtours Agency. The constitutional changes of 1959–64 did little to alter the power structure, for the abolition of plural voting, the grant of the vote to women and the conferment of internal self-government (the latter merely a formal ratification of a *de facto* situation) left untouched a gerrymandered electoral constituency system which, in 1962, permitted the conservative United Bahamian Party to gain 19 seats on the basis of some 26,000 votes and the Progressive Liberal Party only 8 seats on the basis of over 36,000 votes. In such a system reforms ordinarily desirable— the 1957 proposal, for example, that the unofficial members of the Executive Council be appointed by the House—became reactionary tactics, for the House was then, as it still largely is, in the firm control of a closed circuit, with the Negro members slowly growing in numbers, of white businessman politicians. The supreme irony, all in all, of Bahamian politics was that a constitutional system initially, in its seventeenth-century historical origins, a product of the radical Leveller ideas of the early Eleutherian refugees from Royalist Bermuda should have become, long before the modern period, an instrument twisted into the service of a Bourbonese colonial conservatism.

For the Negro majority all this meant a grim struggle for existence in a deceptively idyllic Eden. Denied access to the land by the narrow-minded Crown Lands policy of the British government, they had become, over the years, either squatters living in savage depression in the Out Islands or seafaring boatmen getting what they could from the cycle of 'boom and bust' characteristic of the Bahamian economy. The tourist industry, it is true, provided a more

11

attractive wage employment sector for the New Providence workers.
But, in the first place, the employment (until the post-1945 expansion) was seasonal only, a brief winter season of good wages and
liberal gratuities followed by nine months of precarious existence
in agricultural or fishing pursuits; and, secondly, the improved
wage-rates and living standards thereby made possible, and duly
noted by Major Orde-Browne in his 1939 Report, were rapidly
neutralized by the massive inflationary price-costs structure generated by the tourist economy, by now (1968) the endemic disease
of the economy as a whole. The struggle of organized labour, not
yet completed, to obtain union recognition, improved working
conditions, especially in the special conditions of luxury hotel employment, security against arbitrary dismissal and a democratic
industrial relations machinery continued, with accelerated speed
after 1958. The politicization of the struggle, with the formation
of the Labour Party under Randol Fawkes, as well as of the coloured
middle class Progressive Liberal Party, marked a further stage in
Negro collective action, albeit a quarter of a century behind the
Jamaican development.

It was a war on two fronts. First, of the coloured professional
group, whose limited objectives were summarized in its 1944
memorandum which, adjuring universal suffrage, concentrated
upon the demand for the removal of the 'unseen barrier' frustrating
the social advance of qualified coloured persons and attacking a political system that placed more importance upon social standing in
the white group than upon administrative ability or sense of public
obligation.[10] Second, of the Negro majority, victimized far more
viciously by a double economic and racial subordination. For them,
discrimination against coloured persons in the tourist hotels was an
academic question only. Far more important was the economic
discrimination, the 1942 labour legislation, for example, that denied
collective bargaining rights to domestic and hotel workers. In their
struggle they had to meet ruling class tactics reminiscent of Chartist
England: the house eviction of labour sympathizers, the use of
sedition statutes to silence labour leaders, the invoking of restrictive
immigration legislation, originally intended to deal with undesirable
American hoodlum types, to deport local critics of the regime. Until,
indeed, the ferment of the 1960's, Bahamian society was a three-
tiered structure of the separate worlds of the expatriate residents

and winter tourists, of the domestic white and near-white *élite* and of the Negro masses, ignorant and suspicious of each other. For years it was regarded as positively dangerous for a white person to travel through the Out Islands, and few cared to do it. It is the merit of a travel sketch book like Amelia Defries' *The Fortunate Islands* that, for all of its tone of anthropological naiveté, it braved the opposition of white snobbery to search out, with real curiosity, the ordinary people of the Nassau sponge yards and the desolate Grand Bahama villages.

The key to all this, in the double Bermuda-Bahamas way of life, has been the special character of the power structure in the island societies. Unlike the West Indian islands proper, where British imperial rule, for all its defects, was a continuous reality, the powerful aristocracies of the Atlantic societies were granted almost complete independence of action by London. They became, then, real ruling classes and not mere agents of the imperial centre. Other factors added to the natural intransigence of temper arising from that fact. The relatively large size of the white minority, for example, some forty per cent in Bermuda, made for further self-confidence, reinforced as that balance was by a Bermudian immigration policy deliberately designed to fill even lower income occupations—nurses, teachers, police, hotel staff—with white expatriates. So much was this so that, according to its critics, the police force in Bermuda became nothing much more than a marriage bureau to provide eligible, that is, white husbands for the local white girls.[11] This becomes, from the Negro viewpoint, a white plot to keep the Negro down, so that a great deal of the general complaint of the Negro majority seizes upon the resultant lack of occupational opportunity for Negro candidates rather than emphasizing the disease of a Harlem type of ghetto poverty which, on the whole, does not exist, at least not in Harlem dimensions. There is, too, the American influence, already noted, which continues today by means of official American acceptance of the local segregationist patterns, to the degree that Washington recruits an all white staff in the local consulates, save for chauffeurs, messengers and cleaners.[12] Hence, altogether, a real ruling class mentality, as in Rhodesia and South Africa, which will readily subordinate its traditional 'allegiance' to Britain to an attitude, if need be, of complete and hostile resistance to reforms emanating from London, and especially if the reforms come from any Labour Government of 'labourites and coalminers', to use the contemptuous phrase of a Bermudian white legislator.[13]

Hence, much more than in Barbados, an entrenched white despotism. Its astonishing rule, graphically described by Powles and James Smith some seventy-five years ago, remains basically intact today, although the walls are beginning to crumble. The 1964–65 memoranda forwarded to the United Nations by the progressive forces in Nassau and Hamilton fully catalogued its present character. In both places there is a systematic subversion of democratic growth and a refusal to give effect to majority rule. Coercive legislation, including the restriction of trade union activities to limited statutory purposes only, cripples the trade union movement, while the unions at the same time are denied representation on the vital boards and advisory committees. Social welfare legislation is embryonic only; and even when it appears, as with the recent Bermudian workmen's compensation scheme, it is based upon an archaic form of employers' liability farmed out to private insurance interests. Or, alternatively, there is a 'do nothing' policy, exemplified in the way in which the Bahamas Government has abrogated its right to govern by virtually surrendering its vital powers of control over the massive Freeport luxury tourist-gambling complex to the private Port Authority of the financial interests operating that astonishing tourist ghetto; a surrender which, among much else, leaves the Freeport industrial and tourist promoters almost a free hand in their victimization of labour leaders and their refusal to recognize trade unions in their private empire.[14] A segregationist pattern infects most institutions of the societies, the schools, the civil service, private industry, housing areas, electoral districts, even the peculiar Bermudaian pattern of the so-called workmen's clubs which are, in effect, segregated white and Negro recreation centres. The token integration that has recently taken place certainly has done as yet little to douche the general belief that the dice are loaded against the wearer of a dark skin, politically, socially, economically. It is clear, for example, that in the field of Bermudian secondary education the tiny amount of integration that so far has taken place is of a token character only, occurs mostly in the coloured schools like the Berkeley Institute, and may well be interpreted not as a genuine effort to secure a real integration so much as a mask for securing Government financial support.[15] A close union between business and government produces the spectacle of cabinet ministers doing business with their own firms so that, in the notorious case of the Bahamian Minister of Finance and Tourism, the all-powerful Sir Stafford Sands, it is almost impossible to determine whether he speaks for Government or for his clients and very often he seems to be speaking for both. It is, all in all, a general picture of almost total economic and financial control used ruthlessly against anyone who dares oppose the oligarchies in business or politics.[16] And all of it is capped by a ruling class contempt for public opinion so shameless and unabashed that in 1933 the Bermuda House arbitrarily decided to cease the publication of its debates as an economy measure, thus drawing a smoke screen, in the words of one dissenting member, over its proceedings.[17] Fear and intimidation, indeed, induce a climate of secrecy in the society as a whole so that, in the phrase of one outside observer speaking generally of race relations in Bermuda, racial differences in that colony seem to be a public secret and a private obsession.[18]

There are, of course, concessions to the age, the final abolition, for example, of the iniquitous plus vote for property owners. But such reforms (1) have themselves been extracted very slowly from a recalcitrant ruling *élite* by the riot and strike actions of the 1964–65 period, and (2) in themselves are mild measures that leave untouched the basic social ills. It still remains to be seen whether it will be the liberal Burkian outlook of Sir Henry Tucker or the Eldonian outlook of Sir John Cox that will ultimately prevail in the inner councils of the oligarchy, especially in the matter of party politics.[19] Perhaps even more important, it remains as yet an open question as to whether the coloured populations are ready to launch a root and branch attack against the fundamental economic base of the system and not merely its more indefensible Dickensian trappings. For oligarchical rule has generally conditioned the coloured person to believe that he is generally incapable and irresponsible; and the resultant reluctance to do anything about his situation is strengthened by his own peculiar Bermudian-Bahamian snobbery that looks down on Negroes from elsewhere with different backgrounds. The new religion of party politics, as the 1966 split in the Bermuda Progressive Labour Party between the moderate parliamentary group and its extra-parliamentary radical critics shows,[20] does not in itself guarantee the emergence of a strong popular radical opposition backed by educated leaders who need no longer suffer the harsh fate of the old-style independents of the pre-party era. It may, as a matter of fact, simply bring out in the open the real differences of social class interest between the coloured bourgeois and the black working class.

That last point deserves further emphasis. The election manifestoes of the Progressive Liberal Party in Nassau indicate no enthusiasm in its lawyer leaders for political independence. The Bermudian Labour Party leaders, likewise, argue for nothing more revolutionary than a list of reforms that include night sessions of Parliament, a Bermudian Governor, a new electoral act, abolition of the inefficient and amateur system of Government Boards and• final termination of the Legislative Council as a second chamber.[21] That is to say, the opposition movements as yet want nothing much more than the ending of the various political and constitutional absurdities of the system noted as far back as 1860, in the Bermudian case, in Godet's book.[22] It is not unfair to say, then, that the contemporary climate of opinion in Bermuda and the Bahamas is pretty much at the point where Jamaican opinion stood in 1865 and after. The conservative groups have accepted the new constitutions in the same spirit in which Jamaican conservatives surrendered their rights to the Crown Colony regime in that year.[23] The coloured groups, in their turn, seem to want not so much national independence as a new leadership on the part of the United Kingdom, thus suggesting that many of them still half believe the expatriate myth that without the outsider's guidance the whole structure of things collapse.[24] The old lighthearted tolerance of the system, described in the last century by Bacot,[25] has gone. But a more positive militancy, ready to fight for the full measure of freedom, remains as yet unformed. Whether the astonishing electoral victory of the Progressive Liberals in the Bahamas' election of January 1967, creating the first Negro government ever in Nassau, will change this remains yet to be seen.

The key to all this, perhaps, is the one single cardinal fact that the dominant, almost tyrannical leading feature of Bermudian-Bahamian society is the tourist industry. What sugar once was to the West Indies tourism is today to Nassau and Hamilton. A nineteenth-century writer noted, speaking of Barbadians, that the destruction of the rest of the universe would interest them only as that catastrophe affected sugar prices.[26] Tourism affects Bermudians and Bahamians today in similar fashion. Its phenomenal post-war surge has generated, in its wake, secondary investment by outside capital in the building and real estate fields, all of them stimulated by the handsome tax-exemption structure put together by the business-politicians, including, as in certain select cases such as the massively luxurious Freeport scheme in the Bahamas, guaranteed freedom from customs and excise duties. The ease, too, with which international companies can form non-taxable holding companies in Nassau due to the absence of treaties providing for the exchange of financial information between the Bahamian and other governments, has made of the two Atlantic capitals hospitable centres for tax refugees, both individual and corporate. International finance capitalism, with a firm base in luxury tourism, has thus become the master of the twin economies, promoting with fantastic success the dream of one of the early Nassau entrepreneurs to 'turn this insignificant community into the new Mecca of the world's rich, a metropolis gorgeous enough and luxurious enough to draw the international set away from the Riviera and Biarritz and Palm Beach'.

This dependency on the wealthy United States tourist traffic, fundamentally parasitic, has incalculable consequences for the Bermudian-Bahamian way of life. It has made of the ruling groups paranoid tourist-worshippers. Public policies are shaped by consideration of the traffic's priorities, so that millions have been granted to the Bahamas Development Board for expensive tourist promotion schemes while everything else has languished for lack of funds. The pleasure of the tourist is viewed as paramount and anything likely to upset him is eschewed; hence, in part, the colour bar and hence, too, the active censorship which helps insulate the Bahamian populace against knowing much about outside conditions, about, for example, neighbouring Jamaica where a flourishing tourism manages without colour bar or gambling. The fallacious argument is used, as in the Bermudian case, that the elimination of local segregation patterns would harm the tourist trade, oblivious of the truth that most tourists come because of the island's natural beauty and, being mainly from the eastern United States, themselves belong to a public opinion about race relations that is in fact far ahead of, and not behind local opinion.[27] Tourist development, it is urged, depends on the outside investor; the investor, in turn, will not stay unless he controls hotel operations, whether that involves discriminatory practices or not. A social climate grows up in which money, sex, and snobbishness constitute the major values. The white American tourist and, more latterly, wealthy resident, comes so that, among much else, he may meet European royalty, itself in flight from the European democratic revolution; the local *élites*, in their turn, unashamedly exploit that patronage of European titles by American wealth; and the general result is the moral degradation of all concerned. The presence of a movie company doing a James Bond fantasy; the skilfully advertised ballyhoo accompanying the promotion of things like Sir Victor Sassoon's Heart Foundation; even the Bermuda meeting of President Kennedy and Prime Minister Macmillan: all are pressed into the service of a thoroughly Americanized Madison Avenue sales campaign with Government House and its pathetic British atmosphere playing a servile and quite ornamental role, the Governor, as one legislative critic has observed of the Bermudian situation, sitting with clipped wings in a gilded cage up on Langton Hill.

New and socially undesirable life styles appear, that, for example, of the new 'Freeport crowd' based on the Out Islands real estate and tourist boom, plus licenced gambling, and in which the private airfield becomes the ultimate status symbol. Social marginal types flourish, after the manner of Wallace Groves, the astute Wall Street financier, *persona non grata* to the U.S. Federal authorities, who started the Freeport development. The organized American gangs move in to take over the new gambling industry, after the Las Vegas fashion, producing yet another problem for the Federal Government authorities.[28] Entire departments of local government, the public library, and the police force, for example, are treated as tourist attractions rather than public services. A spurious 'native' culture is sponsored, like Junkanoo in Nassau, or the drab tourist hotel fare of ancient calypsoes sung by bogus calypsonians. A mendacious advertising portrays a 'happy' native society, and anyone who acts to damage the image—the case of Dr Prestwich in the Inagua 'Santa Claus' scandal of 1965 is typical[29]—is fiercely cut down. The local populace are enjoined to sustain the image of a happy-go-lucky paradise 'away from it all', so pleasing to the emotional needs of the tourist, at the same time as the insidious commercialization of social values facilitated by tourism makes it increasingly difficult for them to keep up the pretence. All this, added to the increased awareness of both class and racial differences as change presses in, generally conspires to widen the gap between myth and reality and consequently to weaken the capacity of the general will of the societies to face up to their schizoid character.

# Chapter XIII

# THE PROBLEM OF SIZE
## THE LESSER GROUPS

THERE REMAIN a set of lesser islet groups—the Caymans, the Turks and Caicos, the Grenadines, and the British Virgin Islands—which by reason of their miniscule economies, their anomalous constitutional status and their barren isolation constitute a separate problem all of their own. Published material on them is seriously limited, almost restricted indeed to official publications, due to their having been so unreasonably neglected by scholars until only recently. They have generally attracted the naturalist more than the sociologist, witness a volume like Klingel's 1940 book *Inagua*, an exhaustive study of the ecological web of tropical island life. There are entire periods of their development—the 'Bahamas period' of 1799–1848 of the Turks and Caicos group, for example—of which practically nothing is known. With non-viable economies and grant-aided administrations they have been too small at any time to stand entirely on their own, so that their position, constitutionally, has been that of dependent wards of larger units, a relationship frequently of an astonishing complexity and, perhaps inevitably, unsatisfactory. Lagging behind their parent bodies in general development, and with whom they have had few links of sentiment or economic advantage—the case of the Caymans *vis-à-vis* Jamaica, for example—they have come to constitute aggravating headaches for which so far neither British nor West Indian leadership has been able to find a suitable cure.

Along with British Honduras the Cayman Islands have remained the sole British survivors of the old Central American beach heads established along the Caribbean and Gulf of Campeche shores by the early groups of buccaneers, turtlers, logwood cutters and ship-wrecked mariners. The results, in both cases, have been similar: the establishment, generally, of a nautical culture pattern of a population of ship crews and captains characterized by a real cultural isolation despite their wide travelling habits. The Caymanian isola-tionism can be seen throughout the Caymans story: in the still strong Elizabethan archaisms of the popular speech, in the continu-ing sabbatarianism of a religious-orientated folk, in the habits of social independence, in the low alcoholic intake of the community, in the excessive degree of consanguinity among the closed ethnic clique of the local white families, in, perhaps most notably, the cultural inertia exemplified in the remarkable attachment to the age-old turtle industry, carrying the Caymanian fleets further and further afield in search of a commodity increasingly difficult to obtain but the cultural grip of which upon the insular psychology remains almost as tight as in the earlier heyday of the now legendary green turtle.[1]

It is this cultural traditionalism which today constitutes the basic problem of Caymanian society. For with the post-1945 decline of the turtle industry a serious challenge of cultural adaptation has arisen. The decline was due, in large part, to intractable factors: the decline of maritime traffic and its food needs, the competition of other delicacies in the metropolitan markets, the growing diffi-culties with the Nicaraguan Government concerning Caymanian fishing rights in the Nicaraguan territorial waters. The island eco-nomy thus faces the need for fundamental adjustment to new con-ditions. That adjustment is likely to be of a traumatic quality, when it is remembered that this is a seafaring folk for whom the tradi-tional apprenticeship with the turtling fleets has been the vital training school of its nautical skills, as well as forming an integral element of the basic folk values of the community. If and when turtling fails completely, as it might soon do, not only will the economy receive a shock but, even more, the culture itself will be changed in a fundamental way. Serious problems would then emerge. Indeed, they are already emerging; for whereas the Bar-badian sugar worker can readily desert a work-style that he loathes, the Caymanian sailor has an intimate affection for the sea that no human force, including that of his closely-knit family life, can change.[2] This helps account for the gradual change that has taken place in the employment picture, with an increasing transfer of both crews and officers to Dutch tankers, American merchantmen, and Jamaican steamers. Their remittances, especially from American sources (the export income of the economy is almost entirely in dollars) are basic to island prosperity, although the tax exemption status of the shipping companies makes an adequate evaluation of the economic character of Caymanian maritime employment difficult, if not impossible.[3] But a real gulf is discernible between high shipping profits and low seamen's wages.[4] The inequity is perpetuated by the difficulties of organizing trade unions in a labour force traditionally individualist and perennially absent from the islands. Nor should tourist-like rhapsodical pieces on the society blind the observer to the presence of very real colour-sensitivity in the various racial groups, going so far as to give rise to, first, a definite occupational-colour correlation and, second, a geographical separatism which makes of Grand Cayman island more or less a white, upper class, Presbyterian enclave, and of the Lesser Caymans, Negro Baptist lower class communities. What a burgeoning tourist traffic, based on a free port status, will do to all this is problematical.

The politico-constitutional aspects have been no less troublesome. A century of Jamaican tutelage after 1863 produced a hodgepodge of constitutional arrangements deserving of the fullest Benthamite scorn. The early spontaneous evolution, as in Belize, of a primitive democracy shaped by a community of stragglers lying outside the sphere of official colonial policy was gradually replaced, after 1898, by a system of government by Jamaican administrative and judicial officials. That, of course, was on the executive level. On the legislative level there was the sovereign legislative power of the Jamaican government. But it was rarely exercised, constituting in fact a secondary colonialism of neglect. Individual Commissioners, it is true, generally worked harmoniously with the local Assembly, but the manner in which Mr Gerrard used his powers to impose the strength of his personality upon the local citizenry demonstrated the abuses inherent in a situation governed mostly by half-understood conventions. A long line of Jamaican officials served the dependency well, along with the old Caymanian legislators who had built up the local constitutional tradition. But that was little compensation for absentee government, especially by Jamaican Governors who rarely visited the islands despite the odd fact that official contact, by law, was with them and not with the Jamaican legislature.

All the problems common to dependency status, this is to say, plagued the relationship. It was significant that changes, when they did come after 1945, were the accidental consequence of constitutional developments within Jamaica itself. Thus, the changes of 1958–59 grew out of the implications of the new Jamaican constitution, as well as of the new conditions created by the West Indies Federation. They clarified the rights and powers of the local representative institutions. But they added even more confusion to an already confused constitutional situation for, denying direct Caymanian representation in the new Federal Parliament, they handed the islands over to the administrative responsibility of the portfolio of the Federal Prime Minister at the same time as they confirmed the responsibility of the Government of Jamaica for the Jamaican connection. They thus set up an illogical mixture of official and elected responsibility. To argue that British inventiveness would make the scheme workable[5] overlooked the fact that Caymanians themselves disliked it; for, being now subject to four distinct jurisdictions—the British Government, the Federal Government, the Government of Jamaica, and the new local legislature—a few thousand people on little specks of land, in the words of one Jamaican commentator, must have had more authorities who could make laws for them than any other people in the world. Only the collapse of the Federation and the subsequent grant of separate colony status to the Caymans put an end to that situation.[6]

Situated at the end of the long Bahama chain, the Turks and Caicos Islands have, if possible, been even more neglected. They were arbitrarily annexed by the Bahamas in 1799, mainly to exploit the salt ponds. But the local inhabitants refused throughout to recognize the new authority and finally in 1848 they were made a separate colony of Jamaica, then, later, in 1873, were annexed by the Jamaican Government. The new 1959 constitution instituted a quasi-Crown Colony system based on universal adult suffrage and voluntary voter registration. But it did nothing (as in the Caymans case) to end the unsatisfactory situation in which the Government of Jamaica, along with the Chief Secretary, was placed in an almost feudal authority over the dependency, exercising various vice-regal powers; nor did the promise of consultation with the local Executive Council before Jamaican laws were locally applied meet the difficulties always inherent in the consultatory process. The result was that Jamaica, connected thus with the Turks and Caicos peoples, continued to hang their murderers, hear their appeals, provide their lawyers and judges for them, and incarcerate their long term prisoners. But all those services were rendered irresponsibly, as it were, for there were no clear channels whereby either (1) the Governor of Jamaica was made responsible for his acts to a local authority, or (2) could activate the Jamaica legislature into legislating for the wards, unless he performed the latter function, in the style of the American President, by a 'message' to the legislative house in Duke Street. The establishment of a separate colony status in 1962, as with the Caymans, ended the dilemma.[7]

The early Bermudian adventurers set the socio-economic pattern of salt raking and sailing conducted by a heavily Negro population. Once again, it is an unrecorded history, only occasionally revived by the discovery of local family papers, as in the case of the recently discovered Stubbs family notes and correspondence. Its chief feature has been the one crop salt economy, with all of its attendant risks and dangers: the uncertainty of the overseas markets, especially in Canada and Japan; the absence of any real incentives to regular work habits; the vulnerability of an economy that must literally import almost every item of daily life in its tiny stone walled cottages; the inability of small operators to provide the capital necessary for modernization of extractive processes; the chronic indebtedness of many of the workers to the merchant-middleman and the financial dependence of the latter, in turn, upon American firms. The pressure of those difficulties finally brought about the unorthodox step, in 1951, of the nationalization of the industry, to facilitate the unified control deemed essential to effective reorganization. It remains to be seen whether that step, combined with the recent growth of crayfish exporting for the Miami and New York seafood restaurant trade, and with, too, the remittances of workers employed in Curaçao and the Bahamas (greatly increased by the recent acceptance by employers in those places of the principle of compulsory allotments for dependents) will be enough to rehabilitate the economy. It is at least certain that in these tiny island village economies the small trader looking for quick profits is technologically useless. Sheer necessity, then, rather than social theory, demands his replacement by state trading concerns like the Food Control Department in the field of food and consumers' goods importation.[8]

The social consequences of this changeover to public enterprise will certainly be felt. A recent observer has noted the fact that the departure of the salt owners marked the end of a traditional society in which both white and black, educated and uneducated, 'kept their places' and 'knew their station' and that many islanders have not yet accustomed themselves to the truth that there is no longer an upper layer of society to provide them with jobs, to run the Sunday school and the choir and to set the tone of society in all essential ways.[9] That may be so. But the tradition of self help is strong in these isolated communities; nor should it be overlooked that, in all of them, as Otterbein's *The Andros Islanders* points out with reference to a folk tradition in a more northernly island of the same Bahama archipelago, there is a social family life binding the individual in a web of extended household groups so that he is rarely reduced to being, as in larger societies, an anonymous and isolated individual unprotected against the onslaught of life. The development, in particular, of sexual mores that permit the widows of the community to arrange extra-residential mating relations with a married male 'friend' indicates how the communities invent, in effect, a mode of economic protection for their weaker members. The small island societies are rich in such institutional inventiveness. It will continue to be, as in the past, their one sure sheet anchor of survival.

Nothing better illustrates the illogicality of West Indian political boundaries than the division of the Lesser Grenadines into the St Vincent dependencies on the one hand and the somewhat larger Grenadian dependency of Carriacou on the other. For their social and economic problems are basically similar, arising out of a similar cause; that is, the inability of their inhabitants to press their claims for help as strongly as those who live nearer to the respective seats of government. They are, all of them, isolated communities shaped, historically, by the unique fact that after Emancipation they were abandoned by the Caribbean *élites* and developed, under their own steam, into simple societies of Creole Negro folk in which the constituent elements of the larger West Indian societies—intense racial diversity, sophisticated class stratification, industrialization, efficient communications—were almost completely absent. They became, as it were, Robinson Crusoe communities, living out their way of life almost untouched by outside influences, save as Carriacouan patterns, for example, were influenced by the nearby Grenadian metropolitan system. Their inhabitants, today, regard themselves as distinct entities. The feeling is reinforced by their suspicion that their parent bodies have neglected them; a suspicion only somewhat assuaged when, as in the recent Carriacouan case, one of their citizens, Herbert Blaize, becomes Chief Minister of the ruling party government in Grenada.

Bequia is the leading example of this problem in the Vincentian jurisdiction of the Grenadines dependencies. The Colonial Reports on St. Vincent somehow manage to say practically nothing about the Bequian problems. Yet they are real. Community services are of a low standard and local critics of the St. Vincent government are not averse even to making comparisons with the Grenadian treatment of Carriacou which, it is said, is far better. Carriacou has a good public water supply, electricity, and motor roads. Bequia, in comparison, has practically none of these; people still carry water long distances, they 'race the fowls to bed' because there are only primitive oil lamps, and Port Elizabeth is known as the 'Flashlight Town'.[10] The backward conditions that visitors find 'charming' the local citizenry finds outrageous. An interesting debate, indeed, develops perennially between those who want to keep the 'charm' and those 'locals' who are firmly for 'improvement'. The criticisms that were directed against a visiting Barbadian editor who had deplored the 'Americanization' of Bequia are symptomatic. We need the tourist trade, it is urged. But there is neither capital nor enterprise enough in St. Vincent to undertake the exploitation of the potential tourist appeal. So, foreign venture capital must do what others will not do. In any case, 'it is better to become rich servants to foreigners than to remain poor servants to the poor'.[11] The sense of grievance, of being passed over, is real. It is not without some significance that scholarly work on Grenadines ethnology, anything comparable, say, to M. G. Smith's volume on kinship and community forms in Carriacou, is negligible. One has to go to Bruce Procope's single article for the economics of Grenadines boat building; and one almost knows more, in the work of Father Devas, about the birds of the smaller islands, Canouan, Mayreau, Union, Petit Martinique, than about their human inhabitants.[12]

Carriacou expresses best, perhaps, the capacity for unique development so characteristic of these marginal communities of the general West Indian culture province. The matrifocal family system, prevalent elsewhere, is weak, mainly because of demographic abnormalities, being replaced with a mating system which gives the figures of father and husband dominant roles of a unique kind. The disappearance of the old private plantation system, accelerated by a government purchase policy, has produced a peasant proprietorial economy in which status depends less on crude wealth and more on age, sex, and kinship; and where there is wealth, as with the schooner owner or the landlord, strongly felt community obligations impose real restrictions upon its use, as the Carriacouan ritual of the 'big time' party illustrates. There are, without doubt, certain colour and geographical differentiations, as exemplified by the well-known division between the Scottish and the French enclaves at Windward and Petit Martinique on the one side, and the rest of the island villages on the other side; as late as the 1920's, local opinion reports, no Hillsborough person could set foot in the Windward 'white' section unless he were a Government official. But this does not imply the existence of racial superiority or inferiority feelings of the kind so deeply felt in Grenadian society. Likewise, a high incidence of Carriacouan men emigrating rarely produces, as it might have done, serious cultural disturbance generated by the returning migrant who, in fact, is reabsorbed into the local home and work patterns by a set of ingenious sanctions. It is, all in all, the portrait of an almost idyllic egalitarianism. Yet the fact that much of it copies cultural conditions that existed in the Grenada of sixty years ago suggests that as the new conditions that have promoted change in that senior society come to affect the junior society a similar process, of perhaps tragic consequences, will occur there too. Carriacouan society, this is to say, is as good a test case as any for what is likely to happen to the interplay of the twin factors of uniformity and diversity in the larger West Indian society of the future.[13]

Of all the lesser groups, however, it is the British Virgin Islands that present a grossly anomalous character. For the single dominant feature of the life and economy of the islands is their almost complete economic dependency upon the neighbouring economy of the United States Virgin Islands, combined with their political control, which is increasingly meaningless, by the British government. The roots of that dependency go back to the post-1815 period when the evacuation of the old English estate families left behind a poverty-stricken peasantry of former slaves living precariously on the subsistence production of ground provisions and degenerate scrub stock and for whom St Thomas, first under its Danish rulers and then after 1917 under its American owners, rapidly became the the natural outlet. The period after 1945, with the vast employment opportunities offered by the expanding St Thomas tourist economy, along with something of a Caribbean 'divorce mill' operation, finally cemented the process. The result, today, is that despite Federal immigration restrictions, there is almost complete social and economic integration between the two island groups: in trade, occupations, travel habits, even family and kinship relations. So much so is this the case that the American dollar currency is to all intents and purposes the dominant currency in the British Virgins, and British officials are even compelled to calculate their budget in dollar terms. The 'Americanization' of the folk patterns is almost total in its effects. Wage labour on St Thomas stimulates American-type economic appetites; the British islanders go to Charlotte Amalie for consumer buying in much the same way as American rural dwellers go the the nearest town for shopping; and the alienation of the people from the land is made immensely worse, so that the coastal 'urban' settlements become nothing much more than temporary dormitory areas for a floating population marking time until they can obtain re-entry into the labour market on St Thomas or others of the United States islands. It is even possible that if all Federal restrictions, like the 29-day visiting period as a limit, were eliminated that the local economy of the British Virgin Islands would almost be wiped out.[14]

There thus exists a profound discrepancy between economic reality and political fiction. Politically British, the islands are economically American. Theoretically, London governs the islands, even more directly than before, what with the defederalization of the old Leeward Islands colony in 1956 and the conversion from presidential to colonial status. But the primary concern of everybody, from the British Administrator downwards, is not with London but Charlotte Amalie. There is a constant apprehension as to the effects that any change in American immigration policies—like the deportation epidemic of some years back—may have on local prosperity.

Islanders, both citizens and politicians, inevitably make comparisons between American expenditures on the American Virgin Islands and Puerto Rico and British expenditures, unavoidably miserly by comparison, on their own territory. The general feeling that this, altogether, is a situation where there is a single socio-economic entity divided artificially into two unequal parts thus explains the decision of the British islanders, through their Legislative Council, to remain out of the West Indies federation movement. Their tragedy, of course, is that they are no more wanted by Washington than by London. Even the American Virgin Islands, as American overseas dependencies, themselves are in pretty bad shape, conducting as they do a dispiriting struggle against Congressional conservatism for mild reform measures, a popularly-elected chief executive, for instance. The possibility of Congressional approval of a far more radical notion like the suggested amalgamation between the two entities thus comes to seem utterly remote. 'Members of our Committee,' the Chairman of the House Interior Committee has informed the reform groups in St Thomas, 'have told the Virgin Islanders on innumerable occasions that additional powers and responsibilities would be granted when Congress in its wisdom deems such extension can be justified and managed in a capable manner.'[15] Congress 'in its wisdom' can hardly be expected to promise even that much to a community whose inhabitants are technically British.

The British islanders, consequently, live at the mercy of an American federal bureaucracy, immediately in St Thomas, ultimately in Washington. That economic integration solves, at the moment, intractable local problems does not obscure the fact that it has given rise to its own particular evils. The British Virgin Islands migrant enters a higher wage rate structure when he comes to St Thomas. But it is only high in a comparative sense; in absolute terms he suffers all of the well-known deprivations of alien labour all over the United States. He works at the dirty jobs of the host economy—construction labour, domestic service, cane cutting, menial labour in the hotels—for substandard wages paid, in the main, by unconscionable employers who engage him by means of a 'certification' process which is not a contract in any real sense, and who can easily intimidate him by threats of deportation. He lives, for the most part, in a wooden shack in the slum sections of the island towns. Because he and his kind constitute anything between 50 and 55 per cent of the labour force he places tremendous strain upon community services, for there is a direct causal relationship between the presence of such a large alien labour force and extremely serious housing and medical problems. There is also a scandalous gap between the low living standards of the alien and the increasing affluence of the entrepreneurial segment of the tourist and export industries. There is at work here, essentially, a threefold exploitation: in the first place, that of an employer class making handsome profits out of foreign goods assembled by foreign labour under duty free tariff benefits; secondly, that of the local Virgin Islands Government that has used its lobbying powers in Washington almost exclusively to promote the interests of the entrepreneurs; and, thirdly, that of a local union movement which, for all of its strong labour orientation, has neglected the problems of the alien employee while exhibiting a ready concern for anything adversely affecting the businessman. The end result of all this, as the candid letter of the Acting Director of the Office of Territories to Governor Paiewonsky shows, is a modern version of slave labour incompatible with the current official American vision of the Great Society.[16]

The British Virgin Islander, in brief, is caught between the devil of emigration and the deep blue sea of a depressed existence at home. Des Voeux noted the comic opera style of politics in the last century in the island capital of Tortola;[17] and things have not changed much since. The absence of any powerful spirit of local independence was sufficiently shown by the fact that on two separate occasions, 1867 and 1902, the islanders voluntarily abolished their popular legislative bodies and that the old Legislative Council thus given up in 1902 was in fact not restored until as late as 1950. Politics have thus continued to be fiercely individualist, and it was not until 1966 that faint stirrings in the direction of organizing political parties in Roadtown were heard. Political discussion has continued to revolve around personal scandal more than anything else: why the Director of Public Works clandestinely attends political meetings in a Government jeep, why the local police waste their time playing dominoes, what happened to a missing bull from the Government stock farm, why the Administrator failed to attend the funeral of a prominent civil servant. The business of government has been kept almost exclusively as the special responsibility of the Administrator, in collaboration with an Executive Council whose members are generally regarded by local public opinion as having 'gone over' to Government. The district representational system works badly. The spirit of local civic obligation is so poor that services like the police force are almost wholly imported from the Leeward Islands. How far behind the rest of the West Indies it all is, is evident enough from the fact that Mrs Proudfoot's severely critical report of 1965 suggested nothing more radical than a quasi-ministerial system to help build up the power and prestige of the Legislative Council. In a society where the really important decisions are made by an alien state power down in St Thomas it apparently becomes difficult to invest the local political processes with any real significance.[18]

All of these scattered fragments of British colonial rule face, at bottom, similar problems. They have suffered the neglect that attends obscurity and tinyness and, significantly, have depended for notice by the outside world on, usually, historically minded visiting clergymen, Pusey in the case of the Turks and Caicos, Levo in the case of the Virgins; and such clerical work has itself suffered from a half-patronizing tone on behalf of these children-people, as the clerical mind sees them.[19] With the exception of the Grenadines, all of them must seek politico-constitutional forms that offer an adequate insurance policy for their commercial relationships with the United States economy. Thus the British Virgin Islands have a heavy stake in the ability of manufacturing firms in St Thomas to retain the so-called '50–50 clause' of the United States Tariff Act intact against Congressional interference; while Cayman Islanders have insisted, in the long history of their prolonged constitutional negotiations with Jamaica, upon retaining their separate power over taxes, entry, and employment connections with the United States.[20]

In general terms, such economies as these—trapped within a modern global economy which drains them, by outward movement, of their most active elements, with resultant decline in local economic activity—have three alternatives from which to choose. They can amalgamate with a wealthier economy; they can evacuate; or they can seek development based on indigenous resources. Evacuation, certainly, is unthinkable, for these island propulations possess a fierce passion for their tiny homelands, however much they may leave them in search of better things. Amalgamation, likewise, is difficult, especially if it means amalgamation with the United States. Certainly, too, amalgamation can only have the further consequence of making even worse an already bad emigration pattern; for all of these communities presently suffer from the prolonged male absenteeism that overseas jobs, 'going on the contract', as they say inevitably generate, and family and sex habits are inevitably shaped by that economic phenomenon.

Development, as the final alternative, means, if present trends persist, encouraged by the advice of Keynesian-minded economists, the development of the tourist trade. That might be unavoidable. But it has, as in the Bahamas and Bermuda, its own notorious pitfalls. For it means, frankly, the alienation of the West Indian domain to external corporate shareholders who see tourism, in its varying forms, as a richly speculative growth area. Thousands of acres, even whole islands, become, by sale, the private fiefs of the wealthy English and American family empires, like the Rockefeller holdings in St John and Virgin Gorda in the Virgins group. Places like Caneel Bay and Little Dix become 'rich men's paradises', introducing gross inequalities of living standards hitherto unknown to the island populations. And even where, as in the St John case, a private patron may hand over his acquisitions to the Federal National Park Service for conservationist purposes, the 1962 furore over the attempt of the Federal Government to exercise its power of condemnation to enlarge the park area graphically demonstrated how a force of local residents and small property owners may be defeated by the awesome power of the Federal bureaucracy if they do not have, as the St John people did not have, a Territorial Deputy or a Resident Commissioner in the federal capital to defend their interests.[21] Only, perhaps, the organization of a real Caribbean Economic Community can provide these smaller groups with the investment capital, the organizational skill and the political strength to offset not only the weaknesses inherent in the sensitive tourist industry but also, more importantly, to defend themselves against the danger of having to sell themselves and their tropical birthright to the alien hotel syndicate and the speculative land buyer. Failing that, the fate of the smaller islands is likely to follow that of Anguilla. For the grim lesson of that island's secession from St. Kitts in 1967 is that, without genuine international help, the constitutional vacuums created by such revolts will be eagerly filled by the 'hot' money so plentiful in the Caribbean area since the Cuban Revolution evicted the gambling syndicates from Havana.

# Chapter XIV

## THE FEDERAL VENTURE

### THE FORMATIVE YEARS

THE RECOGNITION of the seminal truth that only a unified Caribbean, politically and economically, can save the region from its fatal particularism is at least a century old. In its particular variant of West Indian federation it certainly goes back to the *Appendix* written in 1860 to the *Lectures on Colonization and Colonies* delivered at Oxford University by Herman Merivale of the Colonial Office between 1839 and 1841. Many of the authors who wrote on the West Indies—Meikle, Darnell Davis, Salmon, de Verteuil, Lamont, Murray, Rippon—advocated federation and drew up their own private constitutional models. Viscount Elibank's lecture of 1911 before the West India Committee in London, speaking in his capacity at that time as Administrator of St Vincent, included a draft bill for a federal constitution prepared by the then Chief Justice of British Honduras which proposed among other things a Federal Council to be indirectly elected from the memberships of the various local legislatures. These private proposals were supported, first, by official British recommendations, from the ill-fated proposals of 1876 to the Colonial Office *Despatches*, respectively, of 1945 and 1947 that laid down the basis of the federal experiment between 1956 (the date of the definitive conference on the federal constitution) to 1962 (the date of the official termination of the Federation). They were supported, secondly, by West Indians themselves, dating at least from the acceptance of Captain Cipriani's resolution at the 1926 Labour Conference (with reservations on the part of the Guianese delegates), through the important Dominica Conference of 1932, to the decisive Montego Bay Conference of 1947 in which British and West Indian opinion came together to accept, in principle, the idea of federal nationhood. Apart from those developments there were peripheral movements: the Leeward Islands Confederation (1871–1956), the various efforts to gain admittance to the

Canadian Confederation, Sir Edward Davson's proposals of 1920 for an advisory joint executive council to provide a body of *expertise* in specialist fields for the individual island legislatures, the manufacture of ingenious constitutional nostrums by enthusiastic amateurs like Ebenezer Duncan of St Vincent. Certainly, if continuous discussion of an idea over a period of eighty years or more is proof of its power then West Indian federation was a powerful issue indeed.

Yet that would be a disastrously erroneous view. For an examination of the prolonged discussion preceding the Montego Bay meeting makes it painfully clear that the federation debate, unlike the earlier Abolitionist debate, possessed no clear purpose, no central driving force to give it energy and direction. In the first place, there was complete absence of agreement as to the scope of the proposed federation. Practically every proposal had its own special conception of what territories should or should not be included. The 1897 Royal Commission limited federation to Barbados and the Windwards, the 1932 Closer Union Commission proposed instead a loose federation of both Leewards and Windwards. The Dominica Conference envisaged a union of Trinidad, Barbados, the Leewards and Windwards, while the later Caribbean Labour Congress proposals of 1938 went further, to include even the Bahamas and the two mainland territories. Some wanted to include Jamaica, others to exclude it. There was, secondly, a comparable confusion as to the very necessity of federation. The Royal Commission of 1882 envisaged some form of ultimate federation, that of 1897 opposed the idea and even saw no virtue in the less ambitious proposals for a unified regional civil serice. Major Wood's 1922 Report emphasized the absence of adequate transportation facilities as a conclusive argument against federation; the 1938 Royal Commission, on the other hand, while reiterating Major Wood's scepticism, accepted federation as an ideal to be worked for, and noted that if West Indian communications were deficient that was because, in large part, the Imperial government had failed to help British shipping companies, by means of subsidies, to compete with the passenger services offered West Indian travellers by the modern and luxurious ships of the foreign lines.

Finally, and in the third place, there was little agreement about the final purposes that federation would presumably serve. With many of its individual West Indian champions, Marryshow, for example, there was little more than a vaguely romantic feeling about West Indian 'unity', and a typically middle class emphasis upon the nationalist content of federation. For the radical groups, the Caribbean Labour Congress, for example, federation meant self-government and dominion status, those concepts in turn being conceived as essential instruments for the overall planning and development of the Caribbean area as an integral part of the larger world economy. For Cipriani, with his strong trade union leanings, it meant the means whereby West Indian social problems such as education and child labour could receive immediate attention in a way that Crown Colony government could not offer. Official British opinion, on the other hand, throughout viewed federation, not as a vehicle for West Indian self-government, but, over-whelmingly, as a problem of colonial administrative convenience. Examination of the voluminous documentation of that opinion in Westminster debates, royal commission reports, Colonial Office memoranda and the published correspondence between the Colonial Secretary and individual West Indian governors shows that the most persistently recurring reason evoked in support of federation was the greater economy and the improved administrative efficiency it was supposed federation would bring about. There was little appreciation of the economic side of federation; which led inevitably to West Indian suspicions about imperial intentions and motives, giving rise to the strong feeling, never at any time really cleared away, that London wanted federation merely to rid herself of continuing obligations in the area;[1] summed up in the alleged remark of a Colonial Office junior official that the general idea behind the official sponsorship of federation was 'to make these scattered legislatures into one compact body in order that the Colonial Office could more expeditiously deal with them in matters relating to the British Government'.[2]

There were, of course, other contributing strains in the general pro-federal movement. There was the contribution of 'functional federalism', that is, the processes of regional co-operation between the various West Indian unit governments on limited matters of common concern: higher education, currency, shipping services, information services, the work of the various Trade Commissioners, judicial co-operation through the West Indian Court of Appeal; and much else.[3] Much of this was 'Federation by conference', the meetings, for example, of the old West Indian Conferences after 1926 or, as an example of one of the many urgent regional problems facing local governments, the first regional Veterinary Conference of 1947 that discussed the question of animal quarantine. Most notably of all, there was the work after 1949 of the Regional Economic Committee, dealing with various matters from shipping services and trade surveys to the United States farm labour programme; the work was especially important because the Committee's habit of rotating its meetings in various island capitals served to educate many local politicians into a regional view of their own insular problems. Yet the conference habit was of limited use. The meetings only involved senior civil servants and a handful of political leaders; they were administration-oriented; they had advisory powers only; and they were no substitute for the single federal agency, with over-riding political powers, which alone could speak and act with authority for the region as a whole. Above all, they suffered from the official touch, being held, up to 1944, under the aegis of the Colonial Office and, after that date, under that of the Anglo-American Caribbean Commission. In the earlier period they assumed, for the West Indies, a sort of tropical extension of the British imperialist mercantilist system after the manner of the old Liberal-Imperialist dream in which, as the English Governor of Barbados told the 1929 meeting, Britain and the West Indies would form one trade unit for marketing purposes and in which the imperial connection would, inferentially, be increased and not diminished. But later developments belied the promise. The general temper of this much-vaunted 'consultative' method may be gauged, altogether, from the fact that the inaugural meeting of the West Indian Conferences of 1926 gathered in the Moses chamber of the House of Lords and was conceived as being an effort to duplicate in the West Indies the conference technique recently developed, at that time, by the British administrations in the East African Colonies and Protectorates; an aim, moreover, described to the delegates by a Colonial Secretary of State who, on his own confession, had never been to the West Indies.[4]

There was, further, as Braithwaite has noted, the contribution of the pre-federal 'federal' associations and institutions of the region. The federal stand of the organized labour movement, going back at least to the 1926 conference, is well known, culminating in the radical pronouncements of the 1945 and 1947 meetings of the newly-formed Caribbean Labour Congress in favour of federal union along with dominion status, both of those essentially political devices being conceived, as in Richard Hart's brief at the 1945 meeting, as instruments to further the cause of regional socialist planning, constituting, as that planning would, so argued the brief, a far stronger basis for the federal state than mere sentiment or traditional loyalty. The Associated Chambers of Commerce, founded in 1917, likewise contributed to regionalist thinking, first by way of their successive conferences that publicized essentially federal concepts like regional shipping services and a regional customs union, and secondly by way of their support, albeit generally lukewarm, of a political federation, going back as early as the pro-federal pamphlet published in 1917 by the West Indian Federal League, a body actually founded by some of the delegates to the foundation conference of the larger Association held in Trinidad.[5] There were, again, the various professional associations organized on a regional basis and concerned with regional problems: the Caribbean Union of Teachers after 1935 seeking support for the ideals of uniform educational standards, increased salaries and the abolition of the dual system of educational control; the Caribbean Bar Association after 1916 concerned with the codification of separate island laws and with the principle of uniformity *in re* the right of admission to practice; most importantly, perhaps, the Civil Service Federation after 1944 fighting against the colour bar in the colonial civil service and working for, among much else, the unification of the service as a regional whole. Finally, there were the federal institutions proper or, to be more exact, extra-federal: the Imperial College of Tropical Agriculture, followed in 1948 by the University College of the West Indies, the West Indian Meteorological Service, and the various churches with their doctrinally universalistic bias calculated to encourage, if not a national viewpoint, at least a regional one. It would be difficult to exaggerate the importance of the one single feature all of those bodies, ideologically so diverse, shared together, that is, their habit of frequent regional meetings, for it was a habit that helped measurably to counteract the disease of insularity in a region so utterly bereft of decent communications that, as Gideon Murray put it, personal interchange of ideas by West Indians on West Indian affairs was almost as rare as the St. Vincent parrot.[6]

Yet there are difficulties in interpreting all this, to see what it means. There is a temptation, perhaps natural, to see any regional body as, *ipso facto*, proof of a burgeoning West Indian nationalism. The University College of the West Indies, for example, as the unitary creation of planned federationist thinking, might have been expected to be such a body, to give some intellectual stimulus to the federal movement. But, as a matter of fact, the UCWI faculty, with a few individual exceptions, did not do so and did not participate at all openly in the federal debate of the 1950's. The West Indian press, again, with exceptions like the Jamaican *Gleaner*, was, as it still largely is, notoriously insularist and failed dismally to carry on the early federal tradition of the old Grenadian *West Indian* under Marryshow's editorship. While it is true, again, that the federal nationalism of the labour movement was throughout diluted by its middle class Anglophilism, thus sharing that characteristic with the business groups, it is nonetheless also true that the essential ideological quality of labour thought was radically nationalist in a way that the business group outlook was not. So, while labour espoused federation as a vehicle for democratic social growth, as the advanced programme of the 1947 meeting of the Caribbean Labour Congress showed, West Indian business thought of federation merely as a device for furthering its own narrow economic interests as primary producers dependent upon an external market and requiring joint lobbying methods in the metropolitan capitals. For labour, it meant a strong federal state. For business, it meant merely a loose confederal association in which, as an early group put it, 'any suggestion of pooling revenues or equalising tariffs with a Lord High Somebody in authority over the whole West Indies would be resented by every colony'.[7] There were, then, qualitative differences in different pro-federal approaches. Some groups embraced a common West Indian loyalty as an act of faith. Others accepted it simply as a necessity of existence; in Braithwaite's phrase, in a sense West Indianism was forced upon the West Indian civil servant as a tactical move in the struggle for senior appointments. The special professional interest, likewise, of the legal profession in federation was perhaps sufficiently indicated in Sir Grantley Adams' observation in one of the early Barbados debates on the subject, that the West Indian lawyer class, like their counterparts in Australia and Canada, might carve a handsome living out of cases of appeal to the Privy Council concerning problems of the constitutionality of local and federal activities within a federal structure.[8] The Caribbean Union of Teachers, again, formed in 1935, espoused with real enthusiasm a West Indian view of educational problems. The business tycoon, on the other hand, who, like Abe Issa, was federalist in his sympathies was so because of his commercial interests spread throughout the islands or, like Sir Robert Kirkwood, saw federation mainly as an improved instrument for negotiating trade agreements with external buyers and investors. For the business groups, obviously, federation, again to quote Murray, was a means to equip the West Indies 'in modern fashion for the commercial battle which is now being waged throughout the civilized world'.[9]

The discussion of the growth of West Indian regional feeling, clearly enough, must distinguish carefully between a West Indianism of groups resident in the area and having a sense of belonging to it, and a West Indianism which is something more, a sense of transcending colonial boundaries and yielding a new loyalty to the larger regional boundaries. The old Creole governing classes of the *ancien régime* before 1834 were thus West Indian in the first sense but not in the second. So, when Père Labat noted in 1700 in the Barbados of that time that many of the English planters and officials spoke a fluent French that fact was due less to any sense of Pan-Caribbean feeling in them than it was to a situation in which both trade and war with the French islands had brought them into intimate contact with the French Antillean culture; a contact subsequently lost. But that, at best, was nothing more than the powerful localist prejudice of the white Creoles of the old West Indian families, usually directed against the 'home' government and its agents, the imported officials, the *métropolitains*. Conversely, the churches were West Indian in the second sense but not in the first; that is to say, being in the main international organizations of expatriate clergy they readily appreciated the fact that a common West Indian culture of family and social habits called for some uniform diocesan structure in the region as a whole, some regional basis of church action. The tremendous life work of the great Bishop Anstey in the West Indian parish after 1911 can be seen, in one way, as an exemplification of that truth. It is therefore necessary to see the later struggle for a native ecclesiastical hierarchy—culminating in Jamaica in 1955 with the appointment of the first native Anglican bishop—not so much as a sign of a larger West Indian regionalism as an indication of the growth of a new class of laity in the individual colonies seeking to set itself up as the heir of the old Anglican plantocracy. Regional identity, this is to say more generally, was frequently not so much an indigenous phenomenon on native grounds as it was the effort of the outsider groups, themselves not sharing, and therefore impatient with individual island loyalties, to impose an abstract ideal upon an intractable insularity, and often for purposes alien to West Indian interests.

The outstanding example of that truth is the series of West Indian Conferences held after 1944 under the aegis of the imperialist Anglo-American Caribbean Commission. For the main purpose of that body was political, to maintain 'stability' in the Caribbean during the war period. That meant, in part, the consolidation of the growing American influence in the region, a purpose aptly summed up in the feeling of American officials at the time that they preferred to set up the Commission's headquarters in Trinidad with an American boss, rather than in St Thomas with a British boss, so that they could have a listening post in the British West Indies.[10] The West Indian Conferences, overcrowded with the Commission's expatriate officials and local government advisers, mostly European, reflected that bias. Their reports were essentially conservative documents, usually advocating common West Indian action on specific subjects such as public works, fisheries and agriculture, tourism, health quarantine, venereal disease, and so on, but failing completely to face up to the problem of the organization of appropriate regional political institutions without which any joint action on those issues would revert to the control of the Commission itself, with its traditional disinterest in organizing independent West Indian action for West Indian purposes. To compare, for example, the 1944 Report of the first such Conference with the Report of the 1945 meeting of the Caribbean Labour Congress is to appreciate the point. For whereas the first document recommended, at its boldest point, mild industrial development to be co-ordinated through the Industries Section of the Caribbean Commission, the second document warned strongly against a policy of heavy capital investment by outside forces which would lead to external economic and political control and could only be avoided by a regional political body democratically accountable to the peoples of the individual territories.[11]

All of this finally culminated, after 1945, in the series of conferences that led up to the establishment of the West Indies Federation in 1958: the Montego Bay founding conference of 1945, and the two London conferences of 1953 and 1956. In the very nature of the case the record was that of a prolonged effort to establish a deliberately conscious act of political construction, for the essence of federation—the process whereby a developing sense of national solidarity is reconciled with the attachment for localist identity, through the setting up of a dual political organization—presupposes a written constitution of some detail. Apart from the long-term causative factors noted above, the period after 1945 brought additional and more immediately pressing factors into being—the intellectual ferment stimulated by the war, for wars, as Marx said of revolutions, are the locomotives of history; universal suffrage and the new popular political movements it threw up; the reconstruction of the civil services on a 'national' basis from the middle 1940's onwards; the wider horizons opened up by professional training and residence abroad; student liberalism learned at McGill and London; the work of the Regional Economic Committee in laying the basis for a federal administrative service; and the rapid development of cheap popular air travel, particularly significant in the light of the observation of the British Guiana observer to the Montego Bay Conference that, hitherto, inter-colonial travel had been restricted to the two categories of visiting cricket teams and civil servants.

The hammering out of the federal constitution—optimistically assumed by the Montego Bay conference to be the work of a brief period only—became, in fact, a tedious process. It produced a mountain of literature: the various conference reports themselves, the Standing Closer Association Committee report of 1949 (the Rance Report), the 1949 report of the Holmes Commission on civil service unification, the 1955 report of the conference of freedom of movement, the reports of the three pre-Federal Commissioners, the Judicial, the Fiscal, and the Civil Service, appointed by the 1953 London conference, the 1957 Mudie Commission report on the controversial matter of the federal capital site, the 1958 report of the Trade and Tariffs Commission, not to mention the endless debates on delegate reports that took place in all of the territorial legislative councils, as well as the academic discussion generated by the federal developments.[12] It was perhaps inevitable, indeed, that the process should have been so maddeningly protracted, for the initial Montego Bay conference did little more than pass a short, simple resolution accepting 'the principle of a federation in which each constituent unit retains complete control over all matters except those specifically assigned to the federal government'. To clothe such a vague directive, itself expressive of the serious divisions of opinion between the radical and conservative forces of West Indian opinion, with the flesh and blood of a full-scale constitutional instrument, of necessity had to take time.

Certain leading features about the process must be noted. In the first place, the federation was the work, almost exclusively, of British officials and West Indian politicians. There was little of a movement of enthusiastic popular opinion behind it. Viscount Elibank had blandly assumed in his book of 1912 that the leading personnel of a federal legislature would be recruited from the class of white managers and planters. That, of course, was no longer possible after, say, 1938. But the federal idea after that date became little more than the plaything of the creole heirs of that class, the new group of coloured politicians thrown up by universal suffrage. The 1947 conference took as its model the Australian federal concept (a choice never really adequately explained), as the Hammond advisory paper on the Australian experience written for that conference shows.[13] But the more democratic aspects of the Australian concept were overlooked, the reference back of successive constitutional drafts to the local electorates, for example, as took place with the plebiscitary approval of the Commonwealth of Australia Act in 1900. Nor was there anything of a serious effort to educate the West Indian peoples of federal association such as the work of the Federal League in, again, the Australian case in the years before 1900. There was, it is true, the remarkable educational effort of Dr Williams in his popular lectures of 1955–56.[14] But that was almost a single-handed Herculean feat and did not have the influence of, for example, the *Federalist Papers* in the popular American debate at the time of the ratification process of 1787. Nor did the new University College of the West Indies, after 1948, fill the gap, for, modelled as it was as a sort of colonial Oxbridge under its English Vice-Chancellors and senior academic staff, and wedded to the imperial intellectual tradition, it did little to fulfil the vision of the

Caribbean Labour Congress in its 1945 meeting of a West Indian university which would become in all its phases a 'centre and focus of West Indian social, cultural, economic, and political aspirations'. The urgent task of mass education in the realities of federation— the task of a lifetime's education, on any showing—was thus left to any odd civic-minded organization that chose to undertake it, the Kingston and St Andrew's Taxpayers and Ratepayers Association, for example, that valiantly tried to penetrate Jamaican popular ignorance of the subject in 1957.[15]

Throughout all of the foundation meetings there reigned an atmosphere, in truth, of official secrecy. The fact, too, that after Montego Bay they were all held in faraway London only added to their general isolationism away from popular life and thought. All of the arguements, moreover, that were advanced by the various conferences—the Federation, in one way, was the child of the conference habit—managed to avoid the seminal question as to what benefits, if any, the new scheme would offer to the West Indian peasant and worker. It was argued that federation would mean a more dignified international personality for the West Indies, that the area's bargaining power on the world economic markets would be enhanced if a single central government replaced a number of weak separate governments, and so on. But none of those could be expected, as reasons, to appeal much to the poverty stricken masses. They certainly could not count on the hope that federation would bring them prosperity or employment. The most that was offered them was Mr Manley's candid admission in his Montego Bay speech that federation by itself would not bring prosperity, only that it would enlarge the area of action and the possibilities of a prosperity which, as he saw it, only West Indians alone could create for themselves: a piece of cold comfort indeed.[16] Or there was the merely sentimental argument, again only of possible appeal to the socially comfortable person, that federation was a 'long hard road with little to gain for the present generation save the knowledge of doing work comparable to the "champions of Magna Carta", the "Founding Fathers of the United States" and all those who by vision, enterprise and sacrifice have wrested freedom and consummated nationhood'.[17] From the proletarian viewpoint, indeed, all of the justificatory reasons in favour of 'closer association' were problematical, even nebulous and, indeed, so pedestrian as to make it

12

impossible to work up any enthusiasm either for or against them. In return for that the man in the street was expected to take on the additional load of yet another structure of government, to accompany a structure already sufficiently burdensome. Federation, as basically a constitutional change, thus had little interest for the masses. Inevitably, then, it became the monopoly of the West Indian civil intelligentsia. And they, naturally enough, as a reading of the various island legislative debates on successive conference delegate reports showed, discussed federation as if it had no real base in the economic lives of their unit territories. Looked at from this viewpoint, Federation marked a stage in which the intelligentsia took over the leadership of the nationalist movement from the popular mass force that had controlled it in the period after 1938.

The second characteristic of the federal venture, allied to the first, was its excessive dependency upon British guidance. Both as an idea and as a set of institutions it was British inspired throughout, even British imposed, imposed, that is to say, in the special British sense in which the colonials were presented with imperial proposals which, they were politely assured, they could accept or not but which were so conditioned that in effect the dependent peoples had no alternative but to accept, the acceptance then in turn being advertised by the colonial officialdom as evidence that federation was the 'free choice' of the governed. The generally disastrous consequences of this could be seen in a number of ways. It was there in the way in which the British, discreetly but firmly, shaped the main outlines of the federal constitutional framework, finally producing an enlarged Crown colony type of constitution which omitted nearly all of the items previously insisted upon by West Indian leaders, including the demand made by a leader as generally conservative as Grantley Adams for (1) a unicameral system, since an upper chamber was an anachronism in modern conditions, and (2) complete excision of any reserve powers for Governors on either unit or federal level, echoing here the radical federation proposals of the 1945 Caribbean Labour Congress meeting, not to mention the proposals of the Pan-African Congress held in Manchester during the same year.[18] It was there in the general atmosphere of all of the main conferences, couched in terms of West Indian leaders assuring the British that they were 'reasonable' people who only wanted British 'co-operation', summed up in Adams' observation, in his Montego

Bay speech, that 'if we put our case before you in a reasonable way, you will see that you can trust the West Indies as much as you trusted the Boers', a rather unfortunate analogy in the light of the fact that the 'trust' placed in the Boers some forty years earlier had been extracted from the British only after they had been defeated in a humiliating war by the Boer farmer-guerrillas, something the West Indians had signally failed to do.[19] It was revealing, indeed, that the only delegate at the Montego Bay conference who attempted to call this elaborate British bluff was Bustamante, speaking, as he put it, as 'an outspoken Jamaican who has come from the gutter'; he alone challenged the Colonial Secretary, as conference chairman, to answer the widespread West Indian suspicion that federation was being imposed upon West Indians as a device for terminating British responsibilities for the general West Indian mess British colonial policy had created; a charge which it is difficult, in the light of subsequent developments, not to dismiss easily.[20] It took other West Indian leaders nearly two decades to catch up with the angry scepticism of the 'Busta' attitude, and it was not until 1966 that a 'small island' leader like John Compton could finally shatter the polite hypocrisies of yet another constitutional conference in Lancaster House with a speech of bitter reprimand directed against yet another Colonial Secretary, this time a Labour minister who seemed to be ignorant even of the elementary geography of the West Indian islands.[21] The same obsequious deference could be seen, again, in the West Indian acceptance, even to the point of signing the documents, of all of the British-made advisory papers and reports. There was, for example, the Rance Committee report of 1949, of which it is not too much to say that it painfully illustrates the dangers of permitting British civil servants, who are dilettantes in matters dealing with problems of federal states, to compose briefs for societies of which they practically know nothing; and only the fact, perhaps, that, as a West Indian newspaper has acidly noted, there is nothing that the average West Indian likes more than to be a civil servant—a post which offers the maximum of security with the minimum of effort[22]—explains why West Indian leadership so timidly accepted their disastrous proposals.

For on every crucial issue the Rance Report was uncannily wrong. It defended the proposed federal Senate with the hackneyed English argument about providing an arena of public service for men who might not want to face the hurly-burly of electoral politics without appreciating that in the West Indian context any second chamber meant, for West Indians, the perpetuation under another name of the nominated seat with all of its evil results. In dealing with the problem of dual sovereignty in a federal state the report assumed, contrary to the grim experience of all modern federal societies, that there would take place a tranquil and reasonable transfer of power from the circumference to the centre of political power, and that facile optimism was compounded by the spirit of haughty disdain in which, with typical English academic parochialism, the American experience was discussed. For, in truth, such transfer has taken place, in actual federal experience in Australia, Canada, and the United States, mostly by means of conflict, often bitter and pro-longed, especially in the controversial area of federal powers. It is worth noting, indeed, that the Rance Report proposals concerning the fiscal foundations of the Federation were rendered largely ob-solete by the far more incisive Report of the pre-Federal Fiscal Commissioner, for whereas the first report restricted the revenue of the federal government to a fixed percentage of unit customs duties as a mandatory levy, the second report sharply exposed the ridiculous inadequacy of such a formula, for the arrangement in effect made the federal government the fiscal prisoner of the in-dividual territorial governments. It is no exaggeration to say that the early demise of the Federation was in large part due to the fact that the later conferences, in debarring the federal government from the strategic income tax field, accepted the Rance Report recommendations despite the demonstrated obsolescence of its proposals. Nor was the Rance Report any more up-to-date in its views on the critical question of continuing United Kingdom economic aid to the new federal nation, for it dismissed the problem with a curiously Victorian assertion that such aid 'would not breed that spirit of self-reliance and that determination to stand on our own feet economically and financially if we are to attain full political independence'; a passage penned, it might be noted, at a time when the British people were receiving massive financial aid from the United States by means of the Marshall Plan without showing any resultant breakdown in their spirit of 'self-reliance'. Political self-government was thus identified with denial of metropolitan financial aid. One grim outcome of that Gladstonian fiscal conservatism, perpetuated by the Treasury mentality, was that whereas in 1834 the imperial Parliament gave a compensation award of some twenty million pounds to the dispossessed West Indian planter class, in 1958 a British Government could only offer a miserly two million dollars to an impoverished West Indian Federation. All in all, it is difficult to agree with Professor MacInnes that the Rance Report was a 'notable State-paper'.[23]

Yet the most intriguing example of the London psycho-complex of West Indians was without doubt the report of the Federal Capital Site Commission of 1956, made at the request of West Indians themselves by 'three wholly impartial persons who have never resided in the West Indies' and whose odd duty it was to recommend a priority list of sites for the federal capital on the basis of a hurried two months' visit which was, inferentially, to make them experts among other things on West Indian 'political and social sentiment'. Their report was no less curious than the manner of their appointment. The mental climate of the chosen capital, it argued, should be metropolitan, not provincial. Yet it proceeded then to nominate Barbados as its first choice, making the choice seem plausible only by the expedient of glossing over the realities of Barbadian life. Only three Englishmen, perhaps, could have opted for a society which, in Leigh-Fermor's words, reflected most faithfully the social and intellectual values and prejudices of a golf club in Outer London or of the married quarters of a barracks in Basutoland, hardly England's most interesting contribution to world civilization. Of the report's passages on Trinidad, in turn, the kindest thing to say is that they were deplorably unsociological. For they managed at once to libel the East Indian community by labelling it a 'disturbing element', thus repeating one of the evil myths of West Indian life, and to fail completely to take cognisance of the new note of positive citizenship introduced into Trinidadian life by the rising PNM. It is difficult not to feel that the Commissioners brought with them the social values of Englishmen for whom the West Indies have traditionally been a promising employment agency or a pleasant vacation spot; certainly, the conditions set out as being necessary to a capital town read quaintly like those that a senior officer of the Colonial Administrative Service might have laid down as conditions of an appointment in the region. At other times the report read like a tourist agency brochure and its final choice was, in fact, the tourist economy of Barbados. On which the proper comment, perhaps, was the remark of Dr Groome of Grenada at the time that the Federal House of Representatives surely did not need an audience of gilded tourists to applaud its deliberations. All in all, the report revealed much, between the lines, of the psychology of the English in the West Indies, even more perhaps than what it said about the capital site controversy. It is not surprising, then, that the 1957 meeting of the Standing Federation Committee jettisoned the report and proceeded to elect Trinidad for the federal headquarters.[24]

What all of this ended in—as the third leading feature of the Federation commencement exercises—was a process in which, somewhere along the way, the earlier West Indian dream of independence, or what more usually was euphemistically called 'self-government within the Commonwealth', was sacrificed to a quite different outcome, a continuing quasi-colonial status under the guise of federation. The one killed the other. How Jamaican nationalism and, later, Trinidadian nationalism allowed itself to be sidetracked into a futile exercise of British manufacture is in fact a whole topic in itself that one day will deserve a West Indian dissertation. In part, it was brought on by the heady optimism of the period after 1945 when the Adams-Manley colonial Fabian axis surrendered its leadership-role to the British Labour Party. It was a fatal tactic, for it grossly overestimated the capacity or perhaps even the willingness of British Labour to implement the sort of massive economic aid—the type of ambitious plan voiced, for example, by the Deputy Leader of the British Labour Party in his address to the foundation meeting of the West Indies Federal Labour Party in Castries in 1956[25]—which federation needed if it was to mean anything concrete. It also misread British Labour's attitude to the colonies, which has always had something of a chauvinistic paternalism about it. To read, for example, the booklet put out on the region at this same time by the Labour Party's Commonwealth Officer, John Hatch's *Dwell Together in Unity*, is to be made embarrassingly aware of how the British socialist has always misconceived the complex nature of West Indian society, trying to fit it into the ideological categories of a Europocentric socialism created out of the special conditions of advanced industrial capitalism. So, every West Indian politician who calls himself 'socialist' receives tendentious approval, while those outside the chosen fold are 'flamboyant' or 'irresponsible' or 'corrupt'; the real significance of PNM radicalism, as distinct from the essentially conservative bias of Barbadian 'socialism', is over-looked because the PNM is not, technically, a socialist movement; the deep power of the 'Busta' personality in Jamaican life cannot be appreciated; while Mr Manley is described in terms more appropriate to the adoration of a saint.[26] All this is worth emphasizing because the internationalist bias metropolitan Labour precluded it from comprehending the emotional power of West Indian nationalism; its white liberal bias precluded it from appreciating the tremendous drive, in Dr Williams, of the idea of *Négritude;* while its essentially United Kingdom-centred framework of reference made it impossible to see that an independent West Indies would have to turn more and more to relationships with the non-English societies of its Caribbean Latin neighbours, the United States and the Latin American countries. Those prejudices in turn were only faintly challenged by West Indian leaders who themselves suffered from the social religion of Anglolatry and so could not break, psychologically, the umbilical cord that tied them to British values.

Hence the relinquishment, early on, of a bold drive for nationalism and independence. The 1945 and 1947 Caribbean Labour Congress programmes had postulated a federal scheme posited on (1) the membership of British Guiana (2) full internal self-government for each unit and (3) dominion status for the federation. The federation finally proposed by Britain lacked all of those terms. It was allowed to do so because, by the Adams-Manley decision, increasingly felt after 1950, to split with the left wing of the nationalist movement, the Caribbean Labour Congress and all that it stood for was rendered impotent; and Richard Hart, indeed, speaking of his experiences at the 1945 meeting, has recorded that Adams spoke in favour of accepting federation on any terms that the British Government would be willing to grant, while later on Manley, as Government leader in Jamaica, failed to take a stand in defence of the Caribbean Labour Congress proposals.[27] The original ideology of the PNP, the extension of democracy in the whole region through winning complete autonomy first for Jamaica, was thus allowed to give way to the pursuit of a federal idea that was not even shaped for West Indian needs. There was about that decision, as W. A. Domingo has pointed out, something of a lack of elementary political sagacity, for it assumed, contrary to all known experience, that a

British imperial government would grant independence and favour federation simultaneously; a prognostication corroborated by later events.[28] It was argued by the defenders of the decision with pontifical finality that no colony in any case could hope separately to achieve independence; a prophecy that proved to be false as later events showed.[29] It is possible, of course, that it was not in itself the idea of federation as such that caused the trouble, despite the convictions of the powerful West India lobby in New York of which Domingo was a leading member. Rather, it might have been that, federation in itself being necessary, what went wrong was the West Indian acceptance of a British-made product drafted by constitutional 'experts' with no real experience of federal problems: the thesis of the PNM-Williams faction. Whatever thesis is correct, the end-result was the same; independence, as a fact, was delayed for years by the endless, tortuous federal negotiations. The decisive 1956 conference sealed the matter with the failure of the West Indian delegates to secure full Commonwealth status, despite the immediately prior example, which was called to their attention, of the wresting of complete self-government from the British Government of the day by Mr Rahman and others for the people of Malaya.[30]

There was, in brief, a fatal ambiguity in the West Indian psychology. It believed passionately in West Indian nationalism. At the same time it accepted uncritically the British belief in the civilizing mission of British imperialism. An early pro-federal pamphlet like Wendell Malliet's *Destiny of the West Indies* (1928) showed how difficult it was for the West Indian middle class patriot to resolve that ideological contradiction, even to see that it existed.[31] Naturally enough, then, the constitutional forms of the Federation based upon that contradiction were at once imperfect and unsatisfactory.

The London Plan of 1953 followed the Consolidated Recommendations of the Rance report in setting up a bicameral legislature. The pragmatic rule adopted by that report for the allotment of seats to the individual units—a broad adherence to the size of population criterion, but in a diminishing proportion—was wisely adhered to, thus preventing the possibility that a territory like Jamaica, with one-half of the federal population, would become a sort of overweening Prussia in the scheme. Equally wisely, the federal constitution eschewed the idea, so popular with earlier federal proposals, in, for example, Darnell Davis' curious scheme of 1890 for colonial consolidation,[32] that the members of the federal House of Representatives should be chosen by their respective local legislatures; for a federal house so chosen would not have been very different from the West Indian Council proposed in the Secretary of State's *Memorandum* of 1947 as an alternative to federation. Such a body would have constituted, to quote Mr Gomes, little more than a debating society where West Indians would have enjoyed themselves by frequent flights into the rhetorical stratosphere.[33] Yet certain local elements still continued to toy with the idea of reducing the federal parliament to exactly such a status of a 'talking shop' with no independent authority, as can be seen in the continuing discussion of alternative schemes such as that of a West Indian League, like the Arab League, operating essentially as a consultative assembly for limited purposes only, 'free from subjection to a central, omnipotent authority'.[34] Such ideas, however, were put aside, to guarantee the independent prestige of the popular federal house. Thus guaranteed, the prestige was further made certain by the 1956 conference decision to reinstate the ban on dual membership of unit and federal legislative and executive bodies, which had been originally recommended by the Rance committee and rejected by the 1953 conference. For dual membership, had it been retained, would have been disastrous. It would have weakened an already weak federation in its effort to compete with the individual unit governments for interest and attention; and also would have delayed the acceptance of an exclusively federal political career as at once a prestigious and full-time occupation. The argument for the dual seats had always been the assertion that there existed a limited quantity of political talent in the region. Yet the 1956 Trinidad elections, in bringing a whole new set of able newcomers into the Trinidadian political field, showed how really empty the argument was. All this, of course, was the literary theory of the lower house. In practice, the fateful decision of both the Trinidadian and Jamaican political leaders to 'stay at home' rather than be drafted into federal leadership meant that the territorial governments tended to send their 'second strings' of talent to Port-of-Spain, so that the federal House, as its debates after 1958 showed, never rose to the level of quality it ought to have shown.

The Senate, of course, was worse. For although the federal architects were right in emphasizing the dangers of an elected second

12*

chamber like the American Senate their alternative scheme of a wholly nominated body was hardly more satisfactory. For in giving the nominating power to the Governor-General, in consultation with the Governors of the respective units (who in turn were required to consult with their respective Executive Councils) the procedure completely insulated the Senate from the elective elements. The experience of the old, unreformed Canadian Senate was warning enough that an executive, if its power to nominate is not curbed, will always be tempted to fill vacancies in a nominated chamber with its own supporters. That, indeed, was what happened in the West Indian case, for most of the Senators appointed after 1958 were 'safe' people whose sole apparent reason for selection was reward by their 'home' governments for services rendered, usually as local nominated members or, as in the case of the two aged Dominican members, the principle of mere longevity. It is of interest that the new Senate of the 1962 Jamaican independence constitution has subsequently shown how a second chamber whose nominees are named by the two main party leaders will rapidly become a place filled by staunch party supporters owing their first loyalty to their party chieftains rather than to the Senate as an entity of some dignity and independence.[35] The justification advanced by the federal planners for a second chamber was the hackneyed one that it could delay 'hasty' decisions on the part of an 'excitable' lower house. This assumes a rash and importunate house impatient of any careful consideration of novel proposals. The West Indian legislative history would hardly seem to prove the point. Slavery emancipation took some fifty years to achieve its end; it took over two decades for the post-1918 constitutional proposals to finally blossom out in the form of the popular constitutions of the 1940's and 1950's; while federation itself, if it be dated from the Secretary of State's Despatch of 1945, took some thirteen years to become a reality. To look at the facts would be enough to persuade any observer to request a technique for accelerating the passage of West Indian legislation rather than delaying it. It hardly makes sense, in the light of this, to speak of the Senate as a 'careful driver' who would put on the brakes if the lower house were going 'too fast' or 'off the road'.[36]

It ought to be noted, finally, that the federal second chamber had the effect of giving a new lease of life to the discredited nominated system at the very moment when the system was being given its *coup de grace* at the individual territorial level. For the Secretary of State's *Despatch* of 1956 to the Governor of Trinidad clearly conceded the point that the nominated members would have to be appointed after consultation with the local Chief Minister and that their appointment, even more, should be made with the view of providing a workable majority for the Government party in the executive council. This effectively compromised the principle which alone had given the system justification, that is, that the nominated member was an independent spirit acting as a check upon the elected element. The *Despatch*, as Mr Hudson-Phillips pointed out at the time for the Trinidadian case, finally applied to the Crown Colony system the established principle of British constitutional law that the party commanding a majority in the popular house must be assured the right to have its leaders placed in office and to expect full co-operation from the executive in the efficient conduct of government.[37] It is odd that the federal arrangements seemed at this point to be putting the clock back. The only way, in any case, to get rid of the constitutional vexations accompanying nominations to a second chamber is to do away with it entirely. The experience of the United States Virgin Islands would appear to indicate that a unicameral legislature best suits these small island societies.

Yet it was the executive-administrative arrangements that underlined most the gross anachronism of the federal constitutional instrument. The principal policy-making body was conceived to be a Council of State constitutionally advisory to the Governor-General as chief executive and appointed by him. Of its 14 members only eight were to be constituted, democratically, the federal Prime Minister and seven colleagues chosen by him, the other six to be made up of three senior civil servants to be designated by the Governor-General at his discretion and three Senators to be nominated by him in Executive Council. This odd procedure produced some odd anomalies. The three Senators chosen to sit on the Council had to suffer a divided allegiance between the Council, as effective Cabinet, and their own parent body, the Senate. It is not for nothing that reform schemes advocating secondment of Senators to the federal Cabinet have always been rejected as unworkable in the American system. The three nominated civil servants, in turn, were liable to behave as the Governor-General's agents in the Cabinet, thus seriously compromising at once the position of the Prime Minister and the doctrine of cabinet collective responsibility. There was everything to be said, as the 1956 conference argued, for allowing the right of officials to attend Cabinet meetings either to fall into desuetude or to be withdrawn from constitution.[38] In 1960 London did in fact finally agree to the abolition of the Council of State in favour of full cabinet government. Yet the matter managed to illustrate the reactionary premises of the constitutional draughtsmen, their conviction that there should be associated with the federal policy-making process men 'who can bring special knowledge and experience to bear on the problems of an entirely new political and administrative structure',[39] which really meant that British senior administrators should be given a niche in the structure because West Indian political leadership inferentially lacked such 'knowledge' and 'experience'. The argument in any case presupposed an administrative rather than a political concept of a modern executive; it failed at any point to conceive the federation as an instrument for propelling rapid social and economic change.

Nothing better illustrated this than the absence of any clear, bold concept of the office of the Prime Minister. Not only was he not master in his own house; the house itself was not in any way an imposing edifice. He was to be elected from the House of Representatives from among its members, a questionable procedure that opened up the possibility, as Mr Mapp noted, that the office would become the object of parliamentary 'lobbying', which could only be avoided by explicitly requiring that the post should be in the power of the Governor-General to offer to the political leader commanding a majority following in the House.[40] The Prime Minister, moreover, had no assurance (until the belated amendments of 1956) that he would be consulted in the choice of candidates to the Senate or that his advice would either be sought or followed in areas like external relations and the maintenance of public order. He had no power to dissolve the federal parliament although the British Prime Minister in effect possesses that power in the British case; indeed, as the exchange of correspondence at much the same time on that point in the London *Times* during 1950 brought out, there was much to be said for making that power explicit in the British case by a formal transfer of the right of dissolution from the Crown to the Prime Minister. The draft constitutions, all in all, seemed not to envisage any really large, imaginative function for the Caribbean Prime Minister. The Rance Report paid as much attention to his function as constitutional adviser to the Governor-General as it did to his function as leading policy maker; yet the latter was surely far the more vital of the two. The *Report* of the pre-Federal Civil Service Commissioner was obliged to speak of his functions as a whole in almost laughably parochial terms, and drew up a curious organizational chart for the federal government which included a Department of the Prime Minister composed of an economic adviser, a public relations officer and a statistician, accompanied with the naïve observation that 'the Prime Minister might wish to concern himself with the general development of the region' and that he could choose to 'concentrate on political and constitutional issues, or to assume wider overall responsibilities for development and planning at the regional level'.[41] Nor was it enough, to offset all this, to enunciate the doctrine of cabinet collective responsibility as the basis of the Prime Minister's prestige, or what there was of it. For that prestige could only be the fruit of function, not of doctrine. And there was little recognizable function. Prestige of any value required, obviously, a quite different concept of the office, seeing it, as the Trinidadian economic planners saw it, as the spearhead of a planned economic development of the region as a whole.

The federal constitution-makers, however, were the prisoners of an astonishingly narrow idea of federation. They saw its West Indian leaders as, primarily, Her Majesty's Ministers overseas, not as the vanguard of a West Indian regional nationalism. That explains why, finally, they invested the office of the Governor-General, not that of the Prime Minister, with most of the panoply of the federal power. At a time when Governor-Generals in the historic Dominions had become overseas replicas of the Crown in England subject, in the main, to the political authority of their respective cabinets, the West Indian federationists managed, almost comically, to revive the office as it had been known before the Statute of Westminster. The 1958 constitution contained some thirty references empowering the Governor-General to act 'in his discretion' or 'in his individual judgment'. He personally appointed all Senators, federal Supreme Court justices, and members of the Public Service Commission. In certain circumstances he could remove any or all of them. He could refuse assent to any bill or reserve it for review by London. He could determine any urgent matter, however important, by himself if time did not permit consultation with the cabinet. The power retained to the Queen, indeed, to legislate for the federation by order-in-Council —a power curtailed in only one detail by the 1956 conference— meant, as Grantley Adams put it, that because of a disturbance anywhere in the federal territory the home government could pass a law prohibiting the holding of a meeting in St John or the holding of a regatta at Oistins.[42] The Governor-General, in brief, had at his disposal powers normally accepted in Dominion constitutional practice as belonging to the Prime Minister—the power to dissolve parliament, the power to set up a 'packed' upper house, even the power to argue his case in cabinet as the recognized master of certain of its members. And all that was accompanied by budgetary arrangements in which, as a Barbadian conservative critic noted, his total salary and emoluments equalled those of the governor of a state of the United States as wealthy as New York.[43] What all this did, in sum, was to transfer to the federal level the very colonialism to which the individual units had been subjected at the territorial level.

All the way, in brief, the decorative elements of the constitutions were given priority over the efficient elements. It produced, as the subsequent short history of the federation showed, a federal establishment controlled by the civil service mentality, the inevitable result of a situation in which, strangely, the administrative officials were enabled to get themselves established into a position of entrenched power almost before the federal political class arrived on the scene. It was a power-bloc insulated against the harsh realities of West Indian life by a public relations apparatus which appeared to believe that what the federal public wanted to hear about was the sartorial style of the Governor-General's wife or West Indian stamps or West Indian coins or the history of the House of Commons mace or even the story of the Royal Military College at Sandhurst. It placed a high premium on the merely entertainment value of the enterprise. The fancy of the West Indian press, understandably, was tickled by the spectacle: 'We can imagine,' wrote the leading St Lucian newspaper *apropos* the appointment of pages for service at the Governor-General's residence, 'His Excellency hailing: "Barbados, bring me some rum; Dominica, some water; and Grenada, nutmeg. Jamaica, what about a banana split." '[44] It fitted all this, then, that the top posts of the federal government should have been filled by London with a whole new set of 'safe' expatriates. Every such post, with the exceptions of the Federal Financial Officer, the Federal Secretary and the Public Relations Officer, was given to an out-sider: the Federal Attorney-General, the Federal Establishment Officer, the Chief Justice and, of course, the Governor-General himself in the form of Lord Hailes. The appointment to the Governor-General's office, indeed, of a former Conservative Party Chief Whip and Minister of Works was especially shocking to West Indian opinion, for it filled that critically important post with an appointee who before coming to the West Indies was merely a minor party hack in Westminster politics, who knew nothing of the West Indies and whose appointment was made without any real consultation with West Indian leaders.[45] The transition from Crown Colony to the representative principle in its fullest form was clearly incomplete even in 1958. 'If you wished to find the Governor-General of the West Indies,' Viscount Burnham had observed in 1923, 'you might have to pace the passages of the Colonial Office until you came to a small room indifferently lighted and there you would find in the person of an excellent head of a department the power behind the throne.'[46] For all of the grand rhetoric that accompanied the prolonged formative period of the federation it was translucently clear that, in the end, the power behind the throne was still there.

# Chapter XV

## THE FEDERAL VENTURE
### THE ROAD TO FAILURE

As is well known, the history of the Federation was one, between 1958 and 1962, of almost immediate decline and fall. The official note, of course, was one of bright optimism. The tone of the academic literature that appeared was somewhat similar, especially when sponsored by the federal bureaucracy, such as the Federal lecture series of 1959.[1] Yet even academic caution was at times overwhelmed by the depressing realities, and a book like *The West Indies Federation* (1961) was a series of essay lectures that mostly dealt, of necessity, with the factors that divided West Indian loyalties, with occasional expressions of pious hope, barely convincing, that the difficulties would be overcome.[2] Every dictate of common sense, it is true, called for the political unification of territories at once so tiny and scattered. The effort, nonetheless, failed. The Federation, in truth, was still-born.

The inevitable post-mortem has spawned a variety of explanations. It is easy enough to dispose of the less plausible. A popular explanation is that it was the fault of the politicians, who 'played politics' with the federal venture. They were, is was said, selfish, grasping men who were too parochial to rise to the heights of federal statesmanship; and Mr Manley's regrettable decision to 'stay home' rather than accept the leadership of federation which he, more than any other single West Indian, had helped create, is cited as only the best-known example of that 'betrayal'. But this is a dubious thesis. West Indian politicians probably did not quarrel among themselves much more than did Americans or Australians in the early stages of their respective federal experiments. There were some sordid moments, true: Bustamante's crass public suggestion, for example, that he and Manley should join forces to 'overthrow' the Adams' government so as to protect Jamaican interests;[3] or the exchange of radio insults between Sir Grantley and Dr Williams; or the unseemly

368

squabbling over the matter of the federal capital site.[4] But they could be matched by comparable episodes in other federal formative periods. In themselves, like all politics, they were symptoms, not original causes. For West Indian politicians, like all politicians in more or less popular systems, are representative men who reflect, and who must reflect if they wish to survive, the basis general prejudices of their electorates. To use them as scapegoats—Manley 'betrayed' us, or 'Busta' deserted the sinking ship—is to indulge the easy temptation of blaming individuals instead of seeing that individuals reflect the social pressures of their time, that, in this particular case, both of the Jamaican leaders were merely mouthpieces for a Jamaican insularity which, as the 1961 referendum vote showed, was overwhelmingly the outlook of the majority of Jamaicans. What was peculiar, perhaps, in the West Indian situation was that the explanation of mere 'politics' was given a special stimulus by the facts that (1) the retention in the federal constitution of the paraphernalia of individual island sovereignty produced an indigestible plethora of politicians so that, in the end, the federal public was weighted down by a costly structure of a Governor-General, five Governors, at least five Commissioners and not less than fifty-five ministers and ministers without portfolio; and (2) the West Indian popular psychology actually encouraged the politicization of everything with its disposition to regard clashes of personalities in the political field with something in the nature of outright cynical amusement. But all this, in and of itself, could not be enough to destroy federation. The thesis of 'politics', thus, is untenable, just as it is equally unreal to blame the West Indian political parties for failing to set up genuinely federal organizations to act as a counterpoise against territorial parochialism (the West Indies Federal Labour Party never really got off the ground) when such a process, the effective federalization of political parties, has literally taken decades to finalize itself in all other federal experiences.

Allied to the argument of 'politics' was the more general argument that the Federation died for want of a powerful spirit of West Indianism to give it drive and energy. That, of course, was true. But it was also largely irrelevant. For such a sense of federal loyalty, historically, has been the result, not the cause of federal enterprise. Indeed, it is precisely the absence of such a sense that necessitates, in the beginning, a federal structure in any case, for otherwise a group of peoples seeking some form of amalgamation could proceed immediately to the stage of a unitary state. The absence of that sense, in the West Indian case, was of course compounded by other special factors. There was no history of popular revolt, of armed struggle against the imperial power to feed it. There was no fear of annexation by an alien power such as helped Canadians after 1812 to grow closer to each other as they looked across the border to the growing expansionist spirit of American Manifest Destiny. The West Indian problem, in one way, was to discover the moral equivalents of colonialist war, the unifying forces which could be as psychologically powerful in peace as those others have been in war. But it is idle to deplore the absence of unity as if unity had to be the *sine qua non* of federal nation-building. It is even more idle to believe that the unity, the shared sense of being West Indian, could be accomplished by things like popular educational campaigns. For such unity, as all federal experience shows, matures out of a long experience of shared effort on the part of individual territories combining to meet particular problems in which all possess a felt concrete interest. That was clearly seen by the Trinidadian PNM leadership at the time. 'These islands,' its brief on *The Economics of Nationhood* cogently argued, 'have a long history of insularity, even of isolation, rooted in the historical development of their economy and trade and the difficulties of communications for centuries. No amount of subjective, that is to say historical, cultural or other activity of the time can be expected to overcome this hertitage. Only a powerful and centrally directed economic co-ordination and interdependence can create the true foundations of a nation. Barbados will not unify with St Kitts, or Trinidad with British Guiana, or Jamaica with Antigua. They will be knit together only through their common allegiance to a central government. Anything else will discredit the conception of Federation, and in the end leave the islands more divided than before.'[5]

The third most popular explanation for failure was the argument of geography. Murray's federal scheme of 1912 had excluded Jamaica for reasons of geographical separation, an exclusion with which Jamaican opinion at that time agreed.[6] The Jamaican Labour Party argument of the later federal period repeated the argument, insisting that there was, in fact, not one West Indies, but two, Jamaica itself and the Eastern Caribbean area. But this, again, was an argument of spurious plausibility only. It confused geography with communications. For the degree of intimacy between societies depends upon the availability of cheap and frequent communications, as the mass transit airline commuting system between New York and San Juan, Puerto Rico, graphically demonstrates. Geographical separation has not stood in the way of the final incorporation of both Alaska and Hawaii into the American Union. It is worth noting, in the Caribbean case, that Murray himself did not make the issue one of absolute debarment to Jamaican inclusion in a federal scheme at some later time when either sea or air communications would have obliterated the separation created by geography;[7] 'Experience proves,' he wrote in another pamphlet, 'that the centralization of government is greater or less in relative proportion to the facilities for communication.'[8] The modern communications revolution has by now made the argument of geographical propinquity quite outmoded. It might be remembered that for a generation after 1867 it was feared that the tremendous distances between the various provinces would bring about the collapse of the Canadian federation, and that the fear was successfully and finally buried with the completion of the Canadian-Pacific Railroad. The theory of the 'two West Indies' will similarly disappear as communications facilitate regular and easy travel within the region. There already exists the nucleus of such a system in the form of the new national airlines of independent units like Trinidad and Jamaica. As such a system takes hold the Caribbean Sea will come to be seen as an avenue and not as a barrier.

This is not to deny that all of these explanations were, to some extent, plausible half-truths. The geographical separation of Jamaica without doubt helped to contribute to the psychological isolationism of the Jamaican national temper. The absence of a felt sense of regional unity—in West Indian life there has always been a sense of common history but little sense of common destiny—certainly, too, aggravated the situation. And it would be idle to deny that the political leaders, on the whole, failed to rise to the occasion. 'The vested interest of ambition in power,' Mr Manley had finely said at Montego Bay, 'is the most dangerous of all the vested interests. It is in the history of every federation that there have always been found men who were unwilling to give up any local root of power for the creation of a larger centre of power itself, and I think we should warn ourselves of the danger and—dare I say?—that we should search our own breasts to discover if there lurks underneath the rationalizations that may be paraded for public consumption that malady which would be, and may yet prove to be, the greatest obstacle to our common ambitions.'[9] It was the supreme irony of Mr Manley's public career that he himself after 1958 should have provided the leading example of that temper. For his decision not to enter federal politics not only brought him the loss, almost overnight, of the veneration and respect he had enjoyed in all the West Indies, but drove him with relentless logic into a path of ultimate desertion of the federal idea. He was thereby trapped in a situation in which he became, in the style of high Greek tragedy, the author of his own misfortune. For the Jamaican electorate not unnaturally felt that if they were to leave Federation it would be more logical to leave it under the guidance of Bustamante, its open enemy, rather than of Manley, its lukewarm friend. The great federationist would fight the Napoleons of Notting Hill. But he would not fight the Confederate rebels of Jamaica. Nor did it add to that inglorious decline that he should have attempted to seek refuge in the very type of evasive rationalization he had denounced in the 1947 speech, in the form of the assertion, never really proved, that he was compelled to 'stay home' because of a sinister anti-federation 'conspiracy' being launched by unnamed forces in Jamaican society. If, this is to say, Federation died on account of political personality factors then Mr Manley must undoubtedly be convicted as the principal offender.

Having said that much, however, it remains clear that no one such theory can fully explain the federal collapse. It would be true to say that all of the factors here enumerated, plus the fact that, as already noted, the Federation was a British-imposed import from the beginning, were all present at the same time. Even more: of all the decisive formative factors common to federal enterprise—a sense of military insecurity necessitating some form of common defence, a desire to be independent of foreign powers, some embryonic political association joining the concerned territories together even before federation, geographical neighbourhood, even in some cases the coagulating experience of anti-colonial armed struggle—few, if any, were present in the West Indian situation. There was no exciting symbol around which federal sentiment might have rallied, save, perhaps, the Chaguaramas capital site issue for a brief moment. There was a real nationalist feeling, beyond doubt, first in Jamaica and then in Trinidad after the rise of the PNM, that could have been harnessed to the federal star in a struggle for federation with full independence. But that was not done; mainly because, as already suggested, Jamaican nationalism, historically antecedent to the Trinidadian, allowed itself after 1945 to be diverted into pro-British channels. The result was, in Marryshow's tart comment, that while other peoples had been fighting to get out of the British Empire the West Indies had been fighting to stay in.[10] The only purpose, then, that could have given meaningful direction and emotional substance to federation, that of hammering out a new West Indian nationalism based upon popular social and economic needs, failed to materialize. There was, in truth, a total absence in any of the various reports put out during the period of drift between 1945 and 1958 of any clear, elevated, comprehensive conception of what Federation was designed or expected to do. That perhaps explains who so much of the endless debating of Federation, so utterly dull, was concerned with form rather than with function. Of necessity, that was a futile exercise, for it is function that determines form, not form that determines function.

What took place, to look at it all from a somewhat different angle, is that a federal scheme conceived in 1945 and brought to fruition in 1958 had to meet the strain, once established as a machinery of government, of the tensions generically inherent in federalism. For by its very nature federalism holds within itself the source of complex and potentially destructive conflicts between the new central government and the individual unit governments. It does not create those conflicts, nor the factors, mostly of vested economic interest, that underly them. But it clothes them with a new politico-constitutional dress. It also gives them fresh virility—as the dispute between the federal government and Jamaica over the issue of retroactive federal taxation showed—for there now exist new political relationships, new forms of political power, even new political *élites*, that enter into the total situation.

The history of the Federation, from this viewpoint, then, was the history of the internal struggle between the nascent federal government and the entrenched territorial economic interests of, variously,

Barbados, Trinidad and especially Jamaica. The leading topics of debate during the period were, in reality, variations on that theme— on federal taxation, on a regional customs union, even on the reform, mandatory after the first five years of its life, of the federal constitution. The leading territories, being colonial economies, were therefore solidly protectionist economies. From the beginning, then, they were joined in a common concern to keep the new federal government as weak as possible. The distribution of legislative powers, the heart and centre of any federal arrangement, reflected that situation. Those powers were divided into two lists, the Exclusive and the Concurrent, the allocation being of such a character as to leave the federal government with an alarmingly narrow area of jurisdiction. Services that obviously require uniform standards on a regional basis, like aircraft and aviation and postal services, were curiously placed on the Concurrent list, that is, under joint local and federal control; and the Trinidad Postmaster-General almost immediately pointed out the distinct danger of perpetuating local anomalies if the postal service was not fully federalized.[11] Items like company law and trade unions, again, were placed on the Concurrent list despite the well-known fact that the trade union movement in the region had been hampered for decades by the power of the individual colonial governments to pass trade union ordinances without reference to any overriding regional sentiment. Even in the vital field of agriculture the federal Government was granted advisory and consultative powers only; and the assumption that agricultural development, when it did take place, would be a sort of federal extension of the existing Development and Welfare schemes of the Colonial Office suggests that concepts of federal economic planning, here, were limited to a social welfare perspective that left untouched the cardinal illness of West Indian agriculture, its weak and conservative technology of production. The fact, above all, that for at least the first five years of its life the federal Government would not be entitled to levy income tax meant that its power at once to spend and to undertake plans of redistributive social justice by means of the tax weapon was drastically curtailed, almost in fact nullified. It meant, too, as the Fiscal Commissioner noted, that the federal Government would start off with a revenue-raising technique that would not only thus arbitrarily circumscribe its policy-making schemes but would also deprive it of a direct relationship with the

federal public. Instead of being conceived, then, as the chief instrument for regional positive economic planning the federal Government emerged, from the very beginning, as a modest administrative
board whose functions were so restricted that the Fiscal Commissioner, again, was constrained to speculate as to whether there would
be enough work for its eight ministers to undertake.[12] The federation
would have been better served, as the 'small island' leaders in particular noted, with a constitution leaving residual powers, of a wide-
ranging character, in the hands of the central government. 'Under
the proposed constitution,' Mr Salles-Miquelle told the St Lucian
Legislative Council at the time, 'there is in my view the danger that
the Federal Government will prove ineffectual in dealing with
matters in which it will be desirable that a strong line be taken.
I fear that at its best the Federal Government is likely to turn out
to be merely an improved version of the Regional Economic Committee, whereas I feel certain that at its worst the Federal Government could well become nothing more than a platform for the
declamation of various and equally negative and indifferent types
of Caribbean politics.'[13]

The prophecy turned out to be correct. There was a concerted
effort to keep the federal centre weak, even make it weaker. On each
seminal issue involving federal power there was some vested territorial interest organized to stand in its way. Thus, the principle
of free movement of persons within the federal territory was compromised early on by the decision of the 1955 conference, called
specifically to deal with the issue, to leave the matter in abeyance
for a five-year period, and further compromised by the later decision
of the 1961 Inter-Governmental Conference to permit only a
gradually phased application of the principle, which would not
then be complete until 1973. That meant a victory for the Trinidadian view that the Trinidadian economy, being a person-importing
economy and not, like Barbados, a person-exporting economy,
could not permit an immediate influx of 'small island' immigrants
to threaten existing wage standards and place fresh strains upon
its embryonic social services. The fear of being swamped by the
'small island' unemployed, clearly enough, was strong enough to
overwhelm a principle absolutely essential to any viable federation,
and could perhaps only be solved in the long run, as Mr Barrow
argued at the time, as the problem of freedom of movement was

seen as a problem of organizing regional full employment.[14] A regional customs union, the *sine qua non* of any federal scheme, as both the McLaghlan Report and the Report of the later Trade and Tariffs Commission emphasized, was likewise rendered null and void by the opposition of the Jamaican leaders on the ground that their economy, being a high protective tariff economy (unlike the Trinidadian), needed protection against the effects of a lower unified tariff of a federal character. They obtained what they wanted at the decisive 1961 conference, ratified by the subsequent London meeting.

Two things are worth noting about the customs union controversy. In the first place, both of the Jamaican party leaderships chose to countenance a brazenly distorted propoganda campaign to the effect that a common external tariff would seriously jeopardize, even destroy, the developing Jamaican industrialization programme. The argument ignored the general consideration that without careful investigation it is never sure in any proposal involving a compulsory free trade entity how the imposition of free trade by means of a regional customs union will affect any particular territory; and that there is probably much less potential conflict of interest than appears on the surface and on a short view because the co-ordination of economic policy, including tariff policy, throughout the proposed region will always permit of measures favourable to the growth of general regional purchasing power and of the capacity of the home market to absorb the products of regional industries.[15] Secondly, the Jamaican propaganda chose to overlook the fact, more particularly, that the customs union proposal finally recommended by the 1958 Commission report went far, perhaps too far, in meeting the Jamaican objections, including the recommendation of a five-year moratorium period to permit the gradual harmonization of existing unit arrangements and an Industrial Commission which would seek to reconcile unit interests upon a federal plane.[16] The Jamaicans rejected even that questionable compromise, going so far as to demand, contrary to all known federal practice elsewhere, that the administration of customs throughout the area should not inhere in the Federal civil service, thus fatally compromising the emergence of a federal administrative process characterized by the twin principles of uniformity and impartiality.[17] In the light of those concessions, not to mention the even more startling proposal of the Fiscal Committee of the Inter-Governmental Conference that for the duration of the proposed transition period Jamaica should remain a separate customs territory[18]—a proposal calculated to make final Jamaican acceptance of any customs union with teeth in it even more problematical—it was palpable misrepresentation to pretend that the special difficulties of the Jamaican high-tariff economy had not been fully considered and met. The truth of the matter was, of course, that since the inception of the federal discussions in 1945 Jamaica had embarked upon an independent industrialization programme of the Puerto Rican type and that by 1958 the protection of that programme had become the cardinal feature of every Jamaican government, PNP or JLP. That meant, among much else, acceptance of an illiberal stand on the general matter of world free trade, emphasized by the Jamaican decision not to subscribe to the General Agreement of Tariffs and Trade (GATT). It meant, too, a new alliance between the Jamaican political forces and the class of businessmen and merchants who exploited the Jamaican consumer behind the shield of a restrictionist import structure, giving rise, incidentally, to a public cynical humour in which the PNP was identified with the Matalon business forces and the JLP with the Ashenheim business forces. It was, perhaps, the final comment upon PNP 'socialism' that its economic views, as this matter showed, were an echo of the narrow philosophy of the Jamaica Chamber of Commerce and the Jamaica Manufacturers' Association.[19] It need only be added that Jamaican intransigence on the issue of free movement of goods only served to intensify Trinidadian intransigence on the issue of free movement of persons.

It was the same with respect to the related matter of the federal tax power. There rapidly developed after 1958 an open fight between the Jamaican view that the federal Government should be denied control over income and profits taxation and the Trinidadian view that there should be built up a joint unit-federal tax system, with unit rates subject to federal approval. The fight, of course, reflected serious differences about the very purposes of federation. For Jamaicans the Federation was to be merely the delegated agent, within defined boundaries, of unit interests. For Trinidadians, it was to become a Hamiltonian central power aiming at the one single purpose that alone could give rationale to the enterprise, that

is, the organization of revenue and spending powers in such a way—
for example, through the planned return of federal monies to the
units by means of the equalization principle—as to facilitate the
gradual closing of the gap of general living standards between
the relatively better-off territories and the poorer territories within
the federal family.[20] The Trinidadian view, naturally, was also the
view of the smaller territories, who clearly feared that federation
could easily become an unequal thing in which they became a
captive consumer market for the expanding industries of the major
territories. It was for that reason that in the 1953 conference proceedings their *Memorandum on Imposed Losses* asked for measures—
a uniform income tax, increased federal services, enlarged grants-
in-aid—calculated to reduce the inequitable burden of federal
membership.[21] The struggle between the two views ended at last
with a complete victory for the Jamaican thesis, as outlined in the
White Paper of 1961, summing up the proposals of the committees
and working parties of the Inter-Governmental Conference of that
year. Those proposals effectively insulated income tax and industrial development from federal Government 'interference' by trans-
ferring them to a curious Reserve List, from which they could not
be taken away except by means of an equally curious and labyrin-
thine amendment process which, in effect, granted the Jamaican
House of Representatives a perpetual Polish veto over any effort
in the future to put some teeth into the federal tax power. The
Jamaican victory was the outcome of (1) a policy of Jamaican
'brinkmanship' in which Mr Manley openly threatened secession
should Jamaica not get all she demanded and (2) the fatal ambivalence of the 'small island' delegations who wanted the financial
help promised by the Trinidadian plan but shied away from the
necessary condition of surrendering their little sovereignties to a
strong centre, a feeling, be it noted, springing out of the general
fact that in the period following the Montego Bay conference a
whole new corps of popularly elected politicians had come into
power who were naturally reluctant to give up their newly-won
ministerial pomp and pageantry to a higher federal power.

In the result, no one cared to call the massive Jamaican bluff.
And bluff it was. For the Jamaican argument rested upon two grave
misconceptions, perhaps deliberately encouraged, of the federal
situation. It insisted, first, that financially Jamaica did not 'get back

anything' from her federal membership dues whereas, in fact, most of the 820,000 pounds contributed by the Jamaican taxpayer to the federal treasury were returned by means of shared federal services— some of which, like the University College, were preponderantly Jamaican in character—which she would still need to have and find money for whether she remained within Federation or not. The Jamaican argument insisted, secondly, that a positive federal tax programme would 'destroy' the Jamaican industrialization pro-gramme. The answer there, of course, was that, as the Federal Prime Minister pointed out, there was no federal intention at any time to interfere with the particular legislation of any unit, pioneer industry and incentive legislation, for example; all that was asked for was a recognition of the 'bounden duty' of the federal Govern-ment so to interfere only if such legislation were to have the effect of creating local monopoly situations that would make impossible the achievement at a later period of a customs union and an effi-cacious federal tax policy.[22] The federal fears about territorial protectionism were, in fact, justified, as was evident from the decision of the Jamaican Government at much the same time to establish an oil refinery which would effectively eliminate the competitive position of Trinidadian oil within the Jamaican economy and thus set a pattern for a disastrous policy of competitive duplication of economic facilities so inimical to the idea of planned regional development on the co-operative basis of unit specialization.[23] The general upshot of all this was that by 1961 the already limited fiscal powers of the federal Government had been so even more whittled down under Jamaican pressure that the federal centre emerged as a weak accounting body relying for its income upon a socially reactionary revenue system that taxed the working class consumer and failed to tax the wealthy industrialist.[24] For its Jamaican mem-bers it was seen, with brutal frankness, as simply a buyers' syndicate in which it suited Jamaica for the time being to pool her resources in order to obtain services she would be ill advised to seek on her own.[25]

The outcome, almost certainly inevitable, of all this was the Jamaican referendum of 1961 in favour of secession and the break-up of the Federation in 1962. It is worth looking at the character of the Jamaican separatist thesis in some detail since it illuminates many continuing Jamaican and, indeed, West Indian attitudes.

For it would be misleading to see the whole thing simply as a comedy of errors, although many of its aspects were comic enough: the way, for example, in which the postponement of each difficult Federal decision was elevated into an almost sacrosanct ritual at each strategic conference, or the lively exchange of newspaper correspondence between Manley and Bustamante in which the two Jamaican leaders sought to outbid each other in their efforts to explain away their earlier passionate moments of pro-federal sentiment.[26] It would be equally misleading to see it all in morally pejorative terms as a Jamaican capitulation to 'selfishness' or 'betrayal' or even just mere 'petty-mindedness', although there was something of all that present. There was much truth in the apt observation of one angry letter writer, speaking of Bustamante's record, that the JLP leader's attitude to the Federation amounted in sports circles to a club leader refusing to join a cricket or a domino league unless his side got the championship trophy in advance.[27] The situation, on the contrary, must be seen sociologically. Jamaican attitudes, essentially, expressed the continuing deep power of *insularismo* in Jamaican and, possibly, West Indian life, feeding on economic interests, both old and new. Nothing less than that could explain the paradox of a mind as sophisticated as Mr Manley's lending its support to the sort of schoolboy rationalizing arguments that were advanced, for example, in his Government's *Ministry Paper* of 1960 in defence of the separatist argument.[28]

That *Paper* reiterated the specious nonsense about 'the inherently natural tendency which is created by water barriers' and cited as evidence the differences between England and Ireland and China and Formosa but discreetly neglected to mention how, in more representative cases, the 'powerful separatist force' of water barriers had not prevented the successful mergers of, for example, Hawaii and the continental United States. It sought to justify its demands for decentralizing the already limited powers of the Federal Government with the argument that in cases like Nigeria and India federation 'has involved a process of decentralizing in an area where more central administration previously prevailed', as if the fact that colonial government was centralized proved that all centralized government is colonial. It repeated, finally, the naïve assumption, similar to that of the discredited Rance Report, that it should be possible to provide an amendment process to enable the Federal

Government 'to grow and expand as convenience and necessity might dictate', thus allowing the centre 'with the consent of the units concerned, to take over the administration of special services in the interests of efficiency and economy'. The presumption of a peaceful coexistence between the central and local governments here postulated, along with the further presumption of a peaceful process of federal expansion, was in fact the sort of Utopian, theoretical reasoning that Mr Manley, as a 'practical politician', affected to sneer at. For, historically, all federal experience shows that the shift of powers to the centre is rarely peaceful, mainly because the units develop vested interests in retaining powers and fiercely resist their surrender. The 'severe dislocations' that the *White Paper* cited as a warning against too heavy a concentration of central power should, indeed, be seen as evidence of the reactionary character of states' rights within a federal system, not as proof of the folly of attempting such concentration. To argue that no attempt should be made because it would provoke the territorial governments into intensified separatist actions was in effect an argument for tolerating blackmail. Federalism, by its nature, encourages conflict, not co-operation, between its twin areas of polarized power. It is for that reason that Sidgwick cited the danger of the independent activity of local governments being used as centres of local resistance to the national will as one of the chief disadvantages of a federal structure.[29] Altogether, the general tenor of the Jamaican argument was to confer upon that local activity a perpetual veto upon the growth of any really powerful federal government in the future.

Yet after all, the point, perhaps, to make is not the logical weakness of the argument but the fact that recourse to it indicated the presence in Jamaica of a virulent nationalism sharper than the internationalist implications of the federal idea, and desperately determined to break federation should federation stand in its way. In one way, as already noted, the nationalism was natural to West Indian society, in a way that federalism, being a British colonial import, was not. From that viewpoint, there was a case to be made for Jamaica, as indeed the Domingo pamphlets showed. The tragedy, in one way, then, was not the existence of Jamaican nationalism but the fact that it operated as a negative and not as a creatively positive force. It chose after 1945 to identify with socially retrogressive developments, first, of a protectionist capitalism based on the profit motive and, second, of a Crown Colony type of federation. Its potentially revolutionary promise thereby failed to materialize. That explains why the early dream of the Jamaica Progressive League leaders like Roberts of a Jamaican nationalism centred in the philosophy of a free and tolerant community emerging out of colonialism, and impregnating the rest of West Indian society by its liberal example, gave way, as they saw it, to an illiberal federationism in which narrow-minded politicians conspired with the British Government, in return for high-flown federal titles, to reverse the course of Caribbean history. It explains, too, why the early internationalist sympathies of the PNP gave way to a xenophobic nationalism turning its back on the colonial freedom movements elsewhere, not to mention the desertion of its smaller West Indian island brethren. It was symptomatic that it was 'Busta' and not the PNP leaders who, alone of all West Indian leaders at the time, openly lent his support to Dr Jagan during the British Guiana 1953 crisis. And even at that, of course, 'Busta's' attitude grew out of temperament, not out of ideological conviction about the evils of colonialism. His own party, save for such characteristic aberrations on the part of its erratic leader, joined with the right wing elements of the PNP to foment the victory of Jamaican nationalism with its emphasis more and more on the theme of material benefits.[30]

The general result of all this was that the prolonged federation discussions ended up with a federation controlled oligarchically by a Jamaican member society that existed almost as a distinct legal personality. It was a federal structure basically dualistic in character, Jamaica, as it were, *versus* the Rest. It was in fact a ridiculous travesty of federation, giving rise, as it did, to periodical harebrained schemes in the Jamaican press in favour, generally, of a dual constitutional structure to correspond to the economic dualism which Jamaica craved: the *West Indian Economist's* idea, for example, of a system of separate provinces each of which would have a special pattern of relationships with the Federal Government, or Mr Manley's scheme of a federal Council of Ministers which, if implemented, would have fatally divided federal executive authority and would have compelled the Federal Prime Minister to lead a Jekyll and Hyde existence between an official and an unofficial cabinet.[31] Minority voices like that of Sir Robert Kirkwood apart, the whole of Jamaican society seemed united in this spirit of gross, inward-turned chauvinism, summed up for all in the shrill declaration of one of the Jamaican federal Representatives, speaking to his fellow-Jamaicans in the Jamaica House of Representatives, that 'Regardless of what you want to say, Jamaica must control Federation. We must have the majority. When we fight here, we can fight; we can cuss; we can do anything we want here. But let us go down to Trinidad as one; let us be united as one when we go to Trinidad; let us go down there as Jamaicans, not divided at all. We are going down there to fight for Jamaica, to protect Jamaica's interest, and when we do that we would have done a good job for Jamaica; we would have been protecting taxpayers of the country.'[32] The decline of the Federation was thus the decline at the same time of the best spirit of Jamaican patriotism. Jamaicans gained their world. But in gaining it they lost their own soul.

In the final resort, it could be possible to see the demise of Federation in terms even broader than those of Jamaican nationalism and its relationship with the rest of the area. It could conceivably be argued that federation, whether of the Trinidadian-Hamiltonian model or of the Jamaican-Jeffersonian model, was in itself a grossly misconceived structure to impose upon West Indian society. It assumed the almost permanent divisibility of the society. It is more justifiable, actually, to see the society as a naturally unitary region for which the appropriate political machinery should be that of a unitary state. For, as a society, it has none of the almost irreparable and profound divisions that fragmentalize, say, many of the contemporary African societies—tribalism, religious fanaticism, deep racial hatreds, regional parochialism. The weakness of the 'pluralist society' thesis, as applied to the West Indian case, has already been noted in that respect. The result is that, in order to justify the federal principle, its advocates were driven frequently into the untenable position of denying that unitary character. As one critic has pointed out, they consequently 'argue about our cosmopolitanism when we are eighty per cent Afro-Asian, they speak about our differences when we are fairly homogeneous in terms of religion and language, they talk glibly of economic disparities when we are all poor, and of our separation by sea when a Sun-Jet can run through the entire West Indian archipelago in between two successive meals'.[33] The proper line of development for the West Indies to have adopted should have been—if this way of seeing the matter is correct—the conscious search for a regional nationalism, along with political independence, that would have built upon those socio-cultural foundations. It would have then appreciated the truth that the federal form, as Dicey insisted, is at best only a halfway house between a status of loose confederation and a full-blown unitary state.

Had the truth been recognized much of the West Indian debate could have saved itself not only from the heartache of the whole fiasco but also from the pedantic wrangling over academic terms that characterized so much of it, especially by the West Indian lawyer class. The whole problem of regional integration was frequently misunderstood because sterile textbook categories were slavishly followed, usually along English academic lines. Thus it was unthinkingly assumed that the leading principle of federalism, following the thesis laid down by an English theoretician like Wheare, was a sort of peaceful coexistence between two equal tiers of constitutional authority; from which it was deduced that anything that detracted from the 'independence' of the unit territories constituted a violation of the federal 'spirit'. This way of thinking could not appreciate, then that the Wheare dichotomy was itself historically provincial, generalizing as it did from the limited experience of eighteenth and nineteenth-century Western communities propelled, ideologically, by classical *laissez-faire* individualism with all its psychotic fear of positive government. The combined pressure in the twentieth century of war, economic depression and welfare state collectivism has rendered the Wheare concept more and more anachronistic. The general trend thus unleashed towards centralization has affected all of the contemporary federal systems, so that, in the case of the United States alone, a new 'federalism' has so redistributed the original allocation of powers that today, in Mr Justice Roberts' sentence, the individual states are not so much co-ordinate sovereigns as they are administrative districts of the federal government.[34]

Functionally, that is to say, there is little if any difference between a unitary state and a federal state under modern conditions. The Trinidadian PNM thesis saw something of this, clearly enough. But it was precluded from pressing the point to its logical conclusion —that what the West Indies needed was a unitary system—by the unavoidable pressures of politics as a government and a party directly involved in the West Indian power struggle. And that the West Indian mind is still enslaved to the textbook pontifications is apparent enough from the 1965 *White Paper* in which the Barbados Government took issue with the St Lucian position that a new Eastern Caribbean federal government should have some degree of centralized control over expenditures as doing 'considerable violence to the federal principle of co-ordinate and independent authority'; from which erroneous maxim it was enabled to deduce, following the old Jamaican argument, that such a federal structure would 'preserve and exercise the same kind of patronizing paternalism which exemplifies the worst aspects of colonialism'.[35] The Federation is dead. But the mental conservatism that in part caused its death still flourishes vigorously in the West Indian frame of reference.

One final point deserves mention. It has become fashionable to label the history of the West Indies Federation a failure of the West Indian political spirit. But it was as much a failure of the British political spirit. That one abortive conference followed another was due, not to West Indian political childishness, but, frankly, to the fact that Great Britain was anxious to use Federation as a means of discarding its now unwanted responsibilities as a colonial power and to the fact, further, that she sought withdrawal from the Caribbean area without providing the sort of economic aid to which, on any showing, the colonies were entitled. The point was aptly summed up in the 1964 statement of the Trinidadian Government's United Nations representative to a subcommittee of the Committee on Colonialism. 'An administering power,' he urged, 'is not entitled to extract for centuries all that can be got out of a colony and when that has been done to relieve itself of its obligations by the conferment of a formal but meaningless—meaningless because it cannot possibly be supported—political independence. Justice requires that reparation be made to the country that has suffered the ravages of colonialism before that country is expected to face up to the problems and difficulties that will inevitably beset it upon independence.'[36] Anything less than that, Sir Ellis Clarke concluded, would constitute something less than the genuine article; it would be trying to fob off West Indians with independence on the cheap. Nor do official protestations from London which only manage, in an evasive fashion, to cite West Indian domestic difficulties as an excuse for British inaction meet the moral issue involved.[37] West

13

Indians, generally, felt this kind of attitude to be shabby treatment. They were, after all, they felt, entitled to something better as, historically, the first of all British colonies to be settled. They quoted the observation of the greatest of all Royal Commissions ever sent out to the region that no other former British colony could claim, as the West Indies could claim, that Britain had placed the labouring population of the West Indies where it was and could not divert itself of the responsibility for its future.

Yet such a divestiture of responsibility was in harsh truth the British motive throughout. It constituted, perhaps, the one single element which, like a key to a mystery, suddenly gives meaning to the seemingly illogical, random moves in the federation charade after 1945. It received its final melodramatic touch, like the epilogue of a bad play, in the treatment that was meted out to the 'Save the Federation' delegation that hurried to London from the federal capital at the very end to ask the Colonial Secretary to intercede to stay the execution. Mr Gomes, as a member of that delegation, has described how the Colonial Secretary, Mr Maudling, his face set angrily, had them lined up like schoolboys brought in for disciplinary action and behaved like an ill-tempered schoolmaster; and that it was only because he, Gomes, was one among many that prevented his remarking on the apparent deterioration of Colonial Office manners.[38] It was the crowning humiliation, for all of the West Indian leaders in the federation struggle, from Marryshow and Cipriani on, had always passionately believed that although British policy might falter, British manners, the code of the English gentleman class they so much adored, would never fail them.

# Chapter XVI

# THE CHALLENGE OF INDEPENDENCE

WITH INDEPENDENCE the West Indian society faces, after the Discovery and Emancipation, its third seminal period. The Discovery set the original pattern of the society as a slave-based sugar monoculture producing massive profits for absentee owners. Emancipation laid the foundations of a changing Creole society of limited commercial capitalism and peasant individualism. The first period, because of its indiscriminate use of imported slave labour, left behind it a legacy of excessive population in relation to the economy's resources. The second period, because of its use of indentured labour, left behind it a legacy of a low-wage economy with living standards artificially kept low by the maintenance of a reservoir of unemployed and underemployed persons. Independence—which, unlike Emancipation, is merely a redefinition of the legal status of the society not necessarily bringing in its wake a profound social metamorphosis such as characterized post-Emancipation society—inherits those problems created by the slave and Creole societies. It is true to say, in essence, that the central reality of independence is the need to convert the patterns set by those earlier social systems into an independent national society run primarily in the interests of its independent citizens.

It is, of course, easy to see what independence, on the surface, means. The new nation takes over the paraphernalia of sovereignty. There are the conventional decisions to join the United Nations and, in the West Indian case, to remain within the Commonwealth; the latter being a decision not made so much out of sentimental regard as out of the need to be represented in a vital trading and finance area. For the crass difference between London's treatment of the Guiana government in 1953 and of the Rhodesian secessionist revolt in 1966 was proof, if it were needed, of the double standard of United Kingdom attitudes to the white and coloured members of the Commonwealth. 'Commonwealth alignment', in any case, must be a meaningless phrase when countries like Trinidad and Jamaica have more in common, speaking now of their basic problems, with countries like Yugoslavia or the United Arab Republic than with Canada or Australia. There is the need for the new nation to set up missions abroad; while, internally, it has to take over the responsibilities of defence and public order by means of new defence forces and control over the police, the last powers yielded up by the imperialist agents. New constitutions must be written, mostly following the Westminster model. The popularly elected minister takes over from the expatriate official. The mass party replaces the individual legislator in the task of organizing and reflecting public opinion. The machinery of government, in brief, becomes adjusted to the new national requirements. Not the least symbolic expression of the change is the final removal of the Colonial Secretary from the colonial arena, thus ending the ridiculous pretension that a whole empire could be effectively governed by a single department in London. That had been seen more than a century ago by the Utilitarian critics of the Colonial Office. 'The Secretary of State for the Colonies,' observed Sir William Molesworth in the period after 1832, 'traverses and retraverses, in his imagination, the terraqueous globe; flying from the Arctic to the Antarctic pole; hurrying from the snows of North America to the burning regions of the tropics; rushing across from the fertile islands of the West Indies to the arid deserts of South Africa and Australia; like nothing on earth, or in romance, save the Wandering Jew.' Independence puts an end at least to that particular absurdity in a society that has been full of absurdities, of ossified institutions existing like so many Egyptian-style mummies in the hospitable colonial climate of opinion.

But all these are the obvious surface phenomena of independence. They indicate little of the more profound metamorphosis of social structure and social attitudes that the traumatic transition from colonial status to freedom ought to mean if it is to mean anything at all. New problems will demand new perspectives, new plans, new mental assumptions about the underlying fundamentals of life. A new sense of urgency will have to make itself felt, for one of the crippling handicaps of West Indian life has been the deceptive sense of security engendered by colonial rule. West Indians have been made to feel, frequently to their own satisfaction, that with paramount responsibility resting with London Britain would always look after things, would always guarantee their safety. So, West Indians have been, like Mr Micawber, incurable optimists waiting for something to turn up. Their capacity for positive action rooted in a frank appraisal of the reality of things was thus seriously undermined. There was lacking the one single incentive, the knowledge that they were on their own in an uncertain and frequently hostile world, calculated to nurture that capacity. That incentive is now there. The real problem of independence is whether the West Indian society can respond creatively to that challenge or will react negatively, seeking in typical colonial fashion to find alibis for inaction or even deliberate evasion of responsibility.

The challenge means a great number of things. It means a new inner strength, both for the individual and the society, the readiness to look inwards, not outwards, for solutions to problems. It means the creation of new institutions, cultural and social as well as political and economic. It means, in brief, the growth of a new positive citizenship, what Rousseau termed in a famous chapter a new civil religion. A new type of public opinion must be organized as the popular base of that citizenship. Equally, a new sense of personal responsibility, of personal involvement, must grow up, for much of what passes for a new national spirit is frequently a sterile anti-colonial prejudice. Even a critic of Caribbean colonialism as left-wing as Daniel Guerin has referred to the temptation, especially in Caribbean politicians, to make the United States into a scapegoat for whatever goes wrong in the area.[1] The game of blaming the ex-colonial power for everything, however historically justifiable it may be, becomes increasingly anachronistic with the passage of time. For it is not enough, with independence, to be merely against something, however justifiably. One must be for something. The social energies of newly liberated peoples, hitherto unutilized in the colonial system, now await the invention of new institutions and new purposes to fulfil themselves. The West Indies, after some early false starts, are thus clearly on the move. The basic questions of their future revolve not around the movement itself but around the direction in which it will propel itself.

Independence, then, means a national stock-taking of heroic proportions. Literally every institution of the society comes in for close re-examination by the new nationalist ethic. Both the political party and the trade union are under pressure to provide answers to the main problems of high unemployment, illiteracy, a dying sugar industry, a high-cost import structure combined with a low-paid and relatively unskilled labour force, a vulnerable production structure dependent on metropolitan preferences, an archaic wages-incomes-profits-prices complex that badly needs rationalization, as the acrimonious Trinidadian debate over the 1965 Industrial Stabilization Bill shows; and so on. The trade union movement, in particular, must face the possibility of new tactics in the industrial struggle as they replace the old tactics; thus, a Trinidadian leader, quoting the United States union leader George Meany, has noted that American unions are now active in politics because they have found that, although the company spy and the professional strike-breaker have just about passed from the scene and although unions have certain protections under the law, the employer has decided that the place to curb the union movement is in the legislative field; with the implication that the West Indian scene is likely to witness a similar development. That is undoubtedly true; and it is interesting to note that the time period during which the West Indian trade union has passed from the status of a social pariah to that of a 'sacred cow' more or less exactly corresponds to the time period, that is to say the period since the 1937 passage of the Wagner Act, during which the American movement has undergone the same metamorphosis.[2] Both political party and union also face the problem of bridging the gulf between their middle class professional leadership and their rank and file. For much of what passes for political 'stability' in the self-congratulatory literature is in reality only a reflection of the traditional apathy of the West Indian masses. The West Indian union leader, in particular, is rarely a proletarian either by birth or inclination and in general knows little more about the proletariat of his locals than a good sepoy colonel of 1856 would have known about the Indian villages from which his recruits came.[3]

The West Indian churches, in turn, face a similar challenge. Their humanitarian record of slavery reform is well known. But for a century or more they have tended to live on the memory of that record. It is suggestive, then, that they are already beginning to take a larger view of their social responsibilities, whether it is in the form of their campaign, as in Antigua and Jamaica, against the introduction of legalized casino gambling as an adjunct to the

tourist industry, or their plea, as with the Caribbean Roman Catholic bishops, for the application of Catholic social justice to the problem of mass subnormal living standards, or even, as with the case
of the 1962 resolution of the Jamaican Presbyterian Church on
foreign policy matters, their concern for a Christian foreign policy
for independent nations.[4] There is, even more than that, the question, peculiarly urgent with the advent of a new political status, of
the West Indianization of the churches, for, as an Anglican canon
of the Trinidad diocese has put it, it would be incongrous in any
developing nationalism to insist on natives serving in the state while
surrendering the churches to the oversight of foreigners.[5] The civil
services, likewise, face the transition from being a colonial power
group to becoming a representative bureaucracy under national
political control. The readjustment of attitudes that will require
in the individual officer has been noted, for the Jamaican service,
in Mr B. St J. Hamilton's book.[6] The ideal of what the civil servant
under the independence regime should strive to be has likewise been
sketched for the Trinidadian case by the exhaustive Lewis Report.[7]
The adjustment will be exacting enough, for the definition of an
able civil servant under the colonial regime, as the Lewis report
points out, was that he attain skills in the art of 'paper passing' to
expatriate officers, thus inhibiting the growth of a positive attitude
to the decision-making process;[8] while no less a person than the
Premier of Barbados has noted, with reference to the privileged
status of civil servants under the same colonial regime, that they have
traditionally regarded themselves as some army of occupation sent
down to the area by the Colonial Office.[9] The new and important
subgroup, finally, of the resident West Indian university faculties,
as well as the annual flow of graduate students now sent down into
the national life, will have to face the challenge of (1) reshaping an
inherited aristocratic concept of education into a democratic one
for new social purposes and (2) rewriting West Indian history to
counterbalance the hitherto existing academic work by either
American-oriented students of West Indian affairs or European
scholars who have considered Caribbean colonialism as most significant because it reflects the economic and political struggles of the
Old World. The adjustment of values and behaviour patterns that
all of these groups, as well as others, must meet reflects, in brief, the
clamant demands of a new citizenship rooted in the obligation to

serve the national community. That citizenship is thus seen as a new social solvent absorbing all groups on a basis of equality in what the Guyanese journalist-essayist P. H. Daly has aptly termed the 'assimilative state'.

The search for a new national interest, it becomes obvious, is the search for a new cultural identity. All newly independent societies seek a positive philosophy to replace the habits of colonial dependency. For, with independence, the society belongs to the resident groups; so, the West Indian society is no longer what Adolphe Roberts once called a semi-barbarous preserve for a small privileged caste of expatriate Englishmen. The logical accompaniment of that, so it seems to the new nation-builders, must be the growth of a new cultural nationalism, a new pride in the hitherto repressed Creole culture fixed upon Captain Cipriani's *dictum* that 'The Englishman has taught us that his home is his castle. We have learned the lesson well, and we must make our home our castle.' The overpowering cultural image of Britain, reinforced by the West Indian mimetic process, and which permeates nearly every nook and cranny of West Indian social psychology, must give way to new concepts of national and even personal identity rooted in West Indian experience itself. Nor is this merely an academic exercise, needful just for the sake of doing it. It is of immediate urgency, for without that new unifying force the independent Antilles, like independent Haiti earlier on, may be destroyed on the rocks of cultural schizophrenia. Much of West Indian opinion already sees this, perceiving clearly that independence goes far beyond questions of a national flag, a national anthem and a national emblem and becomes a question of psychological survival.

West Indians, as persons, this is to say, have to emancipate themselves in their innermost selves from the English psycho-complex. It will not be an easy task. It cannot be seen, as some writers on the area have seen it, as an act of national choice, as if things like social structure, even national character, are commodities, as it were, that new nations can select like so many customers in a food market. It is always easier to give up ideas than to surrender feelings. It will be the task, obviously, of a generation or more, working through education and experience. No one who has seen how difficult it has been for Puerto Ricans to rid themselves of an American psycho-complex will be likely to underestimate the magnitude of this challenge.

For, frankly, West Indians start out on this road with massive, even frightening handicaps. There is little left of the original culture in which to take pride, save for a few scattered artifacts. The Carib Queen of Arima and the Carib reserve villages in St Vincent and Dominica are about all that is left of the original populations. The cultural amalgam of the slave society was no doubt a real thing. But what it was in detail is a closed book, if only because both white planter and mulatto middle class looked on it with contempt. Later Caribbean scholarship, again, has so far done nothing comparable to the tremendous work of American historians on slavery as a social institution. Nor was there, before slavery, a pre-colonial civilization that could serve as the historical base of a rejuvenated nationalism. It would be difficult, certainly, to write for the West Indies the kind of book, like Basil Davidson's *Rediscovery of Africa*, which describes flourishing feudal civilizations pre-dating the arrival of Europeans; and that fact perhaps accounts for the ambivalence and indecisiveness of the West Indian attitude to things African. The West African nationalist can feel himself the inheritor of the great kingdoms of Ghana and Dahomey. The West Indian nationalist has no such refuge. His collective tragedy is that he is, in his cultural self, a schizoid person. He is, in the Martiniquan phrase, *peau noir, masque blanc*, the possessor of a pseudo-European culture in an Afro-Asian environment. It is for that reason that the regional political-constitutional story has seemed at times something of a farcical drama in which the Colonial Office has seemed more eager to give than West Indians have been to receive. There is no first principle of reference, no great martyrology to inspire the new generations. When, therefore, the West Indian playwright is asked, as in the Federal Festival of 1958, to produce a pageant-play on the region's history he has no one great single event, like the Haitian war of liberation or the Cuban Ten Years War, to use as the central *motif* of his production.

Present day attitudes have been shaped by this legacy. There is little conception of government in the national sense. Government, for most people, is something from which to extract special privileges denied to others. Authority is either laughed at, as in Trinidad, or passively deferred to, as in Barbados. There is little understanding

13*

of the idea of creative partnership between citizen and state. The pursuit of individual happiness, of the famous Trinidadian 'freeness', makes itself felt in spendthrift habits and a tradition of gluttony, as can be seen in any Christmas in the West Indies. Those habits, in turn, angrily resist any national fiscal policy that calls for their curtailment, as the frequency of successive austerity budget crises demonstrates. Above all, this is a society deeply impregnated with anti-intellectual attitudes. For, as Père Labat complained bitterly, at the beginning of the eighteenth century, everything was imported into the West Indies except books. Hence the sorry catalogue of general attitudes to things intellectual, only slowly giving way to new and more ideal pressures: the belief in the West Indian student that higher education means education abroad, the low status, financial and social, of the teaching profession, the amusing credulous belief of the West Indian crowd that an 'intellectual' is anybody who writes letters to the local newspaper or possesses a 'certificate' from some third-rate commercial institute run by profit-hungry managers. 'Here, then,' Dr Williams has written with justifiable asperity, 'is the reality of Independence—seeking to deal with our problems on a national scale and in an international context with a mentality conceived in slavery, cradled in indenture, and nurtured in colonialism. The dominant result is the confusion of anti-intellectualism. The slave society had no use for books, the indentured society built jails instead of schools, the colonial system inflicted on us a Director of Education without qualifications. So we, the products of this evil trinity, run all over the place despising qualifications, seeking a special position which has no relevance to our economic realities, aping the customs and attitudes of absentee planters and expatriate officials.'[10]

Nothing, then, is easier than to laugh at the spectacle of the nation-builders of the newly-independent states attempting to reconstruct something out of this dismal heritage. The literature on the region is full of the jaundiced English writer making fun of West Indian follies, without seeing that the joke is on him since they are the reflection of English follies. A critic writing recently from the University of Puerto Rico has managed to dismiss it all, in a piece of entertaining satire, as nothing more than a 'riot of nonsense' and 'fiery irrationalities'.[11] There is much, without doubt, to justify the stricture. To read the discussions in the West Indian press on the need for a distinctive national costume, or to note the bathos of the new national anthems, or to view the passions capable of being worked up over the question as to whether the new Jamaican Governor-General should wear a uniform on ceremonial occasions, is to be made painfully aware of the comedy involved in the effort to set up national rituals and symbols overnight. The same is true of the sort of undignified squabbling that goes on as various groups and individuals seek to claim credit for having been in 'on the ground floor' of the early national struggles, as if there were not 'glory enough for all'; the exchange of correspondence in the Jamaican press between W. A. Domingo and others concerning the genesis of the Jamaican nationalist movement after 1936 is typical.[12] But before all this is seen as raw material for satire two things ought to be remembered. The first is that to expect a growing national consciousness based solely on 'reason' and 'moderation' is to ignore the emotional aspects of human nature in politics. Men are rarely satisfied with merely abstract symbols of a new freedom. They need something more exciting, more tangible, more immediately recognizable. They are, true enough, members of the general army of humanity. But they are, first and foremost, members of their small platoon, through which they experience, as a part, the sense of belonging to the whole. And that this is a generally universal truth of human nature is evident enough from the fact that Kohr has to draw most of his examples of the 'insanity' of nationalism from the established and presumably more 'mature' European countries. If, then, Germans feel that their famous Shakespearian translations are superior to the English original, Puerto Ricans, as a Caribbean example, are surely entitled to compare Rafael Hernandez's patriotic hymn *Lamento Borincano* to Beethoven's Fifth Symphony; and the one as much as the other is an amiable fault easily forgiven.

The second point to make concerns the socio-psychological background of the contemporary efforts of cultural nationalism. For the new nationalism is not simply a mental error or a political mistake. It has real roots in historical experience, being, in fact, the response to the old colonialism. It goes back, in its origins, to the deep sense of shame, humiliation and basic loss of self-respect involved in being ruled by others even when, as with the English Antillean case, it has been a comparatively benign rule. In this sense, as Sekou Toure has put it, nationalism is psychologically inevitable for the liberated colonial peoples. To overlook all this is to be guilty of gross historical naïveté. It is true that symbols may come to be accepted, dangerously, as substitutes for, instead of merely being aids to the solid feelings of national community arising out of common social experience. West Indians themselves, however, are aware of the danger. As Dr Williams has remarked of the Trinidadian case, it takes more than a national anthem, however stirring, a national coat of arms however distinctive, a national flag however appropriate, a national flower however beautiful, to make a nation.[13] There is little evidence that West Indians, who posses the saving grace, in any case, of a pronounced sense of wry humour, are ready to elevate those symbols to the status of the grotesque identity-building absurdities Kohr is concerned to pillory.

Yet there is a real critique to be made of contemporary West Indian nationalism, although it is not the one that critics like Kohr make. It has to do, essentially, with the particular road to social growth and economic development that West Indian governments in the new era have elected to take. For independence is the beginning only. It is not the end. In one way, it merely replaces the national struggle against the external metropolitan power with an internal struggle between the various social and ethnic groups of the new national society, to determine who will inherit the vacuum of power left behind by the departing imperialists. There is nothing in the act of independence that minimizes the fact that the society continues to be a class society in which the Creole commercial and professional groups retain a halo of merit over them and sustain the pose by a sort of psychological confidence trick played by the communications media on the traditionally deferential West Indian masses. The general outcome of the transfer of power from the old empires to the new successor-states thus means little more, in social power terms, than the consolidation of the ruling class hold of (1) a nascent middle class using independence as a ladder to governmental, civil service and diplomatic appointments and (2) a growing business class seeking a new role in the world context of international capitalism. For the West Indian populace as a whole that means simply a change of masters only, and possibly, too, a change in some ways for the worse, for since the bourgeois groups understand them better, psychologically, than did the English officialdom their exploitation by those groups may be made that much easier.

In retrospect, that outcome takes on a certain air of historical inevitability. For after 1938 the potentially revolutionary *élan vital* of the masses was anaesthetized by being canalized into institutions —trade unions, political parties, co-operative societies—controlled by the bourgeois groups. The leadership elements that resisted that process—whether because of a radical racial perspective, as with Garveyism, or because of a radical political perspective, as with individuals like Lennox Pierre and John La Rose in Trinidad and Richard Moore and Reginald Pierrepointe in Barbados—were either pushed aside or purged by the dominant right-wing forces. Others, like George Padmore, who might have fought the process, elected to concentrate on the more promising African scene, not being excited by a West Indian 'revolution' led by a political leadership whose ideas of political emancipation hardly went further than the replacement of the Crown Colony system run by English personnel by a domestic class system run by a native-born *élite*. Others, again, like C. L. R. James, saw clearly enough, in sporadic writing, that no 'revolution' was worthwhile in which peasant and worker did not remain the primary agents, the leading properties of the experiment, for only the submerged classes were capable of genuinely revolutionary activity. But James, in any case, was personally isolated from the West Indian scene, not returning until 1958 (by which time the damage, from the revolutionary viewpoint, had been done) and in any case spoiled his capacity to help by an exaggerated sense of personal importance and, more generally, by his failure to appreciate that far from being a pure revolutionary class the West Indian ordinary people, by the time of independence, had become themselves seriously tainted with colonial bourgeois impurities. All of this, added up, facilitated the bloodless victory of the bourgeois spirit, whether in conservative or reformist garb, in the majority political parties that carried through the passage to independence. That was what took place in all of the West Indian societies, a truth only obscured in the Guyanese case by the Jaganite habit of retaining the orthodox terminology of the traditional Marxist literature.

The result, in the West Indian society of the present day, is the rule of the many by the few. A new vocabulary of nationalist respectability appears in which the fashionable slogan of 'citizenship' really amounts to the general acceptance of goals set by the new governing oligarchy. Ceremonial speechmaking does little but play variations on the theme. A rhetorical passage out of the contribution of the University of the West Indies—'We as citizens must be aware of that thing called political philosophy, as well as be prepared to formulate a particular philosophy to match the political needs and realities . . . of the Caribbean. Do we ever sit and ask ourselves the question, where are we coming from, where are we going, and what do we want now? What body of coherent ideas and principles are our public servants, both politicians and senior civil servants, formulating for the future of this country? And if there are these ideas, have they been passed on to the general populace for acceptance and comment?'[14]—is typical, taking for granted as it does that the role of the masses in the new dispensation is 'acceptance' of ideas made for them by the *élite*. The search for a national interest and a cultural identity, legitimate and desirable as they are, too easily becomes the private game of that same *élite*, so that the important truth—that neither national interest nor identity of any genuine character can be achieved save as they rest on the foundation of social equality and economic justice—is persistently obscured.

Nationalism is thus reduced to a tragic farce in which it is identified with the receipt of empty honorific titles in the British honours award system, solidifying as that does the disease of West Indian social snobbishness; or with the governmental elevation of beauty queens and (as in Jamaica) of vulgarized forms of folk music like the 'Ska' dance into national symbols; or with the official patronage of Decolonization Institutes that preach the lesson of national self-reliance while every other aspect of the official government programme negates the lesson. In every territory, more or less, the population is organized, politically, in 'safe' political parties, the most glaring example being the organization of the *lumpenproletariat* of the West Kingston slums into semi-military political gangs directed by the leaders of both of the Jamaican political groupings. Even the entry of the masses into the national politics, after universal suffrage, can be seen not as the great civic advance West Indian liberals make it out to be but as a process of essentially conservative politicization, since it helped create the new popular belief that politics held the key to all problems and the panacea to every social ill. Hence the West Indian political passion, the amazing fury of the West Indian political partisan, the conviction that 'politics' will cure all. This could only lead to a dead end, since politics is a result, not a first cause. But it was a delusion naturally encouraged by the new class of political office holders who thereby at one and the same time diverted mass energy into a safe outlet and obtained a veneer of legitimacy for their own new status within the West Indian power structure.

The social question, to put this in another way, is thus subordinated to the national question. That subordination, perhaps necessary in the pre-independence era, becomes a tactic of evasion in the post-independence era. The slogans of the national struggle, mostly attacking colonialism, are perpetuated, more and more anachronistically, in the new situation, so that an argument that certainly possesses a manifest degree of historical validity—that the British imperialists are responsible for the legacy they have left behind—is converted into a scapegoat for the frustrations generated by the continuing class-relations of the society. It is tempting to see this, as some indignant English left-wing ideologues in the region see it, as the fruits of a greedy and selfish middle class that lacks a social conscience.[15] But this is to attribute motives to the governing classes (a thoroughly un-Marxian procedure) instead of recognizing that their behaviour is the simple and logical consequence of the system they represent. Or it is possible to see it all, as the Jamaican commentator Frank Hill has seen it, in more optimistic terms, as the outcome of a process in which there has come into power in Jamaica a true governing class in the form of the JLP-PNP political administrators whose full-time energies are devoted to maintaining the state power; who constitute, therefore, a 'natural' governing class in a way that neither the group of mercantile-industrial capitalists nor of the intellectuals constitutes one.[16]

But this second line of argument is hardly convincing unless an unrealistic separation is made between a 'governing' class in the sense of a group of professional politicians exercising the art of statecraft, and a 'ruling' class in the fuller sociological sense of a group controlling the means of production in the economy. To assume such a separation, speaking now of the Jamaican situation, is untenable for two reasons. First, it is so because although the new class of JLP-PNP political leaders were more alike in both educational background and colour distribution to the general population than were the long-established economic *élite*, this did not prevent the acceptance in both political parties of programmes that left untouched the basic principle of the private ownership of production-means; the Federation struggle, as already seen, converted the PNP into the declared defendant of the Jamaican protectionist-minded business interests which the JLP, in any case, always had been. Secondly, there took place in Jamaica, as Bell notes, a process of co-optation of the new political leaderships into the social and asso-ciational life of the older economic *élites*, thereby facilitating, if only partially, a tendency to leave inarticulate or unattended the dis-contents of the lower classes.[17] In the light of these facts it is difficult to accept Hill's defence of the political 'governing' class as an entity of more or less pure Platonic statesmen-administrators whose 'restraint' and 'sense of responsibility' were the main factors for the advance of Jamaican independence. If that in fact were so it would be difficult to find reasons to explain why Jamaica today remains a society deeply divided along both social and racial lines.

Clearly enough, there are limits to the social utility of nationalism. There is much to be said, as already noted, in defence of it. Yet in and of itself it cannot engineer the radical reconstruction of the social order. Like Emancipation before it, it is the necessary con-dition of such reconstruction. But it is not the reconstruction itself. At its best, it promises an end to the colonial psychology of self-contempt. At its worst, it confers a badge of plausible ideological respectability on the identification of the national interest with the sectional interests of the Creole ruling groups. It is true that West Indian nationalism has not done all that it might have done because it has lacked the solidifying unguent of a war of colonial liberation. Writers like Fanon, as in his eulogy of the Algerian Revolution, have argued that the mere experience of violent anti-colonial combat becomes a moral purgative cleansing the colonial spirit with a lasting restorative power. But the decline, after victory, of the Algerian Revolution itself suggests that the memory of colonial comradeship in arms, however evocatively splendid, cannot in itself play that role. The new national society stands in need of more permanent ideas that relate to the continuing experience of its members in the present. That, on any showing, means a socialist ideology so that the nationalist ethic may be married to the planned organization of social equality. Until that ideology emerges, based on the class consciousness of the masses, the West Indian societies will remain the complacent and apathetic communities they have become, lacking the intangible feeling of expectancy, the eagerness to see what the future will bring and the readiness to act to bring the future more rapidly to fruition.[18]

It is at this point that the economic development policies adopted by the new governments of the area become relevant. For the future of the West Indian social order cannot be divorced from the debate on development strategy and regional integration that has taken place in the area since 1940. It has hardly been, in fact, an open debate. For from the beginning it embraced uncritically, both in the structure of its tax incentives and in the character of its domestic income and revenue arrangements, the model of forced manufacturing industrial enterprise dependent mainly upon the capital investment of outside business investors as the best means for transforming the traditional West Indian economic system characterized by long-run stagnation, structural rigidity, and high unemployed rates. The model has flourished for some time in the Caribbean, most famously in the Puerto Rican 'Operation Bootstrap' enterprise. All of the West Indian planners, irrespective of their ideological colouration, have copied the model.

The essential point to make about the model is that in the long run it effectively precludes the pursuit of public policies aimed towards social equality. Internally, it gives new strength to the Creole power structure by giving new opportunities of economic expansion to the existing business units, with the exception of the more inefficient and tradition-oriented family firms. Externally, it facilitates the entry of expatriate capital operations which have the dual effect of (1) increasing the degree of expatriate ownership of resources in the economy, and (2) reducing the local business groups to the status of subordinate partners in a network of international capitalist investment and financial operations, so that they become for all intents and purposes dependent entrepreneurs undertaking a middle class trusteeship of foreign holdings. A new dependent relationship upon outside forces makes itself felt; vital resources, especially in the extractive industries (oil in Trinidad, bauxite in Guyana and Jamaica) are alienated to outside corporate firms that make massive profits accentuated by the location (as in Caribbean bauxite) of the smelting and fabricating processes away from the point of extraction; while production and employment policies are made by overseas head offices unconcerned with local development policies. Nor is all of this offset by rapid or obviously beneficial results for the dependent host economy. Thus, it is notorious in the Puerto Rican case—which enjoys the special advantages, hardly likely to be copied by others, of tariff-free access of goods to the American consumer market and an unrestricted circulatory migration movement—that an intensified industrialization programme along those lines has still left the island economy a system characterized by heavy external ownership of productive facilities, large-scale mass unemployment, a high-cost import structure, a low percentage of trade unionization in the new factories, the sacrifice (characteristic of capitalist enterprise everywhere) of agriculture to industry, and much else; while, in socio-cultural terms, as the work of Rogler, Hollingshead, Seda, Oscar Lewis, and others has shown, the local scene is one characterized by a population large sections of which are at once psychologically depressed and socially disorganized, with alarmingly high percentages of mental retardation, psychosis, incest, prostitution and drug addiction; not to mention a collective inferiority-complex that comes from the habit, reinforced by the externally-controlled industrialization programme, of always looking to the *norteamericanos* to do things, to make decisions as the controlling group in the relationship. Some of this, it is true, is peculiar to Puerto Rico, arising out of the colonial political relationship of the island-dependency to the United States. But most of it springs from the economic factor, the one felt most readily by the mass of the population. There is no reason to believe that a similar process will not take place in other Caribbean economies that place their development eggs in this same basket of American capitalist economic culture.

What occurs, in brief, is a dangerous compartmentalization in the underdeveloped economy between the economic and political spheres of sovereignty. Theoretically, independence confers sovereignty upon the new nation. But economic development of the Puerto Rican type precludes the use of the sovereign police power in implementing any serious programme of social radical change, since nothing must be done, as the local planners see it, to disturb the 'confidence' of the foreign investor in the local financial 'climate'. Certainly nothing must be done, a proposed nationalization programme, for example, that would threaten the place of the foreign-owned sector in the domestic economy; while it is in fact the disparity between the foreign and domestic sectors which embodies most emphatically of all the new inequalities generated by the foreign-capital programme. Local public policy thus becomes affected, in a thousand subtle ways, by the dictates of that programme. In half a dozen fields of policy—foreign aid programmes, government loan projects, mass housing developments, trade union education, even the staffing of the new academic institutions in higher education—the model stimulates afresh the pressure of the foreign 'adviser', the outside 'expert'. The business of the growing public relations machines of the smaller countries becomes more and more that of projecting an 'image' of the country most likely to please the outsider, of making contacts with the strategic elements of the metropolitan economies. The inference is clear; it means, in the blunt language of a gratuitous American adviser in the Jamaican case, effecting friendly relations with 'Congressmen who are on foreign aid subcommittees, Senators who are on Immigration Committees, bankers who underwrite loans in foreign countries, officials of aid agencies, directors of the Export-Import Bank, presidents of foundations who might finance health programmes, people who award international scholarships, editors of magazines and newspapers.'[19]

What this suggests, disturbingly enough, is that the possession of political sovereignty (which Jamaica has, while Puerto Rico does not) is, in fact, of negligible value, since it is rendered largely nugatory by the surrender of large slices of economic sovereignty to outside forces, both financial and political. There develops, in essence, a metropolis-satellite structure in which the satellite develops an export economy, featuring the dominance of the export sector, and precluding the development of any real collectivist planning for domestic purposes. In that process, the satellite loses its right to dispose freely of its own natural wealth and natural resources. The entire principle of equality between states, indeed, is violated; thus, the satellite area of the Caribbean is now in practice characterized by the denial of three rights which important elements of the United Nations Special Committee of 1966 on Principles of International Law identified as essential to the principle of equality : (1) the right to dispose freely of natural resources (2) the right to remove foreign bases and (3) the right to prevent experiments capable of having harmful effects (if the French nuclear-missile programme in French Guiana and the American programme in Puerto Rico are considered).[20]

In the sphere of internal public policy this is expressed in a bifurcation of attitude, for the local reform-minded governments appeal to the ethic of public service in their citizen bodies at the same time as they undertake development policies that appeal, primarily, to the greed and cupidity of the foreign investor. Their attempts at planning inevitably result in state control of the domestic working class (as in the case of the Trinidadian Industrial Stabilization Bill) and little success in any sort of comparable control of, for example, the repatriation of profits and income made in the foreign investment sector. Just as in the cultural field, then, West Indian governments talk about a West Indian 'culture' while in practice they permit the inundation of their societies by the cultural nihilism of American popular amusements, so in the economic and political field they talk about planned development when in reality they pursue policies calculated to perpetuate the underdeveloped satellite status of their countries. This ultimately breeds a double standard of reference slowly poisoning the moral climate of national life. A grave strain is placed upon the democratic principle thus inequitably applied as between the domestic and foreign sectors. 'By trying to reconcile political democracy at home,' it has been argued by West Indian critics of this general policy, 'which demands popular sanction of what is done, with economic dependence upon foreign business, which requires an alien sanction based upon completely different criteria, current public policies are aiming to make the contradictory compatible. It is not that this is impossible—strange as that may sound; it is that it can only be done if a certain duplicity is practised, foreign businessmen being encouraged with promises to be broken in the long run, while popular demands are kept at bay with promises which stand a chance of fulfilment only in the very long run. It is a kind of policy which by its nature has no chance of succeeding if it is publicly articulated. Hence, logically, this policy demands media of publicity which studiously avoid the real issues.'[21]

That kind of contradiction and duplicity is already well enough evident in the post-independence era. It can be seen in the growing conflict between West Indian governments and the West Indian intelligentsia centred, for the most part, in the various centres of the University of the West Indies. The Beckford and Girvan cases demonstrate how the state control of passports and work permits can be used to silence radical critics in the academic community, while there are not wanting signs that research and investigation by the social sciences into the national political and social structure will increasingly meet with official discouragement, even hostility. The contradiction, again, is evident in the frequency with which leftwing advisers, as the Kelshall case in Guyana and the James case in Trinidad exemplify, sooner or later part company with political leaderships which, for all of their anti-colonial rhetoric, embrace the absentee-capital development programme. It is there, too, in the distressing apathy of the general populace as the *élan* of the anti-colonial struggle finds no new purpose of large national vision to identify with and inevitably enters into a decline; with the additional consequence that the mass political parties exhibit more and more an anti-democratic spirit, with leadership coming from the top by way of the personality cult of the leader and not from the bottom by way of creative participation on the part of the rank and file membership.[22] Most significant of all, perhaps, the decline in the moral calibre of life is illustrated by the importation of American political methods, such as the anti-Communist witch-hunting phobia of the McCarthyite period, as witnessed by the Trinidad Government's Commission of Enquiry into 'subversive activities' of 1965, accepting, as did that Commission's report, the dangerous doctrine of 'tendency' as the measure of 'subversive' acts.[23] The supreme irony of Dr Williams' public career, perhaps, is that as Premier of Trinidad he should have countenanced a report by expatriate 'experts' conferring legitimacy upon a concept of governmental control of 'subversive' activity which would have justified every act of hostility and discouragement brought to bear upon his own person, in his capacity as economist to the Caribbean Commission of the 1940's, by the Anglo-American officials of that colonialist body, and against which he himself so finely protested.

It ought to be noted, even so, that it is Dr Williams' own People's National Movement that, almost alone of all Caribbean governments, has attempted a philosophical defence of the non-socialist path of economic development.[24] The argument, to begin with, that PNM policy ought not to be singled out for criticism because in many ways it is far more inherently radical, in its concrete measures, than that of other West Indian governments that label themselves 'socialist' may be promptly dismissed as the mere debating point that it is, for the proper yardstick of measurement is not what bogus socialist movements in Jamaica or Barbados have not done but what a really radical movement could do in Trinidad. More generally, the PNM thesis adumbrates a pragmatic philosophy which, it is claimed, provides for both private and public enterprise and rejects the 'dogmatism' of both state enterprise and private initiative: 'What the PNM has done is to produce a synthesis of ideas both in the liberal and socialist traditions with a strong nationalist and environmental flavour.' Such a view, the argument continues, obtains the best of both worlds: 'it provides for an active and dynamic Government stimulating and guiding at all levels and being ready where necessary itself to enter into the field to preserve or promote enterprises in the interest of the public and of general development.'[25] The Fabian flavour of the argument is self-evident. It is not overtly collectivist; but it supports nationalization on empirical grounds of efficiency and public interest. It is, essentially, the mild reformist outlook of the contemporary Labour Party in Great Britain, the influence of which, apparently, is stronger than the PNM theoreticians, who talk boldly of a New World social philosophy tailored to New World conditions, are willing to admit.

The weaknesses of the argument, however, are equally self-evident. The first weakness is of a general character; in Trinidad, as in the contemporary British welfare state, there has grown up a dual economy, the private and public sectors, operating on two different levels of incentive and reward, the one emphasizing the principle of profitability, the other that of public service. The presumption of a peaceful coexistence between the two is illusory only, for the private sector rapidly tends to create separate labour and administrative *élites*, enjoying higher wage and salary returns, especially by means of numerous fringe benefits, the cumulative tendency being, as Titmuss has pointed out, to divide loyalties, to nourish privilege and to narrow the social conscience, as they have already done in the United States, France and Western Germany.[26] There should be added to that observation the particular fact, peculiar to the contemporary West Indian economies, including that of Trinidad, that the two sectors are hardly in any way comparable, being in fact grossly unequal, as the statistics of their relative contributions to the gross domestic product or to total productive output indicate.[27] The West Indian welfare state, that is to say, is a weak and recent thing that does not have behind it the prolonged political tradition and the massive administrative experience of the British model. The consequent tendency for the more lucrative industries of the long-established private sector to create, hardly without hindrance, a privileged labour force enjoying a level of wage and benefit returns higher than those prevailing outside their sovereignty, plays havoc with the theoretical concept of the public sector as an active and dynamic force stimulating and guiding at all levels.[28]

The second weakness, related to all this, is that the private sector of the neo-colonial export-propelled economy espousing capitalist-directed industrialization, unlike its counterpart in the British economy, is at the same time a foreign-owned sector. Vital decisions on production, employment and sales are made in the metropolitan headquarters. The power of the local government to control these decisions in any meaningful way is correspondingly minimized. It confronts, in fact, in the shape, for example, of the Bookers combine in Guyana and the oil complex in South Trinidad, industrial-financial empires not easily reached by the ordinary Keynesian controls available to metropolitan governments. To talk, then, of nationalization as the final sanction is empty rhetoric, unless the local government is prepared, like the Mexican government in the 1930's, to engage in an open struggle with the private empires. It is suggestive, here, that West Indian governments have generally pursued, in this field, timid and cautious policies. Thus, to revert to the Trinidadian case, government interventionism in the economy as a whole has been restricted to such things as the notorious 'pirate taxi' system in the public transportation system,[29] the disorganized administration of the social services,[30] the anomalous 'dual system' in education,[31] all of them particularly inefficient areas within the domestic sector crying aloud for modernization. The foreign-owned sector, particularly sugar (except Crown Lands policy) and oil, remains substantially untouched. Yet it is clear that the acid test of any government or political party, the criterion by which to judge whether it is genuinely devoted to the cause of national independence and economic development, must be its attitude towards foreign investment. Once such investment is accepted as the prime mover of development, with whatever reservations, the local political force is of necessity hamstrung in its freedom of manœuvre. Thus limited, public policy more and more is turned to modifying human behaviour in the new national citizen body rather than to changing the structural environment.

Yet the most glaring singularity of the Puerto Rican model and its West Indian imitators is that it proposes to cure the ills of economic colonialism by re-establishing the conditions originally producing them. For it repeats all of the leading features of the traditional colonial economy, but set within, of course, the different context of a comparatively free labour market and an embryonic welfare state system: the dependence upon external capital funds, the dominance of the export sector thus financed, the response, in turn, of that sector almost exclusively to external demand patterns, the continuing comparative stagnation of the domestic sector. It is clear enough from Caribbean economic history that those features possess a tremendous tenacity due, in part, to their historical longevity, for they were originally created as part of the early economic process whereby the Caribbean territories, in their sugar-exporting Golden Age, became characterized by the typical structure of a tropical capitalist export economy. That structure, once entrenched, survived both slavery abolition and post-emancipation economic decline, and thus blocked the autonomous generation of an economic development based upon an entirely different structure. The structure, with its various properties, has now become assimilated, under a new guise, to the absentee-capitalist industrial development programme of the modern period. The history of the Caribbean economies as overseas fiefs controlled by expatriate forces is thereby perpetuated, with the single difference that the forces are now those of the modern multi-national business combines. The capacity of the region to break out of the traditional system is, as a result, gravely compromised.

A more or less plausible defence of the new policy can perhaps be made. The new modernizing oligarchy of the developing economies apparently feels that it is a necessary policy whereby they may utilize to their own advantage the expansionist urges of metropolitan capitalism. Capitalism, to quote Muñoz-Marin's apologetic line of reasoning in the Puerto Rican case, is to be seen, utilitarian-wise, as a cow to be milked, not as a 'sacred cow' to be stupidly worshipped. But capitalism, in any of its forms, is rarely that benign, nor that easily amenable to persuasion by forces which, in any case, are parasitically dependent on it. It will export its productive technology to an economic dependency, like Puerto Rico, only when it suits it. Even then, it is only export by a minority sector of the metropolitan system, which must meet at home the hostile pressure of rival industries and trade unions critical of refugee capital, the industrial side being jealous of special privileges granted to the industries, the union side being opposed to a programme in which the host economy exploits as a major incentive the difference in the wage-productivity ratios between the dependent and the superordinate economies. The controversy that raged in 1966 over the new Phillips oil refinery in Puerto Rico, with the national oil industry attacking the special import quota granted by the Department of the Interior to the company as gross favouritism and a dangerous threat to the protected structure of the industry as a whole is symptomatic.[32] At the same time, the West Indian planners emulating the Puerto Rican model must bear in mind that, unlike Puerto Rico, where a docile and largely unorganized labour force is incapable of militant attack upon the anti-labour components of the model,[33] in their own economies they confront an extremely well-organized labour movement much of it, especially in Trinidad, critical of the model. The amiable cow of the Muñoz-Marin metaphor, in brief, may well turn out to be an untameable tiger.

There is, finally, a larger socio-cultural dimension to all this. There is a sort of pre-established harmony between West Indian developmental policy and the general character of the social and economic *élites* that run West Indian governments. Being essentially middle class, the members of those *élites* are at once psychologically disposed to and materially benefited by a policy which (1) tends to increase cultural dependency on the 'higher' external societies, and (2) exaggerates their traditional tendency, as the high income component of the economy, to spend lavishly on imported luxury goods to the detriment of a successful programme of import substitution. Most British and American writers on the area, suggestively, coming themselves from the same social strata in the 'home' societies, have eulogized that middle class as the predestined leaders of the society, as the remarks, variously, of Ayearst, Mrs MacMillan, and Simey demonstrate.[34] Yet it is doubtful if, as a class, they deserve the encomium. Having been shaped, psychologically, by the traditional economic order, they see little amiss in giving it a new lease of life under a different label. Trained and educated in the existentialia of Western capitalist democracy, their world view is limited to the assumptions of that system. They harbour deep class feelings; and those feelings are reinforced in daily life by the relationships they have with their servants, a class of people that has almost disappeared as a Victorian relic in modern British middle class life. They have been culture imitators, rather than culture creators. Frequently charming as individuals, as a class they have learned less to understand their society than to manipulate it. Their general view of the masses, indeed, is composed of a whole series of astonishing and usually hostile stereotypes, only occasionally disturbed by their exposure to the visiting sociologist or anthropologist.

It is natural, then, that the leading West Indian theoreticians, despite their frequent criticisms of the middle class, advocate the Western-type economic development model calculated to strengthen, not weaken, the dominant position of the class. That can be seen, as an example only, in Professor Arthur Lewis' eulogy of that model, couched in almost glowing terms, in his Canadian lectures of 1962. Borrowing, indeed, from Sir Henry Maine's famous distinction between status and contract, those lectures advocated industrialization as a new way of life that promotes equality, since its competitive market economy uses merit wherever it finds it, and thus advances equality of opportunity and social peace; and once launched, the idea of equality penetrates every aspect of social life, removing causes of frustration and bitterness which otherwise poison social relations.[35] It is true enough, of course—as a comment on the argument—that compared with some tribal and rural societies the industrial economy, as Lewis claims, reduces conflicts of race, religion and tribe to the significance of children's games. But it is gross utopianism to imply that that economy, based on the profit motive, does not replace those conflicts with others special to itself, however 'civilized' the rules that govern the conflicts may be. The Lewis thesis, indeed, accepts the optimistic liberal assumptions about the Anglo-American societies at a time when the essential barbarism of their neo-capitalist culture, especially in the United States, is exploding in area after area of their social lives—

racial conflict, ghetto poverty, widespread criminal violence, institutional authoritarianism, the senseless drive for empty status, the general contradiction, in brief, of spiritually purposeless societies between the increasing rationality of their productive and institutional modes and the ever-increasing irrationality in the operation of the system as a whole. The flaw of the thesis is that it confuses industrialization with corporate capitalism, and thereby erroneously concludes that any underdeveloped economy seeking to industrialize itself—a general phenomenon that can hardly be stayed—must embrace the 'free enterprise' model. The irony of the West Indian situation in all of this is that the desirability of the model is usually advanced on the pragmatic ground that in the real, imperfect world no other alternative means of financing the industrialization drive is available when, as a matter of fact, the Cuban Revolution demonstrates, only a hundred miles away from Jamaica, the practicability of a socialist avenue based on central planning, austerity for everybody, and social incentives as against private self-interest. The Puerto Rican and the Cuban models, indeed, today posit a choice between alternative paths for the Caribbean peoples just as the Haitian revolutionary programme after 1792 offered the Caribbean societies of the nineteenth century an effective choice between revolt and acquiescence. The decision that is made will obviously depend upon the capacity and readiness of the masses, in each individual territory, to overthrow the regime of middle class private property which, like slavery before it, obstructs the road ahead to a new freedom.

The internal struggle, finally, takes place within the environment of the international anarchy of the mid-twentieth century. Like all small states the West Indian nations must learn to survive in a world in which there is added to the long-standing legacy of New World colonialism—vulnerable colonial economies, political balkanization, persistent interventionism by the big powers—the new ingredient of global ideological conflict embodied in the open struggle between the Cuban Revolution and the counter-revolution led by the United States. Their geographical position and tiny size have traditionally dictated the necessity of some sort of client relationship with more powerful neighbours. Independence now confronts them with the task of building up their own collective strength, preferably through schemes of regional political and economic integration, so that they may begin to put an end to that situation. They are caught, essentially, between the pressures of two global power struggles: first, the East-West struggle between world revolution and world counter-revolution and, secondly, the North-South struggle between developed and developing nations. External affairs thus become the most urgent priority problem of the new Caribbean states. 'Defenceless,' Dr Williams has told his party conference, 'dependent as we are on external trade for our jobs and our earnings to a greater extent than most countries, what happens in the big world of which we are physically an insignificant part is a matter of life and death to us, and, in the most literal sense of the phrase, we must live by our wits.'[36]

Such an environment inevitably sparks a search for new friends. The old friends, particularly Britain, are slowly withdrawing from the scene as they dismantle their colonial obligations. British foreign policy, certainly in the Western hemisphere, is now largely a timid echo of Washington, and it is even more true today than it was a century ago, as a Trinidadian writer put it in 1856, that 'England will do nothing to save her sinking colonies, but she will do almost anything to court the goodwill of the Americans'.[37] West Indians tend to cite other Commonwealth countries, notably Canada, as potential friends. But they are friends only in the sense that there are, as with Canada, ties of mutual trading interest that go back to 1926. Even at that, in so far as such Commonwealth nations provide aid to the West Indian countries, it is usually designed, whether it takes the form of monetary loans or visiting experts, to improve the external trade picture of the donor nation. The developed economies on the whole, usually discourage the industrialization of the developing economies on the ground that they themselves almost possess a divine right to the processing of raw materials into manufactured goods. Even when there exist no visibly hostile tariff walls there are usually a mass of regulations, as well as shipping requirements made by shipping conferences in which the underdeveloped economies are not represented, that stifle any real free trade exchange. The vanishing trade of West Indian rums on the Canadian market is a case in point.[38] The same applies to Caribbean extractive industries like bauxite, where the primary producers like Jamaica and Guyana are denied the right to process by means of local alumina-producing plants largely for the political reason that the giant North American companies, working with their respective governments, consider the localization of the refining process a risk in an area like the  Caribbean where they have doubts about the 'integrity', that is, the ideological reliability of nationalist governments.[39] The friendship, finally, of the United States is problematical in the light of the fact that the paramount American concern in its Caribbean-Latin American policies is to build up adequate regional military and  political defences against international Communism.

The grant of independence, frankly, merely signalizes the fact that the Caribbean societies have passed from the older British protective umbrella to the new American hemispheric power-system. The implications of that transfer, to say the least, are ominous. It means that the American presence—which by geographical location and historical interest alone will always be there—will shape, for good or ill, the region's future development unless countering forces make themselves felt. The Santo Domingo affair of 1965 served notice that the American police power, with all the massive weaponry that it has at hand, is prepared to intervene unilaterally with crushing effect against any Caribbean threat, however remote, to its hemispheric hegemony. The scope of less dramatic but equally sinister intervention in the domestic affairs of other Caribbean societies, notably Guyana, is by now well documented, having the effect of spreading the Cold War psychology into those affairs; so much so, indeed, that the old-fashioned distinction between 'foreign' and 'local' affairs is practically meaningless in the region's capitals. A not too subtle game of rewarding friends and punishing enemies gets under way, with sanctions of one kind or another always in the background waiting to be used. The 1964 episode in which Washington pressure closed the Nassau, Bahamas, airport to Cuban civilian flights is only one instance of many; but its larger significance was noted at the time by a conservative London paper with the comment that 'It should now be clear to all the islands of the British Caribbean that if they want to share in the Yankee dollar they must be prepared to jump whenever Washington bids them to.'[40] The structural weaknesses of the region are in turn invoked to justify American attitudes; thus, Senator Aiken's special report of 1958 on the West Indies Federal Government's request for the turning over of the American Chaguaramas naval base as the proposed site of the federal capital referred to the 'host of problems' confronting the Federation, including racial tension between the Indian and Negro populations, as part justification for the American refusal to comply with the request; so, weaknesses created in the first place by the colonial powers are then invoked by the imperialist forces as reasons for not helping the region's peoples.[41]

American pressure thus conspires to exacerbate the internal power struggles of the various social and economic groups in the local societies. The domestic politics are increasingly transformed into the vocabulary of anti-American and pro-American factions. A temper of appeasement is felt as the conservative groups see themselves threatened by the rising assertiveness of the mass populations. It is a temper more and more virulent all over. It takes the form, variously, of censorship activities which, as in Jamaica, keep the local populations in a state of permanent quarantine against 'infection' from Cuba; of arguments in favour of Trinidad making itself into the twelfth province of Canada and accepting the role of a 'bastion of the United States defence' in the Cold War;[42] of seeking blatantly to curry American favour, distressingly evident in Sir Alexander Bustamante's unfortunate remark on taking office as first Prime Minister of independent Jamaica, that America was the only republic in the world that he liked, combined with an offer to grant bases to the Americans on Jamaican soil should they ever evacuate Guantanamo; and much else. A climate of fear is sedulously disseminated by the mass media, suggesting dire consequences should American interests be placed in jeopardy by local actions. Ricardo Alegría, speaking of the Puerto Rican case, has noted how that tactic of deliberately fostered fear has been employed by the Creole ruling classes throughout all of Caribbean history, so that the Puerto Rican people have for centuries been intimidated by imaginary or exaggerated dangers: of the English pirates in the sixteenth century, of the Dutch marauders in the seventeenth century, of the popular ideas of the American Revolution in the eighteenth century, and of 'Communist totalitarianism' in the present period.[43] The climate of opinion in the contemporary Caribbean is more and more shaped by this defeatist propaganda. It presents the very real danger that the countries of the region may no sooner achieve their independence than lose it; not necessarily by

way of annexation by a foreign power or re-annexation by the former
colonial power, as was the case with the return of the Dominican
Republic to the Spanish in 1861, but by way of a quiet but relentless penetration, economic and cultural, which ultimately erodes the
substance of independence while keeping it intact as a juridical
fiction—as was, indeed, the case of Cuba between 1898 and 1958.

The future of the region thus presents a grim picture. Release
from this ugly dilemma lies, perhaps, in the long run, in the effective
unification of the entire region within a system of democratic
hemispheric security. For so long as each island, or each island group,
remains jealously detached from its neighbours, constituting a
vigorously preserved set of archaic distinctions made obsolete by
the fact that the only viable system, in the long run, is a single
world system, so long will the region invite intervention, more and
more insolent, by the outside powers. They must, one way or the
other, break out of that shell. They must look even beyond the
Caribbean to effective relationships with Latin American, for it is a
part of their collective tragedy that they have never been considered
as part of the Americas but merely as anomalous colonies in the
area. And they must look, even more imaginatively yet, to the
world stage as a whole, to search out for themselves a viable cultural
identity which will save them from the fate, in Sarmiento's potent
phrase with reference to the status of the new Latin American republics of the nineteenth century, of being trapped between European
civilization and American barbarism. Their future, this is to say,
must ultimately put into reality the dream of Schoelcher's prophecy
of 1852 that 'Upon regarding the West Indies' position in the middle
of the ocean, glancing at the map which shows them to be almost in
touch with each other, one cannot help but think that they may well
come together some day to form a distinct social body in the modern
world . . . They might well unite in confederation, joined by common
interest, and possess a merchant fleet, an industry, arts and a
literature all their own. That will not come about in a year, nor in
two, nor perhaps in three centuries, but come about it some day
shall, for it is natural that it be so.'[44] That prophecy fulfilled, it
could become the starting point for a massive revolution which
would give to a region so long renowned for its natural beauty a
social beauty it has hitherto not known. There, if anywhere, surely
lies the destiny of the West Indies.

# NOTES

Reference carry full data of author, title, publisher, and place and date of publication only when first cited within each chapter. Subsequent references give author's surname and 'short title' of the work cited. Full data are again furnished with each new chapter.

## CHAPTER I

1. Mrs Carmichael, *Domestic Manners and Social Conditions of the White, Coloured, and Negro Population of the West Indies* (London, Whittaker and Co., 1834, 2 vols.), second edition, Vol. II, p. 137.

2. *The Belize Times* (Belize, British Honduras), Section C, 24, 25 December 1965.

3. For Caribbean natural disasters see F. Sterns-Fadelle, *In the Ruins of St Pierre* (Office of *The Dominican*, Roseau, Dominica, 1902); George Kennan, *The tragedy of Pêlée. A narrative of personal experience and observation in Martinique* (New York, The Outlook Co., 1902); C. L. Chenery, *The Jamaica Earthquake*, reprinted from *Barbados Advocate*, 23, 24, 25, January 1907; Robert M. Anderson (ed.), *The St Vincent Handbook, Directory and Almanac for 1909* (Kingstown, St Vincent, 1909), pp. 114–25; Ernest Cain, *Cyclone 'Hattie'* (Ilfracombe, Arthur H. Stockwell, 1964); and Ivan Ray Tannehill, *Hurricanes : their nature and history, particularly those of the West Indies and the southern coasts of the United States* (Princeton, Princeton University Press, 1952). For details of typical hurricane preparations, and how they can become a local political issue, see Barbados, *House of Assembly, Debates*, Official Report, 1962 session (Bridgetown, Barbados, 1 October 1963).

4. Frank Cundall, 'Jamaica', in *British America* (London, Kegan Paul, Trench, Trubner and Co., Ltd., 1900), p. 400.

5. Sir Alan Burns, *Colonial Civil Servant* (London, Allen and Unwin, 1949), p. 142.

6. J. E. Levo, *The West Indian Adventure* (London, Society for the Propagation of the Gospel in Foreign Parts, 1929), p. 55.

7. George I. Mendes, 'Historical Notes of the Early Years of the Island of Montserrat', *The Leeward Islands Review and Caribbean Digest* (Vol. 1, No. 7, May 1937).

8. 'Town Talk', *Evening Post* (Georgetown, British Guiana), 30 July 1965.

9. *The Vincentian* (Kingstown, St Vincent), 5, 21, 28 November 1964.

10. Charles William Day, *Five Years Residence in the West Indies* (London, Colburn and Co., 1852, 2 vols.), Vol. 1, p. 157.

11. Theodore L. Godet, *Bermuda: Its History, Geology, Climate, Products, Agriculture, Commerce, and Government* (London, Smith, Elder and Co., 1860), p. 153.

12. Dr Arthur Lewis, graduation speech, University of the West Indies, reprinted in *The Torch* (Kingston, Jamaica, Ministry of Education, March 1961).

13. For criticism of the social role of the West Indian middle class see Eric Williams, *Some thoughts on economic aid to developing countries; address to the Economics Society of the University of the West Indies.* (Port of Spain, Trinidad and Tobago Government Printing Office, 1963). For the difficulties involved in arriving at a satisfactory definition of 'middle class' in West Indian society see Government Printer, *Report of Middle Class Unemployment Committee* (Kingston, Jamaica, 1941).

14. See for all this, among much else, Richard Frucht, 'Some Notes on a Christmas in the West Indies', *The Democrat* (Basseterre, St Kitts-Nevis), 22 December 1962; Harold F. C. Simmons, 'The Flower Festivals of St Lucia', *The Voice of St Lucia* (Castries, St Lucia), 27 August 1953; Daniel J. Crowley, 'Festivals of the Calendar in St Lucia', *Caribbean Quarterly* (Vol. 4, No. 2, December 1955); Andrew T. Carr, 'A Rada Community in Trinidad', *Caribbean Quarterly* (Vol. 3, No. 1, January 1953); P. A. Brathwaite and Serena U. Brathwaite, *Folk Songs of Guyana* (Georgetown, British Guiana, 1964); Bill Rogers, *Shantos of Guyana* (Georgetown, Guyana, 1966); Institute of Social and Economic Research, University of the West Indies, *The Ras Tafarian Movement in Kingston, Jamaica* (University of the West Indies, 1960); William A. Blake, *Beliefs of the Ras Tafari Cult*, (Kingston, Jamaica, mimeographed, 1961); George Eaton Simpson, *The Shango Cult in Trinidad* (Rio Piedras, Institute of Caribbean Studies, Caribbean Monograph Series No. 2,

1965); selection of Honduran 'breakdowns' in *A History of British Honduras* (anonymous) (New York, Colorite Offset Printing Company, N.D.), pp. 67–70; Joseph G. Moore, *Religion of Jamaican Negroes; A Study of Afro-Jamaican Acculturation.* Ph.D. thesis (Evanston, Northwestern University, 1954); R. B. Le Page and David de Camp, *Jamaican Creole* (London, MacMillan and Co., Creole Language Studies 1, 1960). For brief discussions of the problem of a generic West Indian culture see, from a literary viewpoint, H. L. V. Swanzy, 'Caribbean Voices: Prolegomena to a West Indian Culture', *Caribbean Quarterly* (Vol. 1, No. 2, July-August-September 1949) and, from an anthropological viewpoint, M. G. Smith, 'West Indian Culture', *Caribbean Quarterly* (Vol. 7, No. 3, December 1961). See also Dale Anderson, 'The Reality of a West Indian Culture', *The Social Scientist* (Mona, Jamaica, Guild of Undergraduates, No. 2, 1963–64).

15. For Trinidad Carnival see, among much else, *This Country of Ours* (Port of Spain, PNM Publishing Co., 1962); Trinidad Carnival Issue, *Caribbean Quarterly* (Vol. 4, Nos. 3 and 4, March-June 1956); Kelvin Thomson, *Background to Trinidad's Carnival and Calypso* (Port of Spain, N.D.); Raymond Quevedo, 'Executor' and 'The Golden Era of Calypso Resurgence', *Sunday Guardian* (Port of Spain), 9 February 1964; and Dr F. A. Crichlow, 'The Glory of Our Carnival', *Trinidad Guardian*, 10 February 1964. For typical selections of calypsoes see *Mighty Spoiler 1961 Calypso Booklet* (Port of Spain, Cosmopolitan Printery, 1961) and *Trinidad Calypso Booklet 1964* (Port of Spain, Jet Printing Service, 1964).

16. Barbara E. Powrie, 'The Changing Attitude of the Coloured Middle Class towards Carnival', *Caribbean Quarterly* (Vol. 4, Nos. 3 and 4, March-June 1956).

17. Karl Douglas, 'Carnival Ignores the Local Touch', *Trinidad Guardian*, 26 February 1960. See also Derek Walcott, 'Carnival: Theatre of the Streets', *Trinidad Guardian*, 9 February 1964.

18. Government of Trinidad and Tobago, *Interim Report of the Committee appointed to consider the Role of the Steelband in the National Life* (Port of Spain, mimeographed, N.D. para. 45 (d)).

19. For a typical example of these admonitions see Pete Simon, 'Calypsonians, Take Note', *Trinidad Chronicle*, 31 March 1957.

20. M. G. Smith, 'Social and Cultural Pluralism', *Social and Cultural*

*Pluralism in the Caribbean* (New York, *Annals* of the New York Academy
of Sciences, January 1960), p. 768.

21. For critical discussion of the 'plural society' thesis see *Annals* of the New
York Academy of Sciences, *Social and Cultural Pluralism in the Caribbean*
(New York, January 1960). Smith's thesis is summed up in his *The
Plural Society in the British West Indies* (Berkeley and Los Angeles, Univer-
sity of California Press, 1965).

22. Vera Rubin, *Ibid.*, pp. 782–83.

23. Lloyd Braithwaite, Caribbean Scholars Conference, *Report* (Rio Piedras,
Institute of Caribbean Studies, University of Puerto Rico, mimeographed, July 1961), p. 10.

24. Cecil Clementi, *The Chinese in British Guiana* (Georgetown, The Argosy
Company Ltd., 1915); V. P. Oswald Horton, ed., *Chinese in the Caribbean*
(Kingston, Souvenir, 30th Anniversary of the Chinese Republic, 1911–
1941, 1941); Peter Ruhomon, *Centenary History of the East Indians in
British Guiana*, 1838–1938 (Georgetown, Guiana Edition No. 10); Jacob
A. P. M. Andrade, *A Record of the Jews in Jamaica from the English Con-
quest to the Present Time* (Kingston, The Jamaica Times Ltd., 1941);
Dwarka Nath, *A History of Indians in British Guiana* (London, Nelson,
1950). The *differentiae specificae* of Caribbean society clearly flow from
the seminal fact that it has been an area of rich and intensive culture
contact. For an example in the French Caribbean sub-area see Michel
Leiris, *Contacts de Civilisation en Martinique et en Guadeloupe* (Unesco,
Gallinard, 1955).

25. *Daily Gleaner* (Kingston, Jamaica), 22 June 1959. See also letter to
editor by Rupert R. Chin See, *Daily Gleaner*, 30 June 1959.

26. Jacob A. P. M. Andrade, *A Record of the Jews in Jamaica from the English
Conquest to the Present Time* (Kingston, The Jamaica Times Ltd., 1941),
pp. 110, 117, 162–64.

27. Government of Trinidad and Tobago, *Interim Report of the Committee
appointed to consider the Role of the Steelband in the National Life*, para. 34.

28. Peter Ruhomon, *Centenary History of the East Indians in British Guiana*,
1838–1938 (Georgetown, Guiana Edition, No. 10), p. 280.

29. Christopher Rand, *The Puerto Ricans* (New York, Oxford University Press, 1958), p. 48.

30. Lloyd Braithwaite, in *Social and Cultural Pluralism* ... , p. 825.

31. George Cumper, in Standing Committee on Social Services, *Report of the Conference on Social Development in Jamaica* (Mona, University College of the West Indies, 1961), p. 9.

32. David Lowenthal, in *Social and Cultural Pluralism in the Caribbean*, p. 789.

33. Wendell Bell, *Jamaican Leaders: Political Attitudes in a New Nation* (Berkeley and Los Angeles, University of California Press, 1964).

34. Martin Carter, in *New World Fortnightly* (Georgetown, British Guiana, No. 26, 29 October 1965), p. 27.

35. H. P. Jacobs, in V. P. Oswald Horton, ed., *Chinese in the Caribbean* (Kingston, Souvenir, 30th Anniversary of the Chinese Republic 1911–1941, 1941), p. 27.

36. Pére Labat, *Nouveau Voyage aux Iles de l'Amérique* (1722), quoted in radio script, *The New World of the Caribbean* (Georgetown, British Guiana, Programme No. 4, mimeographed, 1957). An integral, annotated English edition of Père Labat's work is in process of being prepared by Leonard R. Muller of the University of Miami; see note in Current Research Inventory, *Latin American Research Review* (Vol. 1, No. 2, Spring 1966), item 475.

CHAPTER II

1. Bryan Edwards, *The History, Civil and Commercial, of the British West Indies* (London, 1802), 5 vols., Vol. 4, p. 36.

2. Anonymous, *Antigua and the Antiguans* (London, 1844), 2 vols., Vol. 2, p. 141.

3. John Luffman, *A Brief Account of the Island of Antigua, 1786–1788* (London, 1789, 2nd edition). Reprinted in Vere Langford Oliver, *History of the Island of Antigua* (London, Mitchell and Hughes, 1894. 3 vols.) pp. cxxviii–cxxxviii.

4. Richard Schomburgk, *Travels in British Guiana, 1840–1844*, Vincent Roth ed. (Georgetown, the Guiana Edition, *Daily Chronicle*, 1953), Vol. 1, p. 47.

5. Henry Bolingbroke, *A Voyage to the Demerary, 1799–1806* (Georgetown, The Guiana Edition, Daily Chronicle, No. 1, 1947), pp. 149–50.

6. Abbé Raynal, *Histoire Philosophique et Politique des Etablissements et du Commerce des Européens dans les Deux Indes* (London, English translation, 1788), 8 vols., Vol. 5, p. 309.

7. J. J. Thomas, *Froudacity: West Indian Fables Explained* (London, Unwin, 1889), pp. 6–7.

8. For discussion of the 'race question' in the United States see Thomas F. Gossett, *Race. The History of an Idea in America* (Dallas, Southern Methodist University Press, 1963).

9. Benjamin Kidd, *The Control of the Tropics* (London, Macmillan, 1898), pp. 52–53.

10. Albert K. Weinberg, *Manifest Destiny: A Study of Nationalist Expansionism in American History* (Baltimore, John Hopkins Press, 1935), p. 327.

11. *Ibid.*, p. 432.

12. Quoted in Burton J. Hendrick, *Life and Letters of Walter Hines. Page.* (New York, Doubleday, Page, 1922–25), 3 vols., Vol. 1, p. 205.

13. Quoted in Philip Jessup, *Elihu Root* (New York, Dodd Mead, 1938), 2 vols., Vol. 2, p. 513.

14. Weinberg, *Manifest Destiny*, p. 446.

15. Frederick Merk, *Manifest Destiny and Mission in American History* (New York, Alfred Knopf, 1963), Ch. XII. For the resurgence of the 'big stick' policy in the 1960's see, among much else, Institute of International Labor Research, *Dominican Republic. A Study in the New Imperialism* (New York, N.D.). For the fiasco of 'free elections' policy see Theodore P. Wright, Jr., *American Support of Free Elections Abroad* (Washington D.C., Public Affairs Press, 1964).

16. George Fox, *Gospel Family Order, being a Short Discourse concerning the Ordering of Families, both of Whites, Blacks and Indians* (London, 1676). For the Fox visit to the West Indies see George Fox, *Journal* (London, Cash and Joseph Smith, 1852), 2 vols., Vol. II, Ch. IV.

17. Quoted in S. B. Jones, 'Some Pioneers of West Indian Education', in *Antigua Teachers Review* (St Johns, Antigua, January 1940), p. 18. For the Society for the Propagation of the Gospel in the West Indies parish see C. F. Pascoe, *Two Hundred Years of the S.P.G, 1701–1900* (London, S.P.C, 1901). For an Anglican criticism of the Church see J. E. Levo, *The West Indian Adventure* (London, Society for Propagation of the Gospel in Foreign Parts, 1929), pp. 27–29.

18. H. A. Wyndham, *The Atlantic and Emancipation* (London, OUP, 1937), p. 117. See in general Klaus E. Knorr, *British Colonial Theories, 1570–1850* (University of Toronto Press, reprinted 1963).

19. For the 'wrecking' trade in Barbuda in its heyday see series of letters of Barbuda overseers to the Codrington family in Robson Lowe, *The Codrington Correspondence, 1748–1851* (London, Robson Lowe, 1951).

20. Sir Alan Burns, *History of the British West Indies* (London, George Allen and Unwin, 1954), *Preface*, p. 5.

21. W. P. Livingstone, *Black Jamaica: A Study in Evolution* (London, Sampson Low, 1899), p. 233. For and incisive description of the Caribbean area written by a Caribbean historian-politician for an Indian audience in New Delhi, see Dr Eric Williams, 'The Caribbean Today', reprinted, *The Nation* (Port of Spain, Trinidad), 14 July 1961. See also Sidney W. Mintz, 'Caribbean Nationhood in Anthropological Perspective', in *Caribbean Integration*, Third Caribbean Scholars' Conference, 1966 (Rio Piedras, Institute of Caribbean Studies, University of Puerto Rico, 1967).

CHAPTER III

1. Margaret Olivier, *Sydney Olivier: Letters and Selected Writings* (London, Allen and Unwin, 1948), pp. 181–82.

2. F. W. N. Bayley, *Four Years' Residence in the West Indies, 1826–1829* (London, William Kidd, 1832), pp. 499–500.

3. C. S. Salmon, *The Caribbean Confederation* (London, Cassell and Co., Ltd., N.D.), p. 29.

4. *Ibid.*, pp. 126–27.

5. James M. Phillippo, *Jamaica: Its Past and Present State* (London, John Snow, 1843), pp. 395–96, 421–23, 432–41.

6. William G. Sewell, *The Ordeal of Free Labor in the British West Indies* (New York, Harper and Bros., 1861), p. 38.

7. Henry Nelson Coleridge, *Six Months in the West Indies in 1825* (London, John Murray, 1832), p. 281.

8. Wilbur H. Siebert, *The Legacy of the American Revolution to the British West Indies and Bahamas* (Columbus, Ohio, Ohio State University Bulletin, April, 1913); W. Kerr, *Bermuda and the American Revolution, 1760–1783* (London, Oxford University Press, 1936).

9. Described in Ansell Hart, *Monthly Comments* (Newport, Jamaica), Vol. 1, Nos. 6 and 7, August and September 1954.

10. *Ibid.*, Vol. 1, Nos. 10, 11, 12.

11. C. S. Salmon, *Depression in the West Indies. Free Trade the Only Remedy* (New York and London, Cassell and Co., Ltd., 1884), p. 24.

12. Clyde Hoyte, *Sixty Years* (Kingston, Jamaica, 1948).

13. S. J. Fraser, *The Barbados Diamond Jubilee Directory* (T. E. King and Co., Bridgetown, 1905).

14. Henry Kirke, *Twenty Five Years in British Guiana* (Georgetown, Guiana Edition, *Daily Chronicle*, 1948), pp. 6–7.

15. Sir Grantley Adams, quoted from speech to Barbados Workers' Union, Annual Delegates Conference, *Barbados Advocate*, 8 August 1956.

16. Quoted by Canon M. E. Farquhar, 'Candid Comments', *Trinidad Guardian*, 29 July 1956.

17. J. van Sertima, *Scenes and Sketches of Demerara Life* (Demerara, Argosy

Press, 1899). See also E. N. Woolford, *Georgetown vignettes. Sidelights on local life* (Georgetown, Daily Chronicle Ltd., 1917).

18. Her Majesty's Stationery Office, *West India Royal Commission Report* (London, Cmd. 6607, 1945), pp. 94 and 108.

19. *Ibid.*, p. 215.

20. For the social effects of Barbadian nineteenth-century journalism see *Barbados Advocate, Special Independence Issue*, E. R. L. Ward, 'History of the Press' 30 November 1966; and H. A. Vaughan, 'Samuel Jackman Prescod', and Lionel Hutchinson, 'Conrad Reeves: A Kind of Perfection', in *New World, Barbados Independence Issue* (November 1966, Vol. III, Nos. 1 and 2). For the social effects of Barbadian twentieth-century cricket see Dr Bruce Hamilton, 'Emergence of Cricketing Power in Barbados', *Barbados Advocate, Special Independence Issue*.

21. *West India Royal Commission Report, op. cit.*, p. 34.

22. Colonial Office, *Colonial Office Conference, 1927. Summary of Proceedings*, Her Majesty's Stationery Office, Cmd. 2883 (London 1927).

23. Central Statistical Office, Government of Trinidad and Tobago, *Population Census, 1960 Report*, Volume III, Part G (Port of Spain, Trinidad, 1960).

24. Moyne Commission, *op. cit.*, p. 8; and *Trinidad and Tobago Disturbances, 1937, Report of Commission*, Her Majesty's Stationery Office, Cmd. 5641 (London 1938), p. 79.

25. Moyne Commission, *op. cit.*, p. 201.

26. Colonial Office, *Report of the West Indian Sugar Commission*, Her Majesty's Stationery Office, Part IV, Colonial No. 49 (London 1930), para. 434.

27. Colonial Office, *Report on a Financial Mission to the Leeward Islands and St Lucia*, Her Majesty's Stationery Office, Cmd. 3996 (London 1931), p. 77.

28. For the state of West Indian agriculture in general at this time see F. L. Engledow, *Report on Agriculture, Fisheries, Forestry and Veterinary Matters*, Her Majesty's Stationery Office, Cmd. 6608 (London 1945).

14*

29. League of Coloured Peoples, *Memorandum on the Recommendations of the West Indian Royal Commission* (London 1940).

30. T. S. Simey, *Welfare and Planning in the West Indies* (Oxford, 1946) p. 238.

31. *Ibid.*, p. 237. For the general social structure of the West Indies in the post-1945 period see George Cumper, Caribbean Affairs, *The Social Structure of the British Caribbean (excluding Jamaica)*, Part I (Extra-Mural Department, University College of the West Indies, N.D.). The study is based on the statistics of the Report of the 1946 Census.

CHAPTER IV

1. Sir Charles Lucas, *Historical Geography of the British Colonies*, 8 vols., (Oxford, 1887–1920), Vol. II, pp. 70–71. Quoted in Elsa Goveia, *A Study on the Historiography of the British West Indies to the end of the Nineteenth Century* (Instituto Panamericano de Geografia e Historia, Mexico, 1956), p. 138.

2. Adam Smith, *The Wealth of Nations* (London, Everyman Library Edition, 1917), Book IV, Chapter 7, Part ii, pp. 84–85. See for the later period of colonial government D. J. Murray, *The West Indies and the Development of Colonial Government, 1801–1834* (Oxford University Press, 1965), and H. T. Manning, *British Colonial Government after the American Revolution, 1782-1820* (New Haven, 1933).

3. Duke of Buckingham, *Circular Dispatch*, 17 August 1868, quoted in Sir Alan Burns, *History of the British West Indies* (London 1954), p. 656.

4. C. S. Salmon, *The Caribbean Confederation*, Cassell and Co. Ltd. (London, New York, N.D.), p. 64. For another early trenchant criticism of Froude see N. Darnell Davis, 'Mr Froude's Negrophobia', *Timehri*, Journal of the Royal Agricultural and Commercial Society of British Guiana, Vol. II, New Series (Demerara 1888), pp. 85–129.

5. Hume Wrong, *Government of the West Indies*, Clarendon Press (Oxford 1923), pp. 142–43.

6. Vincent T. Harlow and Rita Hinden, *Codicil II : The Case for a Bicameral Legislature*, in *British Guiana : Report of the Constitutional Commission, 1950–51*, Her Majesty's Stationery Office (London 1951), Colonial No. 280, p. 49.

7. N. W. Manley, speech of September 1938 to inaugural meeting of People's National Party, Kingston, reprinted in *Bulletin of the West Indian Federal Labour Party*, Vol. I, No. I (Port of Spain, Trinidad, 1959), p. 16.

8. See as an example remarks of Administrator of Dominica in Legislative Council *Debates*, 24 October 1944, quoted in Morley Ayearst, *The British West Indies. The Search for Self-Government* (NY, New York University Press, 1960), p. 174.

9. The West Indian Conference, convened by the Dominica Taxpayers Reform Association, *Proceedings*, Roseau, Dominica, British West Indies (Castries, St Lucia, Voice Printery, October-November 1932), p. 1.

10. Bessie Harper, *A Short History of the Heads of the Government of the Island of Antigua*, Government Printing Office (St John's, Antigua, 1962), pp. 15–16.

11. L. D. Powles, *The Land of the Pink Pearl or Recollections of Life in the Bahamas* (London, Sampson Low, Marston, Searle and Rivington, 1888), p. 134.

12. Quoted in P. H. Daly, *Story of the Heroes*, third volume, *The Assimilative State* (Georgetown, British Guiana, *Daily Chronicle* series, 1943), p. 351

13. *Daily Chronicle*, 5 January 1905, reprinted in Education and Research Committee of the People's Progressive Party, *Sugar, Yesterday and Today* (Georgetown, British Guiana, N.D.).

14. Henry Taylor, *Autobiography of Sir Henry Taylor*, 2 vols. (London, Longmans, Green and Co., 1885), Vol. I, pp. 249–60.

15. George Price, *Jamaica and the Colonial Office: Who Caused the Crisis?* (London, Sampson Low and Marston, 1866).

16. Eric Williams, *British Historians and the West Indies* (Port of Spain, Trinidad, PNM Publishing Company, 1964). See also the extensive treatment in Elsa Goveia, *op. cit.*

17. Williams, *op. cit.*, p. 163.

18. Sydney Olivier, *Jamaica: The Blessed Island* (London, Faber and Faber Ltd., 1936), Ch. xxxiii.

19. Margaret Olivier, *Sydney Olivier, Letters and Selected Writings* (London, Allen and Unwin, 1948), pp. 12–13.

20. T. S. Simey, *Welfare and Planning in the West Indies* (Oxford, Clarendon Press, 1946), especially Ch. VII: 'Conclusion'.

21. Colonial Office, *Report of the British Guiana and British Honduras Settlement Commission* (London, Her Majesty's Stationery Office, 1948), Cmd. 7533, pp. 9–12.

22. See for this Douglas Hall, *Free Jamaica 1838–1865* (New Haven, Yale University Press, Caribbean Series, 1959), pp. 243-45, and Sydney Olivier, *The Myth of Governor Eyre* (London, Hogarth Press, 1933), Chs. VII and VIII.

23. Speech of Governor Fletcher in *Trinidad and Tobago Disturbances 1937. Report of Commission* (London, Her Majesty's Stationery Office, Cmd. 5641, 1938), pp. 107–14, 118. For the place of James Stephen in the development of the idea of colonial trusteeship see *Memoirs of James Stephen* (ed. Merle Bevington) (London, Hogarth Press). For the efforts of an earlier Governor in the Crown Colony system to make trusteeship a reality see John Brown, 'Sir John Moore as Governor of St Lucia', *The Voice of St Lucia*, 2 December 1961.

24. See correspondence between Governor William Reid and Mr W. C. Redfield in Addison E. Verrill, *The Bermuda Islands* (New Haven, Conn., published by author, 1902), pp. 483–84. Captain Cipriani's trenchant remarks on the Colonial Office 'system', appended to his 1928 speech on his return from the Labour Commonwealth Conference are worth noting; see *Trinidad in the Labour Comity of Nations, being a full report of the activities ... of Captain Cipriani ... at the Labour Commonwealth Conference* (Port of Spain, William Howard Bishop, 1928).

25. Colonial Office, *Report of a Committee on the System of Appointment in the Colonial Office and the Colonial Services* (London, Her Majesty's Stationery Office, Cmd. 3554, 1930), p. 20.

26. Major Sir Ralph Furse, *Memorandum on Post War Training for the Colonial Service*, February 1943, in Colonial Office, *Post War Training for the*

*Colonial Service* (London, Her Majesty's Stationery Office, Colonial No. 198, 1946), p. 31, para. 45.

27. Sir Stafford Cripps, speech to the People's National Party, 1938, quoted in N. W. Manley, *This Jamaica* (Kingston, People's National Party, N.D.), p. 18.

28. Statement of People's Progressive Party, British Guiana, quoted in Audrey Jupp, *Facing Facts in British Guiana* (London, Union for Democratic Control, 1957), p. 2.

29. David H. Bayley, *Public Liberties in the New States* (Chicago, Rand McNally and Company, 1964).

30. Paul Blanshard, *Democracy and Empire in the Caribbean* (New York, MacMillan, 1947), p. 17.

31. Henry Albert Phillips, *White Elephants in the Caribbean* (New York, Robert M. McBride and Company, 1936), p. 155. For a general survey of how all this worked out in the modern period after the First World War, see Jesse H. Proctor, 'British West Indian Society and Government in Transition, 1920–1960', *Social and Economic Studies* (December 1962), Vol. II, No. 4.

CHAPTER V

1. See, for example, C. A. Paul Southwell, *The Truth about 'Operation Blackburne'* (Masses House, Basseterre, St Kitts, 1951) and *Grenada's Monumental Day*, reports and contributions as appeared in *The West Indian* (St Georges, Grenada), 1931. For an earlier expression of this traditional constitutionalism see William Smith's remarks, 'The Government of Nevis in 1745' in *Writings, Past and Present, about the Leeward Islands*, ed. John Brown (University College of the West Indies, Department of Extra-Mural Affairs, 1961), p. 60.

2. Pamphlet No. 37, Antigua-Barbuda Democratic Movement, mimeographed (St John's, Antigua, 23 March 1963) and copies of petitions in *Antigua Star*, 14 November, 1 December 1962.

3. In Alec Waugh, *Island in the Sun* (New York, Farrar, Straus and Cudahy, 1955), p. 92.

4. Colonial Office. *West Indies.* Report by the Hon. E. F. L. Wood, M.P. (London, Her Majesty's Stationery Office, Cmd. 1679, 1922), pp. 17–20.

5. C. A. Paul Southwell, *op. cit.,* pp. 11–12.

6. *Workers Clarion* (Castries, St Lucia), quoted in *Daily Gleaner* (Kingston, Jamaica), 22 November 1957.

7. Wood, *op. cit.,* pp. 6–7.

8. Antigua Labour Party, *Progress Report* (St John's, Antigua, 1951), p. 26

9. For all this see St Kitts Workers League, *Memorandum to the Secretary of State for the Colonies on the subject of Constitutional Reform in the Territory,* reprinted in *The Labour Spokesman,* 31 May 1958; *Daily Gleaner,* 7 March 1958; *Trinidad Guardian,* 18 May 1958; *The Labour Spokesman* (St Kitts), 6, 7 March 1958; text of address of Leeward Islands Governor to Legislative Council, in *St Kitts-Nevis Daily Bulletin* (St Kitts), 17 May 1958; and St Kitts-Nevis-Anguilla, Legislative Council, *Debates,* 5 March 1958.

10. For general constitutional development of the Leeward Islands at this time see 'The Constitutional History of the Leewards', *Caribbean Quarterly* (May 1960), Vol. 6, Nos. 3 and 4.

11. St Kitts Workers League, *Memorandum, op. cit.,* P. 1.

12. For the Baldwin fiasco see Novelle Richards, *The Struggle and the Conquest. Twenty Five Years of Social Democracy in Antigua* (St John's, Antigua, Workers Voice Printer, 1965), Chs. XIII-XVI.

13. Colonial Office. *West Indies. Report of the Closer Union Commission* (London, April 1933), pp. 9–12.

14. *Despatch of Secretary of State for the Colonies to Governor, Leeward Islands,* reprinted in *The Democrat* (Basseterre, St Kitts), 12 January 1957; *Letter of Colonial Secretary to Administrator of Montserrat,* reprinted in *Antigua Star* (St John's, Antigua), 19 December 1962; and for a general discussion, Rawle Farley, *Trade Unions and Politics in the Caribbean* (Georgetown, British Guiana, 1957), pp. 19–28. For a much more critical discussion on the part of radical leadership in the area see discussion in Legislative Council of St Lucia, *Parliamentary Debates, Official Report,* mimeographed (January and February 1963), pp. 16–41, 45–55.

15. *Proposals for Constitutional Reform in Leeward and Windward Islands, 1959,* reprinted in *The Voice of St Lucia* (Castries, St Lucia) 11 April 1959.

16. Union of Students of the Little Eight, *Memorandum,* reprinted in *Antigua Star,* 4 May 1962.

17. For reports of 1965 constitutional conferences on the new 'associated states' status see *Voice of St Lucia,* 9, 13, 16, 20, 23, 27, 30 April, 4 May 1966. See also outline in Institute of Caribbean Studies, University of Puerto Rico, *Caribbean Monthly Bulletin,* January and February 1966.

18. J. W. Fortescue, *A History of the British Army* (London, 1899–1912), Vol. III, pp. 3–4, quoted in Hume Wrong, *Government of the West Indies* (Oxford, Clarendon Press, 1923), p. 45.

19. Arthur P. Watts, *Nevis and St Christophers 1782–1784* (Paris, Presses Universitaires de France, N.D.), pp. 121–56.

20. J. L. Ohlson, 'Barbados', in *British America,* The British Empire Series, Vol. III (London, Kegan Paul, Trench ,Trubner and Co., Ltd., 1900), p. 456.

21. James Grainger, 'Advice to the Planters of St Christopher', in John Brown (ed.), *Writings, Past and Present, about the Leeward Islands* (Department of Extra-Mural Studies, University College of the West Indies, 1961), pp. 40–43.

22. Reports of annual conferences of St Kitts-Nevis Trades and Labour Union (Masses House, Basseterre, St Kitts) ; St Kitts-Nevis Trades and Labour Union, *The Union : What It Is and What It Does* (Basseterre, 1954). For the economics and politics of the annual bonus system see *Labour Spokesman* (Basseterre, St Kitts) 6, 7, 8 November 1962. The issue of 8 November includes summaries of the findings of the Malone Commission of Enquiry, 1943, and the Soulbury Economic Commission of 1948–49.

23. Quoted in Antigua Labour Party, *Progress Report* (St John's, Antigua, 1957). For a general description of the Antiguan economy see 'Economic Change in Antigua', *The West Indian Economist* (Kingston, Jamaica, January 1960), Vol. 2, No. 7.

24. For all this see generally Novelle Richards, *The Struggle and the Conquest. Twenty Five Years of Social Democracy in Antigua., op. cit.*

25. For the economic problem of Montserrat see Colonial Office, *Commission of Enquiry into the Cotton Industry* (London, Her Majesty's Stationery Office, 1953). See also Carleen O'Loughlin, 'Economic Problems of the Smaller West Indian Islands', *Social and Economic Studies* (University of the West Indies), Vol. II, 1962.

26. *Memorandum submitted by the St Kitts-Nevis Trades and Labour Union to the Commission of Enquiry into the Sugar Industry of St Kitts*, mimeographed (Basseterre, St Kitts, 15 September 1961), para. 32.

27. Vere Langford Oliver, *History of the Island of Antigua* (London, Mitchell and Hughes, 1894, 3 vols.).

28. Gordon C. Merrill, *The Historical Geography of St Kitts and Nevis, The West Indies* (Instituto Panamericano de Geografia e Historia, Mexico, 1958), p. 130.

29. Simon Rottenberg and Nora Siffleet, *Report on Unemployment in the Presidency of Antigua, Leeward Islands* (Labour Department, Antigua, 1951)

30. Editorial, *Antigua Star*, 19 February 1958.

31. *Report of Board of Enquiry into the Hotel Industry in Antigua*, mimeographed (St John's, Antigua, 10 January 1962), para. 118. See also in general for all this Andrew P. Phillips, *The Development of a Modern Labour Force in Antigua*, Ph.D. dissertation (Department of Sociology, University of California, Los Angeles).

32. Novelle Richards, *The Struggle and the Conquest. Twenty Five Years of Social Democracy in Antigua*, p. 69.

33. O. W. Flax, 'Experiments in Adult Education in Antigua', *The Mutual Improvement Society Half-Yearly* (St Kitts, June 1947), pp. 37-39.

34. Hubert Maurice Dinzey, 'A Historical Survey of the Mutual Improvement Society', *The MIS Golden Jubilee Magazine* (St Kitts, April 1951), pp. 7-11.

35. Charlesworth Ross, *From an Antiguan's Notebook* (Bridgetown, Barbados, Advocate Commercial Printing, 1962).

36. Extra-Mural Department, Leeward Islands, University College of the

West Indies, *Poems and Stories of St Christopher, Nevis and Anguilla* (St John's, Antigua, 1960); and Extra-Mural Department, Leeward Islands, University College of the West Indies, *Writings, Past and Present, about the Leeward Islands* (St John's, Antigua, 1961).

## CHAPTER VI

1. Hon. E. M. Gairy, letter to Sir Stephen Luke, reprinted in *The Torch-light* (St George's, Grenada), 6 January 1957.

2. *Programme*, West Indies Federal Labour Party, reprinted in *Trinidad Guardian* (Port of Spain, Trinidad), 9 January 1958. For the general constitutional development of the Windward Islands at this time see Coleridge Harris, 'The Constitutional History of the Windwards', *Caribbean Quarterly* (May 1960), Vol. 6, Nos. 3 and 4.

3. George E. Marecheau, 'An Open Letter to the Governor', *Grenada's Monumental Day*, reports and contributions as appeared in *The West Indian* (St George's, Grenada), 1931.

4. F. B. Paterson, in *Debates*, The Legislative Council (St George's, Grenada, Government Printing Office, 1956), 24 February 1955, p. 95.

5. St Vincent, Legislative Council, *Parliamentary Debates* (St Vincent, Government Printer, 1954), Vol. II Third Session, 1 April 1954. For the general political and constitutional development of St Vincent see Wallace Dear, 'The Constitutional Development of St Vincent', *Flambeau* (Kingstown, St Vincent), No. 4, April 1966, and Kenneth John, 'St Vincent: A Political Kaleidoscope', *Flambeau*, No. 5, July 1966. For the critical breakdown of the St Vincent politico-constitutional system in the 1966–67 period see Kenneth John, 'The Political Crisis', *Flambeau*, No.7, March 1967.

6. Dr A. L. Jolly, 'Preliminary Examination of the Economic and Fiscal Structure of St Vincent' in *A Plan of Development for the Colony of St Vincent* (compiled and edited by Bernard Gibbs, adopted by the St Vincent Development Committee, Port of Spain, Trinidad, 1947), p. xvii.

7. 'The Arrowroot Tragedy', *Flambeau* (Kingstown, St Vincent), September 1965.

8. E. L. Jack, 'An Investigation of Credit Facilities for Small Cultivators in the Windward Islands' (1945) in *A Plan of Development for the Colony of St Vincent*, p. 382.

9. For the St Lucian sugar industry see, among earlier reports, Sir Donald Jackson (Chairman), *Report of the Commission of Enquiry into the stoppage of work at the Sugar Factories in St Lucia in March, 1957*. (Castries, St Lucia, 28 June 1957). For the banana industry see *Report of the Commission of Enquiry into the Banana Industry of St Lucia* (Castries, St Lucia, Government Printing Office, 1964), and 'The Banana in St Lucia', *Voice of St Lucia*, 2, 9, 16 March 1963.

10. Simon Rottenberg, 'Labor Relations in an Underdeveloped Economy', *Caribbean Quarterly* (January 1955), Vol. 4, No. 1, p. 54.

11. 'The Banana in St Lucia', *Voice of St Lucia*, 9 March 1963.

12. Grenada, *Debates in the Legislative Council*, 13 October 1954–30 June 1955, pp. 34–37.

13. Ernest Payne, *A Land Tenure Reform Proposal for Grenada, British West Indies*, MA thesis, Michigan State University, mimeographed, 1961, pp. 75–77.

14. 'Report of the Agricultural Commission', *St George's Chronicle and Grenada Gazette* (St George's, Grenada), 28 March, 4, 11 April 1896; and speech of Hon. D. S. Freitas in the Legislative Council, reported in *St George's Chronicle and Grenada Gazette*, 13 June 1896.

15. St Vincent, *Parliamentary Debates*, Legislative Council, Session 1953–54, 5th sitting, 4 February 1954.

16. St Vincent, *Parliamentary Debates*, Legislative Council, debate for 20 August 1964, pp. 19–21; see also remarks of *Memorandum* of the St Vincent Planters Association in *Report of Enquiry into Wages and Other Conditions of Employment of Agricultural Workers in St Vincent* (Kingstown, Government Printer, January 1956), pp. 46–48.

17. Colonial Office, Colonial Development and Welfare in the West Indies, *Agriculture in the West Indies* (London, Her Majesty's Stationery Office, 1942), pp. 51–64.

18. Legislative Council, Grenada, *Report of Inquiry into the Nutmeg Industry*

*of Grenada*, 1951. Council Paper No. 4 of 1951 (St George's, Grenada, Government Printer, 1951).

19. Report of Team of Experts, *The Agricultural Development of St Lucia* (Castries, St Lucia, 1951), pp. 20–21.

20. *Ibid.*, pp. 72–75; and the observations of Dr Arthur Lewis on the question of a land tax in *The Voice of St Lucia*, 29 October 1949.

21. For discussion of this see, for example, St Lucia, *Parliamentary Debates*, Official Report, January-February 1963 (Castries, St Lucia), debate of 30 January 1963, pp. 55ff.

22. See, for example, Dora Ibberson, *Social Welfare, Report on a Visit to St Vincent*, June 1945, in St Vincent, *A Plan for Development*, pp. 691–97.

23. *The Voice of St Lucia*, 9, 13, 16, 20, 23, 27, 30 April, 4 May 1966.

24. St Vincent, *A Plan of Development for the Colony of St Vincent* (Port of Spain, Trinidad, 1947).

25. In Dr Eric Williams, budget speech, reported in *Trinidad Guardian*, 13 April 1961.

26. The West Indian Conference, convened by the Dominica Taxpayers Reform Association, *Proceedings*, Dominica, British West Indies (Castries, St Lucia, Voice Printery, October-November 1932), pp. 1–2.

27. St Lucia, *Report of the Commission of Enquiry under the Chairmanship of Mr Justice J. W. B. Chenery* (Castries, Government Printer, 1962), and *Report of the Commission of Enquiry under the Chairmanship of Sir Eric Hallinan, Kt.* (Castries, St Lucia, 1962).

28. Archibald W. Singham, *Political Crisis and Electoral Change in a Colonial Society*, mimeographed, presented at 1963 annual meeting of American Political Science Association. See for a somewhat different view, Simon Rottenberg, 'Labor Relations in an Underdeveloped Economy', *Economic Development and Cultural Change*, I (December 1952, Chicago). M. G. Smith's separate interpretation of Gairyism rests upon a dubious distinction between the economic and social aspects of the phenomenon which he himself admits is not simple. The whole semi-feudal structure of social relations in Grenadian society rests, after all, on the economic

fact of the planter ownership of estate production (M. G. Smith, 'Structure and Crisis in Grenada, 1950–1954', *The Plural Society in the British West Indies* (Berkeley, University of California Press, 1965).

29. The Rover, 'Our Lawyers and Society', *The Torchlight* (St George's, Grenada), 27 June 1956.

30. 'The St Vincent Riot', collected extracts from *Port of Spain Gazette*, December 1935.

31. Hon. E. Duncan, *Constitutional Development in St Vincent* (Kingstown, Government Printing Office, 13 May 1950). See also Hon. Keith Alleyne, *Memoir of the Constitutional Development of St Lucia* (Castries, Government Printing Office, 1949).

32. Grenada, *Report of the Commission of Enquiry into the Control of Public Expenditure in Grenada during 1961 and Subsequently* (St George's, Government Printer, 8 May 1962). For the politics of Gairyism see, among much else, resignation speech of Hon. R. K. Douglas, Legislative Council, 16 January 1957, reprinted in *The Torchlight*, 18 January 1957; and *Report of Mr Justice J. L. Wills, Commissioner, to investigate circumstances surrounding negotiations between the Government of Grenada and Dr James Ernest Ross*, 15 October 1956, reprinted in *The Torchlight*, 2, 5, 7, 14, 16 December 1956.

33. St Vincent, *Report of a Commission of Enquiry into the Public Works Department* (Kingstown, Government Printer, September 1963).

34. See details of Trinidad Five-Year Draft Plan, covering proposed expenditures for Grenada, and the various reports of the Economic Commission on Unitary Statehood with Grenada in *Trinidad Guardian*, 30 January 1965.

35. Barbados, *The Federal Negotiations 1962–1965 and Constitutional Proposals for Barbados* (Bridgetown, Government Printing Office, 1965), para. 67.

36. The West Indian Conference, *Proceedings*, p. 6.

37. St Lucia, *Parliamentary Debates*, Official Report, January and February 1963 (Castries, St Lucia), debates for 19–22 February 1963, pp. 86–87.

38. See revealing speech of Canadian business leader, K. R. Patrick, partly

reported in *En Ville*, Montreal, 28 May 1966; also in mimeograph form, *A Proposal for a New Canadian-West Indies Relationship*, N.D.

39. Colonial Office. *West Indies*. Report by the Hon. E. F. L. Wood, M.P. (London, Her Majesty's Stationery Office, Cmd. 1679, 1922), pp. 32–33; and Colonial Office, *Governor's Addresses to the Legislative Councils of the Windward Islands* ... (London, 1922).

40. See, for example, *Report of Commission of Enquiry on the Sugar Industry of St Vincent* (Kingstown, Government Printer, April 1955), especially Appendix IV: *Memorandum* submitted by the St Vincent Federated Industrial and Agricultural Workers Union, pp. 33–40.

41. For the record of that episode see *Dominica Herald* (Roseau, Dominica), 9 March 1963.

42. Ebenezer Duncan, *Footprints of Worthy Westindians* (Advocate Co., Barbados, 1946).

43. See, for example, remarks for the year 1920 in *The Grenada Handbook and Directory 1946*, compiled by E. Gittens Knight (Advocate Co., Barbados, 1946), p. 77. A 1924 handbook on the Bahamas even includes an entire chapter on the Kings and Queens of England; see *Tribune Handbook, Standard Guide to Nassau and the Bahama Islands* (Nassau, 'The Tribune', 1924), Section VII.

44. Joseph Alfred Borome, 'George Charles Falconer', *The Dominica Grammar School Magazine* (Roseau, Dominica, September 1955); and Alfred Heldman Richards, *A Gem of Dominica. Memoir of the Hon. J. R. H. Bridgewater* (Bridgetown, Cole's Printery, N.D.).

45. Roderick Walcott, in *The Voice of St Lucia*, 22 March 1958.

CHAPTER VII

1. A. S. Forrest and John Henderson, *Jamaica* (London, Adam and Charles Black, 1906), Ch. XIII: 'The Politics of a Jamaican Negro'.

2. *Ibid.*, Ch. XIV: 'The White Man's Politics'. For this earlier period see, among much else, A. E. Burt, *The Development of Self-Government in Jamaica, 1884–1913* (London, 1960), and Graham Knox, 'Political Change in Jamaica (1866–1906) and the Local Reaction to the Policies

of the Crown Colony Government', *The Caribbean in Transition* (Second Caribbean Scholars' Conference, Mona, Jamaica, published by Institute of Caribbean Studies, Rio Piedras, Puerto Rico, 1965). See also series of useful articles in *Daily Gleaner, Independence Supplement I : Jamaica, The Early Years*, 14 July 1962, and *Independence Supplement 3 : Jamaica, Its People and Institutions*, 28 July 1962.

3. *Jamaica Tomorrow* (Kingston, Jamaica), Vol. I, No. 1, September 1937.

4. *Annual Reports* of Jamaican Union of Teachers, and W. F. Bailey, *History of the Jamaica Union of Teachers* (Kingston, Gleanor Co., 1937). For the Jamaica Agricultural Society see Sir Arthur Thelwell, 'JAS has lost the way', *Daily Gleaner, Independence Supplement 3*, 28 July 1962.

5. R. W. McLarty, *Jamaica, Our Present Condition and Crisis*, published by the author (Kingston, 1919), p. 12.

6. A. A. Brooks, *History of Bedwardism or the Native Baptist Free Church Church* (Kingston, Gleaner Co., 1917).

7. Amy Jacques-Garvey, *Garvey and Garveyism*, published by the author (Kingston, 1963), pp. 43–45.

8. *Daily Gleaner* (Kingston, Jamaica), 10, 12, 18, 20 September 1964.

9. M. G. Smith, 'The Political Implications of Jamaican Social Structure', unpublished paper, University College of the West Indies, pp. 5–6. Smith's analysis of Jamaican society can be followed in M. G. Smith, *The Plural Society in the British West Indies* (Berkeley and Los Angeles, University of California Press, 1965). For the general social structure of Jamaica as it emerged out of the post-1945 period after the Garveyite era, see George Cumper, Caribbean Affairs, *The Social Structure of Jamaica* (Extra-Mural Department, University College of the West Indies, N.D.).

10. For all this see Amy Jacques-Garvey, *op. cit.*, Len S. Nembhard, *Trials and Triumphs of Marcus Garvey* (Kingston, revised edition, 1953), especially Chs. V and VI, and E. D. Cronon, *Black Moses : The Story of Marcus Garvey and the Universal Negro Improvement Association* (Madison, University of Wisconsin Press, 1955).

11. J. E. Levo, *The West Indian Adventure* (London, Society for the Propagation of the Gospel in Foreign Parts, 1929), pp. 7–8.

12. See Richard Hart, *The Origin and Development of the People of Jamaica* (Kingston, reprinted by the author, 1952), pp. 22–25.

13. For the general contribution of trade unionism to the Jamaican story see, for example, Central Bureau of Statistics, *Trade Unionism in Jamaica, 1918–1946* (Kingston, Government Printer, 1946); Jamaica, *Board of Enquiry into Labour Disputes between Trade Unions* (Kingston, Government Printer, 1956); and the critical article by George Eaton, 'Trade Unions Big Boost to Modern Industry', in *Daily Gleaner*, Independence Supplement 2: Jamaica: Its Livelihood, 21 July 1962.

14. Colonial Office, *Labour Conditions in the West Indies*, report by Major G. St J. Orde Browne (London, Her Majesty's Stationery Office, Cmd. 6070, 1939).

15. Sir Alexander Bustamante, letter to editor, *Daily Gleaner*, 6 December 1960.

16. O. T. Fairclough, quoted in Ansell Hart, *Monthly Comments* (Newport, Jamaica), Vol. 5, No. 6, January 1963.

17. Walter G. McFarlane, *The Birth of Self-Government in Jamaica, 1937 to 1944* (Brooklyn, New York, 1957), p. 19. See also J. McFarlane, *Challenge of our time: a series of essays and addresses* (Kingston, New Dawn Press, 1945).

18. People's National Party, *Report of the 2nd Annual Conference*, 28 August 1940 (PNP, Kingston, 1940), p. 14.

19. People's National Party, *Forward March* (PNP, Kingston, 1941), p. 5.

20. N. W. Manley, speech reprinted in *Bulletin of the West Indian Federal Labour Party* (Port of Spain, Trinidad, August 1959), Vol. I, No. 1, pp. 2–18.

21. H. Orlando Patterson, 'Outside History: Jamaica Today', *New Left Review* (London, May-June 1965), No. 31.

22. Sam Brown, letter to the editor, *Daily Gleaner*, 2 April 1962.

23. Text of *Report* of Jamaica Independence Conference, *Daily Gleaner*, 20 February 1962, and Government of Jamaica, *The Jamaica (Constitution) Order in Council 1962* (Kingston, Government Printer, 1962.)

24. People's National Party, *Report of the 2nd Annual Conference*, p. 16.

25. *Forward March*, p. 7.

26. Walter G. McFarlane, *The Birth of Self-Government in Jamaica, 1937 to 1944*, pp. 18–21.

27. W. A. Domingo, *British West Indian Federation. A Critique* (Kingston, The Gleaner Co., 1956).

28. See for all this George W. Roberts, *The Population of Jamaica* (Cambridge, 1957).

29. Alvin Wartel, *Jamaica : Modified Crown Colony Government and the Crisis of 1938* (Rio Piedras, College of Social Sciences, University of Puerto Rico, mimeographed, December 1965), Part IV, p. 26.

30. Sir Robert Kirkwood, quoted, *Daily Gleaner*, 27 May 1961.

31. *Daily Gleaner*, 17 March 1958. The high prestige value of middle-class Standard English, and the way in which it is used as a political control mechanism in Jamaican politics, is discussed fully in Mervyn Alleyne, 'Communication and Politics in Jamaica', *Caribbean Studies* (Rio Piedras, University of Puerto Rico), Vol. 3, No. 2.

32. *Daily Gleaner*, 6, 7 January 1962.

33. *Daily Gleaner*, 20 June 1957, and *Trinidad Guardian*, 23 June 1957.

34. See for all this, among much else, C. Paul Bradley, 'Party Politics in Jamaica', *Sunday Gleaner*, 11, 25 January, 8 February 1959; Frank Hill, 'JLP, PNP, Bulwarks of Two-Party System', *Daily Gleaner*, Independence Supplement 3 : Jamaica: Its People and Institutions, 28 July 1962; People's Freedom Movement, *Freedom Now* (Kingston, 1957); Morley Ayearst, 'Characteristics of West Indian Political Parties', *Social and Economic Studies* (University of the West Indies), Vol. 3, No. 2, September 1954; C. Paul Bradley, 'Mass Parties in Jamaica', *Social and Economic Studies* (University College of the West Indies), Vol. 9, No. 4, 1960.

35. *Spotlight* (Kingston, Jamaica), April-May 1965, November 1965. For the series of articles on the Jamaican economy that helped originate the new PNP programme, written by Dr Arthur Lewis, see *Daily Gleaner*, 6, 7, 8, 9, 10, 11, 12 September 1964. For a West Indian radical criticism of the programme see *New World Fortnightly* (Georgetown, British Guiana), No. 9, 1965, No. 50, 1967.

36. Peter Abrahams, *Jamaica: An Island Mosaic* (London, Her Majesty's Stationery Office, Corona Library, 1957); W. Adolphe Roberts, *Jamaica. The Portrait of an Island* (New York, Coward-McCann Inc., 1955), p. 115.

37. Katrin Norris, *Jamaica. The Search for an Identity* (London, Institute of Race Relations, Oxford University Press, 1962), p. 61. For the general character of Jamaican race relations and race feelings see also F. M. Henriques, *Family and Colour in Jamaica* (London, Eyre and Spottiswoode, 1953), and R. Nettleford, 'National Identity and Attitudes to Race in Jamaica', *Race* (London, Vol. 7, No. 1, July 1965). Henriques notes that while colour prejudice is not a topic of daily discussion in the press, when some incident occurs it acts as a crystallizing agent and accumulated feelings seek to express themselves, *op. cit.*, p. 60.

38. *Daily Gleaner*, 2, 16 April 1961.

39. *New World Fortnightly* (Georgetown, British Guiana), No. 24, 1 October 1965.

40. Quoted, *Daily Gleaner*, 23 June 1964.

41. Jay Monroe, columnist, *Daily Gleaner*, 25 March 1962.

42. James A. Mau, 'The Threatening Masses: Myth or Reality?' *The Caribbean in Transition* (Second Caribbean Scholars' Conference, Mona, Jamaica, published by Institute of Caribbean Studies, Rio Piedras, Puerto Rico, 1965). The liberal commentator likes to see this absence of hostility and aggression feelings as a laudable component of the 'democratic process'. It would be more correct to see it as a deficiency in class consciousness that contributes to the continuing exploitative manipulation of the masses.

43. 'Assets of Great Worth', *Daily Gleaner*, 29 November 1962.

44. W. B. C. Hawthorne, 'Educational Environment of the Jamaican Child', *Sunday Gleaner*, 10 July 1960. For the widely noted speech of the Minister of Development in 1961 emphasizing the tremendous disparities of income and living standards between the 'haves' and 'have nots' in Jamaican society see report, *Daily Gleaner*, 12 April 1961.

45. Jamaica, *Report of the Conference on Social Development in Jamaica* (Kingston, Council of Voluntary Social Services, 1961), p. 175.

46. *Ibid.*, pp. 99–100.

47. *Ibid.*, pp. 170–75.

48. Wendell Bell, *Jamaican Leaders. Political Attitudes in a New Nation* (University of California Press, 1964), p. 69.

49. Rev. Samuel Ebenezer Churchstone Lord, *The Negro and Organized Religion* (Kingston, 1935).

50. G. W. Smith, *Conquests of Christ in the West Indies* (Brown's Town, Jamaica, Evangelical Book Room, 1939), pp. 59–67.

51. Jamaica Christian Council, *Consultation, Resolutions and Recommendations, 1961*, mimeographed (Kingston, Office of the Jamaica Christian Council, 1961). For the history of the Jamaica Christian Council since its formation in 1941 see Rev. J. A. Crabb, M.A. (ed.), *Christ for Jamaica* (Kingston, Pioneer Press, 1951).

52. Jamaica Social Welfare Commission, *Preliminary Report on Socio-Economic Survey of Parts of Western Kingston*, mimeographed, by Horace C. Gordon, M.Sc. (Kingston, 1961).

53. Una Marson, 'Wanted—A Pledge of Loyalty', *Daily Gleaner*, 7 May 1961. The earlier Jamaica this romantic nostalgia looks back to can be read about in things like Claude Thompson, *These My People* (Kingston, The Herald Ltd., 1943).

CHAPTER VIII

1. Eric Williams, 'Education of a Young Colonial', *PNM Weekly* (Port of Spain, Trinidad), Vol. I, Nos. 1, 2, 3, 4, 5, 6, 7, 8, 9, 10, 11, 12, 13, 18 June 1956–13 September 1956.

2. *Ibid.*, No. 1, 18 June 1956.

3. *Ibid.*, Nos. 1, 2 and C. L. R. James, *The Life of Captain Cipriani. An Account of British Government in the West Indies* (Nelson, Lancs., Coulton and Co., Ltd., 1932), p. 54.

4. Quoted, I. M. Cumpston, *Indians Overseas in British Territories 1834–1854* (Oxford University Press, 1953), p. 122.

5. *Ibid.*, p. 110.

6. Eric Williams, *History of the People of Trinidad and Tobago* (Port of Spain, PNM Publishing Co., Ltd., 1962), Ch. 9.

7. William G. Sewell, *The Ordeal of Free Labor in the British West Indies* (New York, Harper and Bros., 1861), pp. 113–15.

8. Colonial Office, *West Indies*. Report by the Hon. E. F. L. Wood, M,P. (London, Her Majesty's Stationery Office, Cmd. 1679, 1922), pp. 22–27. For the point of view of younger radical elements in the East Indian Community at this time see, generally, the *East Indian Weekly* (Port of Spain).

9. Eric Williams, 'Education of a Young Colonial', *PNM Weekly*, No. 9, 16 August 1956; and *The Clarion* (Port of Spain), 12 January 1957. For the growth of the East Indian community in general over this period see, among other things, *Indian Centennial Review, 1845–1945* (Port of Spain, Guardian Commercial Printery, 1945) and *East Indians of West Indian Descent* (Port of Spain, Ibis Publications, 1965).

10. Quoted, Anthony Maingot, *Nineteenth Century Trinidad. A Discussion of the Relative Position within the Society of the French Creole Group* (Rio Piedras, Institute of Caribbean Studies, mimeographed), Ch. IV, footnote 40.

11. City Council speeches in honour of Captain Cipriani, reported in *Port of Spain Gazette*, 19 April 1945.

12. Quoted, C. L. R. James, *The Life of Captain Cipriani*, p. 17.

13. Julian Brathwaite, quoted in interview, *The Nation* (Port of Spain), 8 May 1959.

14. Owen Rutter, *If Crab no Walk. A Traveller in the West Indies* (London, Hutchinson, 1933), p. 114.

15. Eric Williams, *The Case for Party Politics in Trinidad and Tobago* (Port of Spain, Teachers Economic and Cultural Association, Ltd., 1955), *passim*.

16. See series of articles, 'Political Personalities', *Trinidad Guardian*, during August-September 1956.

17. Albert Gomes, 'A Politician Recalls', *Trinidad Guardian*, 1 January 1964. See also issues of 8, 15, 22, 29 January, 12, 19, February 1964.

18. M. E. Farquhar, 'Candid Comments', *Trinidad Guardian*, 27 January 1957.

19. Derek Bickerton, *The Murders of Boysie Singh* (London, Arthur Barker Ltd., 1962).

20. Eric Williams, *The Case for Party Politics*, p. 23. See also Eric Williams, *Perspectives for our Party*, address delivered to *Third Annual Convention of the PNM*, 17 October 1958 (Port of Spain, PNM Publishing Company, 1958), and PNM, General Council, Research Committee, *The Party in Independence* (Port of Spain, PNM Publishing Company, N.D.).

21. Eric Williams, *My Relations with the Caribbean Commission, 1943–1955* (Port of Spain, Peoples Educational Movement of the Teachers Economic and Cultural Association, 1955).

22. Eric Williams, *Premier's Tribute to Tagore* (Port of Spain, PNM Publishing Co., 1961). See also Williams, 'Politics and Culture', *The Nation*, 1 September 1958.

23. C. L. R. James, *Dr Eric Williams. A Convention Appraisal* (Port of Spain, PNM Publishing Co., 1960), pp. 7–9.

24. Office of the Premier and Ministry of Finance, *The Economics of Nationhood* (Port of Spain, September 1959).

25. See for all this *The Economics of Nationhood, passim;* Office of the Premier and Ministry of Finance, *European Integration and West Indian Trade* (Port of Spain, 1960); Dr Eric Williams, *The Pros and Cons of Federation* (Port of Spain, 1955); Dr Eric Williams, 'Statement of Policy on Federation', *Daily Gleaner*, 14 February 1960; Sir Grantley Adams, report of radio speech, *Trinidad Guardian*, 14 March 1961; Dr Eric

Williams, 'The Principal Issues at Stake in the Federal Elections', *PNM Weekly*, 3 February 1958; and Dr Eric Williams, *Revision of the Federal Constitution. Speech by the Hon. the Premier Dr Eric Williams* (Port of Spain, Legislative Council Trinidad and Tobago, 11 September 1959).

26. Albert Gomes, 'A Politician Recalls', *Trinidad Guardian*, 22 January 1964.

27. Legislative Council, Trinidad and Tobago, *Minority Report (B), Report of the Constitution Reform Committee 1955*, Council Paper No. 16 of 1956 (Port of Spain, Government Printing Office, 1956), p. 15.

28. *Despatch from Governor to Secretary of State* in *ibid.*, pp. 49–58.

29. For all this see *Report of the Constitution Reform Committee 1955*, Appendix A, pp. 17–29; People's National Movement, *The People's Charter* (Port of Spain, PNM Publishing Co., 1956); *Trinidad and Tobago (Constitution) Order in Council, 1956* (Port of Spain, Government Printing Office, 1956); Statement on Constitution Reform, *PNM Weekly*, 22 September 1958; Statement on proposed Constitution, *Trinidad Guardian*, 31 October 1958; Dr Patrick Solomon, speech, Legislative Council, reprinted, *The Nation*, 17, 23 30 October, 6, 13, 20, 27 November 1959; *Trinidad and Tobago (Constitution) Order in Council, 1961* (Port of Spain, Government Printing Office, 1961); *Report of the Trinidad and Tobago Independence Conference* (London, Her Majesty's Stationery Office, 1962); *Trinidad and Tobago (Constitution) Order in Council, 1962* (Port of Spain, Government Printing Office, 1962); and Lennox Pierre and John La Rose, *For More and Better Democracy, for a Democratic Constitution for Trinidad and Tobago* (Port of Spain, West Indian Independence Party, 1955).

30. Debate on US bases in the West Indies and British Guiana in *Official Report of the British Guiana Labour Union Silver Jubilee and Third British Guiana and West Indies Labour Conference* (Georgetown, British Guiana, British Guiana Labour Union, 1944), pp. 78–80.

31. For all this see Eric Williams, *History of the People of Trinidad and Tobago*, pp. 268–278; Eric Williams, *The History of Chaguaramas* (Port of Spain, PNM Publishing Co., N.D.); Legislative Council, Trinidad and Tobago, *Statement by the Hon. the Chief Minister on the US Leased Areas in Trinidad and Tobago* (Port of Spain, Government Printing Office, 20 June 1958);

Legislative Council, Trinidad and Tobago, *Speech made by the Hon. the Chief Minister during the debate on the Chaguaramas Joint Commission Report* (Port of Spain, Government Printing Office, 6 June 1958); *Trinidad Guardian*, 19 January 1958. For a fictional account of the uprooting of Carenage residents by the US bases in the 1940's see De Wilton Rogers, *Silk Cotton Home* (Port of Spain, c. 1943).

32. Lloyd Best, 'Chaguaramas to Slavery?', *New World Quarterly* (Mona, Jamaica), Vol. II, No. 1, 1965.

33. Editorial, *Saturday Evening Post*, quoted in *Daily Gleaner*, 21 January 1958.

34. *Official Report of the British Guiana Labour Union Silver Jubilee*, p. 78.

35. Tito P. Achong, *Mayor's Annual Report*, Trinidad, 1942–43, quoted Lloyd Braithwaite, 'The Problem of Cultural Integration in Trinidad', *Social and Economic Studies* (University College of the West Indies), Vol. 3, No. 1, June 1954, pp. 83–84.

36. Quoted in Department of Extra-Mural Studies, University of the West Indies, *The Artist in West Indian Society*, a symposium (Mona, Jamaica), 1964), p. 64.

37. Gertrude Carmichael, *The History of the West Indian Islands of Trinidad and Tobago, 1498–1900* (London, Alvin Redman, 1961), p. 275.

38. Democratic Labour Party programme, *Trinidad Guardian*, 8 December 1957; and 'This is What Capildeo Wants for Us', *Daily Mirror* (Port of Spain), 13 January 1964.

39. For all this see Statement of Workers' and Farmers' Party of Trinidad and Tobago, *Trinidad Guardian*, 11 August 1965; and *We the People* (Port of Spain), 29 October 1965. For the CLR James position see C. L. R. James, 'Dr Williams' Trinidad: An Attack', *Venture* (London, Fabian Society), January 1966. For the earlier history of the DLP splits see, for example, *Trinidad Guardian*, 25, 26, 27, 28, 29, 30, 31 January, 2, 3, 4 February 1959.

40. Statement of Oilfield Workers Trade Union, *Trinidad Guardian*, 21 January 1964. For Quintin O'Connor see Lennox Pierre, *Quintin O'Connor, A Personal Appreciation* (Port of Spain, 1959). For Trinidadian trade unionism in general see Colonial Office, *Trade Union Organization*

*and Industrial Relations in Trinidad, a report by F. W. Dalley* (London, Colonial No. 215, 1947). Later conditions can be sampled in, for example, *The Vanguard* (Port of Spain), 22, 29 October 1965.

41. H. P. Singh, *Hour of Decision* and *Another Congo?* (Port of Spain, Vedic Enterprises, 1962). The stubborn persistency of ethnic stereotypes is fully annotated in two recent studies, Arthur and Juanita Niehoff, *East Indians in the West Indies*, Milwaukee Public Museum Publications in Anthropology 6 (Milwaukee, 1960), and Morton Klass, *East Indians in Trinidad, A Study of Cultural Persistence* (New York and London, Columbia University Press, 1961).

42. Eric Williams, 'The Danger Facing Trinidad and Tobago', reprinted, *Public Opinion* (Kingston, Jamaica), 17 May 1958; Gordon K. Lewis, 'The Trinidad and Tobago General Election of 1961', *Caribbean Studies* (Rio Piedras, University of Puerto Rico,) Vol. 2, No. 2, July 1962. For Dr Capildeo, see Ivar Oxaal, 'Fragments from a Life: Rudranath Capildeo's Triumph over Self', *Trinidad and Tobago Index* (Georgetown, Guyana), No. 4, September 1966. For a fuller survey of East Indian political developments during this period see Selwyn Ryan, 'The Struggle for Afro-Indian Solidarity in Trinidad', *ibid.*

43. Eric Williams, *History of the People of Trinidad and Tobago*, pp. 283–84.

CHAPTER IX

1. Paul Blanshard, *Democracy and Empire in the Caribbean* (New York, MacMillan, 1947) Part II, Ch. V; Patrick Leigh-Fermor, *The Traveller's Tree* (London, John Murray, 1950), Ch. 6.

2. Louis Lynch, *The Barbados Book* (London, Andre Deutsch, 1964).

3. Colonial Office, *Report of the West Indian Sugar Commission* (London, Her Majesty's Stationery Office, Cmd. 3517, 1930), para. 206.

4. Economic Advisory Council. Committee on Nutrition in the Colonial Empire. First Report, Part II, *Summary of Information Regarding Nutrition in the Colonial Empire* (London, Her Majesty's Stationery Office, 1939), pp. 80–81; Colonial Office, Annual Colonial Reports, No. 1913, *Barbados 1938–1939* (London, Her Majesty's Stationery Office, 1939), p. 7.

5. Colonial Office, *Labour Conditions in the West Indies,* report by Major G. St J. Orde Browne (London, Her Majesty's Stationery Office, Cmd. 6070, 1939), pp. 54–61; and remarks of Minister of Health to Public Health Nursing Course, in *Barbados Advocate* (Bridgetown), 1 September 1964.

6. Shirley Gordon (ed.), Mitchinson Report of 1875, in *Caribbean Quarterly* (University of the West Indies), Vol. 9, No. 3, September 1963.

7. Quoted in F. A. Hoyos, *Our Common Heritage* (Bridgetown, Advocate Press, 1953), p. 59.

8. Bishop Hughes, sermon, reprinted in *Barbados Annual Review* (Bridgetown), December 1950–November 1951, No. 9, pp. 1–2.

9. Sir Conrad Reeves, quoted in Hoyos, *Our Common Heritage,* p. 58.

10. N. Darnell Davis, *The Cavaliers and Roundheads of Barbados* (Georgetown, British Guiana, 1887).

11. F. A. Hoyos, 'Federation and the Representative Principle', *Barbados Advocate,* 2 August 1956.

12. William G. Sewell, *The Ordeal of Free Labor in the British West Indies* (New York, Harper and Bros., 1861), p. 71.

13. Henry Nelson Coleridge, *Six Months in the West Indies in 1825* (London, John Murray, 1832), pp. 277–279.

14. Clennel Wickham, *Pen and Ink Sketches, by a Gentleman with a Fountain Pen* (Bridgetown, 1921), *passim.*

15. For all this see Hoyos, *Our Common Heritage, passim.* For an extended survey of the general development of Barbadian freedom see the series of articles by K. D. Hunte, *The Democrat* (Bridgetown), Vol. I, Nos. 1–14, 27 August–26 November 1966.

16. Quoted in F. A. Hoyos, *The Rise of West Indian Democracy. The Life and Times of Sir Grantley Adams* (Bridgetown, Advocate Press, 1963), p. 93.

17. Brigadier Sir Robert Arundell, *Address . . . to the Legislature of Barbados, 1st February, on the Occasion of the Inauguration of Ministerial Government* (Advocate Co., Ltd., 1954), p. 1.

18. See for all this J. M. Hewitt, *Ten Years of Constitutional Development in Barbados, 1944–1954* (Bridgetown, Cole's Printery, 1954).

19. Hon. R. G. Mapp, quoted, Morley Ayearst, *The British West Indies. The Search for Self-Government* (New York, New York University Press, 1960), p. 93.

20. Governor of Barbados, Address to Legislative Council, 5 December 1950, reprinted in *Barbados Annual Review*, December 1950–51, pp. 22–23.

21. Message of Legislative Council to House of Assembly, included in *House of Assembly Debates*, Official Record, 17 September 1963.

22. *House of Assembly Debates*, Official Report, 16 July 1963.

23. Remarks of Barbados Deputy Premier, Hon. M. E. Cox, in *The Nation* (Port of Spain, Trinidad), 17 April 1959.

24. *The Beacon* (Bridgetown), 28 March 1959.

25. Barbados, *Report on Income Tax in Barbados*, by H. R. Howie, O.B.E., 17 June 1944 (Bridgetown, Advocate Co., Ltd., 1944).

26. Barbados Labour Party, *Labour Marches On* (Beacon Printery, 1951), p. 11.

27. Barbados Workers Union, *14th Annual Report* (Advocate Co., 1955), p. 3. See also for general working conditions at this time, Sam Ashby, 'The Negro and the Sugar Rule', *The Democrat*, 5 November 1966, and 'The plight of the worker, 1905–1937', *The Democrat*, 12 November 1966.

28. See for all this the successive *Annual Reports* of the Barbados Workers Union. For the unique Barbadian import-distribution system see Henry Smith, *Report* on cost and structure of distribution in Barbados, serialized in *The Advocate* (Bridgetown) in November-December 1966.

29. William H. Knowles, *Trade Union Development and Industrial Relations in the British West Indies* (Berkeley and Los Angeles, University of California Press, 1959), pp. 107–11. For the remarkable leadership of the Barbados Workers Union see Mitchie Hewitt, 'Dr Springer's Many

Talents' and William Burke, 'Frank by Name is frank by nature', in Barbados *Advocate*, Independence Issue, 30 November 1966. The general contribution of the Union to Barbadian life is summed up in Dr Francis Mark, *The History of the Barbados Workers' Union* (Bridgetown, Advocate Commercial Printing, N.D.).

30. Department of Education, *A Policy for Education* (Advocate Co., 1945); and Elementary Teachers' Association, *Observations on a Policy for Education* (Advocate Co., N.D.). For general surveys of the Barbadian educational system see Dr Elsie Payne, 'Firm Foundation for the Future' and 'The Church has shown Barbados . . .' Independence of Barbados, 30 November 1966.

31. Barbados Workers Union, *Seventeenth Annual Report, 1958* (Bridgetown, 1958), pp. 4–6, 14–15.

32. C. S. V. Petter, *Report of a Survey of Secondary Education in Barbados* (Bridgetown, mimeographed, 1956), para. 11.

33. Hon. F. L. Walcott, in *House of Assembly Debates*, Official Report, 2, 16 April 1963. For the general problem of technical and vocational education in the Caribbean area as a whole, see Colonial Office, Development and Welfare Organization, *Memorandum on Technical Education in the British Caribbean* (Bridgetown, 1956), and Colonial Office, *Report of the Mission on Higher Technical Education in the British Caribbean* (London, Her Majesty's Stationery Office, 1958). With reference to the discussion on breeding habits it must be noted that the remark quoted in the text unfortunately gives further credence to the Barbadian middle and upper class myth that the working class mates and breeds indiscriminately. A recent anthropological report notes how the new campaign for birth control is taking over some of that quality of moral piousness, Constance R. Sutton, *Social and Cultural Factors affecting Family Size Motivation in Barbados*, mimeographed, May 1959.

34. Austin C. Clarke, *The Survivors of the Crossing* (London, Heinemann, 1964). For this general contribution of the Barbados Workers' Union to the Barbadian economy see Barbados Workers' Union, *Seventeenth Annual Report*, August 1958, and *Twenty-Second Annual Report*, August 1963; *Memorandum submitted by the Barbados Workers' Union to the Commission . . . to enquire into the Sugar Industry of Barbados, November 1962*, mimeographed, 1962; *Note prepared by the Barbados Workers' Union at the request of the Chairman of the Commission of Enquiry into the Sugar*

*Industry, on the structure, organization, and finances of the Union*, mimeographed, December 1962; Barbados Workers' Union, *Proposals for a Sugar Workers Rehabilitation and Welfare Fund*, mimeographed, 23 October 1963; Barbados Workers' Union, *Pillars of Security* (Bridgetown, Advocate Commercial Printing, 1963); Barbados Workers' Union, *The Barbados Workers' Union and Economic Planning*, mimeographed, N.D.

35. F. A. Hoyos, *The Rise of West Indian Democracy. The Life and Times of Sir Grantley Adams.*

36. See, for example, Freddie Miller, *Labour Believe* (Bridgetown, 1951).

37. *Barbados Advocate*, 24 November 1964.

38. Sir Grantley Adams, quoted, Hoyos, *op. cit.*, p. 61.

39. International Labour Office, *Report to the Government of Barbados on a Proposed Social Security Scheme* (Bridgetown, Government Printing Office, N.D.).

40. Barbados, *House of Assembly Debates*, Official Record, 21 May 1963.

41. Barbados, *House of Assembly Debates*, Official Record, 27 November 1962, 26 February 1963.

42. Dr Richard M. Jackson, *Report on Local Government in Barbados* (Bridgetown, Government Printing Office, 1963).

43. Remarks of Premier in *House of Assembly Debates*, Official Record, 23 April 1963.

44. Petrov, 'People and Things', *Daily News* (Bridgetown), 3 December 1966.

45. *Voice of St Lucia*, quoted in *Daily Gleaner* (Kingston, Jamaica), 1 November 1957.

46. Radio address, Minister of Education, in *Barbados Advocate*, 13 November 1964.

47. Democratic Labour Party, *Manifesto of the Democratic Labour Party*, Barbados General Election 1961, p. 11.

48. Courtney Blackman, 'Ethnic Groups in Barbados', mimeographed, Conference material, Inter-American University (San German, Puerto Rico), 24 July 1964.

49. Raymond W. Mack, 'Race, Class and Power in Barbados: A Study of Stratification as an Integrating Force in a Democratic Revolution', in Herbert R. Barringer, George I. Blanksten, Raymond W. Mack (eds.), *Social Change in Developing Areas* (Cambridge, Mass., Schenkman Publishing Company, 1965).

50. For the history of the 1961–65 constitutional negotiations see Government of Barbados, White Paper, *Federal Negotiations 1962–1965 and Constitutional Proposals for Barbados* (Bridgetown, Government Printing Office, 1965).

51. *Ibid.*, paras. 77–78.

52. Hon. W. A. Crawford, *House of Assembly Debates*, Official Record, 13 August 1963, pp. 7–14. See also the observations of White Paper, *Federal Negotiations* . . . paras. 110–22.

CHAPTER X

1. Mrs Conway Evans, description of life in British Guiana, in *Daily Argosy* (Georgetown, British Guiana), 3 April 1929, reprinted from *West India Committee Circular*.

2. British Guiana, Legislative Council, *Debates* (Georgetown), motion on British Caribbean Federation, 11, 15 March 1955.

3. 'Roman-Dutch Law in British Guiana and a West Indian Court of Appeal', Appendix IV, *Timehri* (Georgetown), Vol. V, Third Series, 1918.

4. Raymond T. Smith, *British Guiana* (London, New York, Toronto, Oxford University Press, 1962), p. 204.

5. Hon. V. Roth, *Legislative Council on Tour. A Personal Account of the Legislative Council's Tour of the Northwest District and Essequibo, 27–31 March 1952* (Georgetown, Daily Chronicle Printers, 1952).

6. Peter Newman, *British Guiana. Problems of Cohesion in an Immigrant Society* (London, Institute of Race Relations, Oxford University Press, 1964), pp. 83–84. For the general problem of Guyana as a whole see, among much else, Raymond T. Smith, *The Negro Family in British Guiana* (London, Routledge and Kegan Paul, Ltd., 1956); Michael Swan, *British Guiana. The Land of Six Peoples* (London, Her Majesty's Stationery Office, 1957) and *The Marches of El Dorado* (London, Jonathan Cape, 1958). For the aboriginal Indians of the interior see F. W. Kenswil, *Children of the Silence* (Georgetown, Interior Development Committee, 1946), and Nicholas Guppy, *Wai-Wai. Through the Forests North of the Amazon* (London, Penguin Books, 1961).

7. Cecil Clementi, *The Chinese in British Guiana* (Georgetown, 'The Argosy' Company, Ltd., 1945).

8. *Daily Argosy*, (Georgetown), editorial, 9 April 1929.

9. Reverend W. T. Veness, *El Dorado, or British Guiana as a Field for Colonization* (London, Cassell, Peter and Galpin, 1866).

10. Henry Bolingbroke, *A Voyage to the Demerary, 1799–1806* (Georgetown, Daily Chronicle Ltd., The Guiana Edition, No. 1, 1947), pp. 207–8.

11. Collected report of evidence taken before West Indian Royal Commission, *Daily Argosy*, 1939 (Library, Royal Agricultural and Commercial Society, Georgetown), pp. 46–54.

12. René Dumont, *Planning Agricultural Development* (Food and Agriculture Organization of the United Nations, Rome, 1963), pp. 9–11. See also Ian A. McDonald, *Sugar in British Guiana: Challenge and Change*, reprinted from *New World Fortnightly*, No. 10 (Georgetown, 1965).

13. Michael Swan, *British Guiana, The Land of the Six Peoples*, p. 73.

14. Colonial Office, *Report of a Commission of Enquiry into the Sugar Industry of British Guiana* (London, Her Majesty's Stationery Office, Col. No. 249, 1949), pp. 11–12. See also Cheddi Jagan, *Memorandum on the Sugar Industry of British Guiana*, submitted to the Venn Commission, 1948, mimeographed (Georgetown, 1948).

15. Report on Hearings of Labour Commission appointed by the Governor, *Daily Argosy*, 18, 19, 31 December 1935.

16. Collected report of evidence, *Daily Argosy*, p. 77.

17. *Ibid.*, pp. 199–218.

18. *Ibid.*, pp. 135–36.

19. Ian McDonald, *Sugar in British Guiana*, p. 27.

20. Philip Reno, *The Ordeal of British Guiana* (New York, Monthly Review Press, 1964); exchange of correspondence, *Monthly Review* (Vol. 16, No. 8, December 1964); and for the matter of Robert Hart, *Guiana Times* (Georgetown), Vol. 6, No. 2, 1955.

21. Raymond T. Smith, *British Guiana*, pp. 86–87.

22. A. K. Marshall, *Report on Local Government in British Guiana* (Argosy, Georgetown, May 1955), Chs. XII and XIII.

23. Collected report of evidence, *Daily Argosy*, p. 4. For the position, earlier on, of nineteenth-century Governors to the British Guiana plantocracy see remarks of Sir G. William des Voeux, *Experiences of a Demerara Magistrate, 1865–1870* (Georgetown, *Daily Chronicle*, Guiana edition, No. 11, 1948), pp. 86–89. For the generally unsympathetic attitude of Governors to sugar workers' complaints in the 1930's see report of meeting between union representatives and Government officials, *The Daily Argosy*, 10 October 1935. See also *The Daily Argosy*, 24 October 1935.

24. Mr Edun (elective member), in British Guiana, *Legislative Council Debates*, 28 November 1944, Col. 1107.

25. Collected report of evidence, *Daily Argosy*, pp. 183–97.

26. P. H. Daly, *Story of the Heroes*, third volume, *The Assimilative State* (Georgetown, *Daily Chronicle*, 1943), *passim*.

27. A. A. Thorne, Legislative Council, *Debates, 30 May 1944–25 June 1945*, debate of 6 April 1945, Col. 2212.

28. Hubert Critchlow, Legislative Council, *Debates*, debate of 6 July 1944, on Report of Franchise Commission, p. 49.

29. P. H. Daly, *The Assimilative State*, Ch. XXXIV.

30. *Ibid.*, pp. 394–97.

31. British Guiana, *Report of the British Guiana Constitutional Commission, 1954* (Georgetown, Argosy Co., 1954), para. 193.

32. For the People's Progressive Party version of 1953 see Cheddi Jagan, *Forbidden Freedom. The Story of British Guiana* (London, Lawrence and Wishart, 1954); Ashton Chase, *133 Days Towards Freedom in Guiana* (Georgetown, British Guiana, N.D.); Janet Jagan, *History of the PPP* (Georgetown, Educational and Research Committee of the People's Progressive Party, 1963); and Cheddi Jagan, *The West On Trial: My Fight for Guyana's Freedom* (London, Michael Joseph, 1966). The official British version is to be found in *British Guiana. Suspension of the Constitution* (London, Her Majesty's Stationery Office, Cmd. 8980, 1953).

33. *British Guiana. Report of the Constitutional Commission, 1950–1951* (London, Her Majesty's Stationery Office, Colonial No. 280, 1951), para. 49.

34. British Guiana, Governor's Address to Legislative Council, 25 October 1955, *Informatives, Vol. II, May 1955–December 1955* (British Guiana, Government Information Services, 1956), p. 108.

35. Raymond T. Smith, *British Guiana*, p. 173.

36. Dwight D. Eisenhower, *The White House Years: Mandate for Change 1953–1956* (New York, Doubleday and Co., Inc., 1963). Instalment 17 of serialization in *New York Times*, 1 November 1963.

37. Patrick Gordon-Walker, article in *The Star* (London), reprinted in *The Daily Argosy* (Georgetown), 31 August 1955.

38. Rev. Donald Soper, article in *Sunday Chronicle* (Georgetown), 24 October 1954.

39. See remarks of Leader of the Peace and Equality Party, hearings, International Commission of Jurists, in *The Evening Post* (Georgetown), 12 August 1965.

40. Sir Jock Campbell, quoted, Michael Swan, *British Guiana. The Land of Six Peoples*, p. 88.

41. See, for example, *Resolutions* of Third International Conference of West Indian Students, New York, reprinted, *Sunday Gleaner* (Kingston, Jamaica), 19 July 1964. The exaggerated emphasis on personalities is especially marked in the pamphlets written by Norman E. Cameron, *Clearing the Political Air* and *Worrying Features in Our Politics* (Subryanville, British Guiana, Labour Advocate Job Printing Department).

42. *New World Fortnightly*, March 1963, pp. 6–7.

43. Colonial Office, H. C. Sampson, *Report on Development of Agriculture in British Guiana* (London, Her Majesty's Stationery Office, November 1927), p. 14.

44. Raymond T. Smith, *British Guiana*, pp. 141–143, and *New World Fortnightly*, March 1963, Parts V, VI.

45. Philip Reno, *The Ordeal of British Guiana*.

46. Evidence presented to International Commission of Jurists, including Attorney-General's brief, reported in local press throughout August 1965. For the East Indian child marriage system as it stood on the eve of its slow liberalization, see report, *Daily Argosy*, 17 June 1929.

47. *Memorandum* to International Commission of Jurists prepared by British Guiana Teachers' Association, in *Daily Chronicle*, August 1965.

48. Sydney King, unpublished manuscript, (Georgetown, c. 1964), mimeographed, pp. 27–31.

49. Peter Ruhomon, *Centenary History of the East Indians in British Guiana, 1838–1938*, Ch. XXI.

50. Raymond T. Smith, *British Guiana*, pp. 134–43.

51. Quoted, Ruhomon, *Centenary History* . . . , p. 250.

52. *Ibid.*, p. 280.

53. *Ibid.*, Ch. XX.

54. Editorial, *Daily Argosy*, 17 April 1929.

55. See, among much else, Philip Reno, *Ordeal* ...; Ernest Halperin, *Racism and Communism in British Guiana* (Cambridge, MIT, 1964); Peter Newman, *British Guiana* (London, Institute of Race Relations, Oxford University Press, 1964); CISCLA, *Notes and Texts, British Guiana-West Indies Seminar* (San German, Puerto Rico, Inter-American University, mimeographed, 1964); CISCLA, *Report, First Institute on British Guiana* (San German, Inter-American University, 1965); Ved Prakash Vatuk, *British Guiana* (New York, Monthly Review Pamphlet Series, No. 21, 1963); B. A. N. Collins, 'Acceding to independence: some constitutional problems of a poly-ethnic society (British Guiana)', *Civilizations*, Vol. XV, 1965, No. 3; Elisabeth Wallace, 'British Guiana: Causes of the Present Discontents', *International Journal* (Canadian Institute of International Affairs, Vol. XIX, No. 4, Autumn 1964); House of Commons, *Parliamentary Debates*, Official Report (London, Her Majesty's Stationery Office, Monday, 27 April 1964).

56. Educational and Research Committee, People's Progressive Party, *The Racialists of Guyana* (Georgetown, N.D.), p. 7; and *Workers of Guiana, Reunite* (Georgetown, 1964).

57. For all this, see Colonial Office, *Report of a Commission of Enquiry into Disturbances in British Guiana in February 1962* (London, Her Majesty's Stationery Office, Colonial No. 354, 1962); Peter Newman, *British Guiana*, pp. 91–100; Minister of Finance, budget speech, *Parliamentary Debates*, Official Report, Legislative Assembly (Georgetown), 31 January 1962; Cheddi Jagan, *The West on Trial*, Chs. VIII-XVII.

58. For all this see Philip Reno, *The Ordeal* ..., Ch. 6; Cheddi Jagan, *British Guiana's Future: Peaceful or Violent?* (Georgetown, People's Progressive Party, N.D.); Stanley Meiser, 'Dubious Role of AFL-CIO Meddling in Latin America', *The Nation* (New York), 10 February 1964, also in issue of 18 September 1963; *Talk by the Minister of Labour, Health and Housing presenting the facts of the present dispute in the Sugar Industry*, 29 March 1963, mimeographed (Georgetown); Office of the Premier, *Note on the Trade Union movement in British Guiana showing how it is under the dominance of the United States Trade Union movement, whose aim is the overthrow of the Government of British Guiana* (mimeographed, Georgetown, 1963); Francis X. Mark, 'Organized Labour in British Guiana', *The Caribbean in Transition*, Second Caribbean Scholars' Conference, University of the West Indies, April 1964 (Rio Piedras, Puerto Rico, Institute of Caribbean Studies, 1965), pp. 223–33; and Ashton Chase, *A History of Trade Unionism in Guyana* (Demerara, New Guyana Company, 1967).

15*

NOTES

. Cheddi Jagan, *British Guiana's Future : Peaceful or Violent?*; Sydney King, *Genocide in Guiana*, mimeographed (Georgetown, N. D.), and *Next Witness. An Appeal to World Opinion* (Georgetown, Labour Advocate Job Printing Department, July 1962).

60. Guyana Group for Social Studies, series of mimeographed radio talks, 1963–65, especially Dr F. Chandra, 'Cultural Aspects of the Various Ethnic Groups'. See also Rickey Singh, 'A Guyanese Culture?' *New World Fortnightly*, Vol. 1, No. 2, 13 November 1964.

61. Remarks of Attorney-General S. S. Ramphal, in Government of Guyana brief to International Commission of Jurists, in *Guiana Graphic*, 17 August 1965.

62. *New World Fortnightly*, No. 18, 9 July 1965. For the earlier debate on doctrine see Cheddi Jagan, *Speech to PPP Congress, 1956* (Georgetown, mimeographed, 1956), and Sydney King, *Observations on Dr Jagan's Congress Speech* (Georgetown, mimeographed, 1956). For the later debate see various issues of *New World Fortnightly* and *Advance*, People's Youth Organization newsletter. See especially *Advance*, 25 March 1965, for statements on National Unity, Independence, the Cultural Revolution and Socialism.

63. *New World Fortnightly*, No. 9, 5 March 1965, and Sydney King, unpublished manuscript (Georgetown, *c.* 1964), pp. 31–32.

64. For all this, see Statement of People's Youth Organization (PYO), 21 March 1965, in *New World Fortnightly*, No. 12, 15 April 1965; letter of Moses Bhagwan and attached PYO statement, *New World Fortnightly*, No. 18, 9 July 1965; and report of PYO to PPP General Council, in *Evening Post*, 6 August 1965.

65. *Daily Argosy*, 25 June 1929.

66. See particularly 'Guyana at the Crossroads', *Simara*, mimeographed, for Committee for National Reconstruction (Georgetown, November 1965).

67. Colonial Office, *Report of the British Guiana Independence Conference 1965*, Appendix I to Annex B (London, Her Majesty's Stationery Office, Cmd. 2849, December 1965). For the strictly constitutional and administrative aspects of the Guyanese situation see Government of British Guiana,

*British Guiana: Constitutional Instruments, 1961* (Georgetown, 1961);
*Proposed Draft of the Constitution of Guyana* (Georgetown, Government
Printing and Stationery Office, 1962); *British Guiana Conference*, (London,
Her Majesty's Stationery Office, Cmnd. 2203, 1963); *British Guiana
Independence Conference* (London, Her Majesty's Stationery Office, Cmnd.
1870, 1962); B. A. N. Collins, 'La Structure constitutionelle et admini-
strative de la Guyane Britannique', *Civilizations*, Vol. XIII, 1963;
British Guiana, Government Information Services, *Caribbean* and
North Atlantic Territories, *The British Guiana (Constitution) Order, 1964,
1964* No. 921 (Georgetown, 1964).

CHAPTER XI

1. Hume Wrong, *Government of the West Indies* (Oxford, Clarendon Press,
   1923), pp. 99–106. For the nineteenth-century background to the
   Honduran situation see Wayne M. Clegern, *British Honduras. Colonial
   Dead End, 1859–1900* (Baton Rouge, Louisiana State University Press,
   1967).

2. Sir Alan Burns, *Colonial Civil Servant* (London, Allen and Unwin), p. 139.

3. Margaret Olivier, *Sydney Olivier, Letters and Select Writings* (London,
   Allen and Unwin, 1948), Ch. IV.

4. *Report of the Interdepartmental Committee on Maya Welfare* (Belize, British
   Honduras, Government Printer, 1941).

5. N. S. Carey Jones, *The Pattern of a Dependent Economy. The National
   Income of British Honduras* (Cambridge University Press, 1953), p. 18.

6. Colonial Office, *Report of the British Guiana and British Honduras Settlement
   Commission* (London, Her Majesty's Stationery Office, 1948), Cmd.
   7533, pp. 235–239. See also the observations in Colonial Office, *Report
   of the Timber Mission to the British West Indies, British Guiana and British
   Honduras* (London, Her Majesty's Stationery Office, Colonial No. 295,
   1953), paras. 65–77.

7. Major G. St J. Orde Browne, *Labour Conditions in the West Indies* (London,
   Her Majesty's Stationery Office, Cmd. 6070, 1939), pp. 193–199; and
   Colonial Office, *West India Royal Commission Report* (London, Her
   Majesty's Stationery Office, Cmd. 6607, 1945), pp. 400–1.

8. For a selection of the old Honduran 'breakdowns' see *A History of British Honduras* (anonymous) (New York, Colorite Offset Printing Co., N.D.), pp. 67–70.

9. Sydney Olivier, 'British Honduras', in *British America* (London, Kegan Paul, Trench, Trubner and Co., Ltd., British Empire Series, Vol. III, 1900), pp. 476–96.

10. J. C. and M. C. Sologaistoa, *Guide to British Honduras* (Belize, The Trumpet Press and V. Goodrich, 1919), pp. 39–57.

11. Remarks of Member for Toledo District, Legislative Council, *Debates* (Belize), 24 April 1953, pp. 15–16.

12. *Report of the Commission of Enquiry on Constitutional Reform 1951* (Belize, Government Printer, April, 1951), para. 83.

13. Legislative Council of British Honduras, *Minutes of the Proceedings* (Belize, Government Printer), debates of 31 December 1949 and 6 August 1951.

14. See curious discussion on this matter in *Shoulder to Shoulder; or the Battle of St George's Cay, 1798*, compiled by Monrad Sigfrid Metzgen, Chairman, Belize Literary and Debating Society (Belize, 1928).

15. *Report of the Commission of Enquiry* . . . paras. 89–91. For later constitutional developments see Colonial Office, *Report of the British Honduras Constitutional Conference* (London, Her Majesty's Stationery Office, Cmnd. 2124, August 1963).

16. *Report of the British Guiana and British Honduras Settlement Commission*, para. 167.

17. Dr Vernon F. Anderson, 'Why Inertia?' *The Outlook* (Belize, January–March 1945).

18. D. A. G. Waddell, *British Honduras, A Historical and Contemporary Survey* (London, New York, Toronto, Oxford University Press, 1961), p. 115.

19. Stephen L. Caiger, *British Honduras. Past and Present* (London, Allen and Unwin, 1951), p. 185.

20. For the treason charges against the PUP see Colonial Office, *Report of an Enquiry held by Sir Reginald Sharpe, Q.C., into Allegations of Contacts between the People's United Party and Guatemala* (London, Her Majesty's Stationery Office, 1954).

21. Stephen L. Caiger, *British Honduras* . . . p. 145.

22. See, for example, British Honduras, National Independence Party, *Political Song Book*, mimeographed (Belize, Central Office of the NIP).

23. Minister of Natural Resources, speech, Xavier College graduate exercises, *The Belize Times* (Belize), 22 July 1964.

24. *The Premier Speaks* (Government Information Service, Government Printer, Belize, N.D.); *A Collection of Important Speeches and Statements* (Government Information Service, Government Printer, N.D.); *The PUP Government's Manifesto for Belizean Progress : We Head for the Take-Off* (Government Information Service, Government Printer, N.D.). For the background of the Price career see Guardian Staff Reporter, 'Will Price Become Another Jagan?' *Sunday Citizen* (Port of Spain, Trinidad), 1 December 1957.

25. National Independence Party, *The National Manifesto of the National Independence Party* (Belize, N.D.); and *Political Facts about British Honduras, Including Pattern of Betrayal to Guatemala* (Belize, Central Office of the NIP, 1963). For the PUP position on the Guatemalan dispute see *A Collection of Policy Statements by the People's United Party Government on the Unfounded Claims of the Republic of Guatemala to British Honduras* (Belize City, Printing Department, N.D.).

26. Colonial Office, *Land in British Honduras*, Report of the British Honduras Land Use Survey Team (London, Her Majesty's Stationery Office, 1959), p. 35.

27. See replies to critical articles in *Miami Herald* by Chief Information Officer, in *The Belize Times*, 7 November 1965, and by the President, Chamber of Commerce, in *The Belize Times*, 24, 25 December 1965.

28. Thomas W. F. Gann, *The Maya Indians of Southern Yucatan and Northern British Honduras* (Washington, Smithsonian Institution, Bureau of American Ethnology, Bulletin 64. Government Printing Office, 1918). For the position of the Spanish-speaking element see S. R. R. Allsopp,

'British Honduras—The Linguistic Dilemma', *Carribbean Quarterly* (Vol. II, Nos. 3 and 4, September and December 1965). For the 'black Caribs' see Douglas Macrae Taylor, *The Black Caribs of British Honduras* (New York, Viking Fund Publications in Anthropology, No. 17, 1951). For the matter of white immigration see D. Morris, *The Colony of British Honduras, Its Resources and Prospects* (London, Edward Stanford, 1883.)

29. International Bank for Reconstruction and Development, *The Economic Development Program of British Honduras* (Washington, D.C., December 1954), paras. 59–60.

30. *Ibid.*, para. 37. See also the remarks in *Report of the Timber Mission . . .* para. 67.

31. British Honduras (Belize), *Development Plan 1964–1970* (Belize City, Office of the Premier), pp. 57–58,

32. Colonial Office, *Report of the British Honduras Conference* (London, Her Majesty's Stationery Office, Cmnd. 984, 1960). For discussion of the Anglo-Guatemalan dispute see L. M. Bloomfield, *The British Honduras-Guatemalan Dispute* (Toronto, Carswell, 1953); R. A. Humphreys, *The Diplomatic History of British Honduras, 1638–1901* (London, Oxford University Press, 1961); W. J. Bianchi, *Belize: The Controversy between Guatemala and Great Britain over the Territory of British Honduras in Central America* (New York, Las Americas Publishing Co., 1959).

33. British Honduras, *Legislative Assembly. Debates.* (Belize City, mimeographed), 18, 19 June 1962, No. 12, 1961–65 and No. 13, 1961–65.

34. British Honduras, *Legislative Assembly. Debates* (Belize City, mimeographed), 27 June 1961, No. 3, 1961, and 28 September 1962, No. 16, 1961–65.

35. For the later breach of 1958 between Price and Nicholas Pollard, caused by the Guatemalan matter, see Nicholas Pollard, statement, in *Public Opinion* (Kingston, Jamaica), 15 March 1958.

36. William Courtney, in *Daily Gleaner* (Kingston, Jamaica), 5 April 1958; and *Report of an Enquiry . . . passim.*

37. Honduran Independence Party, *Design for Democracy. A Report and a Pledge to the People of British Honduras* (Belize, 1957).

38. Martin Carrabine, S. J., *William Stanton of Belize* (New York, Jesuit Mission Press, Inc., 1932).

39. *The Belize Times*, 12, 15 December 1965. For a general critical summary of the situation as of 1967 see C. P. Cacho, 'British Honduras. A Case of Deviation in Commonwealth Caribbean Decolonization', *New World* (Kingston, Jamaica), Vol. III, No. 3.

## CHAPTER XII

1. G. B. Shattuck (ed.), *The Bahama Islands* (Baltimore, Geographical Society of Baltimore, 1905).

2. Letter of George Washington, reprinted, Walter Brownell Hayward, *Bermuda Past and Present* (New York, Dodd, Mead and Co., 1926), pp. 41–42. For the early American influence see Wilbur H. Siebert, *The Legacy of the American Revolution to the British West Indies and Bahamas* (Columbus, Ohio, Ohio State University Bulletin, April, 1913).

3. L. D. Powles, *Land of the Pink Pearl, or Recollections of Life in the Bahamas* (London, 1888), quoted, Michael Croton, *A History of the Bahamas* (London, Collins, 1962), pp. 215–16.

4. Hayward, *Bermuda Past and Present*, pp. 208–9.

5. John Mitchel, *Jail Journal* (Dublin, M. H. Gill and Sons, Ltd., 1921).

6. Colonial Office, *Labour Conditions in the West Indies*, report by Major G. St J. Orde Browne (London, Her Majesty's Stationery Office, Cmd. 6070, 1939), pp. 213–15.

7. Colonial Office, H. Houghton, Deputy Educational Adviser, *Report on Education in the Bahamas* (1958); H. Houghton, *Report on the Educational System in Bermuda* (Hamilton, Bermuda Press, Ltd., N.D.); H. L. Glyn Hughes, *A Survey of the Medical Services* (Nassau, November 1960).

8. A. Deans Peggs, *A Short History of the Bahamas* (Nassau, Deans Peggs Research Fund, 1959), Appendix: 'Government of the Bahamas'.

9. Duchess of Windsor, *The Heart Has Its Reasons. The Memoirs of the Duchess of Windsor* (New York, David McKay Company, Inc., 1956), Ch. XXXIII.

10. Memorandum, 1944, of Bahamas Civil and Welfare Association, quoted, Paul Blanshard, *Democracy and Empire in the Caribbean* (New York, Macmillan, 1947), pp. 144–45.

11. United Nations, General Assembly, Evidence of W. Brown, Secretary-General of the Constitutional Conference of Bermuda to *Special Committee on the Situation with Regard to the Implementation of the Declaration on the Granting of Independence to Colonial Countries and Peoples* (A/AC. 109/PV. 260, 19 May 1964).

12. *Ibid.*, Hearings of 15 May 1964.

13. Bermuda, *House of Assembly, Debates*, debate on UK Government's White Paper on a petition from the Bermuda Workers' Association, in *The Royal Gazette* (Hamilton, Bermuda), 26 April 1947. See also *Report of the Joint Committee appointed by the Legislative Council and the House of Assembly on Political, Economic and Social Problems raised by Cmnd. Paper Number 7093* (Hamilton, Bermuda, January 1948).

14. *New York Times*, 15, 16 February 1965.

15. Speech, Principal of Berkeley Institute, in *The Bermuda Recorder* (Hamilton), 25 September 1965. See also speech of Headmaster of Whitney Institute, in *The Royal Gazette*, 21 January 1966.

16. *Progressive Liberal Party Memorandum to UN*, reprinted in *Bahamian Times* (Nassau), 28 August 1965; Progressive Labour Party, Bermuda, *Report-UN. Memorandum Committee*, mimeographed, 2 October 1964; *Bermuda Industrial Union Memorandum on the Infringement of Trade Union Rights*, in *B.I.U. News Bulletin* (Hamilton), 21 August 1964.

17. Bermuda, House of Assembly, *Debates, 1933–1934 Session*, debate of 25 October 1933.

18. *New York Times*, 12 February 1965.

19. For the views of Sir John Cox, see report of speech, *The Royal Gazette*, 30 November 1965.

20. For the split in the Bermuda Progressive Labour Party see various reports in *The Royal Gazette*, 16 December 1965, 12, 18 January 1966, and in *The Bermuda Recorder*, 21 January 1966.

21. PLP statement, *Bermuda Mid-Ocean News*, 11 January 1966. See also Bermuda, *House of Assembly. Journals.* Session 1961–62, 15 June 1962, *Interim Report of Joint Select Committee considering the Parliamentary Election Act, 1961;* and Session 1964–65, 12 November 1965, *Report of Joint Select Committee on Constitutional Changes.*

22. Theodore L. Godet, M.D. *Bermuda* (London, Smith, Elder and Co., 1860).

23. Bermuda, House of Assembly, *Debates*, debate on *Constitutional Report of Joint Select Committee*, reported in *The Royal Gazette*, 30, 31 November, 1, 2, 3 December 1965.

24. See letter of G. Gutteridge, *The Royal Gazette*, 15 May 1963, for a typical expression of the expatriate viewpoint.

25. Surgeon Major Bacot, *The Bahamas: A Sketch* (London, Longmans, Green, Reader and Dyer, 1869), p. 103.

26. Greville John Chester, *Transatlantic Sketches in the West Indies, South America, Canada and the United States* (London, Smith, Elder and Co., 1869), p. 92.

27. *An Analysis of Bermuda's Social Problems* (Hamilton, N.D.), pp. 14–16. For a critical account of the socially and culturally depressing consequences of high-powered tourism attuned to the North American affluent society, see the series of reports on Puerto Rican tourism by the Tourism Committee of the Chamber of Commerce of Puerto Rico, reprinted in full, *San Juan Star* (San Juan, Puerto Rico), 13 November 1966, 18, 25 January, 8 February 1967. For a mordant French view of US-oriented tourism in the French Antilles see Jean Raspail, *Secouons le Cocotier* (Paris, Robert Laffont, 1966), Chs. 22, 23.

28. *New York Times*, 13 February 1965. For the structure of the casino gambling empire see series of articles, *Wall Street Journal*, 5, 19 October 1966, 5, 10 January 1967; and *New York Times*, 21 January 1968.

29. *Bahamian Times*, Christmas issue, 1965, 8 January 1966.

CHAPTER XIII

1. See for all this Edwin Beale Doran, *A Physical and Cultural Geography of*

*the Cayman Islands*, Ph.D. thesis, mimeographed (University of California, 1954), and C. Lee Clark, *Grand Cayman, British West Indies. Twenty Years of Socio-Cultural Change*, Ph.D. dissertation (Ohio State University, 1965).

2. David D. Duncan, 'Capturing Giant Turtles in the Caribbean', *National Geographical Magazine* (Vol. LXXXIV, 1943).

3. Edwin Beale Doran, *A Physical and Cultural Geography* . . . pp. 334–36.

4. *Ibid.*, pp. 354–56. For the general economic problems of all of the smaller groups see Carleen O'Loughlin, 'Economic Problems of the Smaller West Indian Islands', *Social and Economic Studies* (University of the West Indies), Vol. II, 1962.

5. Editorial, *Daily Gleaner*, 12 January 1957.

6. See for all this Joint Statement of Cayman Islands Constitution Mission and Chief Minister, Jamaica, *Daily Gleaner*, 12 January 1957; Public Statement, by authority of Colonial Office, *Daily Gleaner*, 10 October 1958; 'Future of the Dependencies', *Daily Gleaner*, 31 January 1958.

7. For the 1958 constitutional proposals see Public Statement, by authority of the Colonial Office, *Daily Gleaner*, 10 October 1958.

8. See generally for all this Colonial Office, various *Annual Reports* on Turks and Caicos Islands (London, Her Majesty's Stationery Office).

9. Doreen Collins, 'The Turks and Caicos Islands—Some Impressions of an English Visitor', *Caribbean Quarterly*, Vol. 7, No. 3 (December, 1961), p. 167. See also *New York Times*, 29 January 1968.

10. Bequia Correspondent, 'In Bequia', *The Vincentian* (Kingstown, St Vincent), 24 October 1963. For the memories of a boy growing up in the sharecropping industry of cotton, plus whaling, in remote Union Island at the turn of the century, see Hugh Mulzac, *A Star to Steer By* (New York, International Publishers, 1963), Ch. 1, 'Recollections of an Island Boy'.

11. Bequia Correspondent, 'In Bequia', *The Vincentian*, 1 August 1964, in reply to Ian Gale, in *Barbados Advocate*, 19 July 1964.

12. Bruce Procope, 'Launching a Schooner in Carriacou', *Caribbean Quarterly* (Extra-Mural Department, University College of the West Indies), Vol. 4, No. 2; Father Raymund P. Devas, *Birds of Grenada, St Vincent and the Grenadines* (Port of Spain, Yuille's Printerie Ltd., 1954). Much of the scanty literature on the smaller islands has been written by the resident expatriate clergyman, who usually sees local life as an expression of cultural childhood on the part of black parish communities. For an example of that attitude see Roscow Shedden (Bishop of Nassau), *Ups and Downs in a West Indian Diocese* (Milwaukee, Morehouse Publishing Co., and A. R. Mowbray, London, 1927).

13. See for most of this M. G. Smith, *Kinship and Community in Carriacou* (New Haven and London, Yale University Press, 1962).

14. John P. Augelli, 'The British Virgin Islands. A West Indian Anomaly', *The Geographical Review* (Vol. XLVI, No. 1, 1955).

15. Quoted, *Daily Gleaner*, 21 March 1958. For later constitutional developments in the US Virgin Islands see Carl J. Friedrich, *Report to the Organic Act Commission of the Virgin Islands Legislature*, mimeographed, (1 March 1957), and Roger Baldwin, *A Report on the Virgin Islands Constitutional Convention*, mimeographed (March, 1965). For details of the new constitutional arrangements of 1966 in the case of the British Virgin Islands, see *The Island Sun* (Roadtown, Tortola, British Virgin Islands), 15 October 1966.

16. Walter S. Priest, 'The Alien: Problem Man in St Thomas', *San Juan Star* (San Juan, Puerto Rico), 4 September 1963; and text of letter of John J. Kirwan, Acting Director of Office of Territories, U.S. Department of the Interior, to Governor of the Virgin Islands, in *San Juan Star*, 17 October 1965.

17. Sir William des Voeux, *My Colonial Service* (London, John Murray, 1903), Vol. II, p. 158.

18. For Mrs Proudfoot's report, see *Daily Chronicle* (Georgetown, British Guiana), 13 August 1965. For later political developments in the British Virgins group, possibly foreshadowing new forms of political activity, see *The Island Sun*, 4 June 1966, 14 January 1967. For a somewhat different view of social problems in Tortola see Robert H. Odell, 'Letter from Tortola', *Virgin Islands View* (St Thomas), Vol. I, Number 9, February 1966.

19. Rev. J. H. Pusey, *Handbook of the Turks and Caicos Islands* (Kingston, Jamaica. Colonial Publishers Co., Ltd.); Rev. J. E. Levo, *Black and White in the West Indies* (London, Society for the Propagation of the Gospel in Foreign Parts, 1930), and, in fictional form, *Virgin Islanders* (London, Hutchinson and Co., 1933). See also fn. 12 above.

20. As an example of the extreme vulnerability of the smaller island economies tied to the United States and dependent upon vagaries of Congressional trade policies, see the Memorandum opinion of Judge Walter Gordon of Virgin Islands District Court in *Virgo Corporation v. Government of the Virgin Islands*, case 165–1965, reprinted *The Daily News* (St Thomas), 25 March 1966.

21. *San Juan Star*, 7, 8, 21 September 1962. For the growth of small island secessionist opinion as an expression of dissatisfaction with their present dependency upon larger island jurisdictions see David Lowenthal, 'Levels of West Indian Government', *Social and Economic Studies* (University of the West Indies), Vol. II, No. 4, December 1962, pp. 385–91. For the particular case of Tobago, and its history of administrative neglect under Trinidad, see Memorandum of group of Tobago citizens to Secretary of State for the Colonies, 'We Want More Representation in the Federal Legislature', in *The Nation* (Port of Spain, Trinidad), 20 May 1960.

CHAPTER XIV

1. See for the matter of federation in general, Eric Williams, *The Pros and Cons of Federation*, text of public lectures (Port of Spain, 1956), and 'The Historical Background of British West Indian Federation', *Caribbean Historical Review* (Historical Society of Trinidad and Tobago, Nos. III-IV, December 1954), pp. 13–69; Jesse Harris Proctor, Jr., 'Britain's Pro-Federation Policy in the Caribbean: An Inquiry into Motivation', *The Canadian Journal of Economics and Political Science* (Vol. XXII, No. 3, August 1956); Lloyd Braithwaite, 'Progress Toward Federation, 1938–1956', *Social and Economic Studies* (University College of the West Indies, Vol. 6, No. 2, June 1957); Jesse Harris Proctor, Jr., 'The Development of the Idea of Federation of the British Caribbean Territories', *Caribbean Quarterly* (Extra-Mural Department, University College of the West Indies), Vol. 5, No. 1; A Correspondent, 'Federation in Review from 1860 to 1956', *Trinidad Guardian*, 7, 9 February 1956; J. M. Hewitt, 'Onwards from Montego Bay', *Barbados Advocate*, 1 August 1956; David K. Easton, 'A Bibliography on the Federation of the

British West Indies', *Current Caribbean Bibliography*, *V* (*1955*), (Port of Spain, Caribbean Commission); *A List of Books on West Indian Federation*, compiled by the West India Reference Library, Institute of Jamaica (Kingston, 1957).

2. Jesse Harris Proctor, Jr., 'Britain's Pro-Federation Policy . . .', p. 322. See also Dr W. A. Osborne, 'The Forces behind Federation', *Trinidad Chronicle* (Port of Spain), 26 August, 2 September 1956.

3. Lloyd Braithwaite, 'Progress Toward Federation . . .', Part B: 'Functional Federalism'.

4. Crown Agents for the Colonies, *Proceedings of the West Indian Conference* (London, May-June 1926), pp. 3–6; and *Proceedings of the First West Indies Conference* (Barbados, January-February, 1929).

5. West Indian Federal League, *What Federation Does Not Mean* (Port of Spain, Trinidad, *c.* 1917).

6. Lloyd Braithwaite, 'Federal Associations and Institutions in the West Indies', *Social and Economic Studies* (Vol. 6, No. 2, June 1957). Murray's contribution to the federal debate is to be found in Hon. C. Gideon Murray, *A Scheme for the Federation of Certain of the West Indian Colonies* (London, The West India Committee, N.D.), and *A United West Indies* (London. The West Strand Publishing Co., 1912).

7. *What Federation Does Not Mean*, p. 5.

8. Sir Grantley Adams, Barbados, *House of Assembly Debates*, 5 November 1951, Col. 1232.

9. Murray, *A Scheme for the Federation* . . . p. 27.

10. Quoted, Eric Williams, *My Relations with the Caribbean Commission, 1943–1955* (Port of Spain, People's Educational Movement of the Teachers' Economic and Cultural Association, 1955), p. 23.

11. *Report of the West Indian Conference*, 1944 (Barbados, Advocate Co., 1944), and Caribbean Labour Congress, *Official Report of Conference* (Barbados, Advocate Co., 1945).

12. For a *resumé* of all this see *A List of Books on West Indian Federation*, compiled by the West India Reference Library, Institute of Jamaica (Kingston, 2nd edition, 1962).

13. S. A. Hammond, *Note on Federation in Australia*, mimeographed, N.D.

14. Eric Williams, *The Pros and Cons of Federation*.

15. Kingston and St Andrew's Taxpayers and Ratepayers Association, *Report on the Federal Enlightenment Campaign*, mimeographed (Kingston, N.D.).

16. N. W. Manley, in Colonial Office, *Conference on the Closer Association of the British West Indian Colonies. Part 2 : Proceedings* (London, Her Majesty's Stationery Office, Col. No. 218, 1948), p. 61.

17. *Report on the Federal Enlightenment Campaign*, p. 2.

18. Sir Grantley Adams, in *Conference on the Closer Association* . . . pp. 37–45; Caribbean Labour Congress, *Official Report of Conference*, and *Statements and Resolutions agreed on by the Caribbean Labour Conference*, September 1945 (Bridgetown, Advocate Co., Ltd.); Report of Pan African Congress held in Manchester, 1945, in *The Masses* (Kingston, Jamaica), 24 November 1945.

19. Sir Grantley Adams, in *Conference on the Closer Association* . . . p. 42.

20. Sir Alexander Bustamante, in *Conference on the Closer Association* . . . pp. 20–27.

21. John Compton, speech, 1966 constitutional conference, in *Voice of St Lucia* (Castries, St Lucia), 7 May 1966.

22. Editorial, *Trinidad Chronicle*, 7 December 1958.

23. C. M. MacInnes, 'British Caribbean Federation', *Developments Towards Self-Government in the Caribbean* (The Hague, W. van Hoeve, Ltd., 1955), p. 158. For the Rance Committee Report see British Caribbean Standing Closer Association Committee, *Report* (Bridgetown, Barbados, Advocate Co., Ltd., and London, Her Majesty's Stationery Office, Colonial No. 255, 1949). See also British West Indies, Development and Welfare Organization, *Financial Aspects of Federation of the British West Indian Territories* (Bridgetown, Advocate Co., Ltd., 1953).

24. *Report of the British Caribbean Federal Capital Commission* (London, Her Majesty's Stationery Office, Col. No. 328, 1956). See also David Lowenthal, 'The West Indies Chooses a Capital', *The Geographical Review* (Vol. XLVIII, No. 3, 1958).

25. West Indies Federal Labour Party meeting, reported in *Trinidad Guardian*, 2, 3, 4 September 1956.

26. John Hatch, *Dwell Together in Unity* (London, Fabian Society, 1958).

27. Richard Hart, letter, *Daily Gleaner* (Kingston, Jamaica), 11 February 1958.

28. W. A. Domingo, *British West Indian Federation: A Critique* (Kingston, Gleaner Co., Ltd., 1956), p. 12.

29. *Ibid.*, pp. 15–16. For a friendly criticism of Domingo by a fellow Jamaican nationalist see Frank Hill, 'Federation—An Act of Faith', *Daily Gleaner*, 8 February 1959.

30. Richard B. Moore, 'Revelations and Reflections on West Indies Federation', *Sunday Gleaner*, 2 November 1958.

31. A. M. Wendell Malliet, *The Destiny of the West Indies* (New York, The Russwurm Press, 1928).

32. N. Darnell Davis, *Colonial Consolidation. The West Indian Dominion* (Demerara, 'Argosy' Press, 1890), pp. 45–46.

33. Albert Gomes, in *Conference on the Closer Association* . . . p. 30.

34. Marco Polo, 'Federation or a West Indian League', *Sunday Gleaner*, 9 November 1958.

35. Critical remarks of Mr Leslie Ashenheim, *Spotlight* (Kingston, Jamaica), Vol. 27, No. 4, April 1966.

36. Supervisor of Elections, West Indies Federal Government, Bulletin No. 3, 'The Federal Elections and You', (Port of Spain, 1958).

37. Mr Hudson Phillips, *Trinidad Guardian*, 1 October 1956.

38. *Report. Conference on British Caribbean Federation* (London, Her Majesty's Stationery Office, 1956, Cmd. 9733), para. 14.

39. Rance Committee, *Report*, para. 89.

40. R. G. Mapp, Barbados, *House of Assembly Debates*. Official Record, 5 November 1951, Cols. 1227–28.

41. *The Plan for a British Caribbean Federation. The Report of the Civil Service Commissioner* (London, Her Majesty's Stationery Office, Cmd. 9619, 1955), Appendix B, paras. 60 and 68.

42. Sir Grantley Adams, Barbados, *House of Assembly Debates*. Official Record, 19 July 1954, p. 1121.

43. Barbados, *House of Assembly Debates*. Official Record, 16 February 1956, p. 1962.

44. *The Voice of St Lucia*, quoted, 'West Indian Opinion', *Daily Gleaner*, 16 January 1958.

45. *Venture* (London, Fabian Colonial Bureau), Vol. 9, No. 2, June 1957. For West Indian press and professional bodies' comment see, for example, *Trinidad Chronicle*, 27 January, 12 May 1957. For earlier anticipatory remarks of T. A. Marryshow on the matter see Grenada, Legislative Council, *Debates*, 26 August 1953, p. 14.

46. Quoted, Henry L. Hall, *The Colonial Office* (London, Longmans, Green and Co., 1937), p. 18.

CHAPTER XV

1. Federal lecture series, in *Caribbean Quarterly* (University College of the West Indies), Vol. 6, Nos. 3 and 4, May 1960.

2. David Lowenthal (ed.), *The West Indies Federation. Perspectives on a New Nation* (New York, Columbia University Press. American Geographical Society, Research Series No. 23, 1961).

3. Sir Alexander Bustamante, letter, *Daily Gleaner*, 8 January 1959.

4. David J. Nelson, *Political Determinants of Federal Capital Location: Inferences for British West Indies*, mimeographed (Port of Spain, 25 February 1957).

5. Office of the Premier and Ministry of Finance, Government of Trinidad and Tobago, *The Economics of Nationhood* (Port of Spain, 11 September 1959), p. 11.

6. See Ch. I, 'Reasons for Excluding Jamaica', in C. Gideon Murray, *A United West Indies* (London, The West Strand Publishing Company, 1912).

7. *Ibid.*, pp. 12–13.

8. C. Gideon Murray, *A Scheme for the Federation of Certain of the West Indian Colonies* (London, The West India Committee, N.D.), p. 29.

9. N. W. Manley, in Colonial Office, *Conference on the Closer Association of the British West Indian Colonies. Part 2 : Proceedings* (London, Her Majesty's Stationery Office, Col. No. 218, 1948), p. 61. For critical observations on Mr Manley's subsequent reversal of attitude, see Norman Girvan, 'The Referendum Exposes the Crisis of Leadership', *Sunday Gleaner*, 24 September 1961.

10. T. A. Marryshow, Grenada, Legislative Council, *Debates* (St George's, Grenada), 21, 22 June 1950, p. 30.

11. *The Plan for a British Caribbean Federation. The Report of the Judicial Commissioner* (London, Her Majesty's Stationery Office, Cmd. 9620, 1955), Appendix 8, pp. 71–72.

12. *The Plan for a British Caribbean Federation. The Report of the Fiscal Commissioner* (London, Her Majesty's Stationery Office, Cmd. 9618. 1955), para. 45.

13. Mr Salles-Miquelle, St Lucia, *Debates of the Legislative Council* (Castries, St Lucia), 20 August 1954, p. 7.

14. Barbados, *House of Assembly, Debates*, Official Record, 22 July 1954, p. 1155. For the 1955 conference on this issue, see *Report of the Conference on Movement of Persons within a British Caribbean Federation* (Port of Spain, Government Printing Office, 1955). For the problem as a whole see

Edwin P. Reubens, *Migration and Development in the West Indies*, No. 3 in series 'Studies in Federal Economics' (Research Institute, University College of the West Indies).

15. *Report of the Trade and Tariffs Commission, Part I.* W.I. 1/58. (Port of Spain, Government of the West Indies, 1958), para. 66.

16. *Ibid.*, paras. 165–67.

17. Statement of Objections of Government of Jamaica to Trade and Tariffs Commission Report, *Public Opinion* (Kingston, Jamaica), 6 December 1958.

18. Report of the Fiscal Committee of Inter-Governmental Conference, 1960, *Daily Gleaner*, 12 July 1960.

19. See report of attitudes of both associations in *Daily Gleaner*, 14 January 1958.

20. *Economics of Nationhood*, pp. 9–11.

21. *Conference on West Indian Federation. Appendix B : Losses Imposed on Windward and Leeward Islands by Federation*, mimeographed (London, April 1953, W.I.F. (53) 12).

22. Statement, Federal Prime Minister, in *Daily Gleaner*, 10 November 1958.

23. For the oil refining issue see *Economics of Nationhood*, Appendix A, i, ii, iii. See also 'Oil in the West Indies—Refinery for Jamaica?', *West Indian Economist*, Vol. I, No. 2 (August 1958).

24. See for all this Federal House of Representatives, debate on Federal Government *White Paper*, in *Trinidad Guardian*, 5, 6 April 1961 ; Mr Manley, text of statement on issue of retroactive fiscal powers, in *Daily Gleaner*, 1 November 1958 ; Jamaica, House of Representatives, debate on 1961 London Conference, in *Daily Gleaner*, 7 July 1961 ; Mr Manley, statement, *Daily Gleaner*, 7 July 1961 ; Government of Trinidad and Tobago, *The West Indies Inter-Governmental Conference on the Federal Constitution, Memorandum for Committee I*, mimeographed, (Port of Spain, September 1959).

25. Louis Marriott, 'Federation a Buyers' Syndicate', *Public Opinion*, 10 June 1961.

26. N. W. Manley, Sir Alexander Bustamante, letters, *Daily Gleaner*, 8 January 1958, 16, 19 March 1958, 17 January 1959, 18 May 1960, 28 June 1961.

27. S. L. Tulloch, letter, *Daily Gleaner*, 22 June 1960.

28. *Ministry Paper on the West Indies Federation*, presented to House of Representatives, Jamaica, full text, *Daily Gleaner*, 27 February 1960. Also reprinted, *The Nation* (Port of Spain, Trinidad), 11, 18 March 1960.

29. Henry Sidgwick, *The Elements of Politics* (London, Macmillan and Co., 1891), p. 518.

30. See, for example, Sir Alexander Bustamante, 'Statement of Policy on Federation', *Daily Gleaner*, 20 November 1958. For a perceptive discussion of the relationship between Jamaican party attitudes to Federation and the internal power-struggle between the various social sections of Jamaican life see M. G. Smith, *The Plural Society in the British West Indies* (Berkeley and Los Angeles, University of California Press, 1965). But the thesis that an anti-Federation vote would set 'new directions of change' and open the way to 'further structural revisions' has not been borne out by Jamaican developments since 1961, *op. cit.*, pp. 317–318.

31. Randolph Rawlins, 'New Thought about Constitution Making', *Public Opinion*, 20 December 1958; Political Reporter, *Daily Gleaner*, 19 January 1958. See also discussion, 'The West Indies Federation—1959 Model', *West Indian Economist* (Kingston, Jamaica), Vol. 2, No. 3, September 1959.

32. Mr Leon, M.H.R., in Jamaica, House of Representatives, reported, *Daily Gleaner*, 7 November 1959.

33. K. R. V. John, 'The Federal Idea and West Indian Political Association', *Flambeau* (Kingston, St Vincent), No. 2 (September 1965), p. 6.

34. Owen J. Roberts, *The Court and the Constitution* (Cambridge, Harvard University Press, 1951), p. 63.

35. Barbados, *The Federal Negotiations 1962–1965 and Constitutional Proposals for Barbados* (Bridgetown, Government Printing Press, 1965), para. 76.

36. Sir Ellis Clarke, quoted, *ibid.*, para. 26.

37. *Ibid.*, paras. 27, 28.

38. Albert Gomes, 'A Politician Recalls', *Trinidad Guardian*, 19 February 1964.

CHAPTER XVI

1. Daniel Guérin, *The West Indies and Their Future* (London, Denis Dobson, 1961), p. 172.

2. John Rojas, in *Evening News* (Port of Spain, Trinidad, 27 November 1961.

3. See, for example, Rawle Farley (ed.), *Labour Education in the British Caribbean* (Extra-Mural Department, University College of the West Indies, 1960). See also the concluding remarks in Francis X. Mark, *The History of the Barbados Workers' Union* (Bridgetown, Advocate Commercial Printing, N.D.), pp. 167–68. The remark in the text about a sepoy colonel of 1856 is taken from the review of the Farley volume by H. P. Jacobs, *Daily Gleaner*, 20 December 1961.

4. Statement of the Jamaica Christian Council on gambling, *Daily Gleaner*, 10 October 1962; exchange of correspondence between Sir Alexander Bustamante and Moderator of the Presbyterian Church of Jamaica, *Daily Gleaner*, 5 November 1962; Statement of the Roman Catholic Caribbean Bishops, *Antigua Star*, 16 February 1962.

5. Canon Farquhar, 'Candid Comments', *Trinidad Guardian*, 23 December, 1956.

6. B. L. St John Hamilton, *Problems of Administration in an Emergent Nation. A Case Study of Jamaica* (New York, Frederick A. Praegar, Inc., Special Studies, 1964).

7. Trinidad and Tobago, *First Report of the Working Party on the Role and Status of the Civil Service in the Age of Independence* (St Ann's, Port of Spain, September 1964).

8. *Ibid.*, para. 32

NOTES 477

9. Hon. Errol Barrow, Barbados, *House of Assembly. Debates*, Official Report, 11 June 1963, p. 22.

10. Eric Williams, 'The Reality of Independence', *The Nation*, Vol. 7, No. 15, 22 January 1965.

11. Leopold Kohr, 'Is Reason Treason? Does economic development signal the end of a country's uniqueness?', *San Juan Review*, May 1965.

12. *Public Opinion* (Kingston, Jamaica), 3 February 1962, 28 July 1962, 20 October 1962.

13. Eric Williams, *History of the People of Trinidad and Tobago* (Port of Spain, PNM Publishing Co., 1962), p. 280.

14. Rex Nettleford, Staff Tutor, University of the West Indies, in *The Torchlight* (St George's, Grenada), 10 June 1962.

15. See, for example, W. I. Carr, speech to Life Underwriters' Conference, in *Spotlight* (Kingston, Jamaica), February 1964.

16. Frank Hill, 'Need for a Governing Class', reprinted, *Caribbean Quarterly*, in 'Editorial Comments and Notes', Vol. 8, No. 3 (September 1962).

17. Wendell Bell, *Jamaican Leaders. Political Attitudes in a New Nation* (Berkeley and Los Angeles, University of California Press, 1964), pp. 74–75. See also M. G. Smith, 'The Plural Framework of Jamaican Society', *The Plural Society in the British West Indies* (Berkeley and Los Angeles, University of California Press, 1965).

18. The emphasis of the nationalist philosophy upon a national consensus framework of reference leads to a dangerous underestimation of its internal contradictions. Thus a recent West Indian statement can write of Eric Williams and C. L. R. James without perceiving that their different ideological ways of looking at West Indian society makes it somewhat misleading to write about them as if they were merely West Indian nationalist ideologues, Philip Sherlock, *West Indies* (London, Thames and Hudson, 1966), pp. 155–58. It is sometimes easier for the outside observer, who is free of local pressures, to see this, for example, Ivar Oxaal, 'C. L. R. James vs. Eric Williams: The Formative Years', *Trinidad and Tobago Index* (The University, Hull, England), No. 2, Fall 1965.

19. Letter, *Daily Gleaner*, 21 October 1962.

20. United Nations, General Assembly, 21st. Session, 1966. *Report of the 1966 Special Committee on Principles of International Law Concerning Friendly Relations and Cooperation among States* (A/6230, 27 June 1966), paras. 404–8.

21. *The Intellectual Tradition and Social Changes in the Caribbean* (Mona, Jamaica, *New World* pamphlet, 1965), p. 15.

22. C. L. R. James, *Party Politics in the West Indies* (San Juan, Trinidad, Vedic Enterprises, Ltd., 1962).

23. Trinidad and Tobago, *Report of the Commission of Enquiry into Subversive Activities in Trinidad and Tobago* (House Paper No. 2 of 1965, Trinidad and Tobago House of Representatives, Government Printery, Port of Spain, 1965), pp. 1–2, paras. 7, 8, 9. See critical observations on this, *New World Fortnightly* (Georgetown, British Guiana), No. 14, 14 May 1965.

24. People's National Movement, General Council Research Committee, *The Party in Independence* (Port of Spain, PNM Publishing Co., Ltd., N.D.); and People's National Movement, *Election Magazine*, 4 November 1966.

25. *The Party in Independence*, pp. 3–4.

26. Richard M. Titmuss, *Essays on the Welfare State* (London, George Allen and Unwin, 1960), p. 52.

27. Trinidad and Tobago, Office of the Prime Minister, *Research Papers, Number I*, December 1963 (Port of Spain, Central Statistical Office), pp. 92–98, 119–120.

28. *The Party in Independence*, p. 4.

29. Arthur Jessop, *Transport in Trinidad* (Port of Spain, Government Printing Office, 1956).

30. A. V. S. Lochhead, *Report on Administration of the Social Services* (Port of Spain, Government Printing Office, 1956).

31. Trinidad and Tobago, *Cabinet Proposals on Education* (Port of Spain, Government Printing Office, 1960). For the failure, by comparison, to deal with the structural ills of the Trinidad sugar industry, see National Union of Sugar Workers, *A Betrayal of the Sugar Workers* (San Fernando, Vedic Enterprises, Ltd., N.D.). For a discussion of the general theoretical model of economic development followed in the West Indies see Lloyd Best, *The Economy of the Commonwealth Caribbean*, mimeographed, N.D. For the PNM position on agrarian reform see Dr Eric Williams, *A Review of the Political Scene*, Address to Special PNM Convention, 11 September 1966, Port of Spain, pp. 13–17.

32. See full report, *San Juan Star*, 16 October 1966.

33. See report of recent information on Puerto Rican trade union membership, *San Juan Star*, 25 April 1966.

34. See Morley Ayearst, *The British West Indies: The Search for Self-Government* (New York, New York University Press, 1960), p. 159; Mona MacMillan, *The Land of Look Behind. A Study of Jamaica* (London, Faber and Faber, 1957), p. 205; T. S. Simey, *Welfare and Planning in the West Indies* (Oxford, 1946), pp. 258–59.

35. Dr Arthur Lewis, 'Industrialization and Social Peace', *Daily Gleaner*, 30 December 1962.

36. Dr Eric Williams, People's National Movement, *Eighth Annual Convention. A Comprehensive Political Report covering all Levels of Government in Trinidad and Tobago, submitted by the Legislative Group* (Port of Spain, September 1964), p. 2, para. 2.

37. L. de Verteuil, *Trinidad* (London, Cassell, 1856), p. 408. For a discussion of present-day British attitudes to independence in the colonies see House of Commons debate on Prime Ministers' Conference, *Parliamentary Debates* (Hansard), Official Report (London, Her Majesty's Stationery Office, 4 July 1960).

38. Address of Hon. Robert Lightbourne to Regional Conference on the West Indies, Dalhousie University, in *Daily Gleaner*, 30 May 1966.

39. Norman Girvan, *Regional Integration vs. Company Integration in the Utilization of Caribbean Bauxite*, mimeographed, Third Caribbean Scholars' Conference (Georgetown, Guyana, 1966).

40. *The Statist* (London), quoted, *Barbados Advocate*, 23 October 1964.

41. Senator George D. Aiken, Special Report to Senate Foreign Relations Committee, reprinted, *Daily Gleaner*, 3 February 1958.

42. E. C. Richardson, *Onward Trinidad, the Solution to Our Economic and Social Problems* (Port of Spain, Enterprise Electric Printery, N.D.).

43. Ricardo Alegría, Director, Institute of Puerto Rican Culture, in *El Mundo* (San Juan, Puerto Rico), 10 January 1963.

44. V. Schoelcher, *Les Colonies Francaises* (Paris, 1852), quoted, Daniel Guérin, *The West Indies and Their Future* (London, Denis Dobson, 1961), p. 174.

# INDEX